Local Remedies in International Law
Second Edition

This work examines the local remedies rule historically and
particularly in modern international law. Not only is the customary
international law discussed but the application, *inter alia*, of the rule
conventionally to human rights protection and generally to
international organizations is also covered. It is as comprehensive a
treatment on the subject as can be. The law is dealt with in the light
of State practice and the jurisprudence of international courts and
tribunals. The author not only examines the jurisprudential basis of
the rule and its established aspects but ventures into some important
areas, such as the incidence of the rule, the limitations on its
application, the burden of proof and the relevance of the rule to
procedural remedies, in which the law is not so clear. The work also
concerns itself with the interests of the international community and
the interests of justice in relation to the rule. While there is a strict
adherence to the requirements of juristic exposition and analysis,
where the law has been more or less determined, the author does not
hesitate to offer criticism and to make suggestions for the
improvement of the law in the light of modern policy considerations.
The work takes into account the recent reports of the International
Law Commission which have not hitherto been examined in relation
to the rule.

   The second edition is a considerably expanded version of the first.
There is not only updating and additional material, but additional
subjects, such as State contracts and bilateral investment treaties, are
included.

Chittharanjan Felix Amerasinghe was formerly Judge of the UN
Tribunal in New York, and of the Commonwealth International
Tribunal in London. He was also Professor of Law and later Honorary
Professor of Law at the University of Ceylon, Colombo. He was
Director of the Secretariat and Registrar of the World Bank Tribunal
in Washington, and is currently a member of the Institut de Droit
International. He has advised governments on international law and
has written extensively on the subject.

CAMBRIDGE STUDIES IN INTERNATIONAL AND COMPARATIVE LAW

Established in 1946, this series produces high quality scholarship in the fields of public and private international law and comparative law. Although these are distinct legal sub-disciplines, developments since 1946 confirm their interrelation.

Comparative law is increasingly used as a tool in the making of law at national, regional and international levels. Private international law is now often affected by international conventions, and the issues faced by classical conflicts rules are frequently dealt with by substantive harmonisation of law under international auspices. Mixed international arbitrations, especially those involving state economic activity, raise mixed questions of public and private international law, while in many fields (such as the protection of human rights and democratic standards, investment guarantees and international criminal law) international and national systems interact. National constitutional arrangements relating to 'foreign affairs', and to the implementation of international norms, are a focus of attention.

Professor Sir Robert Jennings edited the series from 1981. Following his retirement as General Editor, an editorial board has been created and Cambridge University Press has recommitted itself to the series, affirming its broad scope.

The Board welcomes works of a theoretical or interdisciplinary character, and those focusing on new approaches to international or comparative law or conflicts of law. Studies of particular institutions or problems are equally welcome, as are translations of the best work published in other languages.

A list of books in the series can be found at the end of this volume.

Local Remedies in International Law
Second Edition

Chittharanjan Felix Amerasinghe

CAMBRIDGE
UNIVERSITY PRESS

PUBLISHED BY THE PRESS SYNDICATE OF THE UNIVERSITY OF CAMBRIDGE
The Pitt Building, Trumpington Street, Cambridge, United Kingdom

CAMBRIDGE UNIVERSITY PRESS
The Edinburgh Building, Cambridge, CB2 2RU, UK
40 West 20th Street, New York, NY 10011–4211, USA
477 Williamstown Road, Port Melbourne, VIC 3207, Australia
Ruiz de Alarcón 13, 28014 Madrid, Spain
Dock House, The Waterfront, Cape Town 8001, South Africa

http://www.cambridge.org

First published 1990

Second edition 2004

Printed in the United Kingdom at the University Press, Cambridge

Typeface Swift 10/13 pt   *System* LaTeX 2$_\varepsilon$ [TB]

A catalogue record for this book is available from the British Library

Library of Congress Cataloguing in Publication data
Amerasinghe, Chittharanjan Felix, 1933–
Local remedies in international law / Chittharanjan Felix Amerasinghe. – 2nd ed.
      p.   cm. – (Cambridge studies in international and comparative law ; 31)
Includes bibliographical references and index.
ISBN 0 521 82899 6 (hardback)
1. Exhaustion of local remedies (International law)   I. Title.   II. Cambridge studies in
international and comparative law (Cambridge, England : 1996) ; 31.
K2315.A95   2003
341.4'8 – dc21   2003046174

ISBN 0 521 82899 6 hardback

Contents

Preface

In the preface to the first edition of this book I wrote:

> In the introductory chapter of this book I have attempted to justify its publication in spite of the apparently vast literature that already exists on the subject. It is hoped that it will not be regarded as yet another book on local remedies. The primary intention was to bring some element of clarification to and fresh insight into a rather confused but inviting area of the law of State Responsibility. This is all the more important now, particularly in view of the great increase of the flow of investment across national frontiers and the ease with which international travel is possible.

This still remains true for this second edition of the work. It must be emphasized that individuals as aliens, because of the ease of travel, are as much affected by the rule of local remedies as foreign legal persons.

The second edition, like the first, is concerned with the *rule of exhaustion of local remedies* which came into existence in the context of diplomatic protection of aliens. Like the first, again, therefore, this edition does not deal in general with the place of remedies given by national courts in settling disputes involving breaches of international law but is confined to investigating specifically the *rule of exhaustion of local remedies* as it has developed, first, in connection with the diplomatic protection of aliens and, secondly, by extension peripherally to other areas of international law, such as human rights protection and the law relating to international organizations.

Not only has there been updating and revision in the second edition in the light of developments since the publication of the first, but the format has been changed, as will be seen from a reading of the contents pages. Notably, (i) a new Chapter 5 has been introduced dealing with the all important subject of *contracts* involving aliens, (ii) the application of the rule to human rights protection, as updated and revised, has been included in a single chapter (Chapter 13) rather than spread throughout the book, and (iii) the former Appendix, as updated and revised, dealing with international organizations in the context of the rule has been converted into Chapter 14. Moreover, the book has been divided into five parts, which makes the analysis and discussion more systematic and easier to understand. Further, comments made by some reviewers which were thought to be in need of treatment have been taken into account in this second edition.

The bibliography which appeared in the first edition has been omitted. As has been pointed out, a bibliography is unnecessary in a treatise of this nature which to a large extent did break and does break new ground. The references in the footnotes to other material is completely adequate. Indeed, the bibliography was unnecessary for the first edition. It is not proposed to continue to publish what is superfluous.

My thanks go to my friends, Laura and Emily Crow, who typed Chapters 5 and 13 and part of Chapter 10.

Table of cases

Abbreviations

AAA	American Arbitration Association
AALCC	Asian African Legal Consultative Committee
AdV	*Archiv des Völkerrechts*
AFDI	*Annuaire français de droit international*
AIDI	*Annuaire de l'Institut de Droit international*
AJIL	*American Journal of International Law*
Ann. Dig.	*Annual Digest of Public International Law Cases* (now ILR)
Ann. Rep. IAComHR	*Annual Report of the Inter-American Commission of Human Rights*
ArchivDP	*Archivio di Diritto Publico*
ASDI	*Annuaire Suisse de Droit International*
BFSP	*British and Foreign State Papers*
BIT	bilateral investment treaty
BPIL	*British Practice in International Law*
BViss	*Bibliotheca Visseriana*
BYIL	*British Yearbook of International Law*
CAT	Committee Against Torture
CE doc.	Council of Europe document
CERD	Committee on the Elimination of Racial Discrimination
CERN	European Organization for Nuclear Research
CJEC	Court of Justice of the European Communities
CLR	*Columbia Law Review*
COE	Council of Europe

Collection	*Collection of Decisions of the European Commission of Human Rights*
CTC	Commission on Transnational Corporations (UN)
CTS	*Consolidated Treaty Series*
CYIL	*Canadian Yearbook of International Law*
D&R	see *Decisions and Reports*
De La Pradelle-Politis, RAI	*Recueil d'arbitrages internationaux* (1954)
Decisions and Reports	*Decisions and Reports of the European Commission of Human Rights*
EC	European Communities
ECHR	European Convention on Human Rights
EComHR	European Commission on Human Rights
ECOSOC	Economic and Social Council
ECR	*European Court Reports*
ECtHR	European Court of Human Rights
EPIL	*Encyclopedia of Public International Law*
EPO	European Patents Organization
ESO	European Space Observatory
Eurocontrol	European Organization for the Safety of Air Navigation
FAO	Food and Agriculture Organization (UN)
GA	General Assembly of the United Nations
GAOR	*General Assembly Official Records*
GST	*Grotius Society Transactions*
Hackworth, *Digest*	Hackworth, *Digest of International Law* (1943)
Hague Recueil	*Recueil de Cours of the Hague Academy of International Law*
HRC	Human Rights Committee (established under the International Covenant on Civil and Political Rights)
HRJ	*Human Rights Journal*
HRLJ	*Human Rights Law Journal*
Hyde, *International Law*	Hyde, *International Law Chiefly as Interpreted and Applied by the United States* (1945)
IACHR	Inter-American Court of Human Rights
IAComHR	Inter-American Commission of Human Rights
ICC	International Chamber of Commerce
ICCPR	International Covenant on Civil and Political Rights

ICERD	International Convention for the Elimination of Racial Discrimination
ICJ	International Court of Justice
ICLQ	*International and Comparative Law Quarterly*
ICSID	International Centre for the Settlement of Investment Disputes
IJIL	*Indian Journal of International Law*
ILA	International Law Association
ILC	International Law Commission
ILM	*International Legal Materials*
ILO	International Labor Organization
ILOAT	International Labor Organization Administrative Tribunal
ILR	*International Law Reports*
Iran–US CTR	*Iran–US Claims Tribunal Reports*
ITU	International Telecommunication Union
IYIA	*Indian Yearbook of International Affairs*
JDI	*Journal de droit international*
JIA	*Journal of International Arbitration*
JIR	*Jahrbuch für Internationales Recht*
JUNAT	*Judgments of the United Nations Administrative Tribunal*
Lloyd's Rep	*Lloyd's List Law Reports*
LN	League of Nations
LN Doc.	League of Nations document
LNTS	*League of Nations Treaty Series*
LQR	*Law Quarterly Review*
MalayLR	*Malaysia Law Review*
MIGA	Multilateral Investment Guarantee Agency
MLR	*Modern Law Review*
Moore, *A Digest of International Law*	Moore, *A Digest of International Law* (1906)
Moore, *International Arbitrations*	Moore, *History and Digest of the International Arbitrations to Which the United States Has Been a Party* (1898)
NAFTA	North American Free Trade Agreement
NILR	*Netherlands International Law Review*
OAS	Organization of American States
O'Connell	O'Connell, *International Law* (2nd edn, 1970)
OECD	Organization for Economic Cooperation and Development

Oppenheim	*Oppenheim's International Law* (1992)
ÖZÖR	*Österreichische Zeitschrift für Öffentliches Recht*
PAHO	Pan-American Health Organization
PCA	Permanent Court of Arbitration
PCIJ	Permanent Court of International Justice
Proceedings, ASIL	Proceedings of the American Society of International Law
RAI	*Receuil des Arbitrages International*
RBDI	*Revue Belge de Droit International*
RDE	*Rivista di Diritto Europeo*
RDH	*Revista de Derechos Humanos*
RDI	*Rivista di Diritto Internazionale*
RDILC	*Revue de Droit International et Législation Comparée*
REDI	*Revista Española de Derecho Internacional*
Reports	*Reports of the ECHR*
RG de Legis y Jurisp	*Revista General de Legislación y Jurisprudencia*
RGDIP	*Revue générale de droit international public*
RHDI	*Revue Hellénique de Droit International*
RI	*Revue de Droit International*
TAM	Tribunaux Arbitrales Mixtes
UCLR	*University of Chicago Law Review*
UN	United Nations
UN Doc.	UN document
UNAT	United Nations Administrative Tribunal
UNCITRAL	UN Conference on International Trade Law
UNCTC	see CTC
UNESCO	United Nations Educational, Scientific and Cultural Organization
UNICCPR	see ICCPR
UNRIAA	*United Nations Reports of International Arbitral Awards*
UNTS	*United Nations Treaty Series*
US For. Rel.	*United States Foreign Relations*
WBAT	World Bank Administrative Tribunal
WHO	World Health Organization
YBECHR	*Yearbook of the European Convention on Human Rights*
ZaörV	*Zeitschrift für Ausländisches Öffentliches Recht und Völkerrecht*

Part I Prolegomena

1 Introduction

The subject

It is acknowledged generally that local remedies are relevant to the settlement of certain international disputes involving states. The rule that such remedies must be exhausted owes its origin to the diplomatic protection of aliens in which area it was first applied. That the celebrated 'rule of local remedies' is accepted as a customary rule of international law needs no proof today, as its basic existence and validity has not been questioned. The rule has been affirmed in recent diplomatic practice, particularly by developed countries against whom or in regard to whose nationals the rule is most likely to be invoked in regard to the protection of aliens.[1] It has been assumed to exist as a principle of customary or general international law in such conventions as the International Covenant

---

[1] See e.g. statement of the Division of Legal Affairs of the Département politique fédéral of the Swiss Government to the effect that in the case of Swiss citizens condemned to prison abroad 'when feasible and where an effective remedy seems probable, all modes of appellate revision must be exhausted before diplomatic interposition becomes proper', and that it was equally impossible to exercise diplomatic protection while the judicial process was running its course or as long as such process had been resumed: Caflisch, 'La Pratique suisse en matière de droit international public – 1972', ASDI (1973) pp. 359ff.; statement in a memorandum of 1 March 1961 of the US Department of State concerning the treatment of US nationals in Cuba that: 'The requirement for exhaustion of local remedies is based upon the generally accepted rule of international law that international responsibility may not be invoked as regards reparation for losses or damages sustained by a foreigner until after exhaustion of the remedies available under local law': 56 AJIL (1962) p. 167; statement of 18 October 1967 of the Canadian Under-Secretary that under well-established principles of international law the requirement of prior exhaustion of all local remedies must have been fulfilled to justify the espousal of a claim by diplomatic intervention by one state on behalf of one of its nationals against another state: Gotlieb and Beesley, 'Canadian Practice – 1967', 6 CYIL (1968) p. 263.

on Civil and Political Rights, the European Convention on Human Rights and the American Convention on Human Rights.[2] Moreover, in recent history it has been invoked in international litigation before both the International Court of Justice (ICJ) and other arbitral tribunals in circumstances in which such international courts have conceded either expressly or implicitly that the rule exists. For example, the rule was invoked by the respondent state before the ICJ in the *Interhandel Case*, where the Court stated categorically that 'The rule that local remedies must be exhausted before international proceedings may be instituted is a well-established rule of customary international law'.[3] The rule was also accepted by the tribunals as a relevant rule of customary international law in both the *Finnish Ships Arbitration*[4] and the *Ambatielos Claim*.[5] More recently, the existence of the rule was implicitly conceded, albeit by the recognition that it did not apply in the circumstances because of implicit exclusion, by the Iran–US Claims Tribunal in its award in *American International Group, Inc.* v. *Iran*, when it held that 'The Algiers Declarations grant jurisdiction to this Tribunal notwithstanding that exhaustion of local remedies . . . doctrines might otherwise be applicable'.[6] These were all cases of diplomatic protection of aliens by national states.

While it is not the existence or validity of the rule that needs to be supported, there are many aspects and applications of it that need to be clarified. Thus, the statement made in 1956 that 'There is a well established but inadequately defined rule that the alien must exhaust local remedies before a diplomatic claim is made'[7] may still represent a challenging assessment of a situation which requires investigation. Further developments have occurred in the twentieth century, particularly since 1950. For example, the rule has been extended from its original area of application, namely, the diplomatic protection of nationals abroad, to

---

[2] Article 41(c) of the International Covenant on Civil and Political Rights, Article 26 of the European Convention on Human Rights and Article 46 of the American Convention on Human Rights. See also Article 11(3) of the International Convention on the Elimination of All Forms of Racial Discrimination.

[3] 1959 ICJ Reports p. 27. See also the *ELSI Case*, 1989 ICJ *Reports* p. 15, where the rule was applied, without any query, to a case of diplomatic protection under a treaty.

[4] The *Finnish Ships Arbitration*, 3 UNRIAA p. 1479 (1934).

[5] The *Ambatielos Claim*, 12 UNRIAA p. 83 (1956).

[6] Award No. 93-2-3, 4 Iran–US CTR at p. 102 (1983).

[7] Jessup, *A Modern Law of Nations* (1956) p. 104. The rule is being studied and codified by the ILC as a part of its work on diplomatic protection: see Dugard, 'Second Report on Diplomatic Protection', UN Doc. A/CN.4/514 (2001); and Dugard, 'Third Report on Diplomatic Protection', UN Doc. A/CN.4/523 (2002).

the protection of human rights, even though this has been done by express incorporation in agreements between states.[8] The impact of such extensions has been significant, since generally the rule referred to in these conventions is the rule as it is recognized in customary or general international law which pertains to diplomatic protection. A consequence of these developments is that international organs, such as the European Commission of Human Rights which was not essentially a judicial organ, although it acted in a quasi-judicial capacity in dealing with cases alleging violation of human rights, and the European Court of Human Rights, which is, have had to deal with the application of the rule of local remedies. It is important to recognize that it is the rule as accepted in general or customary international law that these organs have been applying.

The significance of the situation which has thus arisen is that the rule, albeit as understood in customary international law, has been applied outside the area of strict diplomatic protection of aliens to areas to which it was not originally intended to apply, namely, the protection of human rights per se, which could and generally do involve the rights of individuals against their own national states or of the stateless against other states. However, the purported content and limits of the rule being applied are those of the customary universal rule of international law. Also, in effect much of the relevant and documented application of the rule has been taking place in regional arenas, although the UN Human Rights Committee also applies it under the relevant instruments. The regional nature of the organs that have most frequently been dealing with the rule may not be critical, in so far as the organs are genuine international organs which are enforcing international obligations. On the other hand, the extension of the rule to areas which are different from the original area of its application, although perhaps still associated with the protection of the individual and therefore not fundamentally unconnected, has not only resulted in the expanded application of the rule but may also have had an influence on the basic theories underlying the rule itself and its nature. In any event, the rule has been developed importantly in its application, its limits have secured greater definition and, as a consequence, the practical effect of the rule in certain areas has been clarified to a large extent. The exposure of the

---

[8] See e.g. Article 26 of the European Convention on Human Rights and Article 41(c) of the International Covenant on Civil and Political Rights, Article 46 of the American Convention on Human Rights and Article 11(3) of the International Convention on the Elimination of All Forms of Racial Discrimination.

traditional rule to these new areas may have had a beneficial effect on it and on the institution of diplomatic protection to which it was originally confined.

It is also true that in the area of diplomatic protection or in the re-lationship between an individual and a foreign state there has been a growing tendency, where possible, to exclude by implication or express agreement the application of the rule of local remedies, as is demon-strated by the Convention on the Settlement of Investment Disputes between States and the Nationals of other States,[9] by many bilateral investment treaties, and by the Claims Settlement Declaration by Alge-ria of 1981 relating to the agreement between the US and Iran.[10] But such exclusion has always been a possibility in the history of interna-tional relations. The lesson to be learnt from this kind of practice is that the rule of local remedies is still regarded as very pertinent to the settlement of international disputes involving aliens and can only be ex-cluded generally by a deliberate act of states involved in a dispute.[11] On the other hand, the fact that the application of the rule to areas other than diplomatic protection and disputes between states and nationals of other states has been developed, albeit by express agreement, signifies that the international community sees some positive use for it. Such considerations, and in particular the application of the rule in fields other than diplomatic protection, warrant a further study of the rule and its development with special emphasis on how it has been applied and defined in the post-Second World War period, having in mind that what has taken place is a proliferated application of the rule relating to the protection of nationals against foreign states which is still a rule of customary international law.

That having been said, it must also be remembered that of special im-portance is the fact that the development of the rule in recent times has

---

[9] See Article 26.

[10] See Article II.1: 1 Iran–US CTR p. 9.

[11] The fact that a state or states may agree to exclude the application of the rule in the settlement of a dispute does not detract from the quality of the rule as a customary rule of law. The incidence of this practice in recent years merely attests to the willingness of respondent states for a variety of reasons to submit disputes directly to international settlement in the interests of peace. That states consciously address the issue of the rule in connection with the settlement of disputes involving the protection of aliens is proof that the rule is otherwise viable and a serious impediment to the direct settlement of a dispute at the international level. It does not in fact reduce the importance of the rule or affect its relevance in the area of the diplomatic protection of aliens. Thus, it is in the interests of the international community that the rule be well defined and reasonably developed even for the purpose of the law relating to diplomatic protection.

been made possible to some extent by its extended applications, albeit by the solemn *fiat* of sovereign states, particularly to the field of human rights protection. While this may be a reassertion of the importance of the original rule, what is of special interest to modern practice and scholarship is how the rule itself has been developed, applied and possibly redefined as a result of this extended relationship to other areas. The fact that the rule relating to diplomatic protection was applicable under customary international law without the conventional agreement of states, while the rule, albeit of customary international law, is applicable in the newer fields to which it has been applied only by the express agreement of states, is not of significance. In effect, in so far as it is the rule of customary international law that is basically being applied, this is what is of relevance, so that it is not untrue to say that what has been developed is basically the rule of customary international law relating to diplomatic protection. Consequently, this study will also attempt to assess the impact of recent developments in the application of what is in essence a customary rule of international law in order to see how the rule has been shaped, how the theory behind it may have been affected, how its nature may have been redetermined and how its application in practice has clarified the ambiguities surrounding it. While the new fields in which the rule has found application will be examined, the developments that have taken place in the area of diplomatic protection will also indubitably be of significance. While the application per se, for example, of the rule of local remedies as an incident in the protection of human rights through international instruments will be examined, the evolution of the rule in its application as a rule of customary international law, originally linked with diplomatic protection, will certainly be a particular focus of attention.

The core of the present study is not the detailed application per se of the rule of local remedies by particular organs or to specific areas outside diplomatic protection. In so far as different areas are considered or the attitudes of international organs are examined, what will be of special interest is how the application of the rule by such organs or in different areas has informed and influenced the development of the rule itself as a customary rule of international law and has led to its clarification or logical and practical definition or redefinition. Recent developments show that the rule of local remedies is regarded not only as an existing rule but also as in many ways a useful one. Hence, it is not excessive intellectualism or a pure academic exercise to examine and discuss its development with particular emphasis on the post-Second World War era.

The question may also be asked whether the customary rule associated entirely and essentially with diplomatic protection, or adaptations of it, have become customary, as opposed to being conventional in one way or another, in other areas outside of diplomatic protection. This is a matter which will be explored later only peripherally, as it requires special attention in its own right. The question is not really *can*, or *is it useful that*, it be a customary rule outside of diplomatic protection, which may validly be asked, but has it become one.

Much of the recent history of the rule has been concerned with the decisions of international tribunals or organs rather than the diplomatic practice of states. Just as in other fields of international law the importance of judicial and quasi-judicial determination has been increasing and has had a decisive effect on the development of the law, so too in relation to the rule of local remedies is such activity of special significance. Thus, naturally, it is the decisions of international judicial and other organs that will constitute the main basis of discussion in the analysis. It is this source of decision-making that has contributed most to the development of the customary rule of international law on local remedies. Indeed, recent diplomatic practice in the matter is virtually non-existent, in so far as it has contributed to new developments in the application of the rule.[12]

A word needs to be said about the literature on the subject. There has been some specialized textual work on the rule in recent years, but this has concentrated to a great extent on the rule as applied in the field of human rights[13] or on limited aspects of the rule's development.[14] What the present volume purports to do is to paint a clearer integrated

---

[12] The development of the rule of local remedies in recent years has been dependent almost entirely on judicial or quasi-judicial determination by international tribunals or organs. Even in the past, diplomatic practice has generally been confined to general statements of the rule or to references to some of the exceptions to the rule such as the non-availability of remedies. There has never been any extensive discussion of the parameters or theoretical basis of the rule in diplomatic practice. For the substance of the rule and its application, the definition of its limitations and the identification of its bases it is predominantly to judicial or quasi-judicial decision that one has to look. For the rest, the rule and its underpinnings have been elaborated in textual authorities.

[13] Some of the works in which the rule of local remedies has been examined with particular reference to the protection of human rights are: Van Dijk and Van Hoof, *Theory and Practice of the European Convention on Human Rights* (1998), Chapter III, pp. 127–53; Castberg, *The European Convention on Human Rights* (1974); Ezejiofer, *Protection of Human Rights under the Law* (1964); Fawcett, *The Application of the European Convention on Human Rights* (1969); Monconduit, *La Commission européenne des droits de l'homme* (1965); Jacobs, *The European Convention on Human Rights* (1975); Nay-Cadoux,

Les Conditions de recevabilité des requêtes individuelles devant la Commission européenne des droits de l'homme (1966); Cançado Trindade, *The Application of the Rule of Exhaustion of Local Remedies in International Law: Its Rationale in the International Protection of Individual Rights* (1983); Amerasinghe, 'The Rule of Exhaustion of Domestic Remedies in the Framework of International Systems for the Protection of Human Rights', 28 ZaöRV (1968) p. 257; Amerasinghe, 'The Rule of Exhaustion of Local Remedies and the International Protection of Human Rights', 17 IYIA (1974) p. 3; Grillo Pasquarelli, 'The Question of the Exhaustion of Domestic Remedies in the Context of the Examination of Admissibility of an Application to the European Commission of Human Rights', in Robertson (ed.), *Privacy and Human Rights* (1973) p. 332; Guinand, 'La Règle de l'épuisement des voies de recours internes dans le cadre des systèmes internationaux de protection des droits de l'homme', 4 RBDI (1968) p. 471; McGovern, 'The Local Remedies Rule and Administrative Practices in the European Convention on Human Rights', 24 ICLQ (1975) p. 119; Monconduit, 'Bilan des conditions de la recevabilité: les tendances de la jurisprudence', 8 HRJ (1975) p. 417; Robertson, 'The European Convention on Human Rights and the Rule of Exhaustion of Domestic Remedies', 4 RDH (1974) p. 199; Ruiloba Santana, 'La Regla de Agotamiento de los Recursos Internos a través de las Decisiones de la Comisión Europea de los Derechos del Hombre', in *Estúdios de Derecho Internacional Público y Privado – Libro-Homenaje al Profesor Luis Sela Sampil* (1970) p. 467; Schaffer and Weissbrodt, 'Exhaustion of Remedies in the Context of the Racial Discrimination Convention', 2 HRJ (1969) p. 632; Sørensen, 'La Recevabilité de l'instance devant la Cour européenne des droits de l'homme – Notes sur les rapports entre la Commission et la Cour', in *René Cassin Amicorum Discipulorumque Liber* (1969), vol. 1, p. 333; Spatafora, 'La Regola del Previo Esaurimento dei Ricorsi Interni nella Giurisprudenza della Commissione Europea dei Diritto dell'Uomo', 11 RDE (1971) p. 101; Robertson, 'Exhaustion of Local Remedies in Human Rights Litigation – The Burden of Proof Reconsidered', 39 ICLQ (1990) p. 191; Cançado Trindade, 'Exhaustion of Local Remedies in Relation to Legislative Measures and Administrative Practices – The European Experience', 18 MalayLR (1976) p. 257; Cançado Trindade, 'Exhaustion of Local Remedies in Inter-State Cases: The Practice under the European Convention on Human Rights', 29 ÖZÖR (1978) p. 212; Cançado Trindade, 'Exhaustion of Local Remedies in the 'Travaux Preparatoires' of the European Convention on Human Rights', RI (1980) p. 73. The Inter-American system of human rights protection was discussed in Cançado Trindade, 'Exhaustion of Local Remedies in the Inter-American System', 18 IJIL (1978) p. 345. Other areas of human rights protection were discussed in Cançado Trindade, 'Exhaustion of Local Remedies under the United Nations International Convention on the Elimination of All Forms of Racial Discrimination', 22 GYIL (1979) p. 374; and Cançado Trindade, 'Exhaustion of Local Remedies under the UN Covenant on Civil and Political Rights and its Optional Protocol', 28 ICLQ (1979) p. 734. Cançado Trindade has also dealt with human rights protection in some of the articles by him referred to below. In the context of human rights protection, the rule is described generally as referring to 'domestic' remedies. References to 'local' remedies in connection with the rule must be taken to include, where appropriate, such 'domestic' remedies and *vice versa*.

[14] Various aspects of the rule of local remedies have been examined in the past, e.g. Amerasinghe, *State Responsibility for Injuries to Aliens* (1967) pp. 169–286; Falk, *The Role of Domestic Courts in the International Legal Order* (1964); García Amador, *Principios de Derecho Internacional que Rigen la Responsabilidad – Análisis Crítico de la Concepción Tradicional* (1963); Amerasinghe, 'The Formal Character of the Rule of Local Remedies', 25 ZaöRV (1965) p. 445; Amerasinghe, 'The Exhaustion of Procedural Remedies in the Same Court', 12 ICLQ (1963) p. 1285; Amerasinghe, 'Limitations on the Rule of Local Remedies', in *Essays in Honour of Professor Manuel Diez de Velasco* (1992) p. 57;

picture of the rule as it now stands in its many ramifications. The object is to demonstrate that the original rule has renewed meaning for international law with a more solid content and a better defined basis and character. There will be less concern for polemics and more emphasis on the viability of the rule today which may also be a partial explanation

Amerasinghe,'Arbitration and the Rule of Local Remedies', in *Festschrift für Rudolph Bernhardt* (1995) p. 665; Amerasinghe, 'Whither the Local Remedies Rule?', 5 *ICSID Review* (1990) p. 292; Ruiloba Santana, 'La Oponibilidad de la Excepción del Inagotamiento de los Recursos Internos en el Arreglo Arbitral de las Diferencias Internacionales', 22 REDI (1969) p. 465; Sand, 'The Role of Domestic Procedures in Transnational Environmental Disputes', *Report to Bellagio Conference* (1974); Sperduti, 'La Recevabilité des exceptions préliminaires de fond dans le procès international', 53 RDI (1970) p. 470; Cançado Trindade, 'The Burden of Proof with Regard to Exhaustion of Local Remedies in International Law', 9 *Revue des droits de l'homme* (1976) p. 81; Cançado Trindade, 'Exhaustion of Local Remedies in International Law: Experiments Granting Procedural Status to Individuals in the First Half of the Twentieth Century', 24 NILR (1977) p. 373; Cançado Trindade, 'The Time Factor in the Application of the Rule of Local Remedies in International Law', 61 RDI (1978) p. 232; Gutierrez Espada, 'La proteccion diplomatica, el agotamiento de los recursos internos y el arreglo de controversias en el Derecho positivo del espacio sobre responsabilidad', 74 RG de Legis. y Jurisp. (1977) p. 531; Stern, 'La Protection diplomatique des investissements internationaux: De Barcelona Traction a Elettronica Sicula ou les glissements progressifs de l'analyse', 117 JDI (1990) p. 897; and Adler, 'The Exhaustion of the Local Remedies Rule after the International Court of Justice's Decision in ELSI', 39 ICLQ (1990) p. 641. See also Doehring, 'Exhaustion of Local Remedies', in Bernhardt *et al.* (eds.), 3 EPIL (1997) pp. 238–42, for a brief account of the rule. Since 1950, there have been some studies of the rule of a somewhat general nature which have purported to examine the rule as a whole or as a complete subject but these have in most cases not considered all the material on the rule either because they are dated or for some other unexpressed reason and, therefore, are now of a limited character: see e.g. Chappez, *La Règle de l'épuisement des voies des recours internes* (1972); Gaja, *L'Esaurimento dei Ricorsi Interni nel Diritto Internazionale* (1967); Haesler, *The Exhaustion of Local Remedies in the Case Law of International Courts and Tribunals* (1968); Law, *The Local Remedies Rule in International Law* (1961); Panayotacos, *La Règle de l'épuisement des voies de recours internes* (1952); Sarhan, *L'Epuisement des recours internes en matière de responsabilité internationale* (1962); and Sulliger, *L'épuisement des voies de recours internes en droit international général et dans le Convention européenne des droits de l'homme* (1979). These works served their purpose and either were useful at the time they were written or were of value for the limited examination they made of the subject. In an article published in 1976 I took a brief and highly condensed look at the rule of local remedies as a whole: Amerasinghe, 'The Local Remedies Rule in an Appropriate Perspective', 36 ZaöRV (1976) p. 727. This did not, however, purport to be an exhaustive or detailed study of the rule as it has developed especially in the post-Second World War era. Mention must also be made of the work on the subject by the ILC, which, however, has been very uneven in quality: see Ago, 'Sixth Report on State Responsibility', 2 YBILC (1977), Part II, pp. 20–43; Crawford, 'Second Report on State Responsibility', UN Doc. A/CN.4/498 at pp. 56–61 and 67–8 (1999); Report of the ILC to the General Assembly, UN Doc. A/56/10 at pp. 304–7, (2001); Dugard, 'Second Report on Diplomatic Protection', UN Doc. A/CN.4/514 (2001); and Dugard, 'Third Report on Diplomatic Protection', UN Doc. A/CN.4/523 (2002).

of why states may want to exclude it in their relations with each other in certain areas to which it may have been applicable, while assigning it a special role in other areas. The difference between this and other specialized studies is that the theme of the present volume is the development, consolidation, delimitation and reaffirmation of the rule of customary international law requiring the exhaustion of local remedies in certain kinds of disputes involving states. There is room for the view that a strong and better defined rule of local remedies will enable states to determine what role it will play or not play in their relations with each other in regard to the treatment of their nationals by other states or even of individuals generally which may, indeed, result in a conscious exclusion of the rule by express or implied agreement or a conscious incorporation of the rule where it was not previously applicable.

This study is directed at the customary rule of international law seen as a rule still basically linked to the diplomatic protection of aliens which at the same time has had an extended application in practice to other important areas of international law concerning the individual. What has specially to be borne in mind is that the recent history of the use of the rule may require or lead to a reassessment of many of the assumptions underlying its basis and nature, and a fresh approach to its limits and content. A significant purpose of the study is to foster a clearer understanding of the rule in its practical application and a deeper appreciation of its theoretical bases. The development of the rule in the twentieth century seems to show a tendency both to rationalize it and at the same time to apply it in the most appropriate practical manner in relation to the policies it is now intended to serve.

Both on account of the recent extended applications of the rule and because of the confusion that surrounded many aspects of the rule previously, there is good reason to re-examine the rule in general. Particularly as a result of the extension of the rule to cover the enforcement of respect for human rights, the nature or formal character of the rule has been profoundly affected with the result that some clarity may have been introduced into that subject around which there had existed a high degree of confusion and obscurity. The development of the law relating to the rule largely in the second half of the twentieth century may also have led to a clearer understanding of the relationship between what is really a denial of justice in a narrow sense and the rule of local remedies itself, while areas such as the scope of the application of the rule resulting from its intrinsic nature and character have come to require a closer examination and more systematic and analytical treatment. The relevance of the principle of consent to the exclusion of the rule has undoubtedly acquired prominence, because of the tendency, already adverted to, of states to try to exclude the application of the rule with regard to their relations in the area of diplomatic protection of aliens. What is at stake here is not the viability or validity of the rule but its fungibility as a requirement in the settlement of a particular kind of international dispute. There may be good reason to believe that developments surrounding the rule in the twentieth century may have led to a clarification and redefinition of the situations in which the rule will be held to be inapplicable because of exceptions based on the principle that one party involved in a dispute should not be caused undue hardship in the pursuit of justice and the settlement of his claims. In short, there are many aspects of the rule that provoke discussion and attract attention.

Paradoxically, although there may be a growing tendency to distrust for a variety of reasons the capacity of the rule effectively to prevent disputes from reaching the international plane of dispute settlement because it fails to produce satisfactory dispositions of disputes at a local or domestic level with the result that it is expressly excluded in some cases of diplomatic protection of aliens, respect for its usefulness and efficacy has been demonstrated in other areas. Not only have the services of the rule been enlisted in the cause of protecting human rights but apparently by analogy since 1927, when the League of Nations Administrative Tribunal was established, a principle that *internal* remedies must be exhausted[15] has become part and parcel of the legal systems of international organizations. This principle has led to qualifications of admissibility *vis-à-vis* international tribunals which settle disputes between staff members of international organizations and the organizations themselves. While the rule applied in this area is not identical or on all fours with the rule of local remedies, it is an example of how international law divides responsibility between jurisdictions and competences and was in all likelihood precipitated by the existence of the rule of local remedies. It is noteworthy, of course, that the extension of the rule to cover human rights protection in general and special areas of human rights, such as freedom from racial discrimination, is explicitly based on the understanding that it is the rule as applied in customary international law, i.e. in diplomatic protection, which is being transposed.

---

[15] See Article VII of the Statute of the LNT: Amerasinghe (ed.), *Documents on International Administrative Tribunals* (1989) p. 179.

This is made clear, for example, in Article 41(c) of the International Covenant on Civil and Political Rights, the former Article 26 and the present Article 35(1) of the European Convention on Human Rights, and Article 46 of the American Convention on Human Rights, all of which refer to 'generally recognized principles of international law'. Mention was also made of the rule in, and it was transposed into, the treaties made after the First World War protecting minorities in Europe.[16] In what the implementation of such provisions by human rights organs, both judicial and quasi-judicial, has resulted is a different question, which will be addressed later.

Scheme and method

While the rule of local remedies is founded on the principal premise that the host or respondent state must be given the opportunity of redressing the alleged injury, to an alien or individual, which constitutes an international wrong, characteristically its application has been influenced and somewhat modified by the consideration of interests other than those of the host or respondent state, and particularly by taking into account the position of the alien or the individual in the settlement of what may be regarded as an international dispute. Consequently, in the application of the rule, specific areas or aspects require detailed analysis. These areas are briefly described here, before they are examined fully, with a reference sometimes to a few of the broad principles relevant to them. A point that needs to be kept in mind is that in these areas the implementation of the rule in the field of human rights protection may require special treatment because special factors come into play. In regard to the material content of the rule, which covers primarily its positive scope and the limitations on it, it will be seen in Chapter 3 that there is *in principle* no room for the influence of any special jurisprudential considerations in the field of human rights protection because of the manner in which the rule has generally been incorporated in the governing conventional instruments. In some other areas, nevertheless, there may be good reason to permit certain special theoretical conceptions to have an impact on the manner in which the rule is applied to human rights protection.

---

[16] See Cançado Trindade, 'Exhaustion of Local Remedies in International Law: Experiments Granting Procedural Status to Individuals in the First Half of the Twentieth Century', 24 NILR (1977) p. 373.

Before these particular areas are considered in Chapter 6 and the following chapters, however, some preliminary matters concerning the evolution of the rule, the bases of the rule, the relationship of the rule to denial of justice, and the special case of contractual wrongs are discussed in Chapters 2 to 5 which with this chapter constitute Part I. Part II, consisting of Chapters 6 to 12, deals with the application of the rule in the customary law of diplomatic protection. Part III, consisting of Chapters 13 and 14, deals with the application of the rule in peripheral contexts, such as human rights protection, particularly under the European Convention on Human Rights which is the principal judicially enforced human rights instrument, and the law of international organizations.

The question in what circumstances the rule of local remedies will or will not be applicable in a dispute involving the protection of an alien, or of an individual, as the case may be, has been raised in cases concerned with the protection of aliens as well as in situations involving the protection of human rights. There may well be situations involving disputes in which aliens or individuals alleging a violation of international law by a state need not exhaust local remedies in accordance with the rule. The issue raised in these circumstances concerns the incidence of the rule. The principles applicable to the resolution of the issue revolve around the function of the rule, and have the effect of containing any perceived over-extension of the rule. In answering the question raised in relation to human rights protection, it remains to be seen whether the difference in the basic considerations has had or can have any particular impact. In the final analysis, what is at issue in determining the incidence of the rule is how far the rule is inapplicable when a state brings a claim against another state on behalf of, or on account of an injury to, an alien or individual, or when an individual himself litigates against a state in respect of an alleged violation of his international rights. The situations involved are such as might on the face of it call for the application of the rule, because the claim is based on an alleged violation of international rights relating to an alien or individual. But conceivably there are limits to the incidence of the rule.[17]

The scope of the rule concerns the issue of to what extent local or domestic remedies must be exhausted in order that the requirements of the rule may be satisfied. The flipside of the coin concerns the limitations on the rule which relate to the issue of whether the alien or the

---

[17] These matters are discussed in Chapter 6.

individual is exempted from exhausting local remedies because of circumstances intrinsically connected with the application of the rule
itself. As regards the positive aspect of the scope and extent of the rule,
the main principle which is relevant flows from the interest of the host
or respondent state in having an opportunity of doing justice through its
own organs. This is a reflection of the respect accorded to the sovereignty
of the host or respondent state. The principle requires that the alien,
in resorting to local or domestic remedies, should give the host or respondent state a fair chance of resolving the dispute. The basic premise
underlying the rule of local remedies – that the sovereign rights of the
host or respondent state should be recognized and respected – controls
the extent of resort to local or domestic remedies. The limitations on
the rule, on the other hand, flow largely from a consideration of the
interests of the alien or individual (and perhaps the national state of
the alien and the international community) in having the rule applied
so as to conform to justice and fairness rather than with an unqualified
emphasis on the sovereign rights of the host or respondent state. The
main principle applicable in determining the limits of the rule of local
or internal remedies relates to the policy of not causing the alien or
individual undue hardship in securing a resolution of what may be regarded as basically an international dispute which it may be possible to
settle at a national level. However, the two principles flowing from the
respect for a state's sovereignty and from the recognition of the alien's
interest in quick and efficient justice without incurring undue expense
and hardship interact so as to modify each other, and to some extent
they are relevant to both the scope of the rule and the limitations on
the rule. To the extent that the scope of the rule is reasonably defined,
the respect for the sovereignty of the state suffers some dilution stem-
ming from the application of the principle of undue hardship to the
alien, while in so far as the limitations on the rule are not permitted
to erode the very rule itself, or to limit it excessively, the principle of
undue hardship to the alien is modified by the principle of respect for
the sovereignty of the state.[18]

In both these areas relating to the scope of, and the limitations on, the
rule there can be seen, in the development of the law, a serious attempt
to give effect to the basic premise of the rule that the sovereign rights
of the host or respondent state in doing justice should be respected,

---

[18] Chapter 7 deals with the scope of the rule, while Chapter 8 examines the limitations
on the rule.

while at the same time taking into account the principle of avoiding undue hardship to the alien or individual, and an endeavour to settle the conflict of interests by the choice of solutions which are often based on compromise, rather than on a rigid conception of the rule as an institutional means of propping up the interests of host or respondent states. The two principles referred to above require reconciliation, particularly in the areas of the scope of and the limitations on the rule. The resolution of the conflicts between these principles in these areas often requires the exercise of fine judgment, since the choices available may seem equally reasonable. What is significant is that the rules applicable in these areas must be seen as a result of an approach which takes into account the conflict of interests, and aims at resolving it in what appears to be the fairest and yet the most practical manner.

Of relevance in considering the scope of and limitations on the rule are several international judgments and arbitral decisions concerning diplomatic protection which have contributed to the jurisprudence on the subject, in addition to state practice, which is also reflected in pleadings before international courts and tribunals where the issues relating to the rule have not been decided.[19] There are also numerous cases decided under the European Convention on Human Rights and other conventions which deal with these matters.[20] On the other hand, the authorities on the incidence of the rule in regard to diplomatic protection are less definitive. The source material consists principally of limited state practice, reflected mainly in the pleadings of states before international tribunals[21] and of the discussions of text writers. Thus, while the law relating to the scope of and limitations on the rule, although not always absolutely settled, may have some cogent precedents to support it, the law relating to the incidence of the rule relies more on deduction from meagre practice and from theory. Nevertheless, it is possible, and necessary, to suggest some solutions to the problem of the incidence of the rule, because of the importance of the issue, taking into

---

[19] Decisions of the ICJ and of arbitral tribunals include the *Finnish Ships Arbitration* (*Finland* v. *Great Britain*), 3 UNRIAA p. 1479 (1934); the *Ambatielos Claim* (*Greece* v. *UK*), 12 UNRIAA p. 83 (1956); the *Norwegian Loans Case*, 1957 ICJ Reports p. 9; the *Interhandel Case*, 1959 ICJ Reports p. 6; the *ELSI Case*, 1998 ICJ Reports p. 15; and the *Arrest Warrant of 11 April 2000 Case*, 2002 ICJ Reports: www.cij-icj.org. Pleadings include those in the *Barcelona Traction Co. Case*, ICJ Pleadings (1962–9).

[20] See e.g. *Nielsen* v. *Denmark*, Application No. 343/57, 2 YBECHR at p. 439; *X* v. *FRG*, Application No. 232/56, 1 YBECHR at p. 143; and *X* v. *Sweden*, Application No. 434/58, 2 YBECHR at p. 354.

[21] See e.g. the *Aerial Incident Case*, ICJ Pleadings (1959).

account the historical antecedents of the rule, its primary purpose as a means of settling an international dispute by giving one party to it, a sovereign state, the opportunity to apply its own means of redress, and other considerations of policy. What is at stake is the right of the host or respondent state to insist on having an opportunity to redress an alien's grievance by its own judicial means in *any* circumstances in which an alien has a dispute with it. In the area of human rights protection, the issue of the incidence of the rule has been raised and pronounced on in some cases,[22] although there, in general, the problem of incidence does not seem to be as acute.

The exhaustion of procedural remedies, particularly in the same court, has been discussed at some length in the case law.[23] Procedural remedies are a special case of local or domestic remedies as such. The scope of the exhaustion required for procedural remedies and the limitations on the requirement of exhaustion have thus, in the circumstances, been given some special attention by the authorities. The real issue in this regard is whether the rules relating to the scope of exhaustion required for procedural remedies, and to the limitations on such exhaustion, are any different from those relating to remedies in general. The issue assumes importance because procedural remedies may involve a somewhat greater degree of technicality than remedies in general. This, however, is a very difficult area in which there is little agreement among the authorities. The fact that there is this disagreement among the authorities, even judicial, would seem to indicate that the subject is more complicated than might appear at first sight. What is in issue is whether the normal resolution of the conflicts of interests in the determination of the scope of, and limitations on, the rule in general should be modified by greater emphasis being given to the principle of avoiding undue hardship to the alien, in contradistinction to the principle which recognizes the sovereignty of the host or defendant state. Whatever the measure of relaxation permitted, if any, there seems to be some attraction in the idea that procedural remedies do deserve special treatment. It would appear that there is no easy solution by way of simply asserting, as some tend to do, that the exhaustion of procedural remedies in the same court is merely another manifestation of the exhaustion of remedies as such, which should, therefore, be governed by exactly the same principles as regards scope and limitations. That there seems to some minds to be

---

[22] See e.g. *Austria* v. *Italy*, Application No. 788/60, *Report of the Plenary Commission* (1963).
[23] See the *Ambatielos Claim* (*Greece* v. *UK*), 12 UNRIAA p. 83 (1956).

a doubt as to the propriety of this method of proceeding is cause for concern that the exhaustion of procedural remedies in the same court needs to be discussed separately, whatever the conclusions reached in answer to the problem.[24]

The principle that consent to the non-application of the rule by the host or respondent state results in the irrelevance of the rule may also be applicable. It is of importance to determine when the principle of consent is applicable, how far it is applicable, what its scope is and, in the case of human rights protection, perhaps whether it is relevant at all. Also related to the principle of consent in a general way is the situation where waiver is implied in the absence of a clear express waiver, as well as the doctrine of estoppel which may operate to relieve the alien or individual of the need to exhaust local or domestic remedies. Implied waiver and estoppel are of particular importance at the present time, since tribunals and courts increasingly seem to show a tendency carefully to investigate circumstances in which it is argued that the rule is inapplicable for these reasons, and to be ready to conclude that the rule cannot apply, where it is reasonable to do so on the basis of the circumstances of the case. The important questions raised concern the circumstances in which waiver will be implied, or where the doctrine of estoppel will be applied, and the presumptions that are relevant to the situation. There is some judicial authority on the principle of consent in relation to the rule of local or domestic remedies.[25]

An issue of some importance which has been considered by the authorities, both judicial and textual, is whether the rule applies when a declaratory judgment is sought from an international court or tribunal. The issue concerns the nature of the rule in the context of dispute settlement. Any discussion of the matter must take into account the consideration that the rule is primarily a means, in the settlement of an international dispute, of allocating functions to be performed by organs that are not international in a situation where the final word properly belongs to an international organ. While the respect shown for state sovereignty is of significance, the conflicting interests that have an impact here are not merely those of the alien and his national state, but also those of the international community in facilitating a solution in accordance with international norms in a manner which, while

---

[24] Procedural remedies are discussed in Chapter 9.

[25] The principles of consent, involving waiver, and of estoppel are dealt with in Chapter 10. The phenomena of bilateral investment treaties and the ICSID Convention are important in regard to waiver.

detracting as little as possible from the sovereignty of the host or respondent state, achieves effectiveness and upholds the primacy of the international legal order. A similar question that has arisen is whether the applicability of the rule depends on the nature of the international judicial forum invoked by the alien or individual or the applicant state in an international proceeding. These matters also constructively relate to implied consent.[26]

An important aspect of the rule of local remedies is the manner in which the exhaustion or non-exhaustion of remedies is to be proved before an international court or tribunal. The issue concerns the burden of proof. There has been some discussion of the matter in the case law in relation to the protection of aliens, but it is in the field of human rights protection that the burden of proof has been considered in some detail by the judicial and textual authorities. What has to be decided in this regard is how in a general way the conflict between the principles recognizing the rights of the host or respondent state flowing from sovereignty and the right of the alien not to be caused undue hardship is to be resolved. These two principles have clashed with particular force in this area, because the rule itself is conceived primarily as a recognition of the sovereignty of the host or respondent state which could lead to placing the total burden of proof on the alien, the individual or the applicant state, while it is also conceded that the proof of exhaustion of local remedies could concern matters which are peculiarly within the control and knowledge of the host or respondent state, and that, since it is primarily the host or respondent state that asserts and benefits from the rule of exhaustion of local remedies, the burden of proof may justifiably rest on that state. The solutions reached in the decisions, or proposed by authorities, have thus been of a practical nature rather than based on any hard and fast theory, and have also taken into account the position of the alien or individual in having to resort to remedies provided by the host or respondent state in a proceeding in reality of an international nature. The manner in which the question of the burden of proof has been dealt with reveals the delicate and complicated nature of the conflict of principles or interests involved in the application of the rule. At the same time, the solutions proposed in the area share so much of a practical character that it becomes difficult to postulate a single theoretical principle as the basis for them. The differences that

---

[26] Declaratory judgments and the nature of the international forum in relation to the rule are discussed in Chapter 10.

may or may not arise in the case of human rights protection have also been faced.[27]

There are a few miscellaneous procedural matters which have been considered by the various authorities. Such issues as when and whether the objection based on the non-exhaustion of remedies must be raised by the defendant state, when the question relating to the exhaustion of remedies may be decided, and the time at which the exhaustion of remedies must be completed, have been adverted to and dealt with in the context of both diplomatic protection and human rights protection. These problems have generally been approached in practical terms with the apparent object of balancing the conflicting interests involved, while the basically international nature of the dispute which demands that solutions appropriate to an international dispute settlement machinery be reached has been kept in mind. This means that, while due consideration is given to the principle relating to the sovereignty of the defendant or host state, other important and relevant principles are also taken into account.[28]

There is a chapter on the application of the rule to human rights protection.[29] The next chapter deals with the adaptation of the rule to the law of international organizations.[30] These two chapters constitute Part III.

Finally, the authorities, both judicial and textual, and state practice have focused on the issue of the formal character of the rule of local remedies. The discussion here centres around whether the rule is procedural or substantive or shares a dual character. The question is by no means entirely academic. On the answers given to the questions raised could apparently depend a variety of consequences of a practical nature, such as what has to be alleged and proved in an international proceeding in which the issue of non-exhaustion of remedies is raised. In this connection, the rule as applied to the protection of human rights has in recent years shed a special light on the problem, and this has tended to defuse some of the speculation surrounding the formal nature of the rule in the context of diplomatic protection, while at the same time restoring the proper perspectives to the discussion of the issue in that context. The nature of the rule is the subject of Chapter 15, in Part IV.

---

[27] The burden of proof is the subject of Chapter 11.
[28] These miscellaneous matters are dealt with in Chapter 12.
[29] Chapter 13.   [30] Chapter 14.

What is of special importance in the investigation of the formal character of the rule is the function of the rule as a mechanism for settling an international dispute at the national level. The policies which form the basis of the rule must be applied in finding a solution to the question in a manner which recognizes the primary purpose of the rule. Over-emphasis on one or the other interest should not be permitted to blur the proper perspective of the rule. The discussion centres around the manner in which the rule operates as a tool of the international legal system designed to achieve certain objectives postulated by the international legal order, rather than as an abstraction committed to one particular end of protecting the concept of state sovereignty or any other concerned interest.

Some concluding remarks are made in Part V, Chapter 16.

2 The evolution of the law relating to local remedies

The origin and historical evolution of the law relating to local remedies provides an interesting instance of how some modern rules of international law came into existence and took their present form.[1] The
requirement that local remedies should be resorted to seems to have
been recognized in the early history of Europe, before the modern national state had been born, in the relations between sovereign territories or individual communities, in regard to the granting of authority
to take reprisals. It is to the ancient practice of reprisals that the historical roots of the modern rule of local remedies is apparently to be
traced. While even in primitive societies there is evidence that reprisals
as an expression of self-help and of communal solidarity were carried
out without the imposition of restrictions,[2] later they became associated with the notion that aliens were entitled to have justice done to
them when they had been wronged. Reprisals consequently came to be
permitted when an alien had suffered a denial of justice as a condition
precedent.[3] Reprisals could no longer be regarded as purely private acts
of revenge. They were taken and became lawful only provided they were
authorized by the sovereign of the injured alien and only when there
was a failure on the part of the sovereign of the wrongdoer to accord

---

[1] The development of the law on local remedies has been reviewed in considerable detail
by Cançado Trindade, 'Origin and Historical Development of the Rule of Exhaustion of
Local Remedies in International Law', 12 RBDI (1976) p. 499. That article attempts to
give a historical account of the birth and establishment of the rule as a rule of
diplomatic protection of nationals.

[2] Spiegel, 'Origin and Development of Denial of Justice', 32 AJIL (1938) at p. 64; McNair,
International Law Opinions (1956), vol. 2, p. 297.

[3] See de la Brière, 'Evolution de la doctrine et de la pratique en matière de représailles',
22 *Hague Recueil* (1928) at pp. 253ff.

22

justice to the alien.[4] Public authority thus became involved to the extent
that it authorized and limited private acts of revenge. Although reprisals
became associated with the notion of a right, such right could only be
exercised if local authorities and judges had refused to recognize the
rights of the alien.[5] There are on record some treaties made as early as
the ninth century between sovereign territories in Italy which clearly
linked the exercise of reprisals to cases where a subject of one party had
been denied justice in the territory of the other.[6] What was envisaged,
it seems, was that the injured party must have suffered in the territory
of the foreign sovereign a private wrong in respect of which the foreign
sovereign had failed to do justice.

In the thirteenth and fourteenth centuries there is more evidence of
both the regulation of reprisals and of the required relationship between
the denial of justice and the practice of reprisals.[7] The case between
Arnald de Sancto Martino and the Castillians[8] which occurred during
this period provides a good illustration of how the system of reprisals
worked at that time. Arnald de Sancto Martino and other Bayonnese
complained to King Edward I of England against the seizure of goods and
injury to property by the Castillians. The English King, in spite of several

---

[4] The practice of letters of marque granted by the sovereign authorizing reprisals
became common at this time: see McNair, note 2 above, at p. 297.

[5] See e.g. Spiegel, note 2 above, at pp. 64ff.

[6] The Treaty of 836 between Sicard of Benevent and the Neapolitans; and the Treaty of
840 between Emperor Lotar I and the Doge Petrus Tradenicus of Venice. The Treaty of
1001 between Venice and Bishop Grausa of Ceneda was of the same kind. For these
treaties, see Spiegel, note 2 above, at pp. 64ff. and 68ff.

[7] See e.g. two decrees of King Alfonso IX of Leon of 1188 and 1230 and a resolution of
1225 in Catalonia (King Jayme I), cited in Spiegel, note 2 above, at p. 66; a letter of King
Edward I of England concerning reprisals against the Portuguese, cited in Clark, 'The
English Practice with Regard to Reprisals by Private Persons', 27 AJIL (1933) p. 694 at pp.
694ff., where reference is also made to subsequent documents linking private reprisals
with the failure of local redress; a treaty of 1265 between the Hanse cities Stralsund
and Demmin for the protection of commerce, cited in *Die Recesse und andere Akten der
Hansetage von 1256–1430* (1870), vol. 1, pp. 5ff.; an Anglo-French Treaty of 1235, cited by
Redslob, *Histoire des grands principes du droit des gens* (1923) p. 189; the treaty of
commerce of 1236 between Tripoli and Geneva and the treaty of commerce of 1256
between Tripoli and Venice, cited in *ibid.*, pp. 189ff.; an agreement of 1195 between
Brescia and Ferrara (in which private reprisals were abolished), cited in Nys, *Les origines
du droit international* (1894) p. 65; and a statute of 1353 in the reign of King Edward III
of England restricting reprisals, cited in Spiegel, note 2 above, at pp. 67ff. In 1333, King
Edward III of England had protested a letter of reprisal issued by the King of Aragon on
the ground that England had not refused reparation: referred to in Redslob, above, at
p. 190 and Nys, above, at p. 67.

[8] See Clark, note 7 above, at pp. 705ff.

efforts, failed to obtain justice for the victim from the authorities in Castille. After the lapse of a considerable period during which the victim failed to get his case settled, in 1316 King Edward II of England, to whom the matter was then referred, ordered that the goods of a Castillian citizen in Portsmouth, as well as all the goods and merchandise of the men and merchants of the Castillian King which came into Vasconia, be seized in order to and to the extent necessary to make full satisfaction to the claimant for his loss. As in this case, there is ample evidence that by the fourteenth century the claimant was expected first to seek justice in the appropriate court of his adversaries' town before applying to his own authorities for help in the event that he failed to obtain it.[9]

In the fifteenth century the practice of restricting reprisals to situations where justice had been denied continued, as seen in the case of de Waghen and the Leydenese.[10] The claimant had failed to get satisfaction for an unpaid debt for a long period, when King Henry V in 1414 espoused his claim and instructed his officers to seize in reprisal the goods of the Leydenese within English territory and hand them over to the claimant on account of his debt.[11] In the sixteenth century the practice in regard to reprisals connected with wrongs done to foreigners was predicated on similar premises, as is illustrated by the letter of reprisal granted by King James IV of Scotland in 1560[12] which stated that the issue of the letter was based on a failure to grant redress for injuries and to restore the goods spoiled. It was made clear at the same time that the claimant should exhaust all local means of redress by suing at law and use all possible means of recovering his ship. So rigid had the general practice become that during this century, while text writers frowned on the practice of reprisals as being hazardous or as acts of war, they agreed that resort could be had to reprisals only where there had been a failure on the part of a state or a sovereign to remedy a prior

---

[9] Gardiner, 'The History of Belligerent Rights on the High Seas in the Fourteenth Century', 48 LQR (1932) p. 521 at p. 538. Clark, note 7 above, at pp. 709ff. gives some examples of treaties relating to the settlement of disputes of nationals abroad and limiting the use of force to cases where justice could not be secured by regular means.

[10] An account of this case is given in Clark, note 7 above, at p. 707.

[11] For other cases of a similar nature which occurred at about the same period, see Clark, note 7 above, at pp. 712ff.

[12] McNair, note 2 above, at p. 297. See also a letter of reprisal granted by Queen Elizabeth I of England in 1565 to some merchants against the Portuguese: Clark, note 7 above, at pp. 717ff.; and an Anglo-French treaty of 1559 which stated in Article XVII that letters of reprisal were to be issued from then onwards only in the event of a manifest denial of justice: *ibid.*

wrong[13] and that they were a solution because that state had through its jurisdiction not prevented the misdeeds of its citizens or had failed to right a wrong.[14]

During this early period when the law relating to alien protection was in its infancy and strictly confined to reprisals, certain significant features were recognizable which, while they marked the law's immaturity, yet showed some signs of its developing into the form which the modern law has taken. First, the record seems to indicate that all the cases in which reprisals were taken involved situations in which the original complaint upon which the ultimate action taken was based was a wrong committed by one private party against another. It was not a wrong committed by the sovereign or the state against an individual claiming protection. It may be noted that the modern law of alien protection concerns both the situation where an alien is initially injured by a private party and that in which the state commits the initial wrong, two situations which may require slightly different treatments.

Secondly, while the public element of the wrong was strongly characterized by the focus of attention being on the failure of the sovereign or state to render justice to the alien, nevertheless, the action taken by reprisal was against the property of private individuals and not against the delinquent state or sovereign. There was no attempt to secure reparation directly from the latter at any point once the claim was taken up by the alien's protector. Rather, action was immediately taken against individuals belonging to the sovereign's or state's community. While action was taken against the community which may be regarded as action against the state or sovereign, the important point is that no attempt was made to take action against, particularly, the state or sovereign *per se*.

Thirdly, in general the authority given in the permission to take reprisals was apparently to recover property only to repair the original damage done by the private party or parties. No account was taken of the delinquency perpetrated by the sovereign or state in whose territory the original wrong was committed in not redressing the wrong through its jurisdiction. In the exercise of reprisals it was redress of the original wrong committed by one private party against another that was considered necessary, not of the total injury committed by the responsible sovereign or state in failing to do justice. This was so, although

---

[13] De Vitoria, *De Jure Belli* (1532), as cited in Scott, *The Spanish Origin of International Law – Francisco de Vitoria and his Law of Nations* (1934) p. lxiv.

[14] Gentili, *De Jure Belli Libri Tres*, as cited in Scott, *The Classics of International Law* (1933), vol. 2, book I, p. 100.

reprisals were directed not simply against the private party or parties who perpetrated the original wrong but against members of their whole community and, therefore, had a public element and character. There was no sophisticated distinction such as appears in the modern law between, for instance, the original private wrong and a manifest denial of justice by state organs which, under the present law, is what requires reparation as a delinquency committed by one state against the national state of the alien over and above the original private wrong.

Fourthly, the cases show that the rule of local remedies was applied almost without exception only in situations where the alien seeking protection was resident or physically present in the territory where the original wrong took place. There are no examples where the rule was regarded as applicable when the original injury did not take place in the territory of the sovereign or state against which reprisals were ordered.

Fifthly, there is practically no evidence of any exceptions being made to the requirement that local remedies should be exhausted. Clearly, where justice was not made available because of the refusal of the local sovereign to have the case heard in his courts, the cases seem to support the view that there was a denial of justice which would have warranted the taking of reprisals. On the other hand, there is no clear example of reprisals being permitted where it was felt or found that a recourse to the judicial means of settlement would have been, for whatever reason, futile.

Finally, it was not entirely clear to what extent the remedies in the territory where the original offence had been committed had to be resorted to nor what was the nature of the remedies to be exhausted. Most of the incidents that took place seem to have involved failure to activate judicial remedies rather than any other kind of remedies. It is also not always clear whether the alien should have exhausted all judicial remedies up to the highest level or whether he should merely have tested them, although in many cases reference is formally made to 'exhaustion' of remedies.

In the seventeenth and eighteenth centuries, with the rise of the nation state, the treaty practice of states indicates that the restriction on reprisals continued and reprisals were permitted only where the claimant had failed to secure justice or there had been undue delay in obtaining justice. Thus, an Anglo-Spanish treaty of 1667 permitted reprisals in case of undue delays in obtaining justice and when no satisfaction had been given within a period of six months from the invocation of the judicial instance.[15] However, with the growing concentration of power in the centralized structure of the state, the practice of private reprisals, albeit authorized by the sovereign in the state, was gradually replaced by governmental action taken exclusively to protect nationals when abroad.[16] As a consequence, by the beginning of the eighteenth century, the taking of private reprisals ceased to be authorized and its place was generally taken by the authorization to take reprisals being granted to ships of the sovereign's fleet.[17] However, the requirement that local means of redress had to be exhausted, which was associated with the earlier practice of private reprisals, survived and continued to persist in the law of public reprisals and the law of alien protection as it developed in the eighteenth century and beyond.

These developments in the law of reprisals and the retention of the requirement that local remedies should be exhausted before even public reprisals were authorized or any other form of action was taken were reflected clearly in the writings of the publicists of that era. For example, Grotius[18] in 1625 confirmed the right of reprisals, while explaining that in the event of a debt due from any civil society or its head all the goods of the members of the society became bound and liable, although reprisals could only be taken if a judgment against a debtor or criminal could not be obtained within a reasonable time or if the judgment obtained had been given plainly against right.[19] Further, by the end of the eighteenth century, there is evidence that the practice of reprisals was beginning to be replaced by diplomatic intervention or settlement by international arbitration, although aliens seeking the intervention of

---

[15] Parry, 10 CTS (1969) p. 116. See, for other examples, a treaty of 1664 between Spain and the Netherlands: 8 CTS pp. 200ff.; a treaty of 1667 between Sweden and the Netherlands: 10 CTS p. 207; a treaty between Great Britain and Spain of 1670: Clark, note 7 above, at p. 711; a treaty of 1673 between Spain and the Netherlands: 13 CTS p. 41; and a treaty of 1678 between France and the Netherlands: 14 CTS p. 404.

[16] See C. de Visscher, *Théories et réalités en droit international public* (1970) p. 299.

[17] See Clark, note 7 above, at pp. 721ff.

[18] *De Jure Belli ac Pacis – Liber Tertius* (trans. W. Whewell) (1853), vol. 3, II, II, pp. 42ff.; II, III, pp. 44ff.; II, IV, p. 48; and II, V, pp. 48ff. The practice as reflected in the legal opinions of the same period follows the view taken by Grotius: see McNair, note 2 above, at pp. 297ff. and 312.

[19] Other authorities who more or less supported the view taken by Grotius were Zouche, *Juris et Judicii Fecialis, sive Juris inter Gentes, et Questionum de eodem Explicatio* (1650) (trans. Brierly, 1911), vol. 2, p. 115; van Bynkershoek, *Quaestionum Juris Publici Libri Duo* (1737) (trans. Franck, 1930), vol. 2, pp. 133ff.; Wolff, *Jus Gentium Methodo Scientifica Pertractatum* (1749) (trans. Drake, 1934), vol. 2, pp. 302ff.; and Vattel, *Le Droit des gens, ou principes de la loi naturelle* (1756) (reprinted, 1863), vol. 2, pp. 62, 83ff., 320ff., 329ff. and 338.

their national state in circumstances in which reprisals would have in the past been considered had still to exhaust local remedies.[20]

During this period, the institution of reprisals became public as opposed to being private, but the pre-condition that local remedies should be exhausted before reprisals were taken was retained. While the law relating to the exhaustion of local remedies had not changed to any appreciable extent and had the same characteristics as before the seventeenth century, it would seem that towards the end of this period there came to be an incipient emphasis on the notion of a manifest denial of justice in relation to the original private wrong as a requirement in addition to the plain exhaustion of local remedies. On the other hand, there is also to be observed the beginning of a detachment of the requirement of exhaustion of local remedies from the practice of reprisals and its transfer to the institution of diplomatic protection as a peaceful means of settling disputes. There can also be detected, at least in the views of publicists, a growing recognition in an explicit manner that there were exceptional circumstances in which local remedies did not have to be exhausted because of the nature of the remedies available. While delay of justice was an obvious example, it may be that the law was beginning to come to terms with the situations which in modern law permit exceptions to the rule of local remedies.

The diplomatic practice of the nineteenth and twentieth centuries shows that the requirement that local remedies should be exhausted by an alien had become a firmly established part of the international law of diplomatic protection. The era of reprisals for wrongs done to aliens had passed and the rule that had been attached as a condition precedent to the exercise of reprisals, whether privately organized or publicly pursued, in an age when the use of force was still a common method of settling disputes was transferred in its entirety to the area of diplomatic protection and judicial disposition of disputes which were essentially peaceful means of settling disputes lacking the resort to force. It is in the early nineteenth century that the rule of local remedies

---

[20] See Article VI of the Jay Treaty of 1794 between Great Britain and the US, which reaffirmed the view that where debts due to creditors were being claimed compensation was not to be awarded when the non-exhaustion of local remedies by the claimants was to be regarded as a predominant cause of the losses incurred. In 1793, shortly before the Jay Treaty, the US Secretary of State wrote to the British Minister that 'a foreigner, before he applies for extraordinary interposition, should use his best endeavours to obtain the justice he claims from the ordinary tribunals of the country': cited in Moore, *International Law* (1906), vol. 6, p. 259.

became established as a part of diplomatic protection, separate from the law of reprisals.

There are numerous examples, beginning in the early years of the nineteenth century, of the practice of the United Kingdom according to which it interposed the requirement that local remedies must be exhausted prior to the exercise of diplomatic protection. Most of those cases involved British citizens abroad, who had sought diplomatic intervention on their behalf,[21] but the requirement had also been insisted on in connection with aliens within the United Kingdom who claimed the protection of their own national states.[22] On a few occasions, the rule was held to have been inapplicable and, therefore, no bar to diplomatic intervention, because local remedies were insufficient, ineffective or futile, as a result of undue delays or procedural irregularities.[23] These latter instances are clear indications that diplomatic practice had come to recognize that there were situations in which the rule could be circumvented or in which there were exceptions to the applicability of the rule. There is further evidence that the United Kingdom has adhered to the rule of exhaustion of local remedies in its twentieth-century diplomatic practice both in cases of protection of its own nationals and where another state has attempted to intervene diplomatically on behalf of its nationals.[24] It may be noted that the rule issued by the UK Foreign and

---

[21] See in particular Parry (ed.), *Law Officers' Opinions* (1970), 12 pp. 53ff.; 17 pp. 5ff.; 22 pp. 414ff., 486ff. and 506ff.; 32 pp. 225ff. and 593ff.; 34 pp. 174ff.; 43 pp. 208ff.; 53 pp. 114ff., 188ff. and 200ff.; 59 pp. 505ff.; 72 pp. 240ff.; 79 pp. 20ff.; 80 pp. 5ff., 73ff., 252ff. and 298ff.; 81 pp. 293ff.; 82 pp. 162ff.; 83 pp. 9ff., 122ff. and 203ff.; 94 pp. 199ff.; and 95 pp. 40ff.; and McNair, note 2 above, at pp. 312ff.

[22] E.g. the *Alexander Newski Case* (1806), in Parry, note 21 above, at 62 pp. 17ff. See also *ibid.*, 54 pp. 225ff.; and Parry and Fitzmaurice (eds.), *A British Digest of International Law* (1965), Part VI, vol. 6, p. 278.

[23] See e.g. Parry, note 21 above, at 79 pp. 380ff., 81 pp. 113ff.; McNair, note 2 above, at pp. 314ff.; Bruns (ed.), *Fontes Juris Gentium (Digest of the Diplomatic Correspondence of the European States – 1856 to 71)* (1932), Series B, section I, vol. I, Part I, pp. 929ff.; and Bruns (ed.), *Fontes Juris Gentium (Digest of Diplomatic Correspondence of the European States – 1871 to 78)* (1937), Series B, section II, vol. II, Part II, pp. 377ff.

[24] In connection with the seizure of some US ships in 1916, the UK government sent a memorandum to the US Secretary of State in which it stated: 'His Majesty's Government attach the utmost importance to the maintenance of the rule that, when an effective mode of redress is open to individuals in the courts of a civilized country by which they can obtain adequate satisfaction for any invasion of their rights, recourse must be made to the mode of redress so provided before there is any scope for diplomatic action.' 10 AJIL (1916), Sp. Supp. p. 120 at p. 139. See also the case of the arrest of a British trawler by Iceland in 1962: E. Lauterpacht (ed.), *The Contemporary Practice of the United Kingdom in the Field of International Law* (1962) pp. 65ff.; the case of a construction contract between British nationals and the US government: *ibid.*, p. 56;

Commonwealth Office in 1971 stated quite categorically that the UK government would not espouse a claim by a UK national against another state 'until all the remedies available to him in the state concerned (i.e. national remedies) have been exhausted' but that, if in the process of exhausting those remedies the claimant had encountered a 'denial of justice', the government might intervene on his behalf to secure redress of injustice.[25]

Among other states in Europe, France has invoked the rule on several occasions both in regard to the protection of its own nationals abroad and in respect of claims of other states on behalf of their own nationals. Thus, in 1934 the legal office of the Ministry of Foreign Affairs decided that, in a dispute between a foreign government and a consortium of French companies, as the latter had not exhausted all local remedies in the foreign country and as a manifest denial of justice had not been established, there remained no ground for diplomatic intervention on their behalf.[26] At the Hague Codification Conference of

report of the Minister of State for Foreign Affairs in 1964 in another case of a British national: Lauterpacht and White (eds.), 2 BPIL (1964) pp. 206ff.; the case of the trial of a British Somali subject in Ethiopia: Lauterpacht, 'The Contemporary Practice of the United Kingdom in the Field of International Law – Survey and Comment', 5 ICLQ (1956) p. 405 at p. 426; and the case of a British national claiming an interest in property which was the subject of an action in the Dutch courts: Lauterpacht and White (eds.), 5 BPIL (1967) pp. 109ff. Rule VII of the UK Government's Rules Applying to International Claims of October 1985 and the comment attached to it state:

> [The UK Government] will not normally take over and formally espouse a claim of a UK national against another State until all the legal remedies, if any, available to him in the State concerned have been exhausted.
>
> *Comment* Failure to exhaust any local remedies will not constitute a bar to a claim if it is clearly established that in the circumstances of the case an appeal to a higher municipal tribunal would have had no effect. Nor is a claimant against another State required to exhaust justice in that State if there is no justice to exhaust.

Cited in Warbrick, 'Protection of Nationals Abroad', 37 ICLQ (1988) at p. 1008.

[25] See Rules VII and VIII: Harris, *Cases and Materials on International Law* (1973) p. 478. A comment attached to Rule VII states that the failure to exhaust local remedies will not be a bar to intervention if it is clearly established that 'in the circumstances of the case an appeal to a higher municipal tribunal would have had no effect'.

[26] See Kiss, *Répertoire de la pratique française en matière de droit international public* (1965), vol. 3, pp. 455ff. Other cases are cited in the same work. One concerns a French national arrested in Haiti: *ibid.*, pp. 499ff. See also *ibid.*, pp. 453ff., 491, 495, 500ff. and 604ff. for other cases. The treaty practice of France which refers to the requirement of exhaustion of local remedies as a condition precedent to diplomatic intervention may also be cited. See e.g. Article 5 of a 1928 treaty between France and the Netherlands and other examples: Kiss, pp. 491 and 499.

1930, the representative of France in addressing the Third Committee declared categorically that 'there can be no action regarding the State's responsibility until the series of available remedies has been entirely exhausted'.[27] The French government has also espoused the view that, where local remedies were not sufficient and adequate and where local legislation left no remedy to exhaust, intervention could take place.[28]

Such nineteenth- and twentieth-century practice of other European states, for example Italy and Switzerland, to which access may be had also shows that there is considerable support in their diplomatic practice for the rule of local remedies as a condition precedent to diplomatic intervention where such remedies are feasible and effective.[29]

The diplomatic practice of the US in the nineteenth century demonstrates that in numerous cases the rule of local remedies was regarded as preventing diplomatic intervention where it had not been observed.[30] On the other hand, the US government was equally emphatic that, as Secretary of State Fish declared in 1873, 'a claimant in a foreign State is not required to exhaust justice in such State when there is no justice to exhaust'.[31] This exception covered situations in which local remedies had been superseded[32] or were deemed insufficient.[33] The diplomatic practice of the US in the twentieth century does not seem to have changed to any significant degree in regard to the applicability of the rule of local remedies. Thus, in a memorandum of 1961 concerning the protection of US nationals in Cuba, the US Department of State affirmed that 'The requirement for exhaustion of legal remedies is based upon the generally accepted rule of international law that international responsibility may

---

[27] See *Acts of the Conference for the Codification of International Law, Minutes of the Third Committee*, LN Doc. C351(c).M.145(c).1930.V, vol. 4, pp. 65ff.

[28] See the 1872 case of a Franco-Italian company operating in Greece: Kiss, note 26 above, vol. 3, pp. 495ff.

[29] For the Italian practice, see the case cited in note 28 above and the cases cited in *La Prassi Italiana di Diritto Internazionale* (1970), vol. 2, pp. 660ff., 663 and 666ff. For the Swiss practice, see the statement of the Swiss Federal Council of 1849, cited in Sarhan, *L'épuisement des recours internes en matière de responsabilité internationale* (1962) p. 33; and the 1972 note by the Division of Legal Affairs of the Département politique fédéral of the Swiss Government: Caflisch, 'La pratique suisse en matière de droit international public – 1972', ASDI (1973) at pp. 359ff.

[30] See the more than fifteen cases cited in Moore, note 20 above, vol. 6, pp. 652ff.

[31] *Ibid.*, p. 677.   [32] *Ibid.*, p. 682.

[33] *Ibid.*, p. 691. The US practice of this period seems to have been in accord with the view that the rule of local remedies was excepted where there had been a denial of justice: *ibid.*, pp. 661 and 666ff. However, the notion of 'denial of justice' was not clearly defined in its entirety.

not be invoked as regards reparation for losses or damages sustained by a foreigner until after exhaustion of the remedies available under local law'.[34]

Canada has also supported the rule of local remedies in its practice. For example, in 1967, in the case of a Canadian claim against an Eastern European state, the Canadian Under-Secretary for External Affairs advised that under the well-established principles of international law the requirement of prior exhaustion of all local remedies must have been fulfilled to justify the espousal of a claim by diplomatic intervention by one state on behalf of its nationals against another state.[35]

The nineteenth- and twentieth-century practice of Latin American states relating to the rule of exhaustion of local remedies has evolved in terms of both the claims of aliens in Latin American states as well as the claims of nationals of such states abroad.[36] In the mid-nineteenth

---

[34] See Kerley, 'Contemporary Practice of the United States Relating to International Law', 56 AJIL (1962) pp. 166ff. There are many examples of diplomatic incidents in the twentieth century in which the US Government supported the rule of local remedies as a preventive factor in the exercise of diplomatic protection: see e.g. Moore, note 20 above, vol. 6, pp. 672ff.; Hackworth, *Digest* (1943), vol. 5, pp. 501, 505ff. and 510ff.; Whiteman, *Digest of International Law* (1970), vol. 8, pp. 769ff. Examples of the application of the rule in early twentieth-century US practice are also given in Borchard, *The Diplomatic Protection of Citizens Abroad* (1916) pp. 817ff.

[35] Gotlieb (ed.), 'Canadian Practice in International Law During 1967 as Reflected in Correspondence and Statements of the Department of External Affairs', 6 CYIL (1968) at p. 263. See also a 1964 case concerning a claim for compensation against the Government of India for loss of income by a Canadian national from interests in India, where the same sentiments were reiterated: Gotlieb (ed.), 'Canadian Practice in International Law During 1964 as Reflected in Correspondence and Statements of the Department of External Affairs', 3 CYIL (1965) at pp. 326ff. For other cases in which the applicability of the rule was reaffirmed, see *ibid.*, p. 327; Gotlieb (ed.), 'Canadian Practice in International Law During 1966 as Reflected in Correspondence and Statements of the Department of External Affairs', 5 CYIL (1967) at pp. 264ff.; and Beesley, 'Canadian Practice in International Law During 1969 as Reflected in Correspondence and Statements of the Department of External Affairs', 8 CYIL (1970) p. 337 at p. 359. In 1968, the Canadian Department of External Affairs stated in general that 'when a Canadian citizen brings to our attention a *prima facie* valid claim against a foreign State in respect of which he has exhausted all local remedies without success, it may be decided to intervene informally through the exercise of good offices or formally through the espousal of the claim in accordance with established principles of international law': Gotlieb and Beesley (eds.), 'Canadian Practice in International Law During 1968 as Reflected in Correspondence and Statements of the Department of External Affairs', 7 CYIL (1969) at pp. 314ff.

[36] See Yepes, 'Les Problèmes fondamentaux du droit des gens en Amérique', 47 *Hague Recueil* (1934) at pp. 107ff.; and Ministério das Relações Exteriores (Brazil), *Pareceres dos Consultores Jurídicos do Ministério das Relações Exteriores 1946–51* (1967) pp. 539ff.

century, the practice was common among Latin American states of enacting legislation incorporating the principle that local remedies should be exhausted.[37] Towards the end of that century a large number of treaties were signed which embodied the rule that local remedies should be exhausted. These treaties recognized that state responsibility was engaged by denial of justice and emphasized the need to resort to local remedies where injuries had been suffered by aliens.[38] There were also numerous international conferences at which the principle of exhaustion of local remedies was firmly and unequivocally asserted by these states.[39] Particular attention may be drawn to the majority opinion delivered in 1961 by the OAS Inter-American Juridical Committee on the contribution of the American continent to the principles of international law governing

---

[37] See OAS Doc. OEA/Ser.I/V 1.2-CIJ-61, January 1962, p. 39; Freeman, *The International Responsibility of States for Denial of Justice* (1938) p. 56; and Yepes, note 36 above, at p. 106. Reference may also be made to the 'Calvo clause', which was an extension of the local remedies rule and which was extensively used in Latin American practice: see Calvo, *Le Droit international théorique et pratique* (1896), vol. 1, pp. 267 and 322ff., vol. 3, pp. 140 and 142ff., and vol. 4, p. 231; Lipstein, 'The Place of the Calvo Clause in International Law', 22 BYIL (1945) p. 130; Shea, *The Calvo Clause* (1955) pp. 258ff.; Law, *The Local Remedies Rule in International Law* (1961) pp. 127ff.; Sarhan, note 29 above, at p. 77; Jiménez de Aréchaga, 'International Responsibility', in Sørensen (ed.), *Manual of Public International Law* (1968) p. 531 at pp. 590ff.; and Chappez, *La Règle de l'épuisement des voies de recours internes* (1972) pp. 76, 81ff.

[38] Treaties with European states are referred to in Yepes, note 36 above, at pp. 104ff.; and Panayotacos, *La Règle de l'épuisement des voies de recours internes* (1952) p. 56. Treaties among Latin American countries themselves are referred to in Yepes, note 36 above, at p. 103. Such treaties are also mentioned in Freeman, note 37 above, at pp. 490ff. and 495; and Irizarry y Puente, 'The Concept of "Denial of Justice" in Latin America', 43 *Michigan Law Review* (1944) at pp. 386ff. and 392ff. It would appear that the rule has also been waived by agreement in Latin American practice: see Nielsen, *International Law Applied to Reclamations* (1933) p. 70; and Feller, *The Mexican Claims Commissions (1923–1934)* (1935) p. 34. Article VII of the Inter-American Treaty on Pacific Settlement of 1948 makes diplomatic intervention on behalf of nationals abroad conditional upon the prior exhaustion of domestic remedies: see OAS Doc. OEA/Ser.I/VI.2-CIJ-61 (1962) p. 40. There were, however, reservations by some states, including the US, to this provision: see *Inter-American Juridical Yearbook (1952–1954)* pp. 60ff., and *(1955–1957)* pp. 96ff.; and Miaja de la Muela, 'El Agotamiento de los Recursos Internos como Supuesto de las Reclamaciones Internacionales', *Anuario Uruguayo de Derecho Internacional* (1963) at pp. 51ff.

[39] See e.g. the First Conference (1889–90), Second Conference (1901–2), Sixth Conference (1928), Seventh Conference (1933) and Eighth Conference (1938), where the rule of local remedies was either referred to or embodied in an Article in a convention: see Scott (ed.), *The International Conferences of American States (1889–1928)* (1931) pp. 45ff.; Yepes, note 36 above, at pp. 93ff.; Fabela, *Intervention* (1961) pp. 156ff. and 178; and OAS Doc. OEA/Ser.I/VI.2-CIJ-61 (1962) p. 39.

the responsibility of the state, which represented the views of sixteen Latin American countries and emphatically made all diplomatic claims subject to the principle of prior exhaustion of local remedies.[40]

The development of the customary rule of local redress in the nineteenth and early twentieth centuries was associated entirely with the exercise of diplomatic protection of aliens. There were significant developments besides. While the applicability of the rule was affirmed, two clear novel concepts associated with it seem to have emerged. First, more frequent mention is made in certain cases of the notion of a denial of justice (manifest or otherwise) as an additional requirement for diplomatic intervention on behalf of aliens. Secondly, at least outside Latin America there has been evident what may be called a growing impatience with the rule which has led to the formulation of exceptions to its applicability or of situations in which local remedies need not be pursued till they are exhausted, while at the same time there can also be seen a clearer emphasis on the relevance of the rule to the law of diplomatic protection of aliens. On the other hand, the requirements for exhaustion, including the reference to a denial of justice, in certain instances have not acquired clearer definition in the diplomatic practice, nor has the exact scope of the rule or the conditions for its incidence been approached to any considerable extent in that practice, although there have been instances when the rule has been regarded as applicable even where the wrong done to the aliens had been committed outside the territory of the respondent state. Furthermore, while reference is made to exceptional situations in which local remedies need not be exhausted, there does not seem to be universal and unequivocal agreement either on the exceptions themselves or on the definition of their content.

While state practice recognized the rule of local remedies in regard to diplomatic protection from the early nineteenth century and there were several instances of arbitral tribunals having to deal with diplomatic

---

[40] OAS Doc. OEA/Ser.I/VI.2-CIJ-61 (1962) pp. 37ff. The US government did not subscribe to this opinion but its views were recorded in a supplementary opinion of the Committee given in 1965: OAS Doc. OEA/Ser.I/VI.2-CIJ-78 (1965) pp. 1ff. The opposition of the US government to the Latin American views is set forth in *Dept. State Bull.* (1959) pp. 666ff. In attempts to codify the law of state responsibility, the view of Latin American countries left clear traces: see Guerrero (rapporteur), 'Report of the Sub-Committee to the League of Nations Committee of Experts for the Progressive Codification of International Law', LN Doc. C.46.M.23.1926.V, in Rosenne (ed.), *League of Nations Committee of Experts for the Progressive Codification of International Law* (1972), vol. 2, pp. 116ff.; García Amador, 'First Report on State Responsibility', YBILC (1956), vol. 2, p. 205.

protection under treaties referring cases to them from as early as 1802,[41] the first case which can be found in which an arbitral tribunal gave judicial recognition to the rule is the *Montano Case*[42] between Peru and the US. The decision in the case was handed down in 1863, i.e. in the second half of the nineteenth century. Thus, recognition in any form of judicial settlement of disputes came some time after it had been assimilated into diplomatic protection by extra-judicial, i.e. diplomatic, means.

There have been other developments, mainly in the twentieth century, which have led to a stronger reaffirmation of the rule and at the same time have amplified, refined and clarified diplomatic practice, where it had been ambiguous, doubtful or silent. Some of these developments may even tend to overshadow the significance, if not the importance, of the recent diplomatic practice in the area.

As already noted in the first chapter, the rule has been extended by conventional agreement, whether directly or indirectly, to the area of human rights protection, which means that the customary rule, originally confined to the law relating to the protection of aliens against states which are not their national states, has become relevant in areas in which nationals are protected against even their own national states. The consequence of this may be to bring to bear on the rule of local remedies certain assumptions and basic premises which are different from those inherent in the law of diplomatic protection, in so far as nationals may be expected to have a closer and more fundamental relationship to their own national states than aliens to states which are not theirs. On the other hand, it is important to keep in mind that even in the field of human rights protection what has been imported is explicitly the rule of customary international law which has been applied to the protection of aliens against states which are not their national states. It is a pertinent observation, however, that those decision-makers who are implementing the rule of local remedies in the context of the protection of human rights, where often a national is complaining against his own national state, have tended sometimes to take an innovative approach

---

[41] This was an arbitration under the Jay Treaty (1794) between Great Britain and the US. It was concluded with a settlement by a treaty of 1802, not with a decision of the tribunal: see Stuyt, *Survey of International Arbitrations 1794–1989* (1990) p. 2, No. 2. Before the *Montano Case*, cited below, there were several other arbitrations involving diplomatic protection: e.g. Stuyt, above, Nos. 5, 6, 9, 10, 33, 47, 50, 55 and 56. None concerned the rule of local remedies.

[42] Moore, *International Arbitrations* (1808), vol. 2, p. 1624.

to the application of the rule. The evidence will be examined later in this work. Suffice it to state here that in the protection of human rights the individual must be considered to be as vulnerable or as safe *vis-à-vis* his own national state as is an alien in relation to a foreign state, as far as the efficacy of justice is concerned, and sometimes even more vulnerable.

An important element of diplomatic practice emerged in 1933 when Germany filed before the Permanent Court of International Justice (PCIJ) an application against Poland concerning the treatment of a Polish national belonging to a minority and protected by the relevant Geneva Conventions. The case was withdrawn before a decision was taken on the preliminary objections or on the merits, although orders were made in the case.[43] The two parties could not agree on whether the rule of local remedies was applicable to the situation, as is shown by the pleadings in the case.[44] The disagreement in the arguments reflects also a disagreement on the practice relating to the incidence of the rule of local remedies. The attitude of the Polish government supported a practice which recognized that the rule of local remedies was applicable by implication to the protection of minorities under the Geneva Conventions, even though the treaties did not specifically incorporate it, presumably on the analogy of diplomatic protection. The attitude of the German government reflected the opposite view of the customary practice. Thus, it is arguable that the diplomatic practice on the particular issue of the protection of minorities was not settled. There are in addition several cases filed before the PCIJ and the ICJ in which conflicting arguments on the application of the rule of local remedies were presented, thus reflecting disagreement on the customary law on the particular points involved or its application.[45] Several cases presented before other courts

---

[43] The *Administration of the Prince von Pless Case*, Orders of 4 February, 11 May, 4 July and 2 December 1933, PCIJ Series A/B Nos. 52, 54, 57 and 59.

[44] See the *Administration of the Prince von Pless Case*, Pleadings, Oral Statements and Documents, PCIJ Series C No. 70 (1933) pp. 134ff., 182ff., 218, 240ff., 270ff., 278 and 290ff.

[45] See e.g. the *Mavrommatis Palestine Concessions Case*, PCIJ Series A No. 2 (1924); the *German Interests in Upper Silesia Case*, PCIJ Series A No. 7 (1926); the *Chorzów Factory Case*, PCIJ Series A No. 9 (1927); the *Serbian and Brazilian Loans Cases*, PCIJ Series A Nos. 20-1 (1929); the *Administration of the Prince von Pless Case*, PCIJ Series A/B No. 52 (1933); the *Affaire Losinger and Co.*, Order of 27 June 1936, PCIJ Series A/B No. 67; the *Borchgrave Case*, PCIJ Series A/B No. 72 (1937); the *Phosphates in Morocco Case*, PCIJ Series A/B No. 74 (1938); the *Panavezys–Saldutiskis Railway Case*, PCIJ Series A/B No. 76 (1939); the *Electricity Co. of Sophia Case*, PCIJ Series A/B No. 77 (1939); the *Anglo-Iranian Oil Co. Case*, 1952 ICJ Reports p. 99; the *Ambatielos Case*, 1953 ICJ Reports p. 13; the *Nottebohm Case*, 1953 ICJ Reports

or tribunals also reflected disagreements on the applicability of the rule or its application.[46]

The question whether resort to exhaustion of local remedies is relevant to other situations was in effect raised before the ICJ in the *Applicability of the Obligation to Arbitrate under Section 21 of the United Nations Headquarters Agreement of 26 June 1947 Opinion*.[47] The issue was whether the UN was under an obligation to submit to the local courts of the US a dispute under the Headquarters Agreement before seeking international arbitration. The Court dealt with the issue succinctly:

> The Court must further point out that the alleged dispute relates solely to what the United Nations considers to be its rights under the Headquarters Agreement. The purpose of the arbitration procedure envisaged by that Agreement is precisely the settlement of such disputes as may arise between the Organization and the host country without any prior recourse to municipal courts, and it would be against both the letter and the spirit of the Agreement for the implementation of that procedure to be subjected to such prior recourse. It is evident that a provision of the nature of section 21 of the Headquarters Agreement cannot require the exhaustion of local remedies as a condition of its implementation.[48]

It is clear that the arbitration, though international in that it was between a state and an international organization, did not arise from diplomatic protection. Hence, the rule was in principle irrelevant in any case. The Court addressed the issue, because some doubt was raised as to what the express words of the agreement meant. Clearly, any international

---

p. 10; the *Norwegian Loans Case*, 1957 ICJ Reports p. 14; the *Interhandel Case*, 1959 ICJ Reports p. 11; the *Aerial Incident Case*, 1959 ICJ Reports p. 132; the *Compagnie du Port, des Quais et des Entrepôts de Beyrouth and the Société Radio-Orient Case*, ICJ Pleadings, Oral Arguments and Documents (1960); the *Barcelona Traction Co. Case*, 1964 ICJ Reports p. 12; the *Barcelona Traction Co. Case*, 1970 ICJ Reports p. 3; the *ELSI Case*, 1989 ICJ Reports p. 15; and the *Arrest Warrant of 11 April 2000 Case*, 2002 ICJ Reports: www.cij-icj.org.

[46] See e.g. the cases brought before mixed commissions and individual arbitral tribunals starting in the nineteenth century and those before the European Commission and European Court of Human Rights. The early cases are to be found in such collections as Moore, *International Arbitrations* (1898), vol. 4; the UNRIAA series; de La Pradelle-Politis; the TAM series; BFSP; and US and Mexican Claims Commission Opinions. Later cases are reported mainly in the UNRIAA series. The most significant twentieth-century arbitration cases in which the rule was placed in issue are the *De Sabla Claim* (*US* v. *Panama*), 6 UNRIAA p. 358 (1933); the *Finnish Ships Arbitration* (*Finland* v. *UK*), 3 UNRIAA p. 1479 (1934); and the *Ambatielos Claim* (*Greece* v. *UK*), 12 UNRIAA p. 83 (1956).

[47] 1988 ICJ Reports p. 12. On this case, see Amerasinghe, 'Arbitration and the Rule of Local Remedies', in *Festschrift für Rudolph Bernhardt* (1995) at p. 669.

[48] 1988 ICJ Reports at p. 29.

agreement can expressly or by necessary intendment include reference to the national courts as a mode of dispute settlement and require exhaustion of local remedies before an arbitration procedure may be invoked. However, that has nothing to do with the rule of local remedies pertinent to diplomatic protection, which is a matter of customary international law. It is clear that the ICJ did not mean to indicate that the rule applied to the Headquarters Agreement as a matter of customary international law.[49] The opposite was the case.

The conclusion to be reached on the basis of what was said by the ICJ in this case is that the rule of local remedies as a rule of customary international law is not applicable as a customary rule as such to international arbitration (or, indeed, to any form of international adjudication), outside the area, in particular, of diplomatic protection. It may, however, be included expressly (or, perhaps, by necessary intendment) in an agreement to submit to international adjudicatory settlement of any kind as a prior condition for such settlement. There is a converse situation to this which will be adverted to below.

Such conflicts in state practice will be discussed, in so far as they are relevant, in the appropriate parts of this work dealing with the various aspects of the rule. But at this point, it is important to consider the importance of judicial, arbitral and quasi-judicial decisions as sources of law in the development of the rule of local remedies, particularly in the late nineteenth and twentieth centuries. Whatever the theoretical approach to such decisions as subsidiary sources of law in terms of the formal sources of law and particularly in relation to customary international law which is based primarily on state practice, at this point in the evolution of international law it cannot be seriously gainsaid that they constitute an increasingly important source of law, especially when there are conflicts in diplomatic or state practice or when such practice has been silent. Consequently, when a dispute on the law relating to the rule of local remedies is settled by judicial, arbitral or quasi-judicial decision, such decision acquires a special status as settling the customary law on the subject and from then on becomes a source for that law, having infused a certain definiteness into that law.

---

[49] Schwebel, 'Arbitration and the Exhaustion of Local Remedies Revisited', in *Festschrift in Honor of Sir Joseph Gold* (1990) p. 373, tries on the basis of the above advisory opinion to make a case for excluding the application of the rule of local remedies to all international arbitration, including those instituted in connection with, in some way, the exercise of diplomatic protection. As regards diplomatic protection, this is a *non sequitur* from what was said by the ICJ.

As will be seen, there is a considerable body of judicial, arbitral and quasi-judicial decisions on the subject of the rule of local remedies in which various aspects of the law relating to the rule, as opposed to the application of the law to the facts or the ascertainment of facts for the purpose of applying the rule in an agreed manner, were discussed and settled. Decisions of this kind have contributed to the development and evolution of the law to a considerable extent. Particular mention may be made here of the *Interhandel Case*,[50] the *Finnish Ships Arbitration*,[51] the *Ambatielos Claim*[52] and certain decisions of the European Commission of Human Rights and of the European Court of Human Rights.

As this work will be concerned with an exegesis and critical analysis of the modern law pertaining to the rule of local remedies, the judicial, arbitral and quasi-judicial cases, particularly since the Second World War, will constitute the main focus of attention, since the development of the customary law has been reflected in the arguments in these cases or in their decisions, rather than in pure diplomatic practice or statements pure and simple. Suffice it here to deal with one example of an area of the law on which there was an unsettled practice and which was apparently clarified by judicial or quasi-judicial decision.

The issue of the applicability of the rule of local remedies to the protection of minorities under treaties in which no explicit reference had been made to the rule, an issue which was raised in the *Administration of the Prince von Pless Case*,[53] was initially not conclusively settled in diplomatic practice but a particular trend seems later to have become apparent in the decisions of judicial and quasi-judicial organs. Such decisions clearly advanced the clarification of the issue to the extent that for all intents and purposes they settled any doubt that was present in the attitudes of governments to the issue.[54] Most of the cases decided on the issue were litigated in the first half of the twentieth century. The trend in those decisions was to recognize that under agreements for the protection of minorities the rule of local remedies or any modified form of it was not automatically or implicitly applicable, where the international agreement was silent on the matter. In short, there was no presumption in

---

[50] 1959 ICJ Reports p. 11. See now also the *ELSI Case*, 1998 ICJ Reports p. 15; and the *Arrest Warrant of 11 April 2000 Case*, 2002 ICJ Reports: www.cij-icj.org.

[51] *Finland* v. *UK*, 3 UNRIAA p. 1479 (1934).

[52] *Greece* v. *UK*, 12 UNRIAA p. 83 (1956).

[53] See Pleadings, Oral Statements and Documents, PCIJ Series C No. 70 (1933) *passim*.

[54] The question has been discussed in some detail in Cançado Trindade, 'Exhaustion of Local Remedies in International Law Experiments Granting Procedural Status to Individuals in the First Half of the Twentieth Century', 24 NILR (1977) p. 378.

favour of the applicability of the rule in such cases. This also raises the question, which will have to be examined later, but unfortunately only peripherally in this work, of whether the rule of local remedies is applicable to areas outside the diplomatic protection of aliens in the absence of explicit reference or necessary implication. The question is undoubtedly an important one. As seen earlier in this chapter, the ICJ has held in effect that it is not a rule which, as one applicable by custom, has any relevance, negatively or positively, to inter-state (or inter-organizational) arbitration as such. It is a possible, though not an inescapable, inference that the Court was also indicating in its own way that the customary rule was in principle confined as a customary rule to diplomatic protection. The broader question is whether, *pace* 'international' arbitration per se, the rule has outside diplomatic protection become already, incipience aside, a customary rule in other areas, such as human rights protection, to mention only one case, not indeed, whether it *can* or *should* become customary in other areas. That the rule or an analogous one is applied by explicit inclusion in international instruments or by necessary implication outside diplomatic protection does not as such prove anything in regard to the answer to this question. What has to be investigated is *practice* and *opinio iuris*.

While state practice per se contributed significantly to the evolution of the rule of local remedies, including those areas of exception, these developments took place largely in the period prior to the late nineteenth century and the twentieth century. By that time, the rule, which had been firmly established, had acquired a certain definition. Nevertheless, differences began to occur in state practice with regard to the applicability of some important aspects of the rule.[55] Thus, from then on, judicial and quasi-judicial decision-making assumed special importance in shaping the rule and its applicability, and in adapting it to more complex situations. It is these developments that are of significance today. No more is the issue whether the rule essentially as relating to diplomatic protection is a part of customary international law, but rather how and when it applies to situations which were not clearly envisaged when it first came into existence.

The history of the rule of local remedies, it must be recognized, shows that the rule itself was created and developed almost entirely in the European world, though the new Latin-American States may have helped

---

[55] Reference to the rule is certainly found in such official government documents as the UK Government's Rules Applying to International Claims (1985): see Rule VII, cited in Warbrick, 'Protection of Nationals Abroad', 37 ICLQ (1985) at p. 1008.

to refine it and contributed to its development, particularly in the late nineteenth and the early twentieth centuries. The rule was certainly not a creation of the interaction of developing countries with developed countries, and was not as such designed to protect developing country interests. Indeed, it was basically a product of the international relations between states of what came to be the developed world. However, now, because the developed world sees the rule as prejudicial to its interests, particularly in the context of foreign investment in developing countries, it has become to a large extent disenchanted with it. The result is that attempts are being made, in the relations between states and in the relations between aliens and host states, to exclude, if possible, the operation of the rule altogether by agreement between the states or parties concerned, as will be seen in Chapter 10 in connection with the examination of waiver, particularly through the instrumentality of the investment treaty.

The disenchantment which was insisted on religiously for a variety of political and ostensibly practical reasons arises from the distrust of the developed world, which for whatever reason sees itself as 'civilized' and the whole developing world as 'uncivilized' in terms of the proper administration of justice, which it regards as the preserve of the developed world. This arrogance has led the developed world to characterize the administration of justice and the legal systems in the whole developing world, regardless, as 'corrupt' and prejudiced against foreign interests in situations where in particular the local state is a party to litigation. Such a general perception may not only be questioned on its merits but is based on the assumption that the administration of justice in developed countries is never corrupt nor prejudiced, not merely against foreign interests, which assumption can clearly not be substantiated and is itself the result of prejudice and poor judgment. Corruption and prejudice are not confined as a function to the process of development but do occur, as is well known, in materially advanced societies, whether administration of justice systems or other areas are in issue.

That having been said, it must be admitted that there is a tendency, particularly in the international relations between developed and developing states, to try to eliminate by agreement the incidence of the rule of local remedies. This is resorted to by substituting some form of non-international (in the sense of inter-state) arbitration for local remedies. Such arbitration involves the participation as arbitrators of persons chosen by the alien party to a dispute, or at least not all appointed or controlled by the host state, whereas local justice is administered by appointees of, or persons chosen by, the host state. The object is osten-sibly to secure impartiality and independence. Arbitral tribunals of the nature conceived are assumed by developed states and their nationals to be 'neutral', while national, i.e. local, courts are regarded as likely to be, for whatever reason, prejudiced in favour of the host state.[56] The assumption of necessary neutrality, impartiality and independence of such arbitral tribunals is, however, open to question. As pointed out by an author from a developed state in regard to ICSID's 'institutional-ized' system, such 'international' arbitration does not inspire confidence, based on neutrality and impartiality, among capital-receiving (develop-ing) nations.[57] The point is that the arbitrators appointed or selected to conduct such arbitrations generally, or by and large, belong to a *club* which is developed-country oriented, whether they themselves are na-tionals of developed states or not, and are likely, or have a tendency, to favour the interests of foreign investors,[58] generally from developed states. While the term 'corruption' has been freely used in the past to describe the justice systems in developing countries when they are con-cerned particularly with foreign interests, 'corruption' becomes a rela-tive term when the tendencies and structure of the existing so-called arbitration system – which is, indeed, not international in the narrow and proper sense, but only transnational – are considered.[59]

---

[56] See Sornarajah, *The International Law of Foreign Investment* (1994) p. 210.

[57] Toope, *Mixed International Arbitrations* (1990) pp. 219–23. Sornarajah, for instance, observes: 'The developing state view is that overseas tribunals are inclined to apply norms developed by jurists from capital-exporting states which are favourable to investment protection and the much vaunted neutrality of the arbitration system in the developed states is but a mirage': Sornarajah, note 56 above, at pp. 210–11.

[58] The notion of a club favouring the interests of its members has been tentatively mooted: see Sornarajah, note 56 above, at p. 211. I would make the point very cogently and seriously. If, as was perceived by foreign investors from developed countries and their national states, the pendulum was in one corner, it has now swung completely to the other.

[59] While it may be the case that certain court decisions involving aliens given in the nineteenth century in Latin-American states may have been questionable from the point of view of absolute justice, this is not logically a ground for characterizing the judicial systems of the approximately 160 developing countries as being incapable of fairly administering justice in relation to foreigners. If this were so, by the same token, based on some experiences of 'natives', it would be necessary to conclude that the administration of justice in colonies was always corrupt and not impartial, when disputes arose between colonizers and 'natives'.

3 Basis of the rule

The development and application of the rule of local remedies have naturally been influenced by the functional considerations which underlie it. These considerations concern the institution of diplomatic protection as such, as well as the rule in a narrower context. It may be useful first to review briefly the basis of the law relating to diplomatic protection, before embarking on an analysis of the underpinnings of the rule of local remedies itself, in order to appreciate the special kind of emphasis which has been inherent in the case of the rule of local remedies. While the rationale for the rule of local remedies should basically be the same as for diplomatic protection in general, it would seem that there are some considerations which enter into the implementation and application of the rule of local remedies which result in certain crucial variations in the importance attached to some of the underlying premises of diplomatic protection. Furthermore, it is important also to examine to what extent the rationale for the rule of local remedies in the context of diplomatic protection may differ from that for the rule as it is applied in the protection of human rights, in order to appreciate whether and how the application of the rule in the protection of human rights has involved, or might involve, departures from the normal practices traditionally associated with the rule as applied in the context of diplomatic protection. Without prejudging results, it may be necessary to bear in mind the premises underlying the two systems of protection in studying how the rule has evolved and in projecting its future evolution.

The basis of diplomatic protection

While the protection of aliens by their national states in one form or another pre-dates considerably the eighteenth century, it was not

43

until the time of Vattel that a clear attempt was made to explain diplomatic protection in any terms. In 1758, Vattel rationalized the position by stating that 'Quiconque maltraite un citoyen offense indirectement l'Etat, qui doit protéger ce citoyen'.[1] He further explained that 'the sovereign of the injured citizen must avenge the deed and, if possible, force the aggressor to full satisfaction or punish him, since otherwise the citizen will not obtain the chief end of civil society, which is protection'.[2]

Vattel's thesis not only asserted the right of the national state of the alien to protect its national, but implied that there was an obligation resting upon the alien's national state to protect him. It is clear that Vattel conceived the right of protection as inhering in the national state of the alien and did not envisage the injury done to the alien as creating any right vesting in the alien at international law to a remedy *vis-à-vis* the host state. A consequence of this view was that the injury done to the alien was regarded as being a violation of an obligation owed by the host state to the alien's national state. Formally, this explanation was the result of the theory that the individual had no rights at international law.[3] On the other hand, it is not clear what Vattel meant by the duty to protect a national abroad which rested upon the national state of the alien. Assuming he was correct in postulating a duty of protection – and this is not certain in the light of subsequent developments in diplomatic protection, the practice of reprisals prior to this time and of diplomatic protection even during his time – the question to be answered is to whom was the duty owed, particularly if the alien as an individual had no rights recognized by international law. Vattel did not venture to answer the question, nor was the issue seriously faced by authorities that followed him. However, the right and duty of states to protect

---

[1] *Le Droit des gens* (1758), Book II, Section 71.

[2] *The Law of Nations or the Principles of Natural Law* (1758) in Fenwick (trans.), *Classics of International Law* (1916) p. 136. Earlier, Grotius had written what appears to have foreshadowed Vattel's bold and outright formulation: see *De Jure Belli ac Pacis* (1625), book II, chapter 17, para. 20, and chapter 21, para. 2. However, it was not until Vattel that the particular formulation discussed here was articulated.

[3] This theory was supported by G. F. Martens, for instance, in the early nineteenth century in *Précis du droit des gens moderne de l'Europe* (1831), vol. 1, pp. 224ff. In the latter half of the nineteenth century and in the early twentieth century, writers such as Pradière-Fodéré, Calvo, Tchernoff, Triepel, Moore, Anzilotti, Hallek, Phillimore, Wheaton, Arias and Oppenheim threw in their support for this view. More recently, Fauchille, Holland, Borchard, Décencière-Ferrandière, Eagleton, Dunn, Freeman. Ralston, Brierly and García Amador, for example, made the same assumption in dealing with diplomatic protection.

their nationals abroad against a host state was strongly asserted later, in discussing diplomatic protection, by authorities such as Fauchille,[4] Oppenheim[5] and Holland.[6]

Although the duty to protect a national against the host state may be questionable, the principle that the right infringed in cases where an alien suffers illegal injury at the hands of a state is the right of the alien's national state and not the right of the alien himself, apparently deriving as it does from the theory that states alone are subjects of international law, has been recognized in several international judicial decisions. Starting with the *Mavrommatis Palestine Concessions Case*, the PCIJ stated that:

It is an elementary principle of international law that a State is entitled to protect its subjects, when injured by acts contrary to international law committed by another State, from whom they have been unable to obtain satisfaction through the ordinary channels. By taking up the case of one of its subjects and resorting to a diplomatic action or international judicial proceedings on his behalf, a State is in reality asserting its own rights – its right to ensure, in the person of its subjects, respect for the rules of international law.[7]

The point at issue in the case was whether the dispute, which originated in an injury to a national of the claimant state, was a dispute involving the Mandatory, the defendant state, and another state member of the League of Nations for the purposes of Article 26 of the British Mandate over Palestine. It was held that the dispute in issue was such a dispute for the reasons given above, even though it arose from an injury to a private individual.

Later, in the *Panavezys–Saldutiskis Railway Case*, which concerned the expropriation of a concession given to an Estonian company by the Lithuanian Government, the PCIJ, in dealing with the preliminary objection based on the nationality of claims rule, confirmed this view when it stated that

In the opinion of the Court, the rule of international law on which the first preliminary objection is based is that in taking up the case of one of its nationals, by resorting to diplomatic action in international judicial proceedings on his behalf, a State is in reality asserting its own right, the right to ensure in the person of its national respect for the rules of international law.[8]

---

[4] *Traité de droit international public* (1922), Part I, p. 884 and pp. 922ff.
[5] *International Law* (1905), vol. 1, pp. 375ff.
[6] *Lectures on International Law* (1933) pp. 165ff.
[7] Jurisdiction, PCIJ Series A No. 2 at p. 12 (1924).
[8] PCIJ Series A/B No. 76 at p. 16 (1938).

In the *Serbian Loans Case*,[9] where the dispute arose from the failure to service certain loans taken by the Serbian Government from French bondholders, and in the *Chorzów Factory Case*,[10] which concerned an expropriation of alien property, the same principle was held to be applicable. In the former case,[11] the application of the principle resulted in the finding that the dispute before the Court was one between states, while in the latter case the Court applied the principle in order to conclude that the damage suffered by the claimant state was not identical with that which its national had experienced, which was a relevant consideration in the calculation of damages.

The ICJ has also affirmed the principle in several cases, either explicitly or impliedly. In the *Reparation Case*, it said of the rule inhering in the institution of diplomatic protection that such protection must be exercised by the national state of the alien:

In the third place, the rule rests on two bases. The first is that the defendant State has broken an obligation towards the national State in respect of its nationals. The second is that only the party to whom an international obligation is due can bring a claim in respect of its breach.

The principle was mentioned only incidentally in this case in the process of establishing another rule of international law, that international organizations too had rights of protection in respect of their officials in connection with the performance of the duties, such rights belonging to the organization and not to the official. Judge Badawi, in the same case, albeit in a dissenting opinion, supported the view taken by the Court when he said:

En reconnaissant à l'Etat le droit de réclamer les réparations des ces dommages le droit international ne le fait pas parce qu'il considére que l'Etat est un représantant légal de la victime mais parce qu'il estime que l'Etat fait valoir son droit propre, le droit qu'il a de faire respecter en la personne de ses ressortissants le droit international.[12]

The principle was reaffirmed by the ICJ in the *Nottebohm Case*,[13] where limitations were placed upon the link of nationality between the individual and his national state, and implicitly in the *Barcelona Traction*

---

[9] PCIJ Series A No. 20 (1929).

[10] Merits, PCIJ Series A No. 17 (1928).   [11] 1949 ICJ Reports at p. 181.

[12] 1949 ICJ Reports at p. 206. It will be observed that Judge Badawi expressly stated that the national state of the alien does not assert a claim as a 'représentant légal de la victime' and thus defends not the right of the alien on his behalf but its own right.

[13] 1955 ICJ Reports p. 24.

Case,[14] where again the application of the nationality of claims rule was in issue.

There are several decisions of other international tribunals in which the principle has been recognized. Thus, in *Administrative Decision No. V* of the US–German Claims Commission, it was stated that

the nation is injured through injury to its national and it alone may demand reparation.[15]

These cases cover injuries arising from the alleged violation of customary international law as well as of treaties involving obligations undertaken *vis-à-vis* aliens. Therefore, there is no reason to distinguish between customary international law and treaties in regard to the basic principle that it is the right of the alien's national state that is infringed when an injury is done to an alien, as a result of which diplomatic protection is exercised. It cannot consequently be maintained that where the substantive obligation is contained in a treaty the corresponding right is that of the national state, whereas in the case of an obligation under customary international law the right is enjoyed not by the national state but by the alien himself.

The principle is also supported by opinions expressed by state legal advisers and in official correspondence. Thus, in 1912 the Solicitor for the Department of State of the US said that 'It should, in the first place, be observed that by espousing a claim of its national for injuries inflicted by a foreign government the espousing government makes the claim its own'.[16] In the *Finnish Ships Arbitration*, the UK Government espoused the same view of diplomatic protection.[17] Many rapporteurs and draft codifications have unhesitatingly conceded that this principle underlies the doctrine of diplomatic protection.[18]

---

[14] 1970 ICJ Reports p. 4.

[15] *US v. Germany*, 7 UNRIAA at p. 140 (1924), *per* Umpire Parker. See also e.g. *Administrative Decision No. II* (*US v. Germany*), 7 UNRIAA p. 26 (1923); the *Finnish Ships Arbitration* (*Finland v. Great Britain*), 3 UNRIAA p. 1485 (1934); the *Spanish Zone of Morocco Case* (*Great Britain v. Spain*), 2 UNRIAA p. 640 (1923); and the *Dickson Car Wheel Co. Claim* (*US v. Mexico*), 4 UNRIAA p. 678 (1931).

[16] Hackworth, *Digest*, vol. 5, p. 488. See also the letter of Secretary of State Frelinghuysen of 11 February 1884, Moore, *International Law*, vol. 6, p. 616.

[17] *Finnish Ships Arbitration* (*Finland v. Great Britain*), 3 UNRIAA p. 1985.

[18] See e.g. García Amador, 'First Report on State Responsibility', YBILC (1956), vol. 2, at p. 192; the Guerrero Report adopted by the Sub-Committee of the League of Nations Committee of Experts, YBILC (1956), vol. 2, Annex 1, p. 222; and the Harvard Draft Convention of 1961, YBILC (1956), vol. 2, Annex 9, p. 229. On diplomatic protection, see also Dugard, 'First Report on Diplomatic Protection' (ILC), UN Doc. A/CN.4/506 at pp. 5ff.

There has been a growing dissatisfaction with this avowed basis of the law of diplomatic protection. Not only has it been attacked because of the analytical inconsistencies the present law on the subject reveals, but it has been severely criticized by text writers on the ground that it is incompatible with the modern conception of fundamental human rights and freedoms.[19]

While the basic principle must be recognized, and it is evident that many consequences which have been reflected in the current law of diplomatic protection flow from it, it cannot be denied that the interests of the alien's national state, which owns the right involved, and those of the host state, which is under the obligations in respect of the alien as a result of the right–duty relationship between those entities, are not the only interests which have shaped the current law. Although the formal incidence of rights and obligations may be established for the current law, the law has been shaped by the influence of other interests involved too. This will be of particular importance in discussing the bases of the rule of local remedies. It is necessary, therefore, to consider how the different interests have affected the particular rules constituting the law of diplomatic protection in order to appreciate the material bases of the law.

The interests of the state of nationality

The interests of the national state have been responsible for certain important and well-established rules in the law of diplomatic protection. Some examples are given here.

First, the rule that the injured alien must have the nationality of the claimant state at the time of the injury[20] flows from account being taken of the national state's interest. Nationality at the time of the injury is the bond which creates rights in respect of the individual at international law. The modification introduced by the *Nottebohm Case*,[21] which required a genuine link between alien and national state, may also from one angle be explained by reference to the genuine interests of the claimant state.

---

[19] See e.g. O'Connell, vol. 2, p. 1115; and García Amador, note 18 above, at pp. 199ff.

[20] See the *Panavezys–Saldutiskis Railway Case*, PCIJ Series A/B No. 76 (1938); the *Reparation Case*, 1949 ICJ Reports at p. 181; the *Nottebohm Case*, 1955 ICJ Reports at p. 23; Hyde, *International Law* (1945), vol. 2, p. 893; O'Connell, vol. 2, p. 1116 and the authorities there cited at note 17. On the nationality of claims rule, see now the Articles drafted for the ILC in Dugard, note 18 above, at pp. 22ff.

[21] 1955 ICJ Reports p. 4.

Secondly, the rule that a Calvo Clause does not have the unqualified effect of depriving the national state of the alien of its right of applying international remedies to violations of international law committed in respect of an alien[22] can only stem from the idea that the interests affected when an alien is injured are those of his national state.

Thirdly, it is an accepted rule that the damage for which reparation must be made is the damage to the alien's national state which is not identical with that which its national has suffered, so that the reparation ordered in a given case need not be simply equivalent to the loss suffered by the alien.[23] This rule also reflects consideration of the interests of the national state.

Fourthly, the reason that the national state has complete control over the disposition of the proceeds of a claim and is not even obliged to hand them to the individual whose claim it has espoused[24] is that the claim has a public character based on the interests of the national state.

Fifthly, the rule that the national state may waive, compromise or discontinue the presentation of the claim irrespective of the wishes of the alien[25] is also derived from the same interests.

Such rules, which reflect the basic principle that the state does not appear as a representative or on behalf of the alien whose claim it espouses, but defends its own rights, are designed directly to protect the interests of the national state of the alien which alone may assert its claim.

The interests of the defendant state, competing national states and entities other than the injured alien

Some of the rules applicable in the area of diplomatic protection are apparently designed to protect the interests of the defendant state,

---

[22] See e.g. the *North American Dredging Co. Case* (*US* v. *Mexico*), 4 UNRIAA at p. 29 (1926); Shea, *The Calvo Clause* (1955) p. 217; Hyde, note 20 above, vol. 2, p. 994; O'Connell, vol. 2, p. 1151.

[23] See e.g. the *Chorzów Factory Case* (Merits), PCIJ Series A No. 17 at p. 28 (1928).

[24] See e.g. *Frelinghuysen* v. *US ex rel. Key*, 110 US 63 (1884); *US ex rel. Boynton* v. *Blaine*, 139 US 306 (1891); *Heirs of Oswald* v. *Swiss Government*, 3 Ann. Dig. (1925–6) p. 244; *US* v. *La Abra Silver Mining Co. Case*, 175 US 423 (1899); *Great Western Insurance Co.* v. *US*, 19 Ct.Cl. 206 (1884); Hackworth, note 16 above, vol. 5, pp. 763ff.; and Feller, *The Mexican Claims Commissions* (1935) p. 84 and the authorities there cited at note 6. In *Administrative Decision No. V* (*US* v. *Germany*), 7 UNRIAA at p. 152 (1924), the Umpire recognized this rule, while stating that in reality states distribute the proceeds of awards on the basis that the interests of individuals are involved.

[25] See e.g. Moore, note 16 above, vol. 6, pp. 1012ff.; Borchard, *The Diplomatic Protection of Citizens Abroad* (1915) pp. 366ff.; and Whiteman, *Damages in International Law* (1937), vol. 1, p. 282.

competing national states and entities other than the injured alien or his national state. As for the defendant state, its interests must naturally and legitimately be considered. On the other hand, as the law has developed, interests other than those of the defendant and claimant states have also been taken into account. A few examples which demonstrate the position are given here.

First, the rule that the alien must not have the nationality of the defendant state, at the time of injury and continuously up to the time of the award,[26] is really a concession to the defendant state. Even though the alien may be a national of the defendant state at the relevant time, there is technically a violation of the right of the other state whose nationality the alien enjoys.

Secondly, it also seems to be recognized that, where an alien has the nationality of two or more states, other than the defendant state, it is only the state with which he has the closest link that may espouse his claim.[27] This rule can only be explained on the basis that the rights of the state of effective nationality are given recognition to the exclusion of the rights of other national states for reasons of convenience. The rule in a way assists the defendant state also, because it cannot be subjected to more than one claim, as it might be if the logic of the principle that it is the right of the national state that is violated were followed to its natural conclusion.

Thirdly, in the case of corporate bodies that are injured, sometimes the national state of the corporation is not regarded as the owner of the claim, but the national state or states of a majority of, or of individual, shareholders are vested with the right of bringing a claim.[28] This rule

---

[26] Jessup, *A Modern Law of Nations* (1956) p. 100; and Van Panhuys, *The Role of Nationality in International Law* (1959) pp. 73ff. The exact rule has been the subject of discussion, although what is reflected above seems to be the better view. See also Award No. 31-157-2, 2 Iran–US CTR pp. 160ff (1983), where the rule was rejected. For a discussion of this rule, see Amerasinghe, *Jurisdiction of International Tribunals* (2003), Chapter 8. Dugard, 'First Report on Diplomatic Protection', UN Doc. A/CN.4/506 at pp. 44ff., proposes a change in this rule for codification and development on the basis of effective and dominant nationality. The reasoning is not clear.

[27] See e.g. the *Nottebohm Case*, 1955 ICJ Reports p. 22; Article 5 of the Convention on Certain Questions Relating to the Conflict of Nationality Laws, 1930, 179 LNTS p. 90. Some doubt has been cast on the rule: see Van Panhuys, note 26 above, at p. 81. However, the rule which has come to be characterized as the 'master' or 'effective' nationality rule seems to be well established: see e.g. Award No. 31-157-2, 2 Iran–US CTR pp. 160ff. (1983). See Amerasinghe, note 26 above, Chapter 8. Dugard, note 26 above, at pp. 54ff., ignoring the closest link theory, proposes a change to this rule.

[28] See e.g. O'Connell, vol. 2, pp. 1128ff. and the literature cited on p. 1124 at note 47.

would rest on a choice between injured states based on convenience. When the corporation is a national of the defendant state and the national states of shareholders are given the right of action,[29] it is the interests of national states, rather than those of the defendant state, that are being given recognition.

Fourthly, the rule that local remedies must be exhausted recognizes the defendant state's interests, by affording such state the opportunity to redress the wrong committed.

Fifthly, the doctrine by which international organizations may grant functional protection to their officers or agents on the basis that an obligation owed to them has been violated[30] may also be mentioned in passing, although it is not strictly a case of diplomatic protection; in this case, the interests of an entity other than the national state are respected.

Where a choice of interests is made between a defendant which is a national state and other national states in favour of the former, the policy behind the choice is the protection of the interests of the defendant state. Where a choice is made between states which do not, perhaps, include the defendant state, the purported object of giving the alien the best protection through one state is coupled with the policy of protecting the defendant state against a multiplicity of claims. In the case of the rule relating to corporations, a choice is made between states that can claim to be national states in the context. This would seem to be based on giving precedence to the interests of the state chosen, perhaps on the understanding that the alien concerned is likely to get the best protection through one state by this choice, although it may not always work out that way. An entity, not a state, is given certain protective powers on a basis completely different from that of the national link, because its interests are regarded as more important than those of the national state. In these cases, it would seem that the interests of all national states, or the interests of the alien, are not always vital. The national state *qua* national state is not given complete recognition, or the best interests of the alien in having multiple sources of protection are overlooked in favour of other interests, although in certain cases the rules purport to give the alien the best protection possible through a single source.

---

[29] For this rule, see the *Barcelona Traction Co. Case*, 1970 ICJ Reports p. 3, where, however, the rule was found to be inapplicable. The separate opinions are particularly important.

[30] The *Reparation for Injuries Case*, 1949 ICJ Reports at pp. 181ff.

The interests and position of the injured alien

Certain rules relating to diplomatic protection that have evolved and been applied in practice display an approach which stresses the important position of the individual in this context. They can only be explained on the premise that the law is basically interested in protecting the rights and interests of aliens themselves. In such cases, the law has not paid much attention to the principle that the right infringed is that of the national state. In a sense the law is interested in protecting the basic human rights of aliens.

There is another aspect of the rule pertaining to the nationality of claims than that which requires the bond of nationality to exist at the time of the injury. The alien must also continuously have the nationality of the claimant state up to the time of the espousal of the claim and, according to some, up to the time of the award.[31] If the right violated is regarded entirely as that of the national state it would be sufficient if the alien were a national of that state at the time of the injury, since the primary right of the alien's national state, on being violated at that time, would be converted into a secondary right to reparation which would vest immediately, and could not be affected by what happened to the alien's nationality thereafter. The rule is to be explained by reference to the fact that the alien's position is being taken into account, though other interests than his are also given importance.

There are certain exceptions to the rule that the alien must have the nationality of the claimant state at the time of the injury. It is possible that a state may espouse the claim of an alien who is not its national as a result of an agreement made before or after the injury with the defendant state.[32] In the same way, aliens may be under the special protection of a state, by agreement with a host state or otherwise, although they are not nationals of the former state.[33] In these cases, it cannot be said that the law merely protects the rights of a particular

---

[31] See the *Panavezys-Saldutiskis Railway Case*, PCIJ Series A/B No. 76 at p. 16 (1938); Oppenheim, vol. 1, p. 347 and the authorities there cited at note 3; Borchard, 'The Protection of Citizens Abroad and Change of Original Nationality', 43 *Yale Law Journal* (1933–4) at pp. 372ff.; Hurst, 'Nationality of Claims', 7 BYIL (1926) at pp. 162ff.; Hyde, note 20 above, vol. 2, p. 893; and O'Connell, vol. 2, p. 1117. This rule too has been questioned, although it has been accepted as a rule of customary international law: O'Connell, vol. 2, p. 1119. For a slightly different view of the rule, see Sinclair, 'Nationality of Claims: British Practice', 27 BYIL (1950) at pp. 125ff.

[32] See O'Connell, vol. 2, p. 1122.

[33] See Hyde, note 20 above, vol. 2, p. 896; O'Connell, vol. 2, p. 1117 and pp. 1135ff.; Schwarzenberger, *International Law* (1957), vol. 1, pp. 592ff.; Panhuys, note 26 above, at pp. 68ff.; and the *Reparation for Injuries Case*, 1949 ICJ Reports at p. 181.

state. Some allowance is being made for the protection of the rights of aliens through representation.

The rule that local remedies must be exhausted by the alien before an alien's claim is taken up at an international level by his national state[34] may be seen as a further indication that it is the alien's position as the victim of the wrong that is being taken into account by the law. If the substantive rights of the national state were alone regarded as having been violated, it is difficult to see why the ensuing remedial rights, which should vest in the national state, should be contingent upon the exhaustion of local remedies by the alien, nor how the satisfaction of the alien's grievance at a national level should wipe out the injury to his national state. Yet, the interests that are given prominence are those of the respondent state.

The injury suffered by the alien is used as a scale for the calculation of damages. Although the ultimate reparation may involve more than the actual loss to the alien,[35] the damage suffered by the alien is the basis for the award of reparation. Such damages awarded may include both damages for material loss and for moral injury suffered by the alien. Although the economic assets of an individual may, by a fiction, be regarded as part of the wealth of his national state, international law does not really treat such assets as being actually the property of the national state. As regards damage through personal injury including moral suffering, it would be difficult to regard the national state as having suffered such damage even by a legal fiction. Thus, it is clear that the law is here paying heed to the interest of the alien rather than to that of his national state.

Such rules, and some of the rules already discussed above, demonstrate that international law recognizes also the nature of the claim as a private claim belonging to the alien, in contradistinction to the recognition given to the public nature of the claim, which has been asserted to be the real basis of diplomatic protection.

Choices among competing interests and essentials

The evolution of the rules relating to diplomatic protection shows that the competing interests involved have been taken into account and given

---

[34] The rule of local remedies, however, is based on regard for more than the alien's interest. As will be seen, the rule was conceived in recognition of the host state's sovereignty. Some Articles on the rule have been formulated for the ILC in Dugard, 'Second Report on Diplomatic Protection', UN Doc.A/CN.4/506 (2001) and Dugard, 'Third Report on Diplomatic Protection', A/CN.4/523 (2002).

[35] See the *Chorzów Factory Case* (Merits), PCIJ Series A No. 17 at p. 28 (1928).

value, so much so that, while recognition has been given to the basic principle that it is the right of the alien's national state that lies at the heart of the institution of diplomatic protection as it has developed, other interests have also been considered in the formulation of some of the applicable rules. In particular, the interests of the injured alien have not been ignored, although it has often been stated that formally it is not the alien's rights that have been violated but those of his national state. The fact that the alien is *per se* involved in the situation has resulted in the formation of certain rules. Moreover, the interests of the host state (the defendant) or other national states have been given preference to the formal rights of certain national states in the context of diplomatic protection proper, while at other times the interests of entities such as international organizations have been given recognition in the extension of protection to individuals. Competition among these interests has been resolved in practice in relation to specific rules by choices in favour of one or the other, without any apparent order or scheme referable to a hierarchy of social policy values. Thus, it is not possible to assert with any conclusiveness that one or the other of these interests is necessarily superior to any of the others. According to the traditional view, the interests of the national state of the alien generally provide the framework on which the law of diplomatic protection is built, and legally speaking this is the formal mould in which the law is cast, although it may not be proper to describe it as the sole basis of the law of diplomatic protection.

The interests of the alien and of the host state are, however, strong elements in determining the precise content of certain rules, so that they too merit consideration as a material basis for the law of diplomatic protection. In the event of competition among the various interests in an area where the rules are not clear, it is difficult categorically to state which might be given preference, although it may be possible to assert that the formal structure of the law of diplomatic protection, resting as it does on the interests of the injured national state, may be given a prominent position in determining the result. On a substantive plane, however, the criticism is cogent that the interests of the injured alien should be given more recognition, especially in the context of modern developments in the law of human rights which are the result of increased concern for the protection of the individual. In the final analysis, as a matter of substance, the institution of diplomatic protection relates basically to a conflict situation involving host states and aliens, although formally the mould in which the law is cast may be limited to a relationship between two sovereign states. The fact that particularly the interests of the alien have shared in shaping the law demonstrates that the formal basis of the law has not always determined the direction of the law. However, the interests of the host or defendant state have called for recognition in addition to those of the injured alien.[36]

It is important to recognize that at any given point in time, even though the formal mould of diplomatic protection was and is a relationship between states, the true essence of the law of diplomatic protection was and is regard for the rights of individuals. This is so, although the category of individuals is restricted essentially to those with an alien nationality and excludes the nationals of the defendant state. It is unimportant that state practice, international case law and text-writers did not as such articulate this truth, or may have explained, when given a chance, the foundations of the rule in a more limited manner. Clearly, while the substantive rights of the individual which were respected may have been limited in terms of what modern human rights coventional (and, perhaps, customary) law protects, the law of diplomatic protection was based on the notion that in effect the interests (and, in reality, the rights) of the individual deserved and required protection. In a sense, there was in diplomatic protection an incipient law of human rights protection. It is foolhardy to deny this observation. The basic concerns in the two areas are really very similar,[37] although legal effectuation of those concerns in the law of diplomatic protection may have been somewhat rudimentary.

This recognition of human rights as deserving protection was and is not related in any direct way, perhaps, to the growth of modern human rights law which is conceivably broader both substantively and procedurally. On the substantive side, modern human rights law, which grew in the latter half of the twentieth century, may influence and may have influenced the content of the substantive rights (or interests) of aliens determined by an international minimum standard which is the basis for such rights in diplomatic protection. However, clearly the awareness

---

[36] Some of the rulings of the Iran–US Claims Tribunal show a tendency to take further account of the relationship between the alien and the host state and consequently to value more the interests of the alien: see Award No. 31-157-2, 2 Iran–US CTR pp. 160ff. (1983). In these decisions, the role played by the interests of the national state of the alien seems to be under-emphasized, although formally the dispute settlement machinery was set in motion by an agreement between the host state and the national state of the aliens and was in essence in the exercise of diplomatic protection.

[37] This point was made by me in 1967 in Amerasinghe, *State Responsibility for Injuries to Aliens* (1967) pp. 11ff.

of the need to respect the (human) rights or interests of individuals (in the persons of aliens only) long pre-dated the modern law of human rights. It was also not connected particularly with the interaction between developed and developing states which can be traced fully to the post-Second World War era.

It would, therefore, be wrong to deny or gloss over the essential similarity of the fundamental purpose and basis of the law of diplomatic protection and modern human rights law, which is often done. This has significance inevitably for the application of the rule of local remedies. At the same time, it is necessary to recognize that the practical approach to both the substantive and the remedial aspects of human rights protection which has derived in one way or another from conventional instruments, regardless of some similarity of purpose and basis, may be different from that taken to such aspects in the law of diplomatic protection as such. This feature has certainly, in one way or another, had some significance for the rule of local remedies.

The interests behind the rule of local remedies

The stage is now set for a closer look at the interests and policies more specifically affecting the rule of local remedies. Just as, in relation to diplomatic protection as an institution, it has been seen that there are competing interests which have profoundly affected the development of the law, so it will emerge that the rule of local remedies has felt in its evolution the impact of particular competing interests and has taken the form it has as a result of the application of certain choices.

The textual authorities, starting principally with Borchard,[38] are agreed that the rule operates as a condition precedent to the exercise of diplomatic protection, although there is disagreement on various aspects of the rule, including the formal nature of the rule.[39] Dunn

---

[38] Note 25 above, at pp. 28, 354 and 817.

[39] See e.g. Dunn, *The Protection of Nationals* (1932) pp. 41 and 55; de Visscher, 'La Responsabilité des états', 2 BViss (1924-II) at pp. 115ff.; 'Le Déni de justice en droit international', 52 *Hague Recueil* (1935) at pp. 421, 427 and 431; Freeman, *The International Responsibility of States for Denial of Justice* (1938) pp. 404ff., 432ff. and 456ff.; Eagleton, *The Responsibility of States in International Law* (1929) pp. 95 and 97ff.; and Ago, 'La Regola del Previo Esaurimento die Ricorsi Interni in Tema di Responsabilità Internazionale', 3 ArchivDP (1938) at pp. 182 and 242ff. These are early authorities. Later, there was general agreement that the rule operated as a condition precedent to the exercise of diplomatic protection.

described the rule as being based on practical convenience,[40] but it would appear that there were more functional reasons behind the rule. It is difficult to speculate on what was the rationale for the rule when it was associated with the institution of reprisals, although even then there were indications that it was a recognition of certain prerogative rights of the host state in its relationship with aliens. However, in the context of diplomatic protection it may now be possible to discern in terms of the interests involved in the situation particular trends in the recognition of interests.

It would seem from the history of the rule that the attitude of the national states of aliens towards the rule was ambivalent. There was a tendency to regard the rule both as an impediment and as an advantage. It was an impediment because it placed a burden upon the alien before he could have his case taken up at an international level. It was an advantage because it relieved national states of espousing claims that might be resolved at a lower level or which were unfounded and frivolous, because the rule acted as a sieve.[41] On the other hand, host states were inclined to regard the rule as a clear benefit to themselves because it reduced the chances of unwelcome interference in the relations between themselves and aliens and of the elevation of disputes to an international level, so much so that sometimes they insisted on a very strict interpretation of the rule.

Borchard saw the reasons for the rule to be that: (i) citizens going abroad are presumed and should ordinarily be required to take into account means of redress for the wrong furnished by the local law; (ii) sovereignty and independence warrant the local state demanding freedom from interference, on the assumption that its courts are capable of doing justice; (iii) the government of the injured alien can be expected to recognize that the local government must have an opportunity of doing justice to the injured alien in its own regular way; (iv) if the injury is committed by an individual or a minor official, the exhaustion of local remedies is necessary to make certain that the wrongful act or denial of justice is the deliberate act of the state; and (v) if the injury

---

[40] Note 39 above, at pp. 156ff. On the issue of the nature of the rule, it is significant that Article 44 of the ILC's Draft Articles on State Responsibility regards the rule as relevant to the *admissibility* of claims in international litigation (see Report of the ILC to the General Assembly (2001), UN Doc.A/56/10 at p. 55) and that the ICJ described the rule as relating to the *admissibility* of an application (*Arrest Warrant of 11 April 2000 Case*, 2002 ICJ Reports para. 40). See also the *ELSI Case*, 1987 ICJ Reports at p. 42, where the rule is described as an important rule of customary international law.

[41] McNair, *International Law Opinions* (1956), vol. 2, p. 197.

is the deliberate act of the state, the exhaustion is necessary to make certain that the state is unwilling to have the wrong put right.[42]

Borchard's view has been criticized by some authorities.[43] In particular, reasons (iv) and (v) do not seem to be special reasons for the rule, apart from the fact that there may be some confusion between situations where the injury is caused by a private individual and those in which the host state is the perpetrator of the wrong, directly or indirectly. Both reasons reinforce the argument that the host state should be given an opportunity to remedy the initial wrong for which it has responsibility, but by themselves they are ambivalent, somewhat insubstantial and unimpressive as explanations for such an important rule as the rule of local remedies. They may point to the convenience of having the alien resort to local remedies, but they do not provide a real justification for a rule that has some very serious implications.[44] On the other hand, the first three reasons reflect to a large extent the underlying justification for the rule, although they state the same premise seen from three different points of view. Perhaps the emphasis should be on reason (ii), in so far as the jurisprudence on the subject seems to refer to it almost exclusively.

It would appear that the rule results mainly from recognition of the respondent state's sovereignty in what is basically an international dispute. There may also be an objective contemplated in the relief of international tribunals from being excessively burdened with litigation. Further, the national state of the alien may have an interest in relief from being unduly burdened with international claims, but this is clearly secondary to that of having the dispute in which its national is involved appropriately settled, if need be, by resort to international litigation. While the interest of the national state of the alien in the existence of the rule may be limited, it may share the interest of the alien in having

---

[42] Note 25 above, at p. 817. See also, for support for this view, *Harvard Research in International Law* (1929) p. 152; García Amador, 'Third Report on State Responsibility', YBILC (1958), vol. 2, at pp. 55ff.; and Law, *The Local Remedies Rule in International Law* (1961) p. 16.

[43] See e.g. Fawcett, 'The Exhaustion of Local Remedies: Substance or Procedure?', 31 BYIL (1954) at pp. 452ff.

[44] Moreover, reason (iv) deals with a substantive point which could as well be settled by an international instance, while reason (v) seems to explain the rule in terms of the assumption that the rule exists, since the host state will probably be unwilling to redress the wrong both before and after the exhaustion of remedies. These are subsidiary grounds for not seriously accepting these reasons as good reasons for the rule. They merely point to factors which may make the rule practically convenient: see further Amerasinghe, *State Responsibility for Injuries to Aliens* (1967) p. 171.

the rule applied equitably. The principal interests involved in the application of the rule are, however, those of the host or respondent state, the alien, his national state as the sponsor of his cause and the international community.

The interest of the host or respondent state

Emphasis has been given in the history of the rule to the interest of the respondent or host state. It is in the interest of the respondent state that it should have the opportunity of doing justice in its own way and of having an investigation and adjudication by its own tribunals upon the issues of law and fact which the claim involves in order to discharge its responsibility. The ICJ gave this as the rationale of the rule when it said in the *Interhandel Case* that

Before resort may be had to an international court in such a situation, it has been considered necessary that the State where the violation occurred should have an opportunity to redress it by its own means, within the framework of its own domestic legal system.[45]

Similarly, in the *Norwegian Loans Case*, Judge Read, albeit in a dissenting opinion, gave the same reason for the rule. He adverted also to the fact that the local courts should give a ruling on the facts and the law involved, when he said:

it is important to obtain the ruling of the local courts with regard to the issues of fact and law involved, before the international aspects are dealt with by an international tribunal. It is also important that the respondent State which is being charged with breach of international law should have an opportunity to rectify the position through its own tribunals.[46]

Judge Córdova, in a separate opinion in the *Interhandel Case*, gave a more elaborate and detailed explanation of the principal rationale for the rule when he said:

This principle . . . finds its basis and justification in reasons which are perhaps more important than the simple possibility of avoiding contradictory procedures and decisions. The main reason for its existence is the absolute necessity of harmonizing international and national jurisdictions – thus ensuring the respect due to the sovereign jurisdiction of States – to which nationals and foreigners

---

[45] 1959 ICJ Reports at p. 27.
[46] 1957 ICJ Reports at p. 97. Judge Read seems later to have restricted adjudication to national law aspects of the case. This was unwarranted. The national courts must settle the total dispute, taking into account international legal issues where relevant.

are subject and in the diplomatic protection of governments to which only foreigners are entitled. This harmony and respect for the sovereignty of States is achieved by granting priority to the jurisdiction of the State's domestic courts in cases where foreigners appeal against an act of its executive or legislative authorities. Such priority is in turn guaranteed only by respect for the principle of the exhaustion of local remedies . . . A State cannot even exercise diplomatic protection still less have recourse to international procedures for redress, unless its national has first exhausted the local means of judicial redress made available to him by the State whose acts he criticizes . . . The basis for the well-established principle of international procedure of the exhaustion of local remedies is the fundamental concept that a claim cannot be submitted, that there is no international claim unless the foreigner who has suffered injury has complied with this principle.[47]

The arbitral commission in the *Ambatielos Claim* endorsed the general emphasis on the respondent or host state's interest when it said that

The Respondent State has the right to require that full use be made of all local remedies before the issues in litigation are brought before an international court by the State whose nationals have allegedly been injured.[48]

Among textual authorities, perhaps C. de Visscher expressed felicitously the *raison d'être* of the rule in stating that

each State must be able to have exhausted in the first instance by its own courts points of fact or of law raised by the claims of foreigners which may possibly engage its responsibility: it is then entitled to await their final decision before it reaches a decision as to the international responsibilities which it may incur.[49]

---

[47] 1959 ICJ Reports at pp. 45ff.

[48] *Greece* v. *UK*, 12 UNRIAA at p. 119 (1956). See also the *Finnish Ships Arbitration* (*Finland* v. *UK*), 3 UNRIAA at p. 1501 (1934), for further support for the interests of the host or respondent state in the rule. Other judicial authorities which identify the recognition given to the sovereign interests of the host or respondent state include: President Klaestad in a dissenting opinion in the *Interhandel Case*, 1959 ICJ Reports at pp. 78ff.; Judge Winiarski in a dissenting opinion in the same case, *ibid.*, p. 83; Judge Armand Ugon in a dissenting opinion in the same case, *ibid.*, pp. 88ff.; Alfaro in a separate opinion in the *Ambatielos Claim* (*Greece* v. *UK*), 12 UNRIAA at p. 124 (1956).

[49] 'Denial of Justice in International Law', 52 *Hague Recueil* (1935) at p. 422. The statement is without prejudice to the question when international responsibility *arises* which is relevant to the discussion in Chapter 15 below. The Institut de Droit International took a similar view in the resolution passed at its Granada session: AIDI (1956) at p. 358. Some other authorities on the point are, e.g. Borchard, note 25 above, at p. 817; Eustathiades, *La Responsabilité internationale des états pour les actes des organes judiciaires et la problème du déni de justice en droit international* (1936), vol. 1, pp. 48ff. and 302; and Law, note 42 above, at p. 15.

There is clearly in such statements a recognition of, an emphasis on and perhaps a concession to the sovereign character of a state. Further, it is also much less expensive for the host state to go through the process of its own courts than to resort to an international instance, particularly if the dispute is settled at the lowest level in the adjudicatory system. There is also the advantage that the publicity of an international adjudication will be avoided by resolution of the dispute by the national courts.

The interest of the alien

However, the alien's interest in having an alleged wrong of an international character adjudicated upon and remedied in the quickest and most efficient way possible cannot be ignored. The rule is of little benefit to the alien if he can obtain quicker, more efficient and cheaper justice through an international adjudication. If resort to local remedies does not result in adequate redress, he will have spent valuable time and money in a pursuit which has been of no avail to him. Thus, a rule which requires resort to local remedies militates against the alien's interest to the extent that he can get more efficient justice through an international adjudication. This interest would, therefore, be relevant in determining the limits of the rule. The alien's main interest is in obtaining good justice at the lowest cost. As was said in the *Finnish Ships Arbitration* in the course of the judgment,

it appears hard to lay on the private individual the burden of incurring loss of money and time by going through the courts, only to exhaust what to him – at least, for the time being – must be a very unsatisfactory remedy.[50]

The interest of the alien's national state

The national state of the alien will share the alien's interest described above. The rule would clearly benefit the alien's national state to the extent that it relieves it from the burden of an international litigation, but it would certainly be interested in such relief only if its national obtains swift and satisfactory justice at the hands of the courts of the host state.

The interest of the international community

An important additional interest may be noted. The fact that the local proceedings are to be envisaged as a stage in the settlement of an

---

[50] *Finland v. Great Britain*, 3 UNRIAA at p. 1497 (1934). See also the *Ambatielos Claim* (*Greece v. UK*), 12 UNRIAA at p. 119 (1956); Alfaro, *ibid.*, p. 125; and Spiropoulos, *ibid.*, p. 128.

international dispute is a relevant consideration. The proceedings are first entrusted to an organ instituted by one of the parties to the dispute. But a basic interest is that of the international community in having a fair and efficient disposition of the dispute. This has an important bearing on the means to be offered by the respondent state in solving the dispute in its local courts. This results, among other things, in requiring the respondent state to do its best to help solve the dispute fairly.

Choices among competing interests

While the rule of local remedies is primarily a recognition of the sovereign rights of, and more or less a concession to, the host or respondent state, it would be inappropriate to conclude that, because it is not clear until the local organs have investigated the matter whether an international wrong has in fact been committed, this is the basis for the rule of local remedies,[51] or that there can be no wrong except through a defect in the administration of justice consequent upon the exhaustion of local remedies.[52] It will be shown in Chapter 4 that the latter view is untenable. The former view is also inaccurate, because not only does it ignore the fact that the rule is that local remedies must be exhausted, and not merely resorted to, in fact the operation of the rule does not lay to rest any doubts about an international wrong if the local courts decide that the respondent state has not committed a wrong. Neither of these theories can justifiably be invoked to explain choices among competing interests in the application of the rule.

Basically, the rule is a recognition of the sovereignty of the host state in so far as such state is in reality being permitted to settle through its own organs a dispute of an international nature to which it is a party. This approach is supported by the fact that the rule seems to have become entrenched in response to an insistence by host states on powers founded on sovereignty rather than because it emanated from a basic principle of justice inherent in the international legal order. Perhaps also of importance is the acceptance given to the rule without protest by national states of aliens, clearly because they found it a practical rule in terms of their own non-involvement in disputes arising from the problems of their nationals in their relations with other states.

---

[51] See e.g. O'Connell, vol. 2, p. 1024.

[52] See Judge Hudson in a dissenting opinion in the *Panavezys–Saldutiskis Railway Case*, PCIJ Series A/B No. 76 at p. 47 (1939); and Judge Morelli in a dissenting opinion in the *Barcelona Traction Co. Case*, 1964 ICJ Reports at p. 114.

It would follow that host states are in some sense being accorded a function by virtue of their sovereign status in the process of international dispute settlement. Local courts and quasi-judicial organs perform functions as agents of the international legal order in settling disputes involving aliens and arising from a violation of international law. Hence, on the one hand, the quest for methods to improve local justice and the investigation of local judicial and quasi-judicial institutions may be warranted, in order to discover how far impartial justice can be expected from the congeries of extant systems, and ultimately to demonstrate that the rule of local remedies can still operate equitably.[53] On the other hand, equally important are the scope and limits of the local remedies rule, which flow from bases comparable to and commensurate with those underlying the rule itself, with the ultimate object that the best interests of the international community are served in ensuring that the adjudication process within its legal order not merely functions, but functions equitably. In this exercise, a basic consideration would be the fact that the rule of local remedies as part of the law of state responsibility is relevant to the promotion and control of private foreign investment and technology flows and, therefore, to economic development.

Although the interests of the host state in protecting its sovereign power to settle disputes with aliens through the adjudicatory processes of its internal dispute settlement mechanisms are significant, the interests of the alien (and its national state) in quick, efficient and economical justice and the interests of the international community in the effective and peaceful settlement of disputes cannot be ignored. In short, the law does take into account the consideration that the alien should not be caused undue hardship. At the same time, it is apparent that there is no established hierarchy of social policy values which is relevant to choices among the competing interests involved when the rule of local remedies becomes applicable. What can be discerned is that, given the importance of economic development rather than the absolute protection of aliens as such in the modern international development process, there is good reason, while permitting the host state to have a fair opportunity to settle through its own organs disputes with aliens, also to recognize the limitations on the application of the rule of local remedies imposed by taking into account the interests of the alien (and his national state) and the international community. This may mean in a

---

[53] See e.g. Dawson and Head, *International Law, National Tribunals and Rights of Aliens* (1971).

given situation leaning towards limiting the rigid application of the rule rather than making unqualified concessions to the rights of sovereignty of host states.[54]

The rule in human rights protection

Since the end of the Second World War, particularly with the promulgation of the Universal Declaration of Human Rights in 1948, there has been a growing interest in the protection of human rights, but it was not until the European Convention on Human Rights came into force in 1953 that the protection of human rights became a practical reality. Many of the instruments relating to human rights incorporate the rule of local remedies, with the result that the rule has been implemented in situations slightly different from those for which the rule was originally designed. As will be seen, the rule applied to the protection of human rights is intended to be the rule of customary international law. Hence, the application of the rule to the protection of human rights may have had a special impact on the development of the rule. Technically, to the extent that the rule applied in the area of human rights protection is meant to be the rule of customary international law, not only should the application of the rule in that area mirror its application in the area

---

[54] There seems to have been some disagreement between the parties on the scope and limitations of the rule in the *Barcelona Traction Co. Case*. The differences arose as a result of emphasis being placed by one party on the rights of the host state to have its total system of dispute settlement invoked to the greatest extent possible, while the other sought a relaxation of the rigidity of the rule in favour of the alien by resorting to arguments based on normal practice, reasonableness and a certain avoidance of extraordinary means of judicial redress: see Spain's written pleadings, *Barcelona Traction Co. Case*, ICJ Pleadings (1962–9), vol. 1, pp. 242 and 254ff., vol. 4, pp. 592, 594, 596ff. and 602ff. and vol. 7, pp. 886ff. and 894ff.; Belgium's written pleadings, ICJ Pleadings (1962–9), vol. 1, pp. 217ff. and vol. 5, pp. 592ff.; Spain's oral argument, ICJ Pleadings (1962–9), vol. 3, p. 817, and vol. 9, pp. 562ff. and 592ff.; and Belgium's oral argument, ICJ Pleadings (1962–9), vol. 3, p. 602, and vol. 8, pp. 569ff. and 575ff. This difference of opinion demonstrates that there can be a real conflict of interests which requires resolution in terms of the values international law protects. In certain circumstances relating to the application of the rule of local remedies, such conflicts may present international law and its courts or organs with very difficult and sensitive choices. On the other hand, it is clear that there is good reason why the rule should be accepted in a modern context, where economic development of less developed nations is a priority, and implemented in an appropriate manner in spite of the differences of opinion that may be prevalent on the various aspects of the rule: see Ago, 'Sixth Report on state Responsibility', YBILC (1977), vol. 2, Part II, at pp. 42ff. For affirmation of the rule in a modern context, see also Dugard, 'Second Report on Diplomatic Protection', UN Doc.A/CN.4/514 at pp. 2ff. (2001).

of diplomatic protection in most respects, but also the evolution of the rule in its application to the protection of human rights could have a developmental impact on the rule as applied to diplomatic protection. In reality, an assessment must be made of the effect of differences in the application of the rule in the area of human rights protection on the rule as applied to diplomatic protection. At this point, the policies behind the rule in the protection of human rights and their relevance will be examined.

It has been said that 'there is a link between respect for freedom within the state and the maintenance of peace between states',[55] so that it follows that the international community has a vital interest in the protection of human rights, and 'the recognition and the protection of fundamental human rights became incumbent upon the international community, inspiring rules which now form an integral part of the international legal order'.[56] Traditionally, there have strictly been no general rules of international law pertaining to human rights, apart from the few there possibly were as a result of the law of diplomatic protection and the disputed rule that a state could justifiably use force 'for the purpose of protecting the inhabitants of another State from treatment so arbitrary and persistently abusive as to exceed the limits within which the sovereign is presumed to act with reason and justice'.[57] The law of diplomatic protection has been limited in general to the protection of a state's nationals against infringements of the law by other states, while the exact scope and very existence of the rule of humanitarian

---

[55] De Visscher, 'Report on the Fundamental Rights of Man', AIDI (1947) at p. 155. See also Hamburger, 'Droits de l'homme et relations internationales', 97 *Hague Recueil* (1959) at p. 298; Cassin, 'Protection internationale des droits de l'homme', *Encyclopédie Française* (1964) at p. 377; and Moskowitz, *Human Rights and World Order* (1958). Recently, the importance and content of the European system of human rights protection was examined in Van Dijk and Van Hoof, *Theory and Practice of the European Convention on Human Rights* (1998). On the Inter-American system, see now in general Cerna, 'The Inter-American Commission on Human Rights: Its Organization and Examination of Petitions and Communications', in Harris and Livingstone (eds.), *The Inter-American System of Human Rights* (1998) at p. 85; Cançado Trindade, 'The Inter-American System at the Dawn of a New Century', in Harris and Livingstone, above, at p. 402; and the bibliography, *ibid*. The Human Rights Committee's approach is presented in McGoldrick, *The Human Rights Committee* (1994). There is no fundamental disagreement in general on the bases of human rights protection in these works.

[56] Golsong, 'Implementation of International Protection of Human Rights', 10 *Hague Recueil* (1963) at p. 10.

[57] Stowell, *International Law* (1931), Part 4, p. 349. See also Grotius, *De Jure Belli ac Pacis* (1625), book II, chapter 25, para. 8(2); and H. Lauterpacht, 'The Grotian Tradition in International Law', 23 BYIL (1946) at p. 46.

intervention has been questioned,[58] although if it were admitted to exist it would give a very limited protection. The systematic protection of the national against his own state or the stateless individual against states can only be based on a broader acceptance of substantive rules and principles relating to human rights which apparently are only coming to be recognized, if at all, in customary international law. In any case, the remedies for the protection of human rights as such come through the medium of conventions and agreements. The implementation of protection remedially can only be determined by the provisions of such instruments, since there is no procedure at customary or general international law to secure the implementation of such protection, particularly against national states of the injured individual. Thus, at present it is to the instruments by which such protection is implemented that resort must be had in order to discover whether and to what extent the rule of local remedies is applicable to the scheme of such protection.

A preliminary question connected with the main issue of policies affecting the rule of local remedies is whether the rule would be implied in the absence of specific inclusion in a human rights treaty or convention. This question cannot apparently be answered by reference to the generally accepted rule that in the case of diplomatic protection the rule is applied in the absence of any indication that it should not apply. The rule as a part of the law of diplomatic protection is arguably distinguishable.

In the case of diplomatic protection, the rule grew up as a result of the practice of states before it came to be recognized as a requirement, but in the case of the protection of human rights there is no such practice that has yet evolved. It may be argued then that, because the provision of remedies for the protection of human rights is dependent on convention or treaty, the presumption would be that the rule is not applicable to human rights protection in the absence of express provision or by necessary implication, unless the protection given takes the form of diplomatic protection, in which case the rule could be implied even within the regime of the express protection of the human rights convention. This could be a formal position. On the other hand, there is a strong case for the view that, where remedial protection is given at an international level in cases of human rights violations, the rule should apply on the analogy of diplomatic protection even in the

---

[58] See R. Chakravarti, *Human Rights and the United Nations* (1958) p. 19.

absence of express or implied provision. If it applies in the absence of express provision, where aliens are the victims of violations of international norms, that is all the more reason why it should apply where a national of the respondent state in the human rights situation is the victim. He is part of and linked to that state, and may be expected to use the local system of remedies for redress before invoking international remedies. That an alien is the victim of a human rights violation and is invoking international remedies outside the institution of diplomatic protection would not entitle him to avoid the rule either. If the rule applies under the general law when diplomatic protection is exercised, he may expect the rule to be applied to him when he invokes remedies under an international instrument outside the institution of diplomatic protection.

The argument that the rule does not apply as such to human rights protection, however, bears further examination and may be elaborated as follows. There is reason to make a distinction between the institution of diplomatic protection and the protection of human rights. The rule of local remedies was developed in connection with the institution of diplomatic protection and prior to that at a time when the state's control was regarded as exclusively appropriate for matters taking place within its jurisdiction.[59] The international community was still tied to a very rigid theory of sovereignty. It is arguable that in situations where the duty to respect human rights is recognized by a state the surrender of what would have been termed sovereignty need not today be conditional upon the recognition of internal methods of settlement before the issue can be examined at an international level. There is a tendency still to revere the exclusive jurisdiction of states, but it would seem logically to follow from the recognition of the fact that individuals have fundamental human rights, even though they may have no connection with foreign states, that a concession has been made which involves the surrender of exclusive jurisdictional rights, so that theoretically there should be a presumption that violations of such rights should be susceptible of examination at an international level without the need for the exhaustion of local remedies.[60] It would follow that, for instance,

---

[59] See e.g. Wittenberg, 'La Recevabilité des réclamations devant les juridictions internationales', 41 *Hague Recueil* (1932) at p. 51; and Eagleton, note 39 above, at p. 95.

[60] See also the Austrian argument before the European Commission of Human Rights, in *Austria v. Italy*, Application No. 788/60, 4 YBECHR at pp. 146ff. The Commission took a different view, though the statement of the view was not necessary for the decision of the case: 4 YBECHR at pp. 148ff.

under the UN International Covenant on Economic, Social and Cultural Rights, since no provision is made for the requirement that local remedies should be exhausted in connection with the enforcement procedure, there would be no need for them to be exhausted before that procedure comes into operation. The position would be different under the International Covenant on Civil and Political Rights, where under Article 41(c) local remedies must be exhausted. Also, under the Charter of the United Nations it would not be necessary that local remedies be exhausted before the United Nations decides to take action under Articles 55 and 56.[61]

The context of human rights protection

The application of the rule of local remedies to the protection of human rights has resulted up to now generally from conventional provisions. There are instances, such as under the OAS Charter, where the rule is applied under resolutions of an international political organ. However, these instances are generically, though derivatively, conventional too, in that the resolutions flow from conventional authority. Thus, what is really important is to understand how the interpretation of instruments providing for such protection has been treated. The approach taken by the European Commission of Human Rights and the European Court of Human Rights in some of the leading cases decided by them is illustrative.

In *Austria* v. *Italy*, the European Commission followed an objective method of interpretation. The view was taken that the obligations undertaken by the parties to the European Convention on Human Rights were essentially of an objective nature intended to protect the fundamental human rights of individuals rather than creative of subjective and reciprocal rights for the parties themselves.[62] In *Golder* v. *UK*, the Commission reaffirmed this view, adding that 'The provisions of the Convention shall not be interpreted restrictively so as to prevent its aims and objects being achieved'.[63] The Commission further stated:

---

[61] It is a different question whether under an instrument which basically incorporates the rule of local remedies the rule could be applied in certain areas by implication where no explicit reference is made to the rule, such as, under the European Convention, to inter-state disputes, or to disputes relating to a prevailing condition. Issues of this nature are dealt with in Chapters 6 and 7 below.

[62] Application No. 788/60, *Report of the Plenary Commission* at p. 37.

[63] Application No. 4451/70, *Report of the Commission* at p. 25.

The decisive consideration here must be that the overriding function of this Convention is to protect the rights of the individual and not to lay down as between States mutual obligations which are to be restrictively interpreted having regard to the sovereignty of these States. On the contrary, the role of the Convention and the function of its interpretation is to make the protection of the individual effective. It is true that it represents only 'first steps' for the enforcement of human rights . . . But this fact cannot be relied upon to justify restrictive interpretations running contrary to its overall purpose.[64]

The European Court in the same case endorsed the views of the Commission that interpretation should be in the light of the ultimate object and purpose of the Convention and as a step towards the collective enforcement of human rights.[65] In two earlier cases, the Court had emphasized the need to interpret the Convention so as to realize its aims and objects and not to restrict to the greatest possible degree the obligations undertaken by the parties[66] and adverted to the fact that the general aim of the Convention was the effective protection of human rights which implied a just balance between the protection of the general interest of the community and the respect due to fundamental human rights, with particular importance being attached to the latter.[67]

The approach to interpretation of the Convention described above reflects some of the basic differences between human rights protection and diplomatic protection. While the former is based at present entirely on conventional law and the latter primarily on customary law, another significant difference between the two institutions is the nature of the connecting link which is a prerequisite for the exercise of protection. In the case of diplomatic protection the connecting link is nationality – the alien must be a national of the protecting state. In the case of human rights protection there is no such requirement. The individual is protected by the enforcement system *qua* individual and not as a national of a particular state. The fact that a person, natural or legal, is injured or a victim as a result of a breach of the Convention gives him a right directly to litigate his grievance before international organs set up under the Convention.

Even where a state takes up a case where an individual's rights have been violated, there is no *vinculum juris* required in the form of nationality. A state party to the Convention which takes up a case does not

---

[64] Application No. 4451/70, *Report of the Commission* at p. 31.
[65] *Golder v. UK*, ECHR Series A, at pp. 9–12 (1975).
[66] *Wemhoff v. Federal Republic of Germany*, ECHR Series A, at p. 23 (1968).
[67] *Belgian Linguistics Case*, ECHR Series A, at p. 32 (1968).

defend its national interest, as happens in diplomatic protection, nor does it act in defence purely of the interests of its national. Not only may a state take up a case where its national is injured but it may do so when any individual is injured, national or not. The collective and mutual guarantee of human rights by all parties to the Convention is a basic premise of the system of human rights protection and empowers a state party to the Convention to act in respect of an injured individual, while also permitting an injured individual to seek protection himself. States may protect not only their own nationals but stateless persons, nationals of the respondent state and nationals of third states. As the European Commission very early on stated in connection with the right of a state party to the European Convention to bring a case before it:

> the High Contracting Parties have empowered anyone of their members to bring before the Commission any alleged breach of the Convention, regardless of whether the victims of the alleged breach are nationals of the applicant State or whether the alleged breach otherwise particularly affects the interests of the applicant State . . . It follows that a High Contracting Party . . . is not to be regarded as exercising a right of action for the purpose of enforcing its own rights, but rather as bringing before the Commission an alleged violation of the public order of Europe.[68]

Unlike in the case of diplomatic protection, not only does the individual initiate action himself, when he makes use of the machinery of protection, but the entire system under the European Convention, involving the Commission, the Court and the states parties to the Convention, is aimed at protecting the individual directly *erga omnes* through the mechanism of the collective guarantee, without the intervention of a national state which may invoke political considerations in taking a decision whether to exercise protection or not, and even against his own national state.[69]

---

[68] *Austria v. Italy*, Application No. 788/60, *Report of the Plenary Commission* at p. 37. The fact that individuals cannot be parties before the European Court further reinforces the theory of the collective guarantee. In proceedings before the Court, the Commission participates in the proceedings *vis-à-vis* the state alleged to have violated the Convention. In this capacity, it represents the public interest: see Mosler, 'The Protection of Human Rights by International Legal Procedure', 52 *Georgetown Law Journal* (1964) at p. 818.

[69] See Eustathiades, 'La Convention européenne des droits de l'homme et le Statut du Conseil de l'Europe', 53 *Die Friedens-Warte* (1955–6) at pp. 68–9; Rolin, 'Le Rôle du requérant dans la procédure prévue par la Commission européenne des droits de l'homme', 9 RHDI (1956) at p. 9; Eustathiades, 'Les Recours individuels à la Commission européenne des droits de l'homme', in *Grundprobleme des Internationalen Rechts – Festschrift für Jean Spiropoulos* (1957) at p. 121; Pilotti, 'Le Recours des particuliers devant les juridictions internationales', *ibid.*, p. 351; Durante, *Ricorsi*

The ability of individuals directly to litigate under the system of human rights protection is also a departure from the practice of diplomatic protection. This power is a basic premise of the systems of human rights protection. It de-emphasizes the role of states, national or otherwise, in the procedure of institutional protection and gives the individual a very direct interest in his own protection. It gives the individual a status which he never really had under the institution of diplomatic protection.

The basis of the local remedies rule in human rights protection

The differences between conventional systems of human rights protection and diplomatic protection may result in a slightly, but only slightly, different orientation in certain respects of the bases of the rule of local remedies as it is applied in human rights protection. In general, the instruments on which such protection is based refer to 'the generally recognized principles of international law' as the point of reference for the rule of local or domestic remedies to be applied. Nevertheless, the implications of this formulation are subject to analysis.

As has been seen, the rule of local remedies in the law of diplomatic protection in general revolves around four groups of interests, and certain values are reflected in the application of the rule. In the case of the protection of human rights, the interests involved are those of the respondent state, the individual, any particular state that may make a claim on behalf of an injured individual, and the international community, particularly of states parties to the instrument. The interests of these entities correspond to the interests of the four groups connected with diplomatic protection.

The rule is applicable to the protection of human rights on the basis, as has been stated, that primary recognition is given to the respondent state's interest in preventing 'la substitution d'une procédure internationale sur voies de recours internes en vue de permettre à l'Etat de réparer ses propres moyens'.[70] This has been recognized by the European

---

Individuali ad Organi Internazionali (1958) pp. 129ff.; Vasak, La Convention européenne des droits de l'homme (1964) pp. 96ff.; Mosler, note 68 above, at pp. 818ff.; Virally, 'L'accès des particuliers à une instance internationale: la protection des droits de l'homme dans le cadre européen', 20 Mémoires publiés par la faculté de droit de Genève (1964) at pp. 67ff.; Müller-Rappard, 'Le Droit d'action en vertu des dispositions de la Convention européenne des droits de l'homme', 9 RBDI (1968) at pp. 491ff., 497ff. and 503; and Economopoulos, 'Les Eléments politiques et judiciaires dans la procédure instaurée par la Convention européenne des droits de l'homme', 22 RHDI (1969) at pp. 125ff.

[70] Eustathiades, 'La Convention européenne des droits de l'homme et le Statut du Conseil de l'Europe', 52 Die Friedens-Warte (1953–4) at pp. 355ff.

Commission of Human Rights on more than one occasion. Thus, in an early case the Commission said that

the rule requiring the exhaustion of domestic remedies as a condition of the presentation of an international claim is founded upon the principle that the respondent State must first have an opportunity to redress by its own means within the framework of its own domestic legal system the wrong alleged to have been done to the individual.[71]

This reason is clearly similar to that which underlies the rule of local remedies in the law of diplomatic protection. Furthermore, the individual, any state that may bring a claim and the international community of states parties to the instrument also have an interest in seeing that the domestic remedies work and provide satisfactory solutions for reasons similar to those which the alien, the alien's national state, and the international community have in seeing that local (domestic) remedies work in the law of diplomatic protection. Indeed, the individual who is not an alien may have a greater interest in seeing that local or domestic remedies work than an alien, because he will generally be more closely connected with the defendant state. On the other hand, the interests of individual states as such may have less importance in the application of the rule to human rights protection, while the collective interest of the parties to the Convention in guaranteeing effective protection might require giving their concern for the proper application of the rule a special emphasis, more so than the interest of the international community in the application of the rule to diplomatic protection.

It is arguable that the interests of the individual should enjoy greater emphasis in certain respects in the context of human rights protection than in the law of diplomatic protection. A factor which perhaps gives some measure of formal support to this view is that in the law of diplomatic protection the right of the alien's national state is regarded as violated, so that the interests of the alien are more obviously identified with those of his national state,[72] which is an impersonal entity. Although the conventional arrangements on human rights provide collective guarantees, there was every intention that the rights guaranteed were to be conferred on individuals; the violation of such rights is not regarded merely as the breach of an obligation owed to the guaranteeing state or states but as an interference with the rights of individuals.

---

[71] Application No. 343/57, *Report of the Commission* at p. 36; and *Austria v. Italy*, Application No. 788/60, *Report of the Plenary Commission* at p. 43.

[72] See Vasak, note 69 above, at p. 10; Robertson, *Human Rights in Europe* (1963) p. 10.

Hence, the individual is given somewhat greater recognition in the protection of human rights, with the result that there is a good case for giving his special interests somewhat greater emphasis. In both diplomatic protection and human rights protection the principal object of the local remedies rule is similar, namely, to enable the respondent state to do justice in a situation which to a large extent it has controlled. There is also a similarity between the two institutions insofar as the affected entity is an individual. On the other hand, in the case of human rights protection the interests of the individual are given special prominence, to the extent that the rights violated are considered to be those of the individual, and he is given direct access to international machinery to enforce the protection of his rights. By the same token, the international community of states parties to the conventional arrangements has a significant interest in the protection of the individual through the system it has established, an interest which may be more pervasive than that of the international community in the protection of the alien through diplomatic intervention.

On the theoretical level, therefore, there may be a good argument for giving more recognition to the interests of the individual and of the international community of states parties to the conventional arrangements, at least to some extent and in certain respects, in the application of the rule of local remedies to human rights protection, than is given to them in the case of diplomatic protection. But this is only a starting point for identifying possible differences in the two situations. There are other factors which will affect the application of the rule to human rights protection, such as the formulation of reference to the rule in the conventional instruments, which could override any of the purely theoretical considerations. On the other hand, it may be useful to recognize that any departures from the principles governing the application of the rule to diplomatic protection could be justified on the premise that it is a particularly important objective in the protection of human rights that the individual should have quick and efficient access to the international forum created under the conventional scheme, so much so that the implementation of the rule of local or domestic remedies should not become an unjustified impediment to such access. Yet, this consideration should not per se result in arbitrary departures from the interpretation of the rule as applied in diplomatic protection, nor does it mean that refined applications of the rule in human rights protection should not be transposed to diplomatic protection, on the ground that human rights protection is different and special. By the same token, it would be incorrect to take the view that human rights protection is interested in 'redress',[73] thus implying that diplomatic protection is not. Both institutions are basically aimed at redress for (ultimately) the individual, whatever may be the formal structure of the law. Both institutions take into account local remedies, as the case may be, for this purpose. Both institutions recognize the ultimate relevance of an international forum for the possible securing of such redress. Hence, why should the assumption be made that human rights protection intrinsically attaches more importance to an international forum than does diplomatic protection? The recognition given, as such, to local remedies in both connections clearly means that they are presumptively a viable means of 'redress' in both cases. The real issue, then, is whether the one institution (human rights protection) prefers or should prefer, for whatever reasons, easier access to the international instance than the other (diplomatic protection).

The formulation of the rule in human rights instruments

General policy considerations are subject to express or necessarily implied contradiction or modification in operative conventions or treaties. As already seen, it is because of express reference to the rule of local remedies in conventions on human rights protection that it becomes necessary that the rule be applied before the relevant international proceeding is commenced. Of the current instruments, the UN International Covenant on Economic, Social and Cultural Rights contains no reference to the rule of local remedies.[74] It is submitted that in this case the rule is irrelevant, as has been stated above. The same applies to the provisions of the Charter of the United Nations relating to human rights.

Four current instruments in which the rule is referred to are examined here as the prime examples of the application of the rule to human rights protection.

First, the UN International Covenant on Civil and Political Rights requires in Article 41(c) that the UN Human Rights Committee shall:

deal with a matter referred to it only after it has ascertained that all available domestic remedies have been invoked and exhausted in the matter, in conformity with the generally recognized principles of international law.

---

[73] Cançado Trindade, note 55 above, at p. 401, stresses redress as an object of human rights protection to the exclusion of diplomatic protection!

[74] The rule was not raised in the discussion of the instrument in the organs of the UN: see UN Doc. A/2929 at pp. 333ff.; and UN Doc. A/6546 at pp. 9ff.

The Article also makes an explicit exception where the application of the remedies is unreasonably prolonged.

It is clear that the rule of local remedies is expressly intended to be applicable. Further, the rule is to be applied in accordance with the generally recognized principles of international law, so that broad recognition must be given to the principle that local remedies must be exhausted and to the principle that there are limitations on this rule. The express provision that the Human Rights Committee must ascertain whether the local remedies have been invoked and exhausted would seem to introduce a somewhat stricter measure for the applicability of the rule than in general international law. In general international law, the rule can only be invoked if the respondent state raises an objection based on it.[75] Under this Convention, it would seem that the matter must be raised by the Human Rights Committee *proprio motu* as a matter of course, if it is not raised by the respondent state, and a finding must be made that the rule has not been infringed before further action can be taken. This has been the practice of the Human Rights Committee since it gave its first decision in 1977 under the Optional Protocol to the Covenant. An exception to the need for fulfilling the requirements of the rule is made specifically in the case of undue delay by the respondent state in the provision of remedies. This merely embodies a recognized exception to the rule that local remedies must be exhausted. The fact that it is expressly mentioned does not mean that the maxim *expressio unius exclusio alterius* can be applied to exclude other possible exceptions to or limitations on the rule. It will be seen in Chapter 13 that the Human Rights Committee has taken a broad view of limitations on or exceptions to the rule under the Optional Protocol to the Covenant. It would also not be possible to argue that the rule of local remedies does not apply when an alien is not involved, as this would defeat the purpose of incorporating the rule in this system of protection of human rights. It is to be noted that Articles 2 and 5 of the Optional Protocol to the Covenant also have a similar requirement relating to the exhaustion of domestic remedies.

---

[75] The practice of the PCIJ and the ICJ has been consistent in this regard. The two courts have always regarded the rule as one that must be invoked by the respondent state as an objection to admissibility: see e.g. the *Chorzów Factory Case*, PCIJ Series A No. 9 (1927); the *Panavezys–Saldutiskis Railway Case*, PCIJ Series A/B No. 76 (1939); the *Norwegian Loans Case*, 1957 ICJ Reports at p. 14; the *Interhandel Case*, 1959 ICJ Reports at p. 11; and the *Barcelona Traction Co. Case*, 1964 ICJ Reports at p. 12.

Secondly, the European Convention on Human Rights states in Article 26 that the Commission 'may only deal with the matter after all domestic remedies have been exhausted according to the generally recognised rules [*principes*] of international law'. The *travaux préparatoires* give little indication of how this Article is to be interpreted.[76] However, the exhaustion of domestic remedies is clearly required according to the generally recognized principles of international law. It is not entirely clear how far the interests of the individual and of the international community may be given greater weight than in connection with diplomatic protection, but there is room for interpretation. The European Commission of Human Rights has taken the view that it must investigate the question of local remedies *proprio motu*, even if the matter is not raised by the respondent state.[77] Under Article 27(3), the Commission must reject any petition which it considers inadmissible under Article 26. The Commission has taken the view that this does not prevent the joinder to the merits of the objection to admissibility.[78] No express mention of the rule of local remedies is made in connection with cases brought before the European Court of Human Rights. However, necessary implication may require the Court to take some account of the rule.[79]

Thirdly, the American Convention on Human Rights states in Article 46 that:

1. Admission by the Commission of a petition or communication lodged in accordance with Articles 44 or 45 shall be subject to the following requirements:
(a) that the remedies under domestic law have been pursued and exhausted in accordance with generally recognized principles of international law;
(b) that the petition or communication is lodged within a period of six months from the date on which the party alleging violation of its rights was notified of the final judgment; . . .
2. The provisions of paragraphs 1(a) and 1(b) of this article shall not be applicable when:
(a) the domestic legislation of the state concerned does not afford due process of law for the protection of the right or rights that have allegedly been violated;
(b) the party alleging violation of his rights has been denied access to the remedies under domestic law or has been prevented from exhausting them; or
(c) there has been unwarranted delay in rendering a final judgment under the aforementioned remedies.

[76] See Eustathiades, note 70 above, at pp. 354ff.
[77] Application No. 524/59, 3 YBECHR p. 354. See also Rule 45 of the Rules of Procedure of the Commission.
[78] Application No. 2991/66, 24 *Collection* at pp. 116ff.
[79] See the *Matznetter Case*, ECHR Series A (1969).

The position seems to be similar to that prevailing under the European Convention on Human Rights, except that there is express provision that the rule does not apply in three situations: (i) where the legislation of the defendant state does not provide for due process; (ii) where there is arbitrary denial of access to the courts by the authorities; and (iii) where there is unwarranted delay in the rendering of a final judgment. In all these situations, under the general international law applicable to diplomatic protection there would be no need to exhaust local remedies. It is doubtful whether the principle *expressio unius exclusio alterius* would apply to prevent the application of other limitations to the rule extant in customary international law, particularly because Article 46(2) does not state that that rule is inapplicable *only* in the circumstances mentioned.

Fourthly, the UN International Covenant on the Elimination of All Forms of Racial Discrimination states in Article 11(3) (and Article 14(1)(a)) that the Committee on the Elimination of Racial Discrimination shall deal with a matter referred to it 'after it has ascertained that all available domestic remedies have been invoked and exhausted in the case, in conformity with the generally recognised principles of international law'. This Article also makes an explicit exception where the application of remedies is unreasonably prolonged. The effect of these provisions is the same as that of Article 41(c) of the UN International Covenant on Civil and Political Rights which has been referred to above.

Finally, in addition there are non-judicial, perhaps quasi-judicial, organs operating under other conventions, such as the Committee Against Torture, acting pursuant to the Convention Against Torture, which apply the rule. Further, sometimes by resolutions made under multilateral conventions constituting international organizations, organs of organizations apply the rule in their work. This is the case with the work of the Sub-Commission on Prevention of Discrimination and Protection of Minorities, operating pursuant to resolutions taken by the ECOSOC, and the work on human rights, outside the American Convention on Human Rights, of the Inter-American Commission on Human Rights which is undertaken pursuant solely to resolutions under the OAS Charter.

Trends in the application of theory in human rights protection as related to diplomatic protection

The rule of local (domestic) remedies, in its application both to diplomatic protection and to human rights protection, has had its supporters and opponents,[80] to the extent that a variety of consequences have been suggested as desirable. But, as the rule is still viable in its application to diplomatic protection, what is relevant is to take note of how far the application of the rule in the area of human rights protection, may be the same as or different from its application to diplomatic protection because of similarities or differences in the basic premises governing the two institutions. As will be seen later, even in relation to diplomatic protection the rule may conceivably have extensive limitations or exceptions to it flowing from its functional basis, so much so that a mechanical approach to the rule as a preventive measure protecting the sovereignty of states may not be warranted, but a more realistic interpretation of the application in practice of the rule may be demanded so as to maintain a certain equilibrium between the interests involved.[81] The question generally is how far is variation of the detailed rules as they have been applied to diplomatic protection called for, when the rule is applied to the protection of human rights.

In regard to the relationship between the institutions of diplomatic protection and human rights protection, textual authorities have taken a variety of views.[82] More specifically, as far as the rule of local remedies is concerned there is a considerable amount of practice, especially

[80] For example, Head favours the application of the rule to diplomatic protection: 'A Fresh Look at the Local Remedies Rule', 5 CYIL (1967) at pp. 142ff.; while Ténékidès opposed it as early as 1933, questioning its foundations as a rule of international law: 'L'épuisement des voies de recours internes comme condition préalable de l'instance internationale', 14 RI (1933) at pp. 514ff. Among ardent supporters of the rule as applied in the protection of human rights may be mentioned Guinand, 'La Règle de l'épuisement des voies de recours internes dans le cadre international de protection des droits de l'homme', 4 RBDI (1968) at pp. 472ff. Opponents of the rule as applied to human rights protection include Drost, *Human Rights as Legal Rights* (1965) pp. 87, 90, 117ff., 122ff. and 133ff.; Antonopoulos, *La Jurisprudence des organes de la Convention européenne des droits de l'homme* (1967) pp. 258ff.; and Castberg, *The European Convention on Human Rights* (1974) p. 191.

[81] See, e.g. the view expressed in H. Friedmann, 'Epuisement des voies de recours internes', 14 RI (1933) at pp. 319ff.; Chappez, *La Règle de l'épuisement des voies de recours internes* (1972) p. 204; and Amerasinghe, 'The Local Remedies Rule in an Appropriate Perspective', 36 ZaöRV (1976) at pp. 728ff.

[82] Cançado Trindade, *The Application of the Rule of Exhaustion of Local Remedies in International Law* (1983) pp. 18ff., has identified five broad categories among the authorities as follows: (i) those who postulate an historical continuum between the two systems (e.g. Kiss, 'La Condition des étrangers en droit international et les droits de l'homme', 1 *Miscellanea W. J. Ganshof van der Meersch* (1972) at pp. 499ff.; and Eustathiades, 'Les Sujets du droit international et la responsabilité internationale: nouvelles tendances', 84 Hague Recueil (1953) at pp. 586ff.); (ii) those who regard human rights protection as absorbed and developed by diplomatic protection (e.g. Dumas, in 37 AIDI (1932) at p. 327, foreshadowed this approach); (iii) those who have stated that

under the European Convention on Human Rights, which shows that the experience of human rights protection has resulted both in variations of the exact practice relating to the implementation of the rule in diplomatic protection as well as in similarities to it. Suffice it here to examine a few examples of what may be described as special features in order to prove the point. More details will emerge when the particular applications of the rule are discussed later.

An important distinction was made by the European Commission of Human Rights in *Austria v. Italy*, when the Commission pointed out that 'by including the words "according to the generally recognized rules of international law" in Article 26 the authors of the Convention intended to limit the material content of the rule and not its field of application *ratione personae*'.[83] The issue raised in the case was whether the rule applied when applications were brought by states (rather than individuals) under Article 24 of the Convention, which did not specifically incorporate the rule. While the Commission held that the rule was applicable under Article 24 as under Article 26, it made it quite clear that in regard to the material content of the rule customary international law was to be followed. The material content covers such matters as the scope of and limitations on the rule. Clearly, in regard to those matters it was the view of the Commission that the customary law relating to local remedies should be followed, irrespective of any argument that may possibly be made in favour of departure from the customary law depending on the slight differences in the basic premises of the two systems of protection. In regard to other matters, such as the incidence of the rule and waiver, the Commission left room for differing approaches, although there was no specific reference to an application of the law so as to favour the individual. Thus, as far as the material content of the rule

diplomatic protection has been absorbed and developed by human rights protection (e.g. García Amador, note 18 above, pp. 199ff.); (iv) those who believe that the protection of aliens is a particularization of human rights protection (e.g. Elles, 'Aliens and Activities of the United Nations in the Field of Human Rights', 7 *Revue des droits de l'homme* (1974) at pp. 296ff.); and (v) those who hold that the two systems are incompatible and not parallel (e.g. O'Connell, vol. 2, p. 1031; Castrén, 'Some Considerations upon the Conception, Development and Importance of Diplomatic Protection', 11 JIR (1962) at p. 40; and Berlia, 'Contribution à l'étude de la nature de la protection diplomatique', 3 AFDI (1957) at pp. 70ff.). This categorization may at times appear to be too facile, as the views taken by each authority may not always be confined to one or other approach. Cançado Trindade himself prefers the last view but in respect of the rule of local remedies this view does not exactly reflect the position adopted in practice. There are areas of parallelism and areas of difference.

[83] Application No. 788/60, *Report of the Plenary Commission* at p. 44.

is concerned, where, as in the European Convention, generally recognized rules of international law are textually invoked, the application of the rule in the context of human rights protection may conceivably be treated as compatible with and, indeed, a development of the rule of local remedies applicable to diplomatic protection, even though in a few other areas differences may appear.

So much having been said for the formal identity of the material content of the rule in the two systems of protection, it remains to consider how in fact the differences in the policies behind the rule as applied in the two systems of protection could affect the implementation of the rule. The European Commission and Court have indicated that the differences may have an impact in certain areas. A few examples are discussed here.

In *Austria* v. *Italy*, the European Commission held that, regardless of the position in customary international law, the argument that, when a state party to the Convention files an application under Article 24 on behalf of a non-national, the rule does not apply, because that Article is silent on the matter and because the state is not exercising its right of diplomatic protection but rather is taking action in regard to a 'direct' injury to it, could not be used to exclude the application of the rule. The rule was found to be applicable by implication and, because, while the applicant state was exercising its rights in regard to an injury resulting from a violation of a collective guarantee, this could not be considered a direct injury, in the same sense that an injury caused to a state, for example by a violation of the rights of one of its diplomats, was a direct injury to which the rule ought not to be applicable, even though there might be some difference between the case in hand and the case of diplomatic protection.

In the *Matznetter Case*,[84] the European Court was confronted with the argument that, because the applicant had not fully exhausted domestic remedies at the time he filed his application with the European Commission, although he had done so by the time the Commission had given its decision, the rule of domestic remedies had not been observed and therefore the application should have been declared inadmissible by the Commission. The Court held in favour of the Commission that domestic remedies should have been fully exhausted only at the time the Commission decided the case and not necessarily at the time the application was filed, in contrast to the requirement of the law of diplomatic

---

[84] ECHR Series A (1969).

protection that the rule should have been observed at the time the case was brought. It is not entirely clear here on the facts whether the Court came to a conclusion which was in conflict with the customary international law of diplomatic protection, as, indeed, it did itself indicate,[85] for the reason that this case concerned a continuing situation, but the statement which was a statement of principle as such must be noted.

In *Ireland v. UK*, the applicant state contended before the European Commission that the rule did not apply to a situation where legislative measures and administrative practices which were allegedly incompatible with the Convention were the subject of the application, because the application was not being brought as a measure of diplomatic protection. The Commission rejected the argument, holding that under the Convention the rule was applicable to cases brought by states under Article 24 of the Convention.[86]

Some observations are in order. It would seem that there is a growing tendency, among text writers and analysts, to invoke the contextual differences in the application of the rule of local remedies to the two institutions of diplomatic protection and human rights protection as reasons for taking a more 'flexible' approach to the application of the rule to human rights protection, in order to bring about the result that it is made easier to avoid the application of the rule or to apply it so as to favour the individual or individuals whose rights have allegedly been violated.[87] However, it is apparent that, as the European Commission has observed, theoretically the rule is to be applied, as regards its *material content*, in the same way pursuant to customary international law in the case of both human rights protection and diplomatic protection. This procedure is clearly subject to modification where, because of express

---

[85] ECHR Series A, at p. 32 (1969). See also the *Stögmüller Case*, ECHR Series A, at p. 42 (1969). In the latter case, the Court took the same view on the same issue as in the *Matznetter Case*.

[86] Application No. 5310/71, 41 *Collection* at p. 85 (1972). There have been cases in which the Commission has opted not to apply the local remedies rule where legislative and administrative measures were in issue: the *First Greek Case*, Applications Nos. 3321/67, 3322/67, 3323/67 and 3344/67, 12 YBECHR at p. 21 (1968). The point was, however, further discussed in the Commission's second decision on admissibility: 12 YBECHR at pp. 21ff.

[87] See in this sense, e.g. Perrin, 'Organisation judiciaire interne et protection des ressortissants étrangers en droit international', 24 *Revue juridique et politique – Indépendence et coopération* (1970) at pp. 52ff.; Spatafora, 'La Regola del Previo Esaurimento dei Ricorsi Interni nella Giurisprudenza della Commissione Europea dei Diritti dell'Uomo', 11 RDE (1971) at pp. 111ff.; and Cançado Trindade, note 82 above, at pp. 45ff.

provision or necessary intendment, a written convention is to be interpreted otherwise. On the other hand, while the principle is clear that the material content of the rule is basically the same in the context of both institutions, the manner in which it is applied in respect of its material content to new situations in human rights protection which have not been faced before in diplomatic protection could conceivably reflect a certain 'flexibility' of approach which may result in a relaxation of the 'rigidity' of the rule even as it is applied to diplomatic protection.[88] This could be a consequence of the impact of contextual differences between the two institutions. While this kind of interaction cannot be ruled out, it would be appropriate to recognize at the same time that, although there may be a presumption in favour of the absence of conflict, in the event of truly conflicting applications respecting the material content of the rule, it would have to be conceded that the rule is not being applied to human rights protection in accordance with general international law, which would mean that as far as the law of diplomatic protection is concerned the conflict must arguably – and this *is* an argument, as will be seen – be resolved in favour of the manner in which it has been or would be properly applied to that law.

As regards areas outside the material content of the rule, there is good reason to believe that in human rights protection an individual approach is being taken to the application of the rule, based on the contextual situation of such protection and the interpretation of the written instruments governing it. As the examples discussed above show, it does not follow from this that the approach taken to the application of the rule will always favour the individual or individuals affected by eliminating or relaxing any so-called 'rigour' that there may be in its application. In *Austria* v. *Italy* and *Ireland* v. *UK*, for instance, the differences in the contextual situation which were noted led to the conclusion that the rule should be applied, thus making it more difficult for the cases to be brought before the international instances, while in the *Matznetter Case* the rule was applied in a less 'rigid' way, with the result that the position of the individual was made easier.

The real issue, in regard to the non-material content of the rule, does not appear to be whether it should be applied less 'rigidly' in order to favour the individual and access to an international forum under the institution of human rights protection. What is at stake is the proper

---

[88] As will be pointed out in the last chapter of this work, the term 'flexibility' (and 'rigidity', as a consequence) is infelicitous.

application of the rule in a given situation in relation to the policies behind it and to differences in the contextual background of human rights protection and diplomatic protection. This may result in preference being given to the interests sometimes of the individual and the international community, or sometimes of the defendant state, on the assumption that the rule is one which primarily favours the defendant state.

With respect to the material content of the rule, the presumption is that, where the written law states that the rule should be applied in accordance with the rules of general or customary international law, it should be applied to human rights protection in the same way as it is applied to diplomatic protection. In this connection, differences in the fundamental premises of the two systems of protection should, therefore, in principle be basically unimportant, though in practice this prescription may not be always followed. Conversely, where the application of the rule to human rights protection develops and refines the rule, there is every reason why such developments and refinements should, where appropriate, be implemented in the law of diplomatic protection.

4 The rule, denial of justice and violation of international law

It is not within the scope of this work to discuss in detail here the concept of denial of justice as it is relevant to the law of state responsibility for injuries to aliens, or definitively to identify its specific coverage. However, since there has been in the past some confusion as to both its meaning and its relationship to the law relating to the exhaustion of local remedies,[1] a brief consideration of the meaning of the concept and of how it is connected to the rule of local remedies in the law of diplomatic protection is required. It may be noted at the outset that the same confusion has not occurred in connection with the application of the rule to the protection of human rights as has been prevalent in regard to the law of diplomatic protection *per se*. This may have some significant bearing on the discussion of the issues involved, as it may show that denial of justice does not by its true nature basically affect the rule of local remedies when the rule is considered in its proper sense and dimensions and when the application of the rule is treated as being confined to the situations to which it is in terms of its purpose and nature meant to be applicable.

Meaning of the concept

Before the connection between denial of justice and the exhaustion of local remedies may be considered, an initial and preliminary question which falls to be considered is how the term 'denial of justice' is appropriately defined for the general purposes of the law of diplomatic protection. Although in principle a term may be used in many senses

---

[1] See e.g. Eagleton, 'Denial of Justice in International Law', 22 AJIL (1928) p. 538; and Freeman, *The International Responsibility of States for Denial of Justice* (1938) pp. 84ff. and 403ff.

provided it is made clear or appears from the context in what particular sense the term is being used, there may be some virtue in trying to identify the most suitable sense in which the term has been or should be used in order to facilitate the understanding and systematic analysis of the law.[2] On the other hand, it may have to be recognized that past usage may defy any attempt to simplify the definition of the term, particularly when the diplomatic practice and jurisprudence on the subject is examined. However, it may, in spite of the variety of usages and manifold meanings given to the term, be possible to identify what may be the most appropriate meaning for the term in the light of the objects of the law and to make some purposive sense out of the confusion, with a view in particular to clarifying the relevance and application of the term to the exhaustion of local remedies and understanding how the concept of denial of justice may affect the rule that local remedies must be exhausted where there has been an injury to an individual, especially when the institution of diplomatic protection is in issue.

As already pointed out in Chapter 2, the law of diplomatic protection for injuries to foreigners grew out of the practice of reprisals which revolved around the 'denial of justice'. The term was ill-defined at the time and could apparently have signified anything from a genuine failure on the part of the courts to administer justice in a case where a

---

[2] The point is well taken that, where the term 'denial of justice' is used in an arbitration treaty as a basis for jurisdiction, the extent of jurisdictional competence granted to the arbitral tribunal will depend on the meaning given to that term and whether it is defined more narrowly or more widely: see the arguments of Jiménez de Aréchaga, 'International Responsibility', in Sørensen (ed.), *Manual of Public International Law* (1968) at pp. 533–5. In a circumstance such as this, the definition of the term becomes singularly important, particularly because the treaty itself would not normally give any indication of how the term is to be defined. Thus, it is clear that for the purpose of determining jurisdiction a uniform definition of the term may be useful. But, more importantly, the definition of the term is pertinent to the question of a state's liability in international law. In so far as certain obligations of a state towards another state in respect of the latter's nationals are described solely by reference to the concept of 'denial of justice', which may or may not be the case, the extent of those obligations would be affected by how much is included in that term. To make the point clearer, there has sometimes been a tendency to assert that a state is liable for denials of justice, implying that these are the only acts of a state's judiciary for which it can be held liable: see e.g. García Amador, 'Second Report on State Responsibility', YBILC (1957), vol. 2, p. 129. If 'denial of justice' is then defined only in a formal sense to include solely the failure to grant an alien access to the courts and subjecting him to unwarrantable delays, the content of a state's obligation in respect of acts of its judiciary would be narrower than if 'denial of justice' were defined so as to cover formal defects as thus described plus substantive defects in the form of manifestly unjust judgments.

foreigner had suffered injury, generally originating in an act or omission attributable to a private person but not necessarily restricted thereto, to a mere failure to redress an injury to a foreigner in similar circumstances. No fine distinctions were originally made, and it was sometimes maintained that even after unsuccessful resort to the courts a failure on the part of the sovereign to redress the injury was a sufficient ground for intervention. Further, no clear distinction appears to have been made among situations where the original injury was caused by a private individual, by the sole action of the courts when the injured alien was the defendant in an action, and by the sovereign himself or the state authorities.[3]

The situation began to be complicated much later when the institution of reprisals was replaced by diplomatic intervention. It was often still asserted that an alien could be protected by diplomatic intervention when he had suffered a denial of justice but there grew up, around a somewhat exaggerated notion of sovereignty, a keener interest in the international duties and responsibilities of states towards foreigners as such, although denial of justice usually signified a failure of protective justice.[4] But, as has also been stated, the term 'denial of justice' did not convey the innate characteristics of the standard.[5] Nor does the term appear to have been used with scientific precision after this.

The case law of international courts and tribunals,[6] attempts at codification,[7] text writers,[8] and the little that exists representing diplomatic practice,[9] all reflect considerable variation in the meaning given

---

[3] While the above statement is true in general and in retrospect, it would appear from the examples available of reprisal that the situations generally encountered were those in which the alien had suffered injury at the hands of some private party. Rarely, if ever, did the circumstance arise that the sovereign or the state had caused the original injury: see Chapter 2 above for the examples.

[4] See e.g. C. de Visscher, 'Le Déni de justice en droit international', 54 *Hague Recueil* (1935) at p. 373.

[5] See Spiegel, 'Origin and Development of Denial of Justice', 32 AJIL (1938) at p. 79.

[6] For the broadest view, see e.g. the discrepancies in the *El Triunfo Case* (US v. El Salvador), 15 UNRIAA p. 459 (1902); *Robert E. Brown Case* (US v. Great Britain), 6 UNRIAA p. 120 (1923); *Interoceanic Railway of Mexico Case* (Great Britain v. Mexico), 5 UNRIAA p. 133 (1931); *Janes Case* (US v. Mexico), 4 UNRIAA p. 82 (1926); *Massey Case* (US v. Mexico), 4 UNRIAA p. 155 (1927); and *Neer Case* (US v. Mexico), 4 UNRIAA p. 60 (1926). For the classical narrow view, see e.g. *Fabiani Case* (France v. Venezuela), 10 UNRIAA p. 83 (1896); *Cotesworth and Powell Case* (Great Britain v. Colombia) (1875), Moore, *International Arbitrations* (1898), vol. 2, p. 2050; *Eliza Case* (US v. Peru) (1963), de La Pradelle-Politis, vol. 2, p. 271; and *Interocean Transportation Co. of America Case* (Great Britain v. US) (1937), 8 Ann. Dig. (1935–7) p. 271. For restricted views that vary, see e.g. (a) *Medina Case* (US v. Costa Rica), Moore, *International Arbitrations* (1898), vol. 2, p. 2317; *Salem Case* (US v. Egypt), 2 UNRIAA p. 1188 (1932); *Yuille, Shortidge & Co. Case* (Great Britain v. Portugal) (1861), de La Pradelle-Politis,

vol. 2, p. 103; (b) *Martini Case (Italy* v. *Venezuela)* (1930), 5 Ann. Dig. (1929–30) p. 153;
(c) *Chattin Case (US* v. *Mexico),* 4 UNRIAA p. 282 (1927); and (d) *Beale, Nobles and Garrison
Case (US* v. *Venezuela)* (1886), Moore, *International Arbitrations* (1898), vol. 4, pp. 3562ff.
More recently, the term has been used in a fairly broad sense to cover refusal by any
means by a state to honour an agreement with a foreigner to arbitrate: see the cases
referred to in Schwebel, *International Arbitration: Three Salient Problems* (1987) pp. 87ff.

[7] Attempts at codification which show no uniformity in the approach to the definition of
denial of justice for the purpose of state responsibility include Article IV of the 1925
Project of the American Institute of International Law, cited in YBILC (1956), vol. 2,
p. 227; Article 3(3) of the 1930 Draft Convention on State Responsibility for Injuries to
Aliens prepared by Deutsche Gesellschaft für Völkerrecht, cited in YBILC (1969), vol. 2,
p. 150; Article 7 of the 1932 Draft Convention on State Responsibility of Professor Roth,
cited in YBILC (1969), vol. 2, p. 152; Article 9 of the 1929 Draft on State Responsibility
for Injuries to Aliens of the Harvard Law School, cited in YBILC (1956), vol. 2, p. 229;
Articles 5 and 6 of the 1927 Resolutions of the Institut de Droit International, 33 AIDI
(1927) pp. 331–2; 1965 Restatement of the Law by the American Law Institute, Foreign
Relations Law of the United States, notes 178–82, cited in YBILC (1971), vol. 2, p. 195;
1926 Guerrero Report to the League of Nations Committee of Experts for the
Progressive Codification of International Law, cited in YBILC (1956), vol. 2, p. 222;
Article 6 of the Draft Treaty on State Responsibility for Internationally Illegal Acts
prepared by Professor Strupp, cited in YBILC (1969), vol. 2, pp. 151–2; 1962 Majority
Opinion on Principles of International Law Governing State Responsibility Delivered by
the Inter-American Juridical Committee, OAS Doc. OEA/Ser.I/VI.2-CIJ-61 (1962) p. 8;
Supplementary Opinion by the US Government in the Inter-American Juridical
Committee, OAS Doc. OEA/Ser.I/VI.2-CIJ-78 (1965) pp. 7–9; and Article 4 of the 1957 Draft
Articles of García Amador on State Responsibility for Injuries to Aliens, YBILC (1957),
vol. 2, p. 129. Some codifications which deal with the subject of a state's international
responsibility for injuries to aliens have avoided specifically using or defining the term
'denial of justice' but have enumerated the various acts, including acts of the judiciary
for which a state may be responsible: see e.g. Bases of Discussion Nos. 5 and 6 of the
1929 Bases of Discussion of the Preparatory Committee of the Hague Conference for
the Codification of International Law, cited in YBILC (1956), vol. 2, p. 223; Article 9 of
the 1930 Provisions adopted by the Third Committee of the Hague Codification
Conference, cited in YBILC (1956), vol. 2, p. 226; and Articles 6, 7 and 8 of the 1961
Harvard Draft Convention on International Responsibility of States for Injuries to
Aliens, cited in YBILC (1969), vol. 2, pp. 143–4. It may be of interest that the
Panamanian–American General Claims Arbitration dispensed with the term 'denial of
justice' altogether: see Briggs, *The Law of Nations* (1952) p. 679. Similarly, there are some
codification drafts which leave the question of the meaning of 'denial of justice' either
untouched or open: see e.g. the 1926 Draft of the International Law Association of
Japan, cited in YBILC (1969), vol. 2, p. 141; the 1956 Resolution of the Institut de Droit
International on the Exhaustion of Local Remedies, 46 AIDI (1956) p. 358; the 1965
Resolution of the Institut de Droit International on the National Character of an
International Claim Presented by a State for Injury Suffered by an Individual, 51 AIDI
(1965) pp. 260–2; and Article 34 of the 1935 'Alejandro Alvarez Project on Leading
Principles of International Law' as amended and adopted by the Académie
Diplomatique Internationale, cited in 15 RDI (1935) p. 538.

[8] Among text writers, the broader interpretation of the term 'denial of justice' is
favoured by, e.g. Hyde, *International Law* (1945), vol. 2, pp. 909ff.; Fitzmaurice, 'The
Meaning of the Term "Denial of Justice"', 13 BYIL (1932) pp. 108ff.; Greig, *International
Law* (1970) pp. 420ff.; and apparently Moussa, 'L'étranger et la justice nationale', 41
RGDIP (1934) pp. 441ff. Most authors, however, support a restricted view of the

definition of the term limiting it to the improper conduct of courts or judges, although there may be variations in the nature of the restrictions required: see e.g. Borchard, *The Diplomatic Protection of Citizens Abroad* (1915) pp. 330ff.; Borchard, 'Theoretical Aspects of the International Responsibility of States', 1 ZaöRV (1929) at p. 246; Durand, 'La Responsabilitè internationale des états pour déni de justice', 38 RGDIP (1931) at pp. 711ff.; Anzilotti, 'La Responsabilité internationale des états à raison des dommages soufferts par des étrangers', 13 RGDIP (1906) at pp. 20ff.; Accioly, 'Principes généraux de la responsabilité internationale d'après la doctrine et la jurisprudence', 96 *Hague Recueil* (1959) at pp. 378ff.; Rousseau, *Droit international public* (1953) pp. 374ff.; Rolin, 'Le Controle international des juridictions nationales', 3-4 RBDI (1967-8) at pp. 10ff. and pp. 181ff.; Oppenheim and Lauterpacht, *International Law* (1967), vol. 1, pp. 359ff.; Brownlie, *Principles of Public International Law* (1979) pp. 529ff.; Kelsen, *Principles of International Law* (1966) pp. 370ff.; Ago, statements in 45 AIDI (1954) pp. 35ff.; Brierly, *The Law of Nations* (1963) pp. 286ff.; Freeman, note 1 above, at pp. 72ff. and 175ff.; Jiménez de Aréchaga, note 2 above, at pp. 553ff.; de Visscher, 'Le Déni de justice en droit international', 54 *Hague Recueil* (1935) at pp. 385ff. and 419ff., and 'La Responsabilité des Etats', 2 BViss (1924) at pp. 99ff.; Kaufmann, 'Règles générales du droit de la paix', 54 *Hague Recueil* (1935) at pp. 431ff.; Guggenheim, *Traité de droit international* (1954), vol. 2, pp. 13ff.; and O'Connell, *International Law* (1970), vol. 2, pp. 945ff. Such authors as Mann and Schwebel would employ the term in a limited sense but so as to include at least failure to arbitrate under an arbitration clause: see Mann, 'State Contracts and International Arbitration', 42 BYIL (1967) at pp. 26ff.; and Schwebel, *International Arbitration: Three Salient Problems* (1987) pp. 61ff. Garcdía Amador also took a narrow view of the definition of the term, although it was a special view and considerably different from that of other authors taking the narrow view: see Article 3 of the Revised Draft on State Responsibility for Injuries to Aliens, YBILC (1961), vol. 2, pp. 46ff. Lissitzyn, for instance, would, because of the imprecision surrounding the term, avoid it as much as possible: 'The Meaning of Denial of Justice in International Law', 30 AJIL (1936) at pp. 638ff.

[9] In the *Affaire Losinger and Co.*, the Swiss government adopted the position that, while the concept of denial of justice had a restricted content including obstruction of access to the courts and undue delays, it was broader than the concept employed in national law which covered only refusal of access to the courts: see the oral argument of the agent for the Swiss government of 5 June 1936, PCIJ Series C No. 78, pp. 313ff. (1936). In the *Electricity Company of Sofia Case*, counsel for the Belgian government pointedly drew attention to the difference between the broader view of the concept and the narrower views, showing a preference for the narrower: see the oral argument of 1 March 1939, PCIJ Series C No. 88, pp. 414ff. (1939). More recently, the subject was discussed by the Spanish and Belgian governments in the *Barcelona Traction Co. Case* (1970). The Spanish case rested on a definition which would confine denial of justice to the formal failure to grant access to the courts and causing absolutely unwarrantable delays but did not restrict international responsibility for acts of the judiciary to such denial of justice, although it maintained that the circumstances of such responsibility had to be carefully defined: ICJ Pleadings (1962-9), vol. 4, p. 463. The equation of denial of justice with a broad notion of absence of 'due process of law' in the sense used in US law was rejected: ICJ Pleadings (1962-9), vol. 4, pp. 498-9. The Belgian attitude apparently changed considerably during the proceedings. The Spanish approach to the definition of 'denial of justice' was finally adopted in principle, although it was specifically mentioned that there were other circumstances in which a state could be responsible for acts of its judiciary, such as where a decision was given that was clearly incompatible with international law or where a decision was manifestly erroneous or *mal jugé*: see Reply, ICJ Pleadings (1962-9), vol. 5, pp. 306ff.; and the oral argument,

to the term 'denial of justice', which may also reveal some disagreement on the substantive content of the duties and responsibilities of states. Suffice it here briefly to identify some of the main connotations given to the term, while at the same time focusing attention on the actual content of the duties and responsibilities of states which clearly persist in spite of a lack of agreement and uniformity in the use of the term 'denial of justice'.

According to the broadest view of the term, a denial of justice would occur whenever there was a breach of international law by any state organ. Not only would the acts or omissions of the judiciary be included in the concept, but any misfeasance or failure on the part of the administrative or legislative authorities would be covered. In this sense, the concept has no special meaning but engulfs the whole range of acts and omissions for which a state is internationally responsible in its treatment of foreigners. As seen above,[10] there are a few authorities, both judicial and textual, which support this usage of the term.

There is a narrower but fairly broad view which would take in under the rubric 'denial of justice' all acts connected with the judiciary or the settlement of disputes. This would amount to including in the concept of denial of justice any failure in due process of law. In this sense not only would all administrative and legislative interference with the administration of justice be included as a denial of justice, although not every act or omission amounting to a breach of a state's international obligations in respect of the treatment of aliens, but such acts as a refusal to arbitrate under an arbitration agreement or under a clause in a contract entered into with a foreigner would be regarded as a 'denial of justice'.[11]

A second narrow view would characterize as a denial of justice any defects in the entire process of the administration of justice. Not only would acts or omissions of the judiciary be denials of justice but all interferences with the judiciary or failure to assist the judiciary in the

---

ICJ Pleadings (1962–9), vol. 8, pp. 43ff. There was considerable discussion of what was a manifestly erroneous decision. The aspect of the debate is examined in considerable detail in Jiménez de Aréchaga 'International Responsibility of States for Acts of the Judiciary', in Friedmann, Henkin and Lissitzyn (eds.), *Transnational Law in a Changing Society* (1972) at pp. 171–87. Some state practice dealing with a state's refusal to arbitrate under an arbitration clause in a contract between a state and an alien as a denial of justice is discussed in Schwebel, note 8 above, at pp. 72ff.

[10] See note 6 above.

[11] See e.g. the view of Mann and Schwebel referred to in note 8 above.

performance of its functions whether by the executive or the legislature would also be so characterized.[12]

There are several variants of the narrow view which concentrate on acts or omissions of the judiciary. According to one of these views, denial of justice covers all wrongs of the judiciary but not those of other organs of the state acting in a judicial capacity.

Another narrow view would have it that it is only refusal of access to the courts or undue delay by the courts in the disposition of a case that could be termed a denial of justice.[13] A further narrow view which is reflected in the 1927 resolution of the Institut de droit international is that a denial of justice occurs when tribunals capable of doing justice do not exist or function, when access is denied to tribunals or when tribunals do not offer guarantees which are indispensable to the proper administration of justice.[14]

The predominant Latin American view of denial of justice was reflected in Articles 6 and 7 of the Guerrero report,[15] to the effect that denial of justice consists only of refusing access to courts, including a refusal of a competent judge to exercise jurisdiction.

A different narrow view is that of the kind supported by authorities such as C. de Visscher.[16] According to this view, a formal denial of justice embraces the denial of access to the courts, while a substantive denial of justice occurs when a manifestly unjust judgment is delivered against a litigant with the result that the latter is subjected to discriminatory or arbitrary treatment.

Finally, the view should be mentioned which describes as a denial of justice any failure of the local redress system to remedy an injury suffered by an alien.[17] The exact scope of this view is not ascertainable, while it would seem to be somewhat circular insofar as it begs the question of when a failure to redress an injury is actionable.

There are other variants of the narrow view propounded mainly by textual authorities. However, they all have in common that they concentrate on one aspect or another of the administration of justice, although with different inclusions and exclusions.

---

[12] This was apparently Freeman's preference: see Freeman, note 1 above.

[13] This seems to have been the view espoused by the Spanish government in the *Barcelona Traction Co. Case*: ICJ Pleadings (1962–9), vol. 4, at p. 463.

[14] See 3 AIDI (1927) p. 331.   [15] See 23 AJIL (1929) Supp. p. 219.

[16] This was clearly the view of the Belgian government in its original Memorial in the *Barcelona Traction Co. Case* (1970): ICJ Pleadings (1962–9), vol. 1, pp. 171 and 174.

[17] Eagleton was responsible for this view: see 'Denial of Justice in International Law', 22 AJIL (1928) pp. 538ff.

While it emerges that there is much disagreement on the definition of the term 'denial of justice' and perhaps to a lesser extent on the exact scope of the obligations of states in regard to the administration of justice in relation to aliens, it is not the purpose here to advocate the choice of one definition in preference to another as a matter of principle. What is important is to draw attention to those definitions that appear to be logically unsatisfactory or fundamentally unacceptable. It would seem that the broad views of denial of justice would only sow confusion and serve no practical purpose, as what require identification specifically are the defects in the administration of justice, other breaches of international obligations by a state aside. At the other extreme the view that a denial of justice is any failure to redress an injury to an alien, whatever its origin, after recourse is had to local remedies or such recourse is attempted provides a more or less circular definition, while it does not define denial of justice in terms of any concrete identifiable acts or omissions in the administration of justice. By focusing on the failure of the alien to secure redress the definition seems to leave unanswered the question which such failures are in issue, and indeed, might well lead to the conclusion that all such failures fall within the definition — which would not reflect the correct position in international law. This problem will be adverted to again later.

Suffice it to say here that without prejudice to the choice of the most serviceable definition, a narrow definition which concentrates on defects in the administrative process of justice as opposed to the acts or omissions of other branches of government unconnected with the judicial process, irrespective of the question of whether there is responsibility for the latter acts or omissions, would seem to be supported by most of the case law and other authorities. This means that when the term 'denial of justice' is used it should connote some specific act or omission connected with the administration of justice. It is unnecessary for our purposes to determine definitively whether such acts and omissions should cover only formal or only substantive aspects or both or indeed whether only some formal aspects should be included. As long as it is understood (i) that denial of justice does not include all acts or omissions for which a state is responsible in international law in its treatment of aliens, (ii) that the term does not describe responsibility for the failure to secure redress per se and (iii) that the term refers only to acts or omissions connected with the process of administering justice whatever they may be, the discussion of the problem of the relevance of denial of justice to the exhaustion of local remedies can proceed. It may be added that the present writer prefers a definition which covers all actionable defects in the administrative process of justice, both formal and substantive. Thus, no such defects would be excluded from the definition. It should also be noted that, where there has been a prior violation by the host state of international law in the treatment of an alien, the mere failure on the part of the judiciary to recognize this violation, and therefore the existence of a judicial decision which is in violation of the international obligations of the host state, is correctly not to be characterized as a denial of justice. Such a situation merely perpetuates the initial violation of international law which has already created international responsibility for the host state. On the other hand, were the judiciary, in deciding a dispute between an alien and another private party, to give a decision involving a violation of the international obligations of the host state, this would be a manifestly unjust judgment and would correctly be characterized as a denial of justice.

A caveat should be entered at this point. While the view has been taken above that 'denial of justice' may be susceptible of more than one acceptable definition, it must not be forgotten that the differences in definition may really conceal a difference of view as to the substantive obligations of states, particularly with regard to the administration of justice *vis-à-vis* aliens. It is not proposed here to settle or, indeed, discuss these differences. What is important is to bear in mind that, whatever definition of 'denial of justice' is accepted, first, it should not be permitted to prejudice the question of the actual substantive content of the obligations of states *vis-à-vis* aliens, and, secondly, it should be a reasonable definition which covers the most important obligations of states *vis-à-vis* aliens relating to the administration of justice. Were it to be accepted that the definition does not cover all the substantive obligations of the host state relating to the process of administering justice, it would then naturally have to be recognized that the liability of host states for injuries committed in the administration of justice may extend beyond 'denials of justice'.

Incidence and relevance of the original injury

As already pointed out, when resort to or the exhaustion of local remedies was made a condition precedent to the taking of reprisals, whether public or private, the distinction between injuries caused by private persons and those caused by acts attributable to the state or sovereign was not clearly made, as far as can be discerned from the documentation on the subject.[18] Nor was the possible difference between the situation where the alien complainant was a plaintiff and where he was a defendant or in an equivalent position particularly noticed. The reason for this could possibly have been that in most cases, as the recorded incidents show, the situation in which an alien calling for protection was involved was one in which he had been initially injured by a private person. Thus, it was natural to express the conditions for the exercise of reprisals in terms of the exhaustion of local remedies resulting in a denial of justice. For there could be no 'responsibility' (i.e. international) attaching to the sovereign or state in the territory of which the injury had been suffered until some act or omission attributable to such sovereign or state had been perpetrated. And this could only happen after the alien had recourse to the system of justice in the relevant state and had thus suffered a subsequent injury at the hands of an organ of the sovereign or the state in failing to secure redress, which was attributable to that sovereign or state. Hence, it was possible to refer to a denial of justice which was attributable to the sovereign or state and which entailed international responsibility. At the same time, no fine distinctions appear to have been explicitly made between the initial injury and the injury consequent on the denial of justice as the redressible injury, nor was there any sophistication about the theory of responsibility for the injury for which reprisals were ordered.

While the connection between denial of justice and the protection granted by the alien's sovereign became established, it was also possible to refer to the requirement that local remedies should first be exhausted, because what was important for the sovereign or state of the alien was to make sure that the other sovereign or state had been given a serious and full opportunity to redress the initial injury of which the alien was complaining, of whatever nature this injury was. Thus, it became necessary to insist on the total system of justice of the other sovereign or state being resorted to or exhausted. Not only had there to be a denial of justice but there had to be an exhaustion of local remedies. In this process the association of denial of justice and the exhaustion of local remedies as a condition precedent to the exercise of protection in the form of reprisals was complete, although there may have been no well-defined concept of what was meant by denial of justice beyond

---

[18] See Chapter 2 above.

the failure of the alien to obtain redress for the original private wrong and no clear idea of what the sovereign or state was being held liable for, whether it was for the original private injury or for the failure to grant redress, beyond the general notion that what was being sanctioned in the eyes of the alien's sovereign or state was the fact that there had been an initial injury caused to the alien which had not been redressed. Indeed, one can but speculate on the theory that governed the action of one sovereign or state against another in the area of alien protection.

When the institution of diplomatic protection replaced that of reprisals, the vagueness and imprecision of the bases of responsibility, which is the term that came to be used later, and of the relationship between denial of justice and the exhaustion of local remedies appears initially to have carried over into the law governing diplomatic protection. It was usual to refer to a denial of justice and the exhaustion of local remedies as two sides of the same coin, as if the one implied the other.[19]

However, the subsequent development of relationships between states and aliens and their national states, the increasing direct dealings between states and aliens, the incursion of judicial methods of settling international disputes in the area of diplomatic protection, including arbitration, and the reflection of textual authorities has, it would seem, led to more sophistication in and rationalization of the law relating to denial of justice and the exhaustion of local remedies. It is consequently no longer possible simply to state that in all circumstances exhaustion of local remedies must result in a denial of justice as reasonably defined, although an exact definition of that term may not be settled, in order that an alien's state may exercise diplomatic protection, nor that the distinction between the kinds of initial wrongs can be ignored for the purpose of the law relating to denial of justice and exhaustion of local remedies.

It is impossible, nevertheless, to identify any specific case or case law which deals especially with or settles the host of questions that arise in regard to the relationship between the exhaustion of local remedies and denial of justice. The task is made no less easy and more complicated

---

[19] This perhaps explains why Eagleton chose to retain the same connection between the concepts and to define a denial of justice as simply the failure of redress after the exhaustion of local remedies. But, as will be seen, with the development of relationships between aliens and foreign states, the concepts could not be dealt with so simply.

as a result of the conflicting views expressed by text writers who have reflected on the issues involved.[20] Without, however, purporting to add to any confusion there may be in the area, a few suggestions may be made on what the observed trends seem to be and how the law has constructively been evolving.

From the point of view of denial of justice a tendency may be observed to accept in principle that there is a distinction between, for example, the situation where the initial injury is a private wrong or the alien is a defendant in a proceeding, and that in which the state commits a wrong which may be equated to an internationally wrongful 'delict' or 'tort' (better described as a *fait internationalement illicite* in French or *lecho internacionalmente ilícito* in Spanish) against the alien. Cases such as the *Interhandel Case*[21] support the view that, where the alleged wrong of this nature is committed by, or is attributable to, the state, this amounts at once to a violation of that state's international obligations *vis-à-vis* the alien. On the other hand, where the alleged initial wrong is, for example, a private one for which the state is not responsible or which is not attributable to the state because of an act or omission on its part, or where the alien is a defendant in a case, there is no violation of its international obligations in respect of the alien by the state until some further act or omission attributable to the state has taken place. Such act or omission occurs when a subsequent wrong is perpetrated during the judicial process or the process of settlement of the dispute concerned. This is usually some act or omission of the judiciary which may properly be characterized as a denial of justice. For example, if access to the courts or to the available procedures is obstructed or if a manifestly unjust judgment is given against the alien, whether he be the plaintiff or the defendant, such denial of access or unjust judgment which is attributable to the state is the violation of international law *vis-à-vis* the alien on which an international claim may be based by the alien's national state.[22] The difference between the two situations is that

---

[20] The same confusing approach is taken by Cançado Trindade, 'Denial of Justice and its Relationship to Exhaustion of Local Remedies in International Law', 53 *Philippine Law Journal* (1978) at pp. 416ff. He appears to favour the view, though, that exhaustion of local remedies must culminate in a denial of justice as such for international responsibility to arise.

[21] 1959 ICJ Reports p. 11. There are earlier cases such as the *Neer Case* (US v. Mexico), 4 UNRIAA p. 60 (1926), and *Janes Case* (US v. Mexico), 4 UNRIAA p. 82 (1926), which recognize the importance of the kind of initial wrong involved.

[22] See e.g. the *Neer Case* and the *Janes Case* cited at note 21 above.

in the one the alleged initial wrong does not by itself generate a violation of international law, while in the other it does.

In the one situation no additional act or omission connected with the administration of justice is necessary to generate an international claim, while in the other the international cause of action is precisely the defect in the administration of justice. If this defect is described as a denial of justice, it is this denial of justice that generates a violation of international law in respect of the alien. Where the alleged initial wrong is directly attributable to the state and an international wrong, this should not and cannot be characterized as a denial of justice, although it is a violation of international law, so that it is not a denial of justice that generates a violation of international law.[23]

In the case of human rights protection, the wrong to the individual which generates a cause of action and is a violation of international law is the initial act attributable to the state which is a breach of the governing convention on human rights.[24] This may be, for example, a false arrest, torture or an improper deprivation of property. Neither has this violation been generally characterized as a denial of justice, nor has a subsequent denial of justice in a narrow sense been regarded as required to create international responsibility.[25] There may be circumstances in which the initial wrong to the individual is a maladministration of justice. If this amounts to a violation of the governing convention, then it is a denial of justice in a narrow sense which is the cause of action. For example, in one case it was held by the European Commission of Human Rights that it was an alleged maladministration of justice by a lower court in Germany that constituted the initial violation of international law, there being no violation of the Convention before this occurrence.[26] Thus, the distinction between injuries which give rise to international responsibility without there being a denial of justice in a

---

[23] 'Responsibility' arises internationally, in strict terms, at the time at which a violation of international norms takes place. As pointed out above, the international legal violation may take place before resort to the local justice system is had. That the responsibility cannot be enforced by resort to diplomatic or legal action at an international level before local remedies have been exhausted does not alter the fact that international responsibility has been incurred. A further point that may emerge is that the existence of the distinction noted above between the initial international wrongs warrants the restriction of the term denial of justice to no more than acts or omissions committed in the course of the administration of justice or the settlement of a dispute that has already arisen.

[24] See e.g. Application No. 1727/62, 6 YBECHR p. 398.

[25] Application No. 788/60, 4 YBECHR p. 148.

[26] Ibid.

real sense and those in which a genuine denial of justice is required to give rise or gives rise to such responsibility is recognized even in this area.

Recognition must be given to the truth that it is always a state's violation of international law which gives rise to international responsibility, whether that violation is a denial of justice in the narrow sense or not. On the other hand, such a denial of justice not only gives rise to responsibility, where it is the initial state violation of international law, but will in certain circumstances also compound responsibility by creating an additional violation of international law, i.e. where the initial state violation of international law is something other than and prior to that denial of justice.

Need to exhaust remedies

Given the difference in situations generating a breach of an international norm, it becomes easier to see how the rule that local remedies must be exhausted will operate in each case.[27] Clearly, where the alleged initial wrong is attributable to the state and is an international wrong, the exhaustion of local remedies will take place in respect of the wrong and will be concerned with rectifying that wrong. The rule would then require that remedies be exhausted up to the highest level. The whole of the dispute settlement procedure relates properly to the application of the rule in this case. It would be important to recognize that, consequent upon the exhaustion of remedies, it is sufficient merely that the initial international wrong remain unrequited or inadequately redressed for the violation of international law to persist and generate a situation that can be subjected to an international claim or to diplomatic protection. There is clearly no requirement that in the process of settling the dispute anything such as a 'denial of justice' in any appropriate sense by the organ or organs responsible for settling the dispute be committed, it being understood that the initial violation of international law, which continues to remain unredressed and therefore subsists, should not and cannot be described as a denial of justice.

In these circumstances, therefore, it is not appropriate to say that there must be an exhaustion of local remedies resulting in a denial of

---

[27] As will be seen in Chapter 15, once the importance of the violation of international law is conceded, it becomes easier also to appreciate the nature of the rule of exhaustion of local remedies.

justice, for this would mean that something more than the absence of satisfactory redress for the initial wrong (such as denial of access to the courts, undue delays in settling the dispute or the rendering of a manifestly unjust judgment) would be required to give rise to a claim based on diplomatic protection. As already pointed out, the fact that the process of internal remedies results in a decision which is contrary to international law or is in violation of the international obligations of the host state cannot appropriately and is not to be characterized as a denial of justice, although it is sufficient eventually to give rise to an international claim based on diplomatic protection. It is to be noted that in respect of the final decision in the process of exhausting local remedies there is no need for proof that that decision was 'manifestly unjust' in any sense of that term in order to give rise to international responsibility. It is sufficient that the decision is inconsistent with the host state's international obligations for a diplomatic claim to be made or international legal action to be taken. What is required in short is that after the exhaustion of local remedies the final decision taken is simply not one which an international tribunal in prospect would take in the case concerned. The fact that the final decision is one which could reasonably be reached by any impartial court deciding the case does not relieve the host state of, or discharge, its responsibility, for instance, on the ground that there had not been a denial of justice.

Where the initial wrong is not a violation of international law by the host state, for example where it is a private wrong or where the alien is made a defendant, or where the state is guilty of a simple breach of contract, as will be seen in the next chapter, resort or an attempted resort to local remedies must take place or local remedies must be activated before an international wrong which is a violation of the host state's international obligations can occur. It is only where such *resort, attempted resort* or *activation* results in an act or omission which is a violation of international law that international responsibility will be incurred, the original wrong not being per se capable of giving rise to responsibility as such. The violation of international law which subsequently takes place may usually be described as a denial of justice. In whatever terms it is described, and whether it is, for example, an act of the executive interfering with the judicial process or denying access to remedies or a failure to make remedies available or an improper act of the judiciary which renders the process tainted or a manifestly unjust judgment pertaining to the substance of the case, this 'malfunctioning' of the judicial process is the international wrong which generates international responsibility. If any such malfunctioning of the judicial process, which is to be determined according to the norms of international law, may conveniently be described as a denial of justice, then the international wrong generating responsibility is properly called a *denial of justice*.[28]

This is, however, not the end of the matter in this particular event. The rule of local remedies is then applicable to this international wrong and the claimant must in accordance with the requirements of that rule *exhaust* (and not merely *resort to*) the means of local redress in respect of that so-called *denial of justice* up to the highest level.[29] Thus, it is true to say that in the above circumstances there must be an exhaustion of local remedies in addition to there being a denial of justice after *resort* to local remedies before an international claim may properly be made, although international responsibility would have arisen once there has been a so-called denial of justice. It is important to emphasize that the international wrong in respect of which responsibility arises and local remedies must be exhausted is the denial of justice, although the measure of the injury done to the alien may in the appropriate case be the initial wrong which did not per se give rise to international responsibility.[30] It is the denial of justice which occurred after the *resort* to local remedies or after such initial *resort* was improperly not made possible, which persists and which has not been remedied after local remedies have ultimately been *exhausted* that is, nevertheless, the cause of action in respect of which responsibility arose and in respect of which an international claim may be made. The failure of redress for the initial denial of justice after *exhaustion* of local remedies makes an international claim legitimate and appropriate, though it is the initial denial of justice after *resort* alone, real or imputed, to local remedies that gives rise to international responsibility.

Three simple examples will illustrate how these principles operate:

First, where the host state confiscates the property of an alien (without any compensation), or tortures him, this is a violation of the host state's

---

[28] Where 'denial of justice' is so defined as not to cover all the substantive obligations of the host state connected with the administration of justice, it is possible that the international wrong generating international responsibility will be an act or omission relating to the administration of justice which is not described as a denial of justice but which is, nevertheless, connected with the administration of justice. As will be seen later, local remedies may have to be exhausted in relation to this wrong.

[29] See the *Ziat, Ben Kiran Case* (*Great Britain v. Spain*), 2 UNRIAA at p. 731 (1924) *per* arbitrator Huber. However, this is only the general principle. As will be seen later, in Chapter 7, there may be certain wrongs which may be termed 'denials of justice' in one of the narrow senses in respect to which no exhaustion of local remedies need take place.

[30] See the *Neer Case* (*US v. Mexico*), 4 UNRIAA p. 60 (1926).

international obligations. Local remedies must be exhausted to redress the wrong. If the wrong remains unredressed or inadequately remedied after such exhaustion, a diplomatic or international judicial claim may be made in respect of the original confiscation or torture. No additional denial of justice in the process of exhausting remedies is required. It is sufficient that exhaustion of remedies has resulted in a decision which perpetuates the violation of international law, which was caused by the original confiscation or act of torture, and does not restore the rights of the alien recognized by international law.

Secondly, where, for example, the alien's property is destroyed by a private citizen, or a private citizen commits a breach of contract *vis-à-vis* the alien, this does not as such cause a violation of the host state's international obligations, although there may be injury to the alien. The alien must *resort* to (not *exhaust* at this stage) local remedies and it is only if, in having such recourse, there is some act or omission amounting to what may be described as a denial of justice that an international wrong attributable to the host state will have been committed. Such a denial of justice may arise, for instance, because of procedural abuses by the courts, or a manifestly unjust judgment. A mere adverse decision will not be a denial of justice or an international wrong. While the denial of justice generates international responsibility on the part of the host state, the alien must then *exhaust* (not merely *resort* to) local remedies in respect of that denial of justice up to the highest level before his national state may espouse a diplomatic claim or take international legal action, which would then be also connected with international 'liability' in a technical or formal sense, as explained later below. After the exhaustion of local remedies, all that is required for international 'liability' to arise, while 'responsibility' would continue, is that the initial denial of justice not be corrected. There is no need for a further aberration in the administration of justice. It is in respect of and to correct the initial denial of justice that local remedies must be exhausted, while, because after the unsuccessful exhaustion of remedies the initial destruction of property or breach of contract will not have been redressed, it will be the measure of the ultimate wrong done the alien.[31]

Thirdly, where the alien is prosecuted for a crime, the initial international wrong in respect of the prosecution will occur only when there has been a miscarriage of justice as a result of some defect in the process of administering justice. This occurrence, which may be described as a

---

[31] A simple breach by a state of a contract with an alien, as will be seen in the next chapter, is on the same footing as a private wrong.

denial of justice, will generate international responsibility. A mere adverse decision will not generate such responsibility, because there would not be a violation of international law. The alien will have to exhaust local remedies up to the highest level in respect of that denial of justice before a diplomatic or international legal claim may be made on his behalf. All that is required for such a claim to be made is that the initial denial of justice or its effects must persist without having been remedied after local remedies have been exhausted. There is no need for the exhaustion of local remedies to result in an additional denial of justice beyond the original denial of justice.

Two consequences emerge from the situations described above. First, in the case where the initial international wrong is the malfunctioning of the judicial process (a denial of justice, so-called), the activation of local remedies before the occurrence of the international wrong does not pertain to the exhaustion of local remedies or to the operation of the rule. The operation of local remedies up to the point of the commission of an international wrong is required in order that an international wrong generating international responsibility for the host state may arise and is not an integral part of the rule. What follows after the 'denial of justice' is the result of the genuine application of the rule of local remedies and is the exhaustion of local remedies required by that rule. There must be *resort* to remedies in order for an international wrong and responsibility to arise from a denial of justice, and *exhaustion* of remedies after that denial of justice in order for the complaint to be espousable or actionable at an international level.

Secondly, if, subsequent to the occurrence of the 'denial of justice' which constitutes the international wrong from which responsibility arises, and in the course of exhaustion of local remedies in respect of this denial of justice, more instances of the malfunctioning of the judicial process or local remedies occur, these would compound the basic international wrong. Such additional occurrences would not be required for the admissibility of a claim or its espousal after local remedies have been exhausted, as already noted, but they would certainly constitute additional wrongs for which the host state would be responsible.

While statements have often been made to the effect that the exhaustion of local remedies resulting in a denial of justice is a condition precedent to the institution of a diplomatic claim, the above analysis, which, it is believed, accurately reflects what now happens in practice, shows that this kind of statement can lead to misunderstanding and confusion and does not correctly describe the modern developments in international law. Where the basis for international responsibility is a so-called denial of justice, international responsibility will continue to exist, international 'liability' will additionally arise, and an international claim will lie or may be espoused after the exhaustion of local remedies according to the requirements of the rule, because that denial of justice subsists or has been inadequately redressed. Where the basis of international responsibility is a violation of the international obligations of the host state other than a denial of justice, all that is required for an international claim to lie or to be espoused subsequent to the incidence of international responsibility is the simple failure to obtain adequate redress after the exhaustion of local remedies.

The practice under the human rights conventions is also in accord with the above explanation. The EComHR has explicitly decided that where the initial wrong is not a denial of justice in a narrow sense but some other violation of international law there need not be a subsequent denial of justice by the highest municipal court after local remedies have been exhausted for a claim to be actionable, it being sufficient that the applicant has failed to obtain adequate redress.[32] This failure, as already noted, is not properly to be characterized as a denial of justice, nor has it been so termed by the European Commission. On the other hand, where the initial wrong is a maladministration of justice, this denial of justice proper would be an original breach of international law and there would be need to exhaust local remedies up to the highest court in respect of this wrong.[33] If the initial denial of justice remains uncorrected, it would be actionable at an international level.

International responsibility and violation of international law

The term 'international responsibility' covers the new legal relations which arise under international law by reason of an internationally wrongful act of a state.[34] The principle that an internationally wrongful act of a state entails its international responsibility referred to above has been applied by the PCIJ in several cases,[35] by the ICJ in contentious

[32] See Application No. 788/60, 4 YBECHR p. 148; and Application No. 1727/62, 6 YBECHR p. 398.

[33] See Application No. 235/56, 2 YBECHR p. 304.

[34] This view is also reflected in the commentary to Article 1 of the Articles on State Responsibility of 2001 of the ILC: see ILC Report to the General Assembly 2001, UN Doc. A/56/10: see http://www.un.org/law/ilc/reports/2001/2001report.htm at p. 63.

[35] E.g. the *Phosphates in Morocco Case* (Preliminary Objections), PCIJ Series A/B No. 74 at p. 28 (1938); and the *SS Wimbledon Case*, PCIJ Series A No. 1 at p. 30 (1923).

cases[36] and by arbitral tribunals.[37] The ICJ has also affirmed the principle in its advisory opinions.[38] Two points emerge. First, there must be an *internationally* wrongful act (or omission), i.e. a violation of international law; secondly, such a violation results in international responsibility.

What 'international responsibility' means may be explained generally in terms of the violation of international law giving rise to 'new international legal relations' (apart from those which existed before the act or omission occurred).[39] The qualification in the parentheses must be understood in exactly the way it is framed.[40] Generally, explanations do not go any further than this. However, what are being referred to as 'new international legal relations' are clearly legal rights and obligations resulting from the incidence or operation of secondary rules, as opposed to primary rules, of international law which specifically relate to remedies or remedial action or inaction.

What is important for the rule of local remedies is that 'responsibility', as defined above, arises at the time at which the violation of international law takes place, not later, not before. *The rule of local remedies applies precisely to this violation.* As a result, local remedies which are intended to identify and implement secondary remedial legal relationships are merely remedial procedures which do not change or affect the existence of international responsibility. At the same time, in certain circumstances, for example if the remedies provided by the local system satisfy the individual affected and there is an acceptance of the remedial action offered by the local system or in effect implement the relevant secondary remedial rules of international law, the 'international responsibility' of the state is discharged and *caedit quaestio*. If not, the international responsibility survives and may properly be litigated before an international forum or diplomatically dealt with at an international level.

---

[36] E.g. the *Corfu Channel Case* (Merits), 1949 ICJ Reports at p. 23; and the *Nicaragua Case* (Merits), 1986 ICJ Reports at pp. 142 and 149.

[37] E.g. the *Dickson Car Wheel Co. Claim*, 4 UNRIAA at p. 678 (1931); and the *British Claims in the Spanish Zone of Morocco Case*, 2 UNRIAA at p. 641 (1925).

[38] The *Reparation for Injuries Case*, 1949 ICJ Reports at p. 184; and the *Interpretation of Peace Treaties* (Second Phase), 1950 ICJ Reports at p. 228.

[39] See the commentary to Article 1 of the ILC's Articles on State Responsibility, para. (3), note 34 above, at p. 65, and the text writers cited in notes 49 and 50 of the commentary to that Article, *ibid.*

[40] The commentary to Article 1 of the ILC's Articles on State Responsibility uses slightly different language: 'and thus gives rise to new international legal relations *additional to those which existed before the act took place*': *ibid.*

In view of the above, it is possible, formally at least, to use the term 'liability' to describe what happens when the international responsibility survives for whatever reason the application of the rule of local remedies (or when the rule is in exceptional cases not applicable). The responsibility which has arisen once there has been a state violation of international law continues to exist. However, it is possible to state further that, in spite of the existence of responsibility, the 'liability' to satisfy, by the application of *international procedures*, the secondary norms relating to remedies arises only when the rule of local remedies has been implemented or does not need to be so implemented because of exceptional circumstances.

This analysis, which introduces the term 'liability', but only at a formal level, does not affect the pervasiveness of international responsibility. All it does is to identify more specifically a point at which there is a change in the procedures, and possibly, as the international system is now framed, in some of the *content* of the remedial rules (e.g. because reparation to the national state of the injured individual may become additionally involved) though not the framework of the rules themselves. 'Liability', then, describes the narrower situation than 'responsibility' which arises when local remedies fail or are not exhaustible, so that procedures at an international level become available, which may also entail a change at that level in the approach to the application of the secondary remedial rules, albeit of the international legal system.

The terminological distinction is not pressed, however, provided the situational differences are not overlooked. What is important is to keep in mind the incidence of international responsibility and its pervasiveness, though procedures may change at a given point and the approach to the implementation of the relevant secondary remedial rules may even also change. Again, where there is no state violation of international law, at that point there can be neither international responsibility nor international liability, whatever may happen later.

The use of the term 'liability' (international, obviously) is not intended to obfuscate but – it is hoped – to clarify. It will not be used frequently in this work, however, in this technical sense and not at all if it can be avoided.

Conclusion: some basic principles

From the above analysis, some conclusions may be drawn relating to the relationship between denial of justice, the violation of international law and the rule of local remedies. The most significant of these are reflected below. Some further, and more direct, judicial authority for these conclusions is also indicated.

First, it is *always* where there has been a violation of international law attributable to the responsible state in the treatment of an alien and to such violation that the rule of exhaustion of local remedies applies. That there is no violation of international law means that at that point the rule is irrelevant, though it may become applicable, if there is such a violation later. There are two aspects to this principle. There must be a violation of international law and that violation must be attributable in one way or another to the responsible state.

This conclusion is clearly further supported by statements of the law in *Swiss Confederation* v. *Federal Republic of Germany (No. 1)*, a genuine international (in this case inter-state) arbitration. *Inter alia*, while emphasizing the need for a violation of international law, in order that the rule may become applicable and to which the rule is applicable, the tribunal said that it was necessary that the 'national of the state which makes the claim has been impaired in his rights *in violation of international law*', that the state against which the claim is made must be responsible under international law for that violation and that the person whose rights had been infringed must have exhausted local remedies, in order to have remedied the wrong done to him.[41]

Secondly, as a result of a violation of an alien's rights merely emanating from the breach of the local law, for example particularly by a private party, which is generally not *per se* a violation of international law by the responsible state, the incidence of the rule of local remedies is not generated, even though there may have been a breach, for example,

---

[41] 25 ILR at pp. 42–3 and *passim* pp. 42–9, particularly p. 49 (1958). Prior to this citation, the tribunal (at p. 42) described the violation of international law as such as a 'denial of justice'. This description must be read in context. The tribunal was dealing with wrongs committed by one private party against another (an alien), in which case correctly there had to be a denial of justice in the narrow sense before an international wrong could be committed by the respondent state. In any case, as explained in the text above, 'denial of justice' has been used, *inter alia*, in a broad, broader and very broad sense. See also *Giorgio Uzielli (No. 229) (Italy* v. *US)*, 16 UNRIAA at p. 270 (1963), where it was said:

> International proceedings in that case were, however, merely subsidiary to the domestic proceedings, and consequently were subordinate to the exhaustion of the remedies provided by the domestic legislation of the State in question; this was because, the claim being of a private domestic nature, international proceedings were admissible only in the case of denial of justice by the appropriate agencies of the State.

of the local law, in the absence of a violation of international legal rights flowing from the international legal system as such.[42]

Thirdly, where there is no violation of international law at the point of the initial wrong complained of, there must be a *resort* to, an attempt to *resort* to or an exempting absence of need to *resort* to a local remedy (not an *exhaustion* of local remedies), as a result of which a 'denial of justice' in a narrow sense occurs. This denial of justice is the violation of international law required for the incidence of the rule of local remedies.

Fourthly, where such a denial of justice occurs, the rule of local remedies would apply to this international wrong, thus requiring *exhaustion* of local remedies (subject, of course, to the exceptions which will be discussed later, particularly in Chapters 7 and 10).

Fifthly, in the above circumstances, no *further* 'denial of justice', properly so-called, is required in order that a violation of international law take place. A failure to secure full redress as requested is sufficient to enable diplomatic action or international proceedings after exhaustion of local remedies.

Sixthly, where the initial wrong complained of is *per se* a violation of international law attributable to the state responsible, the rule of local remedies would apply to that wrong. International diplomatic or judicial action will be legitimate simply after exhaustion of local remedies and failure to obtain the redress sought.

---

[42] *Swiss Confederation* v. *Federal Republic of Germany (No. 1)*, 25 ILR at p. 42 (1958).

5 Contracts, violation of international law, denial of justice and the rule

As will be apparent from the discussion in previous chapters, the rule of local remedies applies, when there is an initial violation of international law by a state in respect of an alien. In connection with the incidence of the initial international legal wrong, with respect to which local remedies must be exhausted, it is necessary to consider contractual relationships. As pointed out in Chapter 4, wrongs committed by private persons against aliens are not as such wrongs which constitute violations of international law. By the same token, breaches of contracts with aliens by private persons do not constitute such violations. Contractual relations between aliens and other private persons, whether national or legal, are entirely in the realm of national juridical relations, while they may involve the application of private international law. Hence, breaches of entirely private contracts by private persons are only breaches of national law, though the application of international private law may take place. For such breaches to have an impact on international law, there must, therefore, be some denial of justice, actual or putative, by the judicial organs of the state concerned which would be the required initial violation of international law in respect of which the rule of local remedies would consequently become applicable in all its facets.

Problems arise with a contract between a state and an alien which is broken (or terminated) by the state party to the contract in whatever manner. The issue is whether, because the breach is by a state, there is a violation of international law by that state in respect of the alien (in regard to which the alien must exhaust local remedies) or whether a violation of international law would occur only at the point at which there is a denial of justice after *resort* to but before exhaustion of the judicial system, or there is some other illegality, as is the case with breaches of contracts between an alien and private persons. In relation to the rule of local remedies, the question is whether local remedies must be exhausted in respect of the original breach of contract or is connected with, for example, the denial of justice, after the original breach has occurred.

The issue could be regarded as one relating purely to whether a violation of a contractual right of an alien by a state party to the contract is to be characterized as a violation of international law similar to delictual violations of an alien's rights. It could also be treated as an issue relating to the nature of a state contract with an alien, i.e. whether it creates mutual rights and obligations for the parties directly within the international legal system as do *treaties* between states, so that a breach of an alien contract by a state is automatically a violation of international law. In both cases, the violation of international law by the contractual breach would activate immediately the rule of local remedies in respect of the contractual breach, with there being no need for a denial of justice or other wrongdoing after an initial reference to the local judicial system for a violation of international law to take place, that violation being the violation in respect of which the rule of local remedies would apply.[1]

The evidence in the authorities is interesting. It is best to consider the trends in the nineteenth and early twentieth centuries and then evaluate what impact on the question the subsequent developments have had.

The earlier authorities

State practice

State practice is of limited assistance in deriving the appropriate rule. On the one hand, there stands the argument adduced by Switzerland in the *Losinger & Co. Case*. This is that a state must be bound by its

---

[1] The matter more recently involved the concept of 'internationalization' and 'delocalization' of state contracts with aliens flowing from the choice of law: see particularly Amerasinghe, *State Responsibility for Injuries to Aliens* (1967) pp. 113ff.; Sornarajah, *International Commercial Arbitration* (1990) pp. 17ff.; Maniruzzaman, 'International Commercial Arbitration: The Conflict of Law Issues in Determining the Applicable Substantive Law in the Context of Investment Agreements', 40 NILR (1993) p. 201; Nassar, 'Internationalization of State Contracts: ICSID, the Last Citadel', 14 *Journal of International Arbitration* (1997) p. 183; and the literature cited in these works. See also Greenwood, 'State Contracts in International Law in the Libyan Oil Arbitrations', 53 BYIL (1982) p. 27; and Bowett, 'State Contracts with Aliens: Contemporary Developments on Compensation for Termination or Breach', 59 BYIL (1988) p. 49.

obligations to an alien under a contract as at the time the contract was made, since the contrary argument would enable a state to free itself of its obligations by enacting special laws:

La validité d'une obligation assumée par un Etat doit évidemment s'apprécier d'aprés la législation en vigueur au moment où l'obligation est née. Cette règle de simple bon sens ne souffre aucune discussion.[2]

The contract was regarded as giving rise to an international obligation, and the breach of contract was seen as a direct breach of international law. This argument was opposed by Yugoslavia, the respondent. The PCIJ did not find it necessary to decide the issue.[3]

In the *Norwegian Loans Case*, a similar argument was raised by France in a case involving public loans, the argument being formulated in general terms so as to cover contracts generally. It was submitted that:

lorsqu'un Etat a conclu avec un particulier étranger un contrat quelconque, il ne peut l'en dépouiller, directement ou indirectement, sans engager sa responsibilité à l'égard de l'Etat protecteur de cet étranger.[4]

Norway opposed this formulation of the rule.[5] The ICJ was not required to decide the issue.

In the *Anglo-Iranian Oil Company Case*, the UK memorial argued in a fashion similar to Switzerland and France that:

a fortiori the principle of respect for acquired rights in the matter of concessions must be regarded as binding upon the Government or Governments of the State granting them when there has been no change of sovereignty over the territory where the concession operates.[6]

Apart from these instances of legal argument, there is little or no evidence in the practice of states of the view that a breach of contract with an alien by a state was regarded as *per se* a breach of international law. The United States, on the other hand, did not seem to espouse that view. In general the United States did not assist its citizens in contract claims of this kind except where there was 'an arbitrary wrong', lack of good

[2] PCIJ Series C, No. 78, p. 32 (1936).
[3] See also the Belgian argument in the *Electricity Company of Sofia Case*, PCIJ Series C, No. 88, p. 54 (1939).
[4] ICJ Pleadings, Oral Arguments and Documents (1957), vol. 2, p. 61. See also *ibid.*, pp. 63, 181 and 182; and ICJ Pleadings, Oral Arguments and Documents (1957), vol. 1, pp. 34 and 404.
[5] *Ibid.*, vol. 1, p. 485; and *ibid.*, vol. 2, p. 134.
[6] ICJ Pleadings, Oral Arguments and Documents (1952) p. 85.

faith or abuse, i.e. where there is some other additional element making the breach of contract a breach of international law.[7] In UK practice, the UK Government was advised not to protect British subjects who enter into contracts with a foreign government 'unless and until they have suffered a denial or flagrant perversion of justice or some gross wrong'.[8] The Latin-American states took the view that a mere breach of contract with an alien by a state was not *per se* a breach of international law.[9] Their approach was reflected at the Hague Peace Conference of 1907. For instance, Argentina maintained that

> [W]ith regard to debts arising from ordinary contracts between the citizen or subject of a nation and a foreign Government, recourse shall not be had to arbitration except in the specific case of denial of justice by the courts of the country which made the contract, the remedies before which courts must first have been exhausted.[10]

El Salvador and Ecuador expressed similar views.[11]

The evidence of state practice reflects some disagreement among states. The weight of authority was, however, heavily in favour of the idea that a breach of contract by a state was not *per se* a breach of international law.

International treaty practice

In view of the uncertainty evidenced in direct state practice, the practice that may have been established by treaties becomes important, as are international decisions.

Cases concerning the establishment of jurisdiction of an international tribunal in contract cases must be distinguished from those which involve or discuss the question of the nature of a breach of contract with

---

[7] See Moore, *Digest of International Law* (1906), vol. 4, pp. 289, 705 and 723; and Hackworth, *Digest of International Law* (1942), vol. 5, p. 611. For other US practice, see Wharton, *Digest of International Law of the United States* (1886), vol. 2, p. 6543; and the material in Wetter, 'Diplomatic Assistance to Private Investment', 29 *University of Chicago Law Review* (1962) p. 275.

[8] McNair, *International Law Opinions* (1956), vol. 2, p. 202. For the UK practice, see further, Hall, *International Law* (8th edn, 1924) pp. 334–6; Phillimore, *Commentaries upon International Law* (3rd edn, 1888), vol. 2; and Parry (ed.), 6 BDIL (1965) p. 359.

[9] Drago, 1 AJIL (1907) p. 692. See also, for the practice of states, Dulon, 38 *American Law Review* (1932) p. 648; for France, *Journal officiel du 8 Juin 1907, Débats Parlementaires, Chambre des Députés* p. 1231; and for Germany, Martens, 1 *Völkerrecht* (1883) p. 379. Further, see *The Suez Canal Problem*, US State Department Pub. 6392.

[10] Scott (ed.), *Reports to the Hague Conferences of 1899 and 1907* (1917) p. 492.

[11] *Ibid.*, pp. 494 and 495.

an alien by a state. Jurisdiction in a case alleging a breach of contract by a state depends on the instrument creating the tribunal, a treaty between the claimant state whose national alleges injury and the defendant state. The question is one of interpreting a treaty.[12] Although the tribunal may decide that the treaty does give it jurisdiction over such a claim, it does not follow that the breach of contract for that reason alone is a violation of international law giving rise to state responsibility. Nor, conversely, is it true to say that there must be a violation of international law giving rise to state responsibility to give a tribunal jurisdiction.[13] Even a stipulation in the *compromis* that claims should be decided according to 'principles of international law' does not change this conclusion. Such a stipulation has been interpreted to mean that the claim must only have an international character. Claims between citizens of one country and the government of another are regarded as being of this character. Thus, claims alleging a breach by a state of a contract with an alien would be of the same nature, and tribunals have assumed jurisdiction in such cases.[14] Also clear is the fact that in such cases tribunals did not focus on establishing whether the breach of contract *per se* was a violation of international law entitling the claimant to redress for such a violation. Instead, they have granted relief for a breach of contract, if such breach could be established according to national law.[15]

In the *Illinois Central Railroad Co. Case*,[16] the United States claimed damages and interest on behalf of a company for non-payment of the price of ninety-one locomotive engines on a contract with the Mexican Government Railway Administration. The defence argued that, because the claim was based on the non-performance of a contractual obligation, it was outside the Commission's jurisdiction. The convention constituting the Commission stated in Article I that the Commission should decide 'all claims against one government by nationals of the other for

[12] See the *Illinois Central Railroad Co. Case* (*United States* v. *Mexico*) (1926), *US and Mexican General Claims Commission Opinions 1926–1927* p. 15.

[13] *Ibid.*, p. 17, interpreting Article I of the General Claims Convention of 1923.

[14] See the *Illinois Central Railroad Co. Case*, note 12 above, where the tribunal discussed at length this concept of 'international character'.

[15] Thus, under the Convention between the US and Mexico of 11 April 1839, the Commission sustained a claim in contract for the furnishing of a war vessel in the *Samuel Chew Case*, Moore, *Digest of International Arbitrations* (1898), vol. 4, p. 3428. See also *ibid.*, chapter 63 *passim*; Hyde, *International Law* (1945), vol. 1, p. 1004; Eagleton, *Responsibility of States in International Law* (1928) p. 160; Ralston, *The Law and Procedure of International Tribunals* (1926) p. 75; and Borchard, *Diplomatic Protection of Citizens Abroad* (1915) p. 298.

[16] *US and Mexican General Claims Commission Opinions 1926–1927*, p. 15.

losses or damages suffered by such nationals or their properties . . . in accordance with the principles of international law, justice and equity'. It was held that the Commission had to derive its powers from a construction of the treaty, that there was no rule that contract claims were cognizable only in cases where some form of governmental responsibility was involved, but that the claims had to be of an international character and the present claim was of that character. There also was an understanding that the fact that the governing instrument might specify that the claims should be decided in accordance with the principles of international law, equity and justice did not mean that a breach of international law must have occurred. It merely meant that the parties to the instrument had chosen special principles to be applied in the settlement of their dispute.[17]

There were cases in which arbitral tribunals refused to assume jurisdiction over contract claims. In the *Hubbell Case*,[18] the claim was on behalf of a US citizen against Great Britain concerning the adoption of a patent belonging to the claimant. Article XII of the arbitration treaty provided for the submission of 'all claims . . . arising out of acts committed against the person or property' of citizens or subjects of either contracting party.[19] Objections to jurisdiction by the respondent were upheld on the ground that claims based on contract did not come within the terms of the treaty. In the *Pond's Case*,[20] it was held, on the other hand, that under an instrument granting jurisdiction over 'claims . . . arising from injuries to their persons or property by the authorities',[21] although claims arising out of contracts came under the cognizance of the tribunal, 'the validity of the contract should be proved by the clearest evidence, and . . . it should also be shown that gross injustice has been done by the defendant'.[22] It is clear that in this case something more than a mere allegation of breach of contract was required for jurisdiction to be assumed. A 'gross injustice' was required.[23]

[17] *Ibid.*   [18] *United States* v. *Great Britain* (1873), Moore, note 15 above, vol. 4, p. 3484.
[19] Treaty of Washington, 8 May 1871 (*Great Britain–United States*), Malloy, *Treaties, Conventions, International Acts, Protocols and Agreements* (1910), vol. 1, p. 700.
[20] *United States* v. *Mexico* (1868), Moore, note 15 above, vol. 4, p. 3467.
[21] Treaty between US and Mexico 1868, Article I, Malloy, note 19 above, vol. 1, p. 1128.
[22] Moore, note 15 above, vol. 4, p. 3467. See also the *Leonard T. Treadwell and Co. Case* (*United States* v. *Mexico*), ibid., p. 3468, where jurisdiction over a claim based on a contract for the sale of arms and munitions was rejected on the same grounds.
[23] In some cases, the tribunal has made its jurisdiction dependent on whether or not the claimant entered voluntarily into the contract. If he had, the tribunal had no jurisdiction: *State Bank of Hartford Case* (*US* v. *Mexico*) (1868), Moore, note 15 above,

These cases show that instruments submitting disputes have differed in their wording and that tribunals have interpreted instruments in different ways. No conclusion can be drawn that points to any uniform rule of interpretation which establishes a presumption that such contract claims were subject to the jurisdiction of international tribunals.[24] Nor is there any evidence in the cases in which jurisdiction was assumed of any rule of interpretation based on the idea that a breach of contract *per se* was a violation of international law. Indeed, the evidence goes the other way.

In spite of the divergent interpretations given to arbitration treaties, it is clear that some cases held or assumed that the governing instrument did confer jurisdiction over claims based on breach of contract by the state party as such.[25] This means that in a large number of bilateral treaties states regarded claims based on breach of contract *per se* by a state as cognizable by international tribunals.[26] Assuming that there was no rule of international law that the breach of contract with an alien by a state was *per se* a violation of international law, the question is whether these treaties represented a practice which gave rise to a new rule of international law that a breach by a state of a contract

vol. 4, p. 3473; see also the *Kearney Case* (*United States* v. *Mexico*) (1875), *ibid.*, p. 3467, where, in the case of a contract for the supply of arms and munitions of war, the tribunal refused jurisdiction. These cases were decided by the same tribunal that decided *Pond's Case* so that the notion of involuntariness may really be a part of the concept of 'gross injustice'.

[24] See the *Illinois Central Railroad Co. Case* (*United States* v. *Mexico*) (1926), *US–Mexican General Opinions 1926–1927* p. 16.

[25] See, for instance, the *Case of Hermon* (*United States* v. *Mexico*) (1839), Moore, note 15 above, vol. 4, p. 3425, *Eldredge's Case* (*United States* v. *Mexico*) (1863), *ibid.*, p. 3460; and *Boulton, Bliss and Dallett's Case* (*United States* v. *Venezuela*) (1903), Morris, *Report of US and Venezuelan Claims Commission* p. 105.

[26] The following treaties are examples of this category: US–New Granada, 1857, Article 1, Malloy, note 19 above, at p. 319; US–Ecuador, 1862, Article 1, *ibid.*, p. 432; US–Peru, 1863, Article 1, *ibid.*, vol. 2, p. 1408; US–Costa Rica, 1860, Article 1, *ibid.*, vol. 1, p. 346; US–Mexico, 1868, Article 1, *ibid.*, p. 1128; US–France, 1880, Article 1, *ibid.*, p. 535; France–Venezuela, 1902, Article 1, Declerq, 22 *Recueil des traités de la France* (1901–4) p. 68; US–Great Britain, 1910, *Treaty Series* No. 573; and US–Great Britain, 1927, *ibid.*, No. 756 (exchange of notes). Contract claims as such were accepted under these treaties.

The following treaties did not admit contract claims as such: US–Mexico, 1868, Article 1 (Umpire Thornton's subsequent interpretation based on expediency, which changed the course of decisions), Malloy, note 19 above, vol. 1, p. 1128; US–Great Britain, 1871, Article XII, *ibid.*, pp. 700 and 705; US–Spain, 1871, para. 5, *ibid.*, vol. 2, pp. 1661 and 1662; and US–Haiti, 1919, Protocol, Article III (four classes of fiscal claims were excepted in this treaty), *Treaty Series* No. 643. See also Hyde, note 15 above, vol. 2, p. 306.

with an alien was *per se* a violation of international law giving rise to state responsibility. It must be noted that the numerical preponderance of those that did not militates against the creation of a new rule of international law. There are other factors, moreover, that clearly indicate that such treaties have not created a new rule of international law.

First, the treaties concerned made no reference to a violation of international law as the basis on which claims were submitted to arbitration. They merely referred to 'claims' by persons against the contracting state. These could very well have been claims based on the breach of national laws. For the creation of a rule of international law an explicit reference to the new rule would be required. Secondly, cases such as the *Illinois Central Railroad Co. Case* stated quite clearly that it was not necessary that an allegation of a violation of international law entailing state responsibility be the basis of a claim in order that the tribunal assume jurisdiction over it;[27] and this, it was said, was so, even though the instrument stated that decisions were to be given according to the 'principles of international law, justice and equity'. This clearly shows that the parties to the treaty did not regard a breach of contract by a state *per se* as a violation of international law, although the tribunal was given jurisdiction in such cases. Thirdly, unless the contrary was stated in the governing instrument, as in the *Illinois Central Railroad Co. Case*, the merits of the case were decided solely by the application of the relevant national law. In the *Frear Case*,[28] for example, the tribunal decided a claim alleging a breach of contract by the application of French law relating to performance and discharge of contracts, as if it were dealing with a case presented to a French court. Thus, these treaties cannot be said to have changed an existing rule of international law that state breaches of contracts with aliens were *per se* not violations of international law.

International decisions

In the decisions of international tribunals there were a few open-ended statements that appear to support the view that a breach of contract with an alien by a state is *per se* a violation of international law.[29] There is little or no evidence, though, that any breach of such a contract by a

---

[27] See also the *Case of Hermon* (*United States* v. *Mexico*) (1839), Moore, note 15 above, vol. 4, p. 3425.

[28] Moore, note 15 above, vol. 4, p. 3488.

[29] See Nielsen's reference to this view in his dissenting opinion in the *International Fisheries Co. Case* (*United States* v. *Mexico*) (1931), *US–Mexico Claims Commission Opinions*

state *per se* has actually been treated as a violation of international law in any case.[30] On the other hand, there is evidence that such breaches *per se* have not been regarded as violations of international law.

The leading case is the *Martini Case*.[31] A concessionary contract for the construction and operation of a railroad between the Venezuelan Government and an Italian company was terminated by the former as a result of a Venezuelan court decision. Italy claimed, *inter alia*, on behalf of the company that a counter-claim by the company before the Venezuelan court to the effect that the Venezuelan Government had broken the contract by granting a monopoly to another individual had been wrongly rejected. The tribunal held against Italy on this count, what is of importance being the tribunal's approach to the contention.

The tribunal did not assert that the Italian company's counter-claim was an allegation of a violation of international law. Further, it did not treat it as one either. It did not examine the merits of the counter-claim virtually as a court of appeal from the Venezuelan court as it would have done if it regarded a breach of contract by a state as *per se* a violation of international law. Rather, it looked for certain other defects in the judgment of the Venezuelan court. The success of the counter-claim had depended largely on the interpretation of the contract, and on this the tribunal said:

As the respondent has emphasized, there exists in several countries a well established jurisprudence by which the rights of a grantee under a contract of concession are interpreted restrictively. If the Court of Caracas, in adopting a restrictive interpretation of the Martini contract on the basis of the Venezuelan law, reached the conclusion that the Feo contract was not contrary to the contract of concession, that conclusion cannot be characterized as erroneous or unjust by an international tribunal.[32]

If the tribunal had been acting virtually as a court of appeal, it would have examined the judgment of the Venezuelan court in order to find out whether that court's notion of the proper rule of interpretation coincided with the arbitral tribunal's opinion of it and whether that court had applied it in the way in which the arbitral tribunal would have applied it. Instead, the tribunal investigated whether the rule of

---

1930–1931 pp. 207 and 242; and Findlay in the *Venezuelan Bond Cases*, Moore, note 15 above, vol. 4, pp. 3616 and 3649.

[30] The *Aboilard Case*, 12 RGDIP, Documents (1905) p. 12, and the *Hemmings Case* (*Great Britain* v. *United States*) (1920), 15 AJIL (1921) p. 292, *seem* to support this view, but even they can be explained.

[31] *Italy* v. *Venezuela* (1903), 25 AJIL (1931) p. 554.   [32] *Ibid.*

interpretation chosen was a *possible* one and whether it had been applied in a *possible* way. Also, the tribunal did not even consider whether international legal principles should be applied to determine whether the alleged breach was a violation of international law and whether the Venezuelan court had chosen those principles and applied them correctly in deciding the issue. Instead, the tribunal seems to have accepted the choice of rules for determining the issue of breach of contract made by the Venezuelan court *ipso facto*. It is to be concluded that the tribunal did not regard a state breach of contract as *per se* a violation of international law.

It is to be noted that the *compromis* restricted the competence of the tribunal to defects in the action before the Venezuelan court.[33] Can it be argued that it was because of this limitation of jurisdiction that the tribunal did not examine the question of whether there had been a breach of contract by Venezuela or whether a breach of contract by a state was per se a violation of international law and not because it did not regard a breach of contract by a state as per se a violation of international law? In discussing its competence, the tribunal said that 'denial of justice' to which its jurisdiction was limited occurred, *inter alia*, 'when a judicial decision, which was final and without appeal and was incompatible with the treaty obligations *or other international obligations*[34] of the State, was given'. If acts of a state which constituted a breach of contract were a violation of international law, they were contrary to the international obligations of that state. If the courts of the state declared that those acts were not a breach of contract and consequently were not a violation of international law, when in fact they were, the judgment of the court was itself incompatible with the international obligations of the state and constituted for that reason a denial of justice within the definition given by the tribunal to that term. Hence, if the tribunal had taken that view of a breach of contract, it would in its own right have examined the acts alleged to have been a breach of contract in order to determine whether there was a violation of international law. The tribunal must have had the competence to inquire into the question whether the acts themselves were a breach of contract and consequently a violation of international law. But it did not. It is clear that the tribunal did not regard a breach of contract *per se* as a violation of international law,

---

[33] 'The Arbitral Tribunal will now examine the question whether in the action brought against Martini & Co., before the Federal Court of Cassation . . . there was a "*denial of justice* or *manifest injustice*".' *Ibid.*, p. 565.
[34] Emphasis added.

while it did not merely regard its jurisdiction as restricted by the terms of the *compromis*.

There is much more evidence in the attitude of international tribunals in favour of the view that a breach of contract *per se* is not a violation of international law. The other relevant cases which support the view were discussed elsewhere by me in 1967.[35] They are the *Illinois Central Railroad Co. Case*,[36] the *International Fisheries Co. Case*,[37] the *General Company of Orinoco Case*,[38] the *Pieri Dominique and Co. Case*,[39] the *Olivia Case*,[40] the *Kunhardt Case*,[41] the *Punchard, McTaggart, Lowther and Co. Case*,[42] the *Cedroni Case*,[43] the *Delagoa Bay and East African Railroad Co. Case*,[44] the *Cheek Case*[45] and the *May Case*.[46] All these cases clearly concluded either that a breach of contract by a state was per se *not* a violation of international law or that something more than a pure breach of contract, such as an arbitrary act, including legislative termination, or denial of access to the courts, was necessary to give rise to a violation of international law.

There are three decisions[47] which have been interpreted to support the contrary view that a breach of contract by a state *per se* is a violation of international law. But on analysis these do not do so. In the *Rudloff Case*,[48] a contract for the construction of a building in the marketplace had been declared null and void by the Municipal Council of the Federal District. The objection was raised by the defendant state that the case was still pending before a Venezuelan court of appeal, that there had been no denial of justice, and that, consequently, there was nothing on which the tribunal could pronounce. In deciding the case against the defendant state, one Commissioner made some statements which may appear to support the view that a breach of contract *per se* is a violation

---

[35] See Amerasinghe, note 1 above, at pp. 79ff.

[36] *US–Mexican Claims Commission Opinions 1926–1927* p. 17.

[37] *US–Mexican Claims Commission Opinions 1930–1931* p. 207.

[38] *Ralston's Report of the French–Venezuelan Mixed Claims Commission* (1906) p. 244.

[39] *France v. Venezuela* (1906), ibid., p. 185.

[40] *Italy v. Venezuela* (1904), *Ralston's Report* p. 771.

[41] *United States v. Venezuela* (1903), ibid., p. 63.

[42] *Great Britain v. Colombia* (1899), La Fontaine, *Pasicrisie internationale* (1902) p. 544.

[43] *Italy v. Guatemala* (1898), ibid., p. 606.   [44] *Great Britain v. Portugal* (1900), ibid., p. 397.

[45] *United States v. Siam* (1898), 1897 US For. Rel. p. 461.

[46] *United States v. Guatemala* (1900), 1900 US For. Rel. p. 659.

[47] The cases on which considerable reliance has been placed by the authorities, such as Eagleton, are the *International Fisheries Co. Case* (Nielsen's dissenting opinion) and the *Venezuelan Bond Cases* (Findlay's opinion). The latter case is referred to below.

[48] *United States v. Venezuela* (1904), *Morris's Report of US and Venezuelan Claims Commission* p. 415.

of international law.[49] It is clear, though, that that was not his view. His opinion shows that he regarded the issue as whether a claim based on a private law breach of contract was cognizable while it was still pending in the national courts under a *compromis* which stated that 'all claims . . . not settled by diplomatic agreement or arbitration' were justiciable. It was not a question of what constituted a violation of international law, which was irrelevant for the purposes of jurisdiction.[50] Further, he did state explicitly that states ordinarily had a right to intervene on behalf of their nationals in the case of contracts only where there was a 'denial of justice',[51] and explained that the *compromis* gave the tribunal exceptional jurisdiction. The Umpire who settled the difference of opinion which occurred between the two Commissioners in this arbitration regarded the matter as entirely one of interpreting the treaty for the purpose of determining the tribunal's jurisdiction in a case where a contract claim was pending before a national court, irrespective of a violation of international law.[52] The case, thus, does not support the view that a state breach of contract with an alien is *per se* a violation of international law.

In the *Beale, Nobles and Garrison Case*,[53] the claimant sued for non-fulfilment of a contract made with the dictator of Venezuela for the establishment of a steamship service involving obligations related to immigration and commerce. The issue was whether the latter had power to contract and whether the contract had been validly concluded. The Commission was confronted with the preliminary question whether it had jurisdiction. One Commissioner said:

It would be difficult, if not impossible, to assign a good reason why, on principles of abstract right and justice, an injury to a citizen arising out of a refusal of a foreign power to keep its contractual engagements, did not impose an obligation upon the government of his allegiance to seek redress from the offending country, quite as binding as its recognized duty to interfere in cases involving wrongs to persons and property.[54]

It is to be noted that the words used were 'injury . . . *arising out of* a refusal of a foreign power to keep its contractual engagements'.[55] Subsequently,

---

[49] *Ibid.*, p. 423 (Bainbridge).   [50] *Ibid.*, pp. 423 and 426.   [51] *Ibid.*, p. 426.
[52] *Ibid.*, p. 431 and especially p. 432.
[53] *United States* v. *Venezuela* (1886), Moore, note 15 above, vol. 4, p. 3548.
[54] Findlay, *ibid.*, p. 3555. It would seem that Findlay was more concerned with the question of whether the state of the injured national has an obligation to intervene, a different aspect of state responsibility. He stated that there was no such obligation, as opposed to a right or power to intervene.
[55] Emphasis added.

he indicated that the additional factor of failing to afford redress was the vital element which constituted the international wrong and not the breach of contract by itself.[56] It is in this light that the passage cited above must be interpreted. Moreover, the conclusion whether there was a cognizable claim or not was reached by an interpretation of the *compromis* to which the question of whether there had been a violation of international law was irrelevant. This means that any statement on the latter point was *obiter*.[57] Further, the analogy between wrongs to persons and property and contractual claims which the Commissioner made was clearly erroneous on the present issue, as has been seen above.[58]

The *Venezuelan Bond Cases*[59] were based on a refusal to pay monies due under certain bonds issued by the old Republic of Colombia and forming part of the Colombian public debt for which Venezuela became responsible. One Commissioner said:

A claim is none the less a claim because it originates in contract instead of in tort. The refusal to pay an honest claim is no less a wrong because it happens to arise from an obligation to pay money instead of originating in violence offered to person or property.[60]

There was in this case a refusal both to adjudicate and to compensate on the part of the respondent. The statement of the Commissioner must, therefore, be taken to include this material fact within the notion of a violation of international law arising from a breach of contract.[61] Thus, it is not the breach of contract *per se* that was characterized as a violation of international law but the breach of contract accompanied by the refusal to adjudicate and to compensate. In addition, the case was in essence regarded as concerning the interpretation of a treaty conferring jurisdiction on the tribunal by the other two Commissioners.[62] In the light of

---

[56] 'Conceding now . . . that good faith as between nations binds the State as a personality to fulfil the terms of its private contracts, *or pay damages for their nonfulfilment* . . .' (emphasis added): Moore, note 15 above, vol. 4, p. 3555.

[57] 'But, however this question may stand on principle it cannot be doubted that, if the present claim was valid in other respects, it would be the duty of the commission, under the Convention between the USA and Venezuela, to make an allowance of damage sufficient to compensate for the wrong, notwithstanding that it originated in a breach of private contract between a citizen of one State and the government of another.' *Ibid.*, p. 3555.

[58] Analogy is not a panacea in the law. The relevance and success of its use depends, among other things, on the similarity of purpose between the relevant fields of law.

[59] *United States* v. *Venezuela* (1898), Moore, note 15 above, vol. 4, p. 3616.

[60] *Ibid.*, p. 3649.

[61] As the reference to 'a refusal to pay an honest claim' indicates.

[62] Findlay: 'The great question that confronts us on the threshold of this case is: Whether by the use of terms under which this commission has been created it was

this fact, the Commissioner's statement must be taken to refer not to the distinction between that which is internationally wrong and that which is not. It is concerned rather with the question of whether claims based on certain kinds of 'wrong' can be distinguished from claims based on other kinds of wrong for the purposes of the treaty. 'Wrong' was not being used in a technical sense to denote an internationally illegal act entailing state responsibility. Hence, the question whether a breach of contract by a state *per se* was an internationally illegal act was not within the purview of this statement. This case also, therefore, does not support the proposition that a state breach of contract with an alien is *per se* a violation of international law.

None of the decided cases, then, in fact supports the thesis that a breach of contract is *per se* a violation of international law. On the other hand, there seems to be some very definite and clear evidence in support of the contrary view. The fact as such that international tribunals assumed jurisdiction in contract cases does not support the view that a state breach of contract *per se* is a violation of international law.

Text writers

Among writers, there was no clear agreement that a state breach of contract with an alien was *per se* a violation of international law. Some held the view that such a breach of contract was *per se* a violation of international law.[63] This view derived mainly from the idea that there should be no distinction between an act by a state alleged to be a delict and one alleged to be a breach of contract. If it was argued, the former was regarded as a violation of international law, then the latter should also be so regarded.[64] *De lege ferenda*, it was suggested that:

> the intention of the United States to demand and Venezuela to assent to a submission of a portion of her public debt to the decision of this body as one of the claims agreed to be referred within the clear intent and purview of the treaty': Moore, *ibid.*, p. 3654; see also Little, *ibid.*, p. 3626.

[63] See e.g. Fauchille, *Traité de droit international public* (8th edn, 1925), vol. 1, p. 529; Clarke, 'Intervention for Breach of Contract or Tort Committed by a Sovereignty', *ASIL Proceedings* (1910) p. 155; Oppenheim and Lauterpacht, *International Law* (8th edn, 1954), vol. 1, p. 344; Hershey, *Essentials of International Law* (1927) p. 261; Cavaré, *La Protection des contractuels reconnus par les états à des étrangers à les exceptions des emprunts* (1956) p. 261; and Brandon, 'Legal Deterrents and Incentives to Private Foreign Investments', 43 GST (1957) at pp. 39, 54 and 55. See also Schwebel, 'International Protection of Contractual Arrangements', *ASIL Proceedings* (1959) p. 266.

[64] Clarke, note 63 above, at p. 155; Fauchille, note 63 above, vol. 1, p. 529, who says: 'Si la responsabilité des Etâts peut avoir pour origines des actes d'un caractére *delictuel*, elle peut résulter égalment d'obligations contactuelles. L'inexécution d'un engagement

It may be that a workable solution of the problem can be found only by generalizing an established principle of international law and at the same time taking a leaf out of the American Constitution and out of the books of authority to which it has given life: without prejudice to its liability for any other tort (such as denial of justice, discrimination, expropriation), the State shall be responsible for the injuries caused to an alien by the non-performance of its obligations stipulated in the contract with that alien if and insofar as such non-performance results from the application of the State's law enacted after the date of the contract; this shall not apply where the law so enacted is required for the protection of public safety, health, morality or welfare in general.[65]

This view was clearly proposed as a modification of what the writer accepted was the international law at the time, namely, that a breach of contract with an alien by a state party to it was not *per se* a violation of international law.[66] The proposal, it is to be noted, related to a specific method of breaking a contract and did not introduce a rule that a breach of contract was always *per se* a violation of international law. The theory of state contracts with aliens in the context of international law was examined by another writer, who concluded that:

There is nothing in the structure of international law and nothing in the relationship between international law and municipal law that inhibits the recognition of international law remedies which relate directly to the contract.[67]

There is no clear statement here or thereafter that a state breach of such a contract was *per se* a violation of international law.[68]

The assumption made by these writers as to the existing law was in keeping with the views of several other writers who regarded a breach of contract by a state *per se* as at the most a simple violation of national

---

qu'ils ont souscrit constitue en effet un manquement à la parole donnée, c'est à dire une violation d'un de leurs devoirs internationaux . . .'

[65] Mann, 'State Contracts and State Responsibility', 54 AJIL (1960) at p. 590.

[66] *Ibid.*, pp. 577–88.

[67] Jennings, 'State Contracts in International Law', 37 BYIL (1961) at p. 181.

[68] See *ibid.*, p. 182. The statement cited above is neither here nor there in relation to the real problem that arises and is being addressed here. In terms of the conclusion, stated above, by Jennings, his article was not specific enough and, more importantly, the analysis was defective and did not raise all the pertinent issues. As will be pointed out later by the present author, it is precisely the present structure of the international legal system that prevents as such the application to alien–state contracts of international remedies, understood to mean remedies provided by tribunals of the international legal system *within* that system and not merely remedies which are available under the secondary rules of public international law and which may be adopted by other tribunals than those of the international system. Jennings completely overlooked the issues raised and the points made below by me.

law and not a violation of international law as well. The latter required something more than a mere breach of contract by the state in order that there might be a violation of international law.[69] Thus, one author wrote:

It may be doubted, however, whether the mere breach of a promise by a contracting State with respect to an alien is generally looked upon as amounting to internationally illegal conduct, or as constituting the violation of a legal obligation towards the State of which he is a national . . . In the estimation of statesmen and jurists international law is probably not regarded as denouncing the failure of a State to keep such a promise, until at least there has been a refusal . . . to adjudicate locally the claim arising from the breach.[70]

It is possible to take the view that whether or not a breach of contract by a state is *per se* a violation of international law depends on whether the government of the state concerned was acting as a sovereign and supreme power or in a private capacity in *entering* into the contract.[71] As an absolute criterion of international responsibility the distinction is both vague[72] and difficult to justify for the purpose in hand. The distinction is predicated on the notion that, where the state acts in its sovereign capacity, it generally does not subject itself to judicial process in its own courts and may avoid its obligations, whereas, when it acts in a private capacity, there is generally redress through the local courts. This is, in fact, not a true representation of the actual situation in states, especially in the Anglo-American jurisdictions. What is more, in practice, where the distinction obtains, the presence of local remedies does not *always* coincide with the private nature of the contract nor

---

[69] E.g. Hyde, *International Law* (1945), vol. 2, p. 988; Jessup, *A Modern Law of Nations* (1948) pp. 104 and 109; Whiteman, *Damages in International Law* (1943), vol. 3, pp. 1555 and 1558; Borchard, *Diplomatic Protection of Citizens Abroad* (1916), Chapter VII; Westlake, *International Law* (2nd edn, 1910), vol. 1, p. 331; Decenciére-Ferrandiére, *La Responsabilité internationale des états* (1925) p. 174; Hoijer, *La Responsabilité internationale des états* (1930) p. 117; Feller, *The Mexican Claims Commissions* (1935) p. 174; Dahm, *Völkerrecht* (1961), vol. 3, p. 210, note 2; and Dunn, *The Protection of Nationals* (1932) p. 165.

[70] Hyde, note 69 above, vol. 2, p. 990.

[71] Dunn, note 69 above, at p. 165. Dunn made a distinction between a state's breaching a contract by the exercise of sovereign power and other situations of breach.

[72] The distinction has been used in the law of sovereign immunity to determine whether a foreign sovereign is entitled to immunity from suit and has taken the form of distinguishing between acts *iure gestionis* and acts *iure imperii*. But the courts have experienced difficulty in applying it to particular situations and, indeed, the answers that the courts of the different countries have arrived at in similar situations have been conflicting. See H. Lauterpacht, 'The Problem of Jurisdictional Immunities of Foreign States', 28 BYIL (1951) p. 220.

does the absence of remedies *always* coincide with the sovereign nature of the contract. Also, there is no good reason of policy for adopting the distinction between contracts made in a state's sovereign capacity and those made in its private capacity for this purpose. However, the distinction between the absence and presence of legal remedies, which is the premise from which such a view would seem to derive, is more relevant to the present problem. It is the same distinction that was inherent in the thesis stated above that international law does not denounce a simple breach of contract by a state until at least there has been a refusal to adjudicate locally.[73]

The opinions of text writers at the time could be divided into two schools: those that maintained that a breach of contract by a state *per se* was a violation of international law and those that required something more than a mere breach of contract for a violation of international law to take place. The latter school had more support.

It is significant that at the Hague Codification Conference of 1930 the basis of discussion relating to contracts was formulated in such a way as to avoid the assumption that the breach by a state of a contract with an alien *per se* was a violation of international law.[74] Most draft conventions then attempted did not expressly embody the rule that a breach of contract with an alien by a state *per se* was a violation of international law, perhaps for the reason that there was no clear agreement on such a rule among states.[75] On the contrary, the Draft Convention prepared

---

[73] Societies of international lawyers also expressed opinions on this question. For instance, in 1958 the US branch of the International Law Association expressed the following view:

> The unsoundness of treating the legal rights arising from contracts between States and aliens as being of a lower order than those arising from agreements between governments or their agencies merits further illustration. Afghanistan recently granted the Soviet Techno-export Organization rights to explore for oil in Afghanistan. A breach by Afghanistan of the pertinent agreement would be a breach of international law. But a contract with a privately owned oil company, for the same object, of the same substance, upon the same terms, breached in the same way, by the same State would not be a breach of international law in the eyes of the formalists.

1957–1958 Proceedings and Committee Reports of the American Branch of the International Law Association pp. 70, 71. The view implicitly advocated here is in favour of regarding a breach of contract with an alien by a state as *per se* a breach of international law. For expressions of opinion by other international societies of lawyers, see 44 AIDI (1952-II) at pp. 251ff.; and *Reports of the Seventh Conference of the International Bar Association* (1958).

[74] YBILC (1956), vol. 2, p. 223, citing from LN Doc C.75. M. 69. 1929 V.

[75] These drafts are conveniently collected in the Annexes to Garcia Amador's 'First Report to the International Law Commission on State Responsibility', YBILC (1956),

by Garcia Amador for the International Law Commission contained a rule which presupposed that such an act was *per se* not a violation of international law.[76]

Functional considerations

Functional reasons which would apply then as now point to the conclusion that a breach of contract by a contracting state *per se* is not a violation of international law, which is also the view better supported by authority. There must be some other factor, such as the refusal of means to secure redress in a national court, to give rise to such a violation of international law. This does not mean that contractual relations between state and alien are outside the purview of international law. Claims arising out of such contracts can certainly be claims alleging a breach of international law, provided they contain the necessary additional features.

The business context

When an alien enters into a contract with a state, he is engaging in a business transaction. In the type of situation that has generally arisen, it is reasonable to expect that an ordinary businessman will acquaint himself with the existing laws of the state with which he contracts concerning the transaction into which he is entering. He freely consents to enter into the transaction. He equally freely consents to the application of the existing laws to that transaction. There is free choice in respect of both, but the two are inextricably linked; the free choice of one involves the free choice of the other. There will be provisions of the law both for determining the validity of a claim that the contract has been broken and for remedying the breach. He accepts those provisions on redress as well.

In business there is an important risk that the transaction will not be fulfilled, although this risk will be attended by remedial rights as provided by the legal system. A businessman can be expected to accept this risk together with whatever rights relating to remedies that there may be. Therefore, where he alleges that there has been a breach of contract, he cannot expect that remedial provisions different from these be applied to his claim. International law can only protect him against

vol. 2, pp. 221–30. For other draft conventions, see e.g. the Abs–Shawcross Convention, *Current Legal Problems* (1961) p. 223, which takes a different view; and the Harvard Draft, 55 AJIL (1961) p. 566.

[76] Article 7, YBILC (1957), vol. 2, pp. 116–17.

abuses of the remedial process or its absence or deprivation of remedies. This would be the usual situation.

The international legal system

In relation to contracts, it is with the questions of whether means of redress are afforded in the state and, if so, how these means are given effect to by the relevant organs of the state that international law normally concerns itself. The alien is entitled to redress according to the national law and to a fair adjudication of claims relating to the contract. It is with these legitimate expectations that international law deals. The substantive rights and obligations connected with the contract, including those of redress, are matters for the proper law of the contract determined at a national level;[77] it is the preservation of the remedial right of redress and the procedural methods by which it is given effect that are within the competence of international law. In this way, it is possible to reconcile the interests of contracting states and aliens.

The delictual analogy

Attempts have been made to assimilate simple breaches of contract to torts or delicts committed against aliens.[78] But the analogy may be questioned. There is more justification for making such injury *per se* subject to international law than there is in the case of contract breaches by a state. In the case of a contract, among other things, the alien has a choice of accepting the transaction, the existing laws applicable to it, and the risk of non-performance subject to the existing remedial rights provided, irrespective of the fact of his entering the territory of a foreign state or the fact of his property being on that territory. In the case of injury to person and property, there is no such act of choice immediately relative to the laws and risk of injury, which is additional to the act of

---

[77] See the *Serbian Loans Case*, PCIJ Series A, No. 20 at p. 41 (1929). Those cases in which tribunals decided cases by reference to 'principles of international law, equity and justice' by virtue of the arbitration agreement did so by the use of general principles derived by analogy which are a source of public international law: see Cheng, *General Principles of Law as Applied by International Courts and Tribunals* (1953) *passim*, especially p. 143, for some general principles which may be applicable; and Meron, 'Repudiation of Ultra Vires State Contracts and the Responsibility of States', 6 ICLQ (1957) at p. 276. But, even so, it does not follow that, whatever the law chosen, the contract is elevated to the international legal system so that particularly a breach of contract *per se* is a violation of international law: see further below.

[78] Findlay in the *Venezuelan Bond Cases* (*United States* v. *Venezuela*) (1898), Moore, note 15 above, vol. 4, p. 3649.

entering the foreign state or introducing property into that state. This difference is important.

There is more justification in not expecting the alien to accept the risk of injury to his person or property subject to adjudication by the local judicial system *only* by his mere choice to enter or keep his property in the territory of the foreign state, as the case may be. That choice is not as significant for this purpose as the choice of entering into a transaction which is so closely connected with law and the risks of business in human experience. Hence it is more plausible in the case of delicts that international law should concern itself with the actual injury, as opposed to restricting itself to the existence and procedure of redress for an alleged infringement of rights under national law, which may include private international legal rules.

Moreover, contract involves mutuality which is irrelevant to delict. The significance of mutuality will be discussed later in this chapter.

Deductions

The weight of authority was in favour of the view that a breach of contract with an alien by a state *per se* was not a violation of international law, in spite of some arguments by states and some opinions expressed by text writers to the contrary. Most state practice and international decisions in general supported this view. Indeed, there was no international decision in which it was held that a state breach of contract *per se* was a violation of international law. There are good functional reasons supporting that view too. This was certainly the original view of the law. It was in the latter half of the twentieth century that serious disputes arose in regard to this view.

Exceptional circumstances giving rise to a violation of international law

In the law as it had developed, there were exceptional circumstances in which a state breach of contract became a violation of international law, without a denial of justice as such having occurred. There were factors which were dealt with as not causing an initial violation of international law and those which were regarded as causing such a violation. The point is that the factors causing an initial violation of international law at the point of the breach of contract were exceptional. For example, an arbitrary act such as a confiscatory breach by legislative act or a breach of contract which was also a breach of treaty was regarded as such a violation. This subject has been adequately discussed by the present author elsewhere.[79] Where such a violation was regarded by international law as having occurred, there was no requirement of an additional denial of justice to cause a violation of international law. The rule of exhaustion of local remedies was applicable to the breach of contract.

The fact that the state breach of contract was also a breach of a treaty to which that state and the alien's national state were parties resulted clearly in the breach of contract being also a violation of international law. The result was occasioned by an international agreement between that state and the alien's national state. The existence of a treaty whose provisions are violated was an additional factor which affects the simple breach of contract.

As was seen in the early cases, that a treaty between the state party to the contract and the alien's national state gives an *international* tribunal established pursuant to the treaty jurisdiction over contracts between an alien and the state concerned did not necessarily by the very fact of the conferment of jurisdiction on the international tribunal convert the state breach of contract into a violation of international law. What the states parties to the jurisdictional treaty did was to confer jurisdiction and give the alien *locus standi* before an international tribunal, in order to have substantive rights and obligations created, *inter alia*, by contracts made at a national (or transnational) level but not at an international level adjudicated upon by an international tribunal. The jurisdictional treaty does not have any impact on the substantive relationship between the parties to the contracts. The arrangements now made under the ICSID Convention and the Claims Settlement Agreement establishing the Iran–US Claims Tribunal, for example, are jurisdictional arrangements of this nature.

Later developments

Particularly in the latter part of the twentieth century, certain practices and features made more articulate the view among certain text writers that a state breach of contract could *per se* be a violation of international law for reasons other than those already established by international law

---

[79] See Amerasinghe, note 1 above, at pp. 89–105.

as it had developed.[80] These reasons relate to the choice of a particular system of law as the proper law of the contract and the choice of jurisdictional forum.

Choice of law

As pointed out frequently,[81] the authorities are in fact divided on the issue of whether the choice of a particular legal system as the proper law can affect at all the issue of whether a state breach of contract amounts to the violation of international law. There are, indeed, several problems with the view that the choice of a particular law does affect the question whether a state breach of contract is a violation of international law.

It was suggested early on, as has been seen, that contracts between states and aliens can be governed by international law, if such law is chosen to be the proper law of contract.[82] Some support for this view was sought from the transnational (not international) arbitral award in the *Petroleum Development (Trucial Coast) Ltd Arbitration*, where the arbitrator referred to a 'modern law of nature' as governing the contract between a state and an alien company.[83] This view was opposed by several writers at the time.[84] The argument against that view was that the 'internationalizing' of a contract would not in practice be carried out because public international law had allegedly not yet succeeded in developing, or sufficiently developing, the necessary legal rules. But this is not an accurate argument.

---

[80] See the discussion in Sornarajah, note 1 above, at pp. 10ff., and the authorities cited therein. Also see Mann, note 65 above; and Jennings, note 67 above.

[81] See the discussion in the works cited in note 1 above.

[82] Mann, note 65 above, at p. 43.

[83] 1 ICLQ (1952) at p. 251. See also Jessup, *A Modern Law of Nations* (1956) p. 139.

[84] See Wolff, *Private International Law* (1950) p. 417; Wolff 'Some Observations on the Autonomy of Contracting Parties in the Conflict of Laws', 35 GST (1950) at pp. 150–2; Fawcett, 'Legal Aspects of State Trading', 25 BYIL (1948) at p. 44, note 3; and Friedmann, *Law in a Changing Society* (1959) p. 472. All in all, there are conflicting views among text writers about the choice of public international law and its effects, but the more accepted view agrees with my conclusions below, though the reasoning may not be the same. See, for more recent writings, e.g. Rigaux, *Droit public et droit privé dans les relations internationales* (1977) p. 435; Wengler, 'Les Accords entre états et ressortissants d'autres états', in *La Contrat économique international: stabilité et evolution* (1975) p. 115; Fatouros, 'International Law and the Internationalized Contract', 74 AJIL (1980) p. 136; Jaenicke, 'Consequences of a Breach of an Investment Agreement Governed by International Law, by General Principles of Law, or by Domestic Law of the Host State', in Dicke (ed.), *Foreign Investment in the Present and a New International Economic Order* (1987) p. 177; Paulsson, 'The ICSID Klöckner v. Cameroon Award: The Duties of Partners in North–South Economic Development Agreements', 1 JIA (1984) p. 154; and Bowett, note 1 above, at pp. 51ff.

The cardinal difficulty in reality is that of *mutuality* which is critical to contractual relationships.[85] This concerns not so much the question whether international law may be the proper law but in what system the rights and obligations of the parties subsist. If the contract whose proper law is international law is placed in the international legal system, it follows that both parties have a right to invoke international law and the facilities afforded by the system to settle any grievances arising out of the contract. Not only would a breach of contract by the state party to the contract be a violation of international law, but a breach of contract by the alien party to the contract must also amount to a violation of international law. From this it would follow that the totality of the contractual relations has its existence in the international legal system and that the alien is given international personality by a mere choice of law. It could then be argued that, where the state party to the contract is in breach of the contract, it has violated international law *vis-à-vis* the alien personally and not necessarily *vis-à-vis* the alien's national state by maltreating one of its nationals. This is a revision of the present law of state responsibility. Moreover, it would also follow that the alien who breaches a contract of this kind may be sued at international law for the breach, which is totally different from the present position.

It would be illogical to say that the alien's national state must be sued as a representative of the alien when it has done no wrong. This would place an unfair burden on states whose nationals enter into contracts with foreign states. Also, it is not sound legal theory. This is so, although in the converse case it may be proper for the alien to be represented in international proceedings when the alien is plaintiff. Clearly, this difficulty, arising from the reciprocal nature of the contractual complex, can be overcome, if it be conceded that the alien has international personality either for these purposes or in general. But it is questionable whether such a concession can be made in the present state of international law, merely by a choice of law. The effect of the choice of public international law would be automatically to give the individual international legal personality with rights and obligations in the international legal system by the state's act of entering into a contract and agreeing to a choice of law. This is not evidenced in state practice as the intention of states. It is also a backhanded way for an individual to acquire international personality.

---

[85] The issue of mutuality in relation to international law and the international legal system was raised for the first time in 1967 by me: see Amerasinghe, note 1 above, at pp. 96–7. That issue has barely been addressed in other text writing.

On the other hand, it is possible to say that, although a contract between a state and an alien may refer to (public) international law as its proper law, it is not thereby raised to a position in the international legal system as such. It still remains a complex of relations belonging to a national level, although it is necessary to import public international legal principles to interpret the contract and give it effect. In other words, such reference would introduce specific rules without altering the position of the contract in the national sphere. The approach taken by the tribunal in the case cited above did not go further than this. The tribunal was right in seeing the reference as an invocation of specific principles, while it did not commit itself to the view that the contract had its existence in the international legal system as such. A choice of international law as the proper law would be possible without affecting the legal system in which the contract is placed.

The arguments made in favour of permitting the internationalization of contracts in the sense described above, i.e. of permitting the contract to be elevated and placed in the international legal system, are not convincing nor does the practice of states warrant the conclusion that such internationalization is possible. The present state of international law and the state of the authorities do not permit such 'internationalization'. Nor can the mere choice of law convert a breach of such a contract by a state into a violation of international law *vis-à-vis* the alien's national state.[86] A significant point is that in the *Anglo-Iranian Oil Co. Case* the ICJ categorically said that a concession contract between a state and

---

[86] I first expounded this view in Amerasinghe, note 1 above, at p. 95ff. The question of the effect of the choice of public international law as the governing law was also discussed there. Verdross, *Varia Juris Gentium* (1959) p. 355, tries to make out a case for the existence of contracts in a quasi-international legal system which is completely outside the national sphere. Though theoretically tenable, the practical difficulties of recognizing that the quasi-international and national legal systems are separate and unrelated remain. Hence, such arbitrations as *Radio Corporation of America* v. *Czechoslovakia* (1932), 30 AJIL (1936) p. 523, *Aramco* v. *Saudi Arabia*, 27 ILR p. 117 (1958), and others which were between states and corporations of private law cannot strictly be said to be arbitrations by tribunals of the international legal system. For a somewhat similar view, see Lalive, 'Contracts Between a State and a State Agency and a Foreign Company – Theory and Practice: Choice of Law in a New Arbitration Case', 13 ICLQ (1964) p. 981.

In *Aramco* v. *Saudi Arabia*, the view was expressed that an agreement between parties both of whom were not states could not be governed by public international law: 27 ILR p. 165 (1958).

See further below for a discussion of the proper law of the contract and the legal system to which it might be subject.

an alien was not comparable to nor was a treaty.[87] Simply interpreted, this statement puts to rest any supposition that a state contract with an alien could create rights and obligations between the parties directly within the international legal system, which would have made such a contract certainly comparable to a treaty. Recent developments in the practice of state contracts with aliens discussed by text writers have not changed that state of affairs.

If the choice of public international law to govern a contract in the international legal system does not make a simple breach of contract *per se* a violation of international law, the question is what does it do. Certain transnational arbitrations which are not international in the sense of belonging to the international legal system have approved the choice of international law as a governing law.[88] It is no argument that public international law has no rules or principles relating to 'contracts'. This is not accurate. Public international law has rules and principles applicable to *agreements* which may in the appropriate case be applied by analogy to contracts between states and aliens, apart from other principles of public international law that may be invoked. Moreover, general principles of law are sources of and part of public international law. Consequently, general principles of *contract* law found in national systems become applicable upon a choice of public international law as the governing law.[89] The choice of public international law as the governing or a governing law can, thus, be construed as no more than a genuine choice of law.

Choice of jurisdictional forum

The authorities have in the past supported the view that a breach of a contract with an alien by a state is not *per se* a violation of international law, there being certain special circumstances which make it such a violation of international law. It is also the case that the choice of

---

[87] 1952 ICJ Reports at p. 112.

[88] See some of the Libyan oil arbitrations discussed in Greenwood, note 1 above. But there are arbitrations in which 'internationalization' depending on a choice of law has been rejected: see e.g. *Aramco* v. *Saudi Arabia*, 27 ILR p. 117 (1958); and *Kuwait* v. *Aminoil*, 21 ILM p. 976 (1982).

[89] No doubt, a choice of general principles of law as such (a source of public international law) is also permissible, because general principles of contract law could be applied.

international legal principles to govern the contract is not such a special circumstance. The recently discovered proposition, dependent on practice, that there may be other principles of law that may govern a contract between state and alien than the national law of the state party to the contract raises only problems with the proper law of the contract. But a related issue is that of jurisdictional forum for disputes arising out of contract. The question that arises is how the modern trend on this issue has affected the traditional view on the nature of a state breach of contract.

In ordinary circumstances, whether a national court or tribunal has jurisdiction over a contract between an alien and a state will depend on the rules relating to jurisdiction of the relevant national legal system. In many national systems, an action against a foreign state may not be possible as a result of the doctrine of sovereign immunity. But, assuming that this immunity is waived, whether a national court which does not belong to the contracting state will assume jurisdiction over a dispute will depend on its own rules relating to jurisdiction. It is possible that a dispute arising from a contract can be submitted to a national court other than that of the contracting state by agreement and that that court will assume jurisdiction over the claim. The same reasoning would apply to submission to an arbitral tribunal within a national system. Also, the jurisdiction of the courts and arbitral tribunals of the contracting state will depend on the rules relating to jurisdiction within that particular legal system. Where the parties to the contract have excluded the jurisdiction of certain courts or tribunals, the effect of such a clause on the jurisdiction of those courts will again depend on the law enforced by those courts or tribunals. Generally, in contract disputes it may be the case that such exclusion clauses are recognized as valid.

These propositions are reasonably clear. The real problem arises when the parties to the contract purport to choose as the forum with jurisdiction a tribunal which is apparently not connected with an identifiable national legal system.

As to the object of this device, it is generally intended that the primary jurisdiction of the national courts of the state party to the contract should be excluded and that the remedies should be provided by an independent tribunal not connected with that legal system. The main reason behind this is ostensibly that the national courts of the party would be bound to give effect to the law of that state. This would include both the conflict rules pertaining to the choice of law governing the contract which might be unfavourable to the alien and more particularly the legislation of that state which might even alter the character of the contract.

As stated by the tribunal in the *Sapphire-NIOC Arbitration,*

Under the present agreement, the foreign company was bringing financial and technical assistance to Iran, which involved it in investments, responsibilities, and considerable risks. It therefore seems normal that they should be protected against any legislative changes which might alter the character of the contract and that they should be assured of some legal security.[90]

Even if an express choice of law were explicitly made excluding the law of such state, if the dispute came before the courts of that state, they would be bound to implement the legislation of that state, which might deprive the choice of law of its full effect, and then they would follow their own conflict rules which might bring about the same or similar results.

The positive effect of such a device is a rather more difficult problem. In general, legal thinking has confined itself to postulating two kinds of legal systems: the international legal system and the national legal systems. Since jurisdiction cannot be conferred on tribunals of the international legal system by the act of a state and an individual, it follows that the jurisdiction conferred by the kind of device envisaged is not conferred upon a tribunal of the international legal system. Traditionally, the alternative is that the tribunal upon which jurisdiction was conferred must be a national tribunal. Thus, where the arbitrator was to be appointed by the President of the Supreme Court of Switzerland,[91] it was to be concluded that the tribunal was part of the national legal system of Switzerland.

However, this kind of solution may not always be possible. For instance, if the arbitrators are to be appointed by agreement between the parties and it is not otherwise apparent that the contract is subject to a national system as such, it might be difficult to identify a national legal system with jurisdiction. The alternative that, where some specific national system with jurisdiction is not apparent, the presumption is that the jurisdiction must be attributed to the national system of the state party to the contract, or if this system does not permit the assumption of jurisdiction, the contract must be regarded as not creating legal relations, may not be attractive to aliens or states. For, it is clear that in

---

[90] 1963; see 13 ICLQ (1964) at p. 1012, where extracts are cited. This was a transnational, not an international, arbitration.
[91] See the Sapphire-NIOC Agreement.

these cases as in others the parties are intent on creating legal relations, although they may wish to avoid the national system of the state party.

A solution would seem to lie in postulating, notionally at least, a third kind of legal system which is dependent to some extent on the choice of the parties for its relevance. It may conveniently be called a 'transnational' (or 'quasi-national') system, the tribunal which has jurisdiction being a tribunal of this system. This system cannot be said to be identical with the international legal system as presently conceived, because it involves states and individuals in the absence of state-to-state relations. On the other hand, it approximates to a national system of a simple nature. It may, thus, be regarded as belonging to the same genre as national systems. Its main characteristics are that resort to it is dependent entirely on choice by the parties to the contract, as resort to national courts and tribunals might not be, such choice having a binding nature apart from the contract itself. It consists entirely of arbitral tribunals created by the parties which are ad hoc, and it must rely on national systems for enforcement. This latter feature is important for determining that the system of law involved is not the international legal system. On the other hand, the system of law which these tribunals administer may or may not be a national system or be of a special kind.[92]

In *Aramco* v. *Saudi Arabia*, the tribunal stated that the contract between alien and state was not governed by public international law.[93] It would follow certainly that the contract was not directly within the international legal system. Also, it is clear that the tribunal which was given jurisdiction over it could not have been a tribunal of the international legal system. On the other hand, in the *Sapphire-NIOC Arbitration*, the arbitrator said that there was a dispute as to whether the law of the seat of a tribunal should be applied as its *lex fori* in determining the proper law of a contract,[94] but avoided deciding it. This approach seems to suggest that the arbitrator refused to commit himself to the view that the tribunal was necessarily a tribunal of the national system of the place of its location. It does lend some support, though negatively, to the view put forward above that the tribunal can belong to a third system – the 'transnational' or 'quasi-national' system. It is to be noted that there was no question of the forum being in the international legal system.

There is no other direct evidence of the 'transnational' system except that in practice there seem to be examples of certain ad hoc tribunals

---

[92] The 'quasi-international' system which is implied in the views of certain writers is of a somewhat different nature. For these views, see e.g. Verdross, note 86 above, at p. 355.
[93] 27 ILR p. 165 (1958).   [94] 1963; 13 ICLQ (1964) at p. 1011.

which operate in isolation from any other national system and do not satisfy the requirements for being characterized as tribunals of the international legal system.[95] Thus, jurisdiction may be assumed in contract cases between states and aliens by tribunals of a 'transnational system' which is different from the international legal system and is not to be identified with any particular national system, though it is comparable to and on the same level as a national system and relies heavily, indeed entirely, on a national system or national systems on a variety of matters.

The relationship between jurisdiction and the choice of the proper law of the contract

There is some connection between the tribunal or court having jurisdiction and the choice of the proper law, though questions of jurisdiction and the problem of the choice of the proper law are separate. Generally, a national court which assumes jurisdiction over a claim will decide what law or laws are applicable to the issue before it by reference to its own conflict (private international) rules. There is some slight variation among national systems regarding these rules. Apart from generally giving effect to an express choice of law provision in the contract, national systems may follow the objectivist theory that the proper law is that of the state with which the contract has 'the most real connexion', while others may choose as the applicable law that to which 'the parties intended to submit themselves'.[96] It was generally the case that national fora would in the past have chosen some national system as governing the contract. This is probably what prompted the PCIJ to say in the *Serbian Loans Case* that 'any contract which is not a contract between States in their capacity as subjects of international law is based on the municipal law of some country'.[97]

While a national tribunal might be more ready to choose a national law as governing the contract, there is nothing which is intrinsically incompatible with the choice by a national tribunal of a law other than a particular national law, such as public international law or a 'transnational law', including general principles of law.

Some difference would arise from the fact that a tribunal which does not belong to any identifiable national legal system but is part of the

---

[95] Greenwood does not characterize the arbitral tribunals in the Libyan oil arbitrations as tribunals of the international legal system: note 1 above.

[96] For these theories, see e.g. Cheshire, *International Contracts* (1948).

[97] PCIJ Series A, No. 20 at p. 41 (1929). See also Jessup, *Transnational Law* (1956) p. 83.

structure of the amorphous transnational legal system assumes jurisdiction in the case. Such a tribunal would naturally find it easier to choose a law that is not a particular national law, such as 'transnational law', as the proper law of the contract, though it is not always bound to do so,[98] but only if the circumstances so warrant. Such a tribunal would not be bound to take cognizance of changes in any national law which purports to affect the contract unless that national law is the applicable law, because there is no overall subjection of such tribunal to the national law of any particular state.

Thus, although the question of jurisdiction is separate from that of the proper law of the contract, the choice of forum with jurisdiction can have some impact on the law applicable to the contract.[99]

Transnational law and breach of contract

The fact that the jurisdictional forum is a transnational tribunal or that transnational law or international law may be the proper law of the contract, as already pointed out, does not affect the nature of breach of contract by the state. The contract not being positioned in the international legal system, breach of such a contract would not *per se* be a breach of international law. At most, the breach would amount to a breach of transnational law, which is comparable at its level to national law.

In accordance with already established principle, a refusal to make available the remedial adjudicatory rights afforded by the transnational system, i.e. by arbitration, would amount to a breach of international law, because it is a denial of justice arising from a failure to grant access to adjudicatory remedial rights upon which there was agreement. Resort to local remedies is also not relevant here in connection with such breach, because by implication the choice of jurisdictional forum by agreement has resulted in a waiver of the application of the rule of local remedies to any denial of justice which may occur. This is an important point which will be discussed later in Chapter 10, in connection with waiver of the rule.

If there were a treaty governing the contract, the breach of contract could in appropriate circumstances be a breach of international law. By definition, legislation could not affect a contract of this kind, so that

---

[98] See *Aramco v. Saudi Arabia*, 27 ILR p. 169 (1958), where Saudi Arabian law was chosen by such a tribunal.

[99] On the possibilities of choice of law, see Amerasinghe, note 1 above, at pp. 113ff.; and Greenwood, note 1 above.

a purported interference by legislation would amount to a breach of contract in the transnational system, as it would be accompanied by a refusal to continue performance. Then also, because of agreement, such a breach of contract would become a breach of international law, only if the appropriate remedial jurisdiction were not respected. Other factors would be irrelevant to converting a breach of such a contract into a violation of international law.

It is evident, therefore, that the postulation of a transnational system with a transnational proper law does not materially change the already established traditional principles concerning breach of state contract. The main difference is that the category of legislative breach is dealt with directly and more easily, because of the separate operation of the transnational system. It becomes merely another example of ordinary breach. A further difference is that an absence of remedies amounting to violation of international law becomes a failure to make available the secondary remedial rights of the transnational system.

Conclusion

The principal conclusion is that a breach by a state of a contract with an alien is not *per se* a breach of international law. There are special circumstances which bring about a violation of international law simultaneously with a breach of contract.

It may be said that the first rule is that only a non-provision of sufficient means of adjudication by a state party to a contract for the purpose of deciding an allegation by the other party that the contract has been breached will cause a violation of international law at the time of the breach. This is still true in principle. An alien's contractual rights are adequately protected, if provision is made by international law for preventing the absence of adequate remedies, when an infringement of those contractual rights has taken place. There are two other circumstances in which international law is clearly and directly infringed in the case of a breach of contract by a state. The first is where express protection is granted to the contractual rights as such by international instruments. This circumstance needs no explanation. The violation of international law is dependent on the express agreement of the states concerned, i.e. the state party to the contract and the national state of the alien. The next circumstance in which a breach of contract is accompanied by a violation of international law is where the state party to the contract attempts to change the contractual rights and obligations outside the existing system of legal rules governing the contractual relationship, i.e. by legislation. The law of confiscation applies in this instance. It is the special nature of the power resorted to in this case that justifies this rule.

Other facts, such as the failure of the state to resort to its courts before cancelling the contract or refusing to perform it, or such as the so-called 'tortious' nature of the breach, do not make the breach of contract a violation of international law. Nor is a breach of contract by a state normally to be treated as a confiscation of property causing a violation of international law. The law of confiscation operates with this effect only in the case of a legislative breach of contract by a state. The purported choice of public international law as the governing law does not insert a state contract into the international legal system so as to make a breach of contract *per se* a violation of international law.

In connection with state contracts with aliens, modern practice has created problems relating to the proper law of the contract and choice of jurisdictional forum over such contracts. It has been shown that it may be possible for the parties to insert the contract into a transnational legal system, different from the international legal system but comparable to national legal systems. This could have the dual effect of vesting jurisdiction in a transnational tribunal and making the proper law of the contract transnational law. The presence of these two conditions would generally mean that legislative changes affecting the contract in the law of the state party to the contract would be ineffective. This combined operation, however, does not materially change the traditional principles relating to breach of state contract. Its main significance is that legislative breach ceases to have a special place in regard to breach of contract by the state and that the meaning of remedies undergoes a slight change. The breach of contract still comes to an international level as a delict in the treatment of aliens caused by other factors than the mere breach of contract.[100] The rule of local remedies would apply to the violation of international law by the state, as it always does, irrespective of whether the violation occurs through an act or omission in the administration of justice or not, unless the application of the rule can be said to have been effectively waived.

---

[100] The issue discussed here was first comprehensively addressed in Amerasinghe, note 1 above, at pp. 66ff. Nothing has changed fundamentally since that discussion except the quantity of writing on the subject: see the other works cited in note 1 above and the works cited in those works.

That it is suggested that transnational law may be selected as the governing law, that a transnational, as contrasted with a purely national, arbitral tribunal may settle a contractual dispute or attempt to settle it, and that, therefore, there is a 'transnational' system does not mean that the so-called transnational system is comparable to the international legal system. As pointed out, it is comparable to national legal systems as far as its level of operation goes. Among other things, it may also have to rely on national systems for enforcement of its arbitral awards which may be treated by national systems as local or foreign arbitral awards. Not only is the system amorphous but it consists generally of *ad hoc* arbitral dispute settlement and has no specific location in terms of territory. It is merely a conceptual creation for permitting certain consequences in the realm of contracts between states and aliens.

To revert to the statement made in the *Serbian Loans Case*, the PCIJ was not wrong in terms of the law as it stood in 1929, nor is the statement fundamentally or intrinsically wrong in a modern context. Seen as an affirmation that the relevant kind of contract cannot be placed in the international legal system as such, it is currently valid and useful. However, on the one hand, developments since the Second World War demonstrate that principles of public international law and general principles of law, whether by themselves or as a part of public international law, have become applicable at the national level as a consequence of the rise of what has been called transnational law. On the other hand, to say that a contract is placed in a transnational system is merely to say that the chosen law is not a particular national law or particular national laws as such, and/or that jurisdiction is vested in a particular kind of *ad hoc* arbitral tribunal.

The effect of referring alien–state contract claims to an international jurisdiction

Sometimes it does happen that contract claims arising from alien–state relations are directly referred to an international arbitral tribunal constituted under an international treaty or convention. This is the case, for example, in regard to tribunals constituted under the ICSID Convention or, sometimes, under investment treaties, both multilateral and bilateral. While it is possible that delictual claims (or comparable claims resulting from contractual violations) arising from 'investments' made in the host state by aliens which are legitimately based on violations of international law may be presented to such tribunals, the issue that arises is what effect the jurisdictional assignment over simple contractual violations, whether committed by states or individuals, to these tribunals which are international tribunals, in that they are created as a result of inter-state agreements, has on the nature of such simple contractual violations.

There is no reason to assume that, solely by creating a jurisdictional forum in an international tribunal and thereby giving individuals, whether natural or legal persons, *locus standi* before such a tribunal, the states concerned had a clear intention to convert a simple breach of contract, whether by an individual or by a state, into an international wrong. What is being done is essentially to create an extra-national forum for the settlement of a dispute involving claims not located in the international legal system and based on national or private international law (i.e. at a national level), even if (public) international law or general principles of law are applicable to the contractual nexus as the directly or indirectly chosen law or otherwise. An international tribunal is explicitly given jurisdiction over contractual violations, whether by states or individuals, which are not *per se* violations of international law. It is purely a special dispute settlement mechanism established for a specific purpose with specific results which may in terms of enforcement of the awards have effects in the international legal system and create international obligations for states, particularly based on the provisions of the governing conventional instruments – but all that is done after judicial decisions have been made. Thus, contractual violations by states over which the tribunals have jurisdiction do not need, in one way or another, to be international wrongs to which the rule of local remedies would normally be applicable as a procedural condition for the exercise of diplomatic protection before an international forum. This is how such treaties and conventions have been interpreted implicitly in their application.

Insofar as, for example, Article 26 of the ICSID Convention explicitly waives the application of the rule of local remedies, the express waiver has really no relevance to simple state breaches of contract which have been regarded as *per se* subject to the jurisdiction of ICSID tribunals in any case. Article 26 must be regarded, however, as certainly applicable, for example, to delictual claims or analogous claims arising from contractual relations against a state *ratione materiae* within the jurisdiction of ICSID tribunals which are based on the violation of international law by the state. That the requirement of a violation of international law basic to diplomatic protection is not critical to the jurisdiction of ICSID and like tribunals is clear. Indeed, such tribunals have jurisdiction over claims against individuals which cannot be based on violations of international law at all. The conclusion is inescapable also that treaties, such as the ICSID Convention, are not confined in their scope to situations where diplomatic protection would be available, though they include them. The waiver of the rule of local remedies would properly be in its essence relevant only where the substantive conditions required for the incidence of diplomatic protection are the basis of jurisdiction for international tribunals.

Part II   Application of the rule

6 Incidence of the rule

Questions relating to the incidence of the rule of local remedies have arisen mainly out of concern that the rule may be applied to situations for which it was not in principle intended. In connection with diplomatic protection, these questions have been discussed largely in diplomatic practice, although there is some judicial precedent on the subject. What has been in issue in the situations which have arisen is whether, in cases where an alien is involved in asserting his rights or having some protection exercised by a protecting state, there are circumstances in which the rule will not be applicable, or whether the rule is applicable in all situations where an alien is involved. The history of the rule in international law has shown that major concerns have in practice been articulated about the over-extension of the rule, rather than about the possibility that it may not be implemented when it should. Although the discussion reflects the clash of interests involved, it has taken the form of invoking such considerations as the intrinsic nature of the rule as an instrument in the settling of disputes essentially concerned with the protection of rights belonging to aliens, rather than of emphasizing the prerogatives of state sovereignty, which could have the effect of highlighting exclusively the interests of respondent states. As a result, the views expressed on these questions have taken into account the historical antecedents and development of the rule and its relevance in inter-state relationships, while there has been some expression of the need to see the rule in the context of its usefulness as a means of protecting what are essentially rights or interests of aliens. The tendency has certainly not been to conclude that the rule is automatically applicable to any context in which an alien's rights or interests are infringed or affected by the acts or omissions of a sovereign state.

The direct injury

The first kind of situation in which the incidence of the rule has been questioned relates to the so-called 'direct injury'. What is implied in this concept is that the injury directly affects the litigating state, even though an alien may be involved, so that, while the latter is concerned indirectly in the legal proceeding, the state is really protecting its own interests, apart from those centring around the right of diplomatic protection, rather than those of the alien. There are two issues that invite attention. The first is whether there are in fact situations involving direct injuries in which legally the rule is not applicable at all. The second concerns the identification or definition of a direct injury. As already pointed out, there are very few judicially decided cases on this issue, although there has been some exchange of arguments on the subject before the ICJ and views impliedly expressed in separate and dissenting opinions in the ICJ.

The existence of the 'direct injury' exclusion

To deal first with the separate and dissenting opinions in the ICJ, these opinions may have differed and dissented from, or been incompatible with, the judgment of the Court on the question whether the rule of local remedies was applicable in the circumstances for the reason that there was no direct injury, but otherwise, on the question of the existence of the 'direct injury' exclusion, there is no reason to infer that they expressed views different from those implied by the Court, because the Court did not expressly take any view contradictory to such views as were expressed in those opinions. In the *Norwegian Loans Case*, Judge Read differed from the Court in holding that one reason why France did not need to exhaust local remedies was that the Norwegian Government or its legislature had impaired the rights of the French bondholders by direct intervention.[1] This was an acceptance of the French argument relating to direct injury. The Court did not deal with the French argument, which will be examined later, on the ground that there were preliminary reasons for dismissing the case unconnected with the failure to exhaust local remedies. Thus, while it is not known how the Court would have held on any issues relating to the exhaustion of local remedies, and even if the view of Judge Read that there was a direct injury in the case was wrong, as it might appear that it was, his opinion supports the contention that there are situations involving direct injuries in which the

[1] 1957 ICJ Reports at p. 9.

rule of local remedies is inapplicable.[2] This support for the view that the local remedies rule does not apply in the case of a direct injury is useful, even though it appears in a dissent which dealt with the rule of local remedies, when the Court decided not to make a pronouncement on the subject, because it is not a lone voice in the wilderness.

Judge Lauterpacht, in a separate opinion in the same case, differed from the Court on procedure and decided the case on the ground that the preliminary objection raised by Norway, that local remedies had not been exhausted, must on the facts of the case be upheld.[3] He dealt with the argument put forward by France, that when there was an initial breach of international law in the treatment of an alien the rule of local remedies was inapplicable, but he dismissed it on the ground that it was precisely where there was an initial breach of international law that the rule operated.[4] Judge Lauterpacht did not discuss the question of whether or not the rule operated where there was a direct injury amounting to an initial breach of international law, but in so far as he did not deny that there was such a principle, but rather stated that there were situations in which there was an initial breach of international law, which were not excepted from the incidence of the rule, he may be taken to have implied that in principle there were situations where the rule was inapplicable, because there had been a direct injury. This implication is warranted because the point was argued by the parties and, had Judge Lauterpacht been of the opinion that there was no limitation of the incidence of the rule in cases of direct injury, he might have been constrained expressly to say so.

In the *Interhandel Case*,[5] where the respondent US Government raised the objection that local remedies had not been exhausted, the ICJ decided the issue and declared the application of the Swiss government inadmissible because the requirements of the rule of local remedies had not been satisfied. In the course of dismissing the action, the Court pointed out that the Swiss contention, that a direct injury had been committed and that, therefore, the rule did not apply, could not be accepted because the circumstances were precisely such that they attracted

---

[2] Judge Read's opinion is not entirely clear. There may have been a confusion between the situation where the alien is exempted from resorting to local remedies, let alone exhausting them, because there are none to exhaust, and that in which the rule is inapplicable because the illegality is a direct injury. The former instance is a limitation on the application of the rule while the latter is one in which the rule is intrinsically inapplicable.

[3] 1957 ICJ Reports at pp. 39ff.   [4] *Ibid.*, p. 38.   [5] 1959 ICJ Reports p. 6.

the application of the rule.[6] In finding that the rule was applicable in the situation before it, the Court did not deny that there could be situations involving direct injury in which the rule by its nature would not be applicable. It is interesting to find that the Court noted the Swiss government's contention that 'the present case is one in which an exception to this rule is authorized by the rule itself'.[7] This language is an indication that the Court acknowledged that the argument was one relating to the incidence of the rule and, thus, by not rejecting it as bad in law in so far as there could not be exceptions to the applicability of the rule on the basis of a direct injury, but rather dealing with the substantive issue of the direct injury, impliedly gave its imprimatur to the idea that there could be exceptions to the incidence of the rule on the basis of a direct injury.

Judge Armand-Ugon dissented from the Court in the same case in holding that the rule of local remedies was not applicable because there had been a direct injury. He stated that:

the rule of the exhaustion of local remedies does not apply to a case in which the act complained of directly injures a State.[8]

Thus, while dissenting on the issue of what constituted a direct injury, he gave clear judicial support to the view that the rule of local remedies was not applicable in the case of a direct injury, however that may be defined.

In both the *Norwegian Loans Case* and the *Interhandel Case*, the applicant governments argued that there had been a direct injury to the state which resulted in the irrelevance of the rule of local remedies. In the former case, the French government referred in its observations to 'le caractère international du différend qui s'est élevé directement entre les deux Etats',[9] and stated that 'une telle réclamation, d'Etat à Etat, . . . n'a pas été soumise à des recours internes'.[10] In its counter-memorial, the Norwegian government referred to the French argument, not denying that there could be situations in which the rule of local remedies was inapplicable because of the nature of the dispute, but contesting the contention that the situation confronting the Court involved a direct injury and not a dispute concerning essentially the obligations of

---

[6] *Ibid.*, pp. 27ff.
[7] *Ibid.*, p. 27. See also the *Elettronica Sicula SpA (ELSI) Case*, 1989 ICJ Reports at pp. 42–3.
[8] 1959 ICJ Reports at p. 89.   [9] ICJ Pleadings (1957), vol. 1, p. 182.   [10] *Ibid.*

Norway relative to the service of its debts owed to French bondholders which basically activated the rule of local remedies.[11]

In the *Interhandel Case*, the Swiss government, while accepting that in principle the rule of local remedies was applicable when an alien was injured, submitted that the rule was not applicable in the case before the Court, because the injury 'constitue une violation *directe* du droit international et lése immédiatement l'Etat demandeur'.[12] It further emphasized that in the instant case 'le dommage a été causé *directement* à l'Etat lésé'.[13] The US government seems to have ignored the issue in its entirety, concentrating its arguments entirely on the fulfilment of the requirements of the rule, because it took the view that the rule was applicable in the case and that there was no possibility that it could be excluded in the circumstances.[14] Thus, in this case, while the applicant state expressly supported the notion that a direct injury would result in the exclusion of the rule, the respondent state neither denied nor supported that argument.

In the *Aerial Incident Case*, the government of Israel observed that the rule of local remedies was inapplicable because the respondent state had violated a right directly vested in the applicant state,[15] thus raising the argument based on the direct injury. The Bulgarian government did not deny the principle that the rule could be excluded where there was a proper direct injury but implicitly took the view that the situation in the case was not one in which the rule could be avoided.[16]

In the *Arrest Warrant of 11 April 2000 Case*, the ICJ held that, where there is a direct injury to the state, even though an alien has been harmed, the rule of local remedies does not apply. The Court held as follows:

The Court notes that the Congo has never sought to invoke before it Mr Yerodia's personal rights. It considers that, despite the change in professional situation of Mr Yerodia, the character of the dispute submitted to the Court by means of the Application has not changed: the dispute still concerns the lawfulness of the arrest warrant issued on 11 April 2000 against a person who was at the time Minister for Foreign Affairs of the Congo, and the question whether the rights of the Congo have or have not been violated by that warrant. As the Congo is

---

[11] *Ibid.*, pp. 277ff.   [12] ICJ Pleadings (1959) at p. 402.

[13] *Ibid.* See also the oral argument of the Swiss government: *ibid.*, p. 547.

[14] ICJ Pleadings (1959) at pp. 315ff. (written pleadings) and 612ff. (oral argument).

[15] *Ibid.*, p. 158. See also the oral argument of the Israeli government at pp. 530ff. and 590.

[16] *Ibid.*, pp. 570ff. (oral argument).

not acting in the context of protection of one of its nationals, Belgium cannot rely upon the rules relating to the exhaustion of local remedies.[17]

It may be concluded from the evidence presented above that there is significant judicial precedent and state practice which generally supports the proposition that a direct injury to the injured state could affect the incidence of the rule where the rights of aliens are concerned by making it inapplicable, however direct injury is defined. Thus, there is no reason to suppose that the principle can be gainsaid.

To add to the supporting evidence, there may be mentioned the opinions of text writers such as Freeman,[18] Eagleton,[19] Hyde[20] and Jessup,[21] among others,[22] who either expressly or impliedly take the view that the direct injury is a valid reason for excluding the application of the rule of local remedies, even though an alien may have been injured.

There is no reason to question the validity of the position which postulates that the rule of local remedies does not become relevant where there is a direct injury to a state even though there may also be an infringement of the rights of one of its nationals. That this is a reasonable qualification of the application of the rule may appear from the history of the rule as having been basically a means of preserving the rights of sovereignty where a state had essentially violated the rights of an alien.

---

[17] 2002 ICJ Reports: see www.cij-icj.org, para. 40. See also the *Air Services Agreement Arbitration (France v. US)*, 18 UNRIAA at p. 432 (1978), where the tribunal referred to the international agreement as containing 'a right granted by one *government* to the other *government*' which is a reference to a right the violation of which results in a direct injury. Earlier, the tribunal referred to an obligation of 'result' (presumably in contrast to an obligation of 'conduct') and for all practical purposes regarded the characterization as an unnecessary fifth wheel (*ibid.*). The distinction invoked is misplaced for the purposes of the local remedies rule, is not universal or general in national laws and was imported by Ago, 'Sixth Report on State Responsibility', YBILC (1977), vol. 2, Part II, at pp. 22ff., as it appears, indiscriminately from the Italian law. Neither is it at all possible to see its relevance to the rule of local remedies nor is it or was it supported by any kind of authority or reasoning in relation to the rule.

[18] *The International Responsibility of States for Denial of Justice* (1938) p. 404.

[19] *Responsibility of States in International Law* (1928) pp. 51 and 103.

[20] *International Law Chiefly as Interpreted and Applied by the United States* (1947), vol. 2, p. 888.

[21] *A Modern Law of Nations* (1956) p. 118ff.

[22] See also Meron, 'The Incidence of the Rule of Exhaustion of Local Remedies', 35 BYIL (1959) at pp. 84ff. There are several authorities, including those who have expressed their views at the Institut de Droit International and the 1956 Granada resolution of the Institut. See particularly Amerasinghe, *State Responsibility for Injuries to Aliens* (1967) pp. 174ff. Cançado Trindade, *The Application of the Rule of Exhaustion of Local Remedies in International Law* (1983) pp. 173–4, also has some remarks on the subject.

The definition of 'direct injury'

It is apparent from the jurisprudence of the ICJ and other international tribunals that the existence of the 'direct injury' exclusion has been recognized. There is also an indication given by the Court of the direct injury which would result in the rule of local remedies not being applicable to a situation involving an alien. The Court has, further, given a negative indication of what the direct injury is not. On the other hand, individual judges have expressed positive views on what could constitute a direct injury, although their views either conflict with those of the Court and are therefore unacceptable, or stand by themselves in circumstances in which the Court has not expressed a view on the matter, so that they have to be evaluated in terms of principle.

As emerges from the *Arrest Warrant of 11 April 2000 Case*, where the issue is whether the rights of a state have been violated in a situation in which the state is not acting in the context of the *protection of one of its nationals*, the rules relating to the exhaustion of local remedies cannot be relied on by the respondent state.[23] This is a positive statement of what is at the heart of the exception of the direct injury.

In the *Interhandel Case*, the ICJ had to adjudicate on whether the US objection that local remedies had not been exhausted in relation to the taking of the property of Interhandel, a national of the applicant Swiss government, should be upheld. The arguments raised by the Swiss government included one based on the direct injury exclusion. The Court said that for the reason adduced by the Swiss government the dispute referred to was not deprived

of the character of a dispute in which the Swiss Government appears as having adopted the cause of its national, Interhandel, for the purpose of securing the restitution to that company of assets vested by the Government of the United States. This is one of the many cases which give rise to the application of the rule of exhaustion of local remedies.[24]

The Swiss government had argued that:

La règle de l'épuisement des voies de recours internes ne s'applique pas, parce que l'inexécution par les Etats-Unis de la décision de l'Autorité suisse de recours fondée sur l'Accord de Washington constitue une violation *directe* du droit international et lése immédiatement l'Etat demandeur. Il ne s'agit donc pas simplement et exclusivement d'une violation des droits d'une personne privée, qui,

---

[23] 2002 ICJ Reports: see www.icj-cij.org, para. 40.   [24] 1959 ICJ Reports at pp. 28–9.

avant de pouvoir être protégée par son Etat national, doit épuiser les voies ordi-
naires des instances internes de l'Etat-violateur. En revanche, quand une décision
internationale n'a pas été exécutée, il n'y a pas de juridictions internes à épuiser,
car le dommage a été causé *directement* à l'Etat lésé.[25]

It is clear that what the Court did, although it was not very explicit,
was to reject the contention that, where an injury to an alien is caused
in the course of violating an international judgment given under an
international agreement between the respondent and applicant states,
the injury caused in that way per se resulted in a direct injury which
would obviate the need to exhaust local remedies. Thus, there was here
a negative pronouncement on what would not constitute a direct injury.

It may be proper to note that this specific view of the Court did not
go unchallenged in that case itself. Judge Armand-Ugon's judgment is
not very clear but it appears that he disagreed with the Court in his
dissenting opinion:

> The Application of the Swiss Government seeks . . . reparation for direct damage
> caused to a State. The unlawful act really derives from the failure of the Ameri-
> can Government (according to Switzerland) to execute the decision of the Swiss
> Authority of Review, which is to be regarded as a judgment by an international
> arbitral tribunal, within the framework of the Washington Accord . . . The rule
> of the exhaustion of local remedies does not apply to a case in which the act
> complained of directly injures a State.[26]

While the opinion came in a dissent which, therefore, must give way to
the opinion of the Court, it does show that the issue of what constitutes
a direct injury is not without its problems. Clearly, however, it must
now be taken as settled that the violation of an international judgment
or an international agreement, binding upon both the host state and
the alien's national state, does not per se cause the act which injures an
alien to become a direct injury to the alien's national state. A Chamber
of the ICJ held in the *Elettronica Sicula SpA (ELSI) Case* that the violation of
a treaty does not necessarily exclude the application of the rule of local
remedies on the basis that the injury caused is direct.[27] In that case
it was found that there was no other injury which was distinct from

---

[25] ICJ Pleadings (1959) at p. 402. The argument was elaborated at pp. 547ff., although not
very progressively, in the Swiss oral argument.

[26] 1959 ICJ Reports at p. 89.

[27] 1989 ICJ Reports at pp. 42–3. In *Swiss Confederation* v. *Federal Republic of Germany (No. 1)*,
25 ILR at p. 42 (1958), the arbitral tribunal stated in effect that the mere fact that the
dispute related to the interpretation of a treaty did not convert the injury caused into
a direct injury. The arbitration was between two states.

and independent of that which arose from the violation of the treaty in regard to the entities in respect of which diplomatic protection was being exercised.

In the *Norwegian Loans Case*, the Norwegian government had, by legislative action, allegedly interfered with the servicing of public loans given by French bondholders to Norway. The French government, in response to the Norwegian government's objection that local remedies had not been exhausted, argued:

La Norvège invoque la règle de l'épuisement préalable des voies de recours internes et affirme que les recours norvégiens ont été délibérément méconnus. Il faut relever, ici encore, la confusion qu'apporte dans le présent litige la prétention du Gouvernement norvégien d'ignorer le caractère international du différend qui s'est élevé directement entre les deux Etats et de ne voir que l'aspect initial du litige, c'est-à-dire la plainte des porteurs français d'obligations norvégiennes.

Le Gouvernement de la République française a montré . . . que sa réclamation vise une attitude propre au Gouvernement norvégien constituant une violation du droit international à propos du traitement appliqué aux ressortissants français . . .

. . . Mais, au surplus, même dans la mesure ou le Gouvernement de la République française, en dehors des réclamations directes de son droit propre vis-à-vis de la Norvège, porte devant le juge international une question d'atteinte aux droits de ses ressortissants, la règle de l'épuisement des recours locaux ne trouve pas application dans cette affaire.[28]

The Norwegian government, on the other hand, opposed this argument, asserting that:

En portant sur le plan international le litige qui s'était élevé entre les détenteurs français d'obligations norvégiennes et leurs débiteurs, le Gouvernement de la République a agi en vertu du droit que posséde tout Etat de fair respecter le droit international dans la personne de ses ressortissants. Un différend interétatique s'est ainsi substitué au différend originaire de droit privé.

Or c'est précisément en pareil cas que la règle de l'épuisement préalable des voies de recours internes trouve son application . . . Le Gouvernement français soutiendrait-il . . . qu'en dehors du litige fondé sur une prétendue atteinte aux droits de ses ressortissants, la Cour serait actuellement saisie d'un différend, qui serait né directement entre les deux Gouvernements et qui aurait une autre base? . . . On se bornera ici à répéter que l'objet du différend dont la Cour est saisie se trouve formulé dans la requête introductive d'instance; que cet

---

[28] ICJ Pleadings (1957), vol. 1, p. 182. The contention was explained in the oral argument: ICJ Pleadings (1957), vol. 2, pp. 74ff.

objet concerne uniquement les obligations de la Norvège relatives au service des emprunts dont sont porteurs certains ressortissants français . . .[29]

The Court did not deal with the objection based on the non-exhaustion of local remedies because the case was dismissed on a different preliminary objection. However, as pointed out earlier, both Judge Read (in a dissenting opinion) and Judge Lauterpacht (in a separate opinion) had something to say about the contention of the French government referred to above. While his judgment is not entirely clear, and the point he took did not answer the French contention in the specific terms in which it was formulated, Judge Read did discuss the objection that local remedies had not been exhausted, stating, among other things, that:

> [I]t has been argued that the rule with regard to exhaustion of local remedies has no application where the rights of the applicant national have been impaired by the direct intervention of the respondent Government or Parliament. If there ever was a case in which the respondent Government and Parliament had intervened to impair the rights of non-resident aliens, it is in the present instance. It is obvious from the terms of the Note of 9th December, 1925, that the Mortgage Bank was not acting under its own motion but under pressure from the Minister of Justice and the Minister of Finance. Further, the Storthing, the supreme legislative authority, in enacting this law was directly intervening so as to impair the rights of the French bondholders.[30]

In view of the fact that Judge Read dissented and decided that the preliminary objections, including the one concerned with local remedies, should be dismissed, while the Court upheld one of the objections, albeit on a point other than the exhaustion of local remedies, it is a difficult question as to what value should be given to his views on the incidence of the rule of local remedies. However, it would seem that he was of the view that, where there is a direct intervention by the respondent government or its parliament which violates the rights of the alien, this by itself is an adequate reason to exclude the application of the rule of local remedies. Judge Lauterpacht, on the other hand, decided, in his separate opinion, among other things, to uphold the preliminary objection based on the non-exhaustion of local remedies, although the Court dismissed the case on the basis of another preliminary objection and did not touch on the issue of local remedies. After stating that there

---

[29] ICJ Pleadings (1957), vol. 1, pp. 277–9. The argument was explained in the oral pleadings ICJ Pleadings (1957), vol. 2, pp. 156ff.

[30] 1957 ICJ Reports at pp. 98–9. As already pointed out in note 2 above, the import of Judge Read's opinion is not very clear.

were many issues of international law which could and should have been raised in the domestic proceedings, he made it quite clear that it was precisely where there was a breach of international law in the treatment of an alien that the rule of local remedies operated,[31] thus implicitly rejecting the French contention that, where the initial act attributable to the host state was also a violation of international law, the rule of local remedies had no relevance, because the dispute involved a claim made by one state against another.

The two individual opinions in the *Norwegian Loans Case* conflict with each other in so far as one upholds the objection based on the non-exhaustion of local remedies and the other dismisses it. Clearly, in view of the ruling of the Court in the *Interhandel Case*, which did not recognize that the rule of local remedies was inapplicable because a treaty or an international judgement had been violated per se, it would seem logical that, *a fortiori*, it cannot be accepted that the rule is inapplicable where there is a violation of customary international law per se. Thus, Judge Lauterpacht's view is sound. To deny this would, as is implied in Judge Lauterpacht's opinion, deprive the rule of any relevance at all. This still leaves the question to be answered whether, accepting the validity of the above two propositions, it can be maintained, as Judge Read seemed to think, that the incidence of the rule would be affected on narrower grounds in either case where a treaty (or international judgment) or customary international law had been violated, purely because there had been direct intervention by a government or its parliament.

At a formal level, it must be recognized that Judge Read's view was implicitly rejected by Judge Lauterpacht in so far as he upheld the objection based on the non-exhaustion of local remedies, unlike Judge Read, and therefore saw no reason to find that in the case, particularly for the reason given by Judge Read, the rule of local remedies was inapplicable. By the same token, since Judge Lauterpacht dismissed the case by upholding one or more preliminary objections, as the Court had done, and since the Court said nothing to contradict Judge Lauterpacht's view of the law on the incidence of the rule, his view has some value as an acceptable one. Thus, formally it may have to be concluded that Judge Read's opinion is not as strong, from the point of view of acceptability, as Judge Lauterpacht's implied rejection of it.

Apart from the formal aspect, Judge Read's view lacks cogency because it does not strictly base itself on a viable theory of direct injury. To make

---

[31] 1957 ICJ Reports at p. 38.

an exception to the incidence of the rule of local remedies because the government of the host state or its legislature has intervened directly with the result that international law has been violated does not relate specifically to the issue of whether there has been a direct injury to the alien's national state. While the limitations on the application of the rule may come into play because there are no remedies to exhaust, which may or may not be the case depending on the internal legal system of the host state, there is no good reason to exclude the application of the rule as a matter of principle in this instance on the ground that there has been a direct injury to the applicant state or, perhaps, on any other ground. It is reasonable to suppose that the concept of direct injury would be defined on the basis of different assumptions and premises, particularly because even in the situation envisaged the applicant state is in essence complaining about a violation of the rights of one of its nationals.

Because, then, the views expressed in the jurisprudence of courts and tribunals which are acceptable are only negative in import – in that they state what is not per se a direct injury – it may be useful to examine the practice of states, conflicting although it may be, as reflected in the pleadings before international courts, in order to discover whether there is anything which can be found which would help to advance the inquiry. Apart from the pleadings in the two cases discussed above, which have already been adverted to and quoted extensively, there is one other case in which the issue was raised but not decided either by the Court or in separate or dissenting opinions, because the case was dismissed on the basis of a preliminary objection not connected with the rule of exhaustion of local remedies, and because neither the Court nor the judges giving separate or dissenting opinions touched on the objection based on the rule of local remedies.

The *Aerial Incident Case* arose out of the shooting down by Bulgaria of an Israeli civilian plane that had penetrated into Bulgarian airspace without authorization. In its application, the government of Israel requested the ICJ 'to adjudge and declare that the People's Republic of Bulgaria is responsible under international law for the destruction of the Israeli aircraft 4X-AKC on 27 July 1955 and for the loss of life and property and all other damage that resulted therefrom'.[32] In its memorial, it further stated:

---

[32] ICJ Pleadings (1959) at p. 7. Similar applications were made by the USA and the UK. The claims were similar, as were the objections raised by the respondent states.

Whereas the Government of Israel has established that the financial loss incurred by the persons whose cause is being adopted by it amounts to the sum of US Dollars 2,559,688.65; MAY IT PLEASE THE COURT to give judgement in favour of the claim of the Government of Israel and fix the amount of compensation due from Bulgaria to Israel at US Dollars 2,559,688.65.[33]

In answering the Bulgarian objection based on the local remedies rule, the Israeli government stated in its observations:

The contention fails to appreciate the nature of the present case. From the fact that 4X-AKC was registered in Israel . . . and was wearing the Israel colours it is the State of Israel which is directly and primarily injured by the improper actions of the military forces of the Bulgarian State acting *jure imperii*. Local remedies are therefore irrelevant, and the particulars of claims contained in Annexes 40, 41 and 42 of the Memorial are also not relevant except in connection with the calculation of pecuniary damages the duty to pay which is one of the consequences of the breach of international law on the part of Bulgaria.[34]

The basis of the contention of the Israeli government was explained more fully in the oral argument:

We can recall no precedent in which a government complaining of actions performed by another government *jure imperii* has been referred to the Courts of the respondent State as a preliminary condition to the obtaining of international satisfaction . . . In our submission there is in this case no ground whatsoever for the introduction of this exception . . . [T]he character of this case as a whole is that the Bulgarian act of which complaint is made affects Israel in its quality of a State. It is the international personality of Israel which has been injured – and sorely injured – by this breach of international law. The action of the Bulgarian authorities has violated rights which are the intrinsic attribute of Israel as a State, the right that an Israel aircraft going about its lawful business should not be improperly obstructed or otherwise interfered with, and certainly not destroyed, in the course of its voyage, and its innocent occupants exposed to the gravest terror and danger . . . [I]t is universally recognized that the rule regarding exhaustion of local remedies is inapplicable to a case of a direct injury caused by one State to another . . . As to types of acts directed against the State and its flag, Professor Eagleton . . . says this . . . 'a public claim is constituted; that is, a claim by a foreign State in its own behalf'. And later . . . he says: 'An important group of such acts is that which includes attacks or insults directed against the State . . . its flag or other emblem.' The aircraft 4X-AKC wore the nationality colours of the State of Israel, a replica of the State flag . . . [T]he injury which has been suffered by the State of Israel is reparable to the State of Israel in a manner appropriate to international law, without regard to the position of individuals, including El Al, who may also have suffered loss as a consequence

---

[33] *Ibid.*, p. 116.   [34] *Ibid.*, pp. 158–9.

of the injury caused directly to the State of Israel . . . This is not a case in which the injuries to the individual preceded the injury to the State and in which the injury to the individual forms the substance, in fact and in law, of the injury to the State . . . In the present case . . . which is *not* a case of diplomatic protection, the starting point is not the particularization of claims . . . but the unity of the aircraft with every person and everything on board, and the link of that unity with the sovereignty of Israel made manifest by the colours as and registration mark it was bearing, by its Israel nationality. Consequently, we conclude, and so submit, that the exception of non-exhaustion of local remedies is unfounded and should be rejected.[35]

The Bulgarian reply to this contention of the Israeli government was not very specific. It consisted, as it appears, mainly of a reference to the judgment of the ICJ in the *Interhandel Case*:

> Cette exception est fondée sur une règle que la Cour, dans son arrêt récent sur l'affaire de l'*Interhandel*, a résumée en ces termes: 'Les recours internes doivent être épuisés avant qu'une procédure internationale puisse être engagée.' Et la Cour a précisé que cette règle était généralement observée 'dans le cas où un Etat prend fait et cause pour son ressortissant dont les droits auraient été lésés dans un autre Etat en violation du droit international'.
>
> Cette règle, Messieurs, je l'ai rappelé dans ma plaidoirie, est applicable aussi bien en matière de responsabilité contractuelle qu'en matière de responsabilité délictuelle ou quasi-délictuelle.[36]

In so far as the Swiss contention in the *Interhandel Case* relating to the substance of the direct injury was rejected by the ICJ, it must be regarded as unacceptable. Similarly, the French contention in the *Norwegian Loans Case* was rejected by Judge Lauterpacht whose opinion, it has been submitted, is the better one since it is a natural corollary of the Court's opinion in the *Interhandel Case*. Thus, the views expressed by states that a violation of an international judgment, an international treaty or international law *per se* results in a direct injury must be regarded as being in conflict with the accepted view of the law. This leaves to be considered only the Israeli view in the *Aerial Incident Case*.

The Israeli argument was based on the theory that the alleged injury was primarily to the sovereignty of Israel made manifest in the nationality colours and markings on the plane which was shot down, and not to the Israeli nationals; the injury to Israel preceded the injury to the aliens and, therefore, this was not a case of diplomatic protection; the claims on behalf of the airline company and the affected individuals were subsidiary to the main claim which related to the violation of the

---

[35] *Ibid.*, pp. 530–1.   [36] *Ibid.*, p. 565; see also *ibid.*, pp. 570ff.

rights of the state of Israel. In principle, the argument that there must be a primary injury to the state rather than to the alien in order that a direct injury be committed seems a reasonable one. The next question, however, is whether in the circumstances of the case there was such a primary injury to the state of Israel. Both the principal idea and the latter question will be considered after a look is taken at the text writers on the subject.

As already seen, text writers who deal with the subject concede that a direct injury to the applicant state could result in the exclusion of the local remedies rule. However, there has been less discussion of how the concept of direct injury, especially for the purposes of the incidence of the rule of local remedies, is to be defined. One text writer who discussed the matter with state responsibility in general in mind and not particularly in the context of the rule of local remedies, has stated:

Nevertheless, various situations in the history of international claims reveal that in addition to the rights of its nationals a state has, in its relations with other states, certain rights which appertain to it in its collective or corporate capacity. The typical cases are those in which injury is done to an official of the state, particularly a consular or diplomatic official. The recognition accorded their special status in traditional international law is extended because of their representative character and not because of their status as individuals, although a supplementary claim may lie for the injury to the individual as such . . . International tribunals have frequently distinguished between a general injury to a state and specific damage.[37]

The author gives many examples of injuries to consular or diplomatic officials but also mentions other injuries, such as damage caused to state-owned ships, which could be considered direct injuries.[38] He concludes:

It should be one of the tasks in the codification of international law to catalogue the types of direct injuries to states for which the state would be privileged to require another state to pay such indemnity as might be determined by an international tribunal to be appropriate to the case. Among these types, in addition to those which have been illustrated by the cases just cited, should be those resulting from direct injury to a state instrumentality engaged in the conduct of commercial and other business activities.[39]

---

[37] Jessup, note 21 above, at pp. 118–19 and 120. The 1956 Granada resolution of the Institut de Droit International also refers to some direct injuries to which the rule of exhaustion of local remedies does not apply. Injuries to Heads of State and diplomats are mentioned.

[38] Jessup, note 21 above, at pp. 119–20.   [39] *Ibid.*, p. 120.

A list of direct injuries might be useful, but it would be very difficult to compile one. Further, a list cannot be exclusive, as room must be left for the inclusion of situations which may not be foreseeable at the time the catalogue is made. What is more important is that some general legal principle be evolved which would govern the situation.

The question has been examined by a text writer who has expressed the general view that:

The principal reason for the non-applicability of the rule of exhaustion of local remedies to cases of direct injury is that in such cases the injured State represents principally its own interests rather than the interests of its nationals and is the real claimant. It follows that a request by the respondent State that the claimant State should exhaust the legal remedies available in the former State would run counter to the principle *par in parem non habet imperium, non habet jurisdictionem* . . .

An attempt to formulate a general theoretical distinction between cases of direct injury and cases of diplomatic protection is bound to be difficult. In the first place it should be observed that there is an extremely close connexion between all the facts of a given case and the classification of that case as one belonging to either of these two categories. A single set of facts giving rise to international legal proceedings may contain elements of both diplomatic protection and direct injury . . . most cases of direct injury contain, in a certain degree, also elements of diplomatic protection. It may well be that at the bottom of almost every international claim there is the motivating factor of interests of individuals which need protection. It is suggested that the classification of a case as one of direct injury or as one of diplomatic protection depends on the element or elements which are preponderant. It is further suggested that once a case has been classified in this way, the international claim, including all its elements, must generally be regarded as a unity and may not be split into its constituent elements, such as those of direct injury and those of diplomatic protection.[40]

As general considerations these are relevant and basically do not create problems. The writer then suggests that regard must be had to two main factors, namely, the subject of the dispute or the action impugned in the proceedings and the nature of the claim.[41] He points out that as regards the subject of the dispute, while injuries caused to private

---

[40] Meron, note 22 above, at pp. 84–6.
[41] *Ibid.*, pp. 86–7. He cites also the present Article 38(1) and (2) of the Rules of Court of the ICJ in this connection, on the ground that those provisions, which deal with the contents of an application instituting proceedings, refer to these two concepts, but points out that the concept of the direct injury concerns substantive factors rather than procedural features.

individuals have usually been considered as cases of diplomatic protection, certain categories of acts, such as, in certain circumstances,
injuries caused by the state to officials of another state, and particularly its consular or diplomatic representatives, violations of treaties or
the destruction of property owned by a state and serving public functions, had been considered to be of a different kind.[42] With regard to
the second element, the nature of the claim, he gave the following
explanation:

[I]t is suggested that the true test is to be found in the real interest and objects
pursued by the claimant State. In this respect there is a distinction of substance
to be drawn between the case in which the claimant State is prompted to bring
the claim in order to secure objectives principally its own, and the case in which
the claimant State is only espousing or adopting the cause of its subject, 'and
is proceeding in virtue of the right of diplomatic protection'. On this basis,
it would appear that when the claimant State is proceeding in virtue of the
right of diplomatic protection, and despite a certain refinement of the doctrinal
position, that State has no distinct interest in the claim apart from the interest
of its national whose cause is thus espoused. But the position would appear
to be entirely different in a case which is not one of diplomatic protection
in that sense, i.e. in a case where the initial act of the respondent State is a
direct infringement of the rights of the claimant State according to international
law . . .

In connexion with this test, consideration of the final submission – the 'precise
and direct statement of a claim' – can be of some assistance. They should give a
clear indication of the relief sought, and hence of the real interests and objects
pursued by the claimant State. Yet this must be met with reserve . . . However,
although the question whether the State is *entitled* to a particular type of relief
is a matter for judicial determination, the fact that the State *desires* a particular
type of relief can be indicative of the real interest of that State in pursuing the
case . . . For instance, in cases of diplomatic protection the State normally seeks
pecuniary compensation or possibly restitution of property, which would satisfy
the claims arising from injuries originally caused to the individuals. But this –
at least by itself – would rarely be an appropriate form of relief to a claim arising
from a direct injury to the State. In such case, an award of pecuniary compensation for its nationals who were incidentally injured by the impugned act is a
secondary object; the primary object is to obtain from an international tribunal
some declaration of the responsibility of the respondent State in international
law, or the establishment of an arbitral tribunal, or some other remedy such as

---

[42] Meron, note 22 above, at p. 87. Ago agrees that such injuries were not subject
to the exhaustion of local remedies rule, because the individuals were state
organs: 'Sixth Report on State Responsibility', YBILC (1977), vol. 2, Part II, at
pp. 39ff.

a binding interpretation of a treaty, or an official apology due to the claimant State in its quality as a State.[43]

The writer explains that international tribunals would have to distinguish between a mere form of words and the real substance of the claim by considering the object of the claim, rather than merely its formulation, in cases where an attempt may be made to represent the claim as being one for a direct injury, when in reality it is based on diplomatic protection.[44]

The approach outlined above poses certain definite problems. For example, in determining whether the subject of the dispute falls into the category of a direct injury, the view discussed suggests that violations of treaties generally fall into this category. But this is prima facie not the case, as is shown by the *Interhandel Case*. Further, the alternative request of the Swiss government in that case was for a declaration that there was an obligation to settle the dispute by arbitration or conciliation.[45] The claim clearly concerned the right of the Swiss government to an arbitration or a conciliation procedure and did not in substance concern the right of the Swiss government to proper treatment for its nationals. A very real object of the Swiss government was the securing of its right to arbitration or conciliation, although it may be said that the ultimate object was the protection of its right to the proper treatment of its nationals. On one interpretation of the 'real object or interest' of this claim it was possible to find that the alternative request was to secure a different international right from the mere protection of nationals to which the state was entitled.[46] The Court, however, did advert to the object of the claim and stated that:

One interest and one alone, that of Interhandel, which has led the latter to institute and to resume proceedings before the United States courts, has induced the Swiss Government to institute international proceedings. This interest is the basis for the present claim and should determine the scope of the action brought before the Court by the Swiss Government in its alternative form as well as in its principal form. On the other hand, the grounds on which the rule of the exhaustion of local remedies is based are the same, whether in the case of an

---

[43] Meron, note 22 above, at pp. 87–9. Cançado Trindade, note 22 above, at pp. 173–4, without discussion, supports the principle that the nature of the claim should determine whether there has been a direct injury.

[44] Meron, note 22 above, at pp. 88–9.   [45] 1959 ICJ Reports at p. 19.

[46] As was held by Judge Lauterpacht, dissenting: *ibid.*, p. 120, and Judge Winiarski, dissenting: *ibid.*, p. 83. It is to be noted that these were dissenting opinions.

international court, arbitral or conciliation commission. In these circumstances the Court considers that any distinction so far as the rule of exhaustion of local remedies is concerned between the various claims or between the various tribunals is unfounded.[47]

Although 'objects and interests' were referred to, it would seem that the Court ultimately took the simple view that the rule of exhaustion of local remedies would have prevented an action being taken for the determination of the main question before an arbitral or conciliation commission just as much as before an international court. Therefore the alternative submission of the Swiss government could not be answered except in the negative, since the failure to exhaust local remedies had been proved.[48] The peculiar nature of the alternative submission made it unnecessary to regard the objection based on the rule of exhaustion of local remedies as a preliminary objection to that submission, since upholding the objection automatically resulted in the giving of a negative answer to it. Nevertheless, it may be stated that at least *obiter* the court did refer to 'objects and interests' as being relevant to the determination of the question of whether the rule of exhaustion is applicable. However, Judge Basdevant in a declaration laid emphasis on the 'subject of the dispute' as the criterion of the validity of the objections put forward.[49]

While there is some conflict of opinion on the proper criterion, it would seem that the concept of the 'subject of the dispute' is not entirely adequate if it refers to categories of acts. On the other hand, the 'nature of the claim', defined as being determined by the 'real objects and interests' of a state, would seem to come closer to a satisfactory solution of the problem.

A possible refinement of this approach may be suggested. While 'objects and interests' of a state in bringing a particular claim may be relevant, it would seem that the real question concerns not so much the 'nature of the claim' as the 'nature of the injury or right violated' on

---

[47] *Ibid.*, p. 29.

[48] Four dissenting judges differed on this point: see Judge Carry, *ibid.*, p. 32; Judge Klaestad, *ibid.*, p. 82; Judge Winiarski, *ibid.*, p. 84; and Judge Lauterpacht, *ibid.*, p. 120. The view taken by the dissenting judges is supported by Law, *The Local Remedies Rule in International Law* (1961) pp. 95ff. The decision in the *Ambatielos Case*, in which it was stated that the Court could not consider whether local remedies had been exhausted in deciding the question whether there was an obligation upon the respondent state to submit to arbitration under treaty provisions, 1953 ICJ Reports at pp. 22ff., also runs counter to the holding in the *Interhandel Case*, even though it does not expressly contradict that case.

[49] 1959 ICJ Reports at p. 30.

which the claim is based. In so far as the former, as determined by the real objects and interests of the state, depends on the latter, it becomes of relevance. It is the 'real objects and interests', which are the essence of the injury committed or the right violated, that govern the answer to the question of whether local remedies should have been exhausted. This is so, because ultimately the claim, whatever it may be, depends on the right violated. The rule of exhaustion relates to the right violated or the injury committed and not to the claim based on it as such, which reflects a secondary or remedial right. It is also the essence of the substantive right violated, as determined by the objects and interests promoted therein, that is of importance.

That an international right belonging to a state has been violated, as has been seen, does not necessarily result in the exclusion of the rule. Indeed, an injury to an alien which violates international law is also a violation of his state's right. What is required is a further inquiry into the essence of the state's right. If the state's right in its essence has for its object the protection of its nationals as such and if this is the main interest sought from it, it may be concluded that the rule of exhaustion applies to it. Hence, a claim based on its violation, whatever the form of that claim, cannot be espoused until local remedies have been exhausted. The claim may be for an apology or for an indemnity for damage caused to an alien, or merely damages for the insult to the alien's state, but this would not make a difference if the essence of the substantive right violated is the right to the protection of the alien. Conversely, if the essence of the right violated is different, then the rule of local remedies would not apply to a claim based on that wrong. Thus, where a diplomat is injured by a state, the diplomat's state can assert that a right has been violated which has for its object the carrying on of functions of state and not merely the protection of nationals. In such a case, no local remedies need be exhausted in respect of any claim based on that violation of international law, although it may be that a claim might be made which purports to recover damages for the personal loss suffered by the diplomat, an alien. Further, it may be that in certain circumstances it is necessary for an international court to weigh conflicting interests and objects behind a substantive right so as to determine whether the predominant interest is that of protecting a national.[50] It is certain that the fact that the protective right is embodied

---

[50] An analogous operation is performed by some, mainly national, courts in determining whether an ordinary offence is a political offence for the purposes of the law of

in a treaty does not make it any less a protective right, as was seen above.

This approach is compatible with Judge Basdevant's theory which stresses the subject of a dispute; for the substantive right is, indeed, the subject of the dispute. However, it goes a little further in attaching importance to the objects and interests which form the essence of that right (not of the claim, as such). Also, it is not incompatible with the theory of 'objects and interests' propounded *obiter* in the *Interhandel Case*, which may in fact seem to support it. Thus, it is the objects and interests underlying a right that really matter, although the claim may be relevant.

That this view of the position is tenable is supported by the fact that, in cases of injury to aliens where local remedies are exhausted and adequate redress is obtained by the injured alien, the delinquent state's responsibility is completely discharged and all claims arising from the injury are extinguished. There is no room for a claim of damages for the international injury to the alien's state or for an apology based on the fact that the alien's state also suffered injury. This shows that, where local remedies must be exhausted, it is the aspect of the state's right that involves protection of the alien which is given emphasis. The protective interest which is inherent in the substantive right that an alien should not be injured is, thus, rightly used as the determining factor in the incidence of the rule of local remedies.

Some examples based on situations that have actually occurred may illustrate the operation of this principle that the incidence of the rule of local remedies depends on the nature of the injury or right violated. In the case of the *I'm Alone*,[51] a Canadian vessel was illegally sunk by a US Coast Guard cutter. The *I'm Alone* belonged to a private company. Since the injury caused was on the high seas, it was an injury to the Canadian flag and Canada successfully claimed an apology and the payment of material amends for the wrong without there having been any prior exhaustion of local remedies. The wrong having been committed outside US territory, the local remedies rule was inapplicable. But had the wrong been committed on US territory, then it is likely that the rule would have been applicable and it would have been a good answer to

<hr/>

extradition: see Amerasinghe, *Studies in International Law* (1969) pp. 164ff.; and Gutteridge, 'The Notion of Political Offences and the Law of Extradition', 31 BYIL (1954) at pp. 430ff.; Evans, 'Reflections upon the Political Offense in International Practice', 57 AJIL (1963) at pp. 11ff.

[51] *I'm Alone Case*, 3 UNRIAA p. 4 (1935).

both demands that the rule had not been satisfied, since the substantive right would have involved a pure interest in protecting nationals. No distinction could have been made by reference to the basis of the claim in order that the claim for an apology and material amends might have succeeded.

In the *Aerial Incident Case*,[52] a civilian aircraft belonging to an Israeli airline penetrated Bulgarian airspace without previous authorization and was shot down by Bulgarian air defence forces. As already seen, the Israeli claim was for damages for the injury to the company that owned the plane by reason of the damage to the property and for the injury to Israeli nationals on the plane. The injury to the state was hardly mentioned in the application as the primary injury for which compensation was claimed. It is only in the memorial and the oral argument, after the objection based on local remedies was made, that the issue of the violation of a right belonging to the state was raised. If the nature of the claim were to be examined by looking at its objects and interests, clearly the object of the claim was to exercise protection over the person and property of Israel's nationals, rather than to assert that a predominant right of the state had been violated.[53] Thus, on the theory based on the nature of the claim, the issue relating to the application of the local remedies rule would have had to be settled in favour of such application, because the substance of the claim related to the protection of aliens. On the other hand, if the alternative theory based on the real interest or right violated, which is a refinement of the above theory, were adopted, the answer would not be so clear. The argument made by the Israeli government in the oral proceedings hinged in substance upon the concept of an injury to the colours of Israel which were worn by the plane. The preliminary issue to be decided was whether, when a private plane was on foreign soil, the fact that it wore the colours of a particular state gave that state a right as such which would have been violated if illegal damage had been caused to the plane. If the answer was in the affirmative, it would then have been possible, on the basis of the theory of the real injury or interest, to conclude that the protection of the state's interest was the primary consideration and the protection of nationals injured in the course of violating that interest a subsidiary

[52] 1959 ICJ Reports p. 127.
[53] It is not clear that this was the point made by the Bulgarian government, which advanced it unequivocally to assert that local remedies should have been exhausted. It is more likely that it was asserting that the injury was not directly done to the state: ICJ Pleadings (1959) at pp. 570ff.

one, so that the rule of local remedies would not have properly been applicable to the protection of the property or person of those nationals. It is clear that, whereas on the basis of a pure 'nature of claim' theory in that case the answer demanded would have been that the rule of local remedies was applicable to the claims on behalf of nationals, on the basis of the theory which additionally requires an inquiry into the real interests protected by the law, the answer would have been that the rule was not applicable. As it is, however, there is no certainty that a state has a right to respect for its colours of the nature contended for by the Israeli government, where the plane is on the territory of another state. The analogy which may occur of respect for a state's flag is generally associated with the high seas and not the territory of a foreign state. However, it is not necessary to decide this issue for the purpose of this exposition. What is relevant is that it is only by the application of the theory based on the real interests or right protected that it is possible to arrive at the conclusion that the local remedies rule was not relevant, whereas the application of the other theory would have resulted in the conclusion that the rule was applicable.[54]

The above approach taken by me in the first edition of this book[55] which is the same as that taken here is definitely supported by the view expressed rather succinctly by the ICJ in the *Arrest Warrant of 11 April 2000 Case*, where it was stated that:

[a]s the Congo is not acting in the context of the *protection of one of its nationals*, Belgium cannot rely upon the rules relating to the exhaustion of local remedies.[56]

---

[54] The preliminary objection based on the rule of local remedies was not decided by the Court because the case was dismissed on the basis of a different objection.

[55] Amerasinghe, *Local Remedies in International Law* (1990) pp. 128–33.

[56] Emphasis added: www.icj-cij.org, para. 40. In the *Air Services Agreement Arbitration (France v. US)*, 18 UNRIAA at p. 431 (1978), the tribunal referred to the core of the rights and duties which are the subject of the dispute, stating that:

> the rule of international law relating to the requirement of exhaustion of local remedies, when making a distinction between the State-to-State claims in which the requirement applies, and claims which are not subject to such a requirement, must necessarily base this distinction on the *judicial* character of the *legal relationship* between States which is invoked in support of the claim. Consequently, with respect to the applicability of the local remedies rule, a distinction is made between 'cases of diplomatic protection' and cases of direct injury.

This statement clearly supports the views expressed in the text above which refer to the nature of the real interests or right protected as the basis of the distinction between what is a direct injury and what is not. See also the statement which is

It is quite clear that this statement emphasizes the 'essence' of the right violated, which is substantially what matters, as is pointed out above, insofar as it points to the 'context of the protection of one of its nationals' as being what is relevant to the incidence of the rule of local remedies.[57] The statement also supports the further conclusion arrived at above that other considerations such as the 'subject of the dispute' without more and the 'nature of the claim', as such, are irrelevant. On the other hand, the 'real objects and interests' of the state, adequately defined, may be synonymous with the 'essence of the right' infringed, but even that requires further refinement.

Jurisdictional connection

Another question that has been raised is whether, in cases where a state is obviously protecting its national, i.e. genuine cases of diplomatic protection, there could arise situations in which the application of the rule of local remedies is excluded. Clearly, there can be little doubt that, where, for instance, state A improperly imprisons a national of state B who is resident in state A, the rule applies, but there may be situations where the applicability of the rule may be questioned where, so to speak, there is doubt as to whether there is an adequate jurisdictional connection. Examples that may be given are (i) where naval officers of state A improperly treat nationals of state B on a ship belonging to state C on the high seas, or (ii) where diplomatic officers of state A in state B treat a national of state C in a manner which violates a treaty between state A and state B. In all cases, especially of this kind, the issue raised is one concerned with jurisdictional connection which would require, in the above examples, the nationals of state B to exhaust local remedies in state A before state B may exercise diplomatic protection over its nationals. On the other hand, the commoner examples of cases where the jurisdictional connection may be assumed to have been established,

somewhat relevant and was made by the arbitral tribunal in *Swiss Confederation v. Federal Republic of Germany (No. 21)*, 25 ILR at pp. 42–3 (1958), that there must be a claim based on impairment of the rights of a national of the claimant state in violation of international law, in order to trigger the rule of local remedies.

[57] It is to be noted that Dugard, 'Second Report on Diplomatic Protection' (ILC), UN Doc. A/CN.4/514 (2001) at pp. 10–15, in draft Article 11, concedes that protection of a national, 'as a preponderant element' is what is important but, first, does not recognize that it is really the 'essence' of the right violated which is the right to protect a national that matters, and, secondly, in the discussion of the subject confuses the issues and elements involved.

apart from the case where the alien takes up residence, either temporarily or permanently, in the territory of the host or respondent state, are those where an alien engages in business in, owns property in[58] or enters into contractual relations with[59] the government of the host or respondent state.

It would appear that in almost all decided cases that have been reported where the rule has been applied the question never arose as to whether there was an adequate jurisdictional connection, because apparently one did exist. In general, most of these cases concerned situations in which the alien was temporarily or permanently resident in, or was physically present in, or had some kind of contractual connection with the host state. The history of the diplomatic practice related to the rule also shows that the circumstances in which the rule was invoked were those in which the alien had some physical connection with the host state. Thus, it is not surprising that Borchard in 1915 expressed the idea that the rule was applicable because the 'alien is deemed to tacitly submit and to be subject to the local law of the state of residence',[60] thus consecrating the requirement of residence. But, as cases like the *Ambatielos Claim* show,[61] the rule has been regarded as being applicable in cases where the alien is not resident or even physically present in the host state but where he has some connection, such as a contractual one, with the host state.

The authorities

The authorities, whether judicial or other, have not generally faced the problem of the jurisdictional connection in any systematic way, although there has been some discussion of the problem. In the cases and arguments before the ICJ there have been a few broad statements of the circumstances in which the rule that local remedies must be exhausted is applicable, without any apparent qualification. Thus, Judge Córdova in a separate opinion in the *Interhandel Case* said that:

---

[58] See e.g. the facts in the *Panavezys–Saldutiskis Railway Case*, PCIJ Series A/B No. 76 (1939), and the facts in the *Interhandel Case*, 1959 ICJ Reports p. 6, where the rule was applied.

[59] See e.g. the type of situation involved in the *Ambatielos Claim* (*Greece* v. *UK*), 12 UNRIAA p. 83 (1956), where the rule was applied, and in the *Norwegian Loans Case*, 1957 ICJ Reports p. 9.

[60] *The Diplomatic Protection of Citizens Abroad* (1915) p. 817. See Harvard Law School, 'Research in International Law II: Responsibility of States (1929)', 23 AJIL (1929) Supplement at pp. 152–3.

[61] *Greece* v. *UK*, 12 UNRIAA p. 83 (1956).

A State may not exercise its diplomatic protection, and much less resort to any kind of international procedure of redress until its subject has previously exhausted the local remedies offered him by the State of whose action he complains.[62]

However, the case before him concerned a situation where injury had been caused to the property of an alien which was located within the territory of the US. In the *Norwegian Loans Case*, Norway argued:

Quel est l'objet de cette règle? Lorsqu'un Etat s'est Plaint d'un acte internationalement illicite, imputé à un Etat étranger et dont la victime est une personne privée, son action sur le plan international n'est recevable que si la personne lésée a préalablement épuisé les voies des recours que le droit interne de l'Etat incriminé met à sa disposition.[63]

In this case, the facts concerned public loans, floated by Norway on the French and other foreign markets, which were to be governed by Norwegian law and with which interference took place in Norway.

On the other hand, there have been more limited statements in the cases and argument before the ICJ such as the one made in the *Interhandel Case*:

the rule has been generally observed in cases in which a state has adopted the cause of its national where rights are claimed to have been disregarded in another state in violation of international law. Before resort may be had to an international court in such a situation, it has been considered necessary that the state where the violation occurred should have an opportunity to redress it by its own means.[64]

This explanation attaches importance to the place where the violation of international law took place. France went further in her view of the limitations in the *Norwegian Loans Case* when she maintained that:

---

[62] 1959 ICJ Reports at p. 46. Some support for a broad view of the circumstances in which the rule of local remedies is applicable is to be found among text writers: see e.g. Reuter, 'La responsabilité internationale', *Droit International Public (cours)* (1955–6) pp. 161ff.; McNair, *International Law Opinions* (1956), vol. 2, p. 219; Gaja, *L'Esaurimento dei Ricorsi Interni nel Diritto Internazionale* (1967) p. 91; and Ago, note 42 above, at pp. 37ff.

[63] ICJ Pleadings (1957), vol. 2, p. 156.

[64] 1959 ICJ Reports at p. 27. There are authors who base the incidence of the rule on (i) the residence of the alien in the territory of the respondent state: e.g. Mummery, 'The Content of the Duty to Exhaust Local Judicial Remedies', 58 AJIL (1964) at pp. 390ff.; O'Connell, vol. 2, pp. 950ff., or (ii) the presence of the alien or his property in the territory of the respondent state: see, e.g. Parry, 'Some Considerations upon the Protection of Individuals in International Law', 90 *Hague Recueil* (1956) at p. 688; Law, note 48 above, at p. 104; and Head, 'A Fresh Look at the Local Remedies Rule', 5 CYIL (1967) at p. 153.

La seule explication de la règle réside dans l'exigence qu'un étranger qui se trouve en litige avec l'Etat sous la souveraineté duquel il a voulu vivre ne puisse provoquer le transfert de son affaire sur le plan international sans avoir épuisé au préalable tous les moyens de la règle par les voies locales.[65]

Here, the emphasis is on residence in the delinquent state as a criterion of limitation. Judge Read in a dissenting opinion in the same case said that the rule was not limited to circumstances in which the injured alien was resident in the delinquent state, but did not state what limitations there were on the incidence of the rule.[66]

In the *Salem Case*, an arbitral tribunal stated, in terms similar to the French argument, that:

as a rule, a foreigner must acknowledge as applicable to himself the kind of justice instituted in the country in which he did choose his residence.[67]

In the *Aerial Incident Case*, Israel argued for a limitation based on some notion of a link. In the oral argument, it was stated:

it is essential, before the rule can be applied, that a link should exist between the injured individual and the State whose actions are impugned. I submit that all the precedents show that the rule is only applied when the alien, the injured individual, has created, or is deemed to have created, a voluntary, conscious and deliberate connection between himself and the foreign State whose actions are impugned. The precedents relate always to cases in which a link of this character has been brought about, for instance, by reason of residence in that State, trade activities there, the ownership of property there – I believe that that covers the majority of the cases – or by virtue of his having made some contract with the government of that State, such as the cases involving foreign bondholders; and there may be other instances. No such link exists in the present case . . . The victims of the Bulgarian action had no voluntary, conscious and deliberate connection with Bulgaria.[68]

The argument of Israel was opposed by Bulgaria on the ground that the link was not part of international law, although it was not indicated whether there were any limitations on the incidence of the rule of local remedies. It was said:

Sans doute, en fait, la plupart du temps, la protection diplomatique est exercée par un Etat à l'occasion d'une rupture de contrat ou bien en raison d'actes gouvernementaux qui portent atteinte aux droits d'un étranger vivant dans le

---

[65] ICJ Pleadings, vol. 1, p. 409.   [66] 1957 ICJ Reports at p. 97.

[67] *United States* v. *Egypt*, 2 UNRIAA at p. 1202 (1932).

[68] ICJ Pleadings (1959) at pp. 531–2. The facts of the case have been described earlier in this chapter.

pays ou possédant des intérêts dans ce pays. Mais rien – absolument rien – ne permet de limiter à ces hypothèses déterminées l'application de la règle que nous invoquons et qui est trés générale . . . Il faut que l'Etat où la lésion a été commise puisse y remédier par ses propres moyens dans le cadre de son ordre juridique interne. On lui donne le droit de corriger ou de faire corriger pas [*sic*] ses tribunaux les erreurs qu'il aurait pu commettre, et je n'aperçois aucune raison valable de faire une distinction, une discrimination, selon que la victime a ou n'a pas avec l'Etat auteur du dommage un lien volontaire, conscient et délibéré.[69]

In diplomatic correspondence too, expression has been given to the view that local remedies must be exhausted in the delinquent state 'in which their rights are infringed, to which laws they have voluntarily subjected themselves by entering within the sphere of their operation, and by which they must consent to abide'.[70] There is here a combination of the idea that the location where rights are infringed is relevant provided there is voluntary subjection to the laws of that state.[71] It may also be mentioned that in early British practice it was asserted that, where an alien suffered injury on the high seas, by seizure or capture of a vessel, local remedies had to be exhausted in the seizing or capturing state.[72] It is doubtful, one may comment, whether the practice would be recognized today.

Text writers who have adverted to the problem also assert in one way or another that there are some limitations on the incidence of the rule. Eagleton refers to the state 'où il [the alien] a choisi à fixer sa résidence'[73] in connection with the rule. Borchard's views have already been mentioned above. One recent writer makes the incidence of the rule rest on voluntary or free submission to the local law and the jurisdiction of the delinquent state.[74]

Largely on the basis of the Israeli argument in the *Aerial Incident Case*, the view has been expressed that there must be a genuine link between the alien and the respondent state in order that the rule of local remedies be applicable. It was explained that:

The most common case in which the genuine link exists and the rule of local remedies is applicable is that involving the physical presence in the territory of

---

[69] ICJ Pleadings (1959) at p. 565.

[70] Secretary of State McLane in 1834: Moore, *International Law* (1906), vol. 6, p. 658.

[71] See also Secretary of State Seward in 1866: Moore, *International Law* (1906), vol. 6, p. 660.

[72] See McNair, *International Law Opinions* (1956), vol. 2, p. 302.

[73] 'L'épuisement des recours internes et le déni de justice', 16 RDILC (1935) at p. 523.

[74] Law, note 48 above, at p. 104.

the wrong-doing State of either the alien or his property. In such a typical case it can be presumed that the link has been properly established. This, of course, is merely a presumption of fact which can be refuted by the circumstances of each specific case. It is in this context that the link theory proves to be particularly helpful. It not only helps us to understand why the rule of local remedies would be applicable to the case of a contractual relationship between a State and a non-resident alien, but is also essential for the necessary exclusion of the applicability of the rule in the case of an alien who, although present in person in the territory of the respondent State, has not established a genuine link between himself and that State. Surely the rule of local remedies is applicable to the case, for instance, of an alien who built a factory in a State, which factory is expropriated by that State without compensation. No question could legitimately be raised as to the existence of the genuine link in such a case. But let us consider the case in which the injured alien came to be in a certain State against his will, for instance, if he was brought there against his will and in violation of international law from the territory of another State or from the high seas by the agents of the former State, or, if his yacht travelling through an international waterway within the limit of the territorial waters of that State was destroyed by a mine illegally planted there by the armed forces of the territorial State. As in neither case a genuine link had been established, there would be no justification for the application of the local remedies rule.[75]

The criterion of the location of the wrong

While an international court or tribunal has not up to now had to decide the specific issue raised here, it appears that the rule has actually been applied in a strictly circumscribed sphere. Simply for the reason that no case has decided that the rule does not apply in every situation in which an alien is injured by a foreign state, it would not be in keeping with the policies behind the rule that it should apply in every such circumstance. Hence, the broad unqualified statements cited above cannot be regarded as properly reflecting the law.

At the other extreme, to insist on the residence or presence of the alien in the delinquent state at the time of the injury would not be compatible with the application of the rule in some of the decided cases. Judge Read was, therefore, correct in rejecting this formulation of the rule by France in the *Norwegian Loans Case*.

---

[75] Meron, note 22 above, at pp. 95–6. Other text writers who apparently support the theory of the voluntary link are Head, note 64 above, at p. 153; Jiménez de Aréchaga, 'International Responsibility', in Sørensen (ed.), *Manual of Public International Law* (1968) at p. 583; and Chappez, *La Règle de l'épuisement des voies de recours internes* (1972) pp. 48ff.

It would seem, then, that the solution lies somewhere in between these two extremes. In terms of the policies behind the rule of exhaustion, it is apparent that it is only where the delinquent state can be said to be entitled to jurisdiction over the issue that the rule may be applied. As is generally known, international law does not for a general purpose define the circumstances in which a state will be entitled to jurisdiction over any particular issue, so that resort to other fields of international law may not be very helpful. In this sense, the analogy of the 'voluntary or genuine link' which may have some relationship to the rules of the nationality of claims may not be so apt, since the policies behind the two fields of law are not identical. On the other hand, such concepts mentioned as 'location of the wrong', 'voluntary subjection to jurisdiction by entering into the sphere of operation' (understood in a general sense), 'tacit subjection to jurisdiction' and 'free and voluntary submission to the jurisdiction' are more relevant to the problem in hand. If we regard these concepts as divisible into two groups, representing respectively the idea of 'the location of the wrong' and the notion of 'free and voluntary submission to the jurisdiction', it will appear that the second is more vague than the first, although it may be difficult sometimes to locate a wrong.

In view of the fact that the ICJ in the *Interhandel Case* distinctly and clearly expressed its agreement with the view that 'the state *where the violation occurred* should have an opportunity to redress it by its own means',[76] the proper starting point for a consideration of the limitations on the incidence of the rule of local remedies is the 'location of the wrong'. If the wrong must be located in the territory of the delinquent state, whatever the difficulties of determining the *locus* of the wrong,[77] then it would generally mean that the person or property must also be located in the delinquent state. *Inter alia*, if a subjective approach to the problem of the *locus* of the wrong were taken, it may be possible to say that the *locus* of the person or property injured may be outside the delinquent state, while the *locus* of the wrong remained within. That would happen where the act constituting the wrong is begun within the delinquent state but terminates on a person or property outside the

---

[76] 1959 ICJ Reports at p. 27 (emphasis added).

[77] The same problem arises in connection with criminal jurisdiction: see the *Lotus Case*, PCIJ Series A No. 10 (1927), which deals with the objective test of the *locus* of a crime. The *locus* of a tort has to be determined for the purpose of the conflict of laws (private international law): see, e.g. Collins (ed.), *Dicey and Morris on the Conflict of Laws* (2000), vol. 2, pp. 1507ff.

delinquent state. This anomaly can be overcome by adopting a test for the *locus* which embodies the objective approach and fixes on the place where the last event necessary to make an actor liable for an alleged wrong takes place.[78] There may still, however, be circumstances in which the alien or his property is outside the territory of the delinquent state, although the wrong is located in the territory of that state, such as where an official of the delinquent state defames an alien who is not in the delinquent state in circumstances in which the wrong is imputable to that state. Nevertheless, it is submitted that it is not out of keeping with the policies behind the local remedies rule that the delinquent state should be entitled to jurisdiction in such circumstances.

There is certainly one circumstance in which the theory of the *locus* of the wrong may have to be modified, and that is, where the determination that the *locus* of the wrong is in the delinquent state is dependent on the presence of the alien's person or property in the delinquent state and that presence of person or property is the result of a seizure made in violation of international law, attributable to the delinquent state. Here the principle *ex iniuria non oritur ius* is applicable.[79] It is to be noted that this exception is not co-extensive with the absence of voluntariness or consent freely given. Although in the incidence of the exception there will be found to be absence of voluntariness or consent, it does not follow that in every case in which there is absence of voluntariness or consent the exception will apply. For instance, the facts of the *Aerial Incident Case* show that the exception did not apply, because the presence of the aircraft in Bulgarian airspace was not attributable to an illegal seizure by Bulgaria, regardless of the question of whether or not it was there voluntarily. On the other hand, the old British view that a seizure on the high seas requires exhaustion of local remedies in the delinquent state cannot be supported in modern law where this exception applies. It is clear also that the principle *ex iniuria non oritur ius* as applied in this context refers only to an *iniuria* attributable to the respondent state.

The application of the theory of the locus of the wrong to a breach of contract, *where such breach is internationally wrongful*, may give rise to apparent difficulties, because such a breach of contract will often be an omission. A solution may be found in regarding a breach of contract in such circumstances as an interference with the alien's rights in the

---

[78] *Restatement of the Law of Conflict of Laws* (1934), section 377.

[79] This principle is applicable to questions of jurisdiction when seizures are made contrary to international law: see Morgenstern, 'Jurisdiction in Seizures Effected in Violation of International Law', 29 BYIL (1952) pp. 265ff., especially at p. 279.

contract, i.e. his right to performance. Since this is in the nature of a *chose in action*, the *situs* of the *chose in action* will determine the *locus* of the wrong. The determination of *situs* will depend on general principles of law as found in the conflict of laws (private international law).[80]

The theory of the *locus* of the wrong, with the exception outlined above, not only has the virtue of recognizing the view of the ICJ and the policies behind the rule of local remedies and of adequately balancing two principal interests involved, but is also compatible with all the decided cases that can be explained by reference to it.

It is quite clear that the broad generic view of 'free and voluntary submission to jurisdiction' as such finds no support in the decided cases or state practice, with the exception of the Israeli argument in the *Aerial Incident Case*.[81] It is also as such an unsatisfactory basis, on a balance of the interests involved and for policy reasons, for establishing an appropriate jurisdictional connection. An example will illustrate the point. If bandits in state A seize an alien (in relation to state B) and bring him across the border to state B, where a delictual violation of international law in respect of the alien in relation to the alien's national state is subsequently committed, there is no reason why there should be no jurisdictional connection for the exercise of jurisdiction on the basis that there had been no free and voluntary submission by the alien to the jurisdiction of state B, where the wrong has occurred. The principle, *ex iniuria non oritur ius*, does not apply, because under this principle the *iniuria* must be committed by state B (in this example). There is clearly no reason why an exception should be made to state B's entitlement to have local remedies exhausted in its territory. Here, state B's interests are clearly paramount.

The conclusion to be drawn on a policy basis is that a broad 'free and voluntary submission' exception is not as such relevant to the law relating to the exhaustion of local remedies. The *ex iniuria non oritur ius* principle by itself – a general principle of law – is an adequate exception legitimately to protect the two principal interests. Conversely, the 'free and voluntary submission to jurisdiction' principle does not have support as such as a general principle of law.

A recent rapporteur of the ILC[82] incorporates in Article 14 of his draft the 'free and voluntary link' principle. The discussion and analysis which

---

[80] See, e.g. Collins, note 77 above, vol. 2, pp. 924ff.
[81] ICJ Pleadings (1959) at pp. 31–2.   [82] Dugard, note 57 above, at p. 26.

follows this draft Article[83] is not merely inconclusive as to the acceptance of the principle in state practice and in judicial decisions or by text writers but rather supports its non-acceptance, because the evidence shows that (i) where such a principle or some variation of it has been recognized as an exception, there has been an explicit or implicit waiver, on the basis of the principle, of the rule of local remedies in the circumstances, (ii) the reference to treaties as establishing the exception does not reveal that such treaties give rise to customary international law, because of a lack of a clear *opinio iuris* in any case, apart from the absence of cogent practice, (iii) existing judicial decisions of relevance as such do not come anywhere near to supporting the principle as an exception, and (iv) text writers are not in agreement at all that the exception as such is applicable but rather ignore it, if at all. The discussion is in fact confused and unsatisfactory. What is eminently clear is that there are judicial decisions, *inter alia*, which categorically support the view that the basic principle of jurisdiction is that of the 'location of the wrong', there being little or no discussion of the exception based on 'absence of voluntary submission'. In any case, unlike the 'location of the wrong' principle, the 'absence of voluntary submission' exception does not have any support in the judicial decisions. The only reference to it is in the Israeli argument in the *Aerial Incident Case*, a reference which is not based on any kind of precedent, authority or a general principle of law nor substantiated by any good reasons of policy. There is undoubtedly more authority and evidence than that required for the acceptance of such a broad exception, apart from good policy reasons.

While the *ex iniuria non oritur ius* principle itself may not have been applied hitherto, *inter alia*, in any international judicial decisions on the rule of local remedies, there are international judicial decisions which have recognized it in other areas[84] and it is clearly an accepted general principle of law. Thus, there is no difficulty in applying it as a general

---

[83] *Ibid.*, pp. 26–35.
[84] That the principle is a general principle of both international law and national law needs no support of authority. In any case, see note 79 above and such cases decided by the PCIJ and the ICJ as the *Jurisdiction of the Courts of Danzig Opinion*, PCIJ Series B No. 15, at p. 26 (1928); the *Legal Status of Eastern Greenland Case*, PCIJ Series A/B No. 53 at pp. 75 and 95 (1933); and the *Namibia Opinion*, 1977 ICJ Reports at pp. 46–7. In the last mentioned opinion, for instance, the ICJ said specifically that a state which does not fulfil its own obligations flowing from an international relationship cannot be recognized as having the rights which it claims to derive from that relationship, thus stating a principle which reflects the broader principle *ex iniuria non oritur ius*.

principle of both international and national law in the context of the rule of local remedies.

The conclusion, based not only on authority or the absence of it but also on considerations of policy, is unavoidable that the criterion of the 'location of the wrong' for jurisdictional connection together with the exception based on the *ex iniuria non oritur ius* principle is adequate to deal with the issue of jurisdictional connection. Certainly, the 'absence of voluntary submission' principle as such is not only too broad, as formulated and explained by the few text writers who mention it, but is unnecessary for a fair and just implementation of the law relating to the exhaustion of local remedies.

7   Scope of the rule

An issue which is crucial to the operation of the rule in practice concerns the extent to which local remedies must be exhausted. As already pointed out, the interplay between the two principal sets of conflicting interests, those of the host or respondent state arising from its sovereignty and those of the alien in securing a fair and equitable solution to his complaint without being put to undue expense or hardship, is significant here, although there tends to be a greater emphasis on those of the host or respondent state in having an opportunity to settle the dispute by its own means. The scope of the rule is inextricably linked with limitations on it which will be discussed in detail in the following chapter, although there will be some overlap between the two subjects. Here, however, the object is to examine how extensive must be the resort to local remedies in order to enable the host or respondent state to have a proper opportunity of settling the dispute. The development of the rule, particularly through judicial decisions, demonstrates that, while great respect is shown for the sovereignty of the host or respondent state, there has been some concern for the interests of the alien, so as not to make the extent of resort required unreasonable.

In this area, as has already been seen,[1] the application of the rule to human rights protection has purported to follow closely its application in the area of diplomatic protection, because, as has been held under the European Convention on Human Rights, the prescription that the rule should apply to human rights protection in accordance with the general principles of international law has required that, certainly as to material content, the rule shall be applied to human rights protection in the same way in which it is, has been or shall be applied to diplomatic protection.

---

[1] See Chapter 3 above.

Thus, the decisions taken under the appropriate human rights conventions would generally be helpful in demonstrating how the rule might be implemented in the area of diplomatic protection, where, of course, fewer conflicts have arisen.

There have been some general statements relating to the extent of the resort to local remedies that is necessary. For example, the 1956 Granada resolution of the Institut de Droit International states that:

Lorsqu'un Etat prétend que la lésion subie par un de ses ressortissants dans sa personne ou dans ses biens a été commise en violation du droit international, toute réclamation diplomatique ou judiciaire lui appartenant de ce chef est irrecevable, s'il existe dans l'ordre juridique interne de l'Etat contre lequel la prétention est élevée des voies de recours accessibles à la personne lésée et qui, vraisemblablement, sont efficaces et suffisantes, et tant que l'usage normal de ces voies n'a pas été épuisé.[2]

In *Nielsen* v. *Denmark*, the European Commission of Human Rights said that:

the rules governing the exhaustion of domestic remedies, as these are generally recognized today, in principle require that recourse should be had to all legal remedies available under the local law which are in principle capable of providing an effective and sufficient means of redressing the wrongs for which, on the international plane, the respondent State is alleged to be responsible.[3]

---

[2] 46 AIDI (1956) at p. 358. In the *Barcelona Traction Co. Case*, the Belgian government cited this resolution in its observations on the preliminary objections: ICJ Pleadings (1962–9), vol. 1, pp. 238–9. There are several codification drafts which incorporate the rule of local remedies. However, while some of these may refer to such concepts as availability and effectiveness, and incorporate some limitations on the rule, they are neither similar in their scope or intent, nor do they deal with the details of the scope of or limitations on the rule: see e.g. Annex 3 (Articles 4 and 9), Annex 6 (para. 3), Annex 8 (Article XII), Annex 9 (Article 8) and Annex 10 (Article 34) of García Amador, 'Report on International Responsibility', YBILC (1956), vol. 2, p. 173; Annex IV, Annex VII (Article 19), Annex VIII (Article 13), Annex X (Article 9), Annex XIV (Section VIII) and Annex XV (Section IX) of Ago, 'First Report on State Responsibility', YBILC (1969), vol. 2, p. 125; García Amador, Addendum (Article 13) to 'Sixth Report on International Responsibility', YBILC (1961), vol. 2, p. 46; Ago, 'Sixth Report on State Responsibility' (Article 22), YBILC (1977), vol. 2, Part I, p. 43. The commentaries to the last two documents referred to above have some discussion on the subject. The more recent draft Articles for the ILC by the rapporteur, Dugard, 'Third Report on Diplomatic Protection', UN Doc. A/CN.4/523 (2002), do not deal at all with the positive aspects of the scope of the rule of local remedies, as is done here, although they deal with limitations arising from undue delay (Article 14(e)) and denial of access (Article 14(f)), at pp. 35–8.

[3] Application No. 343/57, *Report of the Commission* (1961) at p. 37. See also e.g. *X* v. *Ireland*, Application No. 493/59, 7 *Collection* at pp. 94 and 96; and *Syndicat National de la Police Belge* v. *Belgium*, Application No. 4464/70, 39 *Collection* at p. 32.

These statements emphasize the requirements that (i) all remedies must be tested, provided (ii) they are available, (iii) they are sufficient and effective, and (iv) a normal use of such remedies is made. However, apart from questions which are raised concerning the meaning of availability and effectiveness, there may be issues to be confronted with regard to, for instance, how far remedies must be exhausted, who must exhaust them, what kind of remedies must be invoked and how such remedies must be used.

The requirement of availability of remedies

An aggrieved alien is bound only to exhaust those remedies that are available to him. The requirement thus postulated has been described in terms of accessibility. In the Belgian pleadings in the *Barcelona Traction Co. Case*, it was said that 'pour pouvoir entrer en ligne de compte dans la vérification de la conduite de la personne lésée, les recours doivent lui avoir été effectivement *accessible*'.[4] The requirement was explained as follows:

La première condition, à savoir l'*accessibilité* des recours envisagés . . . est dictée par le bon sens. Comme l'indique la sagesse populaire, 'à l'impossible nul n'est tenu'. Un recours inaccessible doit donc être assimilé à un recours inexistant et on ne pourra opposer à l'action d'un Etat l'inaction de son ressortissant lorsque celle-ci est due à une force majeure, *a fortiori* lorsque l'impossibilité a été due à l'attitude des autorités de l'État défendeur.[5]

In the oral argument, the Belgian government elaborated further:

L'accessibilité du recours, c'est la possibilité juridique et matérielle pour la victime d'y avoir recours. Ainsi un individu jeté en prison et mis au secret ne pourra pas se voir reprocher ultérieurement de ne pas avoir adressé à l'autorité compétente, dans le délai prescrit par la loi, les protestations que la loi mettait à sa disposition. Et dans l'affaire qui nous occupe, les sociétés filiales qui ont introduit diverses procédures contre le jugement de faillite, ne pourront pas se voir reprocher de ne pas les avoir poursuivies jusqu'à des décisions finales, alors que diverses manoeuvres, et notamment les substitutions d'avoués, les révocations

---

[4] ICJ Pleadings (1962–9), vol. 1, p. 218.

[5] *Ibid.*, at p. 219. Dugard, 'Third Report on Diplomatic Protection' (ILC), UN Doc. A/CN.4/523 (2002) at p. 38, includes a reference in Article 14(f) of his draft to the need for accessibility, but does not cite the *Barcelona Traction Co. Case* which discussed the views of governments. He bases his conclusion consequently on text writers and the law of human rights protection.

des avoués qu'ils avaient commis par d'autres avoués avec l'approbation des tribunaux, paralysaient complètement ces recours.[6]

As already seen, the European Commission of Human Rights has also referred to the requirement of availability or accessibility in *Nielsen* v. *Denmark* and other cases.

There has in fact been no serious doubt about this requirement, although it is not easy to find cases in which an international court or organ has held that remedies have not been available or accessible. There are, however, some cases in the area of human rights protection in which the concept of availability was invoked. In *Englert*,[7] for instance, the European Court of Human Rights held that no appeal was required because none was available. In *Schmidt*,[8] the Inter-American Commission on Human Rights held that, since the Supreme Court of the state had pronounced on the issue, the remedy of *amparo* was not available and need not have been tested. Thus, availability entailed not only that the remedy be accessible to the particular individual affected, if such remedy existed, but also that that remedy be available as a possible remedy in the specific context of the individual's case.

Ordinary and extraordinary remedies: the requirement of legal nature

There has been some discussion of the question of what remedies must be exhausted in order that the requirements of the rule be satisfied, particularly with respect to extraordinary remedies. The theory of the matter has not been paid much attention in the discussion in the past.

---

[6] ICJ Pleadings (1962–9), vol. 1, p. 602. It may be noted that the Belgian Government's interpretation of accessibility in regard to the case in hand was in dispute and was obviously contested by the Spanish Government.

[7] Case No. 9/1986/107/155 (1987), Judgment. In *Farrell* v. *UK*, Application No. 9013/80, 25 YBECHR (1982) p. 124, the requirement of availability was stressed by the European Commission of Human Rights.

[8] 6 HRLJ (1985) at p. 214. See also *Roach and Pinkerton*, 8 HRLJ (1987) p. 345 (IACHR). The UN Human Rights Committee (HRC) has held that a particular remedy or extraordinary remedies were not available in the case before it, because they were not applicable in the circumstances of the case: see e.g. Communication No. 8/1977, HRC *Selected Decisions* at p. 48; Communication No. 28/1978, *ibid.*, pp. 58 and 59; Communication No. 44/1979, *ibid.*, pp. 77 and 79; Communication No. 70/1980, *ibid.*, p. 131; and Communication No. 73/1980, *ibid.*, p. 134. In Communication No. 70/1980, the HRC held that the fact that the officially appointed defence counsel had not invoked the extraordinary remedies in question indicated that they were not available.

However, it is reasonably clear that in the past practice relating to diplomatic protection the rule has been applied generally to remedies of a judicial nature.[9] Indeed, in 1864 Phillimore in an opinion to the British Crown specifically defined the term local redress which he used as being redress 'through the courts of law'.[10]

It was usual to include remedies available through special courts, provided they were legally constituted, in the concept of 'judicial remedies'. Thus, the US Court of Claims,[11] a Consultative Claims Commission set up by the Mexican Government in 1911,[12] and a Claims Commission set up by the Nicaraguan Government in 1911,[13] have been asserted in diplomatic correspondence to be courts for the purposes of the rule of local remedies. In the case of the Consultative Claims Commission of the Mexican Government, the decree provided that the Commission was to decide 'with reference to the legal foundation or non-foundation of said claims, and upon the amount of the indemnity, if any, to which claimants may be entitled'.[14] It would seem that remedies which could lead to reparation according to rules of law are included among those to be exhausted. For example, resort to a Cour de Cassation with the object of having a claim reconsidered,[15] a recourse to the Quartermaster-General for compensation upon the requisition of goods,[16] an action against judges,[17] a recourse having as its object a declaration that an injurious act and its consequences were unconstitutional,[18] resort to a *recours en requête civile* in order to reopen a process which had ended

---

[9] For decisions, see e.g. *Mavrommatis Palestine Concessions Case*, PCIJ Series A No. 5 (1925); the *German Interests in Upper Silesia Case*, PCIJ Series A No. 6 (1925); the *Chorzów Factory Case*, PCIJ Series A No. 9 (1927); the *Phosphates in Morocco Case*, PCIJ Series A/B No. 74 (1938); the *Panavezys–Saldutiskis Railway Case*, PCIJ Series A/B No. 76 (1939); the *Electricity Co. of Sofia Case*, PCIJ Series A/B No. 77 (1939); the *Norwegian Loans Case*, 1957 ICJ Reports p. 14; the *Interhandel Case*, 1959 ICJ Reports p. 11; the *Finnish Ships Arbitration* (Finland v. Great Britain), 3 UNRIAA p. 1479 (1934); the *Ambatielos Claim* (Greece v. UK), 12 UNRIAA p. 83 (1956); and other cases cited in de La Pradelle-Politis, RAI, vol. 1, pp. 24, 48, 131, 138, 161, 460, 474, 476, 582 and 592; vol. 2, pp. 103, 112, 121, 275, 291, 294, 486, 487, 594, 673, 674 and 710; and vol. 3, pp. 116, 121 and 123. There are also some cases in Moore, *International Arbitrations* (1898) and the UNRIAA series. For some diplomatic practice, see e.g. Moore, *International Law* (1906), vol. 6, pp. 656ff.; Hackworth, *Digest* (1943), vol. 5, pp. 501ff.; and McNair, *International Law Opinions* (1956), vol. 2, pp. 312ff.

[10] McNair, *International Law Opinions* (1956), vol. 2, p. 312.

[11] Moore, *International Law* (1906), vol. 6, p. 676.

[12] Hackworth, *Digest* (1943), vol. 5, p. 506.

[13] *Ibid.*, p. 508.   [14] *Ibid.*, p. 506.

[15] *Electricity Co. of Sofia Case*, PCIJ Series A/B No. 77 (1939).

[16] *Braithwaite Case*, de La Pradelle-Politis, RAI, vol. 3, p. 116.

[17] *Yuille, Shortridge & Co. Case*, de La Pradelle-Politis, RAI, vol. 2, p. 103.

[18] *Pacific Mail Steamship Case*, de La Pradelle-Politis, RAI, vol. 2, p. 476.

in a judgment on appeal,[19] invocation of a *pourvoi en révision* in respect of a special jurisdiction,[20] and passive participation in a procedure for securing reliable evidence,[21] have been held to be remedies that should have been exhausted.

In principle courts have certainly been included in the concept of local remedies, even in the decisions of international tribunals. Thus, in the *Croft Case*,[22] a special court which had jurisdiction over the cancellation of patent rights was held to be a local remedy to which the aggrieved alien should have had resort. Remedies available through a special system of administrative courts are also to be characterized as exhaustible remedies. Thus, in the *Phosphates in Morocco Case*, the French Government contended that local remedies had not been exhausted because it was open to the Italian company 'to have recourse to the civil courts of the Protectorate adjudicating upon administrative questions', and such means of redress had not been exhausted or even tried.[23] The Italian Government did not in its reply contest the French contention on the ground that the administrative courts could not be called 'recours internes', but chose to oppose it on the basis that the remedies available were not effective remedies,[24] thus virtually conceding that administrative courts are local remedies. Although the point was not decided by the PCIJ, the case bears evidence to the agreed practice of states. The fact that resort has already been had to the same courts before would not seem to matter, even if the legal means available are in reality extraordinary ones, provided a legal remedy might be available.[25] In the *Ambatielos Claim*, the tribunal put the matter succinctly by characterizing the remedies to be exhausted as 'legal' when it said: 'It is the whole system of legal protection, as provided by municipal law, which must have been put to the test.'[26]

Text writers generally discuss the rule on the assumption that it is limited to remedies of a judicial or legal nature.[27] Codification drafts of

---

[19] *Salem Case (United States v. Egypt)*, 2 UNRIAA p. 1161 (1932); the separate opinion of Judge Lauterpacht in the *Norwegian Loans Case*, 1957 ICJ Reports at p. 39.
[20] *Yuille, Shortridge & Co. Case*, de La Pradelle-Politis, RAI, vol. 2, p. 103.
[21] *R.T. Roy Case (United States v. Great Britain)*, 6 UNRIAA p. 147 (1925).
[22] *Great Britain v. Portugal* (1856), 50 BFSP (1859–60) p. 1288.
[23] PCIJ Series A/B No. 74 at p. 17 (1938); and the French pleadings in PCIJ Series C No. 84 at pp. 209ff.
[24] PCIJ Series C No. 84 at pp. 439ff.
[25] See the *Interhandel Case*, 1959 ICJ Reports at p. 27.
[26] *Greece v. UK*, 12 UNRIAA at p. 120 (1956).
[27] See e.g. Anzilotti, 'La Responsabilité internationale des états à raison des dommages soufferts par des étrangers', 13 RGDIP (1906) at p. 8; Borchard, *The Diplomatic Protection*

an official nature clearly make the same assumption in general.[28] García Amador's draft is an exception in that it refers to 'all the remedies and proceedings established by municipal law'.[29]

Private bodies have not been so specific in their formulations.[30] Thus, the Institut de Droit International stated in 1927 that '[n]o demand for reparation can be brought through diplomatic channels of a state so long as the wronged individual has at his disposal effective and sufficient means to obtain for him the treatment due to him'.[31] The Harvard Draft of 1961 speaks in Article 19 of 'all administrative, arbitral or judicial remedies'.[32] In the explanatory comment it is stated that: 'By administrative remedies are meant all those remedies which are available through the executive branch of the government, as well as special remedies which may be provided by legislative action if claims are routinely handled through private bills for relief.'[33] There would seem to be some evidence in these exceptional examples that remedies other than those of an essentially judicial nature are contemplated.

Some support is given for this view by a statement made by the PCIJ in the *Phosphates in Morocco Case* to the effect that a failure of local remedies might result 'either from a lacuna in the judicial organization

---

of Citizens Abroad (1916) p. 381; Ralston, *The Law and Procedure of International Tribunals* (1926) p. 95; Eagleton, *The Responsibility of States in International Law* (1929) p. 95; Eagleton, 'Une théorie au sujet du commencement de la responsabilité de l'état', 11 RDILC (1930) p. 643; Hoijer, *La Responsabilité internationale des états* (1930) p. 374; Borchard, in 38 AIDI (1931-I) at p. 424; Dunn, *The Protection of Nationals* (1932) p. 156; Witenberg, 'La Recevabilité des réclamations devant les juridictions internationales', 41 *Hague Recueil* (1932) at p. 50; H. Friedmann, 'Epuisement des voies de recours internes', 14 RDILC (1933) p. 318; Ténékidès, 'L'épuisement des voies de recours internes comme condition préalable de l'instance internationale', 14 RDILC (1933) p. 514; Fachiri, 'The Local Remedies Rule in the Light of the Finnish Ships Arbitration', 17 BYIL (1936) p. 19; Ago, 'La Regola del Previo Esaurimento dei Ricorsi Interni in Tema di Responsabilità Internazionale', 3 ArchivDP (1938) p. 181; Freeman, *The International Responsibility of States for Denial of Justice* (1937) pp. 407 and 422; Fawcett, 'The Exhaustion of Local Remedies: Substance or Procedure?', 31 BYIL (1954) p. 452; Verzijl, in 45 AIDI (1954-I) at pp. 5, 84 and in 46 AIDI (1956) at pp. 13ff.; C. de Visscher, 'Le Déni de justice en droit international', 52 *Hague Recueil* (1935) at pp. 421ff.; Shea, *The Calvo Clause* (1955); Bagge, 'Intervention on the Ground of Damage Caused to Nationals, with Particular Reference to Exhaustion of Local Remedies and the Rights of Shareholders', 34 BYIL (1958) p. 162; Law, *The Local Remedies Rule in International Law* (1961); Mummery, 'The Content of the Duty to Exhaust Local Judicial Remedies', 58 AJIL (1964) p. 389; Haesler, *The Exhaustion of Local Remedies in the Case Law of International Courts and Tribunals* (1968) pp. 28ff.; and Cançado Trindade, *The Application of the Rule of Exhaustion of Local Remedies in International Law* (1983) p. 58.

[28] See YBILC (1956), vol. 2, pp. 221ff.   [29] Article 18, YBILC (1961), vol. 2, p. 48.

[30] YBILC (1956), vol. 2, pp. 227ff.   [31] *Ibid.*, p. 288.   [32] 55 AJIL (1961) at p. 577.

[33] Sohn and Baxter, *Convention on the International Responsibility of States for Injuries to Aliens* (1961) p. 164.

or from the refusal of administrative or extraordinary methods of redress designed to supplement its deficiencies'.[34] Nowhere, in that case,
however, did the parties refer to any remedies except judicial remedies,
which were available through administrative courts. Hence, the statement could consistently be interpreted to cover only 'administrative or
extraordinary methods of redress' of an essentially judicial nature.

An opinion given in 1866 by Jenkins lays emphasis on judicial proceedings but goes on to state that, in the case of a grant of reprisals, it
is necessary that 'all the Instances, first in the Courts of Judicature from
the lowest to the highest, afterwards *with the Prince himself*, have been attempted and pursued without Success or Effect'.[35] This statement seems
to imply that the alien not only must submit to judicial procedures but
must also seek other remedies of a non-judicial nature which do not give
him the assurance of a settlement of his claim on the basis of his strict
legal rights. Apart from the fact that this is a very old precedent, which
in any case stresses the judicial nature of remedies in the earlier part of
the passage, it may be relevant that it refers to the practice of reprisals
and not to that of diplomatic protection proper. That an act of grace
does not come under the concept of remedies to be exhausted seems to
be implied in the reference elsewhere to legal means of redress. Thus,
remedies which would result in a non-binding recommendation given
by the deciding body to an executive organ of the host or respondent
state seem to be excluded from those which must be exhausted.[36]

More recently in the arguments in the *Barcelona Traction Co. Case* some
views were expressed by the contending states on the issue of ordinary
and extraordinary remedies. The Spanish government in its preliminary
objections stressed that, in line with the *dictum* in the *Ambatielos Claim*, it
was the whole system of legal protection (*tout le système*) afforded by the
respondent state that had to be tested.[37] In the case there were certain
remedies arguably involved which may be described as extraordinary
(*recours extraordinaires*). One was the action which could be brought
against a corrupt judge in the event that he was fraudulent in giving a
decision. The second was contentious administrative proceedings in respect of administrative decisions taken by an executive organ, beginning

---

[34] PCIJ Series A/B No. 74 at p. 28 (1938).

[35] McNair, *International Law Opinions* (1956), vol. 2, p. 312.

[36] See the *Neptune's Case* (1797), where an opinion given by the House of Lords to the
British government would not have been binding: Moore, *International Arbitrations*
(1898), vol. 3, p. 3043.

[37] ICJ Pleadings (1962–9), vol. 4, pp. 592–3.

with a hierarchical appeal to the Minister and followed by recourse to the administrative courts. The Spanish argument was emphatic that the first remedy should have been exhausted because it fell within the category of exhaustible remedies:

> Si, par example, un Etat prétend porter une action sur le plan international en raison d'un prétendu déni de justice résultant de la fraude d'un juge interne, il a le devoir de s'assurer au préalable que le particulier, au profit duquel il entend agir, a réellement épuisé les moyens extraordinaires de recours éventuellement prévus dans le système juridique de l'Etat défendeur justement pour l'hypothèse de la fraude d'un juge.[38]

As regards the contentious administrative proceedings, the Spanish government was of the view that these were certainly included as the kind of remedies to be exhausted, although they were extraordinary:

> Le Gouvernement espagnol est donc en droit d'opposer à nouveau l'exception fondée sur la non-utilisation des recours administratifs, et ce exactement dans la même mesure où le Gouvernement belge prétend voir un déni de justice dans les décisions de l'I.E.M.E. Plus particulièrement, l'exception soulevée par le Gouvernement espagnol vise la non-utilisation, dans le cas d'espèce, du *recours hiérarchique* et du *recours contentieux administrative*.[39]

The Belgian government did not dispute the principle enunciated in the Spanish government's argument relating to contentious administrative proceedings but chose to contend that such proceedings would not have been effective in the circumstances because they could not rectify the exercise of discretion by the Minister.[40] Thus there seems to have been agreement on the principle that the extraordinary remedy of contentious administrative proceedings including a hierarchical appeal was not excluded per se from those remedies that had to be exhausted by virtue of its character. In regard to the extraordinary remedy by way of action against a corrupt judge, on the other hand, the Belgian Government objected that this was not a normal case of remedies, although it could have resulted in the overturning of the decision of the judge in question. It was stated that:

---

[38] 'Exceptions préliminaires présentées par le Gouvernement espagnol', ICJ Pleadings (1962–9), vol. 1, p. 242. The Spanish government also referred to the remedy by way of revision of the bankruptcy judgment, which, it argued, although extraordinary, should have been exhausted: ICJ Pleadings (1962–9), vol. 9, p. 923.

[39] ICJ Pleadings (1962–9), vol. 1, p. 242.

[40] 'Observations et conclusions du Gouvernement belge', ICJ Pleadings (1962–9), vol. 1, pp. 267–8.

On peut notamment considérer comme un effet du catactère normal des recours requis, en même temps que de leur efficacité, la dispense très généralement admise d'utiliser les *recours exceptionnels*, tels que l'action en dommages-intérêts contre le magistrat par une prise ou la requête civile.[41]

The Belgian argument concerning the action against a corrupt judge seems to be based on the idea that exceptional recourse is not as such included in the concept of the remedies to be exhausted, rather than that it was not to be expected that the remedy would be invoked because it was not reasonable to demand this of the aggrieved aliens. Thus, here there is an element of disagreement on the character of the remedy that must be exhausted.

Generally, except for a few broad statements, particularly in some codification drafts, the tendency has been to accept some limitations on the nature of the remedy to which resort must be had. The broad definition given in the explanatory comment to the 1961 Harvard Draft seems, therefore, to be unacceptable. The question to be answered relates to the extent of the limitations. Even if the notion of 'l'usage normal', which is reflected in the resolution of the Institut de Droit International, is regarded as the source of some limitations, the Belgian argument in the *Barcelona Traction Co. Case* may seem to go too far. It is interesting to note that most descriptions refer to the exhaustion of legal or judicial remedies as being required, which means that the better view is that only those remedies which are of a judicial or quasi-judicial character must be exhausted, although they may not be confined to those provided by the regular courts of law.

The rationale for the applicable principle in regard to the nature of remedies

In principle it would appear that the policies behind the rule of local remedies would not warrant an unlimited extension of the concept of remedies to all types of remedies. Although the respondent state is given an opportunity of redressing a wrong, it is also relevant that for social ends the alien is being prevented from obtaining direct and less expensive justice from an international tribunal. It would be proper, then, that he should be compelled to use only those means by which he has an opportunity to obtain justice according to law. What international law is interested in is the determination according to law, in an impartial manner, of the alien's rights. Hence, the emphasis on the judicial

---

[41] *Ibid.*, p. 221.

or quasi-judicial nature or remedies cannot be out of place. It would be improper to insist on his seeking remedies from sources which do not operate impartially and have no obligation to decide according to legal principles. Thus, to expect him to approach the administration or the legislature in the hope of having his problem solved as a result of the beneficence of either would be unreasonable. It would seem, therefore, that it is only where remedies enjoy a character which ensures impartial determination of disputes, according to law and not purely by uncontrolled discretion, that the alien must resort to them. This is the test that must be applied to determine the exhaustibility of remedies outside the normal judicial sphere. Thus, administrative tribunals and the like may fall within the category of exhaustible remedies if they share the required character and, particularly, if they are subject to control by the ordinary courts, since this ensures impartiality and determination according to law.

A distinction must, of course, be made between the method of deciding the dispute and the procedure for implementing the decision. It is only the former that is of relevance here. The fact that the implementation of a decision is at the discretion of the respondent state would not affect the position, since this lies within the sovereign powers of the state and a truly judicial determination may in any case be disregarded. The respondent state has a right to determine the alien's right in the proper way, and whatever the subsequent attitude it may adopt towards fulfilling its secondary obligation of reparation, this fact should not affect the classification of a remedy in such a way that it is incumbent upon the alien to resort to it.

That the remedy of a judicial or quasi-judicial nature may not be exhaustible, because it is not adequate and effective is also a different question. It does not affect the issue of whether a remedy falls within the category of remedies which are required to be exhausted. Thus, however effective an uncontrolled and purely discretionary remedy may appear to be because of the particular circumstances of a respondent state or its record of decision-making in similar cases, although this situation is very rarely likely to arise, such a remedy is not subject to exhaustion. Hence, the distinction between legal or judicial and quasi-judicial remedies and those that are not so may be a useful one.

The requirement of adequate and effective remedies

As already seen, the 1956 resolution of the Institut de Droit International referred to the need for exhaustible remedies to be 'efficaces et suffisants'. In a related sense the arbitral commission in the *Ambatielos Claim* referred to the 'essentialness' of remedies[42] even though in that case only procedural remedies were involved. In *Austria* v. *Italy*, the EComHR stated that only a failure to resort to an 'essential' recourse for establishing the merits of a case before the municipal tribunals could lead to the inadmissibility of the claim before an international forum.[43] The notion of 'essentialness' was later explained further as being based on the criterion of whether 'le recours effectivement exercé' enabled the local courts to redress the wrong in the complaint.[44]

In a sense this requirement of adequacy and effectiveness is related to the limitation or exception which operates to make the rule inapplicable and is based on the obvious futility or ineffectiveness of the remedy. Thus, in so far as the limitation is discussed in detail in Chapter 8, what is meant by obvious futility or ineffectiveness will not necessarily be examined here. It is proposed here to investigate generally how international practice has approached the issue of whether a remedy is adequate and effective so as to be exhaustible. In this context, it may also be noted that the question of procedural remedies in the same court has been left for later consideration in Chapter 9, because it is a complicated subject and calls for treatment on its own.

The precedents on the issue of adequacy and effectiveness in the law of diplomatic protection are sparse. In general they have tended to deal with the issue as one concerning the exception to the application of the rule. However, in the pleadings and oral arguments in the *Barcelona Traction Co. Case*, some views were exchanged which may shed light on the nature of the requirement of effectiveness. The contention of the Spanish Government was that, among other things, local remedies had not been exhausted, because resort had not been had to some effective remedies, even though some hundreds of cases had been filed. The Spanish Government conceded that not all remedies, including extraordinary ones, had to be exhausted, but only those which were effective and had some prospect of success. Nevertheless, it argued that, where there was doubt as to whether a given remedy could offer a chance of success, that point should be submitted to the local courts without an assumption being made that the remedy was ineffective, and that consequently two remedies in particular to which resort had not been had should have

---

[42] 12 UNRIAA at p. 120 (1956).

[43] Application No. 788/60, *Report of the Plenary Commission* at p. 57.

[44] *Boeckmans* v. *Belgium*, Application No. 1727/62, 12 *Collection* at p. 47; *Kaiser* v. *Austria*, Application No. 4459/70, 38 *Collection* at p. 55.

been invoked, namely, a timely opposition to the bankruptcy judgment and a request for revision of the judgment within a period of five years, the fact that so many remedies had been sought being irrelevant.[45]

The Belgian Government did not dispute the requirement that any effective remedy must be invoked in stating in its observations on the preliminary objections that effectiveness 'exige de plus que le recours soit susceptible d'apporter la satisfaction cherchée en arrêtant l'action dommageable en cours, ou en effaçant les effets, ou en procurant aux victimes une réparation équitable'.[46] Having generally defined efficacy thus, the Belgian Government in the oral argument illustrated the point as follows:

Quant à l'efficacité que doit revêtir un recours pour être obligatoire, elle doit s'apprécier nécessairement à la fois en fonction du grief que l'on fait valoir, de l'injustice que l'on dénonce et de l'objet que l'on désire atteindre. Ainsi, un condamné à mort ne sera pas tenu à se pourvoir en cassation pour faire valoir l'irrégularité de sa condamnation, si ce pourvoi en cassation n'est pas suspensif de l'exécution et compromet les chances de succès d'un recours en grâce; et si le recours en grâce est rejeté, le défaut de pourvoi ne pourra pas dans ces conditions être reproché à ses ayants-droit lorsqu'ils introduiront une réclamation.[47]

However, the Belgian government did not agree with the Spanish argument that where there was a lack of precedent the courts had to be resorted to because the remedy could not be described as ineffective or without object. There was an inclination on the part of the Belgian government towards the view that in such a case the test of efficacy depended on the expressions of opinion by commentators on the law. General agreement among them that the remedy did not exist would support the ineffectiveness of the recourse.[48]

The views of the parties do not conflict on the requirement of efficacy or its interpretation except with regard to whether in the absence of judicial precedent a remedy could be described as ineffective. In this respect, as will be seen later in Chapter 8, the better view seems to be that of the Spanish government. The general principle that a remedy must be resorted to, if it could achieve the object desired by the claimant, was agreed upon and is the accepted view.

---

[45] ICJ Pleadings (1962–9), vol. 1, p. 256, ICJ Pleadings (1962–9), vol. 3, p. 814, ICJ Pleadings (1962–9), vol. 9, pp. 593 and 609.
[46] ICJ Pleadings (1962–9), vol. 1, p. 220.   [47] ICJ Pleadings (1962–9), vol. 3, p. 602.
[48] ICJ Pleadings (1962–9), vol. 8, pp. 577–8.

There is general agreement in the field of diplomatic protection, it would appear, that local remedies must be exhausted when they are adequate for the object sought or effective. The precedents also show that there seems to be no serious dispute on the interpretation of these concepts, at least in a positive sense. The problems really arise when an exception is sought to the application of the rule on the ground that a remedy is ineffective. This is an aspect which will be considered in the next chapter.

The concept of normal use

As already seen, the 1956 resolution of the Institut de Droit International refers to 'l'usage normal' as being a relevant consideration to the implementation of the rule of local remedies. In the discussion of this resolution at the Institut, Bourquin stated that 'pour apprécier quels sont les recours que le ressortissant doit épuiser, il faut tenir compte de ce que ferait un plaideur normal ayant le souci de défendre ses intérêts'.[49] Guggenheim, referring specifically to the question of time limits imposed by the municipal law in connection with proceedings, thought that there was room for doubt whether there could be an absolute requirement that these be observed, while it was also necessary to recognize that these could not be lightly avoided without giving the injured individual a certain discretion in the pursuit of remedies. He explained that:

En revanche, une solution que permettrait de faire valoir la responsabilité internationale, sans tenir compte des démarches enterprises en vue d'épuiser les instances internes et prescrites au moment de l'invocation de la responsabilité internationale, arriverait à conférer au recours aux instances internes un caractère facultatif, peu compatible avec la substance et le but de la règle telle qu'elle est reconnue par le droit international coutumier. Je pense donc que le juge international, lorsqu'il aura à apprécier l'absence de recours ou de la poursuite de recours ainsi que les conséquences qu'il doit en tirer, appréciera librement les raisons pour lesquelles le recours n'a pas été intenté ou poursuivi; et il examinera en outre la question s'il y a lieu de retenir à la charge de l'Etat, de l'individu ou de la personne morale de droit interne un manque de diligence.[50]

There is also some evidence in early diplomatic practice that the idea of due diligence on the part of the injured individual had been introduced. Thus, a US Assistant Secretary of State said in 1873 that the US would

---

[49] AIDI (1954-1) at p. 61.   [50] AIDI (1956) at pp. 36–7.

not intervene on behalf of one of its nationals unless he had exhausted all recourse to the domestic courts 'with due diligence'.[51]

The Belgian government in the *Barcelona Traction Co. Case* argued that the requirement of normal usage operated in favour of the alien so as to modify somewhat the rigidity of the local remedies rule. As a result, the alien was exempt from using such extraordinary remedies, for instance, as were hardly ever used by litigants, since it was necessary to take into account not only the likelihood of success of the remedies but also the particular circumstances of each case, including the number of efforts made by the litigants in the past and the total lack of success with which such efforts were met.[52] The Spanish government's approach showed a clear disagreement on the meaning of 'normal use'. While conceding implicitly that the concept was relevant,[53] it was argued that it merely meant that the injured alien's company, such as it was, should have seen to it that the actions required of it by the domestic law were taken. The Spanish government argued in its counter-memorial:

En d'autres termes, lorsqu'une règle juridique donnée fait appel à la notion de diligence par l'intermédiaire de certaines expressions typiques – telles que *l'usage normal* des recours et voies internes – il y a là un moyen de contrôle du comportement de certaines personnes physiques ou morales qui se rattache à la façon d'accomplir *une obligation donnée*, et non pas une *obligation quelconque*. C'est donc par rapport à la fonction qu'une telle obligation est appelée à exercer dans le cadre d'un système juridique que la notion de diligence doit être déterminée et que le degré de cette diligence doit être établi. Le recours à des formules stéréotypées, telles que le 'bon père de famille', ne saurait, sans référence aux situations concrètes, donner sa portée exacte au critère de la diligence, tel qu'il a été précisé par la science juridique actuelle surtout dans le domaine des obligations et notamment dans celui de la responsabilité. Or, il s'agit ici de juger la conduite d'un particulier – en l'espèce, une personne morale, une grande société – dont le Gouvernement belge n'a pas manqué de proclamer la haute qualité des administrateurs, alors que dans le cadre de l'exception ici visée il s'efforce, non sans peine, de la présenter comme une société de type patriarcal. D'un groupe de sociétés tel que celui de la Barcelona Traction l'on est en droit d'attendre que sa conduite au cours des procédures internes soit celle d'un plaideur possédant tous les moyens d'assistance technique devant lui permettre de se conformer strictement aux conditions exigées par la loi. Les choses se sont pourtant passées fort

---

[51] *A Digest of the International Law of the United States* (1886), vol. 2, p. 679.

[52] See 'Observations et conclusions du Gouvernement belge', ICJ Pleadings (1962–9), vol. 1, pp. 221–2; and ICJ Pleadings (1962–9), vol. 3, p. 603.

[53] See 'Exceptions préliminaires présentées par le Gouvernement espagnol', ICJ Pleadings (1962–9), vol. 1, pp. 239ff.

différemment, ce qui implique que *sciemment*, on a préféré s'écarter des dispositions légales en vigueur et que l'on ne saurait dès lors échapper aux inéluctables conséquences d'une telle conduite.[54]

There are some decided cases in which it has been stated that the duty to exhaust local remedies must be 'comprise d'une manière raisonable'.[55] As a result, in the *Eliza Case*,[56] where a marshal in Peru was induced by a third party not to proceed to execution of a judgment against a public organization, the Claims Commission held that the alien, a US national, did not need to have recourse against the marshal by way of exhausting local remedies before seeking diplomatic protection, because that recourse would have deferred the justice already done to the alien in an undue manner. Whether the words used are 'normal use', 'reasonable manner' or 'equity' or the like, it would seem that there is some evidence that equitable considerations have sometimes been referred to in the cases that have been decided. But in all the cases concerned, the implication of equity as a modifying influence on a rigid interpretation of the rule of local remedies has been dependent on the express terms of the conventions or *compromis* under which the disputes were submitted to international arbitration.[57] It is, therefore, questionable whether in these cases equity or reasonableness was applied as a modifying influence in the application of the rule which was inherent in the customary international law.

These authorities reveal that there is no unequivocal judicial precedent or practice which warrants the conclusion that an alien may avoid resorting to remedies which would otherwise be covered by the rule of local remedies, because normal practice or use would justify such omission. On the contrary, there is support for the interpretation that 'normal use' refers merely to the obligations of the alien to fulfil the requirements of the local law with respect to such matters as time limits and capacity. The examples of a dilution of the rigidity of the rule

---

[54] ICJ Pleadings (1962–9), vol. 4, pp. 588–9.

[55] The *Eliza Case* (*United States* v. *Peru*) (1863), de La Pradelle-Politis, RAI, vol. 2, p. 275.

[56] *United States* v. *Peru* (1863), de La Pradelle-Politis, RAI, vol. 2, p. 271.

[57] See the *Eliza Case* referred to above in note 55; the *Robert E. Brown Case* (*United States* v. *Great Britain*), 6 UNRIAA at p. 129 (1923); the *Georges Pinson Case* (*France* v. *Mexico*), 5 UNRIAA at p. 351 (1928); the *R.T. Roy Case* (*United States* v. *Great Britain*), 6 UNRIAA at p. 149 (1925); the *David Adams Case* (*United States* v. *Great Britain*), 6 UNRIAA p. 93 (1921); and the *Salem Case* (*United States* v. *Egypt*), 2 UNRIAA at p. 1190 (1932). For some of the *compromis* or conventions concerned, see the Special Agreement of 1910 between United States and Great Britain, Article III, and the Claims Conventions of 1924 between Mexico and France, Article VI(1). See also Haesler, note 27 above, at pp. 31ff.

relate mainly to situations in which there were special provisions in arbitral agreements or *compromis*. There are a few expressions of opinion in state practice and by textual authorities which incorporate a different approach to the problem. It has also sometimes been said by judicial authority that the rule of local remedies is 'not a purely technical or rigid rule'[58] or 'a rule of thumb to be applied in a more or less automatic fashion',[59] but these statements were not intended to introduce equitable or other considerations as such into the application of the rule, given the already established parameters and exceptions to the rule, so as to make it possible for an alien or an individual to avoid the application of the rule by permitting a reference to a liberalizing concept of 'normal use' or reasonableness. Thus, since the internal evidence for the rule, and particularly judicial precedent, do not support the sporadic state practice and textual authorities which take a different approach, these must be discounted. Therefore, it may be true to say that the local remedies rule itself does not contain a feature of its own resulting in a modified application of the rule by reference to such concepts as equity, 'normal use' or reasonableness.[60]

The raising of substantive issues

In the *Finnish Ships Arbitration*, it was held that the individual need only raise in local proceedings the arguments which he raises in international proceedings.[61] He is not expected to raise such arguments in the local courts as the defendant state claims would have given him redress, nor is he bound to raise these in international proceedings. The individual may formulate his case as he thinks fit, but, of course, he will not succeed on

---

[58] Judge Lauterpacht in his dissenting opinion in the *Norwegian Loans Case*, 1957 ICJ Reports at p. 39.

[59] Judge Hudson in his dissenting opinion in the *Panavezys–Saldutiskis Railway Case*, PCIJ Series A/B No. 76 at p. 48 (1939).

[60] See also Haesler note 27 above, at pp. 36–7. In the *Elettronica Sicula SpA (ELSI) Case*, a Chamber of the ICJ held that the respondent had failed to prove that there existed a remedy which the aliens had not exhausted, because the remedy alleged not to have been resorted to was clearly not one which would have resulted in success for them: 1989 ICJ Reports at pp. 46–7. The finding that the remedy in question need not have been used was not based on a concept of 'reasonable use' which would have exempted the aliens from resorting to a viable remedy on the grounds of equity.

[61] *Finland* v. *UK*, 3 UNRIAA at p. 1502 (1934), when it was said that 'all the contentions of fact and propositions of law which are brought forward by the claimant government . . . must have been investigated and adjudicated upon by the municipal courts'. See also the *Ambatielos Claim* (*Greece* v. *UK*), 12 UNRIAA at p. 123 (1956).

his substantive formulation at an international level unless it discloses a cause of action according to international law. Thus, exhaustion of local remedies in connection with arguments of substance is related to the cause of action at international law and not concerned with any special or other feature of the local system of remedies. It is a natural corollary of the above principle that the individual must raise at the local level any arguments which he raises at an international level. In this area exhaustion takes place in relation to substantive arguments, the arguments covering contentions of fact, propositions of law, pleas and claims.

In the recently decided *Elettronica Sicula SpA (ELSI) Case*, a Chamber of the ICJ took a similar view of the law. It was held there that remedies had been adequately exhausted, even though specific issues had not been raised in the particular form in which they were raised in the international proceeding. Court said:

> It is thus apparent that the substance of the claim brought to the adjudication of the Italian courts is essentially the claim which the United States now brings before this Chamber. The arguments were different, because the municipal court was applying Italian law, whereas this Chamber applies international law; and, of course, the parties were different. Yet it would seem that the municipal courts had been fully seized of the matter which is the substance of the Applicant's claim before the Chamber. For both claims turn on the allegation that the requisition, by frustrating the orderly liquidation, triggered the bankruptcy, and so caused the alleged losses.[62]

Thus, it was not a defect that arguments had not been raised in a particular form which the respondent government alleged was likely to have had a greater likelihood of success, and particularly that a reference to the violation of the treaty which was the basis of the international proceeding had not been made in the local court.

The position taken in the *Finnish Ships Arbitration* is still reflective of the law both as regards the need to raise in local proceedings those matters raised in the international proceedings, and in respect of the converse principle that the applicant need only raise in the local proceedings those matters which he raises before the international forum. However, as will be seen in Chapter 13, that position has been clarified by the jurisprudence of the European Commission of Human Rights, in so far as it has been made clear that matters raised before the international forum must only be raised in substance and not necessarily in corresponding form before the local instances.

---

[62] 1989 ICJ Reports at pp. 45–6.

Persons obligated to observe the rule

The issue may arise, particularly where legal persons are involved in a dispute, as to who must exhaust remedies for the purposes of the rule of local remedies. In 1958, Bagge expressed the view that: 'The international claim against the defendant State based on the damage caused to the shareholder is receivable without regard to the exhaustion of local remedies by the shareholder himself as there are no such remedies open to a shareholder.'[63] While this statement does not deny that, if the shareholder has remedies to exhaust in such a situation, he must exhaust them, it does take the view that the shareholder does not have to exhaust remedies, for instance through a bankrupt company or through some other relevant person.

Although, according to a realistic interpretation of the rule of local remedies, it is clear that, wherever possible, the person on whose behalf an international claim is being made must exhaust available, effective and adequate remedies, there is some question as to what the position is in the case of legal persons, particularly when claims are made on behalf of shareholders of corporations. In the *Barcelona Traction Co. Case*, the Spanish government made the objection that the shareholders on whose behalf a claim was being made by the Belgian government should themselves have exhausted remedies which were available to them, which they had not done, irrespective of the remedies exhausted by the bankrupt company or other persons.[64] The Belgian government contended that the shareholders had remedies to exhaust but had done what they should and could through remedies activated by the bankrupt company and that this was a requirement of the rule of local remedies.[65]

The Spanish government's view of the law cannot be gainsaid, it being a question of fact whether there actually were remedies for the shareholders to exhaust. On the other hand, the Belgian government, while disagreeing on this issue of fact, introduced the principle that, in an appropriate situation, a legal person A may be under an obligation to exhaust remedies in order to enable B who is connected with A successfully to invoke diplomatic protection. The issue has not been faced in any judicial decisions, but there is some value in the legal argument submitted by the Belgian government, which was not really contested by the other party to the litigation.

---

[63] Bagge, note 27 above, at p. 70.
[64] Counter-Memorial, ICJ Pleadings (1962–9), vol. 4, pp. 602–4; oral argument, ICJ Pleadings (1962–9), vol. 9, p. 563.
[65] Oral argument, ICJ Pleadings (1962–9), vol. 8, pp. 576–7.

In a complicated situation involving legal persons the degree of dependence and inextricable involvement among the persons concerned may warrant an interpretation of the rule of local remedies which requires some of those persons to exhaust remedies in order to protect others among them. Clearly, this is in the interests of giving the host or respondent state the opportunity of doing justice even in respect of the persons who cannot exhaust local remedies, have none to exhaust or who may have failed to secure redress by exhausting them. On the other hand, much will depend on the particular circumstances of a case, because this, being an extended interpretation of the rule, must not be permitted to cause an alien who is being protected undue hardship. It is, thus, a matter for assessment and determination in each case how the rule is to be applied when it is implemented in this extended manner.[66]

The need for a final decision

In the *Finnish Ships Arbitration*, the point was made that exhaustion of local remedies meant that there must be a final decision of a court which is the highest in the hierarchy of courts to which the injured alien can have resort in the legal system of the respondent or host state.[67] What this means in practice is that the alien must proceed to the highest court in the whole system, which may include more than one line of tribunals or courts where the legal system of the respondent or host state has a multiple hierarchy of fora which can provide redress. The principle has not been disputed.[68] As seen in the *Interhandel Case*,[69] the principle may involve doing more than having recourse in a hierarchical

---

[66] As the issue has not been discussed in any manner in the authorities, judicial or other, it is not intended to deal with it in detail here. What has been done is to provide some guidelines upon which the interpretation of the rule may be based.

[67] *Finland v. UK*, 3 UNRIAA at p. 1495ff. (1934).

[68] Where the alien is unable to have successful access to a higher court because of some failure on his part, such as non-observance of prescribed time limits, he has not exhausted remedies because he has not acted diligently and, therefore, has not made normal use of the local remedies: see above in this chapter. See further the *Electricity Company of Sofia Case*, PCIJ Series A/B No. 77 at pp. 74 and 78–9 (1939), Judge Anzilotti in a separate opinion, at pp. 96–7, Judge de Visscher in a separate opinion, at pp. 138–9, Judge Erlich in a separate opinion, at pp. 144–5, Judge Urrutia in a dissenting opinion, at p. 107, Judge Van Eysinga in a dissenting opinion, at pp. 114–15, and Judge Hudson in a dissenting opinion, at p. 135; and the argument in PCIJ Series C (1939) No. 88 at pp. 393, 427–9 and 432–3; the *C.G. Pirocaco Case* (*United States* v. *Turkey*) (1923), Hackworth, *Digest* (1943), vol. 5, p. 502; and the *Salem Case* (*United States* v. *Egypt*), 2 UNRIAA at p. 1189 (1932).

[69] 1959 ICJ Reports p. 11.

order to the highest court of the respondent or host State. There the alien complainant had secured a judgment from the Supreme Court of the US, but the ICJ found that this was not a final judgment in the hierarchical order because the decision of the Supreme Court reopened the proceedings and sent the case back for further investigation. For this reason the ICJ held that at the time of invoking the international instance the alien had not completed the recourse to local remedies.[70] However, it may also be concluded that from the point of view of the rule of exhaustion of local remedies *per se*, the requirement is clear that an alien or individual needs and is required only to resort to the higher or last court from which he could have obtained an effective remedy.[71]

---

[70] As will be seen in Chapter 13, the European Court of Human Rights has developed considerably the law on this subject.

[71] This point will emerge better from the discussion in Chapter 13 on human rights protection and the application of the rule to domestic remedies.

8   Limitations on the rule

Respect for the sovereignty of the respondent or host state constitutes the foundation of the rule that local remedies must be exhausted. Recognition of other interests, such as those of the alien claimant in avoiding undue hardship and excessive expense in pursuing local remedies, has resulted in limitations being placed on or exceptions being made to the operation of the rule. In its positive form, the rule was not absolute and had certain parameters in so far as exhaustion was initially limited to remedies which were, for example, of a legal nature, available and effective. To some extent these positive requirements imply certain negative qualifications, for it is understood, as has been seen in the previous chapter, that remedies that are, for example, not of a judicial or quasi-judicial nature, not available or not effective do not come within the ambit of those remedies which need to be exhausted. In a sense, the negative requirements are the other side of the coin. The limitations, thus, directly resulting and such others as may have been placed on the rule flow primarily out of consideration for the interests of the alien claimant, but also because of the need to have justice dispensed efficiently and economically, which is an interest of the international community.

In any event, the limitation implied in the positive requirement of effectiveness, which means that those remedies which are ineffective or inadequate need not be exhausted, raises some issues of definition which have been addressed in the various sources of the law. While it may have been less difficult to identify remedies which are effective or adequate, and, therefore, need to be exhausted, and while in practice without too much difficulty it may have been possible to determine what remedies are ineffective or inadequate, because they are clearly so, the question remains what in law is meant by ineffectiveness and inadequacy of remedies for this purpose. Thus, this is one question which requires particular consideration and analysis.

As has been seen in Chapter 3, the interests of the alien claimant are an important consideration in deciding how the rule of local remedies is to be applied. These interests were noted in the *Finnish Ships Arbitration*,[1] particularly in regard to the setting of limits upon the rule. It was also pointed out by the arbitral commission in the *Ambatielos Claim* that the rule could not be strained too far, even though respect for the sovereignty of the respondent or host state required that the whole system of legal protection be tested and exhausted,[2] thus implicitly giving particular value to the interests of the alien claimant. However, identifying the limitations on the rule requires more than mere regard for such interests. The process demands reconciliation of the conflict between the interests of the respondent or host state in having an opportunity of doing justice, and other interests, including those of the alien claimant in avoiding undue hardship and in a quick and efficient dispute settlement procedure. This may sometimes involve walking a tightrope. In the jurisprudence and practice some categories of limitation have been clearly established, although not always without some element of uncertainty. Theoretically, however, there is room for expansion of these categories when new situations arise which may be eligible for consideration. While the outcome of such consideration may not always be foreseeable, it is clear that in each case a careful weighing of the conflicting interests must take place. In this exercise, because of the history of the rule and of the manner in which it has evolved, the important place held by respect for the sovereignty of the host or respondent state, which requires that it be given a fair opportunity of doing justice through its own system, cannot be ignored. Consequently, it is only where the interests of the alien claimant or other interests clearly dominate and require recognition that a limitation will be accepted. Where limitations have been imposed it is because a reasonable case has been made for such limitations. Similarly, where future limitations are canvassed the same principle would apply.

Another consequence of the special respect shown for the sovereignty of the host or respondent state is that the extent of the accepted limitations themselves may be somewhat circumscribed. There seems in the

---

[1] *Finland v. Great Britain*, 3 UNRIAA at p. 1497 (1934).

[2] *Greece v. UK*, 12 UNRIAA at p. 120 (1956). See also at p. 125 (Alfaro) and p. 128 (Spiropoulos) for comparable ideas.

past to have been a general tendency to recognize only those limitations which are really necessary, while laying some constraints on the scope of these limitations. Occasionally, on the other hand, as will be seen, a more liberal influence has more recently been apparent, especially in the area of human rights protection, but this must be regarded as exceptional.

It may also be noted that the special character of procedural remedies, particularly in the same court, may call for and has resulted in a somewhat individual approach, as regards both the scope of exhaustion required and the limitations on such exhaustion. These are discussed in the next chapter.

Early in the history of the development of diplomatic protection, the general statement was made that 'a claimant in a foreign State is not required to exhaust justice in such State when there is no justice to exhaust'.[3] Moreover, earlier, as was seen in Chapter 2, the practice had evolved from the seventeenth or eighteenth century of not insisting in exceptional circumstances on the exhaustion of remedies, whether in the context of reprisals or of diplomatic protection, because of the nature of the remedies available, and perhaps even on account of the conditions of their exercise. But it was only much later that attention was turned to the definition of those exceptional circumstances. Perhaps the first systematic attempt to deal with the problem was in the *Finnish Ships Arbitration*. On the other hand, there are earlier examples of exceptions or limitations being sporadically recognized. What is of importance now is to see how the practice and jurisprudence have dealt with the identification of limitations, taking into account the conflict of interests involved.

Although, as has been seen, the limitations on the rule of local remedies seem to have been described in its early history as being based on the absence of exhaustible justice, this may not be the sole *raison d'être*

---

[3] Secretary of State Fish (US Government) in 1873: Moore, *International Law* (1906), vol. 6, p. 677. The Hague Codification Conference (1929–30) devoted much attention to the question of exceptions to or limitations on the rule of local remedies: see LN Doc. C.75.M.69.1929.V at pp. 136–9, 171–2, 180, 182, 190, 192–3, 195, 206, 209 and 216; LN Doc. C.75(a).M.69(a).1929.V at p. 23; Acts – Minutes, Third Committee, vol. 4, pp. 63, 65, 70–1, 74–6, 78, 162, 164–5 and 168–9; and LN Doc. C.351(c).M.145(c).1930.V at p. 203. Text writers have also discussed the subject, but not very fully: see e.g. Borchard, 'Theoretical Aspects of the International Responsibility of States', 1 ZaöRV (1929) at pp. 241–2; Séfériadès, 'Le Problème de l'accès des particuliers à des juridictions internationales', 51 *Hague Recueil* (1935) at pp. 72–82; Bos, 'Les Conditions du procès en droit international public', 19 BViss (1957) at pp. 232–7; and Amerasinghe, *State Responsibility for Injuries to Aliens* (1967) pp. 192–7.

of all the limitations. In a broad sense, the absence of exhaustible justice may be a highly important consideration, particularly as the inapplicability of the rule is viewed from the point of view primarily of the host or respondent state in so far as the limitations on the rule are related to the inability of that state to do justice. But, as was implied in the *Finnish Ships Arbitration*, it was really consideration also of the alien's interest in not being put to undue hardship that gave rise to the limitation which was found to exist in that case. The tribunal concluded that it was 'hard' (or unjust or unfair) to expect the alien to pursue remedies any further in the circumstances which prevailed in the case. Thus, at the heart of the problem of limitations is the question of justice or fairness, which in turn is inextricably involved with a balancing of the conflicting interests in reality associated with the rule. One consequence of this is that it would be a mistake to regard the rule as rigidly and inexorably established without the possibility of reasonable exceptions being recognized, particularly beyond the existing and accepted limitations. Further, the definition of the currently recognized limitations would properly be dependent on a consideration of the true conflict of interests, although in the ultimate analysis the conclusions reached, whether in regard to the definition of the existing limitations or the validation of new ones, may be a matter of fine judgment. The manner in which the conflict of interests is resolved would also determine what circumstances are characterized as not giving rise to exceptions to or limitations on the application of the rule.

The unavailability and inaccessibility of remedies

As has been seen in the previous chapter, the alien must exhaust only those remedies which are available. This implies that exhaustion is not required of those remedies that are not available. Availability implies, among other things, accessibility. The general notion of availability or accessibility was explored earlier. However, there are specific aspects of inaccessibility which are relevant to the limitations on the operation of the rule. Further, the discussion of inaccessibility and unavailability in Chapter 13 on human rights protection is relevant to the issue.

There may be remedies which, although available, are not in the circumstances applicable to the particular injury of which the alien complains. International courts or organs have then tended to regard the remedy as not available. Apart from the cases discussed earlier in which the remedy was held not to be available in this sense, there have been cases which came before the UN Human Rights Committee in which the remedy was held not to be exhaustible because it was not available according to law.[4] Thus, it is not the theoretical existence of a remedy under the law of the host or respondent state which makes it exhaustible, but rather whether according to that law it is applicable to the claimant's case. By the same token it would follow that it must be quite clear according to the law of the host or respondent state that the remedy in question is inapplicable to the claimant's case.[5]

The ineffectiveness of remedies

The limitation arising from the positive requirement that the remedy be effective or adequate for the object of the claim or application implies that ineffective remedies need not be exhausted. In the law of diplomatic protection, the exception based on ineffectiveness was apparently evolved by a purposeful balancing of the interests of the parties involved, which are inherent in the policies behind the rule. Those interests were taken account of and given effect to, either implicitly or explicitly, in the application of the rule to the problem of appeals from one court to another within the same municipal system in the *Finnish Ships Arbitration*. In that case, it was held that a claimant was not under an obligation to resort to an appeal which was obviously futile. It was insufficient that the remedy merely appeared to be futile for the alien to be exempt from making the appeal. On the other hand, the alien was not absolutely compelled to take his case through to the highest court, whatever the circumstances might be:

As regards finally the third question, whether the local remedy shall be considered as not effective only where it is obviously futile on the merits of the case which are to be taken into account, to have recourse to the municipal remedy, or whether, as the Finnish Government suggests, it is sufficient that such a step only appears to be futile, a certain strictness in construing this rule appears justified by the opinion expressed by Borchard when mentioning the rule applied in the prize cases. Borchard says (a.a. § 383): 'In a few prize cases it has been held that in the face of a uniform course of decisions in the highest court a reversal of the condemnation being hopeless, an appeal was excused; but this rule

---

[4] See e.g. for some early cases, Communication No. 8/1977, HRC *Selected Decisions* at p. 48; Communication No. 28/1978, HRC *Selected Decisions* at pp. 58–9; and Communication No. 44/1979, HRC *Selected Decisions* at pp. 77 and 79.

[5] For some variations on the theme, see Chapter 13 below on human rights protection.

was most strictly construed, and if substantial right of appeal existed, failure to prosecute an appeal operated as a bar to relief.[6]

Accordingly, it was held that, where the finding of fact by a board under an Indemnity Act was final and the success of the claimant's case depended on a different finding of fact, an appeal to a higher court[7] or a reference to a different court or body[8] was obviously futile. Furthermore, it was held that there was no effective remedy by way of petition of right to the King of the respondent state, the UK, since such a remedy lay only in contract cases and there was no contract in that case.[9]

The resulting principle which excused the alien from exhausting remedies in certain circumstances as opposed, on the one hand, to laying upon him the absolute obligation of appeal to all available sources of justice, and, on the other, to excusing him from such appeal in any circumstances in which he chose, whether on a *bona fide* estimate of the effectiveness of the remedies available or not, was evidently reached by a balancing of interests of the respondent state and the alien.[10] It was a compromise between the interests of the respondent state in having a fair opportunity of doing justice by its own means and those of the alien in having the most efficient justice done at the lowest cost in the quickest way. Where it is clear that the resort to an appeal or reference to another court or tribunal would not be a source of adequate redress, the alien is excused from spending his money and time. Also, nothing has been lost by the respondent state, as far as its interest in doing justice by its own means is concerned.

This rule which evolved in the *Finnish Ships Arbitration* was applied more recently by Judge Lauterpacht in the *Norwegian Loans Case*, where the issue of non-exhaustion of local remedies was raised but not decided by the Court. The plaintiff state, France, argued that there were no remedies to exhaust, but Judge Lauterpacht in a separate opinion held that the Norwegian objection was good because it was not clear that resort to the Norwegian courts would have been absolutely futile.[11] In the *Interhandel Case*, the Court similarly held that there was still a possibility of success in the US courts for the Swiss Interhandel Company so that it could not be said that there were no remedies available, and

---

[6] *Finland v. Great Britain*, 3 UNRIAA at p. 1504 (1934). The term 'effective remedy' was used at p. 1495.

[7] *Ibid.*, p. 1543.   [8] *Ibid.*, p. 1545.   [9] *Ibid.*, p. 1550.

[10] Fachiri criticized this particular solution: 'The Local Remedies Rule in the Light of the Finnish Ships Arbitration', 17 BYIL (1936) p. 36.

[11] 1957 ICJ Reports at pp. 39ff.

therefore the Swiss aliens should have exhausted local remedies before having their case taken up before an international tribunal.[12]

As already seen in Chapter 7, the parties in the *Barcelona Traction Co. Case*, while agreeing on the requirement of effectiveness of a remedy, disagreed on the meaning of that term in the context. It would seem that the Spanish government rested its case on a theory of obvious futility, but it is not clear whether the Belgian government took the same view or not; what is evident is that they differed on the circumstances in which the exception for ineffectiveness became operative.

In the law of diplomatic protection the principle that local remedies need not be exhausted where they are obviously futile seems to be established. The *Finnish Ships Arbitration* made it clear that the test is obvious futility or manifest ineffectiveness, not the absence of a reasonable prospect of success or the improbability of success, which are both less strict tests. The absence of a reasonable prospect of success as a test, as will be seen, seems to have found its way into the law relating to the protection of human rights. The test of obvious futility clearly requires more than the probability of failure or the improbability of success, but perhaps less than the absolute certainty of failure. The test may be said to require evidence from which it could reasonably be concluded that the remedy would be ineffective.[13] The test of 'essentialness', which has prevailed in the context of procedural remedies, as will be seen in Chapter 9, on the suggested and apparent interpretation of that term, seems to require less than obvious futility.

The application of the test of obvious futility has resulted in the dismissal of the objection that local remedies had not been exhausted in several kinds of cases. First, it has been held that, where resort to the courts will result in the repetition of a uniform line of decisions adverse to the alien, the remedy is obviously futile.[14] What this means is that the mere likelihood of an adverse decision is insufficient, something

---

[12] 1959 ICJ Reports at pp. 26ff.

[13] Mummery requires that the absence of a proper remedy be 'reasonably clear': 'The Content of the Duty of Exhaust Local Judicial Remedies', 58 AJIL (1964) at p. 401. In the *ELSI Case*, a Chamber of the ICJ held that what was important was whether it could be concluded from all the circumstances that the possibility of success of a remedy was remote: 1989 ICJ Reports at pp. 47–8. In that case, it was found that the remedy identified as not having been exhausted could not have been regarded as possibly relevant to the success of the alien's claim.

[14] *Finnish Ships Arbitration (Finland v. Great Britain)*, 3 UNRIAA p. 1495 (1934), endorsed this principle. In the *ELSI Case*, 1989 ICJ Reports at pp. 47–8, the ICJ found that it was clear that the alien company could not have succeeded in the local courts, because the established law worked definitely against its contentions: see on this point in the case

more than probability of defeat but less than certainty being required. It seems readily to be accepted that a *jurisprudence constante* or *bien établie*, or the existence of a series of decisions which shows that resort to remedies will not end in success, exempts the alien or claimant from exhausting local or internal remedies. This point was either explicitly or implicitly conceded in the written pleadings and oral arguments in the *Barcelona Traction Co. Case*.[15] In that case, there was disagreement, however, on the issue of whether a prevailing consensus among commentators, in the absence of a *jurisprudence constante* on the futility of a remedy, was sufficient to afford an exception. It would seem that the better view is that this by itself would be inadequate to validate an exception to the duty to resort to local or internal remedies.

Secondly, as in the *Finnish Ships Arbitration*, there is no need to resort to a court or body which has no jurisdiction over the issue raised by the alien. This is so whether it is a case of resort to a court of first instance or a court of appeal. However, in such a case this point must be strictly proved, as it was in the *Finnish Ships Arbitration*. In the *Panavezys–Saldutiskis Railway Case*, the argument was raised that it would have been useless to take the matter to the Lithuanian courts because they would not take jurisdiction over an 'act of state', an act *jure imperii*, since this was an act in performance of the government's public function and not a matter 'concerning a civil right' within the meaning of the Lithuanian Code of Civil Procedure. The PCIJ held that it was not satisfied that this was the case in the absence of a Lithuanian court decision on the point.[16] The difference between the two cases is that in the *Finnish Ships Arbitration* the law consisting of statute and common law was quite clear, while in the *Panavezys–Saldutiskis Railway Case* the law, as it stood, was not so clear and therefore the Court refused even to examine it. In the *Norwegian Loans Case*, Judge Lauterpacht's view was similar, namely, that the

---

Adler, 'The Exhaustion of Local Remedies Rule after the International Court of Justice's Decision in ELSI', 39 ICLQ (1990) at p. 651. A similar conclusion exempting the alien from exhausting local remedies was reached for the same basic reason as in the *ELSI Case*, in the *Interpretation of the Treaty of Finance and Compensation Arbitration* between Austria and the Federal Republic of Germany (1972), 32 ZaöRV (1972) at p. 49. See also the *Johnson Case* (*United States* v. *Peru*) (1878), de La Pradelle-Politis, RAI, vol. 2, pp. 593ff.; and Freeman, *The International Responsibility of States for Denial of Justice* (1938) p. 421.

[15] See ICJ Pleadings (1962–9), vol. 1, p. 256, ICJ Pleadings (1962–9), vol. 3, p. 814, ICJ Pleadings (1962–9), vol. 9, pp. 593 and 609 (the Spanish view); and ICJ Pleadings (1962–9), vol. 8, pp. 577–8 (the Belgian view).

[16] PCIJ Series A/B No. 76 at p. 19 (1939). For the argument, see also PCIJ Series C No. 86 at p. 45.

position was not clearly what the French government made it out to be.[17] In the *Interhandel Case*, the ICJ took basically the same stand.[18] The fact that in the *Panavezys–Saldutiskis Railway Case* the Court refused to examine the issue must be explained by the fact that it was not at all clear on the face of it that the Estonian argument was a good one. In the *Finnish Ships Arbitration* the converse was the case and, therefore, the tribunal examined the law to find that the Finnish argument was a good one. Thus, it may further be asserted that unless it appears that there is a clear case that no tribunal has jurisdiction in the case in hand, an international tribunal will not even examine the municipal law.

Thirdly, where it is clear that a national law justifying the acts of which the alien complains would have to be applied by the local organs or courts, thus rendering recourse to them obviously futile, local remedies need not be exhausted. In the *Forests of Central Rhodope Case*,[19] the international wrong was the confiscation of certain forests under a national law permitting such confiscation. Since all state organs would have had to apply that law, it was obvious that recourse to local remedies would have been futile. Hence, the arbitral tribunal held that they did not have to be exhausted.

Fourthly, absence of independence of the courts has been held to exempt the alien or claimant from resorting to the courts. In the *Robert E. Brown Case*,[20] an alien was excused from exhausting local remedies because the courts were at the time completely under the control of the Executive.[21] The obvious futility of recourse to the state judicial organs in these circumstances is based on the absence of justice in the true sense.

Fifthly, where the remedies available clearly will not satisfy the object sought by the claimant, they need not be resorted to because they are ineffective or obviously futile. There are several decided cases concerning the protection of human rights under the European Convention on Human Rights. Where the object of the claimant's action was to prevent

---

[17] 1957 ICJ Reports at pp. 39ff.

[18] 1959 ICJ Reports at pp. 26ff. Where the applicant's appeal is on the facts and a higher court has no jurisdiction except in appeals on matters of law, there is no need to appeal to the higher court: see Communication No. 27/1978, HRC *Selected Decisions* at p. 14, which is a case on human rights protection.

[19] *Greece* v. *Bulgaria*, 3 UNRIAA p. 1405 (1933).

[20] *United States* v. *Great Britain*, 6 UNRIAA p. 120 (1923).

[21] See on the similar position in human rights protection, e.g. Communication No. 63/1979, HRC *Selected Decisions* at p. 102.

his removal from a state's territory in violation of the Convention, a court action which did not have suspensive effect was not a remedy that had to be exhausted because it was obviously ineffective for the object sought by the claimant.[22] Similarly, the EComHR has held that where a claimant finds it impossible to prove before the authorities concerned allegations which are basic to the object of his application, it is obvious that the remedies concerned cannot give the claimant satisfaction and cannot be effective.[23] The case relates to the adequacy of the means provided to achieve the object sought and shows that remedies need not be exhausted where the means available cannot satisfy the desired object. For this same reason, where it is obvious that the reparation available under the municipal remedy would not be adequate in terms of what the alien is entitled to in international law, the remedy would be 'obviously futile' and resort need not be had to it. In the *Finnish Ships Arbitration*, Finland argued that the remedy of the shipowners with the Admiralty Board was ineffective because the rates by which the Board was bound in assessing compensation did not represent fair market rates.[24] The arbitrator rejected the argument because he found that the redress which would be given under the Indemnity Act was adequate redress. The decision does not clearly assert that the international rule is as formulated above, but the point was decided on that hypothesis. The arbitrator did state in passing that:

it appears hard to lay on the private individual the burden of incurring loss of money and time by going through the courts only to exhaust what to him – at least for the time being – must be only a very unsatisfactory remedy, and although the Arbitrator is aware that the contrary opinion has been frequently expressed, the Arbitrator is inclined to find it doubtful whether the fact that such a kind of exhaustion has not taken place always can give the respondent state the right to object to an international interposition.[25]

It is evident that for the exception to operate on the ground that reparation is not adequate for the purpose of satisfying the international claim, the inadequacy of the remedy for the specific object must be proven beyond reasonable doubt.

---

[22] *Becker v. Denmark*, Application No. 7011/75, *Decisions and Reports*, ECHR, vol. 4, pp. 227–8 and 232–3. See also *X v. Denmark*, Application No. 7465/76, *Decisions and Reports*, ECHR, vol. 7, p. 154; *X v. Austria*, Application No. 6701/74, *Decision and Reports*, ECHR, vol. 5, pp. 78–9; and *Zamir v. UK*, Application No. 9174/80, *Report of the Commission*.

[23] *Kornmann v. Federal Republic of Germany*, Application No. 2686/65, 22 *Collection* at p. 10.

[24] *Finland v. Great Britain*, 3 UNRIAA at p. 1496 (1934).   [25] *Ibid.*, pp. 1496–7.

Sixthly, apart from the inaccessibility of remedies, which is a reason for not exhausting them, the absence of due process of law in the legal system of the host or respondent state is clearly a good excuse for not exhausting remedies.[26]

In the *Ambatielos Claim*, it was stated that, where the futility of a remedy otherwise available is the result of the alien's fault, there is no exemption from the application of the rule.[27]

Undue delay

Undue delay in the administration of justice has been held to be a good reason for not exhausting local remedies. This exception may be closely related to the general exception based on obvious futility but it is better considered separately, as delay may not always signify that there is a clear indication that the alien or claimant will not succeed after a lapse of time. However, undue delay in the administration of justice is regarded as a denial of justice in itself and is certainly one which does not require any further exhaustion of remedies. In the *El Oro Mining and Railway Co. Case*,[28] it was held that a court's delay in taking action for nine years was sufficient to make it an ineffective remedy.

The delay necessary to make a remedy ineffective in each case will, of course, vary, it being impossible to lay down a specific time limit

---

[26] The ground has been supported by the Institut de Droit International: see 36(1) AIDI (1935) at p. 435; and 45 AIDI (1954) at pp. 28ff. See also Harvard Law School, *Research in International Law II. Responsibility of States (1929)* p. 134. This ground is specifically referred to in Article 46(2)(a) of the American Convention on Human Rights. Although not all forms of denial of justice may have the result of exempting the alien or claimant from exhausting remedies, certainly this one would seem to have the effect of rendering remedies obviously futile in so far as proper justice and fairness cannot be expected to prevail. The exception would be relevant even in the absence of specific provisions for it in a conventional instrument. The exception was found to be applicable by the Inter-American Commission on Human Rights in Resolution No. 1a/88, where it held that the irregularities pertaining to legal process inherent in Chilean military justice were reflected in the abusive recourse to secrecy in the conduct of the proceedings, with the result that it was initially impossible to gain access to basic elements of the trial and the military authorities were allowed to control the evidence submitted. Therefore the Commission held that due process of law was non-existent and local remedies did not have to be pursued: see Resolution No. 1a/88, Case 9755, *Ann. Rep. IAComHR 1987–88* at p. 137.

[27] *Greece v. UK*, 12 UNRIAA at p. 122 (1956).

[28] *Great Britain v. Mexico*, 5 UNRIAA p. 191 (1931).

for all cases, since several circumstances including the volume of work involved in a thorough examination of the case are relevant.[29] In the *Interhandel Case*,[30] although ten years had already passed since the institution of the action, the Court did not hold that there had been undue delay in the provision of a remedy. Dissenting Judge Armond-Ugon was of the view that, because a further unknown period would have to elapse before remedies were exhausted, ten years already having passed, such remedies were too slow and could not be called adequate or effective and could be dispensed with.[31] There was clearly a difference of opinion on whether there had been undue delay in the case. However, although the Court does not seem to have rejected the view that delay can operate in the alien's favour, it would seem that it did not consider the lapse of time as sufficiently long and important to influence the decision.[32]

While the principle that undue delay would operate in customary international law to exempt the claimant or applicant from exhausting remedies is undisputed, the reason behind it being that justice is being in some way denied the claimant or applicant, even though resort to remedies in the circumstances may not be obviously futile, a more difficult question is how undue delay is to be defined. It is impossible to lay down a definite length of time that would constitute undue delay for all cases, and it would be imprudent to attempt to do so. The circumstances of each case would certainly be a determining factor. Much would depend on the judicial assessment of the situation in each case. As has been seen, in the *Interhandel Case* Judge Armand-Ugon differed from the Court on the question of whether in the circumstances the time that had elapsed since remedies had initially been invoked was sufficient to constitute undue delay. Clearly, such matters as the nature of the wrong would be relevant, it being easier, for instance, to prescribe shorter time limits for violations of personal and civil rights than for injuries to property. The nature of the claimant may also be a pertinent factor, injuries to large corporations, which may give rise to more complicated issues than injuries to individuals, being subject to longer

---

[29] *Ibid.*, p. 198.   [30] 1959 ICJ Reports p. 6.   [31] *Ibid.*, p. 87.

[32] As will be seen in Chapter 13, the principle of undue delay has been applied and elaborated upon in the law of human rights protection. See also Dugard, 'Third Report on Diplomatic Protection' (ILC), UN Doc. A/CN.4/523 at pp. 35–7, Article 14(e) of the draft, and the text writers referred to there.

time limits than injuries to individuals. In the ultimate analysis, such considerations can only provide guidelines, there being no hard and fast rules defining undue delays.[33]

Repetition of injury or likelihood of further damage

It has been suggested that a remedy need not be resorted to, that is, a final decision of the last instance does not need to be waited for, if for some reason or other, further damages are expected or the same injury will be repeated.[34] Some support for this is to be found in a ruling in the *De Sabla Claim*:

> There is great force in the contention of the claimant as to the hardship imposed on her by forcing her to resort to opposition on each application [for grants of the land by others]. The facts of the case show that one opposition, even when successful, accomplished no more than to kill the particular application opposed, and did not even prevent subsequent grants to the identical persons who had previously been successfully opposed . . . The Commission therefore find that the machinery of opposition, as actually administered, did not constitute an adequate remedy.[35]

The situation envisaged may not necessarily compel the conclusion that remedies would be obviously futile, if exhausted, in so far as in each case it is possible to have a final decision given. While the Commission in the *De Sabla Claim* stressed the inadequacy of remedies in the circumstances, the inadequacy seems to have rested directly and specifically on the hardship caused to the alien claimant. Thus, the exception seems to have been derived from a balancing of the interests of the alien claimant and those of the respondent state. Here the scales tipped in favour of the alien claimant.

---

[33] There have been some text writers who have considered the question of defining undue delay in the context of human rights protection: see e.g. Wiebringhaus, 'La Règle de l'épuisement préalable des voies de recours internes dans la jurisprudence de la Commission européenne des droits de l'homme', 5 AFDI (1959) p. 685; Schaffer and Weissbrodt, 'Exhausting Remedies in the Context of the Racial Discrimination Convention', 2 HRJ (1969) at pp. 639ff. See, on the matter of the definition of 'undue delay', the law of human rights protection discussed in Chapter 13. See also the other cases referred to above in this section.

[34] See Freeman, note 14 above, at p. 418; and Law, *The Local Remedies Rule in International Law* (1961) p. 70.

[35] *USA* v. *Panama*, 28 AJIL (1934) at p. 607 (1933).

Other possible exceptional circumstances

There are some limitations or exceptions to the rule of local remedies which have hitherto been applied specifically and only in the law of human rights protection. These relate to (a) the prevailing condition and (b) legislative measures and administrative practices, which are discussed in a later chapter.[36] It is not impossible that these exceptions to the rule be applied in an appropriate manner to the law of diplomatic protection. Their relevance to diplomatic protection has not been raised in practice nor has the jurisprudence of international courts and tribunals dealt with them. The exception discussed earlier, however, relating to the repetition of an injury comes close in appearance to these exceptions. Insofar as the law of diplomatic protection requires an injury to the alien claimant, the requirement laid down in the European Convention of Human Rights, for instance, for individual applicants that the applicant must be a victim of the alleged violation of the law is replicated in the law of diplomatic protection. Given that requirement, the acceptance of the exceptions in the law of diplomatic protection would be based on the policy of recognizing that the hardship caused to the alien in having to exhaust remedies was sufficiently important to warrant a derogation from the respect given to the sovereignty of the host or respondent state in settling the dispute by its legal procedures.

The only argument against the reception of these exceptions into the law of diplomatic protection is that the conflict of interests has already been resolved in favour of nothing less than that remedies must appear to be obviously futile, if they are not to be subject to exhaustion. While no problem would arise in both of the situations in issue where the remedies available are obviously futile, it would be extending the exception based on obvious futility to permit exceptions such as those being contemplated in circumstances in which the remedies were not obviously futile. On the other hand, it must be acknowledged that, although the requirement of obvious futility has been generally established as a principal limitation on the rule, there are already some limitations, such as where there has been undue delay, in which exceptions have been permitted, even where the obvious futility of remedies may not strictly be inherent. To allow an exception for any lesser reason than obvious futility of the remedies available would, however, require that very cogent reasons be given. In the case of the exceptions in issue, both their reasonable and limited nature and the fact that they have been

---

[36] See Chapter 13 pp. 341ff. below.

admitted in the law of human rights protection make their acceptance in the law of diplomatic protection appropriate. As far as such limitations or exceptions which relate to the material content of the rule are concerned, the weight given to the protection of the individual in the area of human rights protection seems equally cogent in the law of diplomatic protection. There is no reason, therefore, to regard them as confined to the conventional law of human rights protection, although their relevance to the law of diplomatic protection seems never to have been tested in state practice or before international courts or tribunals.

Circumstances not limiting the operation of the rule

In the development of the rule of local remedies, in practice and through judicial decision, certain circumstances have been identified as not giving rise to limitations on or exceptions to the rule. In a negative sense, therefore, these circumstances cannot have an effect on the operation of the rule. Such circumstances have been adverted to both in the law of diplomatic protection and in the area of human rights protection, but particularly in the latter. While it has sometimes been said both by judicial and arbitral authorities[37] and by text writers[38] that the rule is flexible and is to be applied in accordance with the circumstances, it cannot be said that there is scope for broad equitable considerations in the formulation of exceptions. The strength of the value attached to the sovereign rights of the respondent state in doing justice in its own way is so pervasive that, as has been seen, it is only when the interests of the alien claimant or individual clearly outweigh those of the respondent state that an exception may be allowed. Consequently, there are many situations in which the argument that the local remedies rule was not applicable has been raised but rejected.

It has been confirmed on more than one occasion that lack of pecuniary means on the part of the alien claimant or individual does not constitute a valid reason for not pursuing local remedies. In the *David Adams Case*,[39] the arbitral tribunal was faced with the argument that the

---

[37] See e.g. the *Norwegian Loans Case*, 1957 ICJ Reports at p. 39 *per* Judge Lauterpacht in a separate opinion; the *Salem Case* (*United States* v. *Egypt*), 2 UNRIAA at p. 1189 (1932); the *Panavezys–Saldutiskis Railway Case*, PCIJ Series A/B No. 76 at p. 48 (1939) *per* Judge Hudson in a dissenting opinion; and the *Electricity Co. of Sofia Case*, PCIJ Series A/B No. 77 at p. 138 (1939) *per* Judge de Visscher in a dissenting opinion.

[38] See e.g. Law, note 34 above, at p. 147; and Jenks, *The Prospects of International Adjudication* (1964) at p. 536. See also Schwarzenberger, *International Law* (1957), vol. 1, p. 604.

[39] *United States* v. *Great Britain*, 6 UNRIAA p. 85 (1921).

owner of a ship confiscated in Canada did not pursue a right of appeal partly because of the absence of pecuniary means. The excuse was not recognized in law as being a reason for not exhausting local remedies.[40]

The better view seems to be that statements by government officials or even in a judgment that in effect there were no further effective remedies available does not excuse the alien claimant or individual from exhausting remedies.[41] However, there may be considerations of estoppel or waiver that may operate in some situations;[42] but then the release from the duty to exhaust local remedies is not to be treated as an exception but as being based on good faith or consent.

Particularly in the area of human rights protection, many invalid excuses have been considered. These are discussed in Chapter 13. There is no good reason why these circumstances, which have been found inadequate to provide an excuse for not exhausting local remedies in the area of human rights protection, should not have the same effect in the law of diplomatic protection. In general, the definition of their inadequacy seems reasonably conceived and appropriate, particularly because as such they bear no relationship to the effectiveness, adequacy or availability of local remedies.

---

[40] See also the *Napier Case* (*USA* v. *UK*) (1921), de La Pradelle-Politis, RAI, vol. 3, p. 121.

[41] See the *Interhandel Case*, 1959 ICJ Reports at p. 27; the *Norwegian Loans Case*, 1957 ICJ Reports at p. 41 *per* Judge Lauterpacht in a separate opinion; and the *Salem Case* (*United States* v. *Egypt*), 2 UNRIAA at p. 1189 (1932). Judge Read in his dissenting opinion in the *Norwegian Loans Case* cast some doubt on this view: 1957 ICJ Reports at p. 98.

[42] See below, Chapter 10.

The rule as applied to the use of procedural resources

In order to pursue a claim against the host or respondent state, an alien will have to use the procedural resources available to him under the local law. Since the decision in the *Ambatielos Claim*,[1] the exhaustion of procedural remedies has called for special attention, not least because in that case an approach was foreshadowed, particularly by some of the arbitrators, which appears to have given the question a special significance. The principal issue which arises is whether the principles which apply in general to the exhaustion of local remedies undergo any modification or change. In the light of in particular the opinions rendered in the *Ambatielos Claim*, and also the views expressed by a few text writers, it is appropriate to examine in some detail the exhaustion of procedural recourse. The principles applicable to the exhaustion of remedies in general, and to the limitations on such exhaustion, are *prima facie* relevant here, so that it is only upon the extent to which they are modified, or require specific explanation because of the manner in which they are applied, that the investigation will focus.

The issue concerns the extent to which and the manner in which the alien claimant must use the procedural resources available to him, primarily in the same court, in order to satisfy the rule that he must exhaust local remedies. The manner in which a litigant conducts his case in this respect is to a great degree a matter of discretion, but for the purpose of the rule of exhaustion of local remedies there may be certain requirements demanded by international law of the manner in which a case is conducted. In practical terms, when an alien claimant

---

[1] *Greece* v. *UK*, 12 UNRIAA p. 119 (1956). This is the landmark case on the subject of this chapter.

has to exhaust local remedies in the host or respondent state, it behoves him to resort to certain resources which constitute the procedure of the courts of that state, such as the calling of witnesses or the presentation of evidence. The problem to be considered is how far international law controls the manner in which he must conduct his case in relation to such procedural resources and more particularly whether this control is any different from that which international law exercises in connection with remedies in general.

In the area of substantive pleas, it has been seen that the rule of local remedies demands that those pleas which are raised before the international forum be raised in substance before the local instances, if local remedies are properly to be exhausted. The answer to the problem connected with procedural resources is not so simple because procedural recourse differs in quality from substantive aspects, being really a means to the broader goal of establishing substantive issues. The use of procedural resources itself calls for forensic skill, but international law, as will be seen, may establish special parameters within which this skill must be exercised, even where a wide element of discretion may be available under the local law.

The category that the concept of procedural resources referred to here represents is not as obvious as it may seem. It would be helpful, therefore, to define it inclusively as well as by reference to certain elements, which, although closely related to the procedures of the judicial machinery, are to be excluded. The concept refers to those methods and means which are available, especially within a particular court of the local legal system, for the conduct of the proceedings on the one hand and for the proof of the factual aspects of the case on the other. Such rules as relate to the representation of the parties by counsel in a lawsuit and stipulate time limitations on various aspects of the proceedings, as well as on the bringing of the action itself, are means available for the conduct of the proceedings, while methods of adducing evidence such as the calling of witnesses and the production of documents would belong to the latter category. Substantive remedies by way of appeal to higher courts or by way of reference to other courts or bodies are outside the scope of the concept being discussed. Such remedies by way of appeal are not strictly speaking procedures of redress. The law relating to these remedies has been referred to in Chapter 7 and is sufficiently clear. Such issues as relate to the raising in local courts of those points or arguments of law which are presented to an international tribunal as the basis of the claim are also not included in the concept. Although the raising of arguments before local tribunals relates to the conduct of the proceedings, it pertains more specifically to the substantive remedies available, in that legal points and arguments that constitute the substance of the claim are in issue. On the other hand, the manner of formally presenting the substantive basis of the claim in the pleadings would relate to the procedural conduct of the case. The choice of the actual arguments concerns the substance of the claim. The submission of a formally correct pleading is a matter of procedure, while the raising of an issue of loss by unjust enrichment, for instance, is not. The requirements pertaining to the substantive aspect of the conduct of proceedings referred to have been dealt with earlier.[2]

There has been little discussion of the exhaustion of procedural remedies in the judicial authorities or by text writers. It has generally been taken for granted that general statements such as those that local remedies (or all local remedies) must be exhausted,[3] or that they need not be exhausted where there are none to exhaust,[4] or that an alien need not resort to remedies which are not effective,[5] obviously futile,[6] or perhaps inadequate in the satisfaction they offer,[7] would cover adequately also the problem of procedural remedies. These statements are of value as statements of principle applicable to the exhaustion of local remedies in general. However, in relation to procedural remedies, problems of a special nature do arise which may make a general solution in terms purely of inadequacy, ineffectiveness or obvious futility somewhat unsatisfactory.[8] On the other hand, it is clear that the rule that local remedies must be exhausted does apply to procedural remedies. The reasoning of the arbitral commission in the *Ambatielos Claim* is in point here:

---

[2] The questions of appeals and substantive pleas were discussed in Chapter 7.

[3] See e.g. Eagleton, *The Responsibility of States in International Law* (1929) pp. 96–7; International Conference of American States, *First Supplement*, 1932–40, p. 90; and García Amador, 'Third Report on International Responsibility', YBILC (1958), vol. 2, pp. 55ff.

[4] See e.g. Borchard, *The Diplomatic Protection of Citizens Abroad* (1915) p. 822; Harvard Law School, *Research in International Law II. Responsibility of States* (1929) at p. 154.

[5] See e.g. Oppenheim, vol. 1, p. 361.

[6] See e.g. the *Finnish Ships Arbitration (Finland* v. *Great Britain)*, 3 UNRIAA at p. 1504 (1934).

[7] See e.g. Eagleton, note 3 above, at p. 96.

[8] Contra Haesler, *The Exhaustion of Local Remedies in the Caselaw of International Courts and Tribunals* (1968) pp. 42ff. and 81ff., who thinks that procedural remedies in the same court are no different from remedies in general in so far as the application of the rule of local remedies is concerned. I made a preliminary examination of the problem of procedural remedies in 'The Exhaustion of Procedural Remedies in the Same Court', 12 ICLQ (1963) p. 1285.

The rule requires that 'local remedies' shall have been exhausted before an international action can be brought. The 'local remedies' include not only reference to the courts and tribunals, but also the use of procedural facilities which municipal law makes available to litigants before such courts and tribunals. It is the whole system of legal protection, as provided by municipal law, which must have been put to the test before a state, as the protector of its nationals, can prosecute the claim on the international plane.[9]

Ironically, it is also as a result of the *Ambatielos Claim* that it has been possible to focus attention on the special problems relating to the exhaustion of procedural remedies which are discussed in this chapter. Indeed, any discussion of the subject must basically derive from that decision and must concentrate on a close analysis of that case and the opinions of the arbitrators.[10] There may, however, be areas in which solely the applicability of general principles must be considered.

The procedural aspects of a proceeding before the local tribunals or courts may be divided into two classes: (a) those that are, according to the local law, obligatory in themselves on a party to the proceeding; and (b) those that, according to local law, are not obligatory but are only permissive or discretionary as means to the conduct of his case.

Procedures that are obligatory under the local law

In the case of obligatory procedural rules or methods, the answer to the question whether an alien claimant must use them in order to exhaust local procedural remedies would depend on general principle. Since they are obligatory on a party to a proceeding if he is to have any chance of succeeding, the alien claimant, like any other party to a proceeding,

[9] (*Greece* v. *UK*), 12 UNRIAA at p. 1200 (1956). The European Commission of Human Rights has taken the view, in reference to procedural means, that the remedies to be exhausted 'comprise the entire system of legal protection established by the *corpus* of municipal law'. *Gussenbauer* v. *Austria*, Application No. 4897/71, 42 *Collection* at p. 47.

[10] The *Ambatielos Claim* has been regarded favourably by many authorities to the extent that it treated procedural remedies differently from remedies in general: see e.g. Hambro, 'The Ambatielos Arbitral Award', 6 AdV (1956–7) p. 167; D. H. N. Johnson, 'The Ambatielos Case', 19 MLR (1956) p. 510, particularly at p. 516; Lipstein, 'The Ambatielos Case: Last Phase', 6 ICLQ (1957) at pp. 654–5; Hulme, 'The Ambatielos Case', 1 *Melbourne University Law Review* (1957–8) at pp. 74–5; and Amerasinghe, note 8 above. On the other hand, there has also been some adverse criticism of the case because it made that distinction: see e.g. de La Pradelle, in 46 AIDI (1956) at p. 307; Resolution of the Institut de Droit International, which excluded any distinction, 46 AIDI (1956) at pp. 302–6; Anonymous, 'Commission d'arbitrage Grèce–Royaume-Uni; sentence du 6 mars 1956, Affaire Ambatielos', AFDI (1956) at pp. 411ff.; Pinto, 'The Ambatielos Award', 84 JDI (1957) at pp. 597–9; and Haesler, note 8 above, at pp. 42ff. and 81ff.

should be bound to observe them. If a decision is given against him because he has failed to observe an obligatory rule, he has not done his best to obtain justice from the respondent state, he has not exhausted local remedies and he cannot be allowed to have his case referred to an international tribunal. Those means not resorted to were essential to the presentation and success of his case, and in so far as he had not invoked all essential remedies or those that were effective and adequate, as required by the rule of local remedies, he must be regarded as having failed to observe the rule. The alien claimant can be expected to do all in his power to obtain justice, since his interest in securing justice is also one that lies behind the rule. It is not an unfair obligation to impose upon him that he should, at least, use all the means which according to the local law he is under a duty to use. Thus, if he fails to institute his case within the time required by the local law after the commission of the alleged wrong or to draft the pleadings as the local law requires, and consequently has a decision given against him, in these circumstances he cannot be said to have exhausted procedural remedies.[11]

The European Commission of Human Rights has endorsed these views in its practice. Thus, it has been held that, where the applicant had been deprived of his civil rights and the law required that he should be represented by a tutor in civil proceedings, for the rule of local remedies to be satisfied he should have been so represented.[12] In an appeal court, the failure to satisfy the requirement that the appeal be filed within one month of the decision appealed was held to have resulted in the non-exhaustion of local remedies.[13] Where the applicant had failed to observe the time limit for filing an action because he could not find a lawyer in the locality to draft his application for legal aid and did not realize that he did not need a lawyer to do this, he was held to have failed to exhaust remedies.[14] In all these cases, the failure to observe obligatory rules of procedure resulted in the non-exhaustion of local remedies.

Two problems may, however, arise. First, if the particular rule disregarded is a doubtful one and the decision against the claimant, resulting from his violation of the rule, is made *primae impressionis*, the question may be asked whether he should bear the consequences of not having

---

[11] In the *Ambatielos Claim*, Spiropoulos supported the view taken above: 12 UNRIAA at p. 128.

[12] Application No. 225/56 (not published), cited by Vasak, *La Convention européenne des droits de l'homme* (1964) p. 128.

[13] X v. *Federal Republic of Germany*, Application No. 352/58, 1 YBECHR p. 342.

[14] *Wiechart* v. *Federal Republic of Germany*, Application No. 1404/62, 7 YBECHR p. 124.

interpreted the rule accurately, considering that the rule was in doubt at least until the decision in his case. It would seem reasonable that in principle he must take the risk, if he has failed to use a remedy required of him, doubtful though it may have been. The solution is inherent in the very nature of the judicial process. The litigant usually takes the risk of a wrong interpretation of a rule. It may be argued against this view that the respondent state is at fault for having doubtful rules in its legal system and that the claimant should not be penalized as a result. However, an answer to this argument is that the claimant is generally expected to take special precautions in his own interest. It is not an unfair burden to lay on him that he should make allowance for such eventualities as are the incidents of any litigation. General principles would seem to require that the procedural remedy in this case be normally regarded as essential.

Secondly, a problem may arise if the obligations imposed on the claimant in respect of the procedures within the local legal system are too harsh for any reason, including a clear lack of clarity, and if he then loses his case because he fails to fulfil a harsh requirement. As an example of a harsh requirement may be taken a rule or directive that certain arguments or evidence should be submitted within a period which is unusually short. By reference to general principles that operate in regard to the treatment of aliens, an alien claimant generally may be said to have exhausted his procedural remedies in a situation of this kind, even though he has failed to fulfil an obligation required by the local procedural law, if his case falls into one of two categories.

The first class of case is where the rule is applied to him in a discriminatory manner so as to increase his burdens, that is to say, where an obligation is imposed on him which for no good reason is not imposed on the nationals of the host state in general. Discrimination as such is illegal in the treatment of aliens. In a suit between the host state and an alien, it is imperative that there should be no improper discrimination in the imposition of procedural requirements, particularly between nationals and aliens. An alien claimant cannot improperly be expected to undertake special burdens in order to obtain justice in the courts of the host state. Equally, a state cannot be permitted to impose procedural obligations of such a kind on alien claimants in order that it may exercise its right of doing justice in connection with alleged breaches of its international obligations. It would seem to follow, therefore, that in such a case the non-fulfilment of a procedural obligation which is discriminatory and contributes to the alien claimant's failure to win his case before the local courts cannot be regarded as a non-exhaustion of procedural remedies.

The second category of case is where the obligation imposed on the alien claimant is contrary to the treaty obligations owed by the respondent state to his national state or falls below the international minimum standard. The reasoning on which is based this exception to the rule that an alien claimant must fulfil all procedural obligations in order to exhaust local remedies is similar to that which applies to the previous exception. Where a treaty lays down some limitation, or international law lays down a minimum standard, an alien claimant cannot be expected to bear heavier burdens in order to find justice in the courts of the respondent state. Conversely, a state ought not to be allowed to impose obligations on alien claimants contrary to its international obligations in order that it may exercise the right of doing justice in cases of alleged violations by it of its own international obligations. Thus, in this case too, an alien claimant must be regarded as having exhausted all the necessary procedural remedies, if his case before the local courts has failed because he has not fulfilled obligations of this kind. It may be difficult to determine what is the international minimum standard in a given case. But this is a difficulty which is encountered generally in the area of international law in which the concept is operative. Suffice it to say that there is in general such a standard and that its application in a given case will depend on numerous factors, including the findings of comparative analyses of the attitudes of legal systems to the relevant problems and the legitimate expectations of the alien claimant in the particular circumstances.[15]

The European Commission of Human Rights has in effect recognized the principle that obligatory procedural remedies need not be resorted to if they fall below the international minimum standard. In *Wiechart v. Federal Republic of Germany*,[16] the Commission discussed the question of whether the circumstances of the case exempted the applicant from observing the time limit set for filing his action. The case involved the drafting of an application for legal aid before the filing of the action.

---

[15] The principles referred to here are generally recognized principles of the law of alien treatment and require no special support from the authorities. The only issue in dispute may be the content of the international minimum standard, but this is a problem of a general nature and is not confined to the area of exhaustion of local remedies. Non-discrimination, it must be recognized, is also subject to qualification on the basis of justifiable differentiation, which may give rise to discussion.

[16] Application No. 1404/62, 7 YBECHR p. 124.

The point was whether the time limit set was too short and, therefore, a harsh requirement because it did not provide for an appropriate exception for the circumstances in which the applicant was placed. The argument was apparently based on the international minimum standard. In so far as the Commission held that the applicant was not exempted from fulfilling the time requirements of the rule of procedure, it took the view that the applicant had not proved circumstances which would have exempted him from observing the rule of procedure on the ground that it failed to permit a generally recognized exception and, therefore, fell below the international minimum standard. There was an acknowledgment that the principle in issue was relevant. It did not apply because of the particular circumstances of the case.

Procedures that are not obligatory but discretionary under the local law

The second category of procedural rules are those that are permissive or discretionary. For example, the rule that witnesses may be called and examined is not an obligatory rule. The rule that counsel must plead in a court of law does not indicate how good counsel must be or whether counsel must have had a certain minimum of experience. Similarly, no indication is given of what kind of evidence must be adduced in order that the claimant may be successful in his case. The action to be taken under rules of this kind is left to his discretion. In the *Ambatielos Claim*, for instance, the procedural remedy in issue was that of calling a witness to give evidence as to the terms of the contract.[17]

---

[17] *Greece* v. *UK*, 12 UNRIAA p. 119 (1956). The case concerned a contract for the construction and delivery of certain ships between the UK government and Ambatielos, a Greek national. Ambatielos alleged that the contract was for delivery on specific dates, that the ships had not been delivered according to contract and that he had suffered loss as a consequence. In proceedings before the English courts in regard to certain of the ships, Ambatielos alleged that the UK government had not produced some interdepartmental minutes relevant to the case on the basis of Crown privilege and had failed to call Major Laing, who gave the assurance as to the specific dates on behalf of the UK government, with the result that judgment was given against Ambatielos. Ambatielos subsequently appealed to the Court of Appeal and asked for leave to call Major Laing, but leave was not granted. The Greek government then brought an international action in protection of Ambatielos for the non-delivery of some and the late delivery of other ships, alleged to be a breach of a Treaty of Commerce between the UK and Greece. The UK government raised the objection, *inter alia*, that Ambatielos had not exhausted his procedural remedies before the local courts by not calling Major Laing.

This category gives rise to a different kind of problem. What is at issue here is how far an alien claimant who is party to a proceeding in a local court must do what he is, under the local law, not under an obligation to do in relation to legal procedures, in order to exhaust local remedies. All other things being equal, two factors seem to be of relevance in determining whether the alien claimant has pursued the appropriate course of conduct in relation to any particular remedy: (i) the effect of the particular remedy in relation to the successful outcome in adequate redress of the case; and (ii) the consideration that legal proceedings are complicated, so that much if not all is left in the hands of counsel, who must exercise a great deal of judgment and forensic skill.

As regards the first factor, it would seem to be necessary that the effect of the remedy in issue must bear some objective relation to the result of the case. The remedy clearly must be of such a kind that, if used, it would have influenced the decision in the case in favour of the alien. But the determination of what the exact influence or relation must be is not easy. The claimant has his case taken up before an international tribunal with a decision against him in a case in which the respondent state points to a particular remedy which he has failed to use. While in broad terms the remedy must be of such a kind that it must be effective, in that had it been used it would have resulted in a decision favourable to the claimant, there are several possible approaches to the definition of effectiveness. It is possible simply to take the view that only such remedies which would *certainly* have brought about a favourable decision need be considered, and that the claimant fails to exhaust his procedural remedies only in circumstances in which he has not resorted to this kind of remedy. Apart from the difficulty of judging the effect of a remedy *ex post facto* in terms of certainty, this criterion appears to weigh the balance too much in favour of the claimant as against the respondent state. Perhaps a more subtle criterion is a degree of probability. This would strike a fair compromise between the interest of the respondent state in doing justice through its own machinery and that of the claimant in having justice done in the most efficient and least expensive way possible. Thus, the proper test to be applied in determining the effect of a remedy seems to be whether its use would *probably* have resulted in success for the claimant. To place the relationship between the remedy and its effect at less than this would pitch the balance too much in favour of the respondent state. If the test were whether there was any *possibility*, however slim, of success through the use of the relevant remedy, the burden on the claimant would be too heavy; for possibilities are unlimited and a vast array of remedies allegedly left unused may be brought within the compass of the rule. The degree of meticulousness expected of the claimant would be excessive.

In the *Ambatielos Claim*, the arbitral tribunal recognized that there had to be some relation between the remedy and its effect on the case, if it was to be characterized as a remedy that had to be used; and in explaining the nature of the rule relating to procedural remedies the tribunal seems to have conceded that there was a danger that the rule might be too widely construed against the interests of the claimant. The tribunal said:

> The rule requires that 'local remedies' shall have been exhausted before an international action can be brought. These 'local remedies' include not only reference to the courts and tribunals, but also the use of procedural facilities which municipal law makes available to litigants before such courts and tribunals. It is the whole system of legal protection as provided by municipal law, which must have been put to the test before a State, as the protector of its nationals, can prosecute the claim on the international plane . . .
>
> It is clear, however, that it cannot be strained too far. Taken literally, it would imply that the fact of having neglected to make use of some means of procedure – even which is not important to the defence of the action – would suffice to allow a defendant State to claim that local remedies have not been exhausted, and that, therefore, an international action cannot be brought. This would confer on the rule of prior exhaustion of local remedies a scope which is unacceptable.[18]

Although the arbitral tribunal recognized that some limitation had to be placed on the scope of the rule in connection with procedural remedies, no clear definition of the limitation was provided. A definition was offered in the following terms:

> the non-utilisation of certain means of procedure can be accepted as constituting a gap in the exhaustion of local remedies only if the use of these means of procedure were essential to establish the claimant's case.[19]

While the essential nature of the remedy was referred to, no explanation was given of 'essentialness'. In his dissenting opinion, Spiropoulos made a similar point when he said: 'Moreover, the remedy must be such as to affect the course of the proceedings; in other words it must be an essential remedy.'[20] He went a little further than the arbitral tribunal in stating that the term 'essential' means 'such as will affect the course

---

[18] *Ibid.*, p. 120.   [19] *Ibid.*, p. 120.

[20] *Ibid.*, p. 128. Spiropoulos also expressed the view that the test of effectiveness applied to procedural remedies was the same as that applied to appeals from a lower to a higher court, and this had implicitly been admitted by the arbitral commission. However, the latter did not necessarily take that view, merely stating the need for 'essentialness'.

of the proceedings'. But even this does not explain specifically how it is to be determined that the proceedings would have been affected.

As far as the *Ambatielos Claim* went, it seems to have been unnecessary for the tribunal to give a specific definition of the notion of 'essentialness' or 'effectiveness' of the remedy, since it was conceded by the claimant in the case that the remedy in question, namely, the calling of the witness, would, if used, have changed the decision of the English court,[21] an admission which the tribunal recognized in its judgment.[22] It is to fill in the gap created by the absence of further explanation, therefore, that it becomes necessary to regard the remedy as effective or essential only if it is probable that its use would have led to success.

The definition suggested of the effect of the remedy for the purposes of the exhaustion of procedural remedies differs considerably from the criterion used in determining whether an appeal must be taken from a lower to a higher court in order that local remedies may be exhausted. The test in the latter case is whether the appeal is not 'obviously futile', as was stated in the *Finnish Ships Arbitration*.[23] That is to say, the remedy of appeal must be resorted to, unless it can be shown that the appeal would 'obviously' not have changed the decision. This is different from saying that an appeal must be taken only if it is probable that an appeal will succeed. Probability of success is the test suggested in the case of procedural remedies. There are good reasons for the difference in standards. The purpose of an appeal is to have a decision reversed by a higher and more experienced tribunal and it is the specific business of appeal courts to reverse decisions. It is not an unfair requirement, therefore, that a claimant should do his best to have a decision reversed in his favour by such a court, unless it is absolutely clear that the court cannot and will not reverse it. In the case of procedural remedies of a discretionary nature within the same court, the object of the remedy is to help the claimant prove his case against the respondent state. It is only those that are likely, therefore, to help him in this task that are

---

[21] 'If there had been Major Laing in front of him, the person who actually conducted the proceedings on behalf of the Ministry, it is quite inconceivable, Sir, we submit on behalf of the Greek Government, that Mr Justice Hill could have come to any conclusion other than that in point of fact it was proved there was a specific contract for delivery of ships on specific dates.' Soskice for the Greek government: *Anglo-Greek Arbitration Minutes*, 2nd Sitting at p. 9.

[22] 12 UNRIAA at p. 121: 'the testimony of Major Laing would have had the effect of establishing the claim put forward by Mr Ambatielos before Mr Justice Hill.'

[23] *Finland* v. *Great Britain*, 3 UNRIAA p. 1495 (1934).

relevant to his case, and not just any remedy which is not obviously useless.

The second factor becomes relevant if it is established that the procedural remedy in issue is effective or essential. There is good reason to postulate that the investigation of the question whether a remedy must be used should not stop with the answer that it is an effective or essential one. Factors connected with the nature of litigation in the modern world, with all its concomitant complications, tactics and specialization, become relevant. In approaching this question, it would be proper to begin by considering the views of the arbitrators in the *Ambatielos Claim*. The tribunal (a majority of three), Alfaro and Spiropoulos took different views on the problem. Both the latter dissented on the issue of whether procedural remedies had been exhausted in the case, although for different reasons.

The tribunal was of the view that, if the procedural remedy in issue was an essential remedy, the failure to use it amounted to a non-exhaustion of local procedural remedies. It said:

It may be that the decision of Mr Ambatielos not to call Major Laing as a witness with the result that he did not exhaust local remedies, was dictated by reasons of expediency – quite understandable in themselves – in putting his case before Mr Justice Hill. This is not the question to be determined. The Commission is not concerned with the question as to whether he was right or wrong in acting as he did. He took his decision at his own risk.

The testimony of Major Laing must be assumed to have been essential for the success of the action of Mr Ambatielos before Mr Justice Hill. It could have been adduced by Mr Ambatielos but was not in fact adduced. Mr Ambatielos has, therefore, not exhausted the local remedies available to him in the proceedings before Mr Justice Hill.[24]

Alfaro, on the other hand, proceeded in his individual opinion to a different extreme in holding that, even if a remedy were essential, there may be circumstances in which its use was not required for the purpose of exhausting procedural remedies:

The 'local remedies' rule . . . means in my opinion that when a claimant appears before municipal courts, either as plaintiff or defendant, he must exhaust the procedural remedies made available to him by the law of the land before each of the several courts in which the case may be tried. The concept of *procedural remedies* must be taken in its general sense. Thus, a claimant may be held not to have exhausted the procedural remedies at his disposal, if he failed, for instance,

[24] *Greece* v. *UK*, 12 UNRIAA at p. 121 (1956).

to adduce evidence despite his necessity to prove the facts of the case, or if he failed to appear in court to argue his case at the stage of the trial in which he had to argue.

But the rule cannot be carried so far as to interfere with the actual or concrete use of a given procedural remedy. Thus a claimant who availed himself of the procedural remedy of adducing evidence, should not be held by an international tribunal to have failed to exhaust local remedies because he did not produce a certain exhibit, or because he did not call a certain witness.[25]

This view allows considerable latitude to the alien claimant. Even if the particular remedy in issue is an effective or essential one, it would appear that provided the claimant has resorted to other remedies of the same *general category*, for example producing evidence, he cannot be said to have failed to exhaust his procedural remedies merely because he failed to use particular remedies, however effective they may be. This places a very light burden on the claimant in the pursuit of his cause. All he need do is to use just one in each general category of procedural remedies in order to exhaust procedural remedies. Apart from the difficulty this view may present in determining the exact scope of each of the general categories, it leaves the door wide open for claimants merely to go through the motions, with no serious intent, of seeking to obtain justice from states against which they may have claims rooted in international law, particularly if they prefer to have an adjudication by an international tribunal. This view does not attach enough significance to the respondent state's interest in being allowed to discharge its international responsibility by means of a decision given by its courts.

The view of the tribunal, on the other hand, seems to err on the side of caution in laying too heavy a burden on the claimant. No room is left for a certain expediency and even good judgment, which may be quite proper in the presentation of a case, especially at the time of trial. An objective 'essentialness' or 'effectiveness', which can be easily determined by hindsight at the time of an international arbitration at a much later date, may not be so apparent at the time of the trial. Thus, the issue arises of whether the risk of a wrong decision must be placed entirely on the shoulders of the claimant, or whether some margin may not be allowed him without detriment to the interests of the host state in doing justice by its own methods. Perhaps Spiropoulos offered an acceptable approach, albeit in his dissenting opinion:

---

[25] *Ibid.*, pp. 124–5.

Whereas, however, in the case of recourse from a lower to a higher court the test to be applied, i.e. the existence and effectiveness, or otherwise, of recourse, is an *objective* one, practical considerations must soften the rigidity of the rule in a case where one and the same court is concerned. The rule, then, becomes one of determining, having regard to the particular circumstances of the case, what counsel would have done in the interests of his client. Moreover, the remedy must be such as to affect the course of the proceedings; in other words it must be an *essential* remedy. But these are, of course, questions which can only be decided by having due regard to the merits of each individual case.[26]

There are two requirements for a finding of non-exhaustion of procedural remedies referred to here. Not only must the remedy be essential, but there is another condition referred to in the statement, namely, that 'The rule . . . becomes one of determining, having regard to the particular circumstances of the case, what counsel would have done in the interests of his client'. This requirement embodies what may be called the objective standard of the 'reasonable counsel'. The question to be asked is whether a reasonable or average qualified counsel, as opposed to a layman, would have taken advantage of the remedy in the interests of his client. In answering that question numerous factors have to be taken into account, depending on the facts of each particular case, as is indicated in the above opinion. A compendious way of explaining it is by saying that the utility of using the measure envisaged must be measured against the risk of not using it. The test makes allowance for such factors as minor errors and the non-obviousness of the essential nature of the remedy, factors which are not lightly to be dismissed in legal practice. The test is not subjective in that it does not give counsel *carte blanche* in the choice of a particular remedy. The mere fact that counsel did not use a given remedy, even for *bona fide* reasons, would not be sufficient in itself to warrant the failure to use the remedy. Nor does it give counsel a similar freedom of choice, provided some action is taken in each general category of procedural remedies, as Alfaro's test would permit. On the other hand, it is not so strict as to require the claimant, as represented by counsel, to act according to the exact objective truth of every situation, as the tribunal's view favours. Where the remedy is an obviously effective or essential one, the application of the second test would not affect the obligation of the claimant to use it. For it could not be argued that a reasonable counsel would, in the circumstances, refrain from using the remedy. It is where the effectiveness

---

[26] *Ibid.*, p. 128.

of the remedy is not so obvious that this test will really be applicable. If it can be shown that the remedy, although in fact effective, is not obviously effective and that reasonable counsel would not think it necessary to use it for his client's benefit, then the claimant need not use it. It would seem that the above view of the law, based on the opinion of Spiropoulos, is most satisfactory as giving adequate weight to the interests of both the claimant and the respondent state. In his search for justice the claimant is under an obligation to observe a certain standard which does not depend on him or his counsel. The respondent state, on the other hand, may not expect perfection on the part of the claimant in his appreciation of the true effect of a remedy.

In the *Ambatielos Claim*, the arbitral tribunal's view of the law on this issue would seem to have been too strict. On the other hand, the result that was reached by the tribunal, on the question of whether the claimant should have called Major Laing in order to exhaust procedural remedies, would have been the same had they applied the more liberal view of the law taken by Spiropoulos and supported here. The decision on the facts of the case does not really conflict with the latter view. Because the application of the test of 'the reasonable counsel' would not have resulted in a finding in favour of the claimant, it was irrelevant whether the test was applied or not. Thus, Spiropoulos' introduction of that test does not have to be regarded as unacceptable, because it was not explicitly rejected by the tribunal and does not require for the case a different result on its facts. On the other hand, although Spiropoulos' view of the law is preferable, a proper application of the test to the facts of the case would seem to have warranted a different conclusion from the one reached by him.

An examination of the facts will show how the decision reached by the tribunal is reconcilable with Spiropoulos' view of the law. As to the effect of the evidence in the possession of the witness, Major Laing, the Greek government conceded that it would have changed the decision of the lower court. It was admitted that the remedy was an effective or essential one. Hence this part of the problem presented no difficulty. It was on the second question, on which in fact argument did take place, namely, whether reasonable counsel would have used the remedy, that the contending parties took differing positions. The UK government argued that the claimant and his counsel believed that Major Laing had important evidence; that the latter had read extracts to the claimant from certain letters which were material, and to which the claimant had no access; that there was no reason to suppose that Major Laing would not have told the truth if he had been called; that Major Laing had not been subpoenaed by the Crown and, even if he had been, that there was no reason why he could not have been called by the claimant; and that in the circumstances it was proper that Major Laing should have been called.[27] It was submitted by the Greek government that the claimant did not call and could not have been expected to call Major Laing as a witness for the following reasons: he was a former officer of the Ministry; he had refused to make a statement to the claimant's solicitors, so that they had not the slightest idea what he would say; as for the letters from which extracts were read to the claimant, the latter had not gathered the import of the letters and it was only when Major Laing read them to him after the first trial that their true meaning was gathered; the plaintiff had called three other witnesses to give evidence on this issue; furthermore, Major Laing had been subpoenaed by the Crown. Most emphasis was laid on the fact that Major Laing refused to make a statement to the claimant's solicitors and that, therefore, since it was not known whether Major Laing would say anything in favour of the claimant, it was in keeping with practice not to call him.[28]

According to the tribunal's view of the law, the fact that Major Laing's evidence was essential was conclusive as to whether he should have been called in order that procedural remedies might be exhausted. On Alfaro's view, some evidence had been called, production of an element of evidence in the category of evidence had been resorted to, and, thus, procedural remedies had been exhausted.[29] Thus, on both these views, the above facts were of little further relevance. However, on the view of the law which was taken by Spiropoulos, these facts are important in answering the question of whether reasonable counsel would have called Major Laing, granting that that remedy was an effective one. Spiropoulos

---

[27] *Anglo-Greek Arbitration Minutes*, 9th Sitting at p. 46; 11th Sitting at p. 45; and 12th Sitting at p. 105.

[28] Especially *Anglo-Greek Arbitration Minutes*, 13th Sitting at p. 90; also 2nd Sitting at p. 33; 3rd Sitting at p. 28; and 6th Sitting at p. 22.

[29] 'Whether Mr Ambatielos or his advisers were right or wrong in not calling Major Laing to testify, I believe is immaterial. Mr Ambatielos, represented by his advisers, made use of the procedural remedy of adducing evidence in court. He adduced such evidence as he thought might prove his case. Whether he was clever or made a mistake, whether or not he lost because of an error in handling the instrumentality of evidence, are questions with which an international tribunal cannot concern itself in dealing with the issue of exhaustion or non-exhaustion of local remedies. Such tribunal should not be called upon to pass judgment on the manner in which the procedural remedies were used, but on the fact that they were used.' *Ambatielos Claim (Greece v. UK)*, 12 UNRIAA at p. 125 (1956).

placed much emphasis on the facts that Major Laing refused to make a statement before the trial, that, therefore, the claimant's solicitors could not know what he would say and that it was in keeping with English practice for counsel not to call such a witness in ordinary circumstances.[30] However, in fact it would seem that the circumstances were not ordinary. From all the circumstances it would have been evident to a reasonable counsel that Major Laing alone had the evidence necessary for the success of the claimant's case.[31] Hence, a reasonable counsel could not have concluded that Major Laing's evidence was unlikely to be of value to the claimant's case so as to warrant his not being called.[32] The utility of calling him outweighed, in the circumstances, the risk of not having some cogent evidence towards the proof of the case. The failure to call him was, therefore, an unreasonable act on the part of counsel and constituted a failure to exhaust procedural remedies.[33] Suppose, on the other hand, that Major Laing, who in fact had important evidence, had indicated that he had none, and there was no reason for the claimant or his counsel to disbelieve him in all the circumstances of the case, then a situation would have arisen in which a reasonable counsel could not have been expected to call him in evidence, even though in fact Major Laing did have cogent evidence and the remedy of calling him would have been effective. Equally, if a witness has shown that he is likely to be so hostile as not to reveal the truth, or if a written document is of such a nature that it is ambiguous by itself, although unknown to counsel and his client and through no fault of theirs there may be some other evidence which could resolve the ambiguity in the claimant's favour, a reasonable counsel could not

---

[30] *Ibid.*, p. 128. See also *ibid.*, p. 128: 'According to English practice, counsel are rarely prepared, *in ordinary circumstances*, to call a witness who has refused to give a statement to the solicitor.' Emphasis added.

[31] That Major Laing had read some extracts from certain important letters to the alien claimant was cogent evidence of this fact. Although the latter may not have gathered the exact import of the letters, counsel ought to have surmised that (a) Major Laing, if anybody, would have the necessary evidence, since he was the responsible officer of the UK government who took part in the actual transaction, and (b) the letter probably contained important evidence of which Major Laing had knowledge.

[32] In an appeal by the claimant, the English Court of Appeal found that the evidence which Major Laing was alleged to have been able to give could have been obtained by reasonable diligence on the claimant's part: *Board of Trade* v. *'Ambatielos', etc.* [1953] Lloyd's Rep 387. This supports the above view.

[33] The finding of Spiropoulos on this point may have been influenced by the fact that, in determining whether reasonable counsel would have called Major Laing, he took into consideration the fact that the UK government was withholding certain relevant documents: 12 UNRIAA at p. 128. However, this fact raised a separate issue.

be expected to resort to either of these remedies as being helpful to his client, effective though they may be in actual fact.[34]

In connection with the above principles which apply to discretionary remedies there are two further problems that arise. The first concerns the verification of the effect of the remedy in question, and the second the time in respect of which the two principles referred to must be applied.

Verification of the effectiveness of the remedy

The question to be answered is how an international tribunal would verify whether the remedy was an effective one and would have changed the decision in the case before the local court. Broadly speaking, there are three possible options: the tribunal may accept the word of the claimant state as to the effect of the remedy; it may accept the word of the respondent state; or it may investigate the matter on the evidence presented to it and come to its own conclusion. Looking to reason and good sense, it would seem that this is a matter of law and fact which the tribunal must ordinarily investigate and decide on the evidence before it. To determine the effect of the remedy, an estimate of probabilities has to be made and there is no reason why a tribunal should not be competent to make such an estimate. It may prove to be a very complicated task, but it is the application of a principle of law to proved facts. On the other

---

[34] A further point was raised in the case which involved the principles discussed above but was not decided by the arbitral tribunal, which had already held that procedural remedies had not been exhausted. The UK government argued that the claimant had failed to exhaust procedural remedies by failing to demand discovery of certain documents which were alleged to have been relevant to the proof of the case, and in respect of which it was alleged that the UK government had claimed the privilege of non-discovery. It was said that such a privilege was asserted by a ministerial certificate and that no steps had been taken to subpoena an official to obtain such a certificate: *Anglo-Greek Arbitration Minutes*, 12th Sitting at p. 114. The Greek government replied that the documents had been called for in the trial court, that counsel for the UK government had said that the documents could not be had and that the trial judge had explained the position in regard to Crown privilege: *ibid.*, 13th Sitting at p. 94; and 6th Sitting at p. 27. In effect, the argument was that, although the formal steps had not been taken, what had happened served to show that such steps would not have had the desired results and would not, therefore, have changed the course of the proceedings and the decision. This issue should have been resolved in favour of the Greek government on the basis that, even if the remedy was in fact an effective one, it was reasonable, in all the circumstances of the case, for the claimant's counsel to assume that a formal request would not have brought forth the documents and would not, therefore, have had effective results. The application of the principle of the reasonable counsel should have operated in favour of the claimant on that issue, although this would not have changed the outcome of the international litigation.

hand, where the claimant state concedes that the remedy concerned is an effective or essential one, there is no reason for the tribunal to go beyond this admission. A finding that the remedy is an effective one, as opposed to a finding that it is ineffective, would not be in the claimant state's favour but to its detriment. If it is willing to concede this result against itself, there is no reason for the tribunal to examine the issue in order to contradict the admission. Similarly, if the respondent state admits that the remedy is not an effective one, then it is denying what is to its advantage and its admission should be accepted by the tribunal.

Difficulties arise, however, when the claimant state concedes the effectiveness of the remedy and the respondent state apparently denies its effectiveness. In short, the parties appear to maintain the converse of what they should in their own interests be maintaining. It is normally for the respondent state to maintain that the remedy which the alien has failed to use is an effective one, while it is for the claimant state to contend that the remedy is an ineffective one so that the alien claimant was not under an obligation to resort to it. The reverse situation seems to have arisen in the *Ambatielos Claim*. Hence, whatever was said by the tribunal and the other arbitrators on this issue must be read subject to this consideration. Their statements would, thus, apply to the general problem only in a limited way. The tribunal said:

The Greek Government further contends that if Mr Ambatielos had called Major Laing as a witness, the decision of Mr Justice Hill would have been favourable to him; this is a contention that is disputed by the United Kingdom Government.

It is not possible for the Commission to decide on the evidence before it the question whether the case would have been in favour of Mr Ambatielos if Major Laing had been heard as a witness. The Commission has not heard the witnesses called before Mr Justice Hill and cannot solely on the documentary evidence put before the Commission form an opinion whether the testimony of Major Laing would have been successful in establishing the claim of Mr Ambatielos before Mr Justice Hill in this respect.

The test as regards the question whether the testimony of Major Laing was essential must therefore be what the claimant Government in this respect has contended, viz., that the testimony of Major Laing would have had the effect of establishing the claim put forward by Mr Ambatielos before Mr Justice Hill.[35]

---

[35] *Ambatielos Claim (Greece v. UK)*, 12 UNRIAA at p. 121 (1956). During the proceedings too, Arbitrator Bagge posed a similar difficulty concerning the tribunal's ability to come to a decision on the substantive issue in the circumstances of the case; *Anglo-Greek Arbitration Minutes*, 12th Sitting at p. 101.

Although it may appear that the tribunal was laying down a general principle that the view of the claimant state as to the effectiveness of the remedy is always to be accepted, it appears to have been dealing only with the situation before it, where the claimant state conceded that the remedy was an effective one, and did not intend to lay down a general principle of that kind. As a general principle, it would defeat the purpose of litigation – for the claimant state would only have to contend that the remedy was ineffective in order to win its point on the issue of procedural remedies. Secondly, the arbitral tribunal's reluctance to investigate whether the remedy was an effective one must be attributed to the fact that the claimant state admitted that the remedy was effective in this case. It is not necessary to suppose that the arbitral tribunal intended to lay down a general principle that an international tribunal does not have the power or ability to decide such a question. It is entirely within the judicial function to decide such questions. In this situation, the tribunal would have to decide whether sufficient evidence had been adduced to prove that the use of the remedy in issue would probably have resulted in a decision in favour of the claimant. If there is insufficient evidence, it means that the respondent state has failed to make its point.

Alfaro adopted a different approach on this issue. The assumption that the Greek view of the effect of the remedy was correct was, in his view, contrary to the realities of the case. He said further:

The evidence before the Commission does abundantly prove that if Major Laing had been called to the witness box, it was extremely doubtful that his testimony, particularly after cross-examination, would have resulted favourably to Mr Ambatielos. Hence, it can hardly be called essential.[36]

He impliedly accepted the view that the tribunal should examine the evidence and reach its own conclusion in regard to the question of whether the remedy was effective. However, unlike the tribunal, he also expressed the opinion that, even where the claimant state admits the effectiveness of the remedy, the tribunal should inquire into the merits of the issue. The view of the tribunal is more in accord with the nature of the judicial process as a means of settling disputes and is, therefore, to be preferred.

The situation that arose in the *Ambatielos Claim* was exceptional and is to be explained by reference to the nature of the litigation. Some confusion arose from the nature of the legal issues involved. The main basis of

---

[36] 12 UNRIAA at p. 125.

the Greek claim was the Treaty of 1866, and the substance of this claim
was that there had been a denial of justice in the proceedings before the
High Court of England in connection with the claimant's breach of contract claim. For this purpose the Greek government argued that there
had been some suppression of evidence by the UK government which
had led to a decision adverse to the claimant. The Greek government
maintained that the breach of contract and the adverse decision resulting in a loss to the claimant contained a denial of justice amounting to
a breach of the treaty. It was also argued by the Greek government that
the breach of contract itself was a breach of international law.[37] The
UK government maintained, on the other hand, that there had been no
denial of justice in the local courts, that no evidence had been unjustly
suppressed, that any evidence that had not been presented in the course
of the proceedings would not have affected the decision and that, therefore, the decision could not have been otherwise. The calling of Major
Laing became relevant to the issue because the Greek government maintained that counsel believed that the UK government would call him as
a witness, so that counsel would have had a chance of examining him
and eliciting the important evidence in favour of the claimant. His not
being called was part of the denial of justice. Implied was the argument
that Major Laing had some useful evidence. The UK government said that
Major Laing had no such evidence as would have changed the decision,
apart from the fact that it had done nothing to prevent him from being
called. For this part of the case the Greek government maintained that
Major Laing's evidence was *effective*, while the respondent state argued
the contrary.

When the defence that local remedies had not been exhausted was
raised by the respondent state, the issue seems to have been argued on
the assumption that the breach of contract was a breach of international law, as being a breach of treaty. For the success of the respondent
state's argument, it now became necessary for it to maintain that the
remedy of calling Major Laing was an effective one which the alien had
failed to use. But this would have been a contradiction of its earlier position. Accordingly the UK government conceded that, *on the assumption*
that the remedy was an effective one, the fault was the alien's for not
having called him.[38] It would not be proper to say, therefore, that the
respondent state rested its case that local remedies had not been exhausted on the assumption that the remedy was ineffective. The Greek

[37] *Anglo-Greek Arbitration Minutes*, 5th Sitting at pp. 1ff.
[38] *Ibid.*, 12th Sitting at p. 112.

government, however, in its reply to this exception does not seem to have gone back on its assertion that the remedy was an effective one. Indeed, it could not very well do so. Instead, it rested its defence on the absence of negligence on the part of counsel in not calling the witness.[39]

Thus, the confusion arose from the fact that the Greek government was placed in a position of having to maintain that it had been prevented from calling effective evidence in connection with the main issue in the claim, while in reply to the objection that local remedies had not been exhausted it would have been to its advantage to maintain that this same evidence was ineffective. This it could not and did not do. The UK government could, on the other hand, contend without inconsistency that Major Laing's evidence would have been effective, if called, but that there had been no denial of justice because the claimant could have called him, while there had been no exhaustion of procedural remedies because he had failed to call him.

The respondent state was really maintaining that the remedy was effective for the purpose of the local remedies issue, while the claimant state not only conceded but strongly contended that the remedy was an effective one for other purposes in the case and did not change its position. The situation was one in which the claimant state conceded the contention of the respondent state that the remedy was effective. Therefore, the conclusion of the tribunal that the remedy must be taken to be an effective one in the circumstances of the case could not have been incorrect. The *Ambatielos Claim*, then, should leave the essential principles governing the determination of effectiveness of a procedural remedy by an international tribunal unchanged.

In the final analysis there are four possible situations that may arise and three principles which govern them:
1. Where the claimant state maintains that the remedy in question is ineffective and the respondent state maintains the contrary, the tribunal must decide the question of the effectiveness of the remedy on the evidence presented to it. This is the normal situation.
2. Where the claimant state expressly concedes the respondent state's allegation that the remedy is effective or there is some implied agreement between the parties that the remedy is effective, the issue is decided by the agreement of the parties and the tribunal merely accepts that position. It was this kind of situation that really arose in the *Ambatielos Claim*, and the above principle was applied in the decision.

[39] *Ibid., passim.*

3. The converse case, where the respondent state concedes the inefficacy of the remedy to the claimant state either expressly or impliedly, is not likely to arise in reality, since that would be incompatible with the raising of the issue by the respondent state. But if it does arise, the same principle as is applicable to category 2 is applicable. The issue is decided by the agreement of the parties.

4. An equally unlikely situation is where the claimant state concedes that the remedy is effective and the respondent state concedes that it is ineffective, such as appeared to be the situation in the *Ambatielos Claim*. As in the *Ambatielos Claim*, it will generally be the case that the true situation is different. If such a case arises, however, it is the concession by the respondent state that should be relevant as a denial of its case. It is more appropriate to accept the admission of the respondent state than that of the claimant state, because, as it is the duty of the respondent state to raise the issue that local remedies have not been exhausted, if it concedes the inefficacy of the remedy it is really contradicting its objection and, thus, denying its case.

The time in respect of which the two principles must be applied

The second question raised relates to the time in respect of which the principles of effectiveness and of the reasonable counsel must be applied. In his separate opinion in the *Ambatielos Claim* Alfaro answered this question when he said: 'Non-exhaustion of local remedies must necessarily take place at the time the local remedy can be resorted to but not afterwards.'[40] This means no more than that the principles discussed above should be applied to the facts of the situation as at the time at which resort could in the ordinary course of affairs have been had to the remedy.

In regard to the principle of effectiveness, the application of the time rule creates no problems. The procedural remedies can only be effective as at the time when they could have been used. No other time could be relevant. Because the tribunal in the *Ambatielos Claim* accepted the statement of the claimant state that the remedy in question was an effective one, it had no need to examine the problem of time in this context. Although Alfaro examined the evidence produced as to the effectiveness of the remedy and concluded that the remedy was not an essential one, since 'it was extremely doubtful that his [Major Laing's] testimony, particularly after cross-examination, would have resulted favourably to

---

[40] 12 UNRIAA at p. 126.

Mr Ambatielos',[41] this aspect of the issue offered no problems as to time for him.

It is in relation to the application of the second necessary principle, that of the reasonable counsel, that the question of time becomes important. As Alfaro indicated, the issue of whether counsel acted reasonably in all the circumstances of the case must be decided with reference to the time at which he had to act in choosing to use or reject the available remedy. It is not appropriate, for instance, that facts which came to light after that time and which were necessarily out of counsel's reach at the relevant time, should be taken into account in applying the principle.

In the *Ambatielos Claim*, as seen above, reasonable counsel would have called Major Laing as a witness on the basis of the knowledge available at the time of the first action, even though the claimant was not fully aware of all the contents of certain letters at the time, but was apprised of them later by Major Laing himself. The absence of detailed knowledge would not have affected the course that counsel should reasonably have taken.[42] In that particular case, therefore, it could not be said that the rule relating to time was of such importance. But it could make a difference where facts coming to light after an action would, if they had been known before, have induced counsel, as a reasonable counsel, to resort to a remedy which he had in his discretion, reasonably exercised, decided to avoid. Then the position must be judged as at the time of the action, and the answer must be given that counsel could not reasonably have been expected to resort to the remedy.

---

[41] *Ibid.*, p. 125.

[42] Alfaro, while admitting the principle, took a different view of the facts in this case. He thought that, although something about the nature of the evidence that Major Laing had may have been conveyed by him to the claimant when he read extracts from letters to him before the first trial, the former really made known the contents of those letters to the claimant only after the decision in that trial; on what was known after the contents of those letters had been made known to the claimant, it was reasonable for counsel to avail himself of Major Laing as a witness but not before; before that event too little was known, so that his hostile or favourable attitude was decidedly doubtful and, therefore, a reasonable counsel could not have been expected to call him: 12 UNRIAA at pp. 125–6. The time at which this test was applied was relevant, according to Alfaro, because, if it were applied to the situation which existed after the trial, the knowledge of the contents of the letters would have weighed the decision on this point against the claimant State, while, if it were applied to the facts as before the trial, the insufficient knowledge would have warranted a decision in favour of the claimant State. But it has been seen above that this difference was not so material as to affect the course that a reasonable counsel would have taken in the circumstances of the case.

Obstruction by the respondent state

If the respondent state prevents a claimant from using an effective or essential remedy, in a manner that is lawful or unlawful according to the law of the respondent state, the claimant is relieved of the obligation of resorting to it and will be regarded as having exhausted procedural remedies even without making use of it.[43] This proposition rests on the principle that local remedies need not be exhausted where there are none to exhaust.

Suppose, however, that the respondent state has evidence in its possession which is useful for the claimant's case before the local courts, and the claimant is not given access to it for the proceedings, a question which arises is whether that fact relieves the claimant of the duty of making use of other effective remedies which may bring about a favourable result and which, taken alone, reasonable counsel can be expected to use. In general terms, the issue is whether the claimant is altogether exempted from exhausting local remedies where there are alternative effective remedies and the respondent state obstructs the claimant in the use of one or some of them.

The problem may arise where a respondent state has failed to fulfil an obligation under its law to provide the claimant with a particular remedy to which he is entitled. In this situation the non-fulfilment of an obligation by the respondent state imposes an unfair burden on the claimant in the proof of his case. The object of the rule relating to the exhaustion of local remedies is to give the respondent state an opportunity of redressing an international wrong by means of its own machinery of justice. If the state is itself unwilling to perform the obligations imposed on it by its own law in the exercise of this right, especially when those obligations touch upon the claimant's right to make his case, there is no justice done. The fact that the claimant can use other means to prove his case or make his case makes little difference then, for the parties are not in a position of equality. It would follow, therefore, that the non-fulfilment of an obligation by the respondent state which deprives the claimant of an effective means of redress exempts the claimant from resorting to other effective means, no matter how much more or less effective than the former means the other means may be. The fact that an effective means of redress has not been resorted

---

[43] This is apart from any other wrong that the respondent state may commit by way of denying the alien justice, if the obstruction is contrary to municipal or international law.

to in these circumstances does not prevent the claimant from success-fully maintaining that the rule of exhaustion of local remedies has been satisfied.

Equally, where the claimant is under an obligation according to the local law to perform some act of a procedural nature, his non-performance of this obligation would not amount to a non-exhaustion of local procedural remedies, if the respondent state is delinquent in performing a procedural obligation which deprives the claimant of an effective means of redress. The basic reason is the same. The object of justice is not to be achieved if one of the parties defaults in the perfor-mance of his share of the obligations which contribute to the making of the other party's case. The right of dispute settlement granted to the respondent state is not being exercised in a manner which befits the purpose for which it was granted.

Where, however, the respondent state deprives the claimant of an effective procedural means of redress, while acting within the rights granted to it by its own law in excess of the rights granted to the ordinary citizen or litigant, and the claimant has an alternative procedural means of an effective nature, the position is different. In the *Ambatielos Claim*, not only was Major Laing's testimony as a witness lacking, but relevant letters in the possession of the UK government were not available for the trial. These letters were alleged by the Greek government to have been vital to the case, so much so that they would probably or certainly have changed the decision in the first proceedings,[44] and, therefore, were an essential remedy. The UK government claimed that it had a legal right at English law to claim that the documents were privileged from discovery.[45] The Greek government does not seem to have contested the validity of this action according to the English law at that time.[46] The answer given by the tribunal to the question was unequivocal:

[44] *Anglo-Greek Arbitration Minutes*, 2nd Sitting at p. 28.

[45] *Ibid.*, 9th Sitting at p. 37. On the claim of privilege, see also *ibid.*, 11th Sitting at p. 51; 12th Sitting at p. 105; and 14th Sitting at p. 27.

[46] *Ibid.*, 2nd Sitting at pp. 66ff. The attitude of the lower (trial) court to a claim of privilege was not characterized as wrong by the Greek government: *ibid.*, 2nd Sitting at p. 73. On the claim of privilege in respect of these documents, see also *ibid.*, 5th Sitting at p. 24 and 6th Sitting at p. 25. The Greek government did raise a question as to whether it was in the public interest required by the privilege that the documents should not be disclosed: *ibid.*, 2nd Sitting at pp. 86–9. However, the Greek contention that the documents should have been produced was based on different grounds from the illegality according to English law of the exercise of the privilege: *ibid.*, 2nd Sitting at p. 87 and 5th Sitting at p. 24.

If a man can secure help by taking course A or course B and is prevented from taking course A, he fails to exhaust his remedies, if he refrains from taking course B.[47]

Applying this principle to the facts, it held that

the question whether Mr Ambatielos was prevented by the United Kingdom Government from adducing other evidence which might have led to the same result does not seem to be relevant to the question whether the failure of Mr Ambatielos to call Major Laing as a witness must be considered as amounting to a non-exhaustion of the local remedy available to him in the first instance.[48]

Spiropoulos, on the other hand, albeit in his dissenting opinion, did not specifically address this problem but merely mentioned the existence of 'documents which the Crown might have in its possession' as a factor in the consideration of the question of whether counsel could reasonably have been expected to call Major Laing as a witness.[49] This view of the law differs from that of the tribunal. Different considerations seem to be relevant to the issue under discussion from those regarded as relevant by Spiropoulos. It would be allowing too wide a latitude to the claimant and imposing too heavy a burden on the respondent state to allow a claimant to avoid an available remedy in these circumstances merely on the basis that a reasonable counsel would not have resorted to the remedy because another effective remedy was being suppressed by the respondent state.

The answer given by the tribunal does not, in spite of its preciseness and succinctness, carry with it any explanation. It would seem that the real content of this particular rule must be determined by reference to the policies behind the rule of exhaustion of local remedies, although basically the rule propounded by the tribunal is valid. An important consideration is that the local proceedings are in the nature of a preliminary procedural requirement in the settlement of a dispute in international law. There is more than just a dispute between state and individual over a purely domestic problem. Thus, there is also an interest of the international community at stake in having justice done. In the light of this factor, the state party to the dispute should do its best to provide adequate means whereby justice may be done in such a dispute.[50] Moreover, the interest of the respondent state in settling an alleged international delinquency by its own means before being saddled with the expense,

[47] 12 UNRIAA at p. 121.   [48] Ibid.   [49] Ibid., p. 128.
[50] See *Anglo-Greek Arbitration Minutes*, 3rd Sitting at pp. 86–8 for a similar idea.

trouble and publicity of an international proceeding must be set off against that of the claimant in having justice done in the best way possible with the greatest saving of such expense as would result from a multiplicity of proceedings. These are cogent considerations for taking an approach to this problem which is less categorical than that taken by the tribunal, which seems to throw the whole burden of the risk on the claimant. In any event, different considerations from those expressed so broadly in the view of the tribunal apply to the case where the respondent state suppresses an alternative means of redress in violation of the obligations of its own or international law. Similarly, although the respondent state may be acting well within its rights according to its law in depriving the claimant of an alternative remedy, the policy considerations set out above may impose some limits on the exercise of these rights. This is a case of proceedings in a state, before the courts of that state, in which that state is a party, an international issue is at stake and that state has control of an alternative effective procedural means of redress. In arriving at a satisfactory definition of the rule two aspects of the situation may require special consideration: (i) the effectiveness of the means of redress as compared with that of the alternative remedy; and (ii) the possibility that a reasonable counsel can make a decision that the remedy in the control of the respondent state is more effective than the alternative remedy.

As to (i) it may be proper to make a comparative estimate of the actual effectiveness of the two remedies. This may be a difficult task, but not impossible. What must be shown is that there is a greater probability of success by the use of the remedy under the control of the respondent state than by the use of the alternative, if the claimant is to be exempted from resorting to the alternative remedy. The second consideration requires that, in addition to (i), it must be shown that a reasonable counsel would have been able to estimate that effectiveness and, therefore, have had some reason for not using the alternative remedy. For, unless counsel has good reason for not using what he could have used and should have used, he cannot be excused. It is insufficient that the remedy being suppressed is in fact more effective than the one available, if counsel does not know this fact or cannot come to a reasonable conclusion on it.[51]

---

[51] Spiropoulos suggested further that, if the alien could not expect to be given the remedy being suppressed in similar proceedings in his national state, he should have no right to expect it as against a foreign state. But, it would seem that this is hardly a consideration of relevance in the light of the policies underlying the law of exhaustion of local remedies.

It will be observed that these principles do not open the door too wide for claimants. They embody firm limitations on the claimant's right to avoid using an alternative remedy which is available. They operate in favour of the interest of the state doing justice by its own means, while they give adequate weight to the interests of the claimant and the international community in having justice done. Prima facie the claimant must resort to the alternative remedy under the ordinary conditions, in order to exhaust procedural remedies in the same court, and to this extent the view of the tribunal in the *Ambatielos Claim* is acceptable. But in an exceptional case the alien may be exempted from resorting to the alternative remedy available. These circumstances arise where it can be shown not only that the remedy of which he was deprived is more effective than the alternative remedy which was available, but also that a reasonable counsel could in the circumstances have come to this conclusion. These conditions are not easily susceptible of proof, and thus it will be seldom that a claimant will gain exemption on these grounds.

In the *Ambatielos Claim* none of the arbitrators examined this aspect of the rule of exhaustion of local remedies in this way. However, it is possible to explain that by reference to the fact that the situation before the tribunal did not involve these exceptional circumstances. It was unnecessary for the tribunal to enter into a detailed analysis of the principles applicable because these issues were never raised, so that it could not be said that the crucial documents which were being suppressed would have been more efficacious than the evidence of Major Laing. Hence, no exemption from the general rule could be granted to the claimant.[52]

---

[52] A further situation that may arise in proceedings before national courts is where the alien cannot produce evidence required by the court for the proof of his case because of the act of his national State. In such a case, the alien's failure to produce the necessary evidence, if detrimental to his case, does not appear to amount to a failure on his part to exhaust his procedural remedies. He has done everything in his power to prove his case. It is his state that has caused the obstruction. In the international proceedings, however, the claim is brought on behalf of the alien by this national state. The claim is regarded as the claim of one state against another. If the alien is regarded as having exhausted local remedies, should not the claimant state be prevented from bringing an international claim on an equitable theory that it must come to an international court with clean hands? Having prevented the respondent state from doing justice in the cause of one of its nationals, should it not be disallowed from claiming justice in the same cause against the respondent state? It will be noted that it is the alien who suffers by this. But there are three entities involved in this situation and at international law each has an interest in relation to the other. It is unfortunate that the solution should work to the detriment of the least responsible of the three. This problem is suggested by the facts of *Société Internationale pour Participations Industrielles et Commerciales SA* v. *Brownell, AG, as Successor to the Alien Property Custodian et al.*, 225 F 2d 532 (1955), certiorari denied, 243 F 2d 254 (1957).

Where the respondent state controls an alternative remedy under the law applying to citizens in general, it cannot be argued that preventing the claimant from access to an alternative remedy has any relevance to the question of whether he may be exempted from using an existing remedy. The respondent state is merely exercising a right available to anyone, including the claimant, equally, so that no question of inequality and unfairness arises. The claimant can be expected to allow for the right of the respondent state to exercise general powers.

It may happen in either case, that is to say, whether the power of suppressing an alternative remedy is granted by the general law or by a special law applicable to the respondent state only, that such power of suppression is contrary to the treaty obligations of the respondent state, or falls below the international minimum standard. In such an event, it is clear that according to the general principles of international law the claimant need not resort to any available remedies, however effective or ineffective they may be, in order to exhaust local remedies, since the remedies provided by the respondent state do not conform to the requirements of international law.

General conclusions

What emerges from the above examination of the issue of exhaustion of procedural remedies in the particular case is that the implementation of the rule of local remedies is not a matter of applying a *strict and inflexible* rule with no variable content for general concepts. Some pertinent observations may be made.

First, while 'ineffectiveness' and 'effectiveness' may be general criteria applicable to the issue, their content is not to be determined simply and in all circumstances, by reference, for example, to 'obvious futility' or, indeed, 'normal use'.

Secondly, there are wrinkles in the application of, for example, the accepted general concept of 'ineffectiveness' (or its opposite), which require a more pragmatic approach.

Thirdly and moreover, complications created by the circumstances of the case, for example of obstruction by the respondent state, raise issues, *inter alia*, of good faith, which require to be addressed individually. Clearly, there may be other special problems inherent in the circumstances of the case which again would have to be addressed on a pragmatic basis, having due regard for the conflicting interests involved.

Fourthly, the instance of procedural remedies which has been considered points also to the possibility that there may be other areas involving, for example, the 'ineffectiveness' or 'effectiveness' of remedies or the 'normal' use of remedies, which have not been dealt with hitherto, in which a similar pragmatic approach would necessarily have to be taken.

Fifthly, the point is that in all situations, while general or indeterminate concepts in the rule may exist, their concretization in terms of law, as well as their application to facts, require not adherence to 'rigidity' but a reasonably sagacious and even imaginative approach, which would achieve the ends of justice, considering all the interests involved.

10   Waiver of the rule and estoppel

The principles of consent and good faith are relevant to the law relating to the rule of local remedies in so far as the rule may be excluded by the operation of either of them. The application of the principle of consent results in the exclusion of the rule on the basis that it has been waived, either expressly or impliedly, by the host or respondent state,[1] while the principle of good faith has the effect of excluding the application of the rule in circumstances such as where the doctrine of estoppel or its equivalent would operate.

Express waiver

Express waiver takes place where the host or respondent state expressly agrees that the rule of local remedies will not apply to a particular dispute or particular disputes. In the law of diplomatic protection, this may take place either before or after the dispute has arisen and may even be by a unilateral act by the host or respondent state. Such waivers have been given in both multilateral treaties and bilateral treaties and do not

---

[1] Waiver has generally been accepted in principle both in judicial decisions and by text writers: see e.g. the *ELSI Case*, 1989 ICJ Reports at p. 42; *De Wilde, Ooms and Versyp*, ECHR, 50 ILR at p. 370 (1971); *Government of Costa Rica Case*, IACHR, 67 ILR at p. 587 (1984); Amerasinghe, 'The Local Remedies Rule in an Appropriate Perspective', 36 ZaöRV (1976) at p. 752; Garcia Amador, 'Third Report on State Responsibility', YBILC (1958), vol. 2, p. 93; Borchard, *The Diplomatic Protection of Citizens Abroad* (1915) pp. 819 and 825; Borchard, 'Theoretical Aspects of the International Responsibility of States', 1 ZaöRV (1929) at p. 240; Witenburg, 'La Recevabilité des reclamations devant les juridictions internationales', 41 *Hague Recueil* (1932) at p. 55; Ipsen, *Völkerrecht* (1990) p. 313; Kokott, 'Report on Exhaustion of Local Remedies', in ILA, *Report of 69th Conference* (2000) at p. 613; and Dugard, 'Third Report on Diplomatic Protection', UN Doc. A/CN.4/523 (2002) at pp. 17ff. and the authorities there cited.

raise any real problems. Examples of such waivers in bilateral treaties are to be found in those that set up the Mixed Arbitral Tribunals and Mixed Claims Commissions between the two World Wars. Particular reference may be made to Article V of the Convention of 1923 establishing the US–Mexican General Claims Commission.[2] A more recent example is the treaty between Canada and the US setting up the *Gut Dam Arbitration* in 1965.[3] The Convention for the Settlement of Disputes between States and Nationals of Other States is an example of a multilateral treaty which excludes the operation *prima facie* of the rule. By virtue of Article 26 of that Convention,[4] where a host state and an alien whose national state is a party to the Convention agree to submit to international arbitration under the auspices of ICSID, established under the Convention, there is no need for the alien to exhaust local remedies before seeking arbitration unless specific provision is otherwise made for such recourse. This is also a case where the waiver has been given before the dispute arises, unlike in respect of most bilateral treaties.[5]

Where the express waiver is given in a bilateral or multilateral treaty and after or before the dispute arises, it is normally irrevocable,[6] although it may be revoked by the agreement of the parties or with the

---

[2] See Feller, *The Mexican Claims Commissions 1923-1934* (1935) p. 34; Nielsen, *International Law Applied to Reclamations* (1933) p. 70; and Eagleton, 'L'épuisement des recours internes et le déni de justice, d'après certaines décisions récentes', 16 RDILC (1935) at pp. 518–19 and 525–6. On the reasons for waiver, see Amerasinghe, *State Responsibility for Injuries to Aliens* (1967) p. 207. The validity of express waiver has been confirmed by text writers: see the writers referred to in note 1 above and e.g. Doering, 'Exhaustion of Local Remedies', in Bernhardt *et al.* (eds.), *Encyclopedia of Public International Law* (1977), vol. 3, p. 240; Briggs, 'The Local Remedies Rule: A Drafting Suggestion', 50 AJIL (1956) at p. 925; and Amerasinghe, 'Whither the Local Remedies Rule?', 5 *ICSID Review* (1990) at pp. 293–4.

[3] See Erades, 'The Gut Dam Arbitration', 16 NILR (1969) p. 161. García Amador recognized an express waiver by agreement in 1958 in Article 17 of his draft to the ILC: see García Amador note 1 above, at pp. 55, 57–8 and 72.

[4] See 55 UNTS at p. 159.

[5] It may be noted that, in the area of adjustment or settlement of environmental disputes, there is a marked tendency towards waiver of the rule. For a discussion of this, see e.g. Hoffman, 'State Responsibility in International Law and Transboundary Pollution Injuries', 25 ICLQ (1976) at pp. 513ff.; Poulantzas, 'The Rule of Exhaustion of Local Remedies and Liability for Space Vehicle Accidents', 17 RHDI (1964) at pp. 103–4; Jenks, 'Liability for Ultra-Hazardous Activities in International Law', 117 *Hague Recueil* (1966) at pp. 191ff.

[6] Clearly, there is a presumption which may be rebutted by evidence to the contrary. On irrevocability as such, see Amerasinghe, *State Responsibility*, note 2 above, at pp. 294–5; Amerasinghe, note 1 above, at p. 737, and the UK pleadings in the *Anglo-Iranian Oil Co. Case*, ICJ Pleadings (1951) at pp. 118–19. In the same case, Iran argued against irrevocability: *ibid.*, p. 501. The grounds on which this argument was made are not clear.

consent of the state of the alien affected. In the case of the ICSID Convention, for example, the express terms in the Convention of the waiver permit revocation by unilateral act of the respondent or host state at any time before it consents to arbitration under the Convention, which consent must be given by a separate act in writing, the other party being required also to give its consent. Thus, while agreement to arbitrate raises a presumption that there has been an express waiver of the rule of local remedies, that presumption is rebuttable by a unilateral act by the host or respondent state, or by agreement between the alien and the state party to the dispute, provided the revocation is done before or at the time that the consent to arbitration is given by the host or respondent state.[7]

Where there is a bilateral or multilateral agreement between states to submit to arbitration or international judicial settlement disputes between their nationals and host states, there is generally no understanding that the rule of local remedies is waived by the very fact of such submission to arbitration or judicial settlement, as is evidenced by the numerous decided cases in which disputes were submitted to such arbitration or judicial settlement under such agreements. No reference was made to the specific inclusion of the rule in the treaties or agreements and the rule was held to be *prima facie* applicable.[8] This issue is discussed further later in this chapter in regard to implied waiver.

Difficulties arise in connection with express agreements made between host states and aliens excluding the rule or express renunciations of the rule. In the case of the above express agreements or renunciations, the question is whether such agreements or renunciations may be unilaterally revoked. Clearly, if the agreement or renunciation is governed by a law other than that of the host state, no revocation according to the law of the host state can take place. But what if, for instance, the agreement appears in a contract governed by the law of the host state which was legally terminated according to the law of the host state? Can the alien or his national state then rely on the express waiver of the rule by the host state? The answer would seem to hinge on whether parts of

---

[7] The provisions of Article 26 apply only to arbitration and not to conciliation under the Convention. Whether the rule of local remedies applies to conciliation proceedings *per se* is a different question. If it did, the rule would not have been waived under the Convention. As pointed out at the end of Chapter 5, the incidence of the rule of local remedies and to what exactly the express waiver applied are not clearly addressed in the ICSID Convention, although the implications of Article 26 can be deciphered.

[8] See e.g. the *Interhandel Case*, 1959 ICJ Reports p. 6.

a contract could be governed by a different law from that which governs other parts. In the case of arbitration clauses in state contracts with aliens, it seems possible to take the view that cancellation of the contract does not result in the cancellation of the arbitration clause, probably on the basis that the arbitration clause stands on its own and is not subject to the total law of the host state. While it may be interpreted in accordance with that law, it cannot be unilaterally and arbitrarily terminated under that law, although there may be refinements of this rule. A similar principle may be applicable to a waiver of the rule of local remedies in a state contract with an alien or a simple renunciation of the rule by a unilateral act in respect of an alien.[9]

Implied waiver

Reference was made earlier to the fact that, where a dispute involving an alien is submitted to international arbitration or adjudication by the states parties thereto, in the context of diplomatic protection, there is no presumption generally that the rule of local remedies does not apply, unless it is expressly invoked or reserved. There is, indeed, considerable evidence to support this view.[10] But, while this view is the better view, it

---

[9] It may be noted that the 1956 resolution of the Institut de Droit International clearly stated: 'La règle ne s'applique pas: . . . (b) au cas où son application a été écartée par l'accord des Etats intéressés.' 46 AIDI (1956) at p. 358. But in fact what is really required is the consent of the host or respondent state, given in any form either generally or to the alien or to his national state. Such consent constitutes an express waiver. On the issue of conciliation and the rule of local remedies there are conflicting views: see e.g. the *Interhandel Case*, 1959 ICJ Reports at p. 29, at p. 45 *per* Judge Córdova in a separate opinion, at p. 84 *per* Judge Winiarski dissenting, at p. 121 *per* Judge Lauterpacht dissenting, ICJ Pleadings (1959) at p. 573 (Swiss oral argument, Guggenheim); Gaja, *L'Esaurimento dei Ricorsi Interni nel Diritto Internazionale* (1967) pp. 157–60; and Cot, *La Conciliation internationale* (1968) pp. 233–4. See further below in this chapter.

Waiver in relation to human rights protection is discussed in Chapter 13.

[10] See e.g. the *Ziat and Ben Kiran Case (Great Britain v. Spain)*, 2 UNRIAA at pp. 731ff. (1924); the *Canadian Hay Importers Case (Great Britain v. US)*, 6 UNRIAA at pp. 142ff. (1925); the *A.G. Studer Case (US v. Great Britain)*, 6 UNRIAA at pp. 149ff. (1925); the *R.T. Roy Case (US v. Great Britain)*, 6 UNRIAA at pp. 147ff. (1925); the *Mexican Union Railway Ltd Case*, 5 UNRIAA pp. 9 and 123 (1926); the *George Pinson Case (France v. Mexico)*, 5 UNRIAA p. 351 (1928); the *Panavezys–Saldutiskis Railway Case*, PCIJ Series A/B No. 76 (1939); the *Electricity Co. of Sofia Case*, PCIJ Series A/B No. 77 at p. 104 (1939) *per* Judge Urrutia in a dissenting opinion; and *Switzerland v. Federal Republic of Germany*, 25 ILR at pp. 42ff. (1958). For text writers, see e.g. Freeman, *The International Responsibility of States for Denial of Justice* (1938) pp. 414ff.; Guggenheim, *Traité de droit international public* (1954), vol. 2, p. 22; Schwarzenberger, *International Law* (1957), vol. 1, pp. 610ff.; Witenberg, note 1 above, at p. 52; García Amador, note 1 above, at p. 60; and Verzijl, 'Rapport supplémentaire sur

has apparently not gone uncontested.[11] In any event, as is evidenced by recent cases which have come before the ICJ, such as the *Norwegian Loans Case* and the *Interhandel Case*,[12] neither state practice nor judicial opinion warrants the opposite view. Thus, though the matter may be regarded as unsettled, it may be concluded that the better view referred to above should prevail in modern international law. This view is also supported by the fact that in most cases of waiver, whether express or implicit, it is waiver of the rule which is not to be found explicitly invoked in bilateral or multilateral agreements between states, or in agreements between states and aliens, that is usually discussed. Further, most of the cases and practice supporting the other view may be explained on the basis that the rule had been for one reason or another implicitly waived in the circumstances of each case.

The question which really arises is whether and when a waiver can be implied. This question obviously raises problems of interpretation, and as a rule each situation should be looked at individually to determine whether there has been a waiver.[13] Clearly, to the extent that there has

la règle de l'épuisement des recours internes', 46 AIDI (1956) at pp. 3ff. On implied waiver now, see also in general Dugard, note 1 above, at pp. 20ff. and the authorities there cited. While the circumstances of the case matter, it must be emphasized that a clear intention to waive the application of the rule must be established: see the *ELSI Case*, 1989 ICJ Reports at p. 42.

[11] See e.g. the *R.L. Trumbull Case* (*US* v. *Chile*) (1889), Moore, *International Arbitration* (1898) p. 3569; the *Selwyn Case* (*Great Britain* v. *Venezuela*), 9 UNRIAA p. 380 (1903); the *Forests of Central Rhodope Case* (*Greece* v. *Bulgaria*), 3 UNRIAA at p. 1419 (1933); the *German Interests in Upper Silesia Case*, PCIJ Series A No. 6 at pp. 13–14 (1925); the *Panavezys–Saldutiskis Railway Case*, PCIJ Series A/B No. 76 at pp. 35ff. (1939) *per* Judge Van Eysinga in a dissenting opinion; the *Lighthouses Arbitration* (*France* v. *Greece*), 23 ILR p. 659 (1956); and the British memorial in the *Anglo-Iranian Oil Co. Case*, ICJ Pleadings (1952) at pp. 122ff. For text writers, see e.g. Borchard, *Diplomatic Protection*, note 1 above, at p. 819; Gaja, note 9 above, at pp. 156ff.; Ténékidès, 'L'épuisement des voies de recours internes comme condition préalable de l'instance internationale', 14 RDILC (1933) at pp. 519ff.; and Schwebel and Wetter, 'Arbitration and the Exhaustion of Local Remedies', 60 AJIL (1966) p. 484. Many text writers do not make a distinction between diplomatic protection and arbitration between states and private individuals who may be legal or natural persons. In the relevant cases, it is not clear that the doctrine of the implied waiver was not being used to explain the position.

[12] *Norwegian Loans Case*, 1957 ICJ Reports p. 9. Neither state argued that the rule had been waived by submission to the ICJ. The Court did not decide the preliminary objection based on the local remedies rule, but none of the judges who dealt with this objection took the view that such submission amounted to a waiver: *Interhandel Case*, 1959 ICJ Reports p. 6. Neither the Court nor the parties took the view that there had been a waiver of the rule of local remedies by submission to an international jurisdiction.

[13] See the argument of the French Government in the *Norwegian Loans Case* which related to the existence of an implied waiver of the rule: ICJ Pleadings (1957), vol. 1, at pp. 407ff.

been a waiver, there can generally be no room for unilateral determination of the waiver. The view taken above of express waivers would support this opinion. Further, while the existence of a waiver will usually have to be determined on the merits of each case, there has been some practice on the question which warrants discussion.

The optional clause

In connection with signatures of the optional clause under Article 36 of the Statute of the ICJ, the PCIJ in the *Panavezys–Saldutiskis Railway Case* took the view that such a signature of the corresponding clause under its Statute did not involve an implied waiver of the rule of local remedies by the signatory.[14] In the same case, Judge van Eysinga disagreed with this view in a dissenting opinion.[15] The issue was not raised as such by the applicant state in the *Norwegian Loans Case*[16] or in the *Inter-handel Case*,[17] where the ICJ was confronted with the question of local remedies, although signatures of the optional clause under Article 36 of the Statute of the Court were involved. Since the acceptance of the compulsory jurisdiction of the ICJ does not basically militate against the preservation of the jurisdiction of national courts, the view may be taken that the opinion of the PCIJ has validity.[18]

Submission by states to international adjudication or arbitration

Submissions to international adjudication or arbitration by agreements between states entered into before the dispute has arisen evidently stand on the same footing as acceptance of the optional clause of Article 36 of the Statute of the ICJ. There is a direct analogy between the two situations. In regard to general arbitration treaties, whether they are entered into before or after the dispute arises, the caselaw is contradictory. There are a few cases which regard the agreement to arbitrate as a waiver of the rule, while the majority seems to take the opposite view.[19] It would seem that the view of the minority, as a general principle, would contradict the cogent analogy to be drawn from the cases decided by the ICJ relating to Article 36, at any rate insofar as the case of the arbitration treaty signed before the dispute arises is concerned. Hence, to this

---

[14] PCIJ Series A/B No. 76 (1939).   [15] *Ibid.*, pp. 35ff.
[16] 1957 ICJ Reports p. 9.   [17] 1959 ICJ Reports p. 6.
[18] Now see the *ELSI Case*, 1989 ICJ Reports at p. 31, where the importance of the local remedies rule for the law of diplomatic protection was asserted and confirmed.
[19] See Law, *The Local Remedies Rule in International Law* (1961) p. 97. The weight of textual authority also favours the latter view: *ibid.*, pp. 95ff.

extent it would be less persuasive. It is to be noted that in the *ELSI Case* a Chamber of the ICJ held that an agreement in a treaty to submit to adjudication by the ICJ, entered into before the dispute arose, did not by itself imply a waiver of the rule of local remedies.[20] The ICJ made it quite clear that implying a waiver in these circumstances was not an easy matter in the absence of a clear intention to do so. On the other hand, the situation is not quite the same in regard to treaties signed after disputes have arisen. In fact, it would seem that the PCIJ and the ICJ have not addressed themselves to this situation, in so far as the situation has not arisen in the cases decided by them. However, in so far as the two Courts have enunciated an undifferentiated general principle which supports the view of the majority taken in other decisions, there is added support for that view. In the last analysis, it is clear that, whether such treaties are signed before or after disputes arise, no waiver of the rule of local remedies may be generally applied.

The question that arises is whether a different principle applies to international arbitration instituted in the exercise of diplomatic protection. Even in the case of general treaties to settle by arbitration, however, it may be possible, in the absence of an express waiver, to find from the natural meaning of the text or the circumstances surrounding the agreement that a waiver of the rule was in fact intended. For example, if it is stated that there shall be *direct* settlement by arbitration or international adjudication, the natural meaning of the text indicates that the rule has been waived.[21]

An example of implied waiver of the rule in an agreement between states which was concluded after the disputes arose is to be found in connection with the agreement which set up the Iran–US Claims Tribunal. Article II of the Claims Settlement Declaration stated that the parties had agreed that an international tribunal would be set up

for the purpose of deciding claims of nationals of the United States against Iran and claims of nationals of Iran against the United States, and any counterclaim which arises out of the same contract, transaction or occurrence that constitutes

---

[20] 1989 ICJ Reports at p. 42.

[21] See *Steiner and Gross* v. *Polish State*, Ann. Dig. (1927–8) at pp. 472ff. Dugard, note 1 above, at pp. 21–3, distinguishes between general arbitration agreements entered into before disputes arise and *ad hoc* arbitration agreements entered into after disputes arise, stating that it is easier to imply waiver in the latter cases than in the former. See also the authorities there cited at notes 100–2. But the distinction is neither of an absolute nature nor is it really useful. In every case it is a question of interpretation. There is no need for additional presumptions.

the subject matter of the national's claim, if such claims and counterclaims are outstanding on the date of this Agreement whether or not filed with any court, and arise out of debts, contracts (including transactions which are the subject of letters of credit or bank guarantees), expropriations or other measures affecting property rights, excluding . . . claims arising under a binding contract between the parties specifically providing that any disputes thereunder shall be within the sole jurisdiction of the competent Iranian courts . . .[22]

Article VII then provided that: 'Claims referred to the arbitration Tribunal shall, as of the date of filing such claims with the Tribunal, be considered excluded from the jurisdiction of the courts of Iran or of the United States, or of any other court.'[23] There was no specific and express reference to or exclusion of the rule of local remedies, but the combined effect of these two provisions led the Tribunal to conclude that the Declaration granted jurisdiction to the Tribunal 'notwithstanding that exhaustion of local remedies . . . doctrines might otherwise be applicable'.[24] The Tribunal did not explain how it came to this conclusion, but it was clear that the waiver of the rule must have been implied from the circumstances surrounding the Declaration and particularly the two provisions cited above, which describe reference to the courts of the two states parties to the arbitration as irrelevant and also exclude their jurisdiction.

While such special situations may be acknowledged, there is no reason to believe that the principles applicable to international arbitrations are any different from those relevant to international adjudication. In effect, international arbitration is a substitute for international adjudication and is given a similar, if not the same, status. For this reason, the same considerations apply to it as were found by the ICJ to be applicable to international adjudication. The arbitrations in which the view was expressed that there was a waiver may be seen as depending on an interpretation of the instrument concerned which resulted in implying a waiver.

In this connection the *Applicability of the Obligation to Arbitrate under Section 21 of the United Nations Headquarters Agreement of 26 June 1947 Opinion*[25] given by the ICJ is not in point. There the Court concluded that the US was under an obligation to submit its dispute under the Headquarters Agreement to arbitration and in doing so stated:

---

[22] *Iran–US CTR*, vol. 1, p. 9.   [23] *Ibid.*, p. 11.
[24] Award No. 93-2-3, *Iran–US CTR*, vol. 4, p. 102.   [25] 1988 ICJ Reports p. 12.

The Court must further point out that the alleged dispute relates solely to what the United Nations considers to be its rights under the Headquarters Agreement. The purpose of the arbitration procedure envisaged by that Agreement is precisely the settlement of such disputes as may arise between the Organization and the host country without any prior recourse to municipal courts, and it would be against both the letter and the spirit of the Agreement for the implementation of that procedure to be subjected to such prior recourse. It is evident that a provision of the nature of section 21 of the Headquarters Agreement cannot require the exhaustion of local remedies as a condition of its implementation.[26]

But this arbitration, though international, did not concern diplomatic protection. The rule of local remedies was irrelevant to it in any case. The Court addressed the issue because some doubt was raised as to what the express words of the agreement meant. Clearly, any international agreement can expressly or impliedly include reference to national courts as a mode of dispute settlement before an arbitration procedure may be invoked, but this is not because the rule of local remedies which generally pertains to diplomatic protection as a matter of customary international law is applicable. It is clear that the ICJ did not mean to indicate that the rule applied to the Headquarters Agreement as such as a matter of customary international law.[27]

In view of the fact that international arbitration resulting from the exercise of the right of diplomatic protection is more or less on a par at the present time with international adjudication the conclusion must be reached that the rule of local remedies is not automatically waived by implication by the simple agreement to submit to such arbitration. There is no evidence that the opposite trend is to be detected in international jurisprudence or practice. The situation is the same, in the absence of evidence to the contrary, whether the agreement to arbitrate is entered into before the dispute arises or after.

The issue of arbitrability

An implied waiver may be construed to take effect as a result of the circumstances surrounding an agreement between states where the issue

---

[26] *Ibid.*, p. 29.

[27] Schwebel fails to see this important point in assuming that it was the rule of local remedies applicable to diplomatic protection that intrinsically applied in this case: see 'Arbitration and the Exhaustion of Local Remedies Revisited,' in Ebke and Norton (eds.) *Festschrift in Honour of Joseph Gold* (1990) pp. 373ff.

to be decided by an international tribunal concerns the arbitrability of the dispute. In this situation the ICJ has held that the rule of local remedies is not applicable.[28] On the other hand, a conflicting decision seems to have been pronounced by the same Court. In the *Interhandel Case*, the Court refused to determine the question of arbitrability because local remedies had not been exhausted.[29] However, in this case there were some strong dissenting opinions[30] which took the view adopted in the earlier *Ambatielos Case* that the local remedies rule was not applicable to the issue of arbitrability. It would seem that the better view is that the question of arbitrability may be decided without local remedies having been exhausted, in particular since the issue does not relate to material compensation or restitution.[31] Also, it is important in this connection that, even if a pronouncement is made on the issue of arbitrability, this does not pre-empt the arbitral tribunal from making a determination on the question whether local remedies had been exhausted.[32] In this situation, however, it must be noted that it may be expressly agreed that local remedies should be exhausted before an international tribunal decided the issue of arbitrability.

Non-inter-state arbitration agreements between states and private parties

The questions of whether and to what extent there has been an implied waiver of the rule of local remedies may arise in connection with arbitration clauses which are included in ordinary state contracts with aliens and which are not also covered in some way by an inter-state agreement between the states concerned. Such contracts would not be on a par with treaties,[33] nor strictly would they be contracts within the international legal system, nor between international persons, although they might be governed by transnational law.[34] A preliminary question that must be answered is whether arbitration clauses included in such contracts would become ineffective, if the contracts themselves are terminated or

---

[28] *Ambatielos Case*, 1953 ICJ Reports p. 16. See also the *Chemin de Fer Zeltweg Case (Austria v. Yugoslavia)*, 3 UNRIAA at p. 1803 (1934).

[29] 1959 ICJ Reports at p. 29.

[30] See 1959 ICJ Reports at p. 32 *per* Judge Carry, at p. 82 *per* Judge Klaested, at p. 84 *per* Judge Winiarski and at pp. 120ff. *per* Judge Lauterpacht.

[31] See Judge Lauterpacht in the *Interhandel Case*, 1959 ICJ Reports at p. 120.

[32] See the *Ambatielos Case*, 1953 ICJ Reports p. 16.

[33] See the *Anglo-Iranian Oil Co. Case*, 1952 ICJ Reports at p. 93.

[34] See e.g. the discussion in Amerasinghe, *State Responsibility for Injuries to Aliens* (1967) pp. 108ff. and the authorities there cited, and now Chapter 5 above.

cease to have effect for some reason. The question is of some importance, because, if arbitration clauses could become ineffective in this way, the question of whether there has been an implied waiver of the rule of local remedies may often become moot. The problem becomes particularly significant where, for example, the contract is governed by the national law of the state party to the contract and the contract is terminated under that law, perhaps by legislation.

In an arbitration between Yugoslavia and a Swiss national, it was argued by Yugoslavia that the cancellation of the contract between Yugoslavia and the alien resulted in the cancellation of the arbitration clause and thus terminated the right of recourse to arbitration. The arbitral tribunal rejected the submission.[35] The decision was by an arbitral tribunal that was not an organ of the international legal system, which it would have been had the dispute been between states, but one instead which was set up by a state and an alien to settle a dispute between them. Hence, its decision probably does not share the prestige and value of an international decision or award. However, in the absence of any international cases on the matter this decision may have some persuasive force. The rationale of the decision would seem to lie in postulating that an arbitration clause in a contract between a state and an alien stands on its own and is separable from the contract as such, whatever may be the position under the law of that state applicable to arbitration clauses in national contracts between the state and an individual or between two individuals. The arbitration clause may have to be interpreted according to a national law, but the issue of its termination falls to be determined outside particular national systems of law, probably by some general principles of law applicable to international contracts or treaties. Importance really attaches to the negative conclusion reached above, even if there is no clear support for the positive suggestion. If the above were not the case, the purpose of having an arbitration clause in a contract between a state and an alien would be defeated.

Because it seems to be the better view that such arbitration clauses survive contracts between states and aliens, the substantive issues of whether and to what extent a waiver of the rule of local remedies can be implied where such an arbitration occurs assumes importance. There appear to be many cases in which arbitration has been resorted to under a state contract with an alien and in which the argument has not been

---

[35] See the *Affaire Losinger and Co.*, *Pleadings, Oral Statements and Documents* (1936), PCIJ Series C No. 78 at pp. 119ff.

raised by the respondent state that the alien has not exhausted local remedies before seeking arbitration.[36] In a few cases concerning this kind of arbitration which came before the PCIJ and the ICJ, the issue was raised by the respondent state, and the plaintiff state argued for a waiver of the rule, but in none of these cases was the issue decided.[37] The fact that the issue of local remedies has not been contested in the majority of cases may lend some support to the view that an arbitration clause does imply a waiver of the rule of local remedies, at least in regard to the merits of the dispute, although it may not be conclusive. The absence of an international decision to the contrary would also not militate against this position. Indeed, it would be reasonable to conclude from the fact that arbitration has been chosen as the means of settling disputes that it was intended to withdraw the merits of the dispute from the jurisdiction of the local courts and institutions at least until the arbitral award had been given. It would be difficult to find acceptable arguments for the opposite view.

There is some support for this view in other transnational (not international) cases. In the award in *LIAMCO* v. *Libya*, the sole arbitrator asserted:

As the arbitration clause and the procedure outlined therein are binding upon the contracting parties, and the procedure outlined therein being imperative, the Arbitral Tribunal constituted in accordance with such clause and procedure should have exclusive jurisdiction over the issues of the dispute. No other tribunal or authority, local or otherwise, has competence in the matter.

The exclusive and compulsory character of the arbitration process in such a case is widely admitted in international law. It has been affirmed by international arbitral precedents . . . and has also been incorporated in the Convention of 1966 on the Settlement of Investment Disputes between States and nationals of other States.[38]

In *Elf Aquitaine Iran* v. *National Iranian Oil Company*, the sole arbitrator made the following statement in response to the argument that the plaintiff company could have used a procedure of redress available under the law of Iran:

---

[36] See Schwebel and Wetter, note 11 above, at pp. 486ff.
[37] The *Affaire Losinger and Co.*, PCIJ Series A/B No. 67 (1936), and *Pleadings, Oral Statements and Documents* (1936), PCIJ Series C No. 78; the *Anglo-Iranian Oil Co. Case*, 1952 ICJ Reports p. 93, ICJ Pleadings (1951); the *Electricité de Beyrouth Co. Case*, 1954 ICJ Reports p. 107, ICJ Pleadings (1954); and the *Compagnie du Port, des Quais et des Entrepôts de Beyrouth and the Société Radio-Orient Case*, ICJ Pleadings (1960). See also Schwebel, note 27 above, at p. 373.
[38] 62 ILR at pp. 179–80 (1977).

The International Court of Justice has declared that 'The rule that local remedies must be exhausted before international proceedings may be instituted is a well-established rule of customary international law', *Interhandel* case (Switzerland v. United States of America) (1959) *ICJ* Reports, at page 27. This rule of local remedies or redress that would require ELF to present its claims to the Special Committee before turning to an international remedy does, however, govern only complaints made by a state in the exercise of its right of diplomatic protection of its national, cf. e.g. Manual of Public International Law, 1958, edited by Max Sorenson, p. 582, and not, as pointed out by Maurice Bourquin in an article in The Business Lawyer, Volume XV (1960) p. 860 et seq., to a request from a party to an agreement on arbitration to initiate arbitral proceedings under that agreement. The parties have by choosing arbitration established a procedure for settlement of disputes which excludes the national legal remedies provided for in national legislation. The established procedure also implies that each party is entitled to have disputes settled by arbitration without evoking diplomatic protection and thus without fulfilling conditions to be met in order for their government to exercise diplomatic protection.

The Sole Arbitrator has therefore reached the conclusion that the rule of local redress does not apply in this case, and that ELF is not obliged to submit its claims to the Special Committee, before these claims can be adjudicated by arbitration under the agreement.[39]

Such opinions as these were given in arbitrations which were neither inter-state arbitrations nor arbitrations established under an arrangement governed by international law as such. However, they merit attention, even though it may be claimed that the arbitrators in such arbitrations may be inclined, on the basis of a material interest, to decide *in favorem jurisdictionis*, whenever possible, because they would prefer to continue an arbitration than refuse to arbitrate at an early stage. There are also some writers who support the view taken that there is an implied waiver, where transnational arbitration is chosen as a means of settling disputes between states and individuals.[40] This view is acceptable, because, as implied in the arbitration above, such arbitrations are not instituted in the exercise of diplomatic protection.

---

[39] 11 *Yearbook of Commercial Arbitration* (1986) at pp. 104–5.

[40] For recent authorities, see particularly Dugard, note 1 above, at p. 23 and the authorities cited in the Report of the International Law Commission on its Twenty-Ninth Session, YBILC (1977), vol. 2, Part II, at p. 49; and Schwebel, *International Arbitration: Three Salient Problems* (1987) pp. 117–21. See also Schwebel and Wetter, note 11 above, at pp. 499ff.; and Schwebel, note 27 above, at p. 373. The latter writer gives two more reasons for the inapplicability of the rule of local remedies to the arbitration situation (*ibid.*, pp. 116–17 and 121–2), but the best explanation is that of the implied waiver.

The rationale of the implied waiver in the above situation results from the substitution of one form of dispute settlement for another. Transnational arbitration is not international (inter-state) arbitration and may be regarded as akin to settlement by national courts or within a national judicial system. By agreeing to this form of dispute settlement the state party to the agreement can legitimately be assumed to have foregone its right to have its courts and judicial system initially invoked to settle disputes. By the same token, given the state's acquiescence to the transnational method, if the method is adhered to and respected, it may also have the right to enjoy freedom from resort to diplomatic protection by the alien or from exercise of such protection by the alien's national state, at least before the arbitration procedure is tested. These seem to be the logical consequences of the choice of transnational arbitration to settle disputes of this kind.

However, not only is the local remedies rule waived, at the point at which it would have been applicable, but the requirement of a denial of justice (in the broad sense) by the state and its judicial system in relation to an alleged breach of contract by the state in order that a violation of international law may occur is not required. What has happened is that breaches of contract which *per se* are not also violations of international law are submitted to transnational arbitration. The need for *resort* to the local courts for a denial of justice to occur, or for a denial of justice to occur in some other manner in respect of such required resort, is completely eliminated. The transnational tribunal becomes a substitute by agreement for the local remedial system. The transnational tribunal *per se* is the remedial system applicable.

If there is a refusal to resort to the transnational arbitration on the part of the host state, there will conceivably be a 'denial of justice', in that access to an agreed remedial system had been denied,[41] which is a violation of an international obligation owed in respect of the alien. It is at this point that the waiver of the local remedies rule would operate to permit, through diplomatic protection, the invocation of an *international* forum or procedure.[42] What would happen, if a defect attributable to the host state in the implementation of the arbitral process takes place, is that, again, there would be a 'denial of justice' through the state's interfering with the process and the result in terms of the waiver of the application of the local remedies rule would be similar.[43] An important

---

[41] See Schwebel, note 27 above.   [42] *Contra* apparently Schwebel, *ibid.*

[43] On the other hand, a mere denial of justice by the tribunal itself, e.g. by a manifest error of law, which is not attributable to the state party to the contract does not result

point is that the waiver of the rule applies to what happens in respect of the agreed remedial measures which have been substituted for the local means of redress, not to an alleged breach of contract by the state *per se*.

Clearly, if the breach of contract by the state is also a violation of international law because of the presence of other factors,[44] the agreed choice of arbitration would result in a waiver of the application of the rule of local remedies in respect of that violation.

While it may be clear that some waiver of the local remedies rule may be readily implied, there has been some discussion of the extent of the waiver. The evidence referred to above is not inconsistent with a partial waiver. It is compatible with the view that, where there is an arbitration clause, resort to local remedies may be required before an international forum is invoked, even though the alien has indicated his willingness to arbitrate, or after the arbitration. The choice of arbitration as a means of dispute settlement does not exclude the possibility that the alien is expected, where possible, to exhaust local remedies in the event of a refusal to arbitrate on the part of the host state, in order to secure enforcement of the obligation to arbitrate, or where the award has been rendered in favour of the alien, in order to secure enforcement or interpretation of the award, or where the award has been rendered against the alien, in order to have the award upset.[45] Whether local remedies need not be exhausted for such purposes would then generally depend on other exceptions to the rule of local remedies, and not on any theory of implied waiver.

On the other hand, the question may be raised whether the implied waiver could not be extended to cover even the situations and remedies excluded above, depending on the nature of the arbitration clause. It has been suggested that, where the arbitral process is intended to be governed by a law other than the national law of the host state, a waiver of all local remedies is implied.[46] This argument may well be based on the view that by choosing a different law from its own for the settlement of disputes by arbitration, the host state has impliedly agreed that resort

in a violation of international law by that state. Then the issue of exhaustion of local remedies does not arise. Indeed, there is no cause for diplomatic protection at all.

[44] See Chapter 5 above.

[45] A similar view is espoused by Sohn and Baxter in the commentary to their draft Convention on the International Responsibility of States for Injuries to Aliens: see García Amador, Sohn and Baxter, *Recent Codification of the Law of State Responsibility for Injuries to Aliens* (1974) pp. 264–5.

[46] See Schwebel and Wetter, note 11 above, at p. 499.

to the remedies offered by its own legal system is not necessary. Be that as it may, this conclusion is not inescapable for the postulated situation, *per se*, in the absence of other indications of waiver. It is quite compatible with such a choice of a different law from that of the host state to govern the arbitral process that the intention was that resort should be had to the remedies of the host state, if available, for the purpose of enforcing the obligation to arbitrate, or of enforcing or interpreting the award, or of upsetting the award. The choice of a different legal system for the particular purpose of the arbitral process does not necessarily involve the renunciation of local remedies, which may be relevant for other purposes, if they are available. Nor can an implied waiver of the remedy relating to the obligation to arbitrate be assumed on the ground that the host state would lack the means to enforce a decision that there is an obligation to arbitrate because enforcement must take place outside its territory. In such a situation the mere decision on the issue may have the desired effect on the host state, and for that reason resort should be had to local remedies on that issue.

Whatever the force of these arguments, the view has also been clearly expressed that there are no limitations at all on the extent of the implied waiver.[47] One reason given for this is that in those situations, where it is envisaged that the implied waiver does not operate, action taken by the host or respondent state would be a 'denial of justice', in relation to which *in any case* there would be no obligation to exhaust local remedies.[48] While this reasoning results in the exclusion of the rule, the exclusion would arise not necessarily from an implied waiver, but from some other limitation in the way of an exception. The theory based on 'denial of justice', obviously used in a very broad sense, has yet to be tested.[49] As emerges from Chapter 4 above, denial of justice by the local courts in any conventional sense is not a ground as such for making an exception to the rule of local remedies.

The above analysis shows that, while the basic notion of an implied waiver in cases of arbitration agreements such as are referred to may be accepted, the nature and extent of the waiver is not only disputed but has been the subject of some obfuscation.

[47] See García Amador, 'International Responsibility, Fifth Report', YBILC (1960), vol. 2, p. 57; Luzzato, 'International Commercial Arbitration and the Municipal Law of States', 157 *Hague Recueil* (1977) at p. 94.

[48] See Schwebel, note 40 above, at pp. 115ff.

[49] This exception is different from those based on absence of access to courts and the like, which give rise to obvious futility. It is evidently a new ground for excepting the rule.

It is suggested that the views expressed by me above prior to the preceding three paragraphs are fundamentally sound. That having been said, what was stated there in relation to local remedies,[50] regarding only the aftermath of an award favouring the alien, enforcement, and the event of an award against the alien, needs to be examined.

Clearly, there is in these circumstances no violation of international obligations by the state party to the dispute which would attract the rule of local remedies. Therefore, there has generally to be some *resort*, or attempt to resort, to local remedies before the rule may apply to a violation of international law. Where there is such *resort*, or attempt, it is only if a denial of justice occurs that there will be a violation of international obligations by that state. There is no reason to suppose that the rule does not apply to such a violation, if it occurs, because of implicit waiver.

The understandings underlying two conventions involving arbitration between states and individuals or their subrogees would seem to support the views expressed above that an agreement to arbitrate between a state and an individual implies a waiver of the requirement that local remedies should be exhausted. The ICSID Convention, in Article 1(2) and later in Article 27(1), makes this clear by providing that a state whose national has agreed to submit a dispute to arbitration under the Convention shall not give diplomatic protection to such national, which indicates that the arbitration under the auspices of ICSID, although described as an 'international' arbitration, is a substitute for arbitration instituted directly in the pursuit of diplomatic protection. While Article 36 explicitly excludes the rule of exhaustion of local remedies where an arbitration under the auspices of ICSID has been agreed to, unless the exhaustion of such remedies had been made a condition precedent to such an arbitration, paragraph 32 of the Report of the Executive Directors on the Convention, which is appended to the Convention and therefore has some interpretative value, states that:

It may be presumed that when a State and an investor agree to have recourse to arbitration, and do not reserve the right to have recourse to other remedies or require the prior exhaustion of other remedies, the intention of the parties is to have recourse to arbitration to the exclusion of any other remedy.[51]

---

[50] See the text above at notes 41ff.

[51] See Doc. ICSID/2 at pp. 10–11 of the Report. As of 26 March 2003 154 States had signed the Convention, while 139 States had deposited instruments of ratification.

It may be concluded both that what is referred to as a rule of interpretation in substance reflects the rule of the implied waiver discussed
above and that its incorporation as the implicit basis of Article 26 of
the Convention reinforces the general nature of that rule. The Report
of the Executive Directors on the Convention may be regarded as part
of the *travaux préparatoires* to which parties to the Convention subscribe
when they sign and ratify the Convention. Thus, the view of the implicit
waiver reflected in that Report may be taken to reflect the practice of
such states at least in relation to the Convention, although, because the
Convention explicitly incorporates the implicit waiver, that view is not
essential for the application of the Convention.[52]

The Convention establishing the Multilateral Investment Guarantee
Agency (MIGA) does not specifically refer to the implicit waiver of the
rule either in its Article 57 or in its Annex II, but there is a reference to
the principle involved in the Commentary on the Convention Establishing the MIGA which may be treated as part of the *travaux préparatoires*
and is of interpretative value. In paragraph 76 of the Commentary, it
is provided that disputes between host states and MIGA as subrogee of
an investor should be settled in accordance with a set procedure or by
special agreement between the parties. In the case of a negotiated agreement, it states that 'the agreement could, for example, provide that the
Agency first seek remedies available to it under the domestic laws of
the host country and seek recourse to arbitration only if it has not obtained relief under such remedies within a specified period of time'.[53]
This statement assumes that an agreement to arbitrate between MIGA
as the subrogee of an alien investor and a host state does not normally
involve the rule of local remedies at all, or is waived, unless reference
to the need for exhaustion of such remedies is expressly made. Here, as
in the case of the ICSID Convention, the understanding reflected is subscribed to by parties to the Convention as being of interpretative value.
The only question is how the rule of local remedies becomes relevant
at all in the situation envisaged. The underlying assumption, correctly
then, may be that it is *not* relevant as such, perhaps because there is no
diplomatic protection involved, but that it may be invoked by agreement.
In the event that diplomatic protection does become relevant, there is

---

[52] The relevance of the local remedies rule to disputes brought to ICSID has been
discussed in Chapter 5.
[53] See Convention Establishing the MIGA and Commentary on the Convention (1985), at
p. 22 of Commentary.

recorded in the statement an understanding that the rule is implicitly waived initially.

These Conventions and their *travaux préparatoires* amply support to the extent relevant the view taken earlier of the implicit waiver of the rule of exhaustion of local remedies, where arbitration is agreed to between a host state and an alien. However, the extent of such implicit waiver, once established, is not so evident. It is significant that in connection with both Conventions, what the interpretative texts purport to refer to is left to customary international law, whatever the terminology used. Therefore, the proper definition of the limits of the rule is left to customary international law and is not affected by anything contained in the *travaux préparatoires* which may be in conflict with such definition. Apart from the general support given to the existence of the rule of implicit waiver in such arbitration cases, these documents do not really provide any assistance in establishing the exact parameters of the rule. In regard to these, whatever disagreement there is has not been dispelled.

Failure to raise preliminary objection

The right to object to the jurisdiction of an international court or tribunal may be waived because of the failure on the part of the respondent state to raise the objections based on the rule of local remedies at the proper time in the international proceedings. This is an implied waiver of the application of the rule on the basis of a procedural position taken by the respondent state and takes place during the international proceedings. Once the waiver has taken place it is irrevocable. The forfeiture of the right to rely on the rule of local remedies is grounded in a general principle that applies to the raising of preliminary objections in general.[54]

Request for a declaratory judgment

As a consequence of two judgments of the PCIJ on jurisdiction it has been concluded that a request for a declaratory judgment precludes the raising of the objection by the respondent state that local remedies have not been exhausted. In the *German Interests in Polish Upper Silesia Case*, the PCIJ held that the rule did not apply where the plaintiff state requested

---

[54] This general principle is mentioned by, *inter alios*, Rosenne, *Law and Practice of the International Court, 1920–1966* (1997), vol. 2, pp. 864–5. See now Amerasinghe, *Jurisdiction of International Tribunals* (2003) p. 303. In the human rights context (see Chapter 13), the principle is often referred to as an 'estoppel'.

only an 'interpretation of certain clauses of the Geneva Convention'.[55] The decision was explained in the subsequent *Chorzów Factory Case* where the Court said that the application in the first case 'only asked the Court for a declaratory judgment between states, which only the Court could give, whereas the present application seeks an indemnity'.[56] The distinction, thus, lies between cases in which a judgment merely declaring a violation of international law is sought and that in which a remedial right is asserted.[57]

This view is based on the notion that, since the initial act alleged to be the cause of the wrong would be a breach of international law by the respondent state, and not merely a breach of local law, a declaratory judgment on that issue would not be inapt and would in fact help to bring about a speedy solution of the dispute. The correlation implied in this reasoning between a judgment by an international tribunal and a breach of international law is easy to accept. So is the idea that, while a judgment on the merits for damages would, in such a case, be barred, it would not be unreasonable to allow a declaratory judgment. The conclusion does strike a compromise between the interests of the respondent state and those of the claimant and his state. By seeking and obtaining a declaratory judgment that the respondent state was in breach of international law, the claimant would be able to establish its position in international law, deriving all the psychological advantage of such a position, while the respondent state would not be prejudiced in its chances of remedying the injury through local means. The plaintiff state retains the advantage of having the law on its side, if the respondent state is in violation of the law, while the latter retains the right of using its own means of redressing the wrong to the individual – a right which is a recognition of its responsible sovereign character – before being subjected to an international directive to perform a secondary obligation of redress in a particular way. However, insofar as the exception is based on the theory of an implied waiver, the waiver could be expressly reversed, provided it is done at the appropriate time.

Among text writers the matter is not regarded as settled,[58] while in its oral argument in the *Interhandel Case* the US government apparently

---

[55] PCIJ Series A No. 6 at p. 20 (1925).   [56] PCIJ Series A No. 9 at pp. 26–7 (1925).

[57] See Beckett, 'Les Questions d'intérêt général au point de vue juridique dans la jurisprudence de la Cour permanente de justice internationale', 39 *Hague Recueil* (1932) at p. 164; de Visscher, 'Le Déni de justice en droit international', 52 *Hague Recueil* (1935) at p. 425; and Kaufmann, 'Règles générales du droit de la paix', 54 *Hague Recueil* (1935) at p. 456.

[58] See the discussion at the Institut de Droit International: 46 AIDI (1956) at pp. 302ff.

did not categorically take the view that the waiver was unqualified.[59] The ILC, on the other hand, appears to have supported the view that the rule of local remedies does not apply where a declaratory judgment alone is sought.[60] The better view seems to be this latter view.

Conciliation proceedings

The implied waiver may also apply to conciliation proceedings, because of the non-judicial nature of the proceedings or their extra-juridical character, and because conciliation does not end in a decision binding on the parties, but there are those who refer to this argument in order to avoid the non-application of the rule.[61] The ICJ in the *Interhandel Case* seems to have taken the view that the rule applies to conciliation.[62] This being an *obiter dictum* in the case, there may be good reason not to accept that view, at least in an unqualified form. However, the matter is undecided, as there is insufficient authority on it. As pointed out by Judge Lauterpacht in a dissenting opinion in the *Interhandel Case*, 'in so far as the procedure of conciliation is concerned, it must not be taken for granted that the legal requirement of exhaustion of local remedies would be fully or invariably applied by a conciliation commission which is not bound to proceed exclusively on the basis of law'.[63] There is a good case for implying a waiver unless there is express contradiction of this implication, or the circumstances of the case require that the implication be rejected.

Waiver and investment treaties

A phenomenon peculiar to the aftermath of the Second World War is the bilateral investment treaty (BIT).[64] Investment treaties may also be

---

[59] ICJ Pleadings (1959) at pp. 501ff.

[60] Report of the Commission to the General Assembly on the Work of its Twenty-Ninth Session: YBILC (1977), vol. 2, Part II, at p. 50. The EComHR has taken the opposite view that declaratory relief, even by way of interpretation, may not be given unless local remedies have been exhausted: *Donnelly and Others* v. *UK*, Applications Nos. 5577–83/72, COE Doc. 43.662-06.2 at p. 83, and see below Chapter 13.

[61] See the disagreement in the *Interhandel Case*, 1959 ICJ Reports at p. 29, *per* Judge Córdova in a separate opinion at p. 45, *per* Judge Winiarski in a dissenting opinion at p. 84, and *per* Judge Lauterpacht in a dissenting opinion at p. 121; Gaja, note 9 above, at pp. 159–60; and Cot, note 9 above, at pp. 233–4. See also the Swiss oral argument in the *Interhandel Case*: ICJ Pleadings (1959) at p. 573.

[62] 1959 ICJ Reports at p. 29.   [63] *Ibid.*, p. 121.

[64] The records shows that the first post-Second World War so-called BIT was signed in 1959. Between 1959 and 2001, there have been 837 BITs signed: ICSID, *Investment Promotion and Protection Treaties*, Release 2001-3 (2001). All these treaties with the

multilateral.[65] There have been drafts of model multilateral and bilateral treaties relating to foreign investment in one way or another by, *inter alia*, the OECD, the AALCC and the UNCTC.[66]

The modern BIT is European in origin. The first was between the Federal Republic of Germany and Pakistan (1959). In 1967, the OECD finalized a Draft Convention on the Protection of Foreign Property. However, the draft was never opened for signature. There are some developed states, such as the US, Switzerland and Denmark, which have model agreements. To reflect the particular interests of developing states in the face of such activity by developed states, the AALCC produced a model treaty with two variants in 1984.

A trend among BITs is to include several different possible forms of arbitration for the settlement of investor-state disputes. Several treaties refer to different kinds of arbitration to which parties may agree. They also provide that in the absence of agreement between the parties on this matter the dispute shall be settled by arbitration according to a particular one of the mentioned forms.[67] Other treaties, for example those concluded by the US, give the host state's advance consent to each of the mentioned forms of arbitration, thus in effect giving the investor the choice.[68] References are common to ICSID, to arbitration under the UNCITRAL rules, and, to a lesser extent, ICC arbitration. There is comparatively little uniformity in this particular area of treaty practice. While the inclusion of an investor–state arbitration clause has become a common feature of BITs, there is variety in the choice of arbitration methods.

Basically, whether an investment treaty (or for that matter any relevant international dispute settlement treaty) includes a waiver, express or implied, of the local remedies rule, where it would otherwise be

exception of one (between Germany and Greece in 1961) have been between developed countries, on the one hand, and less developed countries, on the other. A few of these treaties have been between two less developed countries (e.g. Malaysia and Vietnam (1992), Singapore and Sri Lanka (1980), and Israel and Romania (1991)). Clearly, the BIT is directed at less developed countries and is an instrument to secure special protection, *vis-à-vis* these countries, for investments made in them by nationals of developed states.

[65] Perhaps NAFTA would qualify for this description.

[66] For the OECD, see 7 ILM p. 117 (1968); for the AALCC, see 23 ILM p. 254 (1984); and for the UNCTC, see UN Doc. E/1990/94, Annex.

[67] See e.g. Article 8 of the UK BIT with Czechoslovakia (1990), and Article 10 of the UK BIT with Ghana (1989).

[68] See e.g. Article VI(4) of the US BIT with Armenia (1992), and Article VII(4) of the US BIT with Argentina (1991).

applicable, is strictly a matter of interpreting the treaty. There is no hard and fast rule that BITs, for instance, by their very nature, imply a general waiver of the rule. On the contrary, the correct presumption may be the opposite – that no waiver may have taken place, unless express provision is made for it. The view of the ICJ, as pointed out, is that the rule is an important one whose waiver cannot lightly be presumed. Express waivers, total or partial, have appeared in BITs. More difficult is the answer to the question of when a waiver may be implied where express provision is not made for it. The issue being addressed relates to the incidence of a waiver of the rule.

Where the BIT incorporates ICSID arbitration either as the only dispute settlement procedure[69] or as one alternative,[70] and says no more, it is clear that by virtue of Article 26 of the ICSID Convention the rule of local remedies is waived where it otherwise would apply in circumstances where ICSID arbitration is the relevant means of dispute settlement. A reference to ICSID arbitration as such would involve a waiver of the rule subject to an express and appropriate statement or acceptance of its applicability.

Sometimes the BIT may specifically invoke the local remedies rule or a modified form of it, even where ICSID arbitration is the arbitration procedure chosen. In that case, the provisions of Article 26 are expressly excepted from, a possibility which Article 26 itself contemplates. An example of such an occurrence is the provision in Article 9 of the BIT between the Netherlands and Jamaica (1991) which states:

> 2. If such a dispute has not been settled amicably within a period of three months from the date on which either party to the dispute requested amicable settlement, either party may pursue local remedies for the settlement of that dispute.
>
> 3. If the dispute has not been settled within a period of eighteen months from its submission to a competent body for the purpose of pursuing local remedies, then for the purpose of Article 36 of the Convention on the Settlement of Investment Disputes between States and Nationals of other States opened for signature at Washington on 18 March 1965 (the Convention) the Contracting Party hereby gives its consent to the submission of the dispute to arbitration under that Article.

---

[69] See e.g. the BITs between the UK and Nigeria (1990) and the UK and Congo (1989), and between the Netherlands and Paraguay (1992).

[70] See e.g. the BITs between the UK and Ghana (1989), the UK and Ukraine (1990), the UK and Argentina (1990), Switzerland and Paraguay (1992) and Switzerland and Ghana (1991).

The provision retains an obligation on the part of the investor to accept a reference to local remedies within limits before ICSID arbitration is invoked.[71]

BITs which incorporate other arbitration procedures, such as *ad hoc* arbitration, whether under the UNCITRAL Rules or not, or ICC arbitration, and exclusively so as an alternative, sometimes make no reference at all to the exhaustion or invocation of local remedies as a pre-condition for arbitration. This is the case with such BITs as that between Switzerland and Lithuania of 1992 (Article 9). In such circumstances, the question of whether the rule of local remedies has been impliedly waived becomes one of construction of the BIT. The answer is not crystal clear. It is arguable that, because the host state has agreed to arbitration which is international, being under a treaty, the procedure provided for is in effect the exercise of diplomatic protection by the investor's national state and, therefore, in keeping with the established line of authority discussed earlier, even though the investor is given standing *per se* before the international forum, he has such standing by virtue of the treaty, and the local remedies rule applies in the absence of express waiver. The contrary argument is that, because the host state has agreed to arbitration, even though it is set up by an act of the host state and the investor and not by a direct act of the host state and the investor's national state, the other party to the BIT, although the arbitration flows from an international treaty, it is to be compared to such private arbitrations as took place in the *LIAMCO* and *Elf Aquitaine* arbitrations which imply the exclusion of the rule's application as being substitutes for remedies at the national level. It may be observed that the argument flowing from the conception of the arbitration procedure as one instituted in the exercise of diplomatic protection has considerable force. However, both arguments referred to above are still to be tested in circumstances where in an arbitration set up by the host state and the investor under the BIT the objection to admissibility is raised based on the rule of local remedies.

A situation may arise where the BIT provides for the rule of local remedies by the investor as an alternative to or prior to the institution of arbitration under the treaty. An example of this is the provision in the BIT of 1991 between Argentina and the US which states:

---

[71] See also the BIT between Switzerland and Argentina (1991).

2. In the event of an investment dispute, the parties to the dispute should initially seek a resolution through consultation and negotiation. If the dispute cannot be settled amicably, the national or company concerned may choose to submit the dispute for resolution:

(a) to the courts or administrative tribunals of the Party that is a party to the dispute; or

(b) in accordance with any applicable, previously agreed dispute-settlement procedures; or

(c) in accordance with the terms of paragraph 3.

3. (a) Provided that the national or company concerned has not submitted the dispute for resolution under paragraph 2(a) or (b) and that six months have elapsed from the date on which the dispute arose, the national or company concerned may choose to consent in writing to the submission of the dispute for settlement by binding arbitration: . . .

It is clear that it is the investor who is given the option of resorting to local remedies. Once this option is exercised, the import of the provision would seem to be that local remedies must be exhausted. Failure to exhaust them would then certainly result in the inadmissibility of an international claim based on diplomatic protection, if such a claim were made. Whether such a claim is available is not clear at all from the express terms of the treaty but there is no reason why it should not be.

Where the investor does not exercise the option of referring the dispute to the local courts, it would appear to be implied that arbitration instituted by the investor and the host state under the provision would not be subject to the prior exhaustion of local remedies. Unless this interpretation were given to the text, the provision would not make consistent sense.[72]

There are BITs which provide for submission to arbitration after the investor has exercised an option available to him to have recourse to the local courts. For example, the BIT of 1992 between Switzerland and Paraguay provides in Article 9(2) and (3) that:

(2) Si estas consultas no permitieran solucionar la controversia en un plazo de seis meses, a partir de la fecha de solicitud de arreglo de la diferencia, el inversionista puede someter la disputa tanto a la jurisdicción nacional de la Parte Contratante, en cuyo territorio se realizó la inversión o al arbitraje internacional. En este último caso el inversionista tiene las siguientes opciones:

---

[72] See also, e.g. Article 8(2) and (3) of the BIT between France and Argentina (1991) and Article IX(2) of the BIT between Norway and Indonesia (1991), which are similar.

a) el Centro Internacional de Arreglo de Diferencias Relativas a Inversiones (CIADI), creado por la Convención relativa al arreglo de diferencias entre Estados y nacionales de otros Estados, abierto a la firma en Washington, DC, el 18 de marzo de 1965;

b) un tribunal ad hoc, que salvo otro paracer acordado entre las partes de la controversia, será establecido bajo las reglas de arbitraje de la Comisión de las Naciones Unidas sobre Derecho Mercantil Internacional (CNUDMI).

(3) En caso de que el inversionaista haya sometido la divergencia a la jurisdicción nacional, él no puede apelar a uno de los tribunales arbitrales mencionados en el párrafo (2) del presente Artículo, salvo en el caso que luego de un período de 18 meses no haya una sentencia final del tribunal nacional competente.[73]

It is clear, first, that the rule of local remedies as such has impliedly been supplanted by different rules expressly referred to in the treaty. Secondly, while local remedies are relevant, and that, only if the investor chooses to submit to them, resort to them as a prior condition for arbitration is subject to the express terms of paragraph (3) of the Article. These terms either do not necessarily require an exhaustion of local remedies as such or local remedies are to be regarded as inadequate and ineffective on the basis of undue delay in their implementation.

Provisions which clearly *imply* a waiver of the rule of local remedies in relation to the arbitration provided for are to be found in such BITs as the 1989 treaty between France and Bulgaria which states in Article 8:

1. Tout différend entre l'une des Parties contractantes et un investisseur de l'autre Partie contractante relatif aux investissements est autant que possible réglé à l'amiable entre les deux parties au différend.

2. Si un tel différend n'a pas pu être réglé dans un délai de six mois partir du moment où il a été soulevé par l'une ou l'autre des Parties au différend, il peut être soumis aux juridictions compétentes de la Partie contractante qui est partie au différend et sur la territoire ou dans les zones maritimes de laquelle l'investissement est réalisé.[74]

It is noteworthy that three important international instruments which concern foreign investment and offer models for dispute settlement, though they are not binding treaties, do not jettison the rule of local remedies. Surprisingly, perhaps, the OECD Draft Convention on the Protection of Foreign Property of 1967 uses language in Article 7 (b) which

---

[73] See also e.g. Article 8(1) and (2) of the BIT between the UK and Argentina (1990) and Article 10(1) to (3) of the BIT between the Netherlands and Argentina (1992) for similar provisions.

[74] See for similar provisions, e.g. Article 9 of the BIT between Switzerland and Cape Verde (1991), and Article 12(1) and (2) of the BIT between Switzerland and Ghana (1991).

preserves the exhaustion of local remedies as a condition precedent to arbitration insofar as it states:

(b) A national of a Party claiming that he has been injured by measures in breach of this Convention may, *without prejudice to any right or obligation he may have to resort to another tribunal, national or international*, institute proceedings against any other Party responsible for such measures before the Arbitral Tribunal referred to in paragraph (a) . . .[75]

One of the two 1984 AALCC Model Draft Agreements for Promotion and Protection of Investments provides clearly in Articles 9 and 10 for the requirement of exhaustion of local remedies, whether before diplomatic protection is exercised or before arbitration is instituted at the request of the host state. Those Articles state

Article 9
Access to courts and tribunals

(Alternative 1)
The nationals, companies or State entities of one Contracting Party shall have the right of access to the courts, tribunals, both judicial and administrative, and other authorities competent under the laws of the other Contracting Party for redress of his or its grievances in relation to any matter concerning an investment including judicial review of measures relating to nationalisation or expropriation, determination of compensation in the event of nationalisation or expropriation of losses suffered and any restrictions imposed on repatriation of capital or returns. The local remedies shall be exhausted before any other step or proceeding is contemplated.

[(Alternative 2)
Any difference or dispute between the investor and the host State in relation to any matter concerning an investment including those relating to nationalisation or expropriation, determination of compensation in the event of nationalisation or expropriation or losses suffered and any restrictions imposed on repatriation of capital and returns shall be settled through recourse to appropriate courts and tribunals, judicial or administrative and other authorities competent under the local laws of the host State. Neither contracting Party shall pursue through diplomatic channel any such matter until the local remedies have been exhausted.]

Article 10
Settlement of investment disputes

(i) Each Contracting Party consents to submit any dispute or differences that may arise out of or in relation to investments made in its territory by a national,

---

[75] 7 ILM at p. 132 (1968).

company or State entity of the other Contracting Party for settlement through conciliation or arbitration in accordance with the provisions of this Article.

(ii) If any dispute or differences should arise between a Contracting Party and a national, company or State entity of the other Contracting Party, which cannot be resolved within a period of _____ through negotiations, either party to the dispute may initiate proceedings for conciliation or arbitration after the local remedies have been exhausted.[76]

The provisions on dispute settlement of the Code of Conduct on Transnational Corporations of 1989 formulated by the UNCTC emphasizes the primacy of national courts and tribunals, thus retaining the requirement of resort to and exhaustion of local remedies, while it states in Article 59 that, where the parties so agree, disputes may be referred to other mutually acceptable dispute settlement procedures.[77]

The approach taken in the drafting of BITs without exception, as the examples discussed above show, is based on the assumption that, even if arbitration instituted by the host state and investor is agreed upon in the BIT as a dispute settlement procedure, it does not per se imply a waiver of the rule of local remedies as a pre-condition to such arbitration. It is only, if there is an express waiver or a waiver must necessarily be implied in the interpretation of the treaty, that the application of the rule may be excluded.[78]

BITs generally provide also for the settlement of disputes between the two states parties to the particular BIT. Generally, such provisions refer to disputes relating to 'the application or interpretation' of the treaty. An example of a provision for the settlement of such disputes is Article 10 of the 1989 BIT between France and Bulgaria, which states:

1. Les différends rélatifs à l'application et à l'interprétation du présent Accord sont réglés par voie de négociation entre les Parties contractantes.

2. Si le différend n'est pas réglé dans un délai de six mois à partir dù moment ou il a été soulevé par l'une ou l'autre des Parties contractantes et sauf accord

---

[76] 23 ILM at pp. 263–4 (1984).

[77] See CTC, 'Code of Conduct on Transnational Corporations: Report of the Secretary General', Doc. E/C.10/1989/1.

[78] There is an additional question which may arise in relation to BITs and which was discussed in Chapter 5 in general in regard to international dispute settlement arrangements. That is whether breaches of contract by in particular the host state itself, which are not *per se* violations of international law, are in fact submitted to arbitral settlement under these treaties. Clearly, the answer depends on the interpretation of the particular treaty. The discussion above is of the incidence of the rule of local remedies which relates to exhaustion of remedies, where there has been a violation of international law, and not merely to the resort to or use of local remedies which is usually required before there can be a violation of international law in contract cases.

contraire de ces dernières sur la fixation d'un nouveau délai, il est soumis à la demande de l'une ou l'autre des Parties contractantes à un cour d'arbitrage.

Two questions arise with regard to such disputes which under such provisions are subject to settlement ultimately by arbitration. The first is whether the investor's national state could use these provisions to have disputes settled in the direct exercise of diplomatic protection. The second is whether the inter-state arbitration provided for, if permissible in the exercise of diplomatic protection, is subject to the exhaustion of local remedies by the investor. The answers to both questions depend naturally on the interpretation of the provisions of the particular BIT.

As to the first question, the reference to 'application and interpretation' of the BIT in the provisions cited above, for example, clearly covers the interpretation and application of the treaty to the relationship between investor and the host state. Consequently, the provision must enable the national state of the investor to bring a dispute which involves the application and interpretation of the treaty to arbitration under the provision, even though it may do so in the exercise of diplomatic protection.[79] The only problem is that the treaty specifically provides for the settlement of disputes between investor and host state by specific means. Such express terms, however, do not necessarily imply that provisions such as the one being discussed which refer to disputes between the host state and the investor's national state must exclude disputes the solution of which is sought in the exercise of diplomatic protection directly involving the two states parties to the treaty, provided they concern the application and interpretation of the treaty. It is possible that recourse to diplomatic protection involving the two states in those circumstances is left as a possible *alternative* to the settlement procedures designed to involve the investor directly. On the other hand, it would be reasonable to infer that, once the procedures directly involving the investor are invoked, the treaty does not permit the resort to diplomatic protection directly with the involvement in arbitration of the investor's national state. Otherwise, the settlement procedures provided for would duplicate rather than simplify the procedures for the settlement of disputes which would not be a logically consistent result. The interpretation of the BIT given here, while conceding that the settlement procedures directly involving the investor effectively substitute for the execution of

---

[79] 'Application' of the BIT undoubtedly covers remedies consequent upon such application which could be included in a claim based on diplomatic protection involving the two states directly.

diplomatic protection, also recognizes that Article 10 in addition affords an alternative procedure that can be applied in the exercise of diplomatic protection.

On the assumption that the exercise of diplomatic protection actively and directly involving the investor's state is possible as an alternative to the settlement procedures afforded the investor directly, the next issue is whether such protection by resort to inter-state arbitration procedures is subject to the exhaustion of local remedies by the investor or whether the requirement of such exhaustion has been waived. The answer again depends on the interpretation of the specific provisions of the BIT concerned. Article 10 of the BIT between France and Bulgaria, for instance, does not contain an express waiver of the application of the rule of local remedies in the appropriate circumstances nor does it necessarily imply that the application of the rule has been waived in such circumstances by the host state. The reference to negotiation as a pre-condition for arbitration is a reference to what is required of the parties to the BIT. It does not affect what is required of the investor, if a party to the treaty wishes directly to exercise diplomatic protection. This interpretation of Article 10 is not inconsistent with the provisions of the treaty nor is it illogical. On the contrary, it flows from the importance attached to the rule of local remedies in the settlement of disputes through the exercise of diplomatic protection which was recognized by the ICJ.

The principles of estoppel and good faith

The principles of estoppel and good faith may operate to exclude the application of the rule of local remedies. The doctrine of estoppel in broad terms prevents one party from taking advantage of another when the former by his actions has led the latter to act in a certain manner detrimental to the latter's own interests. The principle of good faith is at the root of this doctrine. The exact scope of the doctrine in international law is not fully defined. For the purpose of the application of the rule of local remedies, the statement in the *Chorzów Factory Case*, which purported to advert to an aspect of this doctrine, may be a good starting point. The PCIJ said:

It is, moreover, a principle generally accepted in the jurisprudence of international arbitration, as well as by municipal courts, that one party cannot avail himself of the fact that the other has not fulfilled some obligation or has not had recourse to some means of redress, if the former party has, by some illegal act, prevented the latter from fulfilling the obligation in question, or from having recourse to the tribunal which would have been open to him.[80]

The Court pointed to an illegal act in particular. However, the principles of good faith and estoppel have a broader coverage than that. In fact, any conduct on the part of one party which is intended to lead and induces the other party to act in a manner which is detrimental to his interests could qualify, there being no special requirement that the conduct be illegal.

While the principles of estoppel and good faith may have a general application to the exclusion of the rule of local remedies in appropriate circumstances, the manner in which they are applicable seems to have a strict definition. There must be cogent evidence that the conduct was not only intended to lead the alien or individual to believe that local remedies need not be further exhausted, for whatever reason, but also that the latter could reasonably be expected to rely on that conduct, did rely on it and for that reason did not resort to the local remedies which were available. Thus, in the *Interhandel Case*, the ICJ did not consider that the conduct of the US government was of this nature when it said:

The Court does not consider it necessary to dwell upon the assertion of the Swiss Government that 'the United States itself has admitted that Interhandel had exhausted the remedies available in the United States courts'. It is true that the representatives of the Government of the United States expressed this opinion on several occasions, in particular in the memorandum annexed to the Note of the Secretary of State of January 11th, 1957. This opinion was based upon a view which has proved unfounded. In fact, the proceedings which Interhandel had instituted before the courts of the United States were then in progress.[81]

It would appear that in the circumstances of the case the Court considered that it was not reasonable to expect that the alien would rely on the opinion of the US government, which was a party to the dispute and had no control on the US courts, and whose opinion on the existence of remedies was not necessarily an expert one. What is required for the principle of good faith and estoppel to operate is not merely that the host or respondent state express a general view about the existence of remedies, but that it conduct itself in such a way that a reasonable opponent would conclude that he was relieved of the duty to exhaust local remedies or that the rule would not be invoked.

---

[80] PCIJ Series A No. 9 at p. 31 (1927).   [81] 1959 ICJ Reports at p. 27.

In the *ELSI Case*, a Chamber of the ICJ dealt with the argument that the rule of local remedies had been excluded by estoppel. While not denying that estoppel could have been relevant to the matter in hand, the Court held that estoppel did not operate to exclude the rule on the facts of the case. It explained the doctrine of estoppel and its application to the facts as follows:

53. There was a further argument of the Applicant, based on estoppel in relation to the application of the local remedies rule, which should be examined. In the 'Memorandum of Law' elaborating the United States claim on the diplomatic plane, transmitted to the Italian Government by Note Verbale of 7 February 1974, one finds that the whole of Part VI (pp. 133 *et seq.*) deals generally and to some length with the 'Exhaustion of Local Remedies'. There were also annexed the opinions of the lawyers advising the Applicant, which dealt directly with the position of Raytheon and Machlett in relation to the local remedies rule. The Memorandum concluded that Raytheon and Machlett had indeed exhausted 'every meaningful legal remedy available to them in Italy' . . . In view of this evidence that the United States was very much aware that it must satisfy the local remedies rule, that it evidently believed that the rule had been satisfied, and that it had been advised that the shareholders of ELSI had no direct action against the Italian Government under Italian law, it was argued by the Applicant that Italy, if it was indeed at that time of the opinion that the local remedies had not been exhausted, should have apprised the United States of its opinion. According to the United States, however, at no time until the filing of the Respondent's Counter-Memorial in the present proceedings did Italy suggest that Raytheon and Machlett should sue in the Italian courts on the basis of the Treaty. The written aide-mémoire of 13 June 1978, by which Italy rejected the 1974 Claim, had contained no suggestion that the local remedies had not been exhausted, nor indeed any mention of the matter.

54. It was argued by the Applicant that this absence of riposte from Italy amounts to an estoppel. There are however difficulties about drawing any such conclusion from the exchanges of correspondence when the matter was still being pursued on the diplomatic level. In the *Interhandel* case, when Switzerland argued that the United States had at one time actually 'admitted that Interhandel had exhausted the remedies available in the United States courts', the Court, far from seeing in this admission an estoppel, dismissed the argument by merely observing that 'this opinion was based upon a view which has proved unfounded' (*Interhandel*, Judgment, ICJ Reports 1959, p. 27). Furthermore, although it cannot be excluded that an estoppel could in certain circumstances arise from a silence when something ought to have been said, there are obvious difficulties in constructing an estoppel from a mere failure to mention a matter at a particular point in somewhat desultory diplomatic exchanges.[82]

---

[82] 1989 ICJ Reports at pp. 43–4. On silence, see also the *Heathrow Airport User Charges Arbitration*, 102 ILR at p. 285 (1996). The distinction between implied waiver and estoppel may be fine. It is suggested that estoppel, as distinguished from implied

There are no clear examples of the application of the principles of estoppel and good faith in favour of an alien or individual. While there is every reason why the principles should be relevant to the operation of the rule of local remedies, it will naturally depend on the circumstances of each case whether the application of the principles should result in the exclusion of the rule.[83]

waiver, be defined as above in this section in order to make the differentiation useful. The fact that the term 'estoppel' may often be used broadly to include true situations of implied waiver, particularly in the context of human rights protection, as will be seen in Chapter 13, does not materially affect the reality.

[83] The most recent work on waiver and estoppel is to be found in Dugard, note 1 above, at pp. 17ff. There the first edition of my present book is cited extensively and the conclusions reached on the subject are identical with mine.

11   Burden of proof

The burden of proof in litigation relates to what must be proved and who must prove it. It is different from production of evidence. The rules relating to evidence, which concern the question of how facts may be proved, do not strictly touch on the burden of proof, although sometimes how a fact may be proved may affect what must be proved, particularly when presumptions of fact come into operation. While proof of facts and production of evidence for such proof constitute an important part of litigation even in international law, the success of a party to litigation will also depend to a large extent on the burden of proof that party carries, in so far as, if he carries the burden, he must adduce adequate evidence to prove on balance what he must prove, whereas if he does not carry the burden, the facts will be assumed to be in his favour until the other party adduces adequate evidence to prove the contrary.

In the case of the local remedies rule, it has been seen that the rule has a certain scope and that there are also certain limitations on the rule, and circumstances in which the rule is inapplicable. When the contention is raised by the respondent, as is usually the case, that the alien has not exhausted local remedies, questions arise as to the burden of proof, particularly because limitations to the rule may be pleaded, but also in relation to the actual scope of the rule.

General principles in customary international law

There are several factors which have influenced, if not determined, the development of the customary international law on the burden of proof which has been applied by international courts and tribunals. An important consideration has been the difference of approach between common law and civil law systems to the character of a judicial proceeding, which has caused some misunderstandings in the deduction of general principles of law. There are two principal methods of judicial proceeding. Proceedings may be founded on the adversarial system, where the establishment of facts depends on presentation by the parties, or on the investigatory system, where facts are established pursuant to *ex officio* inquiries. It has sometimes been assumed that the difference between the two systems has led to a divergence in matters relating to the burden of proof. But it has been shown that in virtually all national legal systems, whether they are adversarial or investigatory, there is generally some division of the burden of proof and that in none of them does one of the parties to a litigation bear the entire burden of proof.[1] There are consequently some general principles relating to the burden of proof which are common to most municipal legal systems.

A general principle which has been referred to in this connection is that *onus probandi actori incumbit*: that it is for the claimant to prove his claim. As has also been pointed out, this does not mean that it is always for the plaintiff to bear the burden of proof, whether positive or negative, because it is sometimes possible for the burden to rest on the defendant to prove relevant contentions in accordance with the maxim *reus in exceptione fit actor*. Hence, the general principle, if there is one, is that the burden of proof lies on him who asserts a proposition.[2] Thus, since the party who makes the allegation must prove his case, it depends on how in a litigation the propositions of law are formulated, with the consequence that the procedural burden of proof may continually shift during the process of trial.[3] It is also important to realize that it is not how the plaintiff formulates his claim, or how the respondent formulates his defence, that will determine how the burden of proof is divided, but that what matters is how the law interprets the claim and the defence or the exception; this will be the deciding factor.

---

[1] Amerasinghe, 'Principles of Evidence in International Litigation', 70 AIDI at pp. 156ff. (2003)); Buschbeck, 'Evidence: Procedures of Judicial Discovery and Burden of Proof', in 3 *Gerichtsschutz gegen die Exekutive* (1971) at pp. 164–6.

[2] See Amerasinghe, note 1 above; Ripert, 'Les règles du droit civil applicables aux rapports internationaux', 44 *Hague Recueil* (1933-II) at pp. 646–7; Witenberg, 'La Théorie des preuves devant les juridictions internationales', 56 *Hague Recueil* (1936-II) at pp. 41–2; Sandifer, *Evidence before International Tribunals* (1939) pp. 92–3 and 97–8; Bin Cheng, *General Principles of Law as Applied by International Courts and Tribunals* (1953) p. 332; and Kazazi, *Burden of Proof and Related Issues* (1996). See also *On a Matter of Diverted Cargoes* (Greece v. Great Britain), 22 ILR at p. 825 (1955).

[3] Sandifer, note 2 above, at p. 92.

That the general principle of law *onus probandi actori incumbit* is recognized by international courts and tribunals is not to be doubted, because there are several decisions in which the principle has been applied. Thus, in the *Queen Case*, it was held that:

One must follow, as a general rule of solution, the principle of jurisprudence, accepted by the law of all countries, that it is for the claimant to make the proof of his claim.[4]

This was further explained in the *Taft Case* as meaning that, on the basis of evidence taken as a whole, the burden rests on the claimant to prove to the satisfaction of the court or tribunal what he asserts, when the tribunal said:

Weighing the evidence as a whole . . . the claimants have failed to discharge the burden resting upon them to prove that the Avon was lost through an act of war.[5]

Some doubt was cast upon the existence of the general principle of law derived from municipal law, by which the burden of proof was, in the sense described, laid upon the party who was the actor, by the statement made in the *Parker Case* by the Mexican–US General Claims Commission that:

The Commission expressly decides that municipal restrictive rules of adjective law or of evidence cannot be here introduced and given effect by clothing them in such phrases as 'universal principles of law', or 'the general theory of law', and the like. On the contrary, the greatest liberality will obtain in the admission of evidence before this Commission with a view of discovering the whole truth with respect to each claim submitted . . . As an international tribunal, the Commission denies the existence in international procedure of rules governing the burden of proof borrowed from municipal procedure.[6]

But, as is shown by another passage in the same judgment, the tribunal was referring to another aspect of proof than the principle *onus probandi actori incumbit*. Immediately after stating the above, the tribunal said:

On the contrary, it holds that it is the duty of the respective Agencies to co-operate in searching out and presenting to this tribunal all facts throwing any light on the merits of the claim presented.[7]

---

[4] *Brazil* v. *Sweden/Norway* (1872), de La Pradelle-Politis, RAI, vol. 2, p. 708 (translation).
[5] *United States* v. *Germany* (1926), German–US Mixed Claims Commission, *Decisions and Opinions* at p. 805.
[6] *United States* v. *Mexico*, 4 UNRIAA at p. 39 (1926).   [7] *Ibid.*, p. 40.

Thus, as has been stated in an explanation of this case, there was no denial of the general principle *onus probandi actori incumbit*:

> From the context of this passage, it is clear that the Commission used the term 'burden of proof' in the sense of a duty to produce evidence, and to disclose the facts of the case. But the term is used in a different sense when it is asked on whom the burden of proof falls, or when it is said that the burden of proof rests upon this or the other party.[8]

The tribunal not only subscribed to the general principle of law relating to the burden of proof *stricto sensu* but went further in interpreting the implications of the principle to mean that *prima facie* evidence adduced by the proponent may be sufficient in certain circumstances when the allegations, if unfounded, could easily be disproved by the opposing party. Thus, the tribunal said:

> The Commission denies the 'right' of the respondent merely to wait in silence in cases where it is reasonable that it should speak . . . On the other hand, the Commission rejects the contention that evidence put forward by the claimant and not rebutted by the respondent must necessarily be considered as conclusive. But, when the claimant has established a prima facie case and the respondent has afforded no evidence in rebuttal the latter may not insist that the former pile up evidence to establish its allegations beyond a reasonable doubt without pointing out some reason for doubting. While ordinarily it is incumbent upon the party who alleges a fact to introduce evidence to establish it, yet before this Commission this rule does not relieve the respondent from its obligation to lay before the Commission all evidence within its possession to establish the truth, whatever it may be.[9]

It appears that the tribunal recognized the general principle of law relating to the burden of proof, but also used the term in a sense different from its accepted meaning. It also went further in maintaining that *prima facie* evidence produced by the proponent could sometimes result in a decision in his favour.

International courts have also implicitly made the point that the plaintiff in a case may not always be the party upon whom the burden of proof is laid. Thus, in the *Rights of Nationals of the United States in Morocco Case*,[10] the United States was in reality in the position of the claimant, in that it claimed special rights and privileges in the French Zone of Morocco, alleging that the Moroccan authorities had violated those rights. France was in fact in the position of the defendant, in denying

---

[8] Bin Cheng, note 2 above, at p. 328.
[9] *United States v. Mexico*, 4 UNRIAA at pp. 39–40 (1926).   [10] 1952 ICJ Reports p. 176.

the existence of those rights and privileges and any violation of them. However, in order to bring the issue before the ICJ, France took the position of the plaintiff by filing an action with the Court. The United States consequently argued that the burden of proof was upon France to prove its case. This was not, however, the view of the Court. The Court examined each of the US claims made in response to the claims of the French Government and rejected them to the extent to which they were not supported by treaties which the United States was entitled to invoke against Morocco. Further, since the United States also invoked custom and usage as a basis for some of its rights and privileges, the Court specifically laid the burden of proof on the United States, and rejected its allegations because it had failed to prove a custom binding upon Morocco. In regard to these allegations, which were intended to establish the special position of the United States, the Court treated the United States as the actor.[11] Thus, it is not the formal position of the parties in the litigation that necessarily determines the burden of proof. It is rather what the law requires to be proved that will ultimately determine who must prove it.

While the general principle prevails that each party is under the obligation to produce whatever evidence is accessible to it and under its control,[12] this does not really affect the incidence or distribution of the burden of proof. On the other hand, there may be circumstances, although only rarely, where the burden of proof lies on each party to establish the arguments upon which it bases its claim, if it wishes to succeed. This is usually the situation in cases concerning sovereignty over territory. Thus, in the *Island of Palmas Case*, the issue was which of the parties had sovereignty over the island. The tribunal took the view that '[e]ach party is called upon to establish the arguments on which it relies in support of its claim to sovereignty over the object in dispute'.[13] In the *Lighthouses Arbitration*, the PCA applied the principle that the burden of proof must be reasonably shared.[14] Thus, it is possible

---

[11] See also Bin Cheng, 'Rights of the United States Nationals in the French Zone of Morocco', 2 ICLQ (1953) at p. 354.

[12] See the *Parker Case* (*United States* v. *Mexico*), 4 UNRIAA at p. 39 (1926), where the Commission said that 'The parties before this Commission are sovereign nations who are in honour bound to make full disclosures of the facts in each case so far as such facts are within their knowledge, or can reasonably be ascertained by them'. See also the *Georges Pinson Case* (*France* v. *Mexico*), 5 UNRIAA at p. 413 (1928).

[13] *Netherlands* v. *United States*, 2 UNRIAA at p. 837 (1928). See also the *Minquiers and Ecréhos Case*, 1953 ICJ Reports at pp. 52 and 67.

[14] *France* v. *Greece*, 23 ILR at p. 679 (1956).

that the respondent in an action may bear the burden of proof, or that the burden may be appropriately divided.[15] This may be of particular importance in the context of the rule of local remedies.

The conclusion to be reached is that, although the plaintiff in an action, as claimant, would generally bear the burden of proving his claims, the respondent may also have to share in that burden, depending on whether it is making a claim or is in the position of making an assertion which is intended to disprove the case of the plaintiff, in which case it assumes the position of actor. What is important for the rule of local remedies is that, once the law determines that the party is in the position of making a claim or an assertion, that party must bear the burden of proof. The burden of proof may, thus, often be divided.

Burden of proof in regard to the exhaustion of local remedies

In relation to the exhaustion of local remedies, the application of the principle *onus probandi actori incumbit* has resulted in the division of the burden of proof. The difficulty is to establish exactly how the burden of proof is divided and consequently which party is to be regarded as the actor in respect of the claims made, which involves deciding what claims are being made by each party.

It is not difficult to appreciate that, according to the basic principle, the burden of proof will be assumed by the respective parties depending on how their respective claims in regard to the exhaustion of local remedies are interpreted. Thus, for example, if the claim made by the respondent is regarded as being that effective local remedies had not been exhausted, when there was no direct injury and there was a jurisdictional connection, it will be for the respondent to prove not only that some local remedies existed but also that they were effective, and had not been exhausted in circumstances in which there was no direct injury and there was the appropriate jurisdictional connection. If, on the other hand, the claim of the respondent is regarded as being that there were some remedies which had not been exhausted, while to the plaintiff are attributed counterclaims to the effect that such remedies

---

[15] For the approach of the ICJ, see the *Corfu Channel Case*, 1949 ICJ Reports at p. 18, the *Asylum Case*, 1950 ICJ Reports at p. 276, and the *Barcelona Traction Co. Case*, 1964 ICJ Reports at pp. 23–4. See also, for comments, Lauterpacht, *The Development of International Law by the International Court* (1953) pp. 595–6, and Rosenne, *The Law and Practice of the International Court 1920–1996* (1997), vol. 3, pp. 1083–92. On the burden of proof in general now, see Amerasinghe, note 1 above; and Kazazi, note 2 above.

were not effective, or that the circumstances revealed a direct injury or the absence of a jurisdictional connection, the burden of proof will clearly be divided. The plaintiff would have to prove to the satisfaction of the court or tribunal that remedies existed which had not been fully exhausted, while the respondent would bear the burden of proving that these remedies were not effective, or that there was a direct injury, or that there was no jurisdictional connection. What is important at this point, moreover, is to recognize also that it is not necessarily the party or parties that determine what the claims are by the manner in which the claims may be formulated. Rather, it is the law that attributes the particular claims made to the parties, so that the burden of proof laid upon each one will be identified accordingly. While there are not many decided cases which have faced the specific problems encountered in regard to the burden of proof in the application of the rule of local remedies, some do exist in which the problems have been at least adverted to, so that it is possible to discuss the trends which have been followed in respect of the burden of proof.

In general, while it has been assumed that there is a *prima facie* distribution of the burden of proof, as was stated by Judge Lauterpacht in the *Norwegian Loans Case*,[16] there is an initial onus on the respondent who raises the objection that local remedies have not been exhausted to 'prove the existence, in its system of internal law, of remedies which have not been used'.[17] The division of the burden of proof was implicitly acknowledged in practice by the PCIJ in the *Panavezys–Saldutiskis Railway Case*.[18] In that case, the respondent, Lithuania, raised a preliminary objection based on the non-exhaustion of local remedies. The plaintiff, Estonia, replied that the Lithuanian courts could not entertain a suit and that in any case, on one particular point, the highest court of Lithuania had already given an adverse decision. The PCIJ took the view that, if either of those claims could be substantiated, the Lithuanian objection would fail,[19] thus recognizing that the plaintiff was bound to prove that the remedies available were not effective. The Court made it quite clear in doing so that, until it had been clearly shown that the Lithuanian courts had no jurisdiction in the matter, the Court could not accept the Estonian contention that the local remedies rule did not apply in the

---

[16] 1957 ICJ Reports at p. 39. See also the *Interhandel Case*, ICJ Pleadings (1959) at pp. 562–3 and 565–6, oral argument of the plaintiff.
[17] *Greece v. UK*, 12 UNRIAA at p. 119 (1956). This view was endorsed by the ICJ in the *ELSI Case*, 1989 ICJ Reports at p. 46.
[18] PCIJ Series A/B No. 76 at p. 18 (1939).   [19] *Ibid.*

case, because there were no effective remedies available.[20] On the same lines, in the *Aerial Incident Case*, counsel for the respondent, Bulgaria, argued that, once the respondent had shown that local Bulgarian courts were largely open and accessible to aliens, it was for the plaintiff to prove that the existing remedies were ineffective, or that they were non-existent.[21]

Further refinements in the distribution of the burden of proof were made by Judge Lauterpacht in the *Norwegian Loans Case*, although the ICJ itself did not deal with the objection raised by the respondent relating to the exhaustion of local remedies. Judge Lauterpacht's expression of views was prompted by a more fundamental disagreement between the parties on the initial distribution of the burden of proof. The respondent, Norway, who lodged the objection, argued that, while it was the claimant (or actor) in the objection,

> sa demande est fondée sur une règle de droit international incontestée, en vertu de laquelle les recours internes doivent avoir été préalablement épuisés pour que l'action du Gouvernement français devant la Cour soit recevable. Si le Gouvernement français soutient que le principe n'est pas applicable, c'est à lui d'établir la raison pour laquelle il en est ainsi.[22]

Norway further stated that:

> Ce n'est donc pas au Gouvernement norvégien qu'il appartient de prouver que les voies de recours ouvertes aux porteurs français par son droit interne offrent à ces derniers des possibilités suffisantes pour que la règle de l'épuisement préalable ne puisse pas être écartée. C'est au Gouvernement de la République qu'il incomberait de prouver le contraire.[23]

In the oral argument, counsel for Norway emphatically stated:

> Une fois l'*existence* des recours internes établie, la règle de l'épuisement préalable devient applicable. Et si l'Etat demandeur veut échapper aux conséquences de cette règle, c'est à lui qu'il incombe alors de prouver que la règle ne joue pas *en raison de l'inefficacité des recours existants.*[24]

---

[20] *Ibid.*, at p. 19.

[21] ICJ Pleadings (1959) at pp. 565–6. The argument was earlier raised that it was sufficient for the respondent to contend that local remedies had not been exhausted for it to be able to claim the benefit of the rule: *ibid.*, p. 559. However, this formulation cannot be interpreted too literally in the light of the argument made later and referred to above that the respondent had proved the existence of remedies which resulted in the onus being placed on the plaintiff to prove the non-existence or ineffectiveness of such remedies.

[22] ICJ Pleadings, vol. 1, p. 280.   [23] *Ibid.*, p. 281.   [24] *Ibid.*, vol. 2, p. 162.

The respondent French government, on the other hand, argued that:

ce n'est pas au Gouvernement de la République française de faire la preuve du caractère inutile du recours aux tribunaux norvégiens. Le Gouvernement norvégien est demandeur dans cette exception, il revendique une compétence nationale, et c'est à lui de prouver l'utilité d'un recours à son organisation judiciaire.[25]

Counsel for France further stated that it was not sufficient for Norway to allege that local tribunals were impartial but that it must prove, in the face of the legislation which had created the situation being complained of, 'qu'il y a devant ses tribunaux une possibilité raisonnable de redresser la situation',[26] and that there should be constant collaboration between the parties in the presentation of evidence, because 'l'un des principes essentiels est l'obligation des parties de collaborer à la preuve'.[27]

The principle that there must be collaboration between the parties in the presentation of evidence has been admitted as a general principle of law. However, presentation of evidence is different from the burden of proof, as already pointed out. The French argument may have gone too far in placing on the respondent the total burden of proving that remedies which were effective had not been exhausted. On the other hand, in the context of the case, there may have been some legitimacy in the French claim that the burden was on the respondent to prove that, in the face of legislation such as was at issue in the case, there was still a reasonable possibility of redress being granted. Judge Lauterpacht in fact supported the latter position, when, while also making some general statements on the burden of proof, he said:

However, some prima facie distribution of the burden of proof there must be. This being so, the following seems to be the accurate principle on the subject: (1) as a rule, it is for the plaintiff State to prove that there are no effective remedies to which recourse can be had; (2) no such proof is required, if there exists legislation which on the face of it deprives the private claimant of a remedy; (3) in that case it is for the defendant State to show that, notwithstanding the absence of a remedy, its existence can nevertheless reasonably be assumed; (4) the degree of burden of proof thus to be adduced ought not to be so stringent as to render the proof unduly exacting.[28]

Judge Lauterpacht, in addition to asserting that, where there was legislation apparently depriving the alien of a remedy, the burden shifted

---

[25] *Ibid.*, vol. 1, p. 184.   [26] *Ibid.*, vol. 2, p. 188.
[27] *Ibid.*   [28] 1957 ICJ Reports at p. 39.

to the respondent, made some points of a general nature, namely, that (i) once the preliminary objection is raised, and the respondent has presumably shown that there were some remedies available to the alien, the plaintiff state must then, as a general rule, prove that those remedies were ineffective, although the degree of burden of proof to be adduced must not then be too stringent, and (ii) this distribution of the burden of proof was only a *prima facie* one. It is clear that Judge Lauterpacht not only regarded the accepted division of the burden of proof as being subject to exceptions but was against laying too heavy a burden on the plaintiff state when the burden shifted to it.

While the exact distribution of the burden of proof must, as Judge Lauterpacht implied, remain to some extent flexible, although it is certain that the burden is not entirely on one party and that, at least initially, the burden is on the respondent to prove certain facts, there are other elements in a litigation which, *prima facie* at any rate, it is clearly the function of the plaintiff to prove. These include the existence of a direct injury and the absence of a jurisdictional connection. The subject is, however, nebulous at present in certain of its aspects, because it has not been considered judicially with any completeness. Since the burden of proof is a matter pertaining particularly to litigation, the importance of judicial precedent relating to it cannot be underestimated. Significantly, therefore, although text writers agree that there is a distribution of the burden of proof,[29] it is neither possible nor desirable to lay down any specific rules for such distribution beyond those already established and referred to above.

Because of the special rules which may apply to the exhaustion of procedural remedies, as has been shown in Chapter 9, it may be useful to consider particularly how the burden of proof may be divided in regard to the exhaustion of discretionary procedural remedies. As has emerged from the earlier discussion, it is apparent that the distribution of the burden of proof in respect of the exhaustion of local remedies in general depends not only on fairness and justice but also to some extent on practical convenience, apart from the formal relevance and applicability of the maxim *onus probandi actori incumbit*.

---

[29] See e.g. Guggenheim, *Traité de droit international public* (1953), vol. 1, p. 81; Fawcett, 'The Exhaustion of Local Remedies: Substance or Procedure?', 31 BYIL (1954) at p. 458, Sereni, *Principi Generali di Diritto e Processo Internazionale* (1955) pp. 30, 40, 76–7 and 90, Law, *The Local Remedies Rule in International Law* (1961) pp. 54–61, Haesler, *The Exhaustion of Local Remedies in the Case Law of International Courts and Tribunals* (1968) pp. 54–5, and Chappez, *La Règle de l'épuisement des voies de recours internes* (1972) pp. 234–7.

As regards discretionary procedural remedies, the law would appear to involve several issues. They relate to (i) the existence of the remedy, (ii) the effectiveness of the remedy, (iii) the reasonable conduct of counsel in regard to the use of the remedy, (iv) the comparative effectiveness of any alternative remedy which has been suppressed and (v) the reasonable conduct of counsel in regard to the alternative remedy. While it may be clear that the existence of the remedy must, according to accepted principles, be proved by the respondent, it is not readily apparent how the burden of proof should be divided beyond that.

In regard to the questions relating to the effectiveness of the procedural remedy, if the burden is on the respondent to prove the facts, it must prove that the procedural remedy in issue was an effective one, in other words one which would probably have resulted in a decision which would have satisfied the alien's complaint. The burden would be on the respondent to adduce sufficient evidence to prove this effectiveness. If it fails to do so, the remedy must be pronounced ineffective. If it adduces evidence which is equally consistent with the effectiveness as with the ineffectiveness of the remedy, it has failed to discharge the onus. If the plaintiff state bears the burden of proof, it must show that the particular remedy was ineffective in that it would probably not have affected the decision given by the local court. The burden would be on the plaintiff state to adduce sufficient evidence to prove the ineffectiveness of the remedy. If it fails to do so, or if it merely adduces evidence which is consistent with either the effectiveness or the ineffectiveness of the remedy, the remedy will be deemed effective and the point will go against the plaintiff state.

According to the principles generally established, taken literally, it is for the respondent, having raised the issue as a preliminary objection, merely to prove that the particular procedural remedy was available. Then it is for the plaintiff state to adduce evidence and prove that the particular procedural remedy was ineffective in so far as it would probably not have affected the local court decision.

Although this approach may be satisfactory with reference to other aspects of the rule of exhaustion of local remedies, such as the exhaustion of substantive remedies or appeals, it is doubtful whether it should be rigidly applied to the question of the exhaustion of procedural remedies in the same court. In the case of the exhaustion of local remedies in general, the respondent points to something which by its very nature raises a presumption that it is effective, such as an appeal not resorted to, so that it is not entirely inconsistent to shift the burden of proving the ineffectiveness of the remedy on to the plaintiff state.

In the case of the exhaustion of procedural remedies in the same court, however, the alien has already availed himself of proceedings before a judge in relation to a specific issue or specific issues of law and fact. There is no reason to presume, therefore, that, because the respondent points to a procedural remedy in the same court which the alien has not used, the alien has failed to conduct his case in the best way possible. The principle *omnia rite esse praesumuntur*[30] would apply in favour of the alien. In that event, the plaintiff state cannot be expected to prove that the remedy referred to was an ineffective one, since that would amount to a denial of that presumption. Hence the burden must lie on the respondent to show that the remedy was not only available but also effective. Therefore, in the case of procedural remedies, the *prima facie* distribution of the burden of proof outlined above should not apply to the issue of whether the remedy is an effective one. The whole burden should rest on the respondent. The exception is explicable by the fact that the exhaustion of procedural remedies is different from the exhaustion of other remedies.

In regard to the issue of whether reasonable counsel could have foreseen that the remedy was an effective one, the same reasoning does not apply. Once it is proved that the remedy is effective, it can justly be said to give rise to a presumption that a reasonable counsel would have used it, so that it is for the party denying this proposition to prove its case, namely, that reasonable counsel could not have foreseen the effectiveness of the remedy. Thus, in respect of this issue, there should be a shift in the burden of proof. The claimant must prove that a reasonable counsel could not in all the circumstances of the case have foreseen the effectiveness of the remedy, effective though it in fact was.

As for the other two issues that may arise in a litigation concerning procedural remedies, they relate to a situation where there are alternative remedies, one of which is being suppressed by the respondent, so that the alien is led not to use the other. Here the respondent has shown that there is an effective procedural remedy which has not been used, while the claimant alleges that there was an alternative which was more effective which, however, was not available through the act of the

---

[30] For this principle of international law, see Amerasinghe, note 1 above; and Bin Cheng, note 2 above, at p. 305.

respondent. It cannot reasonably be presumed that an alternative which is suppressed will always be more effective than the one available so as to lay the burden on the respondent to show that the alternative was of such a kind that the other should have been used. The plaintiff state raises the issue in replication to a defence of non-exhaustion and should be required to prove that both the factors necessary for the success of such a replication are present. Thus, it is the plaintiff state that must prove that the alternative remedy was of greater effectiveness and that reasonable counsel could have acted and did act on this basis.

Briefly, to sum up on the burden of proof in respect of procedural remedies, it is for the respondent to prove that the procedural remedy alleged not to have been used was effective, while it is for the plaintiff state to show that counsel could not reasonably have known or foreseen this fact, and could not reasonably have used the remedy. In a case where the reply is made by the plaintiff state that there was an alternative remedy of which the alien was deprived by the respondent, it is for the plaintiff state to prove both that this alternative remedy was more effective than the other and that counsel could reasonably have, and did in fact, come to this conclusion.

12 Procedural matters connected with the rule

There are a few matters, particularly of procedure, touching upon the implementation of the rule of local remedies which call for consideration. They are important in so far as they may result in various consequences for both the respondent and the claimant, or regulate the manner in which tribunals or organs applying the rule may conduct the proceedings, both as regards the exhaustion of remedies itself and the substantive merits of cases.

The time for raising the objection based on the rule

As already seen in Chapter 10, the benefit of the rule could be forfeited by the respondent by an implication of a waiver, if the objection that the rule had not been observed is not raised in the proceedings when it should be. Thus, it becomes important to determine what is the appropriate time for such action after which the benefit of the rule would be forfeited. In this area, as will be seen from Chapter 13, there are some differences between the law governing diplomatic protection and the law of human rights protection. In the latter, there is a tendency to be open to variation.

The precedents that exist as far as diplomatic protection is concerned are based on the practice of the PCIJ and the ICJ. The objection that local remedies have not been exhausted contests the admissibility of the application and is thus of a preliminary nature. It is not a defence on the merits, the success of which would permanently exclude the case as *res judicata*. As has been pointed out:

[I]n an examination in general of the effect of time on the jurisdiction of the Court, an objection based on the rule regarding the non-exhaustion of local remedies, which has been said to be 'of a temporary and relative character',

293

may therefore be regarded as a dilatory objection *ratione temporis*. If accepted it puts an end, on grounds of prematurity, to the case, but implies the possibility of a renewal of the legal dispute when the temporary obstacle is removed.[1]

It is an objection to admissibility, rather than an objection to jurisdiction or a defence on the merits, which is based on the argument that the case has been prematurely filed and could lead only to a dilatory obstruction to the examination of the merits.[2]

Thus, as to the timing of the objection, the current Article 79 of the ICJ Rules of Court, which has evolved from a more general rule adopted by the PCIJ in 1926, before which the question was not dealt with in the Rules of Court, would govern. Apparently, the PCIJ and the ICJ, before 1972, when the current Article was adopted in its present form, took a more flexible attitude to the issue of timing.[3] The current Article provides:

> 1. Any objection by the respondent to the jurisdiction of the Court or to the admissibility of the application, or other objection the decision upon which is requested before any further proceedings on the merits, shall be made in writing within the time limit fixed for the delivery of the Counter-Memorial.

Hence, a preliminary objection based on the rule of local remedies, because its character as a preliminary objection to admissibility is established,[4] must be raised before the time limit fixed for the delivery of the respondent's counter-memorial. If the respondent fails to raise the objection before the expiration of this period, it forfeits the right to rely on it.

In the case of other international tribunals, it may be assumed that a similar time limit would be fixed for the raising of a preliminary

---

[1] Rosenne, *The Time Factor in the Jurisdiction of the International Court of Justice* (1960) p. 71.

[2] *Ibid.*, p. 70, states that the objection leads only to dilatory obstruction, but this is not so. The alien may subsequently never be able to exhaust remedies because of time limits, the fault being his. In such a case, the objection based on local remedies, upheld in the international proceeding, will have the effect of barring completely the examination of the merits by the international instance. Article 44 of the 2001 ILC Articles on State Responsibility treats the objection based on local remedies as one relating to admissibility of the claim: see GAOR Doc. A/55/10. This assumes in effect that the rule is procedural in nature.

[3] See Rosenne, *The Law and Practice of the International Court 1920–1996* (1997), vol. 2, pp. 864ff.; Grisel, *Les Exceptions d'incompétence et irrecevabilité dans la procédure de la Cour internationale de justice* (1968) pp. 26ff. These works discuss preliminary objections in general.

[4] See the *Panavezys–Saldutiskis Railway Case*, PCIJ Series A/B No. 76 at p. 22 (1939).

objection founded on the non-exhaustion of local remedies. Once the preliminary nature of the objection based on the local remedies rule as one to admissibility is conceded, it must also be acknowledged that there is such a time limit for the raising of the objection.

The time of decision on the objection based on the rule

The view has been expressed both judicially and by textual authorities that, unless a certain order for the decision of objections is imposed by logical necessity, an international tribunal such as the ICJ may determine the order that may suitably be followed, such determination being based even on criteria of economy and not governed by the attitude of the party or parties.[5] There has additionally been an expression of the opinion which requires a certain consistent order in the disposition of preliminary objections which is clearly based on logic. In particular, judges of the ICJ have espoused the view that the objection of non-exhaustion of local remedies, as one to admissibility, should be decided after and not before questions of competence or of jurisdiction have been settled in favour of competence or jurisdiction.[6] As was stated by President Klaestad in the *Interhandel Case*:

In its Third Preliminary Objection the United States Government challenges the jurisdiction of the Court on the ground that Interhandel has not exhausted the local remedies available to it in the United States courts. The Court has held that an objection of this kind is not a plea to the jurisdiction of the Court, but a plea to the admissibility of the Application. Sharing this view I am further of the opinion that an adjudication upon this Objection presupposes that the Court has first established its jurisdiction, when that jurisdiction is challenged, as it is in the present case. This Objection is of a temporary and relative character, dependent on the outcome of the lawsuit of Interhandel in the United States courts. It is not, as are the absolute objections to the jurisdiction of the Court, directed against that jurisdiction, which in the present case is governed by Article 36, paragraph 2, of the Statute, and the Swiss and United States Declarations made thereunder. The true legal nature of this Preliminary Objection becomes

---

[5] See Judge Morelli in his dissenting opinion in the *Barcelona Traction Co. Case* (Preliminary Objections), 1964 ICJ Reports at pp. 98–9, and in his separate opinion in the *Barcelona Traction Co. Case*, 1970 ICJ Reports at pp. 226–31; C. de Visscher, *Aspects récents du droit procédural de la Cour internationale de justice* (1966) pp. 104–5.

[6] See in the *Interhandel Case*, Judge Sir Percy Spender in a separate opinion, 1959 ICJ Reports at p. 54; President Klaestad in a dissenting opinion, *ibid.*, pp. 78–9; Judge Armand-Ugon in a dissenting opinion, *ibid.*, p. 91; and Judge Lauterpacht in a dissenting opinion, *ibid.*, p. 100.

clear when it is considered that the dispute may, under certain conditions and in a modified form, again be submitted to the Court as soon as the remedy available to Interhandel in United States courts is finally exhausted.[7]

Juristic writing has supported these views expressed by the international judiciary.[8] However, while it has been observed that generally the ICJ has tended, first, to examine objections to jurisdiction or competence before objections to admissibility, particularly because examination of questions of admissibility implies an exercise of jurisdiction or competence, and, second, to examine *exceptions péremptoires* before dilatory exceptions, in order to dispose first of the more radical grounds of objection, leaving for a later stage the objections which could result in a subsequent examination of the case, it is also clear that the main tendencies thus observed have not always been adhered to in practice by the Court.[9] However, it is certain that international tribunals do not consider the merits until they have adjudicated on dilatory preliminary objections based on the rule of local remedies, because upholding the objection would have the effect of rendering the application inadmissible and precluding consideration of the merits by the tribunal.

Joinder to the merits

It has been the practice in the law of diplomatic protection for international tribunals and organs to join an objection based on the non-exhaustion of local remedies to the merits of the case. While this practice does not affect the character of the objection as one to admissibility, and the necessity for it to be adjudicated upon before the merits, it does raise questions as to when this procedure is appropriate or inappropriate.

   In the case of the PCIJ and the ICJ, the possibility of joining a preliminary objection to the merits was first expressly permitted in 1936 by the introduction of a new provision in the Rules of Court of the PCIJ. Before that, there are no instances of joinder. Since then, there have been several cases in which joinder of an objection based on the local remedies rule has been permitted by the Court, while sometimes joinder has been refused. In the *Panavezys–Saldutiskis Railway Case*, the PCIJ

---

[7] 1959 ICJ Reports at pp. 78–9.
[8] See Abi-Saab, *Les Exceptions préliminaires dans la procédure de la Cour internationale* (1967) pp. 229–31; and Chappez, *La Règle de l'épuisement des voies de recours internes* (1972) pp. 154–6. Rosenne, note 3 above, vol. 2, pp. 864ff. does not deal specifically with preliminary objections based on the local remedies rule.
[9] Abi-Saab, note 8 above, at pp. 229–32.

asserted its authority to order the joinder of a preliminary objection to the merits in the interests of the good administration of justice, and decided to join to the merits, among others, an objection based on the local remedies rule.[10] Earlier, in the *Affaire Losinger and Co.*, a preliminary objection based on the rule had been joined to the merits, in order that the Court might adjudicate in the same judgment on the objection and, if need be, on the merits.[11] In the *Barcelona Traction Co. Case* (Preliminary Objections), the objection based on the rule was joined to the merits. The Court stated:

this is not a case where the allegation of failure to exhaust local remedies stands out as a clear-cut issue of a preliminary character that can be determined on its own. It is inextricably interwoven with the issues of denial of justice which constitute the major part of the merits. The objection of the respondent that local remedies were not exhausted is met all along the line by the applicant's contention that it was, *inter alia*, precisely in the attempt to exhaust local remedies that the alleged denials of justice were suffered. This is so obvious on the face of the pleadings, both written and oral, that the Court does not think it necessary to justify it further at this stage, by any statement or consideration of the events in question, which can be left until the merits are heard.[12]

In the *Norwegian Loans Case*, the objection based on the rule of local remedies was joined to the merits by agreement between the parties.[13] In the *Interhandel Case*,[14] however, the Court's majority of nine decided the case by upholding the objection based on the local remedies rule without joining it to the merits, although the possibility of doing so had been raised by the claimant.[15] Four of the dissenting judges thought that the objection should have been joined to the merits.[16]

While it is clear that an international tribunal has considerable discretion to join to the merits an objection based on the local remedies rule, it is not entirely certain how this discretion will be exercised. Some indication of the basis for joinder was given in the *Barcelona Traction Co.*

---

[10] Order of 30 June 1938, PCIJ Series A/B, and PCIJ Series A/B No. 75 at pp. 55–6 (1938).

[11] Order of 27 June 1936, PCIJ Series A/B No. 67 at pp. 24–5 (1936).

[12] 1970 ICJ Reports at p. 46. The issue of joinder had been discussed extensively in the oral pleadings: see particularly, ICJ Pleadings (1962–9), vol. 2, pp. 309–11 (Spain); and ICJ Pleadings (1962–9), vol. 3, pp. 652ff. (Belgium).

[13] Order of 28 September 1956, 1956 ICJ Reports at pp. 73–5. The issue was also discussed in the *Aerial Incident Case*, ICJ Pleadings (1959) at pp. 523–4 and 593 (Israel) and pp. 445, 559, 564 and 572 (Bulgaria). In the *Elettronica Sicula SpA* (*ELSI*) *Case*, the objection was also joined to the merits by agreement of the parties: 1989 ICJ Reports at p. 42.

[14] 1959 ICJ Reports p. 6.   [15] ICJ Pleadings (1959) at pp. 553–6.

[16] 1959 ICJ Reports at p. 81 (President Klaestad), p. 84 (Judge Winiarski), p. 89 (Judge Armand-Ugon) and p. 124 (Judge Spiropoulos).

Case (Preliminary Objections), as was seen above. The matter has been further discussed by text writers;[17] but perhaps the simplest explanation of how joinder to the merits will be decided upon, in the absence of agreement between the parties, was given in the oral argument on behalf of the respondent in the *Barcelona Traction Co. Case* (Preliminary Objections), where it was pointed out that an analysis of practice showed that in principle the Court asked itself three questions: (i) whether the plea submitted was really a preliminary objection; (ii) if so, whether a decision could be taken on this preliminary objection without pre-judging the merits; and (iii) if the answer to those questions was in the affirmative, then, without necessitating a pre-judgment of the merits, whether an examination of the question did not touch upon the facts mentioned in the claim to such an extent that in the interest of justice it was better that the Court should not decide without first obtaining the further information that could be furnished to it by the full exchange of the four written pleadings provided for by the Rules of Court for an adjudication on the merits.[18]

The time at which remedies must be exhausted

It may be important to determine at what point in time local remedies must be exhausted. The issue is whether the exhaustion of local remedies must be completed before the date of filing of the application with the international organ, or whether the critical date may occur later.

In general, the critical date would not be so crucial, because even if it has not occurred at the appropriate time, it is possible for another action to be filed after that date occurs, as the effect of dismissal of the action on the ground that it is inadmissible for failure to exhaust local remedies is not to render the matter *res judicata*. But sometimes, particularly in the law of human rights protection, it may matter what date is chosen as the critical date, because a second application may be excluded by operation of the six-months rule, or by some provision in the *compromis* or other instrument giving the tribunal's jurisdiction.

In the law of diplomatic protection, it is generally assumed that the critical date is no later than the date on which the application is filed with the international tribunal. That is to say, the exhaustion of remedies must be completed before the application is so filed. A relevant

---

[17] See particularly C. de Visscher, note 5 above, at pp. 106–11.
[18] ICJ Pleadings (1962–9), vol. 2, pp. 658–9 (Belgium).

decision in this regard is that in the *Electricity Co. of Sofia Case*.[19] There it was argued by the respondent that when the application was filed the Bulgarian Court of Cassation, which was the last in a series of recourses available, had not given a decision with final effect and that, therefore, the rule of local remedies had not been observed. On this point the PCIJ agreed with the respondent and upheld the objection. The date of completion of exhaustion of remedies was important for this purpose, because by the time the Court of Cassation did give its final decision, the bilateral treaty on which the claimant founded the Court's jurisdiction had terminated by denunciation, so that the claim could not be made under that treaty.[20] It is significant that Judge Van Eysinga in his dissent took the view that the objection should not have been upheld because to uphold it thus was a pure formality, considering that the claim could have been submitted again after the critical date under the Optional Clause declaration.[21]

---

[19] PCIJ Series A/B No. 77 (1939).

[20] In that case the claimant, however, succeeded partially in founding the Court's jurisdiction on the signature of the Optional Clause.

[21] PCIJ Series A/B No. 77 pp. 113ff. (1939). Judge Anzilotti, in agreeing with the Court's view, said in a separate opinion that, although the rule of local remedies had only a suspensory effect, the critical date was relevant because the objection that the rule had not been observed was based on a treaty.

Part III   Peripheral and analogous applications of the rule

13   The rule and human rights protection

The rule of local remedies has been expressly incorporated, as has been seen in Chapter 3, in the European Convention on Human Rights (ECHR), the American Convention on Human Rights (the 'American Convention') and the International Covenant on Civil and Political Rights (ICCPR). That domestic remedies must have been exhausted 'according to the generally recognized rules of international law' is a requirement of admissibility under these Conventions, as is exemplified by Articles 26 and 27(3) of the former European Convention (see Article 35(1) of the new Convention).[1] Because the application of the rule of domestic remedies to the protection of human rights under the European Convention is conventional, it is important to understand how the Convention which provides for such protection has been interpreted. The approach taken by the European Commission of Human Rights (EComHR) and the European Court of Human Rights (ECtHR) in some of the leading cases decided by them is illustrative. There are a few cases of the Inter-American Court of Human Rights (IACHR) which may also be considered. The application of the rule by the IACHR is directly conventional. The UN Human Rights Committee (HRC) has also applied the rule. The Inter-American Commission of Human Rights (IAComHR) has applied the rule directly or indirectly on account of international agreement. Further, as has been seen in Chapter 3, the Sub-Commission on Prevention of Discrimination and Protection of Minorities, which examines complaints relating to human rights violations under authority of resolutions of ECOSOC taken

---

[1] The new Convention reflects the same provisions as the old Convention contained in Articles 26 and 27(3). Thus, the application of Articles 26 and 27(3) of the old Convention by the EComHR and ECtHR still holds good for the new Convention. See also e.g. the American Convention on Human Rights (Article 46(1)(a)), and the ICCPR (Article 41(c)). Provisions are referred to in Chapter 3 above.

pursuant to provisions of the UN Charter and, thus, operates under the UN Charter, also applies the rule of domestic remedies under those resolutions. Pursuant to the ICERD, the CERD applies the rule, as is done under the Convention Against Torture by the CAT.

It is important to recognize that the work of the above Sub-Commission is not ultimately judicially controlled by a court (as, for example, the work of the EComHR was controlled by the ECtHR). In the same way, the work of the HRC, which clearly acts only quasi-judicially, albeit directly under the ICCPR or the Optional Protocol, is not ultimately judicially controlled. The work of the IAComHR outside of the framework of the American Convention on Human Rights but pursuant to the OAS Charter, whether before or after the American Convention came into force, is likewise not judicially controlled (by the IACHR, which functions only under the American Convention). While these bodies may be acting quasi-judicially in performing these functions, because they are not judicially controlled (e.g. by courts such as the ECtHR or the IACHR) in these functions, their precedents are of less worth from the angle of *judicial* settlement of international human rights disputes than the jurisprudence of the EComHR and the ECtHR, and that of the IAComHR, acting under the control of the IACHR (i.e. under the American Convention) and the IACHR. That having been said, the work of the HRC on the domestic remedies rule will be included peripherally in this survey (for what it is worth), and reference will be made occasionally to the decisions of the IAComHR acting outside the American Convention.

The object of this chapter is to present and elucidate the basic principles that have been applied in connection with the implementation of the rule of local (domestic) remedies mainly under the European Convention, because the jurisprudence of the organs which have applied the rule under that Convention is the leading and most important and extensive jurisprudence, and it is genuinely judicial in character.[2] That jurisprudence has also had by far the longest life and shows, for that reason, among others, considerable development and maturity. The decisions of organs acting under other international agreements are also

---

[2] McGoldrick, *The Human Rights Committee* (1991) p. 188, agrees with this observation and also adverts to the reference in the ICCPR and Optional Protocol to public international law. The work of the HRC, in applying the domestic remedies rule is examined in the above work (pp. 187 ff). See also Joseph, Schultz and Castau, *The International Covenant on Civil and Political Rights* (2000), which is a casebook (pp. 74–96). The analysis is poor in this work.

considered, though perhaps peripherally and incidentally. It is also principally with the prior example of diplomatic protection in mind that the analysis is made. It is certainly not a purpose to list exhaustively all the cases and decisions of all human rights organs which deal with the rule, a futile exercise in a work of this nature, nor merely to multiply examples. It will suffice to refer to case authority which establishes the relevant principle.

It must also be borne in mind that, while conventions or other governing instruments, without exception practically, refer to the exhaustion of remedies according to 'the generally recognized rules or principles of international law', they may also, as is the case of Article 24(2) of the American Convention, expressly, though not exclusively, state how in relation to specific contexts the rule of international law is to be interpreted for the purposes of the convention in issue. Without a doubt, the specific convention or instrument must be applied in terms of such express provisions. However, none of these express provisions have diluted, as far as is known, the 'generally recognized rules or principles of international law' relating to the rule of local remedies, as applied to human rights protection. Nor can it be contended that they have as such expanded such basic rules and principles. What remains to be examined, therefore, is to what extent these rules and principles have been recognized or modified in the application of the conventions or instruments which show basically a remarkable similarity as far as the reference to general principles of international law is concerned and the tendency not expressly to dilute or expand them as such.

The direct injury

In regard to the protection of human rights, the relevance of the direct injury exclusion for the rule of local remedies would seem less apparent. However, there are situations in which the concept of the direct injury may be relevant in order to *exclude* the application of the rule. Some cases have arisen under the European Convention on Human Rights.

First, in connection with applications made under Article 24 of the Convention by states, the argument has been made that the rule does not apply. This argument is based on a theory which seems to bear a relationship to the doctrine of the direct injury in its application to the rule of local remedies in the area of the protection of aliens. In *Austria* v. *Italy*, the applicant government, which had filed a claim under Article 24 of the Convention, argued that applications from states under the

Convention were not subject to the rule that domestic remedies must be exhausted because they were not based on diplomatic protection, but rather were brought on behalf of individuals under special international protection and were based on the concepts of collective guarantee and the general interest.[3]

In its examination of this Austrian contention, the EComHR[4] first recounted the basis and status of the rule of local remedies in general international law and stated that the system of protection of the Convention extended to nationals of the respondent state; that, therefore, the rule of local remedies should apply *a fortiori* to a system of international protection which extends to a state's own nationals as well as to foreigners; and that the system of collective guarantee did not weaken the case for the applicability of the rule. The Commission then decided that Article 26 covered inter-state applications because of the express internal evidence contained in Article 27(3) and the absence of any limitations in Article 26. The Commission treated the matter as one primarily of interpretation of the Convention. It is significant that Article 26, which incorporated in the Convention the rule of local remedies, did not make any distinction between the various kinds of application. But it also had been held that the rule of domestic remedies is inapplicable to applications by states based on a prevailing condition which amounts to a violation of the Convention,[5] although in Article 26 this category of application was not *explicitly* excluded from the purview of the rule. The question then is whether the kind of state application under discussion could also be excluded from the coverage of Articles 26 and 27(3). In both cases individuals in reality are particular victims of the violation of the Convention who can exhaust domestic remedies. Therefore, while the words of Articles 26 and 27(3) may be interpreted to make the rule of local remedies applicable to this kind of state application, the issue is whether an exception should not be made.

It does not seem arguable that for the purposes of interpreting Articles 24, 26 and 27(3) of the Convention a difference is to be made in the case of such state applications, because they are founded on the concepts of collective guarantee and general interest. There is nothing

---

[3] Application 788/60, *Report of the Plenary Commission* at pp. 42ff.
[4] *Ibid.*, at p. 44.
[5] *First Cyprus Case (Greece v. UK)*, Application 176/56, 2 YBECHR p. 184; *First Greek Case (Denmark/Norway/Sweden/Netherlands v. Greece)*, Applications 3321–3323/67 and 3344/67, 12 YBECHR p. 21.

inherently incompatible between these notions and the applicability of the rule of domestic remedies to such state applications under Articles 24, 26 and 27(3) as they stand. Under these Articles, there is room for the application of the rule whenever an individual's rights are violated under the Convention. In this kind of state application such a situation does arise. Moreover, the internal structure of Article 27 supports the interpretation proposed above. Article 27(3) made it necessary for the Commission to reject any petition that it considered inadmissible under Article 26. No distinction is made between state applications filed under Article 24 and individual applications governed by Article 25. On the other hand, Article 27(1) and (2), which dealt with other grounds on which the Commission must reject a petition, referred specifically to petitions filed under Article 25. The conclusion is therefore warranted that, for the purposes of Article 27(3), both state applications and individual petitions were to be rejected, if they were inadmissible under Article 26.[6]

While, however, the Commission decided, and cold logic may demand, that the rule of domestic remedies be applicable to the inter-state dispute, although the Convention is not explicit on the matter, the reference in Article 26 to the general principles of international law may prompt the question of whether the incidence of the rule should not be affected by the fact of the collective guarantee and the general interest, even though, as seen in Chapter 3, the Commission has taken the view that that reference strictly relates only to the material content of the rule. Even if an analogy were drawn from the exclusion of the rule in the customary international law of diplomatic protection in the case of the direct injury, it is not certain that the injury to the applicant state in an inter-state dispute under the Convention could be characterized *per se* as a direct injury purely on the ground that there is a collective guarantee and a general interest underlying the Convention. Clearly, the only basis for distinguishing state applications in inter-state disputes from individual applications is that in the former case individuals are placed

---

[6] The reasoning and decision in *Austria v. Italy* have been criticized: see Vasak, *La Convention européene des droits de l'homme* (1964) p. 114; Eustathiades, 'Une Nouvelle experience en droit international – les recours individuals à la Commission des droits de l'homme', in *Grundprobleme des internationalen Rechts – Festschrift für Jean Spiropoulos* (1957) at pp. 111ff. See further, on inter-state cases, Cançado Trindade, 'Exhaustion of Local Remedies in Inter-State Cases: The Practice Under the European Convention on Human Rights', 29 ÖZÖR (1978) at pp. 214ff.

under special protection because of the existence of a collective guarantee and a general interest. What this means is that states are given the right of instituting proceedings on behalf of non-nationals because it is in the general interest of the community of states parties to the Convention and because each state party guarantees on a collective basis that every other party will observe its obligations under the Convention, even in respect of individuals who are not nationals of the complaining state. The guarantee is given to the individuals concerned upon whom rights are conferred by the Convention and to every other state party which is not the respondent state. States parties to the Convention have substantive rights in regard to non-nationals, and not merely the right of representation. The above theoretical basis for the right of states to institute the proceedings on behalf of non-nationals should not, however, critically affect the rule of local or domestic remedies. Whether the complaint is brought by a state or by an individual, the individual concerned can exhaust domestic remedies. The fact that in the former case a state asserts its own right does not alter the position. For, in diplomatic protection too this is the case; nevertheless, the rule is applicable. Moreover, in both diplomatic protection and the case of a non-national state exercising protection under the Convention, it is the right of the state to protect the individual that is violated which is the normal basis for the incidence of the rule. In short, there is as such no interest other than the interest in protecting an individual, which has been violated and forms the basis for the application in an inter-state dispute. Thus, the analogy of the direct injury in the customary international law relating to the incidence of the rule is not viable.

Nor can an argument be based on the Granada resolution of the Institut de Droit International of 1956 which makes the rule inapplicable where persons who are under *special international protection* are injured. The exceptional cases to which this resolution refers involve injuries to such persons as heads of state and diplomats, which are direct injuries to the state. The characterization of these injuries as direct injuries is based on the notion that the state's interest involved is not purely that of protecting a national or individual but entails the furtherance of other objectives such as maintaining its own functions or dignity, which predominate in the situation.

While the rule of local remedies is applicable to the protection of human rights in inter-state disputes according to the general principles of international law, the exclusion based on the direct injury could conceivably become relevant in *certain* circumstances.[7] Thus, where a state wished to bring before the EComHR a case in which one of its diplomats had been maltreated in violation of the European Convention, it should not have been necessary for the diplomat first to exhaust domestic remedies, because the injury was in substance an interference with the carrying on of functions of state and not merely an interference with the state's right to protect its nationals. It would seem to be irrelevant that the state is making use of procedural protection given by the Convention to protect its own interests, or that its right of redress will be limited by the terms of the Convention on redress and it will, therefore, only be able to claim under the Convention a remedy for the violation of human rights. There is no reason why the principles applicable should be other than those relevant to general international law, although, of course, the fact that a state takes up a violation of the Convention on behalf of an individual does not *per se* convert the injury into a direct injury. In all cases, it would be required to establish that there was in fact a direct injury capable of being so characterized under the general principles of customary law applicable to diplomatic protection. By the very nature of the system under the Convention, however, the instances of direct injury that can arise are likely to be rare.

A different situation which may arise under a conventional system for the protection of human rights, such as that which exists under the European Convention, is where the injured diplomat, for instance, in the circumstances outlined above tries to secure a remedy for himself by bringing an individual petition under the Convention. The question then is whether the rule of local remedies applies to his claim. The claim brought by the state in customary international law is in theory based on the violation of a right belonging to the state. In the case of proceedings instituted, for instance, by a state under the Convention, the state also claims for a violation of its own rights. How can it be otherwise? Where the diplomat institutes proceedings, however, he is not asserting the rights of his appointing state under the Convention. He is only asserting his own rights, although granted to him by an agreement between states. Besides, the injury would be a direct injury only *vis-à-vis* the state that has appointed the diplomat, because only the

---

[7] The view that there may be a direct injury is not inconsistent with the theory that human rights instruments are concerned with *rights* of individuals. The latter truth does not gainsay the eventuality that the rights of states may also be directly violated, as pointed out above: *contra* Cançado Trindade, 'Book Review', 86 AJIL (1992) at p. 627.

state has the right relating to the carrying on of state functions. Thus, it would seem that the diplomat would not be able to rely on the direct injury to the state which has appointed him.[8]

Jurisdictional connection

In the area of human rights protection the problems arising from issues related to jurisdictional connection do not appear to be so acute as in regard to diplomatic protection, partly for the reason that the conventional instruments are limited in their area of application. Under the old European Convention on Human Rights, for example, Article 1 stated that the parties 'shall secure to every one within their jurisdiction the rights and freedoms defined in Section I of this Convention' (Article 1 of the revised Convention is identical). The Convention, therefore, applies only in respect of persons within a state's jurisdiction. The ICCPR imposes in Article 2(1) an obligation to respect and ensure human rights in regard to persons within the territory and subject to the jurisdiction of the state. It is clear that in these Conventions and others like them a state is at the most under an obligation to respect human rights only in respect of persons within its jurisdiction. In the case of the ICCPR, the area of application is limited further to the territory of the state concerned. Thus, where state A prevents X, a national of state B who is in its territory, from having access to his family who are nationals of state B and are in state B, under both the ECHR and the ICCPR state A violates the family rights of X but not those of X's family, because the family is not within the jurisdiction of state A. In the case of the ICCPR there would be an added reason that X's family is outside the territory of state A.

---

[8] However, such an applicant may claim that the rule of domestic remedies does not apply because he can claim diplomatic immunity from the jurisdiction of the respondent state. This claim would only be maintainable if the appointing state has not waived the immunity. Thus, in a situation where a direct injury has been committed, an individual may under the conventional situation be indirectly exempted from resort to domestic remedies. It should be noted that the question of the direct injury has not been raised before the IACHR. As far as inter-state disputes under Article 45 of the American Convention on Human Rights are concerned, Article 46(a) specifically makes the rule of local remedies applicable to them. For the rest, the same principles would be applicable as apply under the European Convention on Human Rights. The discussion above of the direct injury shows that the concept results, when applicable, in the exclusion of the incidence of the rule. This helps the state's case which involves an individual to come before the international instance without the exhaustion of domestic remedies. Why should its application, where appropriate, not be considered, then, in the case of human rights protection?

Problems arise in connection with the rule of domestic remedies, under the European Convention in particular, where jurisdiction and territory are not co-extensive. Thus, where Y, a national of state C, who is in state D, is arbitrarily deprived of his liberty by officers of state C acting officially in state D, state C has interfered with the rights of Y. Because Y is a national of state C, it may be contended that he is within state C's jurisdiction and that state C has violated the Convention. In such a case the question that arises is whether Y must exhaust local remedies in state C before he can bring his case before an international instance. From a more general point of view the issue is whether the incidence of the rule of local remedies is co-extensive with any violation of the relevant convention.

The principles discussed in relation to diplomatic protection will be applicable to the protection of human rights, where the rule of local remedies is made applicable by reference to the general principles of international law. Thus, the argument may legitimately be made that it would at least be necessary for the violation of the convention concerned to take place on the territory of the respondent state for the rule of domestic remedies to become applicable. Where state A commits a wrong against Y on the territory of state B, or anywhere outside its territory, the rule would not be applicable to that wrong, even though the injury may be actionable under the convention. This is an important point, especially since jurisdictional connection in this sense may not be the same as 'jurisdiction' for the purpose of determining whether the relevant convention has been violated so as to make it possible to invoke its machinery. Thus, under the European Convention, while it would be possible for proceedings to be instituted against state A, where state A commits a wrong in respect of X, one of its nationals, in state B, because state A has jurisdiction over X, it should not be necessary for X to exhaust local remedies anywhere, because there is no jurisdictional connection between state A and the wrong for the purposes of the incidence of the rule. Again, even if the violation of the relevant convention takes place on the territory of state A, and if the victim had come to be there as a result of a seizure made in violation of international law by state A, there should be no need for the exhaustion of local remedies, although state A may have sufficient jurisdiction over the victim for proceedings to be instituted.

The analogy drawn from customary international law in regard to the incidence of the rule of local remedies where there is no adequate jurisdictional connection is relevant, because it may be reasonable in terms of policy to apply it. On the other hand, the applicability of the relevant principles depends on the interpretation of the particular convention in issue. It has also been observed that the reference to the generally recognized principles of international law has been interpreted under the European Convention to be confined to the material content of the rule. This does not mean, however, that principles not related to the material content of the rule cannot be applied under the relevant convention, if it is warranted by policy. In the case of the principles relating to jurisdictional connection, it may be desirable, for practical and other reasons connected with the nature of the rule, to apply them to human rights protection, when and if they become relevant. It may be noted that the result of the above view is to restrict the application of the rule. It operates in favour of the individual, not against him.[9]

Scope of the rule

In *Nielsen* v. *Denmark*, the EcomHR said that

the rules governing the exhaustion of domestic remedies, as these are generally recognized today, in principle require that recourse should be had to all legal remedies available under the local law which are in principle capable of providing an effective and sufficient means of redressing the wrongs for which, on the international plane, the respondent State is alleged to be responsible.[10]

This statement emphasized the requirements that all remedies must be tested, provided they are available, they are sufficient and effective, and a normal use of such remedies is made. These requirements are in principle the same as in the law of diplomatic protection.

Availability and accessibility

There has in fact been no serious doubt about the requirement of availability or accessibility. In *Englert*,[11] for instance, the ECtHR held that no appeal was required because none was available. In *Schmidt*, the IAComHR held that, since the Supreme Court of the respondent state

---

[9] The view expressed by Cançado Trindade that the analogy is not applicable not only shows a misunderstanding of the implications of applying the analogy but does not make any sense. Cançado Trindade, note 7 above, at p. 627.

[10] Application 343/57, *Report of the Commission* (1961) at p. 37. See also *X* v. *Ireland*, Application 493/59, 7 *Collections* at pp. 94 and 96; *Syndicat National de la Police Belge* v. *Belgium*, Application 4464/70, 39 *Collections* at p. 32.

[11] Case No. 9/1986/107/155 (1987), Judgment. In *Farrell* v. *UK*, Application 9013/80, 25 YBECHR (1982) p. 124, the requirement of availability was stressed by the EComHR.

had pronounced on the issue, the remedy of *amparo* was not available and need not have been tested. Thus, availability entailed not only that the remedy be accessible to the particular individual affected, if such remedy existed, but also that that remedy be available as a possible remedy in the specific context of the individual's case.[12]

Ordinary and extraordinary remedies

There is evidence that the EComHR was aware of the issue of the nature of the remedy that needs to be exhausted, although its general approach has been rather to determine whether the remedy was effective as a criterion of whether it should be exhausted.[13] In regard to extraordinary remedies, the Commission has taken the view that the extraordinary nature of the remedy does not affect the requirement of exhaustion, because the answer to the question of whether the remedy should have been exhausted depended entirely on whether the remedy was adequate and effective.[14] There are several cases decided from very early on in which the Commission took the view that the remedy was exhaustible, although it was an extraordinary one. Thus, the right to petition the Special Court of Revision in Denmark for the reopening of proceedings and for an order for a new trial, although an extraordinary remedy, was held to be a legal remedy to which resort should have been had.[15] It is not clear what is meant by 'legal nature', but it would seem that this concept is compatible with the concept of 'judicial nature' current in customary international law. The remedies

---

[12] 6 HRLJ (1985) at p. 214. See also *Roach and Pinkerton*, IACHR, 8 HRLJ (1987) p. 345. The HRC has held that a particular remedy or extraordinary remedies were not available in the case before it, because they were not applicable in the circumstances of the case: see Communication No. 8/1977, HRC *Selected Decisions* at p. 48; Communication No. 28/1978, *ibid.*, pp. 58 and 59; Communication No. 44/1979, *ibid.*, pp. 77 and 79; Communication No. 70/1980, *ibid.*, p. 131; and Communication No. 73/1980, *ibid.*, p. 134. In Communication No. 70/1980, the HRC held that the fact that the officially appointed defence counsel had not invoked the extraordinary remedies in question indicated that they were not available. In *C.F. et al.*, Communication 118/1981, para. 10.1, the HRC stated in effect that 'remedies the availability of which is not reasonably evident' are not available, but found in the case that this was not the situation.

[13] See Danielus, 'Conditions of Admissibility in the Jurisprudence of the European Commission of Human Rights', 2 HRJ (1969) at p. 292.

[14] See *Nielsen* v. *Denmark*, Application 343/57, *Report of the Commission* at pp. 36–7. The HRC has implicitly taken a similar view. In Communication No. 44/1979, HRC *Selected Decisions* at p. 79, an exceptional remedy was held not to be exhaustible not because it was exceptional but because it would not have been effective.

[15] *Nielsen* v. *Denmark*, Application 343/57, *Report of the Commission*.

may include, for example, reference to a special constitutional court,[16] or to administrative courts of different kinds, such as administrative courts of first instance,[17] superior administrative courts,[18] administrative courts of appeal,[19] a federal administrative court[20] or an administrative Detention Commission.[21] They may include a disciplinary action of a special nature against the officer concerned before a person or committee with judicial powers,[22] an appeal to the Attorney-General acting in a quasi-judicial capacity,[23] an application for the transfer of a case to another court on the ground of prejudice which would have resulted in a rehearing,[24] or an appeal which would have resulted in the rehearing of the case.[25] In these cases, the remedies available were held to be determinable according to law and not to rest on pure discretion exercised in a non-judicial manner. It may also be necessary to seek alternative judicial remedies successively. Thus, where in a federal state there is a federal Constitutional Court and a state Constitutional Court, both of which have jurisdiction over the same matter, it will be necessary to litigate in both courts.[26]

There were some cases in which the EComHR held that an extraordinary remedy was not subject to exhaustion; but this was not on the ground that it was an extraordinary remedy, but rather because the remedy was not adequate and effective. Thus, in *Brückmann* v. *Federal Republic of Germany*,[27] it was held that a petition filed with the Court of Appeal after a decision of the German Federal Constitutional Court, in order

---

[16] X v. *Federal Republic of Germany*, Application 27/55, 1 YBECHR p. 138; X v. *Federal Republic of Germany*, Application 254/57, 1 YBECHR p. 150; X v. *Federal Republic of Germany*, Application 605/59, 3 YBECHR p. 296; A et al. v. *Federal Republic of Germany*, Application 899/60, 5 YBECHR p. 136.

[17] X v. *Federal Republic of Germany*, Application 1197/61, 5 YBECHR p. 92.

[18] X v. *Federal Republic of Germany*, Application 289/57, 1 YBECHR p. 148.

[19] X v. *Federal Republic of Germany*, Application 254/57, 1 YBECHR p. 150.

[20] X v. *Federal Republic of Germany*, Application 232/56, 1 YBECHR p. 143.

[21] X v. *Federal Republic of Germany*, Application 423/59, 4 YBECHR p. 302.

[22] X v. *Federal Republic of Germany*, Application 297/57, 2 YBECHR p. 204.

[23] X v. *Federal Republic of Germany*, Application 254/57, 1 YBECHR p. 150. The HRC has also referred to such administrative remedies of a quasi-judicial nature as exhaustible: see Communication No. 79/1980, HRC *Selected Decisions* at p. 32.

[24] *Boeckmans* v. *Belgium*, Application 1727/62, 5 YBECHR p. 370.

[25] X v. *Sweden*, Application 434/58, 2 YBECHR p. 334. Other cases in which extraordinary remedies were not distinguished for the purpose of the rule of local remedies are e.g. X v. *Ireland*, Application 493/59, 7 *Collections* p. 96; X v. *Sweden*, Application 3788/68, 35 *Collections* p. 72.

[26] Application 302/57 (not published), cited by Vasak, note 6 above, at p. 120.

[27] Application 6242/73, 46 *Collections* p. 207.

to re-open proceedings in the case, was not an effective and adequate remedy and, therefore, did not have to be exhausted.[28]

However, it is not necessary to resort to a merely discretionary extraordinary remedy of a non-judicial nature, such as one whose object is to obtain a favour and not to vindicate a right. In the *De Becker Case*, it was concluded that an action for reinstatement under a statute, which should have enabled the complainant to resume his profession, if it had succeeded, was not a remedy to which he should have had recourse, because 'its purpose is to obtain a favour and not to vindicate a right'.[29] Similarly, resort need not be had to other administrative remedies of a discretionary and non-judicial nature. Application for release by giving a promise which was not provided for by law that the applicant would respect the laws and constitution, was held to be merely a discretionary remedy.[30]

It may also be noted that special remedies provided by constitutional courts in such countries as the Federal Republic of Germany and Austria are also subject to exhaustion, although they are not ordinary remedies. The EComHR consistently affirmed this. In *X and Y* v. *Austria*, for example, the Commission found that, while the applicant had exhausted remedies available in the ordinary courts by appealing to the Supreme Court, 'this does not absolve him from pursuing the remedy available for an alleged breach of his human and constitutional rights by means of a direct appeal to the Constitutional Court within the time prescribed'.[31]

---

[28] See also *X* v. *Federal Republic of Germany*, Application No. 918/60, 7 *Collections* p. 110; *X* v. *Sweden*, Application 1739/62, 13 *Collections* p. 102; *X* v. *Denmark*, Application 4311/69, 37 *Collections* p. 96; *X* v. *Federal Republic of Germany*, Application 6049/73, 1 D&R p. 56. See also comments by Wiebringhaus, 'La Règle de l'épuisement préalable des voies de recours internes dans la jurisprudence de la Commission européenne des droits de l'homme', 5 AFDI (1959) at p. 695.

[29] Application 214/56, 2 YBECHR at p. 238.

[30] *Lawless* v. *Ireland*, Application 332/57, 2 YBECHR p. 326. Other decisions where the remedy has been regarded as discretionary include *Greece* v. *UK*, Application 299/57, 2 YBECHR p. 192 (petition to the Queen which was a measure of grace); *X* v. *Belgium*, Application 458/59, 3 YBECHR p. 234 (appeal for pardon). See also, *Ellis*, Communication No. 276/1988 (HRC), which agrees with this approach of the EComHR.

[31] Application 2854/66, 26 *Collections* at p. 54. See also e.g. *X* v. *Austria*, Application 1135/61, 11 *Collections* p. 22; *X* v. *Austria*, Application 2370/64, 22 *Collections* p. 101; *X* v. *Austria*, Application 4511/70, 38 *Collections* p. 85. There were several cases against the Federal Republic of Germany in which a similar conclusion was reached: see e.g. *X* v. *Federal Republic of Germany*, Application 1086/61, 9 *Collections* p. 16; *X* v. *Federal Republic of Germany*, Application 2201/64, 16 *Collections* p. 75; *Soltikow* v. *Federal Republic of Germany*, Application 2257/64, 27 *Collections* p. 24; *X* v. *Federal Republic of Germany*, Application 4046/69, 35 *Collections* p. 115; *X* v. *Federal Republic of Germany*, Application 4445/70, 37

However, the need to exhaust constitutional appeals may not exist, if that recourse does not afford an effective remedy for the particular complaint.[32] Thus, constitutional appeals are *per se* within the concept of remedies to be exhausted, although in given circumstances they may not be subject to exhaustion for other reasons.[33]

Effectiveness and adequacy

The EComHR dealt with the issue of effectiveness and adequacy on more than one occasion. Thus, on the issue of adequacy (*suffisance*) the Commission held that, where the applicant was seeking compensation and damages for unlawful imprisonment after his release, the right of recourse to an Internment Commission, which did not have the power to grant compensation and damages but could only recommend release, was not an adequate remedy with respect to the applicant's claim for damages and compensation. Thus, it did not have to be invoked for the purposes of the rule of domestic remedies.[34] By the same token, the Commission held that, where the remedy could satisfy the object of

---

Collections p. 121; *X* v. *Federal Republic of Germany*, Application 5172/71, 44 *Collections* p. 125. On constitutional appeals, see Verdussen, 'La Cour européenne des droits de l'homme et l'epuisement préalable de recours au juge constitutionnel', in *Liber Amicorum Marc-André Eissen* (1995) p. 435.

[32] See e.g. *Ringeisen* v. *Austria*, Application 2614/65, 27 *Collections* at pp. 53–4.

[33] In another unreported case against the US before the IAComHR, not covered by the American Convention, the Commission had before it the issue of exhaustion of multiple remedies, including administrative remedies. The issue of whether the resort to some such remedies could be excepted under the rule of domestic remedies (because exhaustion became unduly onerous) was not settled by the Commission, because the case was closed before it could be decided: see Cerna, 'The Inter-American Commission on Human Rights', in Harris and Livingstone (eds.), *The Inter-American System of Human Rights* (1998) at pp. 88–9. The question of whether an exception lies where exhaustion becomes unduly onerous was left open. There is also the question of whether, where alternative remedies are available, opting for one results in exhaustion of remedies: see McGoldrick, note 2 above, at p. 194. It is likely that the correct approach is to hold that in principle it would. The HRC's approach is to be more cautious about 'non-judicial' remedies, i.e. those that are administrative or extraordinary in that they are not court remedies. However, while emphasizing the need to exhaust 'judicial' remedies, it has recognized that other remedies, excluding those which are purely discretionary, such as a petition for mercy, which was in issue in *Ellis*, Communication No. 276/1988, may, in appropriate circumstances, need to be exhausted: see *Patino*, Communication No. 437/1990; *Vicente*, Communication No. 612/1995; and *Muhonen*, Communication No. 89/1981.

[34] *Lawless* v. *Ireland*, Application 332/57, 2 YBECHR (1958–9) p. 318. See also *X* v. *Sweden*, Application 1739/62, 13 *Collections* p. 102; and *X* v. *Austria*, Application 3972/69, 37 *Collections* at p. 19. See also *Van der Sluijs, Zuiderveld and Klappe* v. *The Netherlands*, Applications 9362/81, 9363/81 and 9387/81, 25 YBECHR p. 212. On the adequacy and effectiveness of remedies, see also the *De Jong and Baljet Case*, Applications 8805/79 and

the applicant's claim, it should have been invoked and exhausted. In *X* v. *Federal Republic of Germany*, the applicant's complaint was against the Public Prosecutor for having violated his right of defence. Because this complaint could have been satisfied by recourse to a disciplinary action to which the applicant had not resorted, the Commission held that domestic remedies had not been exhausted.[35]

The notion of effectiveness (*efficacité*) attracted the attention of the Commission more obviously and, as has been observed,[36] is one of the salient concerns of the Commission with respect to the rule of domestic redress. This feature of the rule is closely connected with that of adequacy for the object sought but is totally distinct from the concept of manifest lack of foundation.[37] As a rule, the Commission took the view that, if a remedy is likely to be effective, resort must be had to it. Thus, where no appeal in a formal sense was open to the applicant, but where there was a possibility that counsel could request his release from his obligations as a legal aid counsel, the Commission found that there was a remedy which theoretically might have provided an effective means of redressing the alleged wrong.[38] In *X* v. *Ireland*, the Commission held that an application to the Detention Commission of the respondent state was a legal remedy which would have secured the applicant's early release from the alleged illegal detention and, therefore, resort should have been had to it.[39] Conversely, where a decision of the Secretary of State of the UK was undeniably unquestionable before the courts by

8806/79, 24 D&R (1981) at p. 150; *Z* v. *The Netherlands*, Application 10400/83, 38 D&R (1984) at p. 150; *M* v. *France*, Application 10078/82, 41 D&R (1985) at p. 119; *Moution* v. *France*, Application 1192/84, 52 D&R (1987) at p. 235; the *Civet Case*, Judgment of 28 September 1999, 42 YBECHR (1999) p. 166; and the *Selmouni Case*, Judgment of 28 July 1999, *ibid*.

[35] Application 297/57, 2 YBECHR at p. 214. See also *X* v. *Sweden*, Application 3788/68, 35 *Collections* p. 72.

[36] See Nay-Cadoux, *Les Conditions de recevabilité des requêtes individuelles devant la Commission européenne des droits de l'homme* (1969) pp. 97ff. The HRC has referred to an 'effective' remedy as one which 'offers reasonable prospect of success': see e.g. *Patino*, Communication No. 437/1990, para. 5.2. It has also affirmed its established jurisprudence that effective remedies must be exhausted: see *Ominayak et al.*, Communication No. 167/1984, para. 13.2.

[37] See, e.g. *X and Y* v. *Belgium*, Application 1661/62, 10 *Collections* at p. 19, Danielus, note 13 above, at p. 293; and Cançado Trindade, *The Application of the Rule of Exhaustion of Local Remedies in International Law* (1983), p. 73.

[38] *Gussenbauer* v. *Austria*, Application 4897/71, 42 *Collections* at p. 47.

[39] Application 493/59, 7 *Collections* at p. 95. See also *X* v. *Ireland*, Application 4125/69, 37 *Collections* p. 50; *X* v. *UK*, Application 5006/71, 39 *Collections* p. 93; *Kamma* v. *The Netherlands*, Application 4771/71, 42 *Collections* p. 20; and *Svenska Lotsförbundet* v. *Sweden*, Application 4475/70, 42 *Collections* p. 13. See also on the proof of effectiveness the

way of *certiorari*, resort to the courts would not have been effective and was unnecessary,[40] or, where raising the issue of constitutionality would clearly not have provided an effective remedy in a criminal case, the issue did not have to be raised by the applicant in order to exhaust local remedies.[41]

There can be no question that there is general agreement in respect of human rights protection (as in the field of diplomatic protection) that local or domestic remedies must be exhausted when they are adequate for the object sought or are effective. The precedents also show that there seems to be no serious dispute on the interpretation of these concepts, at least in a positive sense. The problems really arise when an exception is sought to the application of the rule on the ground that a remedy is ineffective. Inefficacy will be discussed later in this chapter.

Normal use

'Normal use' has also been referred to in the caselaw of the EComHR on the local remedies rule. In *Austria* v. *Italy*, the Commission said that the rule required 'the normal use of remedies likely to be effective and adequate'.[42] In *Ringeisen* v. *Austria*, the Commission stated that 'if remedies which seem effective and sufficient are open to an individual within

---

Farrell Case, Application 9013/80, 30 D&R (1983) at p. 83; and the *De Jong and Baljet Case*, Applications 8805/79 and 8806/79, 24 D&R (1981) at p. 150. On effectiveness in general, see e.g. *Remli* v. *France*, Application 16839/90, 77-A D&R (1994) at p. 29; the *Cardot Case*, Judgment of 19 March 1991, 34 YBECHR (1991) at p. 195ff.; and the *Guzzardi Case*, Judgment of 6 November 1980, A.39 (1981) at pp. 21ff.

[40] *Kaplan* v. *UK*, Application 7598/76, *Report of the Commission* (1976).

[41] *Ventura* v. *Italy*, Application 7438/76, *Report of the Commission* (1982). The Commission followed its jurisprudence in *Lithgow and Others* v. *UK*, Applications 9006/80, 9262/81, 9263/81, 9265/81, 9266/81, 9313/81 and 9405/81, *Report of the Commission* (1984), in finding that remedies that were not effective and sufficient need not be pursued. This case is discussed in Mendelson, 'The United Kingdom Nationalization Cases and the European Convention on Human Rights', 57 BYIL (1986) p. 33. The case went up to the European Court of Human Rights but the issue of local remedies was not raised there: see *Lithgow and Others* v. *UK*, ECHR Series A, No. 102 (1986). The European Court of Human Rights has held that only remedies that are effective and sufficient need be exhausted: see *Airey* v. *Ireland*, ECHR Series A, No. 32 at p. 11 (1979); and *Van Oostewijck* v. *Belgium*, ECHR Series A, No. 40 at pp. 13–14 (1980). The HRC also has held that complaints were inadmissible before it, because remedies that were effective, such as applications for *habeas corpus*, appeals to the Supreme Court, to Crown Prosecutors, higher police authorities and the Attorney General, had not been canvassed: see Communication No. 27/1978, HRC *Selected Decisions* at p. 14; Communication No. 2/1976, *ibid.*, p. 22; and Communication No. 79/1980, *ibid.*, p. 32. In the *Velasquez Rodriguez Case* (Judgment), Decision No. 4, IACHR Series C, para. 55 (1988), the IACHR stressed the need for an adequate remedy, defined as one 'suitable to address an infringement of a legal right'.

[42] Application 788/60, *Report of the Plenary Commission* at p. 57.

the legal system of the respondent State, he must use and exhaust such remedies in the normal way'.[43] But for the Commission the normal use of remedies has meant no more than that 'time limits laid down in domestic law for the introduction of appeals must be observed by applicants',[44] or that the applicant must exercise remedies in a manner that was valid, taking into account his capacity.[45] There does not seem to be any indication in the jurisprudence of the Commission that the concept of 'normal use' is a means of introducing 'flexibility' into the application of the rule of local remedies by reference merely to reasonableness or equity.[46] The jurisprudence of the Commission, in particular, supports the interpretation that 'normal use' merely and generally refers to the obligations of the alien or individual to fulfil the requirements of local law with respect to such matters as time limits and capacity.

Raising of substantive issues

The EComHR applied the principles stated or implied in the *Finnish Ships Arbitration* relating to the raising of substantive issues which were discussed in Chapter 7. An application was declared inadmissible for failure to exhaust domestic remedies because the complaint raised before the Commission, namely, that the proceedings before a *Landgericht* (regional court) in the Federal Republic of Germany had been conducted in such a

---

[43] Application 2614/65, 27 *Collections* at p. 53. See also *Simon-Herold* v. *Austria*, Application 4340/69, 38 *Collections* at p. 33. Some other decisions to the same effect are referred to in the latter case.

[44] See *X* v. *Federal Republic of Germany*, Application 352/58, 2 YBECHR at p. 344; *X* v. *Federal Republic of Germany*, Application 945/60, 8 *Collections* at p. 105; *Inhabitants of Alsemberg and of Beersel* v. *Belgium*, 12 *Collections* at pp. 27–8; *X* v. *Norway*, Application 2002/63, 14 *Collections* at pp. 27–8; *X* v. *Federal Republic of Germany*, Application 2366/64, 22 *Collections* at p. 122; *X and Y* v. *Austria*, Application 2854/66, 26 *Collections* at p. 53; and *X and Y* v. *Federal Republic of Germany*, Application 3897/68, 35 *Collections* at p. 80. The HRC also has stressed the need to observe time limits and has declared complaints inadmissible for failure to do so: Communication No. 27/1978, HRC *Selected Decisions* at p. 14; and Communication No. 26/1978, *ibid.*, p. 19.

[45] See *X* v. *Federal Republic of Germany*, Application 225/56, 1 YBECHR at pp. 145–6.

[46] See the comments by Monconduit, *La Commission européenne des droits de l'homme* (1965) at p. 315. However, the view has been expressed that the test of reasonableness or 'normal use' should be introduced to modify the application of the rule of local remedies: see Directorate of Human Rights, CE Doc. H (64) 1 (1964) at p. 20; and Vasak, note 6 above, at p. 130. Normal use clearly requires that the procedural requirements of the domestic law be fulfilled: see e.g. *A.P.A.*, Communication No. 433/1990. The CERD agrees with this view: see e.g. *C.P. and M.P.*, CERD 5/1994; and *Barbaro*, CERD 7/1995. However, there are circumstances, such as the failure of a state-appointed lawyer to advise of a remedy in time so that time limits could be met, which the HRC has held may exempt a petitioner from this requirement: see e.g. *Griffin*, Communication No. 493/1992; and *Mpandanjila*, Communication No. 138/1983.

manner as to violate certain provisions of the European Convention on Human Rights, had not been raised on appeal before the *Bundesgerichtshof* (federal court).[47] There are many cases in which the Commission took the same stand and declared the application inadmissible for failure to exhaust domestic remedies.[48] On the other hand, the Commission made it clear in *X v. Austria* that the requirement is that the matter be raised in substance before the relevant local courts:

> the mere fact that the applicant has, in pursuance of Article 26, submitted his case to the various competent courts does not constitute compliance with this rule: . . . it is also required that any complaint made before the Commission and relating to lower courts or authorities should have been substantially raised before the competent higher court or authority.[49]

The Commission applied the principle in *Ringeisen* v. *Austria* and found that the applicant had, indeed, exhausted local remedies, where he had raised in substance before the constitutional court the issue underlying a complaint made to the Commission, although that court refused on formal legal grounds to deal with the question.[50] Thus, as a result of the application of the law by the Commission, the point has been clarified that the requirement relating to the raising of substantive pleas is not essentially one of form. What is required is that the matter be substantially raised before the relevant domestic courts.

The position taken in the *Finnish Ships Arbitration* is still reflective of the law both as regards the need to raise in local proceedings those matters raised in the international proceedings, and in respect of the converse principle that the applicant need only raise in the local proceedings those matters which he raises before the international forum. That position has been clarified by the jurisprudence of the Commission, in so far as it has been made clear that matters raised before the international forum must only be raised in substance and not necessarily in corresponding form before the domestic instances. Moreover, in *Austria* v. *Italy*, the Commission held that:

---

[47] *X* v. *Federal Republic of Germany*, Application 627/59, 8 *Collections* at pp. 23–4.

[48] To mention only a few, see *X* v. *Federal Republic of Germany*, Application 263/57, 1 YBECHR p. 146; *X* v. *Belgium*, Application 1103/61, 8 *Collections* p. 124; *X* v. *Austria*, Application 3001/66, 26 *Collections* p. 59; *Samer* v. *Federal Republic of Germany*, Application 4319/60, 39 *Collections* p. 18; *Kamma* v. *The Netherlands*, Application 4771/71, 42 *Collections* p. 19; and *X* v. *Austria*, Application 5560/72, 45 *Collections* p. 64.

[49] Application 3001/66, 26 *Collections* p. 64.

[50] Application 2614/65, 27 *Collections* at p. 55. On the recent practice, see Van Dijk and Van Hoof, *Theory and Practice of the European Convention on Human Rights* (1998) pp. 142ff.

the question of presumed innocence raised by the Austrian Government in paragraph I(2) of their written conclusions was submitted in substance to the Court of Cassation of Italy . . . if they had expressly invoked Article 27(2) of the Italian Constitution and Article 6, paragraph (2) of the European Convention, the young men of Fundres/Pfunders would therefore not have submitted any supplementary argument but would simply have put forward one more argument which in practice coincides, by its intention, with those which they effectively promoted.[51]

The argument raised in the Italian court was based on a section which stated that criminal responsibility was personal. The argument raised in international proceedings related to the presumption of innocence. The Commission thought that the former in substance covered the latter. In so far as the former argument contained the notion that the accused had to be proved personally guilty, it substantially covered the presumption of innocence. The Commission apparently derived the principle involved from the broader principle that:

only the non-utilisation of an 'essential' recourse for establishing the merits of a case before the municipal tribunals leads to non-admissibility of the international complaint.[52]

The issue has been raised before the Commission of whether the applicant can rely on the duty of a local court to examine an issue *ex officio* in order to avoid the necessity of raising a particular issue before that court. Although in *Delcourt* v. *Belgium* the Commission was reluctant to deal with the question,[53] in the same case, which came up before it later, and in other cases decided both before and after the case, it has held that the failure of the applicant to raise an issue before a local court which must deal with the question *ex officio*, nevertheless results in the non-exhaustion of local remedies.[54]

---

[51] Application 788/60, 4 YBECHR at p. 176.   [52] *Ibid.*, at p. 172.
[53] Application 2689/65, 22 Collections at p. 84.
[54] See, e.g. *X* v. *Belgium*, Application 2322/64, 24 *Collections* at p. 42; *Delcourt* v. *Belgium*, Application 2689/65, 24 *Collections* at p. 84; and *X* v. *Norway*, Application 2002/63, 14 Collections at p. 270. The HRC has also dealt with the issue of raising substantive issues before domestic courts. In keeping with general principle it has held that it is the *substance* of the petitioner's complaint that must be raised before the domestic fora, the specific form being irrelevant, just as much as references to the specific conventional provisions violated are not required: see e.g. *Grant*, Communication No. 353/1988; *Perera*, Communication No. 541/1993; and *B.D.B.*, Communication No. 273/1989. It is not required that the petitioner ensure that the issues are considered by such fora: see e.g. *Little*, Communication No. 283/1988.

Need for a final decision

The EComHR has had to deal with the issue of the final decision on more than one occasion, both in order to determine whether the rule of domestic remedies had been observed and for other purposes. It has not been disputed by the Commission that an applicant must have recourse to all competent domestic courts and obtain a final decision from the highest court before the Commission may pronounce on his case. In *Ringeisen* v. *Austria*, the ECtHR implicitly endorsed this view, when it held that, while a final decision was necessary before an international forum such as the Commission could pronounce on the dispute, in the case of the Commission it was sufficient if that decision was given before the Commission was called upon to pronounce on the question of admissibility of the application, even though the final decision may not have been delivered before the application had been filed with the Commission.[55] Needless to say, domestic remedies must have been exhausted before the ECtHR may assume jurisdiction.

The Commission has held that proceedings must be completed, in the sense that they must neither be still pending nor have been discontinued, and that appeals must have been carried to the highest court. Where an appeal in a court was still pending,[56] where proceedings had been previously discontinued because of the applicant's health and at his request,[57] and where the applicant had lost his case in the court of first instance and an appeal could have been taken which would have led to the rehearing of the case,[58] it was held in each case that local remedies had not been exhausted. Where an appeal had been withdrawn and a plea of nullity had been raised with the result that the decision of the court had become *res judicata*, it was held that, because the original appeal had not proceeded, local remedies had not been exhausted.[59] However, where a final decision has been given by the highest court and no further recourse is available, local remedies will be regarded as having been exhausted, as was held by the IACHR. In *Schmidt*, the IACHR held that, once the Costa Rican Supreme Court had disposed of the applicant's case which involved his detention, no remedy was

[55] ECHR Series A No. 13 at p. 38 (1971).
[56] *X* v. *Federal Republic of Germany*, Application 115/55, 1 YBECHR at p. 137.
[57] *X* v. *Federal Republic of Germany*, Application 722/60, 5 YBECHR at p. 104.
[58] *X* v. *Sweden*, Application 434/58, 2 YBECHR at p. 354.
[59] *X* v. *Austria*, Application 1234/61, 5 YBECHR at p. 96.

available by way of *habeas corpus*, with the result that remedies had been exhausted.[60]

It is in connection, however, with the application of the provision relating to the six-month time limit in Article 26 of the (old) ECHR that the EComHR really had to deal with the question of the final decision. That provision requires that the Commission deal with a dispute within a period of six months of the date on which the final decision was made. The final decision for this purpose has been held in *Nielsen v. Denmark* to be exclusively 'the final decision resulting from the exhaustion of all domestic remedies according to the generally recognized rules of international law'.[61] Thus, the Commission's view of the final decision for the purposes of the six-month rule will also be relevant to the definition of that concept for the exhaustion of local remedies proper. There are many occasions on which the Commission has identified the final decision as being the decision of the relevant court in a given national legal system,[62] but what is of importance for the purpose of determining whether domestic remedies have been exhausted is the distinction made between those situations in which recourse to a higher court is still available, with the result that exhaustion would take place only when that court has taken a decision, and those in which such recourse is obviously not available, so that exhaustion has already taken place. For the purpose of the six-month rule the fact that further recourse is available would result in time not having begun to run, while, if there is

---

[60] *Schmidt*, 6 HRLJ (1985) at p. 214. The HRC has pointed out that domestic remedies must be 'properly exhausted': *R.T. v. France*, Doc. A/44/40 at p. 277, paras. 5.3 and 7.4. In that case and also in *N.S. v. Canada, Selected Decisions* p. 19, and *S.H.B v. Canada*, Doc. A/42/40, p. 174, para. 7.2, the HRC found on the facts that, according to generally recognized rules of international law, domestic remedies had not been properly exhausted. On the other hand, in *J.R.T. v. Western Guard Party*, Doc. A/38/40, p. 231, the HRC found that because of the 'ambiguity ensuing from the conflicting time limits, the applicant had made a reasonable effort to exhaust remedies and they had been exhausted'. There are cases in which the HRC has addressed the issue of ongoing proceedings and decided that the facts showed that complete exhaustion had not taken place: see McGoldrick, note 2 above, at pp. 190–1.

[61] Application 343/57, *Report of the Commission* at p. 35.

[62] See e.g. *X v. Federal Republic of Germany*, Application 918/60, 7 *Collections* at p. 110; *X v. Federal Republic of Germany*, Application 968/61, 8 *Collections* at p. 28; *X v. Austria*, Application 1053/61, 8 *Collections* at pp. 7–8; *X v. Sweden*, Application 1739/62, 13 *Collections* at p. 102; *X v. UK*, Application 3505/68, 29 *Collections* at p. 63; *X v. Denmark*, Application 4311/69, 37 *Collections* at pp. 95–6; *X v. Austria*, Application 3972/69, 37 *Collections* at p. 20; *X v. Federal Republic of Germany*, Application 4438/70, 39 *Collections* at pp. 24–5; and *Svenska Lotsförbundet v. Sweden*, Application 4475/70, 42 *Collections* at p. 13.

no further recourse available, the final decision would have been taken and time would have begun to run from the time that decision had been taken, regardless of whether the applicant was making or had made further efforts to invoke other remedies.

The Commission has had to make its determinations on the basis of its estimate of the adequacy and effectiveness of recourse to a given court. Thus, in *X v. UK*,[63] the Commission upheld the view that the remedy by way of appeal to the High Court for a writ of *habeas corpus* would not have been an effective one where detention was consequent upon a conviction by a court of competent jurisdiction, while it was apparent that no leave to appeal to the House of Lords would have been given, because there was no issue of public interest, with the result that the decision of the Court of Appeal, to which the applicant had appealed his conviction, was the final decision. Thus, the time for the purposes of the old Article 26 had begun to run from the date of the latter decision.[64] In certain circumstances, it may be a difficult decision for an applicant to take as to whether a recourse to another higher court is effective or adequate, which recourse may put him at a disadvantage when time limits are an element to be considered.[65] From the point of view of the rule of exhaustion of domestic remedies *per se*, however, the requirement

---

[63] Application 3505/68, 29 *Collections* at pp. 62–3.

[64] There are other cases in which a similar conclusion has been reached: see e.g. *X v. Sweden*, Application 3893/68, 33 *Collections* at p. 10; *X v. Federal Republic of Germany*, Application 3979/69, 33 *Collections* at p. 13; *X v. Austria*, Application 3972/69, 37 *Collections* at p. 19; and *X v. Austria*, Application 5560/72, 42 *Collections* at p. 64.

[65] There are several problems that may arise, e.g. what should an applicant do when he has reached the highest court but there may be some extraordinary court available, the effectiveness of which is not clear, or when there is a continuing situation and the highest court has already been reached, or when the applicant has decided to reopen the case in the municipal courts in the hope of securing a remedy? The decision in *Ringeisen v. Austria*, ECHR Series A No. 13 at p. 38 (1971), where it was held that remedies must have been exhausted at the time when the Commission pronounces on admissibility, and not at the time the application has been filed, tends to mitigate some of the hardship that may be caused in so far as the applicant may, after the highest court has given an apparently final decision, file a case with the Commission while still pursuing remedies in the domestic courts, with the object of having a decision from the new source of recourse before the Commission pronounces on admissibility: see also, for discussion of these issues, Cançado Trindade, note 37 above, at pp. 101–5; and *X v. Belgium*, Application 4859/71, 44 *Collections* at pp. 6–7; *Nielsen v. Denmark*, Application 343/57, *Report of the Commission* at pp. 32–5; *X v. Sweden*, Application 1739/62, 13 *Collections* at p. 102; and *X v. Denmark*, Application 4311/69, 37 *Collections* at p. 95. It may not always be possible for an applicant to take advantage of the ruling in *Nielsen v. Denmark*, as much may depend on chance. On the other hand, it may not be desirable to use or extend that ruling so as to deprive the six-month rule of any real significance by trying to accommodate applicants who may like to

is clear that an individual needs and is required only to resort to the higher or last court from which he could have obtained an effective remedy.

Limitations on the rule

Unavailability or inaccessibility of remedies

As has been seen, the individual must exhaust only those remedies that are available. This implies that exhaustion is not required, if those remedies are not available – the converse of the requirement of availability relevant to the scope of the rule. Availability implies, among other things, accessibility. The general notion of accessibility or availability was explored earlier in connection with diplomatic protection. However, there are specific aspects of accessibility relevant to the limitations on the operation of the rule which have been discussed by human rights organs.

There may be remedies which, although available, are not in the circumstances applicable to the particular injury of which the individual complains. International human rights courts or organs have then tended to regard the remedy as not available. Apart from the cases discussed earlier in which the remedy was held not to be available in this sense, there are several cases which came before the HRC in which the remedy of *habeas corpus* was held not to be exhaustible because it was not available according to the law to persons arrested under prompt security measures in Uruguay.[66] Thus, it is not the theoretical existence of a remedy under the law of the respondent state which makes it exhaustible, but rather whether according to that law it is applicable to the claimant's case. By the same token, it would follow that it must be quite clear according to the law of the respondent state that the remedy in question is inapplicable to the claimant's case. On the other hand, in Communication No. 70/1980,[67] the HRC held that, where defence counsel who had been appointed by the respondent state advised that the extraordinary remedies of annulment and review were not available, this was sufficient to satisfy the limitation of unavailability.

---

gamble on resort to internal remedies: see for similar comments Jacobs, *The European Convention on Human Rights* (1975) p. 242.

[66] See Communication No. 8/1977, HRC *Selected Decisions* at p. 48; Communication No. 28/1978, HRC *Selected Decisions* at pp. 58–9; and Communication No. 44/1979, HRC *Selected Decisions* at pp. 77 and 79.

[67] HRC *Selected Decisions* at p. 131.

This approach to unavailability is interesting. It warrants the conclusion that counsel's advice is conclusive on the availability of a remedy, regardless perhaps of the factual situation, only where a person pursuing remedies has had to have such counsel appointed by the respondent state. It does not open the floodgates to the opinions as such of any counsel retained by a claimant. It is because the respondent state assumed the responsibility of appointing the applicant's counsel that it is bound by his opinion. In this situation, the doctrine of estoppel or the principle of good faith may more properly be invoked.

Apart from such action on the part of the respondent state as prevents the claimant or applicant from access to remedies, for example by refusing to allow him to have legal representation, there have been some cases brought before the HRC in which the respondent state has obstructed the course of justice and thus made remedies inaccessible. In Communication No. 29/1978,[68] the HRC held that, where the defence lawyers had either been imprisoned or disappeared, remedies were not accessible, evidently because the failure to exhaust remedies was attributable to the obstructive actions of the respondent state. There are also cases decided by the EComHR in which a similar conclusion was reached on the facts of each case.[69]

The HRC has explained that, where the alleged victim needed legal assistance and 'had no effective contact with lawyers' for advice or assistance, that was a relevant factor in determining whether remedies were available, although this was said in a case where the relevant remedy of *habeas corpus* was not available to the victim in any case.[70]

The HRC's approach to legal assistance suggests that its absence is a factor to be taken into consideration in deciding whether remedies were available. It depends clearly on the circumstances of the particular

---

[68] HRC *Selected Decisions* at pp. 11–12. See also Communication No. 63/1979, HRC *Selected Decisions* at p. 102; and *Bleir* v. *Uruguay*, *ibid.*, p. 109. It is still a moot point whether refusal of the opportunity to appear personally to present a case is a denial of access to remedies: see *X* v. *Sweden*, Application 434/58, 2 YBECHR (1958–9) at p. 354, where it was said that the matter should be given serious consideration.

[69] See e.g. *Greece* v. *UK*, Application 299/57, 2 YBECHR (1958–9) at pp. 194–6; and *Denmark, Norway, Sweden and the Netherlands* v. *Greece*, Applications 3321–3/67 and 3344/67, 26 *Collections* at pp. 107–8. See also *Donnelly and Others* v. *UK*, Applications 5577–83/72, 43 *Collections* at p. 147. For some decisions of the IAComHR where absence of access to remedies was held to release the complainant from exhausting remedies, see e.g. Resolution No. 19/87, Case 9429, *Ann. Rep. IAComHR* (1986–7) at pp. 126–7; and Resolution No. 1a/88, Case 9755, *Ann. Rep. IAComHR* (1987–8) at pp. 137–8.

[70] See Communication No 8/1977, HRC *Selected Decisions* at p. 48.

case whether its absence is such a factor. The HRC has concluded that remedies need not be exhausted in effect where abnormal or onerous conditions have been attached to their exhaustion.[71]

Under Article 46 of the American Convention, a consistent pattern of gross human rights violations may sometimes create a presumption against the state that domestic remedies did not exist or were ineffective.[72]

An exception to the application of the rule has also been made by the IACHR in certain circumstances of *indigence* of the individual affected. The ECtHR and the HRC had earlier taken a different view.[73] The ECtHR very early in its existence found that the failure of the applicant to contest a violation of his human rights resulted in an operative non-exhaustion of internal remedies, even though the failure was due to lack of means.[74] In the case in which the HRC was faced with the excuse that the failure to exhaust internal remedies in connection with the protection of his human rights was due to the applicant's lack of means, it found that internal remedies had not been exhausted, although it did not specifically discuss the issues of impecuniosity.[75] Thus, it impliedly agreed that the lack of means in the circumstances of the case, at any rate, was not a good reason for not exhausting internal remedies. In the case before the ECtHR, the applicant had failed to explore the possibility of legal aid. This certainly influenced the Commission in reaching its decision on the issue of exhaustion of internal remedies.

The IACHR was required by the IAComHR to render an advisory opinion on the relevance of indigence to the rule of exhaustion of internal remedies.[76] The questions put were as follows:

---

[71] See *Montero* v. *Uruguay*, Communication No. 106/81, Doc. A/38/40, p. 186, para. 6.1.

[72] See Vivanco and Bhansali, 'Procedural Shortcomings in the Defense of Human Rights', in Harris and Livingstone, note 33 above, at p. 431. Another circumstance causing inaccessibility which has been adverted to by the HRC is the 'fear' of victimization of the petitioner, presumably if it is legitimate: *Phillip*, Communication No. 594/1992, para. 6.4.

[73] The issue of indigence as an exception based on inaccessibility to the application of the rule of domestic remedies in, *inter alia*, human rights protection has been discussed in Amerasinghe, 'Indigence and Inaccessibility as Limitations on the Rule of Local Remedies', in *Hacia un Noevo Order Internacionel y Europeo, Estuchios en Homenaje al Profesor Don Manuel Díez de Velasco* (1993) p. 57.

[74] X v. *Federal Republic of Germany*, Application 181/56, 1 YBECHR (1955–7) p. 139.

[75] Communication No. 19/1977, HRC *Selected Decisions* p. 23. In *P.S.*, Communication No. 397/1990, the HRC more openly stated that indigence was irrelevant (para. 5.4).

[76] Advisory Opinion OC-11/90, 10 August 1990, *Annual Report of the Inter-American Court of Human Rights* (1990), p. 39.

1. Does the requirement of the exhaustion of internal legal remedies apply to an indigent, who because of economic circumstances is unable to avail himself of the legal remedies within a country?
2. In the event that this requirement is waived for indigents, what criteria should the Commission consider in making its determination of admissibility in such cases?[77]

The IACHR regarded the issue as requiring an interpretation of Article 46 of the American Convention which deals with the rule of local remedies including specific situations in which the rule is inapplicable. Article 46(2) of the American Convention makes exceptions to the application of the rule where:

a. the domestic legislation of the state concerned does not afford due process of law for the protection of the right or rights that have allegedly been violated;
b. the party alleging violation of his rights has been denied access to the remedies under domestic law or has been prevented from exhausting them; . . .

The Court thought that Articles 1(1), 8 and 24 of the American Convention were relevant to the issue. These Articles provide:

Article 1
Obligation to Respect Rights
1. The States Parties to this Convention undertake to respect the rights and freedoms recognized herein and to ensure to all persons subject to their jurisdiction the free and full exercise of those rights and freedoms, without any discrimination for reasons of race, color, sex, language, religion, political or other opinion, national or social origin, economic status, birth, or any other social condition.
    . . .

Article 8
Right to a Fair Trial
1. Every person has the right to a hearing, with due guarantees and within a reasonable time, by a competent, independent, and impartial tribunal, previously established by law, in the substantiation of any accusation of a criminal nature made against him or for the determination of his rights and obligations of a civil, labor, fiscal, or any other nature.
2. Every person accused of a criminal offense has the right to be presumed innocent so long as his guilt has not been proven according to law. During the proceedings, every person is entitled, with full equality, to the following minimum guarantees:
    . . .

---

[77] *Ibid.*, p. 40, para. 2.

d. the right of the accused to defend himself personally or to be assisted by legal counsel of his own choosing, and to communicate freely and privately with his counsel;

e. the inalienable right to be assisted by counsel provided by the state, paid or not as the domestic law provides, if the accused does not defend himself personally or engage his own counsel within the time period established by law;

. . .

Article 24

Right to Equal Protection

All persons are equal before the law. Consequently, they are entitled, without discrimination, to equal protection of the law.

By interpreting Article 26(2) in the light of these Articles, the Court came to the conclusion that:

If it can be shown that an indigent needs legal counsel to effectively protect a right which the Convention guarantees and his indigence prevents him from obtaining such counsel, he does not have to exhaust the relevant domestic remedies. That is the meaning of the language of Article 46(2) read in conjunction with Articles 1(1), 24 and 8.[78]

The reasoning of the Court was dependent on the provisions of Article 8(2), but also relied on the proscription of discriminatory treatment stipulated in Articles 1(1) and 24. The Court finally laid down some general principles relating to the effect of indigence. The Court stated that:

25. Sub-paragraphs (d) and (e) of Article 8(2) indicated that the accused has a right to *defend himself personally or to be assisted by legal counsel of his own choosing* and that, if he should choose not to do so, he has *the inalienable right to be assisted by counsel provided by the state, paid or not as the domestic law provides* . . . Thus, a defendant may defend himself personally, but it is important to bear in mind that this would only be possible where permitted under domestic law. If a person refuses or is unable to defend himself personally, he has the right to be assisted by counsel of his own choosing. In cases where the accused neither defends himself nor engages his own counsel within the time period established by law, he has the right to be assisted by counsel provided by the state, paid or not as the domestic law provides. To that extent the Convention guarantees the right to counsel in criminal proceedings. But since it does not stipulate that legal counsel be provided free of charge when required, an indigent would suffer discrimination for reasons of his *economic status* if, when in need of legal counsel, the state were not to provide it to him free of charge.

---

[78] *Ibid.*, p. 47, para. 31.

26. Article 8 must, then, be read to require legal counsel only when that is necessary for a fair hearing. Any state that does not provide indigents with such counsel free of charge cannot, therefore, later assert that appropriate remedies existed but were not exhausted.

27. Even in those cases in which the accused is forced to defend himself because he cannot afford legal counsel, a violation of Article 8 of the Convention could be said to exist if it can be proven that the lack of legal counsel affected the right to a fair hearing to which he is entitled under that article.

28. For cases which concern the determination of a person's *rights and obligations of a civil, labor, fiscal or any other nature*, Article 8(2) for criminal proceedings does not apply. It does, however, provide for *due guarantees*; consequently, the individual here also has the right to the fair hearing provided for in criminal cases. It is important to note here that the circumstances of a particular case or proceeding – its significance, its legal character, and its context in a particular legal system – are among the factors that bear on the determination of whether legal representation is or is not necessary for a fair hearing.

29. Lack of legal counsel is not, of course, the only factor that could prevent an indigent from exhausting domestic remedies. It could even happen that the state might provide legal counsel free of charge but neglect to cover the costs that might be required to ensure the fair hearing that Article 8 prescribes. In such cases, the exceptions to Article 46(1) would apply. Here again, the circumstances of each case and each particular legal system must be kept in mind.

30. In its advisory opinion requested, the Commission states that it *has received certain petitions in which the victim alleges that he has not been able to comply with the requirement of exhaustion of remedies set forth in the domestic legislation because he cannot afford legal representation or, in some cases, the obligatory filing fees.* Upon applying the foregoing analysis to the examples set forth by the Commission, it must be concluded that if legal services are required either as a matter of law or fact in order for a right guaranteed by the Convention to be recognized and a person is unable to obtain such services because of his indigence, then that person would be exempted from the requirement to exhaust domestic remedies. The same would be true of cases requiring the payment of a filing fee. That is to say, if it is impossible for an indigent to deposit such a fee, he cannot be required to exhaust domestic remedies unless the state provides some alternative mechanism.[79]

The Court clearly reached its decision that indigence and poverty may be a ground for exempting an individual from exhausting internal remedies on the basis of provisions contained in the American Convention. The reasoning was that, if substantive provisions of the Convention made it obligatory for the state to provide certain opportunities for justice for an individual and also prohibited discrimination for reasons of economic status, then situations could arise in which the inability of the

[79] *Ibid.*, pp. 46–7, paras. 25–30.

individual to have fair access to remedies by reason of his indigence or impecuniosity would exempt him from exhausting the internal remedies. In the case of the American Convention, violation of any human rights provisions of the Convention would not require resort to internal remedies before the jurisdiction of the Commission (or the Court) was invoked, if the individual were indigent, and the indigence prevents him from accessing remedies in circumstances in which the unavailability of access to remedies because of indigence is also a violation of the substantive provisions of the Convention by the respondent state. In the case of the American Convention, whether indigence would create such a situation, depends on a variety of circumstances, such as whether the proceeding is civil or criminal, whether legal representation is required or necessary for the case, whether court costs are payable and how much, and whether there is available legal representation free of charge as through legal aid, among others. The important point, according to the Court, is whether the circumstances of the individual's indigence, in connection with the legal framework for the administration of justice – such as legal representation and legal costs – result in the respondent state being in violation of its obligations under the provisions of the American Convention, particularly Articles 1(1), 8 and 24. It is important that the Court rested its conclusion regarding the exception arising from indigence to the requirement that internal remedies be exhausted on the interpretation of specific substantive provisions of the American Convention, as supplemental to the application of the provisions of the Article of the Convention dealing specifically with the exhaustion of internal remedies.

A similar approach could be taken under both the European Convention on Human Rights and the ICCPR[80] with similar results. Thus, Article 26 of the old European Convention may be interpreted as permitting an exception to the requirement that internal remedies be exhausted, on

---

[80] The Optional Protocol to the ICCPR is also relevant. It should be noted that the HRC has also clearly indicated that the non-availability of legal aid constituting a contravention of the ICCPR (Article 14(1)) and leading to non-exhaustion of a remedy because of indigence would exempt the petitioner from the need to exhaust remedies: *Currie*, Communication No. 377/1989. This is so, even where the failure to provide legal aid is not such a contravention, at least in certain circumstances: *Henry*, Communication No. 230/1998; and *Gallimore*, Communication No. 680/1996. However, the impact of indigence or lack of means cannot be absolute. The assessment of the lack of means and the circumstances of the case play a significant role in the conclusions reached: see e.g. *R.W.*, Communication No. 340/1988; *Faurisson*, Communication No. 550/1993; and *G.T.*, Communication No. 420/1990.

the ground that it is reasonable to permit such an exception where provisions of the Convention itself relating to the right to remedies have been violated, even though, unlike in the case of the American Convention, no specific reference is made to exceptions other than those permitted by general international law. Because it is a requirement of general international law that remedies be available or accessible, 'availability' or 'accessibility' of remedies may in the case of the European system be interpreted by reference to the terms of the Convention itself. The relevant substantive provisions of the old Convention were Article 6 and 14. The former referred to the right to a 'fair hearing' in both civil and criminal cases and prescribes that in criminal proceedings free legal assistance should be provided where the interests of justice so requires and the individual has no means to pay for it. Article 14 which is also critical provided that the enjoyment of rights set forth in the convention should be ensured without discrimination 'on any ground such as sex, race, color, language, religion, political or other opinion, national or social origin, association with a national minority, property, or other status'. 'Other status' clearly included economic status, as in the American Convention where it is specifically mentioned. Thus, the results reached in the case of the European Convention as regards an exception to the rule of local remedies based on indigence or impecuniosity could be similar to, if not identical with, those reached by the IACHR.

In this connection, it should be noted that in the case in which the ECtHR held that the individual's poverty did not excuse him from exhausting local remedies it was specifically stated that the individual had not attempted to seek legal aid which may have been available. Thus, there was no established violation by the respondent state of Article 6 of the old Convention.

In the case of the ICCPR, Article 5(2)(b) of the Optional Protocol could be interpreted in such a way as to permit an exception in the case of impecuniosity where the provisions of the ICCPR have been violated. These provisions are Articles 14 and 26, which are similar in formulation and content to Articles 6 and 14 respectively of the old European Convention. Thus, the same result could be reached under the ICCPR by the HRC as was proposed under the European Convention.

While the effect of impecuniosity on the incidence of the rule of local remedies may be established in general terms in the case of human rights protection under the express provisions of the three human rights instruments discussed above, the exact dimensions of this exception to the rule of local remedies may not be defined. The question also arises of whether impecuniosity is relevant without other specific conventional provisions being invoked than the exception based on inaccessibility. An argument in favour of the application of an exception may be made on the basis of the general provisions relating to the rule of domestic remedies in the conventional law, in these cases. In the Conventions it is recognized that remedies must be both 'accessible' and 'available' to the individual affected and that they must be 'adequate and effective'. It is not difficult to conclude that where, whether in criminal or civil proceedings, the provisions of the local law are such that the alien cannot make use of them because his access to them is *unreasonably* prevented by his indigence or impecuniosity, the requirements referred to above are not fulfilled. In these circumstances, there is no reason not to permit an exception to the rule of local remedies.

In construing the requirement of reasonableness, it may be postulated that the provisions of the human rights instruments relating to remedies discussed above reflect general requirements relevant to the interpretation of the provisions referring to the exceptions to the rule. Thus, there should not be any difficulty in applying the conclusions of the IACHR generally in order to permit an appropriate exception to the application of the rule of local remedies where an individual's impecuniosity or indigence affects his ability to have recourse to the remedies which he would under the rule be normally obliged to exhaust. That having been said, while the principle that indigence is a factor that affects accessibility may be admitted, the circumstances of each case, as the subsequent practice of the HRC adverted to earlier shows, will determine whether indigence has affected accessibility.

The existence of a generalized fear in the local legal community of representing the individual affected has been regarded by the IACHR as a ground for recognizing an exception to the application of the rule. Generally, the situation in issue is the result, directly or indirectly, of the conduct or omissions of the respondent state, but the individual does not apparently need to prove this. The exception relates to inaccessibility and not necessarily to the acts or omissions of the respondent state resulting in that inaccessibility. What is relevant is the impact of a situation prevailing in the respondent state. In the caselaw the situation is not labelled as one of inaccessibility of remedies, but clearly it may be so characterized with propriety.

The issue came up before the IACHR for the first time in the request for the advisory opinion discussed above.[81] The question raised was whether domestic remedies need to be exhausted, when the claimant was unable to obtain the necessary legal representation because of a general fear in the legal community of the respondent state. This situation may occur where an atmosphere of fear prevails and lawyers do not accept cases which they believe would place their own lives and those of their families in jeopardy. The Court held that the same basic principles were applicable to this issue as to the case of indigence or impecuniosity. Thus, if for the reason stated above the individual is prevented from availing himself of the internal remedies necessary to assert or protect his human rights guaranteed by the American Convention, he should not be required to exhaust those remedies. The Court said:

34. Article 1 of the Convention provides not only that the States Parties have an obligation to *respect the rights and freedoms recognized (t)herein* it also requires them *to ensure to all persons subject to their jurisdiction the free and full exercise of those rights and freedoms.* The Court has already had occasion to emphasize that this provision imposes an affirmative duty on the States. It is also important to note that the obligation *to ensure* requires the state to take all necessary measures to remove any impediments which might exist that would prevent individuals from enjoying the rights the Convention guarantees. Any state which tolerates circumstances or conditions that prevent individuals from having recourse to the legal remedies designed to protect their rights is consequently in violation of Article 1(1) of Convention . . .

35. It follows therefrom that where an individual requires legal representation and a generalized fear in the legal community prevents him from obtaining such representation, the exception set out in Article 46(2)(b) is fully applicable and the individual is exempted from the requirement to exhaust domestic remedies.[82]

The Court relied on Article 1(1) of the American Convention, but it is clear that on a more general basis the exception could be related directly to the conventional 'denial of access' to remedies. It is important to note that in the view of the Court the *tolerance* by the respondent of the circumstances which prevent an individual from retaining counsel because of a generalized fear with the result that he does not have access to remedies was regarded as a denial of access to remedies. There is significantly no requirement of positive obstruction of access in this case – a more passive attitude could result in the denial of access required to trigger the exception. This may be important for the definition of the exception based on the denial of access in other circumstances as well

---

[81] Advisory Opinion OC-11/90, note 76 above.   [82] *Ibid.*, at p. 48, paras. 34–5.

as that based on a generalized fear as described. The development and elaboration by the Court in this way of the principle of inaccessibility must be recognized as a distinct contribution. Of course, the secondary principle explained by the Court in this way needs to be fleshed out by being applied to practical situations.

Clearly, because the exception applied by the IACHR is rooted in the recognized limitation to the rule of local remedies based on accessibility of remedies, the same exception could in principle be applied under the other two conventional instruments by the EComHR, the ECtHR and the HRC.

The relationship of this principle enunciated by the IACHR in this advisory opinion to the general exception to the rule of domestic remedies based on 'inaccessibility' of remedies is important for the law of human rights in general. While in the case of the human rights conventions this principle which permits the non-exhaustion of remedies may often be justified by reference to express substantive provisions of the conventions which lay upon the respondent state certain duties *vis-à-vis* the provision of remedies and the operation of its legal system, in some situations the general provision of the law that domestic remedies need not be exhausted, where such remedies are inaccessible to the individual, would justify the application of the principle being discussed so as to permit an exception to operate in the appropriate circumstance. In the law of human rights, there is evidence that the inaccessibility of remedies would as a general rule, deriving from whatever source, be a situation in which domestic remedies need not be exhausted. The principle is one that implements the exception based on inaccessibility.

Inefficacy

In addition to the inaccessibility or unavailability of remedies as a reason for not exhausting them, the absence of due process of law in the legal system of the respondent state is a sufficient excuse for not exhausting remedies. This ground is specifically referred to in Article 46(2)(a) of the American Convention and was also supported in the Institut de Droit International.[83] Although not all forms of denial of justice may have the result of exempting the alien or claimant from exhausting remedies, certainly this one would seem to have the effect of rendering

---

[83] 36(1) AIDI (1935) at p. 435; and 45 AIDI (1954) at pp. 28ff. See also Harvard Law School, *Research in International Law II. Responsibility of States (1929)* p. 134.

remedies obviously futile in so far as proper justice and fairness cannot be expected to prevail. The exception would be relevant even in the absence of specific provisions for it in a conventional instrument. The exception was found to be applicable by the IAComHR in Resolution No. 1a/88,[84] where the Commission held that the irregularities pertaining to the legal process inherent in Chilean military justice were reflected in the abusive recourse to secrecy in the conduct of the proceedings, with the result that it was initially impossible to gain access to basic elements of the trial and the military authorities were allowed to control the evidence submitted. Therefore, the Commission held that due process of law was non-existent and local remedies did not have to be pursued.[85]

The IAComHR has taken the position in its reports that the absence of an independent judiciary, such as could result for a variety of reasons from the maintenance of a military regime of a state of emergency, even after the emergency has ended, renders remedies ineffective.[86] The IAComHR has also taken the view that, where the remedies available do not cover, and therefore cannot satisfy, all complaints, the remedies are not effective.[87]

Where the remedies available clearly will not satisfy the object sought by the claimant, they need not be resorted to because they are ineffective. There are several decided cases concerning the protection of human rights under the European Convention on Human Rights. Where the object of the claimant's action was to prevent his removal from a state's territory in violation of the Convention, a court action which did not have suspensive effect was not a remedy that had to be exhausted because it was obviously ineffective for the object sought by the claimant.[88]

---

[84] Resolution No. 1a/88, Case 9755, Ann. Rep. IAComHR (1987–8) at p. 137.

[85] The HRC has held that the absence of procedural guarantees for a fair and public hearing by a competent, independent and impartial tribunal (required by Article 14 of the ICCPR) rendered remedies ineffective: *Gilboa* v. *Uruguay*, Doc. A/41/40, p. 128. Clearly, this particular requirement does not apply to all domestic remedies. Special security regimes may render a remedy ineffective: *Santullo (Valcada)* v. *Uruguay*, Doc A/35/40 at p. 107 (HRC). See also for ineffectiveness: *G. Barbato* v. *Uruguay*, Doc A/38/40 at p. 124 (HRC), and the cases referred to in McGoldrick, note 2 above, at pp. 190ff. and note 681 therein.

[86] See Cerna, note 33 above, at p. 87 and note 90 therein.

[87] This was in a case brought to its attention outside the American Convention (Case 3228 involving the US as respondent): see Cerna, note 33 above, at pp. 87–8.

[88] *Becker* v. *Denmark*, Application No. 7011/75, 4 D&R, at pp. 227–8 and 232–3. See also *X* v. *Denmark*, Application 7465/76, 7 D&R at p. 154; *X* v. *Austria*, Application 6701/74, 5 D&R at pp. 78–9; and *Zamir* v. *UK*, Application 9174/80, *Report of the Commission*.

Similarly, the EComHR has held that, where a claimant finds it impossible to prove before the authorities concerned allegations which are basic to the object of his application, it is obvious that the remedies concerned cannot give the claimant satisfaction and cannot be effective.[89] The case related to the adequacy of the means provided to achieve the object sought and shows that remedies need not be exhausted where the means available cannot satisfy the desired object.

While such categories as are referred to above may be established in the jurisprudence of human rights organs, there is no reason why the other categories, applicable to diplomatic protection, discussed in Chapter 8 should not be applied to human rights protection. Further, the question has been raised by some decisions of the EComHR as to whether the general requirement of 'obvious futility' has been abandoned for the application of the rule of domestic remedies in the context of the protection of human rights and particularly under the European Convention on Human Rights. There is some element of doubt in the jurisprudence of the Commission. There are cases in which the Commission apparently supported the test of obvious futility in regard to limitations on the rule of local remedies, while in other cases a less stringent test of absence of a reasonable prospect of success of the remedies in question was applied. The difference between the two tests is that under the former test what must be shown in order to trigger an exception to the application of the rule is that it was clear beyond reasonable doubt or that it was manifestly clear that remedies could not result in a successful outcome, while in the case of the latter test all that need be shown for an exception to operate is that the remedy in question would probably not have resulted in successful reparation.

There were cases decided by the EComHR in which, on the one hand, it has been said that 'if there is any doubt as to whether a given remedy is or is not intrinsically able to offer a real chance of success', it should be canvassed so that the issue may be decided by the local courts.[90] In

---

[89] *Kornmann* v. *Federal Republic of Germany*, Application 2686/65, 22 *Collections* at p. 10.

[90] *X* v. *UK*, Application 3651/68, 31 *Collections* at p. 90. For this reason, an appeal to the Court of Appeal in the UK was held to be subject to exhaustion in this case. See also *Retimag* v. *Federal Republic of Germany*, Application 712/60, 4 YBECHR at p. 400; *X* v. *Federal Republic of Germany*, Application 8961/80, 24 YBECHR p. 74; and *McVeigh, O'Neill and Evans* v. *UK*, Application 8022/77, 8025/77 and 8027/77, *Report of the Commission* at pp. 112–13. There is a certain relativity, in any case, about the notion of 'obvious futility', if that is the proper test. Much depends on the circumstances of both the applicant and the context in which he is operating, whatever the test: see e.g. the *Akdivar Case*, Judgment of 16 September 1996, 15 Reports 1996-IV para. 70, which deals

Kjeldsen v. *Denmark*,[91] one part of the application was held to be inadmissible because the remedy indicated by the respondent against certain directives issued by the Danish Ministry of Education and against certain other administrative measures could not *clearly* have been said to lack any prospect of success, while the other part of the application, which related to measures taken under an Act of Parliament, could not be contested in court because no proceedings could be taken against such an instrument, and therefore was held to be admissible.

On the other hand, there are numerous cases in which the test applied has been whether the remedy 'soit efficace et offre des chances raisonnables de succès'.[92] In *Lawless* v. *Ireland*,[93] the applicant had failed in his bid to secure a writ of *habeas corpus* in regard to his detention so that it was clear that he could not succeed in an action for damages for false imprisonment. The Commission held that such action had no reasonable prospect of success and was, therefore, an ineffective remedy.

It is not apparent whether in all the cases in which the test was said to be absence of a reasonable prospect of success, with the result that the rule of domestic remedies was found to be inapplicable, the facts showed that, while this test was met, the decision would have been different if the stricter test of obvious futility had been applied. At the same time, it is not always clear in many of the cases in which the Commission held that local remedies should have been exhausted, because they were not obviously futile or there was some doubt about their effectiveness, that the decision would have been different if the less strict test of absence of a reasonable prospect of success had been applied. What emerges, therefore, is that there was a lack of clarity in the jurisprudence of the EComHR. Further, it is not entirely clear that the general trend in its decisions is to apply the less strict test in favour of the exception,

---

with inefficacy. The exception of ineffectiveness must, therefore, be applied with some degree of 'flexibility' and without excessive formalism: *ibid.*, para. 69; Judgment of 19 March 1991, the *Cardot Case*, 34 YBECHR (1991) at pp. 195ff.; and Judgment of 16 December 1992, the *de la Pradelle Case*, 35 YBECHR (1992) at p. 219.

[91] Application 5095/71, 43 *Collections* at pp. 54–5. On administrative practices in particular and the domestic remedies rule, see McGovern, 'The Local Remedies Rule and Administrative Practices in the European Convention on Human Rights', 24 ICLQ (1975) p. 119.

[92] X v. *Federal Republic of Germany*, Application 968/81, 8 *Collections* at p. 27. See also *Austria* v. *Italy*, Application 788/60, *Report of the Plenary Commission* at pp. 55ff.

[93] Application 332/57, 2 YBECHR p. 318.

although there are many cases in which it has ostensibly been applied. Consequently, it cannot with certainty be asserted that the *established* rule in the jurisprudence of the EComHR is that the less strict test applies generally as determining the limitations on or exceptions to the rule of domestic remedies.[94]

Undue delay

In the field of human rights protection, undue delay has been acknowledged to be a reason for excusing the applicant from exhausting remedies. In some conventions, the exception is referred to explicitly. The ICCPR in Article 49 and the Optional Protocol in Article 5, the UN International Covenant on the Elimination of All Forms of Racial Discrimination in Article II, and the American Convention on Human Rights in Article 46, all make express reference to the exception to the rule of exhaustion of local remedies where there is unwarranted delay in the application of remedies. But the explicit reference seems to have been made *ex abundanti cautela*. Even under the European Convention

---

[94] This is an observation made on the basis of the decided cases. Cançado Trindade noted that the less strict test was more widely applied, and concluded that this had *replaced* the stricter test in the jurisprudence of the EComHR: note 37 above, at p. 97. This conclusion is not clearly supported, particularly in light of some of the more recent cases. Moreover, neither the ECtHR nor the EComHR has categorically overruled the adoption of the more strict test in principle. It is also evident that in general, where an application has been declared admissible, the facts show that it would have been obviously futile to resort to or exhaust the remedies in question. The converse would also seem to be true. These organs have generally confined themselves to stating that the remedies were 'ineffective' or 'inadequate'. It may, on the other hand, be *desirable* that the less strict test be adopted as the rule where there is a doubt as to obvious futility. On the application of the principle of ineffectiveness in the cases, see also now, *Buscarini* v. *San Marino*, Judgment of 18 February 1999, 38 ILM at p. 743; *Selmount* v. *France*, Judgment of 28 July 1999, 38 ILM at pp. 1506ff.; and van Dijk and van Hoof, note 50 above, at pp. 137–42 and 144–7. In the two cases cited above herein it was quite clear that the resort to remedies or exhaustion of remedies was absolutely (obviously) futile. The HRC has used the criterion of absence of 'prospect of success' as a test of efficacy: see, e.g. *Pratt and Morgan*, Communications Nos. 210/1986 and 225/1987, para. 12.3. The test is objective (see e.g. *Pratt and Morgan, ibid.*) and is not dependent on the subjective belief of the victim (see e.g. *R.T.*, Communication No. 262/1987; and *Kaabar*, Communication No. 674/1995). The CAT and the CERD have described the remedy as 'futile' but have not used the term 'obviously futile': see e.g. *P.M.P.K.*, CAT No. 30/1995; and *Barbaro*, CERD No. 7/1995. The CAT has indicated by implication that ineffectiveness (futility) is not easily presumed: see *P.M.P.K.*, CAT No. 30/1995. There is certainly no problem with accepting the less strict test of inefficacy as the applicable test in the context of human rights protection.

on Human Rights, where the old Article 26 made no such reference, the exception based on unreasonable delay was recognized.

Although, as already pointed out in the context of diplomatic protection, what is unreasonable delay may depend on the circumstances of each case, there are several cases in which the HRC has held that remedies need not be exhausted because there had been such delay. In Communication No. 28/1978,[95] where the applicant had been arrested and detained, since final judgment had not been rendered in the case after a lapse of four and a half years, the HRC decided that the application of the remedy in question was unreasonably prolonged and that, therefore, the non-exhaustion of remedies was not a bar to its considering the case.[96] The IAComHR has also implemented the provisions of the Convention governing it by deciding in several cases that unreasonable delay in the application of remedies had had the effect of exempting the applicant from the duty to exhaust local remedies.[97]

The EComHR has often held that local remedies need not be exhausted where there was unreasonable delay in the administration of justice, even though the European Convention does not specifically refer to this exception. It had obviously done so in carrying out the prescription to apply generally recognized rules of international law. In X v. *Federal Republic of Germany*, decided in 1959, the Commission stated that 'les lenteurs de procédure' before the Federal Constitutional Court could be a circumstance which would relieve the applicant of the duty to exhaust that remedy,[98] although in the case itself it held that delay had not been proved. In *De Becker* v. *Belgium*, the Commission held that one reason why a particular remedy did not have to be exhausted was that the applicant

---

[95] HRC *Selected Decisions* at p. 59.
[96] For other decisions of the same order, see e.g. Communication No. 44/1979, HRC *Selected Decisions* at p. 79; Communication No. 73/1980, HRC *Selected Decisions* at pp. 134–5; *Pietroroia* v. *Uruguay*, Doc. A/39/40, p. 153; *Hermaoza* v. *Peru*, Doc. A/44/40, p. 200; *Weinberger* v. *Uruguay*, Doc. A/36/40, p. 114; and *Hammel* v. *Madagascar*, Doc. A/42/40, p. 130. There are cases in which the HRC has on the facts rejected the application of the exceptions: see e.g. *H.S.* v. *France*, Doc. A/41/40, p. 169; and *N.A.J.* v. *Jamaica*, Doc. A/45/40, Appendix, para. 10.3.
[97] See e.g. Resolution No. 16/84, Case No. 7951, Ann. Rep. IAComHR (1984–5) at p. 103; Resolution No. 15/87, Case No. 9635, Ann. Rep. IAComHR (1986–7) at p. 62; Resolution No. 17/87, Case No. 9425, Ann. Rep. IAComHR (1986–7), p. 118; Resolution No. 20/87, Case No. 9449, Ann. Rep. IAComHR (1986–7) at p. 130; Resolution No. 1a/88, Case No. 9755, Ann. Rep. IAComHR (1987–8) at pp. 132–9; and Resolution No. 14/89, Case No. 9641, Ann. Rep. IAComHR (1988–9) at pp. 104–15.
[98] Application 222/56, 2 YBECHR (1958–9) at p. 350.

would have had to wait five years after his release in order to canvass it, which was too long.[99]

Repetition of injury or likelihood of further damage

In the law of diplomatic protection, as has been seen, the better view is that a remedy need not be resorted to, that is, a final decision of the last instance does not need to be awaited, if for some reason, further damages are expected or the same injury will be repeated. There is no reason why the same exception should not be applicable to human rights protection.

Limitations applied in human rights protection

In the area of human rights protection, the ECtHR, *inter alios*, has referred to three situations in which the rule of domestic remedies is inapplicable because of the nature of the particular situations. These limitations on the applicability of the rule relate to (i) the prevailing condition, (ii) legislative measures and administrative practices, and (iii) the continuing situation.

The prevailing condition

In *Austria* v. *Italy*, the parties virtually agreed that local remedies did not have to be exhausted where there was a prevailing condition which violated the European Convention on Human Rights.[100] The EComHR agreed with this position.[101] The exact scope of this exception is not

---

[99] Application 214/56, 2 YBECHR (1958–9) at p. 238. Other cases in which undue delay has been referred to as a ground for releasing the applicant from the duty to exhaust remedies are *Nielsen* v. *Denmark*, Application 343/57, 2 YBECHR (1958–9) at p. 440; *X* v. *Federal Republic of Germany*, Application 297/57, 2 YBECHR (1958–9) at pp. 213–14; *X* v. *Federal Republic of Germany*, Application 538/59, 2 *Collections* at pp. 348–9; *X* v. *Federal Republic of Germany*, Application 704/60, 3 *Collections* at p. 6; *Orchin* v. *UK*, Application 8435/78, *Report of the Commission*; and *Ventura* v. *Italy*, Application 7438/76, *Report of the Commission*. There are *special circumstances* which are cautiously conceded in which domestic remedies may not be exhausted. These are all related to the practical aspects of 'effectiveness': see van Dijk and van Hoof, note 50 above, at pp. 152–3. The HRC has not only recognized undue delay as a ground for not requiring exhaustion of remedies (see e.g. *Ominayak et al.*, Communication No. 167/1984; *Fillastre and Bizoarn*, Communication No. 336/1988; and *Hendriks*, Communication No. 201/1985) but has established also that the delay must not be attributable to the fault of the petitioner (*H.S.*, Communication No. 184/1984) and that mere fear of delay is inadequate (*R.L. et al.*, Communication No. 658/1959). What is undue delay also depends on the circumstances of the case: *H.S.*, Communication No. 184/1984.

[100] Application 788/60, 4 YBECHR at p. 146.   [101] *Ibid.*, p. 148.

clear, nor, indeed, is the question whether it is the same as the next one to be considered, which concerns legislative measures and administrative practices. There is also the question of whether it applies equally to inter-state cases as to individual applications. It may be difficult to apply it in individual cases, because in these the individual must be a victim of the alleged injury or must have suffered an injury. A more difficult question is how different this exception is from that which has been recognized in the case of legislative measures and administrative practices.

Legislative measures and administrative practices

In the *First Cyprus Case*,[102] the applicant government charged that the respondent government had violated the European Convention on Human Rights on account of the latter's legislative measures and administrative practices in Cyprus. In its decision, the EComHR stated that the rule of local remedies as recognized in general international law did not apply to the application in the case, 'the scope of which is to determine the compatibility with the Convention of legislative measures and administrative practices in Cyprus'.[103] This was an inter-state case and in many subsequent inter-state cases the Commission has followed the ruling in this decision.[104] The reason given for this exception is basically that, whereas the local remedies rule was based on the effectiveness and availability of remedies, in the kind of case under consideration 'judicial remedies prescribed would tend to be rendered ineffective by the difficulty of securing probative evidence, and administrative inquiries would either be not instituted, or, if they were would be likely to be half-hearted and incomplete'.[105]

While the exception may be based on the ineffectiveness and inadequacy of the remedies likely to be available, it is not clear that in the kind of case envisaged the remedies would be obviously futile, although

---

[102] *Greece* v. *UK*, Application 176/56, 2 YBECHR (1958–9) at p. 182.

[103] *Ibid.*, at p. 184.

[104] See the *Second Cyprus Case* (*Greece* v. *UK*), Application 299/57, 2 YBECHR (1958–9) at pp. 188–92; *Austria* v. *Italy*, Application 788/60, 4 YBECHR p. 182; the *First Greek Case* (*Denmark, Norway, Sweden and the Netherlands* v. *Greece*), Applications 3321–3/67 and 3344/67, 11 YBECHR p. 710 and 12 YBECHR p. 194; the *Second Greek Case* (*Denmark, Norway and Sweden* v. *Greece*), Application 4448/70, 13 YBECHR p. 108; *Ireland* v. *UK*, Application 5310/71, 41 *Collections* p. 25.

[105] *First Greek Case* (*Denmark, Norway, Sweden and the Netherlands* v. *Greece*), Applications 3321–3/67 and 3344/67, 12 YBECHR at p. 194.

there may be no reasonable prospect of their succeeding. Further, it may be that in a given case there is no injury to an individual in the case of an impugned legislative measure, which would make the exception a very special one.

The complicated and difficult nature of the exception is attested to by the problems encountered with identifying 'administrative practice' for the purposes of this exception. It was laid down in the *First Greek Case*[106] that not all administrative practices would be covered by the exception, but only such practices as involved both the repetition of acts and official tolerance which were subject to proof, and it was explained further that such administrative practice did not require merely the repetition of administrative decisions, but consisted rather of repeated factual events which were tolerated. In circumstances, however, in which such administrative practices are proven to exist, there does not seem to be a further requirement that local remedies be shown to be ineffective, at least in the sense of not providing a reasonable prospect of success, if not obviously futile. Nor is it a question of presumptions; for the exception seems to operate regardless of whether the respondent state provides contrary evidence that there were local remedies which were both available and effective.

In regard to individual applications under the European Convention, the applicability of the exception has been regarded as being dependent both on whether the applicant has been affected by the situation as a victim and on whether administrative practice in the sense defined could be proven to exist.[107] Thus, in the case of an individual application, it is insufficient that the situation merely exists; it must have a definite adverse impact on the applicant. On the other hand, the Commission elaborated elsewhere on the notion of 'victim' and asserted that the term covered not only direct victims or victims of the alleged violation but also persons 'who would indirectly suffer prejudice as a result of such violation or would have a valid personal interest in securing the

---

[106] *Denmark, Norway, Sweden and the Netherlands* v. *Greece*, Applications 3321–3/67, 12 YBECHR at pp. 195–6. See also on administrative practices *Ireland* v. *UK*, Application 5310/71, 41 *Collections* p. 25; and Judgment of 16 September 1996, the *Akdivar Case*, 15 Reports 1996-IV, para. 67.

[107] See e.g. *Kjeldsen* v. *Denmark*, Application 5095/71, 43 *Collections* at pp. 46ff.; *Pedersen* v. *Denmark*, Application 5926/72, 43 *Collections* at pp. 93ff., *Busk Madsen* v. *Denmark*, Application 5920/74, cited in 44 *Collections* p. 93 note 1; and *Donnelly and Others* v. *UK*, Application 5577–5583/72, 43 *Collections* p. 122. See also *G* v. *Belgium*, Application 9107/80, 22 D&R (1983) at p. 79; *X and Y* v. *UK*, Application 9471/81, 36 D&R (1984) at p. 61; and the *Aksoy Case*, Application 21987/93, 37 YBECHR (1994) at pp. 117ff.

cessation of such violation'.[108] Thus, while the exception is applicable
to individual applications, although in a limited way because of the
requirements laid down by the Commission, those requirements are not
so restrictive.[109] It is clear, however, that the exception is applicable
under the European Convention, whatever the practical application of
the exception may be.[110]

The continuing situation

The issue in the case of a continuing situation is not so much the time of
exhaustion of remedies, in the sense discussed in the previous section,
as the time at which the domestic remedies are deemed to have been
exhausted for an application to be lodged without an objection based on
the rule of exhaustion of local remedies being tenable. This situation has
arisen in connection with the protection of human rights, for example
where there has been a detention while on remand for an unreasonable
length of time.[111]

It was held by the ECtHR in *Stogmüller* v. *Austria* that, where there has
been such a continuing detention, domestic remedies will be deemed
to have been exhausted when the first final decision has been given
without securing the release of the applicant, it being unnecessary for
the applicant to continue thereafter to resort to remedies in order to
secure his release in order that remedies may be fully exhausted. It

[108] *X* v. *Federal Republic of Germany*, Application 4185/69, 35 *Collections* at p. 142. See also *X*
v. *Federal Republic of Germany*, Application 282/57, 1 YBECHR (1955–7) at p. 166; and
Koolen v. *Belgium*, Application 1478/62, 13 *Collections* at p. 89. On the jurisdictional
significance of the concept of 'victim', see Amerasinghe, *Jurisdiction of International
Tribunals* (2003) pp. 739ff.

[109] There is a fairly lengthy discussion of the exception which is the subject of this
subsection and its scope in Cançado Trindade, note 37 above, at pp. 187–212. For
others who have discussed the issue, see e.g. Waldock, 'General Course on Public
International Law', 106 *Hague Recueil* (1962) at pp. 209ff.; Müller-Rappard, 'Le Droit
d'action en vertu des dispositions de la Convention européenne des droits de
l'homme', 4 RBDI (1968) at pp. 489–90; Danielus, note 13 above, at pp. 286–7; Boyle
and Hannum, 'Individual Applications under the European Convention on Human
Rights and the Concept of Administrative Practice: The Donnelly Case', 68 AJIL (1974)
at pp. 440–53; Castberg, *The European Convention on Human Rights* (1974) pp. 46–8; and
McGovern, note 91 above, at pp. 119–27.

[110] See Application 8007/77, 13 D&R (1979) p. 152. The practice of the IAComHR in regard
to 'general' cases as opposed to 'individual' cases is similar. In the practice of the
HRC, the existence of 'practices' has been referred to (see McGoldrick, note 2 above, at
p. 196), but their relevance for the rule of domestic remedies is a different matter.

[111] See e.g. Article 5(3) of the European Convention on Human Rights; and Article 7(5) of
the American Convention on Human Rights; and Article 9(3) of the ICCPR.

becomes apparent also in these circumstances that the application may relate to a situation which persists after the filing of the application, in respect of which domestic remedies, it may be argued, have not been exhausted. The Court said in *Stogmüller* v. *Austria*:

As to the point whether the proceedings instituted may embrace complaints concerning facts which occurred after the lodging of the application, international law, to which Article 26 refers explicitly, is far from conferring on the rule of exhaustion the inflexible character which the government seems to attribute to it. International law only imposes the use of the remedies which are not only available to the persons concerned but are also sufficient, that is to say capable of redressing their complaints. Thus, in matters of detention while on remand, it is in the light of the circumstances of the case that the question is, in appropriate cases, to be assessed whether and to what extent it was necessary, pursuant to Article 26, for the detained applicant, who had exhausted the remedies before the Commission declared his application admissible, to make later on further appeals to the national courts in order to make it possible to examine, at international level, the reasonableness of his continued detention. But such question only arises if the examination of the reasons given by the national courts in their decision on the appeals made before the lodging of the application has not led to the conclusion that, at that date, the detention had exceeded a reasonable time. Indeed, if the opposite be the case it is clear that the detention while on remand which is held to have exceeded a reasonable time on the day when the application was lodged must be found, except in extraordinary circumstances, to have necessarily kept such character throughout the time for which it was continued.[112]

In regard to the absence of the need for several applications in the case of continued detention, the ECtHR had earlier held in *Neumeister* v. *Austria* that:

It would be excessively formalistic to demand that an applicant denouncing a situation should file a new application with the Commission after each final decision rejecting a request for release. This would pointlessly involve both the Commission and the Court in a confusing multiplication of proceedings which would tend to paralyse their working.[113]

Some non-limiting circumstances

In the area of human rights protection particularly, many invalid excuses have been considered. Some examples are mentioned here. Ignorance of the existence of a remedy or of the conditions for its invocation does

---

[112] ECHR Series A No. 9 pp. 42–3 (1969).   [113] ECHR Series A No. 8 p. 38 (1968).

not constitute an excuse for not exhausting remedies:[114] *ignorantia juris non excusat.* Consequently, mental disability or lack of knowledge of the law is not an excuse.[115] Mere doubts as to the existence or effectiveness of a remedy do not exempt the individual from exercising a remedy,[116] nor does bad advice given by counsel or his opinion[117] or the personal opinion of the individual as to the probability of success of a remedy[118] or as to expediency and tactics in handling his case.[119] Alleged lack of facilities for the purpose of exhausting remedies is not an excuse.[120] Other circumstances which have been held not to be reasons for the failure to exhaust remedies are the applicant's ill-health,[121] his advanced age,[122] wrong information given by a court official,[123] detention *per se* of the applicant[124] or his extradition or expulsion from the respondent state's territory.[125]

Use of procedural resources

The EComHR has in effect recognized the principle that resort need not be had to obligatory procedural remedies, if they fall below the international minimum standard. In *Wiechart* v. *Federal Republic of Germany*,[126] the Commission discussed the question whether the circumstances of the case exempted the applicant from observing the time limit set for filing his action. The case involved the drafting of an application for

---

[114] See e.g. *Wiechart* v. *Federal Republic of Germany*, Application 1404/62, 15 *Collections* at p. 23; and *X* v. *UK*, Application 5006/71, 39 *Collections* at p. 93.

[115] *X* v. *UK*, Application 6840/74, 10 D&R at pp. 15ff.

[116] See e.g. *X and Y* v. *Belgium*, Application 1661/62, 10 *Collections* at p. 19; *23 Inhabitants of Alsemberg and of Beersel* v. *Belgium*, Application 1474/62, 12 *Collections* at p. 28; and Communication No. 79/1980, HRC *Selected Decisions* at p. 32.

[117] See e.g. *X* v. *Belgium*, Application 1488/62, 13 *Collections* at p. 96; and *Simon-Herold* v. *Austria*, Application 4340/69, 38 *Collections* at p. 33. See also by implication Communication No. 19/1977, HRC *Selected Decisions* at p. 23.

[118] *X* v. *Federal Republic of Germany*, Application 289/57, 1 YBECHR (1955–7) at p. 149.

[119] See *Austria* v. *Italy*, Application 788/60, *Report of the Plenary Commission* at p. 55.

[120] See e.g. *Wiechart* v. *Federal Republic of Germany*, Application 1404/62, 15 *Collections* at p. 23; and *X* v. *Belgium*, Application 4930/71, 40 *Collections* at p. 41.

[121] See e.g. *X* v. *Federal Republic of Germany*, Application 181/56, 1 YBECHR (1955–7) at pp. 140ff.; and *X* v. *Federal Republic of Germany*, Application 289/57, 1 YBECHR (1955–7) at p. 149.

[122] See e.g. *X* v. *Federal Republic of Germany*, Application 568/59, 2 *Collections* at p. 3.

[123] See e.g. *X* v. *UK*, Application 4133/69, 36 *Collections* at p. 64; and *X* v. *Federal Republic of Germany*, Application 5594/72, 44 *Collections* at p. 133.

[124] See Cançado Trindade, note 37 above, at p. 120.

[125] See e.g. Communication No. 2/1976, HRC *Selected Decisions* at p. 22.

[126] Application 1404/62, 7 YBECHR p. 124.

legal aid before the filing of the action. The point was whether the time limit set was too short and, therefore, a harsh requirement, because it did not provide for an appropriate exception for the circumstances in which the applicant was placed. The argument was apparently based on the international minimum standard. In so far as the Commission held that the applicant was not exempted from fulfilling the time requirements of the rule of procedure, it took the view that the applicant had not proved circumstances which would have exempted him from observing the rule of procedure on the ground that that rule failed to permit a generally recognized exception and, therefore, fell below the international minimum standard. There was an acknowledgment that the principle in issue was relevant. It did not apply because of the particular circumstances of the case.

Waiver

In the field of human rights protection, where the rule of local remedies applies in the system of protection, no provision is expressly made for its waiver in any way.

Express waiver

There are cases in which the express waiver of the rule has been recognized. International organs such as the EComHR, the HRC and the IAComHR are not conciliation organs but organs acting judicially. Hence, the question of whether the local remedies rule is applicable to complaints brought before them may be moot. In any event, as it is, their constitutive instruments made the rule a condition of admissibility for cases brought before them.[127] While these organs have the power *ex officio* or *proprio motu* to ascertain whether domestic remedies have been exhausted, it is apparent that they do recognize express waivers of the application of the rule. In several cases, the EComHR has acknowledged that express waiver at the time of the proceedings by the respondent state has the effect of excluding the application of the rule. In *57 Inhabitants of Louvain and Environs* v. *Belgium*,[128] for example, the

---

[127] On the issue of conciliation and the rule of local remedies, there are conflicting views: see e.g. the *Interhandel Case*, 1959 ICJ Reports at p. 29, at p. 45 *per* Judge Córdova in a separate opinion, at p. 84 *per* Judge Winiarski dissenting, at p. 121 *per* Judge Lauterpacht dissenting, ICJ Pleadings (1959) at p. 573 (Swiss oral argument); Gaja, *L'Esaurimento dei Ricorsi Interni nel Diritto Internazionale* (1967) pp. 157–60; and Cot, *La Conciliation internationale* (1968) pp. 233–4. See also Chapter 10 above.
[128] Application 1994/63, 13 *Collections* p. 109.

respondent maintained that it did not intend to invoke the objection that domestic remedies had not been exhausted because the application was directed at Belgian legislation. The EComHR, therefore, decided that it did not have to examine whether the applicants should have seised the Belgian *Conseil d'Etat* before appealing to the Commission. In *Christian Müller* v. *Austria*,[129] the respondent expressly waived the rule of domestic remedies by submitting that it waived its right of contesting the admissibility of the application. The Commission noted the waiver of conditions of admissibility and declared the application admissible. More recently, in *Van der Musselle* v. *Belgium*, the express waiver of the rule at the proceedings was noted and the application declared admissible.[130] The IACHR has also stated that the requirement of exhaustion of domestic remedies could be waived, expressly or tacitly, because it was a means of defence, and that such waiver could be irrevocable.[131] In the case of human rights protection, it is rarely that an express waiver of the rule would be given before the proceedings, the usual form of such waiver being the renunciation of the right to raise an objection to admissibility based on the rule.

Implied waiver

Because in the area of human rights protection international organs such as the EComHR have the power to investigate *ex officio* or *proprio motu* whether the rule of exhaustion of local remedies has been satisfied, the problem of the effect of a failure on the part of the respondent state to raise the objection that local remedies have not been exhausted is somewhat more complex. While the objection may not be raised, the Commission may take up the issue *ex officio*. Thus, the initial failure of the respondent state to raise the objection may not be fatal. On the other hand, once the issue is raised by the Commission, if the respondent state refuses to take up the case that domestic remedies have not been exhausted when it is requested to do so by the Commission, it is deemed to have waived the benefit of the rule. Thus, where in a case in which the Commission raised the issue of domestic remedies, the Belgian government consistently maintained throughout the oral

---

[129] Application 5849/72, *Report of the Commission* at pp. 120ff.
[130] Application 8919/80, 24 YBECHR p. 360.
[131] *Viviano Gallardo Case*, No. G/181, IACHR Series A at p. 88 (1981); the *Velasquez Rodriguez Case*, Decision No. 1, IACHR Series C at p. 77 (1987); the *Fairen Garbi and Solis Corrales Case*, Decision No. 2, IACHR Series C at pp. 82ff. (1987) and the *Godinez Cruz Case*, Decision No. 3, IACHR Series C at pp. 75ff. (1987).

hearing that it did not intend to rely on the rule of domestic remedies, because the application was directed not against a ministerial decision but against legislation as such. The Commission found that the respondent government had waived its right to rely on the rule and, therefore, that the Commission did not have to examine whether the applicants should have had resort to the Belgian *Conseil d'Etat* before seizing the Commission.[132] But the practice of the Commission has not been consistent. In *X* v. *Austria*, for instance, where the respondent government had objected to the failure of the applicant to resort to certain remedies, the Commission found the application inadmissible, while noting that the applicant should have resorted to a remedy which had not been referred to by the respondent government as being exhaustible.[133] It is, thus, not entirely clear how far the doctrine of implied waiver as a result of the failure of the respondent state to take up the objection based on domestic remedies is applicable, where an international organ must investigate *ex officio* whether the rule has been satisfied.

On the other hand, the practice of the ECtHR showed that, once the issue of exhaustion of domestic remedies had not been raised or dealt with before the EComHR, the issue could not be raised before the ECtHR. The ECtHR also explained that it was not for it (or the EComHR) to identify *ex officio* additional remedies to exhaust[134] or to cure of their own motion any want of precision or shortcomings in the respondent state's submissions.[135]

Estoppel and good faith

Estoppel in the narrow sense of the term, as used in the *Interhandel Case* and the *ELSI Case*, could apply to the application of the rule in human rights protection. There is no reason why it should not.[136]

---

[132] *57 Inhabitants of Louvain and Environs* v. *Belgium*, Application 1994/63, 13 *Collections* at p. 109.

[133] Application 2547/65, 20 *Collections* at pp. 80ff. The Court has more recently resorted to the concept of waiver (or estoppel), where the objection relating to domestic remedies has not been raised in time: see *Hasan* v. *Bulgaria*, Judgment of 26 October 2000, 40 ILM at p. 20.

[134] *Deweer* v. *Belgium*, ECHR Series A No. 35 (1980); *Foti* v. *Italy*, ECHR Series A No. 56 (1982); and *De Jong and van der Brink* v. *The Netherlands*, ECHR Series A No. 77 (1984).

[135] *Bozano* v. *France*, ECHR Series A No. 111 (1986).

[136] For the use of the term in these cases, see Chapter 10 above. There are human rights cases in which the term 'estoppel' or its variants has been used but these cases do not deal with estoppel in the narrow sense. They are concerned rather with implied

The HRC has in effect conceded that the respondent state could be estopped from relying on the application of the rule, when it held in *Y.L.* v. *Canada*[137] that the fact that the victim had not been advised that he could have resorted to judicial review was not relevant to the issue of whether his claim was subject to judicial control and supervision. That the question was one of estoppel proper, in that what was being faulted was the conduct of the state which led to the victim's actions in regard to remedies, is apparent from the circumstances alleged to have led to the non-exhaustion of remedies. Further, the dissenting members of the HRC took the view that the respondent was estopped as a result of its conduct from asserting that domestic remedies had not been exhausted.[138] However, the HRC has held that, where the victim has 'already been given to understand that there was no further remedy', the respondent could not claim that remedies had not been exhausted.[139]

While the general principles relevant to estoppel as referred to by the ICJ in the *Interhandel* and *ELSI* cases are applicable to human rights protection and there is no reason to conclude that the principles applicable are different, it has yet to be seen whether the human rights organs would take a different view of the application of those principles in relation to the particular circumstances that prevailed in those two cases. There is no reason to suppose that they would not or should not. The two ICJ cases dealt with circumstances in which it was evident that according to general principles there could not be an estoppel.[140]

The burden of proof

Questions relating to the burden of proof in the application of the rule of domestic remedies have arisen in connection with the implementation

---

waiver: see e.g. *Granger* v. *UK*, ECHR Series A No. 174 (1990); *Bozano* v. *France*, ECHR Series A No. 111 (1986); *De Jong, Baljet and van der Brink* v. *Netherlands*, ECHR Series A No. 77 (1984); and *Ciulla*, v. *Italy*, ECHR Series A No. 148.

[137] Doc. A/41/40, p. 145.   [138] *Ibid.*, p. 150.

[139] *Mahonen*, Communication No. 89/1981.

[140] Cançado Trindade takes issue with this approach: see note 7 above, at p. 630. However, there is no evidence that the human rights organs have rejected, after addressing, such general principles. Clearly, as was demonstrated in *Y.L.* v. *Canada*, decided by the HRC and discussed above, there can be disagreement on the application to the facts of the principle of estoppel. Cançado Trindade, note 7 above, at p. 630, asserts that, if facts similar to those in the *ELSI Case* came before the ECtHR in connection with a human rights violation, the finding on estoppel would have been different. This conclusion is not only an assumption but does not affect the content of the principle of estoppel or the possibility that there may be disagreement among the judges on the application of the principle to facts or on the findings of fact.

of the protection of human rights, particularly in the practice of the European Convention on Human Rights, of the IACHR and of the HRC. The general practice is significant in that it has evolved pragmatically. A brief survey is provided here.

The European Convention on Human Rights

Because Article 26 of the old European Convention on Human Rights referred to the 'generally recognized rules of international law' (see now Article 35(1) of the new Convention) and, as has been pointed out in Chapter 3, this has been interpreted to cover only the material content of the rule of local remedies,[141] it may possibly be inferred that the generally recognized rules of international law relating to the burden of proof in the application of the rule of domestic remedies would be applicable in the area of human rights protection, on the assumption that the burden of proof pertains to the material content of the rule. This approach has not been totally rejected by the ECtHR, where in *Johnston and Others*[142] the Court held that the respondent in a case filed by an individual must show with sufficient certainty the existence of remedies which should have been exhausted. Although the Court did not refer to the shift in the burden of proof thereafter, because the respondent had failed to discharge its burden of proof, there is no reason to suppose that the Court was not in agreement with the practice in the law of diplomatic protection. The same approach had earlier been taken in *Foti and Others*,[143] where the Court held that the application was admissible because the respondent had failed to establish the availability of remedies which had not been utilized.

The importance of these cases cannot be underestimated, because attempts have been made to show that at one time, under the Rules of Procedure of the EComHR, the Commission took the view that, at least in cases filed by individuals, the applicant bore the entire burden of demonstrating that he had exhausted all remedies available to him.[144]

---

[141] See e.g. the view taken by the ECtHR in *Austria v. Italy*, Application 788/60, 7 *Collections* at p. 62.

[142] Case No. 6/1985/92/139, *Report*.

[143] 25 YBECHR p. 32 (1982). See also the argument of the EComHR in the *Vagrancy Cases*, ECHR; Series B, *Pleadings, Oral Arguments and Documents* at p. 293 (1969–71).

[144] See especially Wiebringhaus, note 28 above, at pp. 688–9; Cançado Trindade, note 37 above, at pp. 143–5. Rolin, in discussing the burden of proof, had also indirectly adverted to the tendency of the Commission to limit itself to evidence adduced by the claimant: 'Le Rôle de requérant dans la procédure prévue par la Convention européenne des droits de l'homme', 9 RHDI (1956) at pp. 9–11.

It is to be noted that Rule 41(2), adopted in 1955,[145] referred to the duty of the applicant to show that all domestic remedies had been exhausted. This formulation, while expressly or implicitly placing upon the applicant the burden of showing that he had exhausted all remedies, or that available remedies were ineffective, was not necessarily inconsistent with a duty being placed upon the respondent to show that there were remedies available which had not been exhausted. However, most of the cases which came before the EComHR which implemented this rule were equivocal, even if they did not openly contradict a division of the burden of proof. They held that the applications were inadmissible because the applicants had failed to demonstrate either that they had no remedy or remedies open and available to them, or that there were circumstances relieving them of that obligation to exhaust remedies according to the generally recognized principles of international law.[146] On the other hand, there is at least one case, filed by a state, in which the Commission held that the respondent must first establish that there existed remedies which had not been exhausted. In *Greece* v. *UK*, the EComHR held that 'it is the duty of the government claiming that domestic remedies had not been exhausted to demonstrate the existence of such remedies'.[147] It could very well be that in the other cases referred to above the Commission felt that it was patently clear that these were remedies ostensibly available, so that there was no need for the respondent to prove that this was so.

Whatever the correct position at the time, it was realized that Rule 41(2) may have been improperly drafted,[148] because it was amended in 1960 so as to require the applicant to provide information which would enable it 'to be shown that the conditions laid down in Article 26 of

---

[145] 1 YBECHR at p. 74.
[146] See e.g. X v. *Federal Republic of Germany*, Application 232/56, 1 YBECHR at p. 144; Application 307/57, cited in Wiebringhaus, note 28 above, at p. 688; X v. *Federal Republic of Germany*, Application 222/56, 2 YBECHR at p. 351.
[147] Application 299/57, 2 YBECHR at pp. 190–2.
[148] Writers have criticized what they believe to be the earlier practice of the European Commission: see e.g. Monconduit, note 46 above, at p. 318; Nay-Cadoux, note 36 above, at p. 88; Eissen, 'Le Nouveau règlement intérieur de la Commission européenne des droits de l'homme', 6 AFDI (1960) at pp. 774–5 and 783–6; Antonopoulos, *La Jurisprudence des organes de la Convention européenne des droits de l'homme* (1967) p. 68; Grillo Pasquarelli, 'The Question of the Exhaustion of Domestic Remedies in the Context of the Examination of Admissibility of an Application to the European Commission of Human Rights', in Robertson (ed.), *Privacy and Human Rights* (1973) p. 335; Cançado Trindade, note 37 above, at p. 144.

the Convention have been satisfied'.[149] Following the amendment, the Commission followed its earlier decision in *Greece* v. *UK* by holding in another inter-state case, *Austria* v. *Italy*, that:

According to the generally recognized rules of international law to which Article 26 of the Convention refers, it is incumbent on the respondent government, to prove the existence in their municipal legal system, of remedies which have not been exercised.[150]

The Commission thus reaffirmed the burden lying upon the respondent. At the same time, the Commission confirmed that, once the respondent had discharged its burden, the burden shifted to the applicant to show in the particular circumstances that 'this remedy was unlikely to be effective and adequate in regard to the grievance in question'.[151] The same principles relating to the burden of proof were applied in *Alam and Khan*, a case brought by an individual. The Commission said that

according to the generally recognized rules of international law to which Article 26 refers, it is incumbent upon the respondent government, if they raise the objection of non-exhaustion, to prove the existence in their municipal legal system of a remedy which has not been exhausted.[152]

There are other cases brought by individuals in which the same approach was taken by the Commission.[153] Even in cases brought by individuals it was never disputed that in any case the applicant shared the burden of proof, once the respondent had proved that local remedies existed.

The burden of proof is of importance in cases in which it is alleged that legislative measures and administrative practices exist which are a violation of the European Convention. It will be recalled that under the Convention the existence of such measures or practices results in an exception to the applicability of the rule of local remedies. Clearly, the existence of such measures or practices, which the applicant claims renders the rule inapplicable, is subject to proof by the applicant, but in the jurisprudence of the European Commission the question has arisen of whether, for the exception to succeed, there must be substantial proof of the existence of such measures, or whether *prima facie* evidence is sufficient. In *Ireland* v. *UK*, it was held that, because the applicant state had

---

[149] 3 YBECHR at p. 24.
[150] Application 788/60, 7 *Collections* at p. 62.   [151] *Ibid.*, pp. 63–4.
[152] Application 2991/66, 24 *Collections* at p. 133. The objection was joined to the merits in this case.
[153] See e.g. *X* v. *Belgium*, Application 1727/62, 6 YBECHR at p. 398; *23 Inhabitants of Alsemberg and of Beersel* v. *Belgium*, Application 1474/62, 12 *Collections* at p. 25.

failed to produce substantial evidence to show that an administrative practice existed, the application was inadmissible insofar as it related to that administrative practice, on the ground that domestic remedies had not been exhausted in regard to the alleged violation of the Convention.[154] In *Donnelly and Others* v. *UK*, however, which was a case brought by individuals, it was held that *prima facie* evidence in support of an administrative practice violating the Convention was sufficient to render the application admissible on the basis that the domestic remedies rule was inapplicable.[155] The former case was brought by the state, while the latter application was filed by individuals. But it is difficult rationally to explain on this basis the difference in the Commission's rulings on the burden of proof. It is suggested that, in accordance with the theory that there is only a *prima facie* distribution of the burden of proof, where legislative or administrative practice is adduced as a reason for the absence of the duty to exhaust domestic remedies, *prima facie* evidence of such facts should suffice to shift the burden of proof to the respondent.

A further problem apparently arose in the jurisprudence of the European Commission when the applicant was in detention. The problem has also been raised by text writers.[156] The question was whether because a person had been detained, the burden of proof borne by an applicant to show that remedies were not effective was affected, once it had been shown by the respondent that remedies were available. The Commission seems to have taken the view that, even when a person was detained, he must bear the burden of proving that he had been deprived of access to remedies, or that the remedies available were ineffective,[157] but that the circumstances of detention may affect the amount of evidence required to prove these facts.[158] It is not entirely clear that the *burden of proof* to show that remedies were effective or accessible shifted to the respondent.

The American Convention on Human Rights

The IACHR has taken a slightly different approach to the burden of proof. While conceding that the burden of proof is determined according

---

[154] Application 5310/70, 41 *Collections* at p. 85.
[155] Applications 5577/72–5583/72, 43 *Collections* at p. 148. See also the discussion in *Denmark, Norway, Sweden and the Netherlands* v. *Greece*, Applications 3321/67–3323/67 and 3344/67, 11 YBECHR at pp. 770–8.
[156] See Cançado Trindade, note 37 above, at pp. 158–61.
[157] See *X* v. *Federal Republic of Germany*, Application 4065/69, 35 *Collections* at p. 120; *Kornmann* v. *Federal Republic of Germany*, Application 2004/63, 20 *Collections* at p. 53.
[158] See *Kornmann* v. *Federal Republic of Germany*, Application 2686/65, 22 *Collections* at p. 53.

to generally recognized principles of international law, the Court held in *Velasquez Rodriguez* that 'the State claiming non-exhaustion has an obligation to prove that domestic remedies remain to be exhausted and that they are effective'.[159] The Court placed the burden of proving that the remedies were effective on the respondent rather than have the applicant prove that the remedies were ineffective. In the case itself and in others like it, the exception of non-exhaustion of remedies was joined to the merits, because the alleged failure to provide judicial remedies was also a direct violation of the American Convention.

The approach of this Court to the burden of proof contrasts with the law of diplomatic protection. It must, therefore, be regarded as different and based on a desire to help the individual. It is not the same as the approach taken under the European Convention.

The Human Rights Committee

Early in its history the HRC took a position on the basic approach to the burden of proof. It generally accepted that the respondent state must at least provide evidence that the applicant had remedies available to him which he had not exhausted.[160] However, the Committee also consistently, since its inception, took the view that the respondent state must not only give details of the remedies which it submits have been available to the applicant in the circumstances of his case, but also provide 'evidence that there would be a reasonable prospect that such

---

[159] Series C, Decision No. 1 at p. 77 (1987). See also *Fairen Garbi and Solis Corrales*, Series C, Decision No. 2 at pp. 82ff. (1987); and *Godinez Cruz*, Series C, Decision No. 3 at pp. 75ff. (1987). See also the judgments on the merits in these cases: Series C, Decision Nos. 4, 5 and 6 (1988–9). The distribution of the burden of proof in such a way as to place a heavier burden on the respondent state was affirmed by the IACHR in Advisory Opinion OC-11/90, para. 41. The distribution of the proof under the American Convention has been described as follows:

> The petitioner must show that a good faith effort was made to exhaust domestic remedies when filing a petition with the Commission. This includes presenting specific information as to how, where and when the petitioner sought a remedy at the domestic level and failed to obtain redress. At this point, if the state so chooses, it may argue that the petitioner has failed to meet his or her burden; that is, that there remain remedies to be exhausted. The state may meet its burden by explaining *which* remedies might have been exhausted, and *how* that ought to have been accomplished. The state must essentially show that domestic remedies were available, adequate and effective: Vivanco and Bhansali, note 72 above, at p. 429.

[160] See e.g. Communication No. 1/1976, HRC *Selected Decisions* at p. 18; Communication No. 5/1997, HRC *Selected Decisions* at p. 41; and Communication No. 8/1977, HRC *Selected Decisions* at p. 48.

remedies would be effective'.[161] Then the applicant must show that he has exhausted any allegedly available remedies, or that the remedies were ineffective or inaccessible, or that there were other circumstances absolving him from exhausting them.[162]

These views of the HRC on the burden of proof seem, as in the case of the IACHR, to contrast with the law of diplomatic protection. They are based evidently on the desire to give more assistance to the individual in making his case.

Matters connected with procedure

The time at which remedies must be exhausted

It may be important to determine at what point in time domestic remedies must be exhausted. The issue is whether the exhaustion of domestic remedies must be completed before the date of filing of the application with the international organ, or whether the critical date may occur later.

In general, the critical date would not be so crucial, because even if it has not occurred at the appropriate time, it is possible for another action to be filed after that date occurs, as the effect of dismissal of the action on the ground that it is inadmissible for failure to exhaust domestic remedies is not to render the matter *res judicata*. But sometimes in the law of human rights protection it may matter what date is chosen as the critical date, *inter alia*, because a second application may be excluded by operation of the six-months rule.

The ECtHR has faced the problem in the law of human rights protection. The Court took the view in *Ringeisen v. Austria*[163] that, provided the applicant had resorted to domestic remedies before he filed his application with the EComHR, it did not matter that he had not received a decision with final effect from the last court before the date of filing the application, although it was necessary for such a decision to have been

---

[161] E.g. Communication No. 4/1977, HRC *Selected Decisions* at p. 4. See also e.g. Communication No. 6/1977, HRC *Selected Decisions* at p. 53; Communication No. 10/1977, HRC *Selected Decisions* at p. 106; Communication No. 22/1977, HRC *Selected Decisions* at pp. 5–6; and Communication No. 29/1978, HRC *Selected Decisions* at p. 11. See also *C.F.*, Communication No. 118/1981, paras. 6.2 and 10.1; and *S.H.B. v. Canada*, Communication No. 192/1985.

[162] See e.g. *T.K. v. France*, Doc. A/45/40, Appendix, para. 8.2. The position taken by the HRC on the burden of proof is not entirely clear: McGoldrick, note 2 above, at p. 189.

[163] ECHR Series A No. 13 (1971).

given by the time the Commission was called upon to pronounce on the admissibility of the application. Whether because of the existence of the six-months rule, or because of the formal nature of the issue or for some other policy reason, the ECtHR agreed that 'there was a need for flexibility in the application of the rule'.[164]

The time for raising the objection

Generally speaking, the human rights instruments, as has been seen, merely state in effect that the international organ should deal with the matter after all domestic remedies have been exhausted. They do not advert to the procedure of raising an objection founded on the rule of domestic remedies. Thus, there is no fixed time limit in these instruments for the submission of such an objection.

In practice, however, some time limits do operate. The fact that international organs concerned with human rights violations have assumed the role of raising *ex officio* the issue of domestic remedies, even if the defendant has not raised it, means that any normal time limit may be superseded by the decision of the organ concerned to raise the issue, which theoretically it may do at any stage in the proceedings. But apart from this, these organs have established a procedure under their rules for the raising of objections based on the rule of domestic remedies which involves certain time limits, although these happen to be fairly extended.

According to the Rules of Procedure formulated under the European Commission of Human Rights, for instance, in an inter-state case brought before the EComHR, the President of the Commission notified the defendant through the proper channels of the application and invited observations on its admissibility. In the case of an individual application under Article 25 of the old European Convention, the rapporteur appointed by the President of the Commission to examine the application must report on its admissibility to the Commission, but might in doing so request information from the applicant or the defendant state. On the basis of this report, the Commission might have at once declared the application inadmissible. It was possible that such a declaration of inadmissibility might occur after the defendant had been invited to make submissions on the exhaustion of domestic remedies and

---

[164] ECHR Series A No. 13 at p. 37 (1971). Judge Verdross was unable to agree with the Court on the critical dates: *ibid.*, at p. 49. For comments on this case, see Cançado Trindade, note 37 above, at pp. 214ff. For a similar approach by the HRC, see *Pietroroia v. Uruguay*, Doc. A/36/40, p. 153.

the applicant had had a chance of replying. But, if such a declaration had not been made, the Commission could request further information from the parties, including written observations. At this point an adversarial procedure was followed, and an oral hearing could be held to hear further observations before a decision was taken on the admissibility of the application. During this whole procedure, time limits were fixed by the rapporteur. But an oral hearing was at the discretion of the Commission. However, generally no decision was taken on admissibility without an oral hearing.

It would seem that time limits for the raising of the objection based on the rule of domestic remedies were to some extent flexible under the European Convention. There was apparently no fixed time limit for the submission of such an objection, provided it was made in the course of the examination of admissibility.[165] Clearly, the objection must be raised at some point during the admissibility stage in accordance with the general principle that all points must be pleaded at the proper time.[166]

In several cases, the objection based on the domestic remedies rule was accepted, although it was only raised at the oral hearings.[167] The Commission, thus, held that there was no requirement that a preliminary objection such as this one should be raised at the stage of the written proceedings, it being possible for the objection to be raised later at the oral hearings. While in practice the objection was raised in the written proceedings,[168] whether or not it was also raised in the oral proceedings,[169] the fact that the defendant could delay the raising of the objection until the stage of the oral hearings shows that the approach of the European Commission favoured the applicant.[170]

The time of decision on the objection

In the case of human rights protection, there are generally several grounds of inadmissibility listed in the relevant jurisdictional

---

[165] See Grillo Pasquarelli, note 148 above, at p 336. See now on this subject in respect of the EComHR, van Dijk and van Hoof, note 50 above, at pp. 149–50.

[166] Morrison, *The Developing European Law of Human Rights* (1967) p. 86.

[167] See e.g. *Retimag* v. *Federal Republic of Germany*, Application 712/60, 8 *Collections* at pp. 36–7; and *Boeckmans* v. *Belgium*, Application 1727/62, 12 *Collections* at p. 45.

[168] See *57 Inhabitants of Louvain* v. *Belgium*, Application 1994/63, 13 *Collections* at pp. 108–9.

[169] See *23 Inhabitants of Alsemberg and of Beersel* v. *Belgium*, Application 1474/62, 11 *Collections* at p. 55.

[170] There is here noticeably a greater inclination to help the applicant than in the law of diplomatic protection.

instruments, including the non-exhaustion of domestic remedies.[171] The question in connection with the protection of human rights is whether there is any order of priority that applies to the disposition of objections, it being generally recognized that preliminary objections, such as that based on the non-exhaustion of domestic remedies, should in any case be disposed of prior to the judgment on the merits.

The conventions and the rules of procedure of the relevant organs do not generally deal with this question of priority, nor does the jurisprudence of these organs show any clear pattern, although suggestions have been made by text writers on how such priority may be established.[172] The conclusion to be drawn is that in the practice of organs enforcing human rights law there is considerable latitude in the treatment of the order in which preliminary objections may be decided, while the principle that objections based on the rule of domestic remedies should generally be decided before the merits are adjudicated upon has been respected.

Joinder to the merits

It has been the practice in the law of human rights protection as in the law of diplomatic protection for international tribunals and organs sometimes to join an objection based on the non-exhaustion of domestic remedies to the merits of the case. Organs enforcing human rights instruments have easily adopted the practice of joining to the merits an objection based on the domestic remedies rule. Here, as in the law of diplomatic protection, the power of joinder is discretionary and is exercised on grounds which are in principle no different from those that prevail in the law of diplomatic protection. In the case of human rights protection, joinder has generally been adopted where, while the defendant objects that domestic remedies have not been exhausted, or the issue is raised *ex officio* by the international organ, the substantive question is also raised of whether a protected human right invoking the duty of the defendant state to provide impartial remedies and due

---

[171] See e.g. Article 27 of the old European Convention on Human Rights (Article 35 of the new Convention); and Articles 46 and 47 of the American Convention on Human Rights.

[172] Fawcett, *The Application of the European Convention on Human Rights* (1969) p. 313; and Robertson, 'The European Convention on Human Rights and the Rule of Exhaustion of Domestic Remedies', 4 RDH (1974) at p. 202. The relationship between the objection based on the rule of local remedies and other objections was adverted to in *Donnelly and Others* v. *UK*, European Commission of Human Rights, COE Doc. 43.662-06.2 at p. 83 (1975).

process has been violated, so that the two issues depend on interrelated matters.

There are certainly cases in which the EComHR disposed at an early stage of the objection based on the rule of domestic remedies without joining it to the merits.[173] However, there are numerous examples of joinder of such an objection to the merits. In *Ireland* v. *UK*, the Commission joined to the merits the objection based on the rule of domestic remedies in circumstances in which the issue was raised of whether the rule was applicable because an administrative practice existed which was alleged to be in violation of the substantive provisions of the European Convention.[174] In *Austria* v. *Italy*, the Commission also asserted its power to join to the merits an objection based on the domestic remedies rule.[175]

The reasons for joinder vary from case to case, but all depend on a close relationship between the substance of the objection and the merits of the case. For example, in *Greece* v. *UK*, the Commission said that inquiry into allegations that domestic remedies had not been exhausted related to the merits of the case and could not be undertaken before argument on the merits had been heard.[176] In *Alam and Khan* v. *UK*, the Commission stated more extensively that:

> The question whether there was in English law an effective remedy against the refusal of the immigration authorities to allow the entry of Mohamed Alam into the United Kingdom is in the circumstances of the present case closely linked with the question arising under Article 6(1) whether or not the applicants had access to an independent and impartial tribunal for the determination of their right to respect for family life; . . . in these circumstances the Commission finds that the issue under Article 26 cannot be decided without an examination of questions which concern the merits of the applicants' complaint.[177]

In Donnelly and Others v. *UK*, the Commission explained that:

> In the present case, the question of the effectiveness of the remedies available to the applicants is, for the reasons set out above, closely linked with the alleged existence of an administrative practice in breach of Article 3. In these

---

[173] See e.g. *Lawless* v. *Ireland*, Application 332/57, 2 YBECHR at pp. 330, 334 and 340; *Denmark, Norway and Sweden* v. *Greece*, Application 4448/70, 34 *Collections* at p. 69; and *Svenska Lotsförbundet* v. *Sweden*, Application 4475/70, 38 *Collections* at p. 76. The same has happened in the IAComHR.

[174] Application 5310/71, 41 *Collections* at pp. 87ff.

[175] Application 788/60, *Report of the Plenary Commission* (1963) at pp. 64ff.

[176] Application 299/57, 2 YBECHR at pp. 190ff.

[177] Application 2991/66, 10 YBECHR at pp. 504ff.

circumstances, the Commission finds that the issue under Article 26 cannot be examined without an examination of questions which concern the merits of the applicants' complaint concerning the alleged administrative practice. The Commission has already found that the determination of the part of the application relating to such administrative practice should depend upon an examination of the merits. Accordingly, the Commission finds it appropriate to join to the merits the issue under Article 26 of the Convention relating to the applicants' allegations that each of them was a victim of specific acts in breach of Article 3.[178]

In *Velasquez Rodriguez*, the IACHR, in joining to the merits an objection based on the rule of domestic remedies, referred to the relationship of the substance of the objection to the substantive allegation that the absence of remedies had resulted in a violation of the American Convention on Human Rights, while at the same time giving other pertinent reasons:

Thus, when certain exceptions to the rule of non-exhaustion of domestic remedies are invoked, such as the ineffectiveness of such remedies or the lack of due process of law, not only is it contended that the victim is under no obligation to pursue such remedies, but, indirectly, the State in question is also charged with a new violation. Thus, the question of domestic remedies is closely tied to the merits of the case . . . Of course, when the State interposes this objection in timely fashion it should be heard and resolved. However, the relationship between the decision regarding applicability of the rule and the need for timely international action in the absence of effective domestic remedies may frequently recommend the hearing of questions relating to that rule together with the merits, in order to prevent unnecessary delays due to preliminary objections . . . In such cases, given the interplay between the problem of domestic remedies and the very violation of human rights, the question of their prior exhaustion must be taken up together with the merits of the case . . .

If the Court, then, were to sustain the Government's objection and declare that effective judicial remedies are available, it would be prejudging the merits without having heard the evidence and arguments of the Commission or those of the Government. If, on the other hand, the Court were to declare that all effective domestic remedies had been exhausted or did not exist, it would be prejudging the merits in a manner detrimental to the State. The issues relating to the exhaustion and effectiveness of the domestic remedies applicable to the instant case must, therefore, be resolved together with the merits.[179]

---

[178] Application 5577/72–5583/72, 43 *Collections* at p. 148. See for joinder to the merits by the HRC, *Fals Borda* v. *Colombia*, Doc. A/37/40, p. 193, para. 7.2.

[179] IACHR, Series C, Decision No. 1 at pp. 79ff. (1987). As a matter of interest, the HRC has in its practice stated that it may reverse a decision finding non-exhaustion in the light of subsequent information: see *C.F. et al.*, Communication No. 118/1981, Doc. A/40/40, p. 217.

The six-months rule

Under some human rights instruments, there is a time limit for the submission of applications. For example, the old European Convention on Human Rights provided in Article 26 that an application to the EComHR is inadmissible, if it is not brought within six months from the date of the final domestic decision.[180]

In an early case,[181] the EComHR held that, where the injury, which was in that case a continuing one, had taken place before the entry into force of the Convention for the defendant state, the six-months period began to run not from the date of the first commission of the injury but from the date of the entry into force of the Convention for the defendant state and the acceptance by it of the right of individuals to apply to the Commission under Article 25 of the (old) Convention. As a result, the application in that case was held to have been filed in time.

There are many cases in which the EComHR has applied the principle that the *terminus a quo* for the running of the six-months period is the final decision in the last 'effective and sufficient' remedy. This prevents the applicant from resorting to remedies which are not effective and sufficient after such a final decision, with the result that the running of time may be delayed. In *X* v. *Federal Republic of Germany*, the Commission said that the remedies to be taken into account were:

Those which are capable of providing an effective and sufficient means of redressing the wrongs which are the subject of the international claim; . . . it is for the Commission itself to appreciate in the light of the particular facts of each case whether any given remedy at any given date appears to have offered to the applicant the possibility of an effective and sufficient remedy for the wrong of which he complains and, if not, to exclude it from consideration in applying the six-months time limit in Article 26.[182]

In *X* v. *UK*,[183] the Commission held that the final decision to be considered for the running of the six-months period was the decision in the applicant's unsuccessful appeal to the Court of Criminal Appeal and not

---

[180] Now see Article 35(1) of the new European Convention. See Article 46(1)(b) of the American Convention. See also Application 15213/89, *M* v. *Belgium*, 71 D&R (1991) at p. 234, for the reason for the rule which relates to the premise that the longer the delay the more difficult the establishment of facts becomes.

[181] *De Becker* v. *Belgium*, Application 214/56, 2 YBECHR p. 236.

[182] Application 645/59, 7 *Collections* at pp. 4–5. See also *X* v. *Federal Republic of Germany*, Application 968/61, 8 *Collections* at p. 27.

[183] Application 3505/68, 29 *Collections* at pp. 62–3.

the subsequent refusal of an order of *habeas corpus* which occurred as a result of the applicant's resort to this remedy. As a result the application was found to have been filed out of time. There are several other cases in which the Commission had to determine, for the purposes of the running of time, which decision was the final decision on the basis of effectiveness or the absence of it.[184]

In many cases, the Commission was faced with the problem of reopening a case for retrial. In *Nielsen v. Denmark*,[185] for instance, the Commission held that the decision of the Special Court of Revision of Denmark given after the decision of the Danish Supreme Court was the *terminus a quo* for the running of time because the remedy before the Special Court of Revision offered the applicant an opportunity of an effective and efficient means of redress. On the other hand, in the later case of *X v. Denmark*,[186] the Commission held that recourse to the Special Court of Revision did not in the applicant's particular case afford an effective and sufficient remedy and the decision of that court could not, therefore, be considered in determining the point from which the six-months period began to run. In circumstances such as these, the Commission has consistently applied the test of effectiveness of the domestic remedies concerned in determining whether they could be considered as the *terminus a quo* for the running of time.[187]

The continuing situation has also been the focus of attention in connection with the determination of the *terminus a quo* for the application

---

[184] See e.g. *X v. Belgium*, Application 512/59, 1 *Collections* p. 4; *X v. Federal Republic of Germany*, Application 1216/61, 11 *Collections* p. 5; *X v. Federal Republic of Germany*, Application 2694/65, 23 *Collections* p. 97; *X v. Sweden*, Application 3893/68, 33 *Collections* p. 10; *X v. Austria*, Application 3972/69, 37 *Collections* at pp. 19–20; *X v. Sweden*, Application 4475/70, 42 *Collections* p. 13; and *X v. Austria*, Application 5560/72, 45 *Collections* p. 64. In cases where there is no remedy, for example, the running of time would commence from the time at which the applicant was actually affected. The time limit cannot be deferred, for example, by lodging a request for pardon, applying to an incompetent organ or asking for the reopening of the case: see e.g. the *Christians Against Racism and Fascism Case*, Application 8440/78, 21 D&R (1981), at p. 147; *X v. Sweden*, Application 10230/82, 32 D&R (1983) p. 303; and *Altern v. Federal Republic of Germany*, Application 10380/83, 36 D&R (1984) p. 209.

[185] Application 343/57, *Report of the Commission* at pp. 32–9.

[186] Application 4311/69, 37 *Collections* at p. 96.

[187] See e.g. *X v. Federal Republic of Germany*, Application 918/60, 7 *Collections* p. 110; *X v. Sweden*, Application 1739/62, 13 *Collections* p. 102; and *X v. Austria*, Application 3591/68, 31 *Collections* p. 46. On the exact *terminus a quo* which may vary given the particular circumstances of the case, see e.g. *Bozano v. Italy*, Application 9991/82, 39 D&R (1984) p. 147; the *Aarts Case*, Application 14056/88, 70 D&R (1991) p. 208; *X v. France*, Application 9908/82, 32 D&R (1983) p. 266; and *C v. Italy*, Application 10899/84, 31 YBECHR (1988) at p. 37.

of the six-months rule. The Commission took the view that restrictive provisions such as those which imposed a time limit on the filing of applications could not be interpreted broadly.[188] In *De Becker* v. *Belgium*, where the applicant was complaining of a continuing state of affairs which was infringing his rights, the Commission said:

when the Commission receives an application concerning a legal provision which involves a permanent state of affairs for which there is no domestic remedy, the problem of the six months' period specified in Article 26 can arise only after this state of affairs has ceased to exist; . . . in the circumstances, it is exactly as though the alleged violation was being repeated daily, thus preventing the running of the six months' period.[189]

As a result of this approach, the Commission has held that, in a continuing situation, where the applicant had no domestic remedy to which he might resort, the six-months rule was not *exactly* applicable.[190]

There were circumstances in which the Commission did not reject the objection based on non-exhaustion of domestic remedies by reference to the six-months rule. Although rejection of such an objection was not automatic, it was only good for the reasons that the Commission upheld. In *X* v. *Austria*,[191] the applicant contended that the delay in filing was due to his ill-health and morale during the period at issue. The Commission found that the applicant had not produced evidence to support these contentions and therefore had not filed his application within the required six-months period.

The Commission on occasion examined the question of whether the running of time under the six-months rule could be interrupted or suspended as such. There were cases in which the Commission proceeded on the basis that the running of time may be suspended or interrupted and examined the question of whether there were any justifying circumstances.[192] More recently, the EComHR and the ECtHR have absolved the

---

[188] See *De Becker* v. *Belgium*, Application 214/56, 2 YBECHR at p. 238.

[189] Application 214/56, 2 YBECHR at p. 238. See now *Agrotexim Helles SA* v. *Greece*, 14807/89, 35 YBECHR (1992) at p. 46; and van Dijk and van Hoof, note 50 above, at pp. 160–2.

[190] See e.g. *23 Inhabitants of Alsemberg and of Beersel* v. *Belgium*, Application 1474/62, 11 *Collections* at pp. 57–8, *Denmark, Norway, Sweden and the Netherlands* v. *Greece*, Applications 3321/67, 3322/67 and 3344/67, 11 YBECHR at p. 778; *Huber* v. *Austria*, Application 4517/70, 38 *Collections* at p. 113; and *X* v. *Federal Republic of Germany*, Application 6181/73, 43 *Collections* at p. 196.

[191] Application 6317/73, 2 D&R at pp. 87–8.

[192] See e.g. *X* v. *Belgium*, Application 613/59, 3 *Collections* p. 2; *X* v. *Sweden*, Application 3071/67, 26 *Collections* p. 76; and *X* v. *Federal Republic of Germany*, Application 4149/69, 36 *Collections* p. 67. Recently, the Court held that the filing of a letter could effectively be the *terminus ad quem*: *Buscarini* v. *San Marino*, Judgment of 28 July 1999, 38 ILM at p. 742.

applicant from observing the six-months rule because of special circumstances.[193]

The Commission in many cases determined the final decision from which time began to run. Thus, in *Krzycki v. Federal Republic of Germany*,[194] it was held to be the decision dismissing a claim for compensation, while in *X v. Norway*[195] the relevant decision, in criminal proceedings, was found to be the decision on the last appeal against conviction.

There is also the question of the *terminus ad quem* in relation to the six-months rule. The Commission has held that this is the date of filing of the pleading with the Secretary General of the Council of Europe.[196]

---

[193] See the *Toth Case*, Judgment of 12 December 1991, 34 YBECHR (1991) p. 258, ECHR Series A No. 224 at pp. 22–3.

[194] Application 7629/76, 9 D&R at pp. 175ff.

[195] Application 6930/75, 9 D&R at pp. 37ff.

[196] See *X v. Norway*, Application 1468/62, 12 *Collections* at pp. 104–5. The rule was derived from the Rules of Procedure of the European Commission. See on this aspect, van Dijk and van Hoof, note 50 above, at pp. 156ff.

14 The rule and international organizations

Exhaustion of local or internal remedies may also be discussed in regard to the relationship between states and international organizations (or between international organizations themselves) and in regard to the employment relationship between international organizations and their staff. International organizations are a comparatively recent phenomenon. Hence, the rule of local remedies, which has a much longer history than the life of international organizations, cannot be regarded as intrinsic to the law of international organizations. If the rule is to be applicable in any way in that area, it will be by analogy or on the basis that in specific situations it may be appropriate to apply the rule itself or a similar rule in a different form. What must be discussed then is how far the law of international organizations, in terms of its policies and objectives, requires that the rule of local or internal remedies or an analogous rule be applied to certain situations which arise in the functioning of such organizations. The position is somewhat complicated, because there seem to be no judicial decisions or agreed or accepted practice in the area of the relations between organizations and states. In the area of employment relations, on the other hand, the situation is different, as the relevant basic premises are distinct.

In the case of the relationship between states and international organizations, it is only since the international legal personality of such organizations was formally recognized in the *Reparation for Injuries Case*[1] that the question was seriously asked whether it was proper that the rule of local or internal remedies be applied in that area. The question arises both where the international organization is a claimant on behalf of an individual against a state and where a state claims on behalf of a

[1] 1949 ICJ Reports p. 174.

national or individual against an international organization. A third situation which has involved the exhaustion of internal remedies is where
a staff member brings a claim against an organization under the internal law of the organization[2] in regard to his employment relationship.
This situation concerns a relationship which is entirely internal to the
organization.

Claims by international organizations against states

Since the decision of the ICJ in the *Reparation for Injuries Case*,[3] it has
been established that international organizations such as the UN have
the capacity at international law to bring claims, particularly against
states in situations in which a right relating to a staff member and
vested in the organization has been violated. This followed the recognition of the international personality of the UN in the same case.[4] After
the decision in this case, it was suggested that the rule of local remedies
should be applied, apparently without qualification, to claims on behalf
of staff members, because it would save the UN much trouble and give
to the respondent state an opportunity to repair through its own means
the injury caused by it.[5] This view is based on the idea that the reason
for applying the rule of local remedies to the case of claims by international organizations against states is similar to that which underlies the
rule which applies in the case of the relations between aliens and host
states.

While in the proceedings before the ICJ in the *Reparation for Injuries
Case* counsel for the Secretary General of the UN merely stated that,
in the context of claims by the UN against states for injuries to its
officials, there was 'room for consideration' whether the rule of local
remedies was applicable,[6] in the memorandum of the Secretary General to the General Assembly of the UN, explaining what procedures

---

[2] On the nature of the law, see Amerasinghe, *The Law of the International Civil Service*
(1994), vol. 1, pp. 3ff.

[3] 1949 ICJ Reports p. 174.

[4] Prior to this case there had been some opposition to the recognition of the
international personality of an international organization: see Quadri, 'Cours général
de droit international public', 113 *Hague Recueil* (1964-III) at pp. 476ff.

[5] See Eagleton. 'International Organization and the Law of Responsibility', 76 *Hague
Recueil* (1950-I) at pp. 351ff.; Brownlie, *Principles of Public International Law* (1990) p. 504;
and Cançado Trindade, 'Exhaustion of Local Remedies and the Law of International
Organizations', 57 RI (1979) at pp. 82–3.

[6] *Reparation for Injuries Case*, ICJ Pleadings (1949) at p. 89.

should be taken pursuant to the case, no mention was made of the rule. Consequently, no reference is made to the rule in the resolution of the General Assembly dealing with the matter.[7] However, it has been submitted subsequently that, where a staff member of the organization has been threatened with a private nuisance, he should first have recourse to local remedies, no waiver of immunity being necessary because the acts are of a private character over which local courts would have jurisdiction in any case.[8] One author has suggested in this connection that after exhausting remedies a staff member of an international organization should be able to seek the protection of the organization which he serves rather than that of his national state, because of the primary allegiance which he owes to the organization.[9]

The matter has not been laid to rest in that there are several problems connected with the view that the rule of local remedies applies to claims by international organizations on behalf of their staff members. First, it must be recognized that in the *Reparation for Injuries Case* what the ICJ acknowledged was that as a result of the according of international personality to international organizations such as the UN, such organizations had the right to bring claims on behalf of their staff members for injuries suffered in the performance of their official functions. The ICJ said:

In order that the agent may perform his duties satisfactorily, he must feel that this protection is assured to him by the Organisation, and that he may count on it. To ensure the independence of the agent, and, consequently, the independent action of the Organisation itself, it is essential that in performing his duties he need not have to rely on any other protection than that of the Organisation (save of course for the more direct and immediate protection due from the State in whose territory he may be). In particular, he should not have to rely on the protection of his own State. If he had to rely on that State, his independence might well be compromised, contrary to the principle applied by Article 100 of the Charter. And lastly, it is essential that – whether the agent belongs to a powerful or to a weak State; to one more affected or less affected by the complications of international life; to one in sympathy or not in sympathy with the mission of the agent – he should know that in the performance of his duties he is under the protection of the Organisation.[10]

---

[7] See UN General Assembly Resolution 365 (IV) of 1 December 1949.

[8] Hardy, 'Claims by International Organizations in Respect of Injuries to their Agents', 37 BYIL (1961) at pp. 525ff.

[9] Grieg, *International Law* (1970) p. 626.   [10] 1949 ICJ Reports at p. 182.

The Court made a clear distinction between a staff member acting in his official capacity and the treatment of such a staff member in his personal capacity. As one writer has pointed out:

It seems to be implicit in the Court's view as stated above, that while an international official in no way ceases to owe allegiance to his own country in his personal capacity, in his official capacity and in the performance of his functions his first and only allegiance must be to his organization; and in case of conflict this must prevail. Similarly, an international official must, in his private life, conform to the laws and regulations of the country of his official residence; but in his official capacity his duty to the organization remains.[11]

It would seem, therefore, that, where a staff member is injured while performing his official duties, the organization would have the exclusive right of protection, while, where the injury takes place when he is in his private capacity or in his private life, his national state would have the right of protection. Although some may believe that it is undesirable that a staff member should have to rely on his national state for protection in his private life, if he is to be able to maintain his independence in the performance of his official duties, as the law now stands, the better view, in the light of the *Reparation for Injuries Case*, seems to be that the organization has the right of protection only where the staff member is acting in an official capacity.

Assuming that the correct position is that an international organization has a right of protection only where a staff member is acting in his official capacity, the next question is whether the rule of local remedies is applicable where the organization is a claimant against a state. In the situation envisaged, the ICJ made it clear that the organization was not subrogated to the rights of the staff member against the respondent state but was asserting its own right to have international law respected in respect of its staff members. The Court stated:

Only the party to whom an international obligation is due can bring a claim in respect of its breach. This is precisely what happens when the Organisation, in bringing a claim for damage suffered by its agent, does so by invoking the breach of an obligation towards itself . . . The question . . . presupposes that the injury for which the reparation is demanded arises from a breach of an obligation designed to help an agent of the Organisation in the performance of his duties. It is not a case in which the wrongful act or omission would merely

---

[11] Fitzmaurice, *The Law and Procedure of the International Court of Justice* (1986), vol. 1, p. 81.

constitute a breach of the general obligations of a State concerning the position of aliens; claims made under this head would be within the competence of the national State and not, as a general rule, within that of the Organisation.[12]

The reasoning of the Court has been explained as follows:

The Court's thinking is here very compressed. The problem evidently is to see why, in bringing a claim in respect of a breach of an international obligation due to itself, the organization should be able to do anything more than claim for the damage caused directly to itself, *qua* organization, and why it should be entitled also to make a claim on behalf of the agent personally. The national state of the injured party can do this because it is held itself to have suffered injury in the person of its national and because it has suffered a breach of the general obligation of states to one another under international law to afford certain treatment of aliens in their territory. Can an international organization equally be held to have suffered an injury in the person of its agent or servant, and if so, what is the international obligation owed to it the breach of which gives rise to this injury? This, as the Court said, must be something other than the general international law obligation to afford certain treatment to aliens. The answer appears to be . . . that the nature, functions, and requirements of an international organization normally make it necessary that its agents should be able to look to it (and not to any state, even their national state) for protection and for the preferment of personal claims on their behalf arising out of any wrong or injury done to them in the course of carrying out their duties on behalf of the organization. On the question of what was the obligation to the United Nations Organization the breach of which gave rise to a right to make such a claim, the Court found that a duty of affording protection to agents of the Organization in the performance of their functions arose as a general inference both from the Charter and certain related instruments, and from particular provisions . . . A breach of an obligation to the Organization being thus involved, the Organization was (as in the case of the national state of an injured party) invoking its own right in making the claim, even though the claim was in respect of personal damage to the agent or his dependents.[13]

The conclusion to be deduced is that the organization in protecting a staff member primarily asserts a right vested in itself to be able to achieve its objectives through its staff members. This is slightly different from the right a state asserts to have international law respected in the person of its nationals. The right which an organization has is more akin to that which a state has of protecting its diplomats or officials. In both cases, the claimant's right pertains to the achievement of some broad objective connected with its functions. The protection of the staff

---

[12] 1949 ICJ Reports at pp. 181–2.   [13] Fitzmaurice, note 11 above, vol. 1, pp. 86–7.

member, as with the protection of the diplomat or official, is inciden-
tal to the claim asserted on the basis of a direct interference with the
rights of the international organization. Thus, this is a situation which
must be likened to the direct injury caused a state and involving also
an injury to one of its nationals – a situation to which the rule of local
remedies is inapplicable. On this basis, then, the rule of local remedies
would in any case not be relevant to claims by international organizations in which they seek, among other things, to protect their staff
members.

If the view is taken that international organizations have the right to
protect their staff members against injuries incurred outside their official functions, the issue would arise of whether the rule of local remedies should apply to a claim by an international organization against a
state. In this regard, it may be argued that respect for the sovereignty
of the respondent state warrants the exhaustion of local remedies, since
the international organization is asserting what is, indeed, its right, but
a right only to protect its staff member, which may legitimately be compared to the right of a state to protect its nationals from injury by the
respondent state. In both cases, the sole object of the right is the protection of an individual. In both cases, the protection is from injury by
a state. Therefore, the same rationale based on respect for sovereignty
should result in the application of the rule to a claim brought by an
international organization as forms the basis for the application of the
rule in a claim brought by a state.

Claims against international organizations

The converse situation, where the international organization is the respondent in a case involving the protection of a national, raises different
problems. The question is whether, where the international organization
does provide internal means of settling disputes between such persons
and itself, they have an obligation to exhaust such remedies before their
national states may exercise diplomatic protection.

The view has been expressed that diplomatic protection *vis-à-vis* an
international organization is subject *mutatis mutandis* to the prior exhaustion of internal or local remedies. Thus, the explanation has been
given that, once the international personality of an international organization is recognized by a state, diplomatic action by that state in respect
of a national allegedly wronged by the organization can only take place
after the individual has exhausted the means of redress provided to him

by the organization.[14] It has been said that exhaustion of internal remedies is one of several possible alternative means of settlement before
diplomatic protection is exercised:

> S'agissant d'une organisation internationale dont l'appareil administratif et ju-
> diciaire est naturellement plus rudimentaire que celui d'un Etat; les instances
> 'internes' ne se dérouleront pas nécessairement à l'intérieur du système ju-
> ridique de l'organisation. La règle citée signifie en réalité que le réclamant de-
> vra user de toute procédure judiciaire, arbitrale ou administrative qui aboutit à
> statuer sur sa demande d'indemnité et à laquelle l'organisation internationale
> accepte de se soumettre. Ces voies de droit pourront être assurées soit par un
> organe judiciaire ou administratif de l'organisation, s'il en existe un qui soit
> compétent pour examiner une réclamation individuelle, . . .[15]

Other authors recognize that it may be difficult for organizations to
provide internal or local remedies for this purpose,[16] but offer other
means of settling disputes between organizations and individuals, even
though organizations may have procedural incapacity before international courts and tribunals.[17] It is significant that one author took the
view that the local remedies rule was inapplicable in such cases on the
ground that it was impracticable, if not impossible, for an organization,
such as the UN, to provide local or internal remedies in claims against
itself, and that, if the argument was raised that there was no reciprocity
as between a state and the organization in the applicability of the rule
of local remedies, it should be rejected on the basis that convenience
and practicability should prevail over any theoretical or technical requirement of reciprocity.[18]

The argument based on reciprocity is not a very convincing one. On
the other hand, the contention referred to above based on practicability
and convenience seems more realistic. But even this argument would
prove inadequate, if an organization did take the trouble to provide
a system of local or internal remedies to which an individual could
have access. What is at issue is the theoretical basis for insisting on the
application of the rule of local remedies to the situation.

---

[14] Ritter, 'La Protection diplomatique à l'égard d'une organisation internationale', 8 AFDI
(1962) at pp. 454ff.

[15] *Ibid.*, pp. 454–5; see also *ibid.*, pp. 427 and 456.

[16] See Brownlie, note 5 above, at p. 504, note 67.

[17] See Jenks, 'Liability for Ultra-Hazardous Activities in International Law', 117 *Hague
Recueil* (1966-I) at pp. 190ff. See also Fitzgerald, 'The Participation of International
Organizations in the Proposed International Agreement on Liability for Damage
Caused by Objects Launched in Outer Space', 3 CYIL (1965) at pp. 268ff.

[18] Eagleton, note 5 above, at pp. 351ff.

It will be recalled that one of the basic requirements for the incidence of the rule of local remedies is the jurisdictional connection between the individual and the respondent state.[19] Whatever the accepted criterion for this connection, which, it was suggested on the basis of the evidence, should be the right according to accepted principles of the respondent state to exercise jurisdiction over the individual which was primarily dependent on a territorial link, although there could be exceptions to this, it would seem that an international organization, although it has international personality, lacks the capacity in ordinary circumstances to exercise such jurisdiction over an individual, whether he be a national of a state or not, when an injury is inflicted by it on that individual. That being the case, it seems difficult to postulate that, when an individual has been injured by an international organization, he must first exhaust the local or internal remedies provided by the organization before invoking the protection of his national state.

While international organizations may have international personality and the capacity to have rights and obligations at international law, they are not states, as was pointed out by the ICJ in the *Reparation for Injuries Case*.[20] Thus, it is conceivable, as is the case in reality, that they do not have jurisdictional rights or powers over individuals in the same way that states have. The fact that such organizations do not have developed judicial systems, apart from their own internal systems for settling disputes with their staff members, supports the view that they do not have jurisdictional powers over individuals in general, even if they may purport to exercise such powers, in situations where individuals who are not staff members have been injured by them, by providing internal or local remedies. For these reasons also it is difficult to see how the rule of local remedies would be applicable to the situation being discussed.

The view taken above that the local remedies rule does not apply where an individual is harmed by an international organization found some support from the Institut de Droit International, when it dealt with the question of injuries caused by UN forces. In its 1971 resolution, the Institut stated that:

The United Nations is liable for damage which may be caused by its forces in violation of the humanitarian rules of armed conflict, without prejudice to any possible recourse against the State whose contingent has caused the damage. It is desirable that claims presented by persons thus injured be submitted to bodies composed of independent and impartial persons. Such bodies should be

---

[19] See Chapter 6 above.   [20] 1949 ICJ Reports at p. 179.

designated or set up either by the regulations issued by the United Nations or by the agreements concluded by the organization with the States which put contingents at its disposal and, possibly, with any other interested State. It is equally desirable that if such bodies have been designated or set up by a binding decision of the United Nations, or if the jurisdiction of similar bodies has been accepted by the State of which the injured person is a national, no claims may be presented to the United Nations by that State unless the injured person has exhausted the remedy thus available to it.[21]

It will be noted that the duty to exhaust remedies is made dependent on the acceptance of the jurisdiction of the adjudicating body by the national state of the injured individual or on a binding decision of the UN. Thus, there is an understanding that there is no general principle that the rule of local remedies is automatically applicable to the situation, in the absence of agreement on the part of the national state of the individual or of a binding decision of the UN, which could only flow from the provisions of the Charter of the UN, to which the state upon which the decision is binding must be a party. The rapporteur made this aspect of the application of the rule quite clear in his report when he stated that exhaustion of remedies would be a condition precedent to diplomatic protection 'only if the regulations of UN forces where they were provided for had either been accepted by that State or imposed by means of an obligatory decision of the organization (conceivable in relations between the organization and member States)'.[22] There were some objections in the discussions at the Institut to the reference to the rule, because it was not certain that the rule of local remedies was applicable to the claims of individuals against international organizations.[23] Further, it was explained in answer to some problems raised that the rule would not apply in the case of direct injuries to the state by UN forces.[24] In the result, however, it was clear that the incorporation of the rule was based on the agreement of the national state of the individual, whether it had been given directly or indirectly.[25]

---

[21] Article 8: 54 AIDI (1971-II) at pp. 469–70.

[22] P. de Visscher, 'Les Conditions d'application des lois de la guerre aux opérations militaires des Nations Unies', 54 AIDI (1971-I) at pp. 58–9.

[23] See 54 AIDI (1971-II) at p. 220.

[24] See P. de Visscher, 54 AIDI (1971-II) at pp. 219–20.

[25] In the context of relationships between individual states and international organizations, it may be mentioned in passing that in the EC system the rule does not seem to be applicable, whether the action is being brought by an individual against a State or by an individual against an organization: see Cançado Trindade, note 5 above, at pp. 98ff. This is also the case in the conventional system of the ILO: see, e.g. *ibid.*, pp. 97–8.

Claims by staff members against international organizations

Claims arising from the employment relationship by staff members against international organizations are generally settled judicially by administrative tribunals or courts established by, or under the constituent instruments of, such organizations. The employment relationship is governed by the internal law of the organization concerned which is a particular type of international law.[26] While the administrative tribunals or courts are international in character, they decide disputes essentially between staff members as individuals and the organization, disputes which arise from the employment relationship. Further, the disputes are between individuals and organizations, no states as such being involved. A state does not exercise protection over the staff member when he brings an action against the organization.

The courts or tribunals which settle these disputes are generally, except in the case of the European Court of Justice, established specifically by the organizations themselves or by their constituent instruments, although they are intended to be impartial and independent judicial bodies. Their decisions are generally binding on the organization. The system is such that the staff member is always the claimant and the organization the respondent.

In these circumstances, the question whether the rule of internal (local) remedies is applicable requires interpretation. What is being asked is whether internal means of settlement, whatever their nature, must be exhausted before the independent judicial body may be invoked. In practice, the internal means of redress available to staff members are not strictly comparable to the remedies which must be exhausted by an alien as an individual in the context of diplomatic protection, or in the area of human rights protection. As has been seen in Chapters 7 and 13, where diplomatic protection or human rights protection is involved, the remedies which must be exhausted are of a judicial or legal nature. In the case of the employment relationship in international organizations, the remedies provided, prior to the invocation of the judicial remedy, through the international administrative tribunal are essentially of a non-judicial and non-legal character. Such remedies may include direct review by the same or another administrative authority of an administrative decision affecting the staff member, or review by a different,

---

[26] For a discussion of the nature of the legal system and the law governing the employment relationship in international organizations, see Amerasinghe, note 2 above, vol. 1, pp. 3ff.

hierarchically superior authority after advice is taken from an advisory investigative body which may be expected to act quasi-judicially. Review, nevertheless, takes the form of a discretionary administrative decision, although it may involve advice from an investigative body. Moreover, these bodies or authorities are staff members themselves, or are composed of staff members. They do not generally provide a means of independent or impartial judicial or legal determination of disputes, which is the case in the context of diplomatic and human rights protection. These internal remedies are really of an entirely administrative nature and are intended to give the administration or management an opportunity of changing its mind after a procedure which is more akin to mediation or conciliation than to judicial settlement. For example, Article XI of the UN Staff Regulations refers to administrative machinery with staff participation set up to advise the Secretary General in case of appeals by staff members against an administrative decision, while Rules 111.1 and 111.2 of the Staff Rules which implement the Staff Regulations establish a Joint Appeals Board composed of staff members to consider appeals and advise the Secretary General.[27] Such bodies advise the administration, which takes the final decision in revision, which becomes the subject of appeal to the independent judicial body, the administrative tribunal. It is the final administrative decision that is appealed. Administrative tribunals do not sit in appeal over the advisory recommendations of investigative bodies, as if they are acting as judicial organs, as has been pointed out by the World Bank Administrative Tribunal.[28] Thus, the whole context and substance of such internal remedies are very special. There is really no analogy between them and the local remedies which must be exhausted in the law of diplomatic protection or of human rights protection. There is also no question of respect for the sovereignty of a state.

As a consequence, while it is probably the case that in the absence of an express written requirement there is no general principle of law to the effect that applicants to administrative tribunals or courts must exhaust, or indeed seek, internal means of redress as a prior condition of admissibility for their applications, the written internal law of international organizations as a rule makes specific provision for the exhaustion of internal remedies and spells out the remedies to be sought.

---

[27] See Amerasinghe (ed.), *Staff Regulations and Staff Rules of Selected International Organizations* (1983), vol. 1, pp. 13 and 94.
[28] See e.g. *Van Gent* (No. 3), WBAT Reports [1985], Decision No. 18 at p. 7.

Thus, Article 7 of the Statute of the United Nations Administrative Tribunal[29] makes provision for the exhaustion of internal remedies which are described in the Staff Regulations and Staff Rules of the UN, while Article II of the Statute of the World Bank Administrative Tribunal provides that no application shall be admissible, except under exceptional circumstances as decided by that Tribunal, unless 'the applicant has exhausted all other remedies available within the Bank Group, except if the applicant and the respondent institution have agreed to submit the applications directly to the Tribunal'.[30]

A further point to be noted is that it is not clear that the principle of exhaustion of internal remedies in the law of the international civil service has been based on analogy with the rule of local remedies in diplomatic protection, although it may be possible that the concept of internal remedies and the need to exhaust them may have been derived from the example of diplomatic protection. There is also absolutely no reference to the law of local remedies in diplomatic protection in the provisions of the written law of international organizations relating to internal remedies, nor do international administrative tribunals or courts invoke the law by analogy in deciding issues relating to internal remedies. The law relating to internal remedies in this area has evolved separately and on its own. The rules relating to the exhaustion of internal remedies are, therefore, of a very special nature and would repay at least a cursory examination, although a detailed examination may be out of place here.[31] It must be recognized, however, that there are certain similarities between the implementation of the rule in this area and its implementation in the law of diplomatic protection. To the extent that these similarities exist, they may indicate that ideas have been borrowed from the law of diplomatic protection or of human rights protection, although the functional connection between the rule as applied in these areas and in the law of the international civil service may be less certain.

In regard to complaints procedures as internal remedies, the League of Nations Tribunal has said: 'As a general rule, this principle seems to answer to a legal necessity . . . inasmuch as, while reconciling the interests of the officials with those of the Administration, it gives the latter an opportunity of verifying the facts alleged to be the cause of the damage to be made good.'[32] The European Court of Justice has stated that the

---

[29] Amerasinghe (ed.), *Documents on International Administrative Tribunals* (1989) at p. 8.
[30] *Ibid.*, pp. 45–6.   [31] See further Amerasinghe, note 2 above, vol. 1, pp. 235ff.
[32] *Perrasse*, LNT Judgment No. 14 (1935) at p. 3.

object of such procedures is to enable and encourage an amicable settlement of the differences which have arisen between officials and the administration, and that in order to comply with this requirement it is essential that the administration be in a position to know the complaints or requests of the person concerned.[33] Clearly, the purpose of internal remedies in general is to facilitate the settlement of disputes by informal, non-judicial means before they are subject to the more rigorous test of judicial scrutiny. Furthermore, as will be seen, some internal bodies could serve as a sound means of fact-finding, which may be of special assistance later to the judicial organs because of inherent limitations on their powers to compel discovery and the giving of evidence by witnesses.

Tribunals have on several occasions been confronted with the objection that internal remedies had not been exhausted and have held that the applicant had fulfilled the requirement that internal remedies be exhausted. Thus, for example, it has been held that remedies had been exhausted because the internal appeals board concerned had in fact given a report before the applicant filed his application with the tribunal,[34] or that the administration, having been given an opportunity to review the complaint, had in fact replied to the applicant.[35] The European Court of Justice has been rather liberal in applying provisions relating to the exhaustion of internal remedies. It has held, for instance, that, where it is not readily apparent that an internal complaints procedure should be pursued, but the applicant has spent time pursuing it, it should not be held against the applicant in relation to the time-limit for filing an application before the Court that he had pursued a remedy to which he did not have to resort.[36] On the other hand, tribunals have also held on the facts that internal remedies had not been exhausted.[37] Thus, if internal remedies are to be deemed to have been exhausted, the applicant must have made a proper complaint in the required manner

---

[33] *Sergy*, Case 58/75, [1976] ECR at p. 1152.

[34] *Vassiliou*, UNAT Judgment No. 275 (1981), JUNAT Nos. 231–300, p. 457.

[35] *Ditterich*, Case 86/77 [1978] ECR p. 1855; *Breuckmann*, ILOAT Judgment No. 270 (1976) (Eurocontrol).

[36] *Marcato*, Case 44/71, [1972] ECR p. 427; *Orlandi*, Case 117/78, [1979] ECR p. 1613; *Detti*, Case 144/82, [1983] ECR p. 2421.

[37] See e.g. *Ambrozy*, ILOAT Judgment No. 119 (1968) (FAO); *De Buck* ILOAT Judgment No. 279 (1976) (ESO); *Ali Khan* (No. 3), ILOAT Judgment No. 614 (1984) (ILO); *Denis*, UNAT Judgment No. 260 (1980), JUNAT Nos. 231–300, p. 294; *List*, Case 124/78, [1979] ECR p. 2499; and *Harrison*, WBAT Reports [1987], Decision No. 53.

and form.[38] It cannot be argued that the applicant had resorted to an alternative means of redress, which was not extended under the written law, as a substitute for an internal remedy that was required by the written law.[39] However, the respondent may agree to exempt the applicant from resorting to internal remedies so that he could directly seize the tribunal of his application; but such agreement must be clearly proved and will not be lightly presumed.[40]

There is general agreement that internal remedies need not be exhausted where the written law does not require it,[41] or where there are in effect none, or no more, to exhaust.[42] Thus, where the respondent misled the applicant because it had made a reply to his complaint conditional upon the signature of his appraisal report, the ILO Administrative Tribunal (ILOAT) held that he could file directly with the tribunal.[43] Where the appeals body of the organization fails to report within a reasonable time, the ILOAT has held that the applicant is exempted from pursuing internal remedies to their conclusion.[44] On the other hand, in allowing an exception to the rule that internal remedies must be exhausted, because in effect there are none to exhaust, tribunals are cautious. Exceptions are not lightly to be presumed. In *García and Márquez*,[45] the ILOAT found that, while the organization had tried to delay the internal proceedings, the appeals body was able to hear the applicant's appeal and was ready to give a decision within a reasonable period. In these circumstances no exception to the rule was held to be permissible. As one reason for caution in dispensing with the requirement of internal recourse, the ILOAT has explained that in many instances material evidence obtainable from the hearings of internal appeals bodies, which were more familiar with the position of the staff in the organization, might not be available to the tribunal.[46] At the same time, as pointed out earlier, tribunals do not sit in appeal from the decisions of these appeals bodies.

---

[38] See *Roelofsen*, ILOAT Judgment No. 423 (1980) (Eurocontrol).

[39] See *Misra*, ILOAT Judgment No. 213 (1973) (ITU).

[40] See *Gaba*, ILOAT Judgment No. 458 (1981) (UNESCO).

[41] See e.g. *Saravia*, OASAT Judgment No. 47 (1979); *Grassi*, Cases 6 and 97/79 [1980] ECR p. 2141; *Mavridis*, Case 289/81 [1983] ECR p. 1731.

[42] See e.g. *Ali Khan* (No. 2), ILOAT Judgment No. 565 (1983) (ILO).

[43] *Ozorio* (Nos. 1 and 2), ILOAT Judgment No. 185 (1971) (WHO).

[44] *Tarrab* (No. 9), ILOAT Judgment No. 499 (1982) (ILO); *Ido*, ILOAT Judgment No. 588 (1983) (WHO).

[45] ILOAT Judgment No. 408 (1980) (PAHO).

[46] *García and Márquez*, ILOAT Judgment No. 408 (1980) (PAHO) at p. 6.

In order that internal remedies may be properly exhausted so as not to render an application inadmissible, allegations and claims raised in the application before the tribunal must be raised before the internal body.[47] The subject-matter of the application and of the internal appeal need not, however, be identical, provided it is substantially the same.[48] The essential facts must be the same, although the submissions made may be different, and the claims made in the application before the tribunal may be different from those made in the internal appeal, provided they are narrower in scope.[49] Indeed, it is sufficient if the claims in both proceedings are substantially similar, even if they are not identical and those presented in the application to the tribunal are not narrower than those of the internal appeal. This is so, even to the extent that a claim for damages as an alternative to annulment may be regarded as having been implied in a claim for annulment by itself made in the internal appeal.[50]

Where the applicant has failed to observe the time-limits for the submission of internal complaints or appeals, with the result that his appeal before the appeals body had been rejected as inadmissible, he will be deemed not to have exhausted internal remedies.[51] Tribunals will examine the decision relating to time-limits of the internal appeals body in order to determine whether the law had been correctly applied, which may involve an interpretation of the written law, and, if it has not been correctly applied, rule that internal remedies had been exhausted by the applicant.[52] There are circumstances in which the time-limit for the bringing of an internal appeal will not be strictly applied and an exception be made, for example where the respondent has misled the applicant and is in breach of good faith.[53] But generally such time limits are unlikely to be extended lightly, even if equitable considerations

---

[47] See *Foley*, ILOAT Judgment No. 452 (1981) (FAO); *Glorioso* (No. 2), ILOAT Judgment No. 550 (1983) (PAHO): *Zang-Atangana*, UNAT Judgment No. 130 (1969), JUNAT Nos. 114–166, p. 155; *Kahale*, UNAT Judgment No. 165 (1972), JUNAT Nos. 114–166, p. 406.

[48] See *Bode*, Cases 45 and 49/70 [1971] ECR p. 465; *Küster*, Case 23/74 [1975] ECR p. 353; *Miss B*, Case 152/77 [1979] ECR p. 2819.

[49] See *Zihler*, ILOAT Judgment No. 435 (1980) (CERN) at p. 6; *Gubin and Nemo*, ILOAT Judgment No. 429 (1980) (Eurocontrol).

[50] See *Herpels*, Case 54/77 [1978] ECR p. 585.

[51] See e.g. *Schulz*, ILOAT Judgment No. 575 (1983) (EPO); *Michl*, ILOAT Judgment No. 585 (1983) (EPO); *Ho*, UNAT Judgment No. 189 (1974), JUNAT Nos. 167–230, p. 170; *Deshormes*, Case 17/78 [1979] ECR p. 189.

[52] See *Francis*, UNAT Judgment No. 105 (1967), JUNAT Nos. 87–113, p. 189; *Denis*, UNAT Judgment No. 315 (1983); *Ziante*, ILOAT Judgment No. 548 (1983) (WHO).

[53] See *Decroix*, ILOAT Judgment No. 602 (1984) (EPO) at p. 5.

may warrant an extension, because any other conclusion would impair the stability of the position in law of the parties, which it is the object and point of time-limits to preserve.[54] Tribunals have pointed out that, for instance, the late discovery by the applicant of the illegality committed[55] or even involvement in a serious accident[56] does not delay the running of time for the purpose of the time-limits for internal remedies. Some tribunals have held that the reliance on the time-limit for internal appeals may be waived by the respondent by agreement or by its conduct,[57] while the European Court of Justice has referred to the mandatory nature of such time-limit in the Staff Regulations of the EC, with the result that it could not be altered even by agreement.[58] The ILOAT has also held that, where the issue of timeliness had not been raised by the respondent in the internal appeal, it was acting in bad faith to raise the issue before the tribunal and therefore the respondent was estopped from contending that the application was inadmissible because internal remedies had not been exhausted.[59]

Where an application has been dismissed, because it was inadmissible as a result of the failure to exhaust internal remedies, the application is not *res judicata* and may be introduced again, once internal remedies have been properly exhausted, if this is still possible.[60]

---

[54] See *Decroix*, ILOAT Judgment No. 602 (1984) (EPO); *Meyer*, ILOAT Judgment No. 612 (1984) (EPO).

[55] See *Meyer*, ILOAT Judgment No. 612 (1984) (EPO).

[56] *Ziante*, ILOAT Judgment No. 548 (1983) (WHO).

[57] See *Grangeon*, UNAT Judgment No. 159 (1972), JUNAT Nos. 114–166, p. 373.

[58] *Schiavo*, Cases 122 and 23/79 [1981] ECR p. 473.

[59] *Nielsen*, ILOAT Judgment No. 522 (1982) (UNESCO).

[60] See e.g. *Reinarz*, Case 29/80 [1981] ECR p. 1311.

Part IV Nature of the rule

15   Nature of the rule

There has been some discussion and disagreement in the past on the nature of the rule of local remedies, as such, or its formal character. The issue has generally been formulated in terms of whether the rule is one of substance or procedure. Sometimes the discussion has been centred more specifically on when the 'responsibility' at international law of the respondent state arises,[1] which may or may not be the identical question involved in the consideration of the nature of the rule as one of substance or procedure depending on how the terms used are defined.

It has also been stated that the differences of opinion, found also in state practice and judicial statements, are 'of theoretical rather than practical interest'.[2] As will be seen, while this may to a large extent be a plausible assessment, there are certain matters which could in practice be affected by the view taken of the nature of the rule. On the other hand, it is necessary to define what exactly the discussion is about, as often some of the disagreement may appear to stem from a confusion about what are the parameters of the subject, while it has to be acknowledged that there is some genuine difference of opinion on substantive matters connected with the formal character of the rule.

Apropos the contents and limits of the discussion, the question relates primarily to when the breach of international law giving rise to liability on the part of the respondent state to repair the injury to the alien or

---

[1] See the discussion in the *Report of the ILC to the UN General Assembly on the Work of its Twenty-Ninth Session*, YBILC (1977), vol. 2, Part II, pp. 34ff.; Ago, 'Sixth Report on State Responsibility', YBILC (1977), vol. 2, Part I, pp. 22ff., where the rapporteur refers to the rule as applying necessarily 'to the genesis of international responsibility'. See now also Dugard, 'Second Report on Diplomatic Protection' (ILC), UN Doc. A/CN.4/514 at pp. 15ff., who touches on the issue.

[2] See *Report of the ILC on the Work of its Twenty-Ninth Session*, YBILC (1977), vol. 2, Part II, p. 35.

individual takes place. That is to say, what is of interest is whether the liability *at international law* to make reparation arises before local remedies have been resorted to and exhausted, or only after recourse has been had, without satisfaction, to all the local remedies which need to be exhausted. If the liability arises after the exhaustion without satisfaction of local remedies, then because international law has not been violated prior to that or at the time the initial injury to the alien or individual was committed, the rule of local remedies would operate as one of substance. This is because substantive liability at international law for an international wrong arises only after the rule has been applied. If the liability to make reparation at international law arises at the time of the initial injury to the alien or individual, because international law was violated at that time, and such liability arose before the rule of local remedies was applicable, the rule of local remedies would operate as one of procedure. In this case, the resort to local remedies becomes a matter of orderly procedure in the process of international dispute settlement arising from a violation of international law. Local remedies would be a procedural step in the settlement of an international dispute engendered by the violation of international law inherent in the initial injury to the alien.

In Chapter 4 above, a possible distinction was made, in the discussion of the relevance of denial of justice, between liability for the international wrong in respect of the alien or individual, and 'responsibility' for that wrong. This was essentially a formal distinction and is not pervasive nor is it used in general or in this work except for practical purposes. Although it helps to identify when the violation of international law actually takes place, while at the same time acknowledging that the international mechanism of dispute settlement, as opposed to the national means of settlement, does not normally come into operation until after this means has been exhausted, this cannot conceal the problem that exists of determining when the violation of international law takes place and, therefore, whether the rule of local remedies is a rule essentially of procedure or of substance. The formal distinction made was not intended to evade the issue that remains of when the responsibility or the liability, as the case may be, for the international wrong comes into existence. Its purpose was to underline the fact that there could be a difference between the time at which international responsibility arises as a result of the violation of an international norm and the incidence of the obligation, in respect of which there is a corresponding right, to have the liability determined by an international as opposed to a national mechanism. What is at the heart of the discussion in this chapter is when international responsibility to make reparation for a violation of international law arises, regardless of what means, whether national or international, are required to be used to establish that responsibility, and whether the term 'liability' is used or not. The answer to that question should intrinsically settle the dispute relating to the formal character of the rule, because upon it depends, by definition, the characterization of the rule as one of substance or procedure, although there may be other relevant factors which merit consideration in connection with the problem.

The prevailing views in theory

As the rule of local remedies is a very practical matter which concerns largely international litigation, it will be appropriate carefully to examine state practice and in particular the caselaw on local remedies, in order to establish the nature of the rule. But before this is done the prevailing theoretical views expressed by text writers, most of whom will be identified, need to be considered.

While the findings of the Institut de Droit International at its sessions in 1927, 1954 and 1956 were somewhat inconclusive,[3] views expressed in the debates on state responsibility at its 1927 session,[4] the preliminary and definitive reports of the rapporteur (Verzijl) on the local remedies rule for its 1954 session,[5] the supplementary report on the rule by Verzijl for its 1956 session[6] and the debates on the rule at its 1954 and 1956 sessions[7] seem unequivocally to support the view that the rule is only a procedural prerequisite for the settlement of what is basically an international claim by international means. The procedural view was consistently maintained by de Visscher, starting in 1927, in so far as he stated that the rule affected less the existence of responsibility than the conditions of exercise of the claim.[8] The procedural view identifies

---

[3] 33 AIDI (1927-I) at pp. 455ff.; 33 AIDI (1927-III) at pp. 81ff.; 45 AIDI (1954-I) at pp. 5ff.; and 46 AIDI (1956) at pp. 1ff., 265ff., 314–15 and 364.

[4] See the views expressed by Séfériadès, d'Erlach and Jacquemyns: 33 AIDI (1927-III) at pp. 158–60.

[5] See 45 AIDI (1954-I) at pp. 14–16, 21–2, 24–32, 84, 88–9, 91–2, 95–6 and 104.

[6] 46 AIDI (1956) at p. 3.

[7] See the views expressed by Bourquin, Muûls, Salvioli and Scelle in 1954: 45 AIDI (1954-I) at pp. 45–6, 49–55, 73, 78 and 79–81; and by Guggenheim, Huber, Rolin, Verdross and de Visscher in 1956: 46 AIDI (1956) at pp. 31–7, 39, 42–4, 47 and 49.

[8] See C. de Visscher, Note on the 'Responsabilité internationale des Etats et la protection diplomatique d'après quelques documents récents', 8 RDILC (1927) at pp. 245ff.; 'Le Déni de justice en droit international', 52 *Hague Recueil* (1935) at pp. 421ff.; and *De l'équité dans le règlement arbitral ou judiciaire des litiges de droit international public* (1971) p. 91.

the incidence of the international responsibility of the respondent state as at the time at which the violation of international law takes place, when the alien or individual is injured by an act imputable to that state, although the enforcement of that responsibility by means of diplomatic protection is not permitted until local remedies have been exhausted. Freeman apparently also took the view that international responsibility arose upon the commission of the internationally illegal act which injured the alien or individual, and that the requirement that local remedies be exhausted was a procedural prerequisite for the admissibility of an international claim, which was intended to give the respondent state an opportunity of redress before the claim became justiciable at an international level.[9] There has been much support for the procedural view of the rule from other textual authorities who have examined the matter in some detail.[10] There are also writers who have at various times in general terms supported the view that the incidence of responsibility takes place before, and is not contingent upon, the exhaustion of local remedies.[11]

---

[9] *The International Responsibility of States for Denial of Justice* (1938) pp. 407ff.

[10] The principal supporters of the view are Amerasinghe, *State Responsibility for Injuries to Aliens* (1967) pp. 330–54; Amerasinghe, 'The Formal Character of the Rule of Local Remedies', 25 ZaöRV (1965) pp. 445ff.; Amerasinghe, in the first edition of the current work (1990) pp. 319ff.; H. Friedmann, 'Epuisement des voies de recours internes', 14 RDILC (1933) at pp. 318–21, 323–4 and 326–7; Kaufmann, 'Règles générales du droit de la paix', 54 *Hague Recueil* (1935) at pp. 413ff. and 423ff.; Basdevant, 'Règles générales du droit de la paix', 58 *Hague Recueil* (1936) at pp. 662ff.; Cohn, 'La Théorie de la responsabilité internationale', 68 *Hague Recueil* (1939) at pp. 250, 301 and 313ff.; Panayotakos, *La Règle de l'épuisement des voies de recours internes, en théorie et en pratique* (1952) pp. 29ff. and 113; Urbanek, 'Das völkerrechtsverletzende nationale Urteil', 9 ÖZÖR (1958–9) at pp. 213ff.; Law, *The Local Remedies Rule in International Law* (1961) p. 141; Haesler, *The Exhaustion of Local Remedies in the Case Law of International Courts and Tribunals* (1968), pp. 92ff. and 131ff.; Chappez, *La Règle de l'épuisement des voies de recours internes* (1972) pp. 9ff.; and Strozzi, *Interessi statali et interessi privati nell' ordinamento internazionale: la funzione del previo esaurimento dei ricorsi interni* (1977) p. 104.

[11] See e.g. Hyde, *International Law* (1945), vol. 2, p. 911; Ross, *A Text-book of International Law* (1947) pp. 242 and 265; Rousseau, *Droit international public* (1953) p. 366; Bin Cheng, *General Principles of Law as Applied by International Courts and Tribunals* (1953) p. 180; Reuter, 'Principes de droit international public', 103 *Hague Recueil* (1961) pp. 590 and 613; Waldock, 'General Course on Public International Law', 106 *Hague Recueil* (1962) p. 208; Brierly, *The Law of Nations* (1963) p. 282; Delbez, *Les principes généraux du droit international public* (1964) p. 381; Kelsen, *Principles of International Law* (1966) pp. 370ff.; Vallat, *International Law and the Practitioner* (1966) pp. 33ff.; and Lauterpacht, *International Law – Collected Papers* (1970), vol. 1, p. 398. The 1961 Harvard Law School Draft Convention on State Responsibility espoused the procedural view of the rule: 55 AJIL (1961) p. 548. In 1965, the Inter-American Juridical Committee, in explaining the US view on the principles governing state responsibility, stated that it was the

There are also some text writers who support the substantive view of the rule. This view is that responsibility arises only when the alien or individual cannot obtain reparation in the state where he suffered the injury, either after he has resorted to local remedies or because there are none to exhaust. Anzilotti explained the incidence of responsibility in terms of a denial of justice after the exhaustion of local remedies,[12] while Ago maintained that an international illicit act 'well characterized' came into existence only when the state organs had failed to give effect to an international obligation, thus causing responsibility to arise at that time.[13] Ago substantially reaffirmed his view in his 1977 report to the ILC,[14] and the ILC, in its report to the UN General Assembly of the same year, did not specifically reject his views, though its statement was non-committal. The ILC stated:

Before having, as it does, obvious consequences in regard to the procedure for claims, the principle of the exhaustion of local remedies necessarily operated at the level of the actual mechanism of fulfillment of an international obligation and, consequently, at the level of determination of the existence of a breach of an international obligation.[15]

Recognition was apparently given to the procedural view of the rule in this statement, which obviously is at variance with Ago's substantive view of the rule, in that an attempt was made to acknowledge that the rule had a procedural significance, but, in so far as the violation of international law was associated with the absence of satisfaction after the exhaustion of local remedies, the substantive view was also recognized. This was made abundantly clear in the later statement that

In other words, the finding that the right of the State to demand reparation exists only after the final rejection of the claims of the private individuals concerned inevitably leads to the conclusion that the breach of the international obligation has not been completed before those remedies are exhausted, that is to say, before the negative effects of the new conduct of the State in regard

enforcement and not the birth of responsibility that was subordinated to the rule of local remedies: OAS Doc. OEA/Ser.I/VI.2.-CIJ-78 at pp. 7 and 10ff.

[12] *Cours de droit international* (1929) pp. 518ff. Anzilotti first propounded his view much earlier in 1906: 'La Responsabilité internationale des états à raison des dommages soufferts par des étrangers', 13 RGDIP (1906) at pp. 5ff. and 291ff.

[13] 'La Regola del Previo Esaurimento dei Ricorsi Interni in Tema di Responsabilità Internazionale', 3 ArchivDP (1938) at pp. 181ff.; 'Le Délit international', 68 *Hague Recueil* (1939) at pp. 514ff.; and 45 AIDI (1954-I) at pp. 34ff.

[14] Ago, note 1 above, at pp. 22–33.

[15] *Report of the ILC on the Work of its Twenty-Ninth Session*, YBILC (1977), vol. 2, Part II, p. 35.

to those remedies have been added to those of the initial conduct adopted by the State in the case in point, thereby rendering the result required by the international obligation definitively impossible of achievement.[16]

The approach is not only confused but clearly equivocal.

Borchard[17] and the 1929 Harvard Draft Convention on State Responsibility for Damages to Aliens[18] supported the view that the rule was one of substance. It may also be noted that, while an impasse on the question of the nature of the rule was reached at the Hague Codification Conference of 1930, most governments seem basically to have adhered to the view that the rule was a substantive one with the consequence that responsibility both commenced and was enforceable only after local remedies had been exhausted.[19] There are some other text writers who have supported the substantive view.[20]

A third view has been expressed. This view is best explained by one of the few writers who support it.[21] It is based essentially on a threefold analysis. A distinction is made between breaches of international law

---

[16] *Ibid.*, pp. 35–6.

[17] See 'Theoretical Aspects of the International Responsibility of States', 1 ZaöRV (1929) at pp. 237ff.; and the report in 36 AIDI (1931-I) at pp. 424ff.

[18] Harvard Law School, *Research in International Law (Nationality – Responsibility of States – Territorial Waters)* (1929) at pp. 149ff. The Inter-American Juridical Committee in an opinion of 1961 stated that, in the view of sixteen Latin American countries, in the American continent the rule of local remedies was not merely procedural but substantive: OAS Doc. OEA/Ser.I/VI.2-CIJ-61 at p. 37.

[19] See the account given of the consideration of the matter at the Hague Conference in Cançado Trindade, 'The Birth of State Responsibility and the Nature of the Local Remedies Rule', 58 RDI (1978) at pp. 158ff.; and in Ago, note 1 above, at pp. 24ff. There were states which supported the procedural view of the rule.

[20] See Strisower in 33 AIDI (1927-I) at pp. 492ff.; Durand, 'La Responsabilité internationale des états pour déni de justice', 38 RGDIP (1931) at p. 721; Accioly, *Tratado de Direito Internacional Público* (1933), vol. 1, p. 352; Fenwick, 'The Progress of International Law During the Past Forty Years', 79 *Hague Recueil* (1951) at p. 44, and *International Law* (1965) pp. 330 and 334; Hackworth, in 45 AIDI (1954-I) at p. 69; Cavaré, in 46 AIDI (1956) at p. 276, and 2 *Le Droit international public positif* (1962), vol. 2, p. 363; Durante, *Ricorsi individuali a organi internazionali* (1958) p. 137; Simpson and Fox, *International Arbitration Law and Practice* (1959) pp. IIIff.; Monaco, *Manuale di Diritto Internazionale Pubblico* (1960) p. 374; Sarhan, *L'épuisement des recours internes en matière de responsabilité internationale* (1962) pp. 257ff. and 542; Sereni, *Principî Generali di Diritto e Processo Internazionale* (1955) p. 1534; Morelli, 'La Théorie générale du procès international', 61 *Hague Recueil* (1937) at p. 350; Jiménez de Aréchaga, 'International Responsibility', in Sørensen (ed.), *Manual of Public International Law* (1968) at pp. 583ff.; O'Connell, *International Law* (1970), vol. 2, pp. 945ff., 951 and 1053; Doehring, 'Does General International Law Require Domestic Judicial Protection Against the Executive?', in *Gerichtsschutz gegen die Exekutive* (1971), vol. 3, pp. 243ff.; Giuliano, *Diritto internazionale* (1974), vol. 1, p. 593; and Gaja, *L'Esaurimento dei Ricorsi Interni nel Diritto Internazionale* (1967) at pp. 5ff.

[21] Fawcett, 'The Exhaustion of Local Remedies: Substance or Procedure?', 31 BYIL (1954) at pp. 452ff. See also Fitzmaurice, 'Hersch Lauterpacht – The Scholar as Judge', 37 BYIL

and breaches of local law. In the first class of case, where there is only a breach of international law, in other words a breach of treaty or other international obligation, the local remedies rule does not apply, since there are no remedies to exhaust. The second situation is that in which there is a breach of local law but no breach of international law. Here the rule operates substantively and a denial of justice is required for international responsibility to arise:

[responsibility] can only arise out of a subsequent act of the State constituting a denial of justice to the injured party seeking a remedy for the original action of which he complains.[22]

Thirdly, where the action complained of is a breach of both international law and local law, the rule is a procedural one which operates merely to regulate the order of judicial action at different levels.

This analysis, although it uses the notion of dual legal systems as a starting-point, includes within the rule both those situations in which *resort* to local redress (and not *exhaustion* of local remedies) is necessary to the cause of action, because without it no defect in the administration of justice can be shown, and those in which such resort is not required for the cause of action but is part of the procedure of international redress. As already shown in Chapter 4, causes of action arising from wrongs, between private individuals or otherwise, which require a denial of justice in the administration of justice for the international wrong to be consummated, do not really result from the application of the rule of local remedies, although some resort to local remedies may be required in order to give rise to the cause of action. Thus, the situations in which the rule of local remedies would, according to this view, operate substantively are eliminated, leaving only the other two situations. Of these, that in which the cause of action arises from a violation of international law which is not, however, a breach of national law, results in fact in the non-application of the rule, because of a limitation inherent in the rule arising from the absence of local remedies.[23] Thus, the rule would conceptually operate in a procedural manner in

---

(1961) at p. 53; and Brownlie, *Principles of Public International Law* (1998) p. 497. Dugard, 'Third Report on Diplomatic Protection' (ILC), UN Doc. A/CN.4/514 (2002) at p. 32, supports this view, although inconsistently in Article 11 of the draft Articles on Diplomatic Protection he refers to the exhaustion of local remedies as a 'procedural' precondition to international action: *ibid.*, p. 15.

[22] Fawcett, note 21 above, at p. 456.

[23] This category has been criticized in the Norwegian argument in the *Norwegian Loans Case*, ICJ Pleadings (1957), vol. 1, pp. 457–8, mainly on the ground that in some countries international law prevails over national law before local courts.

this situation, as in the remaining situation, but would not be applicable because of limitations on the application of the rule. In effect, therefore, this view, which attributes both a substantive and a procedural character to the rule and specifically takes into account situations in which the rule is inapplicable, because of the limitations inherent in the rule, can be reduced, when examined, to a basically procedural view of the rule.

García Amador, among others, took a similar view of the rule, which postulated that it could work as one of procedure or of substance, when he said that the rule was a suspensive condition for the enforcement of responsibility which 'may be procedural or substantive, but to which the right to bring international claims is subordinated'.[24] There are a few other authors who make a distinction between the rule as giving rise to a denial of justice, where it would operate substantively, and the rule as a means to the enforcement of an international obligation, where it would operate procedurally.[25] This distinction has been shown to be unwarranted and unnecessary.

Theories explanatory of the rule

While there is disagreement among text writers on the character of the rule as one of substance or procedure, a question which will be adverted to again later, at this point it may be useful briefly to examine some theories explaining the rule which may have some bearing on the question, although they do not directly answer the issues raised.

Ago distinguished between two kinds of international '*fait illicite*' which resulted in there being simple and complex international delicts. When one organ of the state caused damage which was a violation of international law, this constituted a simple international delict which was

---

[24] 'State Responsibility – Some New Problems', 94 *Hague Recueil* (1958) at p. 449.

[25] See e.g. Eagleton, *The Responsibility of States in International Law* (1928) at pp. 95ff.; 'Une Théorie au sujet du commencement de la responsabilité internationale', 11 RDILC (1930) at pp. 643ff.; Eustathiades, *La Responsabilité internationale de l'état pour les actes des organes judiciaires et le problème du déni de justice en droit international* (1930) pp. 243ff. and 331ff.; Starke, 'Imputability in International Delinquencies', 19 BYIL (1938) at pp. 105ff.; Castberg, in 45 AIDI (1954-I) at pp. 64–5; Briggs, 'The Local Remedies Rule: A Drafting Suggestion', 50 AJIL (1956) at pp. 925–6; and Fitzmaurice, 'Hersch Lauterpacht – The Scholar as Judge: I', 37 BYIL (1961) at pp. 53ff. There are others who support one of the other views who are, however, rather equivocal in that at times they appear to support the view discussed here: Freeman, note 9 above, at pp. 407 and 410; Bin Cheng, note 11 above, at pp. 178 and 180; and Haesler, note 10 above, at pp. 131ff.

attributable to the respondent state according to international law, but when in addition the total structure of the state subsequently failed to bring about the result desired by international law, what resulted was a complex international delict. It was only when the latter arose that the breach of international obligation became definitive.[26] Thus, he could state:

Si un organe de l'Etat internationalement obligé accomplit un acte non conforme à la tâche d'obtenir le résultat dû, et cause par là un dommage à un particulier étranger, cet acte ne suffit pas pour fonder l'Etat national de la victime du dommage à affirmer la responsabilité internationale de l'Etat auquel appartient l'organe; il faut encore qu'il soit établi que son ressortissant ne peut plus obtenir la réalisation de ce résultat par appel à d'autres voies de l'ordre juridique interne; en d'autres termes, il faut que le fait illicite international complexe soit réalisé dans tous ses éléments. C'est là le sens véritable et la portée extrèmement importante de la *local redress rule*.[27]

Because what was important was the failure of the respondent state to achieve, by its own means, a certain final result concerning the treatment of aliens and not the initial injury to the alien, which may have been an international illegality, it was the *délit international complexe* that determined the character of the rule of local remedies. This led Ago to conclude that the rule was substantive. Ago's view which was reflected also in his work for the ILC referred to earlier included in the discussion a distinction between obligations of 'conduct' and obligations of 'result', which was unfamiliar before to international law, not a universal or common distinction made in national laws so as to merit being treated as a general principle, and was, perhaps, imported indiscriminately and out of context from the Italian law (not, as far as I know, even from the Roman law). To cut a long story short, it is an unnecessary fifth wheel in the discussion of the rule of local remedies and was and is totally unwarranted on the basis, not only of the lack of any kind of authority at the time, but also of the lack of any kind of current authority. It does not help in the interests of clarity nor does it have any basis in reason or considered analogy for the purposes of the rule of local remedies.

While the analysis made by Ago may also be faulted on the grounds that it makes an invalid and unnecessary distinction, what appears to

---

[26] See Ago, 'Le Délit international', 68 *Hague Recueil* (1938) at pp. 506ff. Anzilotti had already developed the notion of the international illicit fact: *Cours de droit international* (1929) pp. 426ff.

[27] Ago, note 26 above, at p. 516.

be inaccurate is the interpretation of the legal situation involved. What international law probhibits is the initial injury to the alien. To say that international law merely prohibits the perpetuation of the injury after resort to local remedies, and therefore does not take particular note of the initial injury as a violation of international norms, provided the result is brought about that satisfaction is given to the injured alien, seems to twist the truth to suit the theory. In short, it seems difficult to accept an interpretation of the situation which requires the state merely to fulfil its secondary obligation, of making reparation through whichever means it chooses, as the result to be achieved by the obligation imposed by international law, and therefore characterizes this secondary obligation as the only one that has not been fulfilled, while not attaching special importance to the primary obligation not to cause a certain kind of injury to the alien in the first place. The local remedies rule really pertains only to the secondary obligation, leaving the fact of the violation of the primary obligation substantially unaltered. Thus, the consequences drawn from the distinction between simple and complex international delicts, if such distinction must be made, seem ill-conceived and unwarranted. Moreover, to distinguish between a violation of law, in this case international law, that gives rise to responsibility and one that does not seems jurisprudentially unsound.

Scelle proposed the theory of *dédoublement fonctionnel* in order to explain the performance of certain functions by states which were intended to achieve results in the international legal order. He took a dualist approach to the relationship between the municipal and international legal orders and explained that:

Les agents dotés d'une compétence institutionnelle ou investis par un ordre juridique utilisent leur capacité 'fonctionnelle' telle qu'elle est organisée dans l'ordre juridique qui les a institués, mais pour assurer l'efficacité d'un autre ordre juridique privé des organes nécessaires à cette réalisation, ou n'en possèdent que d'insuffisant.[28]

Therefore, the local remedies rule enabled state organs to perform functions in order to achieve results in the international juridical order. The respondent state had the right of priority to make reparation effective in the international legal order through its own means, thus performing

---

[28] 'Le Phénomène juridique du dédoublement fonctionnel', in *Rechtsfragen der internationalen Organisation – Festschrift für Hans Wehberg* (1956) at p. 331.

a dual function within two legal orders.[29] The consequence of this view, which focused on the remedial function at international law of local remedies in the context of the rule, was to attribute to the rule a procedural function.

There have also been text writers who regard the rule as a conflict rule. Thus, according to one writer it is a rule

for resolving conflicts of jurisdiction between international law and municipal tribunals or authorities; the rule determines when and in what circumstances the local courts, on the one hand, and international tribunals, on the other, must or may assume jurisdiction over the issue.[30]

This approach is of a somewhat more practical nature. It led the writer to opt for a mixed nature of the rule, as has been seen, which, as was also seen, can be reduced to a basically procedural character.[31]

There are others who regard the rule as one of practical convenience which results in a derogation from the theoretically superior jurisdictional competence of the international legal order. It resulted from a practice which was more opportunistic than based on fundamental principles. In this respect it was a recognition of the sovereignty of the respondent State. Verzijl thus stated that:

Si, malgré le fait qu'un Etat a déjà encouru une responsabilité internationale ensuite d'une lésion infligée à un étranger sur son territoire, cet Etat pouvait éluder provisoirement les conséquences normales de sa responsabilité par un renvoi de l'étranger à ses tribunaux internes, cela pourrait s'expliquer uniquement par une pratique internationale qui aurait introduit une dérogation aux principes normaux de responsabilité pour délits internationaux, rien que pour des motifs d'opportunité qui n'ont rien à faire avec des considérations de principe.[32]

---

[29] Scelle explained his theory particularly in 45 AIDI (1954-I) at pp. 79ff., but also deals with it in *Précis de droit des gens – principes et systématique* (1934), vol. 1, pp. 43ff. and vol. 2, pp. 319ff. Scelle's theory was accepted also by many other authorities, such as Freeman note 9 above, at pp. 408–9; Rolin, 'Les Principes de droit international public', 77 *Hague Recueil* (1950) at p. 450; Verzijl, in 45 AIDI (1954-I) at p. 88; Guggenheim, in 46 AIDI (1956) at p. 33; and Bourquin, in 45 AIDI (1954-I) at pp. 52–3.

[30] Fawcett, note 21 above, at p. 454. See also Castberg, note 25 above, at pp. 64–5.

[31] Ténékidès also regarded the rule as a conflict rule, but was not so concerned about the impact of this characterization on the nature of the rule: 'L'épuisement des voies de recours internes comme condition préalable de l'instance internationale', 14 RDILC (1933) at pp. 527ff.

[32] Verzijl, in 45 AIDI (1954-I) at pp. 22–3. Ténékidès, who criticized the rule heavily, also inclined to this explanation of the rule: note 31 above, at pp. 515ff. See also Jenks, *The Prospects of International Adjudication* (1964) p. 536.

Verzijl's view led him to conclude that the rule was procedural in character.

All the explanations of the rule are not necessarily exclusive of each other. However, in so far as they have led to certain conclusions about the nature of the rule based on the incidence of international responsibility, apart from liability as defined, such conclusions are open to examination, as is any theory concerning the nature of the rule.

Possible practical consequences of the different views of the nature of the rule

While the distinction between substance and procedure in relation to the nature of the rule may in a sense be regarded as pertaining to theory, whether the rule is regarded as substantive or procedural does have some practical consequences. The manner in which the rule has been understood and implemented in practice does, therefore, have some reverse impact on the question.

The cause of action

Upon whether the rule is substantive or procedural depends the determination of the international cause of action. If the rule that local remedies must be exhausted is to be regarded as merely procedural, the cause of action arises before resort to local remedies becomes necessary or is made and is independent of the working of the local remedies in the respondent state. Resort to local remedies by the alien would then be no more than a condition precedent to the international right of action of the alien's national state. The international *cause* of action and the international *right* of action are thus to be distinguished. The rule would operate to create a system of appeals of which the international tribunal would be the last in the hierarchy. The *cause* of action would have to be taken to the local courts as primary courts before a *right* of action before an international court could arise. On the other hand, if the rule is to be regarded as one of substance, the cause of action arises after the local remedies have been exhausted and not before, and without such exhaustion there could be no international cause of action. Also, the cause of action then coincides with the right of action – unlike the situation where the rule is regarded as one of procedure. Moreover, if the rule were regarded as substantive, the deficiency in the local remedies provided would be a material factor in the cause of action.

There is evidence in the case law and practice that supports the view that the international cause of action arises before local remedies are resorted to or exhausted. On the other hand, there is what appears to be an anomaly. Although the international cause of action arises with the commission of the original injury attributable to the respondent state, and the claimant state is vested with a right to remedial action on the part of the respondent state, international law takes a different view of the duty of reparation depending on whether or not satisfactory reparation is provided by the exhaustion of local remedies. If the injured alien or individual is satisfied by resort to local remedies, the injury to the alien or individual, as well as the injury to the claimant state, is regarded as having been repaired and the secondary right of action vested in the claimant state disappears without any particular additional reparation being made to the claimant state for the injury done to it in the person of its national or the individual. Thus, the substantive remedial right at this stage is only to requite the injury to the alien or individual. However, if local remedies are exhausted without satisfaction being obtained, the substantive remedial right of the claimant state, which it may assert through the exercise of diplomatic protection, is not only to have the injury to the alien or individual remedied but also to have the injury to itself repaired. In these circumstances, the remedial right becomes enlarged.

This apparent anomaly is to be explained not by reference to the choice of a substantive or procedural character for the rule but by the tribute paid by international law to the sovereignty of the respondent state. When the respondent state repairs the injury, a violation of international law, by its own means, it is regarded as having provided adequate satisfaction to the claimant state even in respect of the injury done to that state. When it fails to cure the ill by its own means, the claimant state's right to additional reparation for the injury to itself, which had been held in suspense, revives, because in spite of the opportunity given to the respondent state to repair the injury to the alien or individual it has failed satisfactorily to discharge its secondary obligation. Thus, this apparent anomaly need not influence the incidence of the cause of action. That cause of action, therefore, could arise at the time the initial injury is perpetrated.

The time of incidence of international responsibility

The time when international liability or responsibility arises is also determined by the decision whether the rule is one of substance or of procedure; and this may be important in deciding the jurisdiction of international tribunals where this depends on a *compromis* or other instrument of submission. Thus, where the *compromis* states that only international disputes which arise after a certain date are cognizable by the tribunal, if the rule of local remedies were regarded as procedural, the dispute would arise at the time the initial wrong was committed, which may occur before the relevant date; whereas, if the rule were regarded as substantive, the dispute would arise at a different time, namely, after the exhaustion of local remedies, which may occur after the relevant date. There is evidence, as will be seen, that the time of incidence of international responsibility, as opposed to liability, according to the distinction made, is the time at which the initial injury attributable to the respondent state was caused to the alien or individual.[33]

The manner in which the issue is treated internationally

From the point of view of the procedure of international tribunals, the characterization of the rule as substantive or procedural may determine the manner in which, in the proceedings, the objection that local remedies have not been exhausted is treated. If the rule is regarded as a matter of substance, then the non-exhaustion of local remedies is relevant to the merits, although it may be dealt with as a preliminary objection, since without that factor there could be no *cause of action*. Hence, it would always have to be dealt with as a matter relating to the merits. Judge Hudson adopted this view in his dissenting opinion in the *Panavezys–Saldutiskis Railway Case* before the PCIJ, where he said:

I cannot agree with the conclusion reached by the court that the second Lithuanian objection, based upon the alleged 'non-observance by the Estonian Government of the remedies afforded by municipal law', has a preliminary character which requires it to be dealt with apart from the merits, and which in this case justifies a holding that the Estonian claim cannot be entertained. In my view the objection lacks that character and it ought to be rejected; hence the Estonian claim should be entertained, even if the principal Estonian submission should later have to be rejected because of the non-exhaustion of local remedies.[34]

---

[33] As e.g. in the *Phosphates in Morocco Case*, PCIJ Series A/B No. 74 (1938), which is discussed below. This difference in the time of incidence of responsibility could also affect the admissibility of the claim through the operation of the nationality of claims rule. For instance, if the time of incidence occurs prior to a change of nationality, the claim will not be admissible, while if the change of nationality takes place before the time of incidence, the claim will be admissible.

[34] PCIJ Series A/B No. 76 at p. 47 (1939).

In the very next passage the reason for this view appears: 'This is not a rule of procedure', he says, speaking of the rule of local remedies, 'it is not merely a matter of orderly conduct. It is part of the substantive law as to international, i.e. state-to-state, responsibility.'[35] Thus, he based his opinion as to whether the question was one to be dealt with as relating to the merits, or as relating only to an objection to admissibility, on whether the rule had a substantive or procedural character.

A logical consequence of the view that the rule is substantive is also that the upholding of an objection based on the rule would result in the case being *res judicata*, because the objection pertains to the substance of the claim. The objection would then not operate purely as a dilatory procedural bar to admissibility.

If, on the other hand, the rule is classified as procedural, then the issue must be dealt with as a preliminary objection to admissibility, even though it may be joined to the merits. It is clear that the Court differed from Judge Hudson on the nature of the rule and regarded it as procedural, thereby making it possible for it to deal with the issue arising from it solely as a preliminary objection to admissibility. The holding of the Court was that

the second Lithuanian preliminary objection having been submitted for the purpose of *excluding an examination by the court of the merits of the case*, and being one upon which the court can give a decision without in any way adjudicating on the merits, must be accepted as a preliminary objection within the meaning of Article 62 of the Rules.[36]

Although the objection was joined to the merits in this case, it was decided and upheld as a preliminary objection which did not pertain to the merits.[37]

---

[35] *Ibid.*, Judge Armand-Ugon in a dissenting opinion in the *Barcelona Traction Co. Case* (Preliminary Objection) was of the opinion that the distinction between substance and procedure was irrelevant to the question of when the objection based on the non-exhaustion of local remedies was decided: 1964 ICJ Reports at p. 164. The question when the objection may be decided, i.e. whether it should be considered with the merits or not, is slightly different from the question of how it should be regarded. It is conceivable that, even though it is regarded as *concerning* the merits, it may be decided as a preliminary objection, just as an objection that a claim is manifestly unfounded may be.

[36] PCIJ Series A/B No. 76 at p. 22 (1939). See also Neilsen in the *International Fisheries Co. Case* (*United States* v. *Mexico*), 4 UNRIAA at p. 713 (1931), who maintained, albeit in an opinion which dissented on the main issue in the case, that the rule of local remedies does not concern the fundamental question of 'whether a wrong was initially committed by authorities of a respondent government'.

[37] The ILC Draft on State Responsibility (2001) treats the objection based on the rule as relating to admissibility: ILC Report to the General Assembly (2001), Chapter IV, at

Waiver and estoppel

It has been seen that the rule of local remedies may be waived impliedly or expressly for a variety of reasons, or that the respondent state may be estopped from relying on it. One situation in which the rule is said to be impliedly waived by the respondent state is when the claimant state requests a declaratory judgment that there has been a breach of international law. This view is based on the idea that, because the initial act alleged to be the cause of the wrong would be a breach of international law by the respondent state and not merely a breach of local law, a declaratory judgment on that issue would not be inapt and would help in fact to bring about a speedy solution of the dispute. The correlation implied in this reasoning between a judgment by an international tribunal and a breach of international law is evident. Whatever the conditions that might be required for the grant of a declaratory judgment, it is only if the rule of local remedies is conceived as having a procedural nature that such a judgment will be available before local remedies have been exhausted. If the rule were of a substantive nature there would be

---

p. 65. Crawford, the rapporteur on this subject for the ILC, in referring to the decision on admissibility in the *Phosphates in Morocco Case*, PCIJ Series A/B No. 74 (1938), regards it as contradicting the substantive view of the rule of local remedies. However, in the process, he (i) confuses objections to jurisdiction with objections to admissibility, (ii) does not recognize clearly that the PCIJ did not explicitly refer to the rule as being procedural in nature but, because of what it did in upholding the objection to admissibility based on local remedies on the basis of the reasoning it adopted, rejected outright the substantive view of the rule and unequivocally opted for a solely procedural view of the rule, and (iii) does not acknowledge the conclusion that it was what the PCIJ did and not what it specifically said which conclusively supported the procedural view of the rule and was completely inconsistent with any partial or total substantive view of the rule. This conclusion was not apparent on the surface but was the result of a careful analysis of the case made for the first time by me and which appeared in the first edition of this book in 1990 (pp. 347–50). For Crawford's work, see his *The International Law Commission's Articles on State Responsibility* (2002) p. 23, and particularly note 68. The *Phosphates in Morocco Case* is cited as if it is an *obvious* historical source for the procedural view as opposed to the substantive view, which it is not and was never considered by text writers to be before my work published in 1990. Dugard, note 21 above, at pp. 15ff. and 26ff., conceded that it was what the PCIJ did in the *Phosphates in Morocco Case*, though it never used the term 'procedural' or explained the nature of the rule, which supported the procedural view of the rule, and rightly referred fairly extensively to the analysis made by me of the case which extracted and justified this conlcusion: *ibid.*, p. 23. However, he came to the conclusion in the end that the rule was both procedural and substantive in nature (*ibid.*, pp. 31–2), which is a conclusion, as will be seen at the end of this chapter, that is not tenable and is based on a confusion between *resort* to local remedies and *exhaustion* of local remedies in different situations.

no internationally illegal act involving international responsibility (and also liability) upon which an international court or tribunal could properly pronounce.

There may be waiver of the rule in other circumstances too. The general mode of doing this would be by agreement, express or implied, between the national state of the alien and the state alleged to be in the wrong, either before or after the injury occurs. There are numerous reasons why states may agree to waive the requirement of reference to the local courts, most important among which is that the political or social climate in a foreign state may be adverse to the interests of the nationals of a particular state and decisions of courts may tend to be influenced crucially by this climate. Another reason is that states regard direct reference to international tribunals as a saving in time and money resulting from the avoidance of a multiplicity of proceedings. But whatever the reasons, and these must remain largely political, it is certainly the case that there are numerous instances of states agreeing to waive the requirement of reference to the local courts.

If the rule of local remedies is one of procedure, then such a waiver is possible and comprehensible. Because the rule is only a means of establishing the orderly conduct of international litigation, an exception may be made to the rule and steps in the order may be excluded. The character of the alleged wrong will in no way be affected. It is only the method of settlement that undergoes a change. The wrong, which remains the same, is conclusively determined and redressed, by an international court directly, rather than by the usual preliminary methods available in the respondent state.

If the rule is one of substance, it would follow logically that a waiver of the requirement that local remedies should be exhausted would not be possible. The resort to local remedies becomes a material part of the wrong being alleged before the international tribunal. Without that resort there would be no cause of action. If a waiver of the requirement were allowed, no cause of action involving international responsibility could be proved before an international tribunal. Either remedies will have to be exhausted, or the absence of adequate remedies amounting to a failure of remedies will have to be proved. To speak of a true waiver is incongruous in such a case.[38]

---

[38] In examining the historical evidence, care must be taken to distinguish two sets of situations. There are several treaties in which clauses eliminating recourse to the local courts are found, e.g. the Claims Convention between the United States and Panama,

The same arguments apply to forfeiture of the benefits of the rule by estoppel.[39] The rule is dispensed with in this manner before an international tribunal, if after it is forfeited there is still an international wrong which an international tribunal can redress. This can only be so if the rule is not substantive but is rather of a procedural character.

Judicial and state practice

An examination of the decisions of international courts, statements made by international judges and arbitrators and state practice reflected in arguments before international courts and tribunals reveals a conflict similar to that present in the textual authorities, without perhaps the same exploration of the theoretical background. However, there is cogent evidence which favours the procedural view of the rule, in so far as decisions themselves can best, or, indeed, only, be explained on this basis, while there is no evidence of such a nature supporting the substantive view. It is not merely statements that must be looked at but also what courts, tribunals and judges in fact did, particularly in the light of the conclusions reached in the previous section.

28 July 1926, Article 5, US Treaty Series No. 842. One category contains genuine waivers of the rule of exhaustion of local remedies in relation to a claim giving rise to international responsibility. The other embodies quasi-waivers. The claims are admitted to be independent of a basis in international law, although they are of an international character in that they originate in injuries done to aliens; international principles may be applied by international tribunals in the settlement of these disputes, but they are not claims based on breaches of international law; they are really claims rooted in national law which are decided through agreement between the parties by international tribunals applying international principles: see the *Illinois Central Railroad Co. Case (United States* v. *Mexico)*, 4 UNRIAA p. 23 (1926). Any waiver of resort to local remedies that may be included in treaties involving this situation is not really a waiver of the rule that applies to international wrongs. It is a waiver of a requirement of international law based on analogy, obviously made and explicitly included in such treaties to avoid misunderstanding. The truth of the matter is that normally such national wrongs could not be brought before international tribunals unless some 'denial of justice' had been perpetrated by or in relation, to the local courts, because there could not be an international wrong in the absence of such a denial of justice. Occasionally, when it is agreed to bring national wrongs before international tribunals to be decided by the application of international principles, an express clause is included in the treaty whereby the absence of a 'denial of justice' resulting from resort to the local courts ceases to be a ground for the tribunal's abdicating its jurisdiction.

[39] For an argument based on estoppel, see the French argument in the *Norwegian Loans Case*, ICJ Pleadings (1957), vol. 2, p. 407.

Support for the substantive view

In the *Mexican Union Railway Case*, the tribunal said that 'the responsibility of the State under international law can only commence when the persons concerned have availed themselves of all remedies open to them under the national laws',[40] thus supporting the substantive view of the rule. Judge Morelli, in a dissenting opinion in the *Barcelona Traction Co. Case* (Preliminary Objections), stated:

The local remedies rule, as a rule of general international law, is in my view substantive and not procedural. It is indeed a rule which is supplementary to other rules, which also themselves possess the character of substantive rules, namely the rules concerning the treatment of foreigners. Those rules require from the State to which they are directed a particular final result in respect of the treatment of foreign nationals, leaving the State which is under the obligation free as regards the means to be used. Consequently, if an organ of the State which is under the obligation performs an act contrary to the desired result, the existence of an internationally unlawful act and of the international responsibility of the State cannot be asserted so long as the foreign national has the possibility of securing, through the means provided by the municipal legal system, the result required by the international rule.[41]

This is perhaps the best judicial expression of the substantive view. Judge Hudson, in a dissenting opinion in the *Panavezys–Saldutiskis Railway Case*,[42] and Judge Córdova, in a separate opinion in the *Interhandel Case*,[43] also made statements which clearly espouse the substantive view of the rule. Both judges were certain that international responsibility (and liability, then) did not arise until local remedies had unsuccessfully been exhausted.

Among arguments made by states before international courts, that made by the Polish government in the *Administration of the Prince von Pless Case* before the PCIJ, when it raised a preliminary objection based on the local remedies rule, is perhaps the earliest modern example of support for the substantive view of the rule. The respondent state said that 'until the legal means made available by internal legislation to individuals to defend their interests have been exhausted, there can be no question of the international responsibility of the State'.[44] The French government in the *Norwegian Loans Case* apparently took a position which supported

---

[40] *Great Britain v. Mexico*, 5 UNRIAA at p. 122 (1930).   [41] 1964 ICJ Reports at p. 114.
[42] PCIJ Series A/B, No. 76 at p. 47 (1939).   [43] 1959 ICJ Reports at pp. 45–6.
[44] PCIJ Series C No. 70 at pp. 134–5 (1933) (translation).

the substantive view in a different way. In interpreting the Norwegian argument that local remedies should have been exhausted, it said that the argument required that a denial of justice by the courts of Norway should be shown before the responsibility of Norway could be incurred.[45] It is not clear that this was what Norway was saying but, that apart, the French view amounted to maintaining that, where the rule of local remedies applied, the resort to local remedies must result in a 'déni de justice' in order that international responsibility may arise. This reflects a substantive view of the rule, because there can be no international responsibility, where the rule is applicable, before local remedies are exhausted or at the point of the initial injury. A statement of the Swiss government in the *Interhandel Case* also seems to support the substantive view of the rule, although elsewhere in the case the same government took a different view of the rule, as will be seen. It was said that the rule of local remedies operated as a condition precedent to establishing international responsibility for an act attributable to the state – 'avant qu'on puisse faire valoir la responsabilité de l'Etat'.[46] Thus, international responsibility was assumed to arise only after the exhaustion of local remedies.

Direct support for the procedural view

The most explicit reflection of the view that the rule is procedural is to be found in the separate opinion of Judge Tanaka in the *Barcelona Traction Co. Case*, where he, unlike the Court, considered the objection that local remedies had not been exhausted and found that the rule had been observed and local remedies exhausted. His view was that:

There can be no doubt that the local remedies rule possesses a procedural character in that it requires the person who is to be protected by his government to exhaust local remedies which are available to him in the State concerned, before his government espouses the claim before an international tribunal.[47]

In explaining the procedural nature of the rule, he stated further:

Thirdly, this procedural rule appears to express a higher conception of equilibrium or harmony between national and international requirements in the world community. The intention of this rule is explained as follows by Professor Charles De Visscher: 'Il s'agit donc ici avant tout d'une règle de procédure propre a réaliser un certain équilibre entre la souveraineté de l'Etat recherché

---

[45] ICJ Pleadings (1957), vol. 2, p. 185.
[46] ICJ Pleadings (1959) at p. 402.   [47] 1970 ICJ Reports at p. 143.

et, d'autre part, les exigences supérieures du droit international . . .' ('Le déni de justice en droit international', 52 *Académie de droit international, Recueil des cours,* 1935, II, p. 423).[48]

Judge Armand-Ugon, in a dissenting opinion in the *Interhandel Case,* took the approach that a plea based on the rule was essentially an objection to admissibility, and made it clear that international responsibility had already arisen before the resort to local remedies in stating that

The purpose of the local remedies rule is simply to allow the national tribunals in the first stage of the case to examine the *international responsibility* of the defendant State as presented in the Application.[49]

It is clear that, if the national courts pronounce on the international responsibility of the state, such responsibility must already have arisen, and that what the national court does is discharge a procedural function by providing a remedial process not affecting the incidence of that responsibility.

Judge Lauterpacht in the *Norwegian Loans Case* also appears to have lent support to the procedural view of the rule in so far as he explained how in his opinion the rule operated, but his views are better considered in the next section which deals with what courts and judges have done.

In the *Norwegian Loans Case,* although Norway did not specifically state that the rule was procedural, its arguments show that it accepted that theory in principle rather than a substantive view of the rule. The first indication of the Norwegian attitude is to be found in the fact that it regarded the rule as pertaining to the admissibility of the claim and not to the merits. The preliminary objection was argued on the basis that it should be decided as a preliminary objection and not as a matter which had to be considered at the stage of the dispute when the merits were decided. Thus the objection was phrased in terms of 'recevabilité' and not by reference to the basis of the dispute:

Lorsque l'Etat intervenant comme protecteur de ses nationaux, se plaint d'un acte (ou omission) illicite, imputé à un Etat étranger et dont la victime est une personne privée, son action sur le plan international n'est recevable qu'à la condition que le prétende lésé ait préalablement épuisé les moyens de recours que le droit interne de l'Etat incriminé met à sa disposition.[50]

Formulated thus, it is apparent that it was not argued that the rule operated substantively so as to deprive the French government of a cause of action 'au fond'.

---

[48] *Ibid.*   [49] 1959 ICJ Reports at pp. 88–9.   [50] ICJ Pleadings (1957), vol. 1, at p. 138.

Second, in explaining the reasons behind the rule of local remedies and the basis of the rule, the Norwegian government took the view that it was purely to enable the competent organ of the state concerned to clarify the issues involved that the rule prevented an international jurisdiction from being invoked.[51] There was no implication that there must be some kind of judicial misconduct before the rule of exhaustion was satisfied. An element of confusion was, however, introduced later in the argument, when it was said that the dispute became an inter-state dispute when local remedies had been exhausted and it was taken up on the international plane by the national state of the injured individuals.[52] In such circumstances, an inter-state dispute was substituted for an original dispute of private law.[53] These statements seem to imply that the original wrong was founded entirely on private law and had no basis in international law. It may be, however, that it was understood that, although a dispute may originate in private law, this did not preclude it from being founded in international law as well, although it may not have been an inter-state dispute in the sense that the national state of the alien could appear as a party in litigation.

Third, in keeping with the original stand of Norway was its clarification of the relevance of denial of justice to its objection based on the failure to exhaust local remedies. At one stage in its argument the French government raised the question of a possible confusion between the two concepts and clarified its own position.[54] In reply, the Norwegian government stated quite clearly that it was a mistake to confuse the two notions; it was not true to say that, in the event that the Norwegian courts had been resorted to and no redress had been obtained, the remedy for the French government would have been by way of alleging a 'denial of justice' by the Norwegian courts:

Les tribunaux norvégiens ont certes le devoir d'appliquer le droit norvégien, mais dans le cas ou le droit norvégien serait contraire aux prescriptions du droit international, il n'est pas douteux que l'Etat norvégien en serait internationalement responsable.[55]

Thus, Norway seems to have regarded the local remedies rule as a procedural rule not to be confused with rules relating to denial of justice by the judiciary of a state.

Finally, in replying to the French argument that the right to rely on the rule of local remedies had been forfeited by the fact that it had not

---

[51] *Ibid.*, pp. 276–7.   [52] ICJ Pleadings (1957), vol. 1, pp. 277–8.
[53] *Ibid.*, p. 278.   [54] *Ibid.*, pp. 182ff.   [55] *Ibid.*, p. 219.

been insisted on from the beginning of the dispute, the Norwegian government chose to base itself on the non-existence of such a principle of forfeiture, and alternatively on the argument that, even if the principle were admitted, on the facts there could be no forfeiture.[56] In no respect was the argument raised that, because the rule of local remedies was of a substantive nature, France, in order to prove its case on the merits, must have resorted to local remedies, there being no possibility of anyone forfeiting rights under the rule. Such an argument would have been appropriate had Norway taken its stand on the substantive nature of the rule.

There are indications that the Swiss government in the *Interhandel Case* took a procedural view of the rule, in so far as it contended that a declaratory judgment could be given, even if local remedies had not been exhausted,[57] although elsewhere in its argument, as was seen, it seems to have supported the substantive view of the rule. But more interestingly it was the US government that seems to have adopted a procedural view of the rule in replying to the Swiss arguments in the case. First, it argued that, even assuming the direct violation of international law by the breach of a treaty, the doctrine of exhaustion would still apply, and the international wrong would not give rise to a claim between states unless local remedies had been exhausted.[58] While the language used in delineating the argument is ambiguous, its substance involves the notion that the rule is of a procedural character. Although it was said that the wrong would not be 'sufficiently definite and complete' before local remedies had been resorted to, it is implied that it is the original international wrong that forms the subject matter of the international claim and that it is not altered by the failure of the local courts to give redress. Similarly, in regard to the point made by the Swiss government that since the application was for a declaratory judgment the rule did not apply, the US replied by accepting that principle but contesting the issue that what was being requested was a declaratory judgment.[59] The acceptance of that principle could have been made, only if the rule was conceived as a procedural one.

The action taken by courts and judges

There are several instances where courts (or tribunals) and judges, in dealing with the issue of whether local remedies had been exhausted, have followed a course of action which indicates that they supported the

---

[56] *Ibid.*, pp. 448ff.   [57] ICJ Pleadings (1959) at pp. 405 and 564.
[58] *Ibid.*, p. 505.   [59] *Ibid.*, pp. 316ff., 501 and 618.

procedural view of the rule. The arbitrator in the *Finnish Ships Arbitration* analyzed the nature of the rule and made certain significant remarks which support the thesis that the rule is procedural. His approach to the problem displayed a firm conviction that the rule of local remedies had a procedural character.

The arbitrator squarely faced the fact that there were differences of opinion as to the nature of the rule.[60] He conceded that there was a view that the rule of exhaustion of local remedies was of a substantive nature which predicated the responsibility of a state on the rejection of the alien's claim by the national courts. He also went so far as to say that the acceptance of this view would not result in any difference in certain respects.[61] But the general tenor of his judgment is against that view.

In the first place, he said that the basis of the claim in the case was an initial breach of international law committed at the time the damage complained of was caused, and not a subsequent failure of the UK courts or legal system to mete out justice.[62] Both the UK government and the Finnish government agreed that this was the basis of the claim. In the tribunal's holding is reflected a decisive attitude to the cause of action in a case involving the exhaustion of local remedies. It was accepted that the international cause of action arose at the time the initial injury was committed and not at the time the UK courts failed to give a remedy. Implicit is the distinction between the cause of action and the right of action made earlier in this chapter. Thus, the arbitrator's approach is consonant with the view that the rule of exhaustion merely affects the incidence of the right of action and does not pertain to the cause of action.

The arbitrator also implicitly agreed with the UK Government's contention that a condition precedent to the bringing of an international claim, namely, that all the judicial remedies available be exhausted, had not been fulfilled:

If the private persons concerned had failed to exhaust their municipal remedies, there was no foundation for any diplomatic claim. In the present case, the essential condition precedent – the exhaustion of municipal remedies – not being fulfilled, it followed that, under this well established rule, the Finnish Government had not, and never had had, any right under international law to make any diplomatic claim with respect to this matter at all.[63]

---

[60] *Finland v. UK*, 3 UNRIAA at p. 1502 (1934).   [61] *Ibid.*
[62] *Ibid.*, p. 1501.   [63] *Ibid.*, p. 1488.

This statement refers to the exhaustion of local remedies as a condition precedent to the *right* to make a diplomatic claim, and not as a condition precedent to the existence of a basis for an international claim. Had the view been accepted that the rule is of a substantive nature, exhaustion of local remedies would have been a condition precedent not merely to the right of bringing an international claim but to the existence of an international cause of action.

It was clearly stated that the failure to provide remedies on the part of the UK judicial system was not an international wrong.[64] In regarding the failure to provide judicial remedies as irrelevant to the cause of action, the arbitrator took the view that the rule of local remedies could not be of a substantive character. A distinction was made between claims based on denial of justice by the courts, where there is a decision of a court that is 'grossly unfair and notoriously unjust', and claims where local remedies have simply not been successfully exhausted. In the former case, it was said that there must not only be a judgment of a court, in order to predicate liability, but it must also be shown that it was grossly unfair and notoriously unjust, whereas in the latter case liability existed on the merits of the claim itself.

The arbitrator's opinion on the purpose of the local remedies rule is revealing. He made two points: (i) the rule exists to give the respondent state an opportunity of redressing an alleged wrong irrespective of the question of whether a wrong has actually been committed or not; (ii) the respondent state is entitled to its own appreciation of the questions of law and fact involved in the claims.[65] Underlying this analysis is the notion that the alleged wrong is not principally subject to the adjudication of the national tribunals of the respondent state but belongs to a different regime, namely, the international legal order. Both the above points testify to the fact that the rule is a tribute to the respondent state, and is not intended to control the administration of justice by the respondent state as the rules relating to the denial of justice purport to do. They are in accord with the view that the rule establishes something like an appellate system, in which the national courts are the primary courts and the international tribunal is the court of last resort, and which is therefore of a procedural character.

While the arbitrator apparently took the view that the rule of exhaustion was of a procedural nature and his reasoning and decision were in all respects consistent with that view, the question remains whether

---

[64] *Ibid.*, p. 1501.   [65] *Ibid.*, p. 1501.

it was his opinion that the rule of exhaustion could not be of a substantive character. Although he may be said to have rejected the view that the structural character of the rule is totally substantive, he did not explicitly support the approach that the rule is entirely procedural. It would seem, however, from the foregoing examination of the judgment, that a great deal of what was said was consistent with the view that the rules relating to the denial of justice are of a separate nature and should be regarded as belonging to a different department of the law. Equally, the approach adopted appears to be inconsistent with the notion that issues relating to the denial of justice are just another aspect of the one rule relating to the exhaustion of local remedies. In this connection, the analysis of the purposes of the rule is particularly important. It implies a recognition that the policies underlying the law of denial of justice are different. Also, the insistence on the idea that it is the initial breach of international law that constitutes the subject of an international adjudication where the rule of local remedies is invoked, and not the failure of the local courts to provide a remedy, lends special support to the view that the rule has only a procedural character.

Some light is shed on the problem by the arbitral decision in the *Ambatielos Claim*. There were three claims submitted by the Greek government in respect of which the objection was raised by the United Kingdom that local remedies had not been exhausted. If these claims were to be regarded as being subject to the rule that local remedies must be exhausted in the procedural sense, they should have been based directly on breaches of international law. The tribunal took this view of the Greek allegations when it said that:

> the question raised by the United Kingdom government (relating to exhaustion of local remedies) covers all the acts *alleged* to constitute breaches of the treaty. The Commission will, therefore, examine the validity of the United Kingdom objection independently of the conclusions it has reached concerning the validity of the Ambatielos Claim under the treaty of 1886.[66]

The tribunal examined the application of the rule of local remedies to each claim. In other words, the mere fact that certain acts had been alleged in the claim of the Greek government to be breaches of the treaty was sufficient for the tribunal to deal with them in relation to the objection that local remedies had not been exhausted. An allegation of a breach of international law was the only relevant consideration. Thus,

---

[66] *Greece* v. *UK*, 12 UNRIAA at p. 118 (1956).

the rule was apparently treated as a rule of procedure to be applied to an initial breach of international law alleged by the claimant government, namely, a breach of treaty.

The decision in the *Phosphates in Morocco Case*[67] gives the most cogent and even, indeed, conclusive support to the view that the rule of local remedies is procedural. In its preliminary application of 30 March 1932 to the PCIJ, the Italian government requested the Court to hold that the decision of the Mines Department dated 8 January 1925 and the denial of justice which had followed it were inconsistent with the international obligation incumbent upon France to respect the acquired rights of the Italian company Miniere e Fosfati. The French government had accepted the compulsory jurisdiction of the Court by a declaration dated 25 April 1931 for 'any disputes which may arise after the ratification of the present declaration with regard to situations or facts subsequent to this ratification'. The question, thus, arose of whether the internationally wrongful act of which the Italian government was complaining could or could not be regarded as a 'fact subsequent' to the critical date. The Italian government contended that the breach of an international obligation initiated by the decision in 1925 only became a completed breach following certain acts subsequent to 1931, particularly a note of 28 January 1933 from the French Minister for Foreign Affairs to the Italian Ambassador and a letter of the same date addressed by the same Minister to the Italian individual concerned. The Italian government saw the note and the letter as an official interpretation of the acquired rights of Italian nationals which was inconsistent with the international obligations of France. It saw in them a confirmation of the denial of justice to the Italian nationals concerned, constituted by the refusal of the French Resident-General to permit them to submit to him a petition for redress in accordance with the terms of Article 8 of the *dahir* of 12 August 1913. The new denial of justice now consisted in the final refusal of the French government to make available to the claimants an extraordinary means of recourse, whether administrative or other, in view of the lack of ordinary means. On the basis of these facts, the Italian government clearly opted for the theory that an internationally wrongful act, although initiated by original conduct contrary to the result required by an international obligation, is completed only when the

---

[67] PCIJ Series A/B No. 74 (1938). The analysis of this case presented here is *substantially* the same as that to be found in the first edition (1990) of this book, at pp. 347–50, as are the conclusions reached as a result of the analysis.

injured individuals have tried unsuccessfully to make use of all existing appropriate and effective remedies. It was thus from that moment that, in its view, the responsibility came into existence.

In opposition to the Italian government, the French government maintained that if, as the former affirmed, the decision of 1925 by the Mines Department really merited the criticisms levelled against it – violation of treaties, violation of international law in general – it was at that date that the breach by France of its international obligations had been committed and completed, and at that date that the alleged internationally wrongful act had come into being. The French representative affirmed that:

Here, the rule of the exhaustion of local remedies is nothing more than a rule of procedure. The international responsibility is already in being, even if it cannot be enforced through the diplomatic channel or by resort to an international tribunal and appeal to the Permanent Court of International Justice until local remedies have first been exhausted.[68]

In its judgment of 14 June 1938 the Court indicated that it did not discern in the action of the French government subsequent to the decision of 1925 any new factor giving rise to the dispute in question, and that the refusal by the French government to accede to the request to submit the dispute to extraordinary judges did not constitute an unlawful international act giving rise to a new dispute. The Court went on to say:

The Court cannot regard the denial of justice alleged by the Italian Government as a factor giving rise to the present dispute. In its Application, the Italian Government has represented the decision of the Department of Mines as an unlawful international act, because that decision was inspired by the will to get rid of the foreign holding and because it therefore constituted a violation of the vested rights placed under the protection of the international conventions. That being so, it is in this decision that we should look for the violation of international law – a definitive act which would, by itself, directly involve international responsibility . . . In these circumstances the alleged *denial of justice*, resulting either from a lacuna in the judicial organization or from the refusal of administrative or extraordinary methods of redress designed to supplement its deficiencies, merely results in allowing the unlawful act to subsist. *It exercises no influence either on the accomplishment of the act or on the responsibility ensuing from it.*[69]

---

[68] PCIJ Series C No. 85 at p. 1048.
[69] PCIJ Series A/B No. 74 at p. 28 (1938). Emphasis added.

The PCIJ clearly held that the initial act, which was a violation of international law, gave rise to international responsibility, and that such responsibility did not arise solely after the later actions, relating to the exhaustion of local redress, alleged by the claimant state to have taken place. The time at which international responsibility arose was critical for this case and, therefore, the decision in the case is based on the understanding that international responsibility arose before any resort to local remedies might have taken place. This is clearly based on a procedural view of the rule of local remedies.[70] There was absolutely no room left for any inference that the rule is at all substantive. It is undoubtedly *conclusive* judicial authority for the procedural view, and is the leading case on the nature of the rule, though it becomes so as a result of close analysis, which, it is to be noted, provides a *conclusive* and *ineluctible* answer to the problem.

A strong element of support for the procedural view is to be found in those cases in which the objection based on local remedies, even if joined to the merits, was decided purely as a preliminary objection to the admissibility of the claim and not as pertaining to the merits at all.[71] Further, in so far as the PCIJ has accepted the principle in the *German Interests in Upper Silesia Case*[72] that, at any rate in certain circumstances, a declaratory judgment could be given, even if local remedies had not been exhausted, it lent its imprimatur to the procedural view of the rule.

In the *Interhandel Case*,[73] the ICJ came out more positively in favour of the view that the rule of local remedies is to be conceived as a rule of procedure. The case sprang from the confiscation by the US government of shares belonging to the Société Internationale pour Participations Industrielles et Commerciales (Interhandel, a Swiss company) in the General Aniline and Film Corporation. This was done under the Trading with the Enemy Act during the Second World War, on the ground that the shares were property belonging to an enemy-controlled company. Subsequently,

---

[70] Ago tries quite unconvincingly to reconcile this decision with his view that the rule is substantive: note 1 above, at p. 29. The Court's conclusion clearly identifies international responsibility with a violation of international law, which is the basis of the procedural view, and not with the subsequent failure of local remedies (whether accompanied by a denial of justice or not) which is the basis of the substantive view.

[71] See e.g. the *Administration of the Prince von Pless Case*, PCIJ Series A/B No. 54 (1933); the *Affaire Losinger and Co.*, PCIJ Series A/B No. 67 (1936); the *Panavezys–Saldutiskis Railway Case*, PCIJ Series A/B No. 76 (1939); the *Electricity Co. of Sofia Case*, PCIJ Series A/B No. 77 (1939); and the *Interhandel Case*, 1959 ICJ Reports p. 6.

[72] PCIJ Series A No. 6 (1926).   [73] 1959 ICJ Reports p. 6.

an agreement, known as the Washington Accord, was reached between the US government and the Swiss government, among others, according to which Swiss assets in the US were to be released. Acting under the terms of the Accord, the Swiss Authority of Review confirmed a finding of the Swiss Compensation Office that Interhandel was not controlled by Germans. The Swiss government requested the release of the assets of Interhandel in the US, in accordance with the terms of the Washington Accord, on the basis of this finding, while the US government contended that this decision was not binding on it. In the meantime, Interhandel took proceedings in the US courts for the recovery of its property, but these proceedings had not been concluded since, after the initial dismissal of the action in the Court of Appeal, the Supreme Court granted *certiorari* for the reinstatement of Interhandel in its suit. Proposals of the Swiss government for settlement by arbitration under certain treaties were rejected by the US government. The Swiss government then instituted proceedings before the ICJ for the release of the property of Interhandel, or in the alternative for the submission of the dispute to an arbitral tribunal. In reply, the US government raised several preliminary objections, among them the objection that, since Interhandel had not exhausted local remedies, the court could not examine either of the Swiss claims.

The Court upheld this particular objection and dismissed the action without examining any of the other objections. Two important points are borne out by its reasoning. First, it said that the objection was directed against the admissibility of the application of the Swiss government, which would be devoid of object if the requirement of prior exhaustion of local remedies were fulfilled.[74] To the extent that the plea was not regarded as pertaining to the merits of the case, and that it was decided as a preliminary objection and not as a defence on the merits at the stage at which the preliminary objections were considered, it is clear that the rule of local remedies was conceived not as performing a substantive function, but rather a procedural one.

Second, the Court took the view that the rule 'had been generally observed in cases in which a State has adopted the cause of its national whose rights are claimed to have been disregarded in another State in violation of international law',[75] and that the object of the rule was to enable the state where such violation occurred to redress it by its own means, within the framework of its own domestic legal system.

[74] *Ibid.*, p. 26.   [75] *Ibid.*, p. 27.

This view, that the cause of action is a violation of international law occurring at the time of the original wrong and not a failure of the local courts amounting to a breach of international law, can only be in accord with the procedural nature of the rule of local redress.[76]

The Court's approach reflects a positive attitude to the character of the rule in the case before it, in that it laid down that the rule performed a procedural function. It may also be said that the procedural character of the rule was admitted without any kind of concession being made as to the possibility of its also having a substantive function. Thus, there is no reason to assume that the Court would necessarily have agreed that the rule should be characterized in that way as well or at all.

In the *Norwegian Loans Case*, Judge Lauterpacht considered in a separate opinion the objection that local remedies had not been exhausted. Judge Lauterpacht's approach is instructive in that he paid special attention to two aspects of the rule of local remedies which are particularly relevant to the view that the rule is procedural. These were the nature of the defence, that local remedies had not been exhausted and the relevance of denial of justice to it. On the second matter, Judge Lauterpacht was of the opinion that a denial of justice was not the foundation of an action where the rule of local remedies was implicated. The exhaustion of local remedies without success merely opened the way for international proceedings relating to the initial breach of international law, denial of justice being irrelevant.[77] This view could only have been based on a procedural interpretation of the rule.

As to the nature of the defence, Judge Lauterpacht could not have been more explicit that the defence was only relevant where an initial breach of international law formed the basis of a claim. Its function was not to convert into a breach of international law an act which was initially not such a breach by altering its content, nor to make possible a finding that there was a breach of international law as an essential prerequisite of international proceedings. It was essentially to be conceived as a bar to the jurisdiction of the court, not affecting the question of whether Norway had violated international law. This stand is expressed in a striking passage:

---

[76] Four of the six dissenting judges did not openly disagree with the Court on this issue. Of the two who did, Judge Lauterpacht held that the case should be dismissed on a different objection and Judge Armand-Ugon agreed that the objection was one to admissibility, while he held that the rule did not apply in the case in hand because the injury was direct.

[77] 1957 ICJ Reports at p. 41.

The relevance of these questions of international law cannot properly be denied by reference to the fact that unless and until Norwegian courts have spoken it is not certain that there has been a violation of international law by Norway. The crucial point is that, assuming that Norwegian law operates in a manner injurious to French bondholders, there are various questions of international law involved. To introduce in this context the question of exhaustion of local remedies is to make the issue revolve in a circle. The exhaustion of local remedies cannot in itself bring within the province of international law a dispute which is otherwise outside its sphere. The failure to exhaust legal remedies may constitute a bar to the jurisdiction of the Court; it does not affect the intrinsically international character of a dispute.[78]

The view expressed there of the nature of the defence supports the theory that the rule of local remedies is procedural.

Although Judge Lauterpacht did not commit himself to the view that the rule of local remedies is solely of a procedural nature, there is every indication that he preferred to think of it in this way and also to regard denial of justice as a separate ground for responsibility. On the other hand, his approach was clearly a denial of the theory that the rule of local remedies was solely a rule of substance.[79]

A further factor of importance is that the success of an objection based on the rule has never been regarded as rendering the case *res judicata*, as might otherwise be logically required if the rule is considered truly one of substance pertaining to the merits of the case. The success of such an objection has always had the effect of delaying the justiciability of a claim on the basis that it is inadmissible because of a defect in the procedure of litigation, as was seen in Chapter 12.

Deductions

This survey of what courts, tribunals and judges have done when faced with an objection that local remedies had not been exhausted shows that the evidence conclusively favours the view that the rule of local remedies is procedural and neither substantive nor a combination of the two. Judges or states may have made statements supporting the view that the rule is substantive, but the practice of judicial bodies relating to the rule leads overwhelmingly to the conclusion that the rule has not been treated as substantive or as both substantive and procedural but as solely procedural in character. In fact, there is no decision of an

---

[78] *Ibid.*, p. 38.
[79] Judge Read in a rather confusing opinion does not seem to have taken a clear stand on the issue: *ibid.*, pp. 97ff.

international court or tribunal that supports the substantive view or a combination of the substantive and procedural views.

The view of the rule in human rights protection

In the human rights conventions, human rights are regarded as substantive rights corresponding to substantive obligations undertaken by the signatories. Thus, in the European Convention on Human Rights the parties undertake in Article 1 to 'secure to everyone within their jurisdiction the rights and freedoms defined in Section 2'. Also, in the International Covenant on Civil and Political Rights, Articles 1 to 27, which deal with human rights, such rights correspond to substantive obligations. Failure to respect a right provided for in these conventions is therefore a breach of the relevant convention and a violation of international law for which there is international liability. There is no reason to suppose that a further element is required, by way of failure of local remedies after exhaustion, for the international wrong to be consummated, whether by denial of justice or some other means. In these circumstances, the rule of local remedies would operate procedurally and not substantively.

In most decided cases the general view taken by the European Commission of Human Rights, when it has adverted to the issue, has been that, because the rule of local remedies is in customary international law a procedural condition precedent to the exercise of diplomatic protection, under the European Convention it is a procedural condition precedent to the invocation of the jurisdiction of the EComHR.[80] In one case, however, the EComHR did state that 'the responsibility of a state under the Human Rights Convention does not exist until, in conformity with article 26 (of the old Convention), all domestic remedies have been exhausted'.[81] But this is an anomalous statement which is in conflict with the other statements of the Commission. Moreover, in this case the Commission in effect took the approach that the rule was one of procedure; for it held that it was the alleged initial maladministration of justice by a lower court in the Fedearl Republic of Germany that constituted the original breach of international law in respect of which local remedies had to be exhausted. There was no violation of the European

---

[80] See e.g. *Austria v. Italy*, Application No. 788/60, 4 YBECHR at p. 148.
[81] *Mr and Mrs X v. Federal Republic of Germany*, Application No. 235/56, 2 YBECHR at p. 304.

Convention prior to this. It was not the view of the Commission that the subsequent failure to mete out justice on the part of the higher local courts was the source of the breach of international law or that the initial breach of the Convention was only consummated and became a completed international wrong only after the failure of local remedies.

As a result of Article 27(3) of the European Convention (Article 35 of the new Convention), the Commission always treated the matter of local remedies as one of procedure, because that Article required the Commission to reject any petition which it considers inadmissible because local remedies had not been exhausted.[82] This implies that the objection based on the rule relates to a procedural matter and not to the substance of the claim. The objection does not concern itself with the lack of a substantive element creating responsibility on the merits of the claim, which may be dealt with at a preliminary stage in the proceedings.

The Commission has decided that for responsibility to arise in addition to the initial wrong there need not be a denial of justice by the highest municipal court after the exhaustion of local remedies, it being sufficient that the applicant has failed to obtain adequate redress.[83] Thus, the adequacy and the effectiveness of a remedy depend on whether the individual would have been able to secure the result he desired by its use.[84] This position is based on a procedural view of the rule.

Further, the fact that the rule may be waived by the respondent state, even after the Commission has adverted to the rule *proprio motu*, seems to indicate that the rule is regarded as procedural. The possibility of waiver implies that there was an initial violation of international law giving rise to international responsibility.

The situation does not seem to be complicated, as in the case of diplomatic protection, by the presence of an additional compensatable element *vis-à-vis* the claimant state itself once domestic remedies have been exhausted without success. Under the human rights conventions not only may individuals who have successfully resorted to domestic remedies litigate before the international body but sometimes states whose rights have been violated under the collective guarantee may take up their cause. In either case, states parties to the conventions do not claim damages or compensation for the violation of their own rights. The system is intended essentially to protect the individual who has

---

[82] See *Austria v. Italy*, Application No. 788/60, 4 YBECHR at p. 116.

[83] See *Austria v. Italy*, Application No. 788/60, 4 YBECHR at p. 148; and *Boeckmans v. Belgium*, Application No. 1727/62, 6 YBECHR at pp. 398–402.

[84] *Boeckmans v. Belgium*, Application No. 1727/62, 6 YBECHR at pp. 398–402.

been injured. Therefore, the absence of the additional element of compensatable injury to the state makes it easier to postulate a procedural character for the rule of local remedies as applied in the area of human rights protection. It is less complicated to accept the interpretation that the initial infringement of the convention by an injury to an individual is a violation of international law for which the respondent state incurs immediate responsibility at international law, thereby rendering the exhaustion of domestic remedies essentially a procedural matter.

Concluding observations

The substantive view of the rule of local remedies is based principally on one of two postulates: either that an additional denial of justice by the local courts is required for the international wrong to be committed, because the initial injury is never a violation of international law; or that, although the initial injury may be an international wrong, the violation of international law is somehow not completed till local remedies have been unsuccessfully exhausted.

It has been seen that there are situations in which the initial injury attributable to the respondent state is a violation of international law and that, as shown in Chapter 4, an additional denial of justice by the local courts is not required to create an international wrong. Thus, the evidence shows that it is not accurate to base the substantive view of the rule on the first postulate, since it is precisely where an initial injury, by whatever organ of the state it is committed, can be characterized as an international wrong that the rule of local remedies applies. The evidence, both of judicial and state practice, shows that, where there is an initial violation of international law, no additional denial of justice need be shown after local remedies have been unsuccessfully exhausted for a cause and right of action at the international level to arise. Where an act of the courts which is a denial of justice constitutes the initial violation of international law, international responsibility for the wrong would arise at that point because of the violation of international law, and the exhaustion of local remedies in respect of the denial of justice, if required, would properly constitute a procedural pre-condition for the exercise of the international right of action by way of diplomatic protection, or for the protection of human rights.

The alternative postulate depends on what appears to be a distinction between an international wrong which creates international responsibility and one which does not. This seems a logically and functionally

difficult distinction, not to say an artificial one, which at the same time
defies jurisprudential analysis. Jurisprudential theory admits of a distinction between a cause of action which is unenforceable, temporarily
or permanently, and one which for some reason is not, the cause of action being a separate concept from the right of action, but it does not
make the kind of distinction envisaged in this postulate. Moreover, the
evidence, apart from some scattered statements to the contrary, supports
strongly the view that the distinction is not demonstrable in the judicial and state practice, whereas there is overwhelming support for the
theory that international responsibility arises and the actual violation
of international law takes place at the same time. The distinction also
seems to be an unnecessary fifth wheel, which makes the explanation of
international responsibility rest on a dubious fiction. Even though the
ILC seems originally not to have criticized or openly rejected this theory, it seems to be neither logically sound nor supported by the practical
evidence.

The procedural view of the rule of local remedies, on the other hand,
not only has the virtue of being compatible with jurisprudential and
functional logic, but also has the greater and patently conclusive support
of the practical evidence. It explains the function of the rule without
derogating either from the sovereignty of states, which it is important
to respect, or from the practical rationality and convenience of the rule.

The view that the rule of *exhaustion* of local remedies is one of substance in some circumstances but of procedure in others is just as
patently wrong as the view that the rule is one of substance. It fails to
distinguish between *exhaustion* that takes place in respect of an initial
wrong which is a violation of international law, whether it is a violation
of the local law or not, and mere *resort* to the first available local remedy,
which may be so described, and which is usually necessary before any
international wrong may occur by a denial of justice, and takes place
when the initial wrong is a wrong in terms of only the local law and is
not a violation of international law. The conclusion has been advanced
that this view that the rule of *exhaustion* of local remedies is sometimes
one of procedure and at other times one of substance 'is logically, the
most satisfactory'.[85] In fact, 'logically' it is the most unsatisfactory and
untidy, because it fails to distinguish between *exhaustion of* and mere
resort to local remedies, and consequently does not recognize that the
rule as understood in current international law is of the '*exhaustion of*

---

[85] Dugard, note 21 above, at p. 32, para. 63.

local remedies' and not merely or at all of the '*resort* to local remedies', but confuses the two situations.

To sum up, it is useful to recapitulate the gist of the procedural view of the rule of local remedies which is clearly the correct and only possible view of the rule. The conclusions offered here are dependent also on the findings made in Chapter 4.

1. The rule operates in respect of a state violation of international law (not merely of local or national law).

2. Such a violation immediately generates the international responsibility of the offending state.

3. The rule pertains to secondary norms relating to remedies and is concerned with procedures for the settlement of disputes.

4. The rule prescribes a certain *procedure* in the orderly settlement of a dispute relating to a violation of international law by a state which requires exhaustion of remedies through the local legal system (subject to exceptions) as a condition precedent to settlement by international methods at the international level.

5. The application of the rule does not require an additional denial of justice within the local legal system before an international procedure may be invoked, the mere failure of the local legal system finally to settle the dispute being sufficient to enable the reference to international procedures.

6. Thus, it is the original international wrong which is ultimately actionable at the international level, though an additional denial of justice within the local system could compound that international wrong.

7. Where an initial state wrong is perpetrated (whether by commission or omission) which is not also an international legal violation (e.g. where it is a wrong only according to the local or national law), because there is no initial international wrong (also generating international responsibility), a denial of justice within the local legal system is necessary to generate a state violation of international law. This denial of justice calls for and is the result of only a *resort*, and not an *exhaustion*, of local remedies, in order that the conditional procedural requirement of exhaustion of local remedies be triggered.

8. Such a denial of justice, as a state international wrong generating international responsibility, would require that local remedies be exhausted in respect of *it* as a condition precedent to its being taken up at an international level as a violation of international law.

Part V   Epilogue

16 A concluding appraisal

The rule of local remedies has in some respects had a distinguished history. It can hardly be said that in the context of modern international law it is defunct or has ceased to be relevant, although a tendency may have arisen to try sometimes to circumvent it by various techniques. Moreover, its explicit incorporation in the law of human rights protection, which is basically conventional at the present time, has resulted in its extension beyond its original sphere of application, thus attesting further to its importance. It may also be mentioned that an analogous rule is applied in connection with certain disputes involving international organizations. The question is not whether the rule should be jettisoned because of objections to it which certain interests that may regard the rule as an unnecessary fifth wheel in the international system of settling what are basically international disputes may have. The rule is too firmly established. Moreover, its *raison d'être* is still to be deemed unchanged and viable. But a question that may be raised is whether it is being applied and developed in the most appropriate way.

Balancing of interests

The rule sprang up primarily as an instrument designed to ensure respect for the sovereignty of host states in a particular area of international dispute settlement. Basically, this is the principal reason for its survival today and also for its projection into international systems of human rights protection. Whether in the modern law of diplomatic protection or in the conventional law of human rights protection, the *raison d'être* of the rule is the recognition given by members of the international community to the interest of the host state, flowing from its sovereignty, in settling international disputes of a certain kind by its

425

own means before international mechanisms are invoked. The utility of this policy value underlying the rule cannot be denied, whether in the context of diplomatic protection or of human rights protection. Even though the disputes concerned, involving individuals as they do, are international disputes, the same reasons that led to the formation of the rule and have supported the rule through the years have really survived the development of more sophisticated systems of international dispute settlement. The response to the possibility of shortcomings in the application of the rule resulting from a, so called, 'rigid' approach is not to throw the baby out with the bath water, but to condition limitations on the rule and the development of the rule to accommodate as far as possible the legitimate concerns of affected interests.

Functionally, to date, the accelerated interaction between aliens and foreign states because of the ease of international travel, the growing sense of community in the world and the demands of economic development, in both developed and developing nations, means that the rule could be important in the settlement of international disputes that may arise from the exercise of, or in the context of situations which may lead to, diplomatic protection, just as the rule has been given further prominence as a result of the increasing concern for the protection of human rights which has manifested itself in the establishment of conventional systems of enforcement. The respect, shown by reference to the rule, for the sovereignty of the respondent state in conflict situations involving diplomatic protection in general international law has not waned, while in human rights protection the invariable incorporation of the rule in conventional systems is a recognition of its viability as a preliminary means of dispute settlement which leaves room for the exercise of certain sovereign rights by the respondent state.

Although the value attached to respect for the sovereignty of the host or respondent state is at the heart of the implementation of the rule, there is evidence in the evolution of the rule that international law attaches importance, in the rule's application, to values other than the interests of the host or respondent state. Such interests as those of the alien or individual, of the national state of the alien and of the international community have been taken into consideration. In different situations, the conflict between or among the various interests has been resolved in favour of one or other of the interests besides those of the host or respondent state, while sometimes the roll of the dice has favoured the latter. Generally, it may be concluded that there has been a judicious weighing of conflicting interests, particularly by judicial or quasi-judicial organs of the international community, before a solution has been reached. The only query, perhaps, is whether sometimes in the application of the rule the decision-makers have tended to lean unreasonably against the alien or individual.

It is apparent that local remedies operate as a step or steps in the orderly procedure of settling international disputes. The rule is no more and no less than a method of ascribing to sovereign states a dispute settlement function in international disputes to which they are parties. While states are surely capable of responsibly and constructively discharging the trust placed in them by the international community in conferring on them a role which flows from respect for their sovereignty, it is reasonable to expect that the rule should operate essentially as a means of securing economically and efficiently the settlement of international disputes in the areas relating to the protection of aliens and of human rights. Thus, while, on the one hand, a sovereign state is given every opportunity of settling such disputes equitably through its own organs, and it is in the interests of all concerned that such disputes should be settled at the earliest possible opportunity at a local level, on the other hand, it is logical that some recognition should also be given to the countervailing interests of all parties concerned in efficient justice without, *inter alia*, financial waste.

The importance of respect for the sovereignty of the host or respondent state has been attested to in many areas of the law relating to the rule of local remedies and it is right that this should be so. Particular mention may be made of the approach to the scope of the rule. The law relating to extraordinary remedies, to the raising of substantive issues and to the persons who should exhaust remedies, for instance, has resulted in a substantial role being assigned to the local or domestic system of dispute settlement, as has the conclusion that in the usual case what is required is a normal use of remedies, but not in the sense that what reasonable counsel might have done was necessarily adequate. In certain respects the stringency with which waivers are implied from agreements by the host or respondent state, and the rather strict manner in which the doctrines of estoppel and good faith have recently been applied, particularly in the *ELSI Case*, also flow from regard for the sovereignty of the host or respondent state.

On the other hand, consideration for other concerned interests has led to limitations on the incidence of the rule by reference to the concepts of direct injury and jurisdictional connection. While these limitations do not in reality inappropriately detract from the sovereignty of the host or respondent state, they have clearly arisen from the policy objective of containing the application of the rule and confining it to situations which the host or respondent state may justifiably claim to be subject to its system of dispute settlement. Other limitations, such as the requirement that only remedies of a legal nature need to be exercised, also flow from a rational approach to the balancing of the conflicting interests involved, which recognizes and gives effect to interests other than those of the host or respondent state. The recent application, by the ICJ, of the law relating to the raising of substantive issues and to the availability of remedies in the *ELSI Case* also reveals some concern that the rule should not be applied in such a manner as to rob it of its balanced effectiveness by over-protecting the interests of the host or respondent state.

The principle of avoiding undue hardship to the alien or individual, which has been clearly recognized in international jurisprudence and practice, and was explicitly acknowledged in the *Finnish Ships Arbitration*, has, it appears, especially been applied to impose limitations upon the operation of the rule. To the extent that the quality of the remedies offered is controlled, the principle has been effective, and on the basis of the opinions in the *Ambatielos Claim* it is possible to see and anticipate a further relaxation of strict requirements in regard to procedural remedies. On the other hand, in so far as the general limitation relating to the quality of remedies propounded in the *Finnish Ships Arbitration* has been strictly construed, there has been a tendency to lean towards the sovereignty of the host or respondent state. Even though there are indications that in the law of human rights protection a conflicting approach had emerged in some of the cases, particularly because it has been held that in respect of the material content of the rule its application in the field of human rights protection is identical with its application in the law of diplomatic protection, it cannot be conclusively asserted that the interests of the individual have as a rule been given greater recognition in the human rights area than in the law of diplomatic protection, though this has certainly happened sometimes. Furthermore, the rejection of many excuses which clearly favour the interests of the alien or individual, in both diplomatic and human rights protection, confirms the respect accorded the sovereignty of the host or respondent state. It is understood that the principle of avoiding undue hardship to the alien or individual has a specific and important relevance and is tempered by the basic principle of respect for the sovereignty of the host or respondent state. However, it cannot be said that the interests of the alien or individual have necessarily been prejudiced.

There is, however, a tendency which has been observed to avoid the application of the rule by express or implied waiver, more recently through the instrument of the BIT. Jurisprudence and practice have been found to have considerably developed the implication of waivers. While explicit waivers tend to be strictly construed, as already pointed out, the implication of waivers has been more liberal in connection with certain specific situations, just as the doctrines of estoppel and good faith have also to a large degree worked in favour of excluding the application of the rule. Perhaps these trends indicate a certain impatience with the rule, particularly on the part of protecting states. The approach to implication of waivers and estoppel or good faith, however, has not been overly protective of the interests of aliens or individuals and of protecting states, although such interests have clearly been considered. Generally, waivers have been implied and estoppel or good faith has been effective only where the circumstances justify a conclusion which requires a modification of the recognition of the sovereign interests of the host or respondent state. While waivers of the rule may sometimes be given after the injury has been committed, the numerous decided cases involving the application of the rule in the area of human rights protection and the numerous cases involving the rule in the field of diplomatic protection which have come before the PCIJ, the ICJ and other tribunals, such as the *Interhandel Case*, the *Norwegian Loans Case* and the *ELSI Case*, prove that waivers are not automatic and that the doctrines of estoppel, in the narrow sense, and good faith do not often operate to exclude the application of the rule. Indeed, in 2002, as a result of NAFTA, there has been agitation and discontent both among US investors and other interest groups, and concern in the US Government, that the exclusion of the local remedies rule under NAFTA and other BITs in general has backfired. Thus, there is now a move to retain in investment agreements some control by local law and courts, or, at any rate, its effect.[1] The short point is that the US is unhappy with the position that foreign investors are not subject to US law, believed to be compatible with international law and applied by the US courts, in relation to the treatment of investment.

---

[1] *Financial Times*, 2 October 2002, p. 7. The reasoning behind the new position does not appear clearly from this report.

The rule may, thus, still be regarded as an important instrument of dispute settlement in the international system. Nor has the point been reached at which it may be concluded that the rule is not a useful mechanism for defusing international disputes before they reach an international level, provided there is always a judicious balancing of the interests involved.

By the same token, a similar balancing of interests is to be seen or may be implemented in the analogous application of the rule to disputes involving international organizations. This is so particularly in the area controlled judicially by international tribunals relating to staff matters. But it also applies to other areas involving international organizations. There is no evidence that the contrary is the case nor is there any reason to believe that in the future the contrary will be the case, where the law has not already been developed or needs to be developed.

The rule in human rights protection and its impact

It must be recognized that the *domestic* remedies rule, so called, is not an invention of international human rights law. Not only do the relevant instruments generally refer to 'general international law' (which obviously means the law of diplomatic protection in particular), but (i) human rights organs, particularly those operating judicially or under judicial control, invoke general international law, and (ii) there is no substantial evidence that, in the event that there is a customary law applying the rule to human rights law as such, the rule applicable would not be based on the rule in diplomatic protection as is the case with the conventional law and that applied by human rights organs mentioned above. Consequently, it would be foolhardy to postulate differences as a basic assumption, rather than to recognize that human rights law starts with an awareness of the relevance of the principles of the general international law of diplomatic protection and proceeds to use them, while at the same time implementing the law with refinements and even, perhaps, differences, where such are called for by the particular circumstances of human rights protection. This approach which is pragmatic appears to be the one taken by all human rights organs virtually without exception. They do not, as the evidence shows, take the view that the rule as applied to diplomatic protection is 'rigid', as opposed to 'flexible', as such, or that the rule as applied to human rights protection is original and has an existence of its own or that they must ignore the principles found in the law of diplomatic protection.[2] It may be possible to identify a narrowing of scope or broadening of limitations, for example, especially in applications to particular situations when legitimate comparisons are possible, but that is not to say that basic approaches, whether of principle, of conceptual content, or of applications, are fundamentally and always different, or can never be similar or comparable, or that comparisons and analogies are irrelevant.

It must be emphasized that there is a difference between changing or not recognizing a *principle*, in this case as applied in diplomatic protection, and giving the principle development (i.e. of conceptual content) which may be different. When the latter takes place, the principle remains, though the conceptual development may be narrower. Indeed, conceptual concretizations cannot be characterized as narrower or different, unless identical or, at least, similar contextual situations are being considered. When a situation has never been faced under one convention but has been under another by the relevant organ, or has not been encountered in the law of diplomatic protection but has been in the law of human rights protection, it is not appropriate to say that there has been a narrower development or application of the *principle*, or, even more so, that the *principle* is different or has been changed. What is taking place is a development in application. That having been said, where principles or their conceptual development or contextual application are different, whether from those recognized in the law of diplomatic protection or from those recognized by another organ or other organs operating under other instruments, this must be recognized.

The above distinctions and realities are noted, because there are what are properly termed specific contextual applications as well as what are properly characterized as differences of principle and differences of conceptual content in the implementation of the rule of domestic remedies

---

[2] Cançado Trindade disagrees in effect with this approach, believing virtually that the rule as applied to human rights protection has a total life of its own. This is the burden of his argument in 'Book Review', 86 AJIL (1992) *passim*. In any case, 'flexibility' and 'rigidity' are relative terms – relative to the point of view being used. What is flexibility from the respondent state's angle is rigidity from the individual's point of view and *vice versa*. This is so, even though, as has become apparent, some human rights organs and bodies do use this terminology, obviously with a bias against states and in favour of individuals. It makes sense and accords more with reality to talk, for instance, in terms of expansion or narrowing of the scope of, and narrowing or expansion of the limitations on, the rule.

by human rights organs. It will be apparent, though, that the incidence of differences in principle is much less than the incidence of conceptual development or contextual applications, though sometimes these phenomena are confused or, at least, not kept distinct by text writers.[3] Furthermore, while differences or similarities in broad principle are easy to identify, it is often not easy to distinguish conceptual development from contextual application, but this is the appropriate manner in which to approach the matter.[4]

It is evident that in principle human rights organs have implicitly accepted that the starting point is the law of diplomatic protection. This is evidenced by their recognition of such basic principles, broad and conceptually indeterminate in a sense though they may be, such as, for example, those relating to availability, accessibility, normal use and effectiveness of remedies, to ordinary and extraordinary remedies, to the need for a final decision, to full exhaustion, to unavailability, inaccessibility and inefficacy of remedies (the converse of some concepts mentioned above), to undue delay, to repetition of injury and to waiver and estoppel. The principles relating to such procedural matters as the time of exhaustion, the time for raising the objection, the time of decision on the objection and joinder also are clearly related in the two institutions.

What has happened in the law of human rights protection in most areas is that (i) general concepts included in principles have already been filled out and given narrower definition (e.g. full exhaustion, use of ordinary or extraordinary remedies, including alternative remedies, and inaccessibility) and (ii) there has been application of principle and general concepts included in them to situations which have not been encountered at all in the law of diplomatic protection (e.g. inaccessibility).

---

[3] E.g. Cançado Trindade, note 2 above, at p. 626, does not keep these distinctions separate. The working of conceptual development (concretization) and contextual application in relation to principles of law is explained in greater detail by me in my treatise *Principles of the Institutional Law of International Organizations* (2nd edition) chapter 6.

[4] Cançado Trindade is obsessed with 'flexibility' and 'adjustment' at the expense of recognizing new applications of the rule: see *ibid.*, p. 631; and Cançado Trindade, 'The Inter-American Human Rights System at the Dawn of a New Century', in Harris and Livingstone (eds.), *The Inter-American System of Human Rights* (1998) at p. 401. A more helpful and objective, and less dogmatic and assumptive, approach to the implementation of the American Convention is taken by e.g. Cerna, 'The Inter-American Commission on Human Rights', in *ibid.*, pp. 85–92, and Vivanco and Bhansali, 'Procedural Shortcomings in the Defence of Human Rights', in *ibid.*, pp. 429–32.

It is unnecessary here to examine in detail where the law of human rights protection differs from or is similar to the law of diplomatic protection in regard to the rule of local or domestic remedies. These differences and similarities have already been pointed out or are apparent. Suffice it to say that in the area of burden of proof there are generally considerable differences between the approach of human rights bodies and the law of diplomatic protection, as also there may be in the conceptual content of effectiveness of a remedy.

However, it is equally important to recognize that just as there are clear similarities of principle in other areas, e.g. availability of remedies and undue delay, there are also (i) areas, such as inaccessibility, in which there has been further conceptual development in the experience of human rights bodies and (ii) areas, such as extraordinary remedies and alternative remedies, in which there have been new contextual applications to situations which have not been encountered in the law of diplomatic protection. In both of these categories, the proper and useful approach is to regard the approach of human rights bodies as a possible source for the development of the law relating to local remedies in diplomatic protection. Thus, for instance, the application in human rights law of the concept of inaccessibility to the situation where in a given social context the legal profession is virtually coerced into not advising an individual is a development which can inform the law of diplomatic protection. That development also highlights to some extent the possibility that inaccessibility may result not only from conduct or situations attributable to the respondent state but also from societal phenomena.

In the same way, as for conceptual development, the application of principles to new fact situations could inform the law of diplomatic protection. The approach taken by human rights bodies to extraordinary and alternative remedies is a good example of this.

It is not being suggested that there be a wholesale and indiscriminate importation to the law of diplomatic protection of developments in these senses in the law of human rights protection, nor that a converse process of limitation or expansion of the law of human rights protection on account of the law of diplomatic protection be envisaged. What is necessary is that a close look be taken at the developments referred to above, in the context of diplomatic protection, before they are accepted as being relevant or rejected as being irrelevant, just as much as in the converse case a similar kind of evaluation must take place.

That there are differences between the law of human rights protection and the law of diplomatic protection in certain areas of the application of the rule of local remedies must also be recognized. The burden of proof appears to be one of these areas. It is not suggested that it is always desirable that the gap be bridged. Nevertheless, the lessons learned in one area may be useful in the other area. A good example is the conceptual development of inaccessibility to include the indigence of the individual who is the victim as a factor to be considered. In some early cases in the law of diplomatic protection, impecuniosity or indigence of the alien was regarded as a factor which was not relevant to the issue of inaccessibility. It may be possible that the irrelevance of indigence in these cases depended on the circumstances of each case. A similar treatment of indigence is to be found in the jurisprudence under the European Convention and in the practice of the UN Human Rights Committee, as has been seen. However, the advisory opinion of the IACHR has now indicated that indigence is a factor which *in principle* is relevant (to inaccessibility) for the purposes of the rule of domestic remedies. This precedent is clearly one that could inform not only the law of human rights protection as applied by other human rights bodies or organs, which, as has been seen, was interpreted differently by some of them, but also the law of diplomatic protection which was apparently in principle interpreted differently. Here is an instance where differences could result in a closer look being taken at the conceptual content of principle even to the extent of changing it or its approach.[5]

The important point is that, though it is possible that there be differences in the content or application of the rule in the two areas, which must exist because of the possible differences that there may be in the perception of the rule as it is relevant to the two areas, there is no need to regard the development of the rule in the two areas as incurably separate nor is there a justification for such an approach in the light of the bases of the rule as applied in the two areas. While valid differences must be accepted, there is every reason why the experience in one area could inform the development of the law in the other.[6]

[5] The issue of indigence and impecuniosity in relation to the limitations (based on inaccessibility) on the rule of local remedies, both in diplomatic protection and in human rights protection, is discussed at length in Amerasinghe, 'Indigence and Inaccessibility as Limitations on the Rule of Local Remedies', in *Hacia un Nuevo Orden Internacional y Europeo, Estudios en Homenaje al Profesor Don Manuel Diez de Velasco* (1993) p. 57.

[6] In the light of the above analysis, the implication is open to question that generally recognized rules of international law relating to the application of the rule in

That having been said, it is also clear that the development of conceptual content in like principles and the contextual application of such principles are subject to the influence of several different factors which become relevant on account of the diverse phenomena in modern international society, such as the existence of tyrannical dictatorships as opposed to truly just democracies or other polities, of endemic judicial inefficiency and corruption even in democracies or polities of whatever kind, and of a distinction made in conventional human rights law between non-derogable and derogable rights, though there are no absolute and invariable conclusions to be reached because of such differences. That this is the position in the context of international human rights protection is easily conceded.[7] On the other hand, there is no reason why similar factors which may exist could not have an impact on the rule of local remedies in diplomatic protection.

It has been pointed out recently by the IAComHR that the Inter-American system (under the American Convention particularly) of providing an 'international remedy' is subsidiary compared to the primary role of national courts.[8] The Commission made clear that, where petitioners can litigate before domestic courts and do have access to justice, they must do so in compliance with the rule of domestic remedies. This is an unequivocal admission that the domestic remedies rule has a significance in the context of human rights protection just as it does in the law of diplomatic protection. There is no implication that domestic remedies may be side-stepped at the drop of a coin or that the object of the human rights protection system is to get the matter at any cost to an international forum, simply because international human rights dispute settlement procedures are available. In short, the general principles are still valid that the rule of domestic remedies applicable in human rights law *derives* from the rule of local remedies of the law of diplomatic protection and bears a significant resemblance to the latter, while appropriate differences may be recognized, and that the development of the rule in the two areas are interconnected and need not *necessarily* be different, or, conversely, the same.

---

diplomatic protection must 'suffer adjustment or adaptation' in the context of the law of human rights protection in general and necessarily, resulting in unbridgeable and consolidated *differences*. This implication is found in Cançado Trindade, note 2 above, *passim*, and note 3 above, at p. 403.

[7] See Vivanco and Bhansali, note 4 above, at pp. 429–31.
[8] *Marzioni v. Argentina* (1996), Report No. 39/96, Case 11.673 at paras. 50–2.

Relevance of theory

A word needs to be said about theory. Theory is important in so far as it has an impact on the practical application of the rule. It has become apparent that there are some loose ends which need to be tied up. A case, and a cogent one at that, has been made out for distinguishing situations where the rule operates as a result of an initial violation of international law in respect of an alien or individual and those in which the initial international wrong is a denial of justice by or in respect of judicial organs, where the rule for a variety of reasons does not apply immediately to the initial wrong as such which is not *per se* a violation of international law. The distinction is important in practice, because its consequences include the dissociation from the former situation of denial of justice connected with a judicial organ as an additional requirement to the initial violation of international law in respect of the alien or individual. Judicial and state practice strongly support the distinction.

Regarding theories as to the nature of the rule, it has been shown that the acceptance of one theory or the other does have some consequences for the implementation of the rule. In spite of the view originally and apparently adopted by the ILC in particular, it is abundantly clear that not only does the weight of the evidence support the purely procedural view of the rule rather than any substantive view at all, but – following the analysis, made by me and published in 1990 in the first edition of this work, of the *Phosphates in Morocco Case* – the PCIJ decided in effect quite unequivocally that the rule was *only procedural* and could not be substantive, partially or fully, thus, laying to rest any controversy about the nature of the rule. The development of the rule in the area of human rights protection has in effect given added support to the procedural theory of the nature of the rule. Moreover, the procedural view would appear to enjoy a logical coherence and completeness which the substantive view or any view combining the two views does not.

Undue 'strictness' as a problem

Finally, the question of whether the rule has been applied too strictly, whether in the law of diplomatic protection or in regard to human rights protection (or, indeed, analogously, in other areas), may be broached. As already pointed out, the primary purpose of the rule is to give the host or respondent state (or sometimes an organization, as the case may be)

an opportunity of rectifying a situation which is alleged to be in violation of the law.[9] Consequently, it would defeat that purpose, if the rule
were implemented in such a manner or if such an approach were taken
as to make it too easy for aliens or individuals to have direct access to international fora, particularly judicial (or, sometimes, quasi-judicial), by
avoiding recourse to local, domestic or internal remedies without giving the host or respondent state a fair chance of doing justice. What is
required is that the rule be applied in such a way that justice is not trav-
estied by too much regard for the interests of host or respondent states
and too little consideration of the other interests involved, particularly
of the alien or the individual, as the case may be. There is no evidence
that decision-makers in the international system of dispute settlement
have not hitherto tended to respect the demands of justice in the implementation of the rule. It is chiefly in the area of limitations on the rule,
particularly by reference to the principle of avoiding undue hardship to
the alien or individual, and in the application of the principle of consent to the non-application of the rule, that the legitimate parameters
of the rule need to be kept in mind. The development of the rule has
shown that these parameters have generally been judiciously and saga-
ciously established and may be maintained in the future by prudent
interpretation. There is no reason to believe that, when decision-makers
are confronted with the application of the rule to new situations, they
cannot duly apply the rule, having considered all the relevant interests,
in such a way as not to over-emphasize or ignore certain interests in
relation to others. It is really a matter of balancing interests and finding
a result which would ensure justice, which after all may be a question
of common sense and reason.

Analogous applications

This appraisal would not be complete without special mention of the
analogous application of the rule in relation to certain areas of the law
of international organizations which testifies to the respect given to it.

---

[9] What is said here applies *mutatis mutandis* to the rule as applied to organizational
relationships.

Index